D0075461

THE UNITED STATES
IN LATIN AMERICA

THE UNITED STATES IN LATIN AMERICA

A Historical Dictionary

David Shavit

Greenwood Press

New York • Westport, Connecticut • London

Library of Congress Cataloging-in-Publication Data

Shavit, David.
    The United States in Latin America : a historical dictionary /
David Shavit.
      p.   cm.
    Includes bibliographical references and index.
    ISBN 0–313–27595–5 (alk. paper)
    1. Latin America—Relations—United States—Dictionaries.
    2. United States—Relations—Latin America—Dictionaries.
    3. Americans—Latin America—History—Dictionaries. I. Title.
F1418.S494 1992
303.48′28073′03—dc20   91–32403

British Library Cataloguing in Publication Data is available.

Library of Congress Catalog Card Number: 91–32403
ISBN: 0–313–27595–5

First published in 1992

Greenwood Press, 88 Post Road West, Westport, CT 06881
An imprint of Greenwood Publishing Group, Inc.

Printed in the United States of America

∞

The paper used in this book complies with the
Permanent Paper Standard issued by the National
Information Standards Organization (Z39.48–1984).

10 9 8 7 6 5 4 3 2 1

Contents

Preface

Contacts between the United States and Latin America began in the seventeenth century when sea captains and merchants began to trade with the islands in the Caribbean. They were followed by consuls and diplomats; filibusters and adventurers; army, naval, and marine officers; explorers and travelers; government officials; missionaries; journalists; businessmen; colonists; engineers; colonial administrators; physicians; educators; economists; naturalists; scientists and scholars; archaeologists and anthropologists; authors and artists; and other American institutions, organizations, and business firms which established a whole gamut of relationships between the United States and Latin America.

The entries in this dictionary provide information about persons, institutions, and events that affected the relationships between the United States and Latin America; specifically, persons who actually have been in Latin America, and particularly those who have left written or visual records of their stay; organizations and institutions that functioned in Latin America; and events that occurred in that area.

The dictionary covers all the countries of Latin America south of the United States, including Mexico, Central America, the islands of the Caribbean Sea, and South America, excluding those parts of Mexico that were later annexed to the United States. Geographical names used in a specific entry are the ones relevant to the period covered. A list of variant place names appears in the front matter.

The dictionary attempts to provide comprehensive coverage of persons, institutions, and events that brought the United States into contact with Latin America. However, with limited space, some omissions were necessary. U.S. diplomats who served in Latin America are included only if they contributed to U.S.–Latin American relations in some way or if they left some record, such as a book of memoirs, about their service in the area. A complete list of all chiefs of U.S. diplomatic missions in Latin America is included in an appendix. Moreover, only those travelers whose travel reports are of particular interest and influence are included.[1] Although many governmental agencies, in addition to the Department of State, were involved with Latin America, only a few had establishments in the area.[2] Finally, only those business firms that had the biggest impact on the countries of Latin America and on U.S.–Latin American relations are included. Lists of firms that invested or marketed their products in Latin America are available in several sources.[3]

The references at the end of each entry note whether the subject is listed in the general biographical dictionaries, such as the *Dictionary of American Biography, National Cyclopaedia of American Biography, Appleton Cyclopaedia of American Biography, Notable American Women, Who's Who in America, Who Was Who in America, Current Biography,* and *Contemporary Authors.* The references also attempt to list every book and article written about the subject, but references that appear in the *Dictionary of American Biography* and *Notable American Women* have not been duplicated. Volume and page numbers are provided only for the *National Cyclopaedia of American Biography* because it is not arranged in alphabetical order. Asterisked names and topics indicate that the subject is covered in a separate entry in this volume.

Efforts have been made to include complete and accurate information, but this was not always possible because some information is no longer available and other information could not be located. Unfortunately, mistakes are inevitable in a work of this scope. The author would appreciate receiving corrections and emendations.

Many individuals provided assistance, especially librarians, archivists, and officials of missionary societies. The dictionary would have been far less complete without their help. Special thanks are due to Professor Jack Wiener, who helped with the Spanish- and Portuguese-language sources, and to the staff of the Interlibrary Loan Office of Northern Illinois University, DeKalb, Illinois.

NOTES

1. Sources of additional information on travel accounts include Harold F. Smith, *American Travels Abroad: A Bibliography of Accounts Published before 1900* (Carbondale, Ill., 1969); Thomas L. Welch and Myriam Figueras, comps., *Travel Accounts and Descriptions of Latin American and the Caribbean, 1800–1920: A Selected Bibliography* (Washington, D.C., 1982); Bernard Naylor, *Accounts of Nineteenth-Century South America: An Annotated Checklist of Works by British and United States Observers* (London, 1969); A. Curtis Wilgus, *Latin America in the Nineteenth Century: A Selected Bibliography of Books of Travel and Description Published in English* (Metuchen, N.J., 1973); and G. Cole, *American Travellers to Mexico, 1821–1972: A Descriptive Bibliography* (Troy, N.Y., 1978).

2. A comprehensive list of current governmental agencies involved with Latin America is available in Michael Grow, *Scholars' Guide to Washington, D.C., for Latin American and Caribbean Studies* (Washington, D.C., 1979).

3. Martin H. Sable, *Master Directory for Latin America: Containing Ten Directories Covering Organizations, Associations, and Institutions in the Field of Agriculture, Business-Industry-Finance, Communications, Education-Research, Government, Interna-*

tional Cooperation, Labor-Cooperatives, Publishing and Religion, and Professional, Social and Social Services Organizations and Associations (Los Angeles, Calif., 1965); *Directory of American Firms Operating in Foreign Countries* (New York, 1955/56–   ); "Multinational Investments in Latin America," in Berger Burbach and Patricia Flynn, *Agribusiness in the Americas* (New York, 1980), pp. 253–281; and "U.S. Transnational Corporations and Their Subsidiaries Operating in Central America, 1985," in Tom Barry and Deb Preusch, *The Central American Fact Book* (New York, 1986), pp. 319–348, provide more comprehensive lists.

Abbreviations

AA	*American Anthropologist*
AAAG	*Annals of the Association of American Geographers*
ACAB	*Appleton's Cyclopaedia of American Biography* (New York, 1888– 1901)
AmAntiq	*American Antiquity*
Amherst	*Amherst College Biographical Record* (Amherst, Mass., 1973)
AMWS	*American Men and Women of Science*
AN	*American Neptune*
AndoverTS	*General Catalogue of Andover Theological Seminary* (Boston, 1908)
BAAPG	*Bulletin of the American Association of Petroleum Geologists*
BDABL	*Biographical Dictionary of American Business Leaders*, John H. Ingham (Westport, Conn., 1983)
BDAC	*Biographical Directory of the American Congress 1774–1971* (Washington, D.C., 1971)
BDAE	*Biographical Dictionary of American Educators*, ed. John F. Ohles (Westport, Conn., 1978)
BDC	*Biographical Dictionary of the Confederacy*, Jon L. Wakelyn (Westport, Conn., 1977)
BE	*Brethren Encyclopedia* (Philadelphia, 1983–1984)
BGSA	*Bulletin of the Geological Society of America*
BMNAS	*Biographical Memoirs of the National Academy of Science*
BRDS	*Biographical Register of the Department of State*
CA	*Contemporary Authors* (Detroit, 1962–)
CB	*Current Biography*
CDCWM	*Concise Dictionary of the Christian World Mission*, ed. Stephen Neill et al. (Nashville, Tenn., 1971)
CE	*The Catholic Encyclopedia* (New York, 1967)

Cutolo	*Nuevo Diccionario Biografico Argentino (1750–1930)*, Vicente Osvaldo Cutolo (Buenos Aires, 1968–1985)
DAB	*Dictionary of American Biography* (New York, 1928–)
DACB	*Dictionary of American Catholic Biography*, John J. Delaney (Garden City, N.Y., 1984)
DADH	*Dictionary of American Diplomatic History*, John E. Findling (Westport, Conn., 1980)
DAMB 84	*Dictionary of American Medical Biography*, ed. Martin Kaufman, Stuart Galishoff, and Todd L. Savitt (Westport, Conn., 1984)
DAMIB	*Dictionary of American Military Biography*, ed. Roger J. Spiller (Westport, Conn., 1984)
DANB	*Dictionary of American Negro Biography*, ed. Rayford W. Logan and Michael R. Winston (New York, 1982)
DAS	*Directory of American Scholars*
DCB	*Dictionary of Catholic Biography*, John J. Delaney and James E. Tobin (Garden City, N.Y., 1961)
DH	*Diplomatic History*
DLB	*Dictionary of Literary Biography* (Detroit, 1978–)
Drees	*Americans in Argentina: A Record of Past & Present Activities of Americans in Argentina: Rodney to Riddle*, ed. Charles W. Drees (Buenos Aires, 1922)
DSB	*Dictionary of Scientific Biography* (New York, 1970–1976)
ELA	*Encyclopedia of Latin America*, ed. Helen Delpar (New York, 1974)
EM	*Encyclopaedia of Missions* (New York, 1891–1904)
EMCM	*Encyclopedia of Modern Christian Missions: The Agencies*, ed. Burton L. Goddard (Camden, N.J., 1967)
ESB	*Encyclopedia of Southern Baptists* (Nashville, Tenn., 1958–1982)
EWM	*Encyclopedia of World Methodism* (Nashville, Tenn., 1974)
Figueroa	*Diccionario Biografico de Estranjeros en Chile*, Pedro Pablo Figueroa (Santiago de Chile, 1900)
GR	*Geographical Review*
HAHR	*Hispanic American Historical Review*
Hanrahan	*The Bad Yankees—el Peligro Yankee: American Entrepreneurs and Financiers in Mexico*, Gene Z. Hanrahan (Chapel Hill, N.C., 1985)
Hill	*Emissaries to a Revolution: Woodrow Wilson's Executive Agents in Mexico*, Larry D. Hill (Baton Rouge, La., 1974)
IAB	*Indiana Authors and Their Books*, R. E. Banta and Donald R. Thompson (Bloomington, Ind., 1949–1974)
IAEA	*Inter-American Economic Affairs*
JIAS	*Journal of Inter-American Studies*
JISWA	*Journal of Inter-American Studies and World Affairs*

Langley	*The Banana Wars: An Inner History of American Empire, 1900–1934*, Lester D. Langley (Lexington, Ky., 1983)
LC	*Lutheran Cyclopedia*, rev. ed. (St. Louis, 1975)
Luiggi	*65 Valiants*, Alice H. Luiggi (Gainesville, Fla., 1965)
Manthorne	*Tropical Renaissance: North American Artists Exploring Latin America, 1839–1879*, Katherine E. Manthorne (Washington, D.C., 1989)
MDPC	*Ministerial Directory of the Presbyterian Church, U.S., 1861–1941*, comp. E. C. Scott (Austin, Tex., 1942)
Musicant	*The Banana Wars: A History of United States Military Intervention in Latin America from the Spanish-American War to the Invasion of Panama*, Ivan Musicant (New York, 1990)
NAW	*Notable American Women* (Cambridge, Mass., 1971–1980)
NCAB	*National Cyclopaedia of American Biography* (New York, 1898–)
NYHSD	*New York Historical Society's Dictionary of Artists in America*, George C. Groce and Davis H. Wallace (New York, 1957)
NYT	*New York Times*
OAB	*Ohio Authors and Their Books*, William Coyle, ed. (Cleveland, Ohio, 1962)
PGSA	*Proceedings of the Geological Society of America*
PHR	*Pacific Historical Review*
Pletcher	*Rails, Mines, and Progress: Seven American Promoters in Mexico, 1867–1911*, David M. Pletcher (Ithaca, N.Y., 1958)
PolProf	*Political Profiles*, Nelson Lichtenstein, ed. (New York, 1976–1978)
PrincetonTS	*Biographical Catalogue of the Princeton Theological Seminary 1815–1932* (Princeton, N.J., 1933)
RCHG	*Revista Chileana de Historia y Geografía*
S	*Supplement*
SDAE	*Seventh-Day Adventist Encyclopedia*, rev. ed. (Washington, D.C., 1976)
Simpson	*Discoverers of the Lost World: An Account of Some of Those Who Brought Back to Life South American Mammals Long Buried in the Abyss of Time*, George G. Simpson (New Haven, Conn., 1984)
TA	*The Americas*
Udaondo	*Diccionario Biografico Argentino*, Enrique Udaondo (Buenos Aires, 1938)
USNIP	*United States Naval Institute Proceedings*
Willey	*Portraits in American Archaeology: Remembrances of Some Distinguished Americanists*, Gordon R. Willey (Albuquerque, N.M., 1988)
WSSW	*Who's Who in the South and Southwest*

WWA	*Who's Who in America*
WWAP	*Who's Who in American Politics*
WWAW	*Who's Who among American Women*
WWE	*Who's Who in the East*
WWLA	*Who's Who in Latin America: A Biographical Dictionary of Notable Men and Women of Latin America*, ed. Ronald Hilton (Chicago, 1945–1951)
WWWA	*Who Was Who in America*

Place Names

Current Name	Former Name
American Virgin Islands	Danish West Indies
Argentina	United Provinces of the River Plate
Baja California	Lower California
Belize	British Honduras
Colombia	Gran Colombia
Colombia	Granadian Confederation
Colombia	New Granada
Colombia	United States of Colombia
Dominican Republic	Santo Domingo
Guyana	British Guiana
Puerto Rico	Porto Rico
Suriname	Dutch Guiana

Chronology

1794–1804	Revolution in Saint-Domingue (Haiti)
1799	Toussaint Louverture captured Santo Domingo
1804	Haiti declared its independence
1804–1806	Jean-Jacques Dessalines, emperor of Haiti
1808	Great Britain and United States abolished slave trade; Portuguese court fled to Brazil
1810	Autonomous governments set up in Argentina, Chile, Colombia, and Venezuela
1811–1820	Henri Christophe, king of Haiti
1815	Brazil declared a kingdom
1817	José de San Martin defeated the Spaniards at the Battle of Chacabuco
1818	Chile became independent
1819–1831	Gran Colombia
1820	Expeditionary force commanded by José de San Martin landed on coast near Lima, Peru, to begin final stage of Peruvian liberation
1821	Victory of Simón Bolívar at Carabodo, last major engagement of war in Venezuela; Mexico, Costa Rica, Honduras, Nicaragua, and Santo Domingo became independent
1822	Brazilian Empire declared independent under Pedro I
1822–1823	Agustin de Irubide, emperor of Mexico
1822–1831	Emperor Pedro I of Brazil
1822–1844	Haiti occupied Santo Domingo
1823	Bernardo O'Higgins forced to resign as head of government; slave revolt in British Guiana
1823–1838	Central American Federation
1824	Battle of Ayachucho, Peru, last major engagement in South America; Peru became independent

1825	Revolt of Uruguay against Brazilian rule
1825–1828	War between Argentina and Brazil
1825	Bolivia became independent
1826	Panama Congress
1828	Uruguay became independent
1829–1830	Gran Colombia dissolved
1829	Venezuela became independent
1829–1832, 1835–1852	Juan Manuel de Rosas, dictator of Argentina
1830	Ecuador became independent; death of Simón Bolívar
1832–1837	Francisco de Paula Santander, president of New Granada
1833	British forces seized Falkland Islands
1833–1836, 1841–1844, 1853–1855	Antonio López de Santa Anna, president of Mexico
1836	Texas became independent
1837	"Pastry War" between Mexico and France
1839	Central American Union collapsed
1840–1889	Pedro II, emperor of Brazil
1844	Santo Domingo became independent
1846–1848	U.S.-Mexican War
1849–1852	Narciso López expeditions against Cuba
1855	Panama Railroad completed
1855–1857	William Walker filibustering expedition in Nicaragua
1858–1860	Civil War in Mexico
1858–1872	Benito Juárez, president of Mexico
1862–1868	Bartolomé Mitre, head of the Argentine government
1864–1867	Maximilian, emperor of Mexico
1865	Santo Domingo declared its independence
1865–1870	War of Triple Alliance—Argentina, Brazil and Uruguay against Paraguay
1868	Grito de Lares in Puerto Rico
1868–1874	Domingo Sarmiento, president of Argentina
1868–1878	Ten Years' War in Cuba
1870–1888	Antonio Guzmán Blanco, dictator of Venezuela
1873	*Virginius* affair in Cuba
1876–1880, 1884–1911	Porfirio Díaz, president of Mexico
1879–1883	War of the Pacific—Chile and Bolivia against Peru

1883–1929	Tacna-Arica controversy between Chile and Peru
1887–1899	Venezuela boundary dispute between Venezuela and Great Britain
1895–1898	Second Cuban war of independence
1898	Spanish-American War
1899	Treaty of Paris; Spain ceded Cuba and Puerto Rico to the United States; United Fruit Company formed
1899–1902	U.S. military occupation of Cuba
1900	Puerto Rico became U.S. territory
1902	Republic of Cuba established
1903	Panama became independent
1906–1909	Second U.S. intervention in Cuba
1908–1935	Dictatorship of Juan Vicente Gómez in Venezuela
1911–1920	Mexican revolution
1911–1913	Francisco Madero, president of Mexico
1912–1925	U.S. Marines occupied Nicaragua
1914	Panama Canal opened; Victoriano Huerta, president of Mexico; United States occupied Veracruz, Mexico
1915–1921	Venustiano Carranza, president of Mexico
1915–1934	U.S. Marines occupied Haiti
1916	U.S. punitive expedition into Mexico
1916–1922, 1928–1930	Hipolito Irigoyen, first popularly elected president of Argentina
1916–1924	U.S. Marines occupied the Dominican Republic
1917	Danish Antilles sold to the United States
1919–1930	Augusto Leguía, president of Peru
1920–1924, 1932–1938	Arturo Alessandri Palma, president of Chile
1921–1924	Alvaro Obregón, president of Mexico
1923	Adolfo de la Huerto revolt in Mexico
1925–1933	Gerardo Machado y Morales, president of Cuba
1926–1933	U.S. Marines occupied Nicaragua
1928–1933	Agustino Sandino insurrection in Nicaragua
1929	Settlement of the Tacna-Arica question; Gonzalo Escobar insurrection in Mexico
1930–1945	Getulio Vargas, president of Brazil
1930–1961	Rafael Leonides Trujillo, dictator of the Dominican Republic
1932–1934	Leticia dispute between Ecuador and Peru
1932–1935	Chaco War between Bolivia and Paraguay
1933	United States initiated the "Good Neighbor Policy"

1933–1959	Fulgencio Batista, dictator of Cuba
1934–1940	Lázaro Cárdenas, president of Mexico
1937–1956	Anastasio Somoza, dictator of Nicaragua
1946–1955	Juan D. Perón, president of Argentina
1948	Puerto Rico elected its first Puerto Rican governor
1952	Bolivian revolution
1954	Guatemalan crisis
1957–1971	Francois "Papa Doc" Duvalier, dictator of Haiti
1959	Fidel Castro triumphed in Cuba
1961	Rafael Trujillo assassinated in the Dominican Republic; Bay of Pigs invasion of Cuba
1962	Jamaica and Trinidad and Tobago became independent; Cuban missile crisis
1964	Riots in Panama
1965	United States invaded the Dominican Republic
1966	Barbados and British Guiana became independent
1966–1983	Military rule in Argentina
1967–1979	Anastasio Somoza Debayle, dictator of Nicaragua
1968–1981	Colonel Omar Torrijos, dictator of Panama
1969	"Futbol war" between Honduras and El Salvador
1970–1973	Salvador Allende, president of Chile
1971–1986	Jean Claude "Baby Doc" Duvalier, dictator of Haiti
1973	Bahamas became independent; coup d'état in Chile
1973–1989	General Augusto Pinochet, dictator of Chile
1974	Grenada became independent
1977	Panama Canal treaties signed; St. Lucia became independent
1978	Panama Canal treaties ratified; Dominica became independent
1979	St. Vincent and the Grenadines became independent; popular resistance led by the Sandinista National Liberation Army forced Anastasio Somoza out of power in Nicaragua
1980	*Mariel* boat lift from Cuba to the United States
1981	Antigua and Barbuda and Belize became independent
1982	Falkland Islands War between Argentina and Great Britain
1983	St. Kitts–Nevis became independent; United States invaded Grenada; Argentina returned to civilian rule
1983–1989	Colonel Manuel Noriega, de facto ruler of Panama
1986	Jean Claude Duvalier overthrown in Haiti
1989	United States invaded Panama
1990	Sandinistas defeated in general election in Nicaragua

Introduction

Contacts between the British colonies of North America and the Latin American colonies of the several European powers were established in the eighteenth century mainly through trade with Latin American ports carried out by American merchants, in spite of various regulations barring such activities. Trade increased greatly after the establishment of the United States, which soon began sending consuls to these ports to aid and protect U.S. traders, ships, and sailors. When the Latin American colonies began their struggle for independence from Spain, the United States looked favorably on the establishment of independent nations in Latin America, and Americans joined the struggle and fought in the revolutionary armies. Between 1822 and 1825, the United States recognized the independence of Colombia; United Provinces of La Plata; Mexico; Chile; Brazil; the Central American Federation; and Peru. The Monroe Doctrine of 1823 was a significant milestone in U.S. relations with Latin America which stated that the United States would oppose any attempts by European powers to help Spain regain its lost colonies and restore colonial rule in Latin America. U.S. expansionist policies and its attempts to establish economic and military hegemony in the Caribbean led to several conflicts with Latin American countries, particularly the War with Mexico in 1846–1848, to various filibustering expeditions to Cuba and Central America, and to unsuccessful attempts to annex Cuba and the Dominican Republic. The 1850s also began a long period of U.S. involvement in exploring and developing land and water routes across the isthmuses of Central America. The period began in 1846, when the United States secured from New Granada the right to transit across the Isthmus of Panama, followed by the building of the Panama Railroad, and culminated in the construction of the Panama Canal, which was completed in 1914.

During the period following the Civil War, U.S. entrepreneurs began to function in Latin America and to invest in various enterprises. They built railroads and developed silver and copper mines, utilities, and sugar and banana plantations, initially in Mexico, Central America, and the Caribbean (particularly in Cuba), and later in other parts of Latin America. They worked to secure markets for U.S. products and to foster trade between the United States and the countries of Latin America. In the twentieth century, economic relations were greatly expanded, and many U.S. corporations became involved in large-scale investments in Latin America and in developing various new resources, such as petroleum, aluminum, and rubber.

The Spanish-American War established the United States as the most important political power in the American hemisphere. The Roosevelt Corollary declared the right of the United States to intervene in the affairs of Latin American countries that were unable to govern themselves, trying to eliminate political disorder and financial mismanagement in these countries and preventing the possibility of intervention of European governments. The United States played an increasingly decisive role in the Caribbean and Central America. It acquired Puerto Rico, the Panama Canal Zone, and the American Virgin Islands, exercised a protectorate over Cuba, and began to use military as well as economic power to implement its policies. Between 1900 and 1950, the United States invaded or occupied countries within the Caribbean Basin seventeen times, including Cuba, Honduras, Panama, Nicaragua, Haiti, and the Dominican Republic. It also became involved in various activities during the Mexican revolution.

In the 1930s, the United States adopted the "Good Neighbor Policy," which repudiated intervention and adopted a new approach to Latin America, moving away from unilateral actions by the United States to collective action by all the nations of Latin America. The United States, however, supported a military coup in Guatemala in 1954, intervened in Cuba in 1961 and in the Dominican Republic in 1965, supported a military coup in Chile in 1973 and military activities in Nicaragua during the 1980s, and intervened in Grenada in 1983 and in Panama in 1989.

The Good Neighbor Policy led to closer and more friendly relationships between the United States and the Latin American countries. As a result, most Latin American countries gave the United States valuable aid during World War II. In the period following the war, however, U.S. concern with the communist threat diminished the importance of Latin America. While the inter-American system was strengthened, the Organization of American States was created, and the United States provided technical aid and military assistance to Latin American countries, little economic aid was offered. Relations also worsened when some Latin American countries began to nationalize and expropriate the holdings of U.S. corporations. The Alliance for Progress, established by the U.S. government in 1961, involved a program to vitalize the social and economic development of Latin American countries but became moribund in 1969. In later years, with few exceptions, the United States accorded its relations with Latin American countries a low priority.

A

ACCESSORY TRANSIT COMPANY. The American Atlantic and Pacific Ship Canal Company* (formed in 1849 and controlled by Commodore Cornelius Vanderbilt) received a charter from the Nicaraguan government in 1851 with exclusive right to transport passengers and cargo across the isthmus of Nicaragua. It operated as the Accessory Transit Company until 1855. Following William Walker's confiscation of the company's property, Vanderbilt closed the firm in 1856. *References*: *DADH*; and David I. Folkman, Jr., *The Nicaragua Route* (Salt Lake City, Utah, 1972).

ADAMS, CHARLES BAKER (1814–1853). Naturalist, born January 11, 1814, in Dorchester, Massachusetts. Adams graduated from Amherst College and attended Andover Theological Seminary. He was a tutor and lecturer in geology at Amherst College in 1837, professor of chemistry and natural history at Middlebury (Vt.) College from 1838 to 1847, state geologist of Vermont from 1845 to 1848, and professor of astronomy and zoology at Amherst College from 1847 until his death. He was in Jamaica in 1843–1844 and 1848–1849 and made collecting trips to Panama in 1849–1850 and to St. Thomas, Virgin Islands, in 1852–1853. He wrote *Catalogue of Shells Collected at Panama with Notes on Their Synonymy, Station, and Geographical Distribution* (New York, 1852). Died January 18, 1853, in St. Thomas, Virgin Islands. *References*: *ACAB; DAB; NCAB* 5:311; and *WWWA*.

AGASSIZ, JEAN LOUIS RUDOLPHE (1807–1873). Naturalist, born May 28, 1807, in Môtier-en-Vuly, Switzerland. Agassiz attended the universities of Zurich and Heidelberg, and graduated from the universities of Munich and Erlangen. He was professor at the University of Neuchâtel (Switzerland) from 1832 to 1846. He came to the United States in 1846 and was professor of natural science at the Lawrence Scientific School of Harvard University from 1848. In 1859, he founded the Museum of Comparative Zoology at Harvard University. He led the Thayer expedition to Brazil in 1865–1866. In 1873, he led an expedition through the Strait of Magellan. Died December 14, 1873, in Cambridge, Massachusetts. His wife, **ELIZABETH CABOT CARY AGASSIZ** (1822–1907), accompanied her husband on the Thayer expedition to Brazil, and they both wrote *A Journey in Brazil* (Boston, 1867). *References*: Louis Agassiz Papers, Houghton Library, Harvard University, Cambridge, Mass.; *DAB*; *DSB*; Edward Lurie, *Louis Agassiz: A Life of Science* (Chicago, 1960); Edward Lurie, *Nature and the American Mind: Louis Agassiz and the Culture of Science* (New York, 1974); *NAW*; Louise H. Tharp, *Adventurous Alliance: The Story of the Agassiz Family of Boston* (Boston, 1959); and A. Curtis Wilgus, "Nineteenth Century Travelers: Louis and Elizabeth Agassiz," *Americas* 24 (February 1972): 25–32.

ALCOA. Organized as the Pittsburgh Reduction Company, and later renamed the Aluminum Company of America, it began production in 1888. As early as 1912, it acquired bauxite deposits in British Guiana. During World War I, it increased its bauxite holdings in British Guiana and made investments for the first time in Dutch Guiana. By 1925, it secured virtual monopoly control over available bauxite deposits in the British and Dutch Guianas. *References*: Charles C. Carr, *Alcoa: An American Enterprise* (New York, 1952); Charles W. Parry, *Alcoa, a Retrospection* (New York, 1985); and George D. Smith, *From Monopoly to Competition: The Transformations of Alcoa, 1888–1986* (New York, 1988).

ALL AMERICA CABLES, INC. Began as the Mexican Cable Company (later Mexico Telegraph Company), established in 1878, and Central and South American Cable Company (later Central and South American Telegraph Company), established in 1879. The name of Central and South American Telegraph Company was changed in 1920 to All America Cables, Incorporated. It was acquired by the International Telephone and Telegraph Company (I.T.T.) in 1927. Mexico Telegraph Company was sold to Western Union Telegraph Company in 1927. *Reference*: All America Cables, Inc., *A Half Century of Cable Service to the Three Americas* (New York, 1928).

ALLEN, CHARLES H(ERBERT) (1848–1934). Banker, born April 15, 1848, in Lowell, Massachusetts. Allen graduated from Amherst College. He was engaged in the manufacture of wooden boxes and in the lumber business in Lowell, Massachusetts. He was a member of the Massachusetts House of Representatives in 1881–1882 and the Massachusetts Senate in 1883, member of the U.S. House of Representatives from 1885 to 1889, Massachusetts prison commissioner in 1897–1898, and assistant secretary of the navy from 1898 to 1900. He was the first civil governor of Puerto Rico from 1900 to 1902. He was later vice president of the Morton Trust Company and of the Guaranty Trust Company of New York, and president of the American Sugar Refining Company. Died April 20, 1934, in Lowell, Massachusetts. *References*: *BDAC*; and *WWWA*.

ALLEN, HEMAN (1779–1852). Public official and diplomat, born February 23, 1779, in Poultney, Vermont. Allen graduated from Dartmouth College, studied law, and was admitted to the bar in 1801. He practiced law in Colchester, Vermont, was chief justice of Chittenden County court from 1811 to 1814, and served in the state house of representatives from 1812 to 1817 and in the U.S. House of Representatives in 1817–1818. He was U.S. marshal for the district of Vermont from 1818 to 1823. He was the first U.S. minister to Chile from 1823 to 1827 and established the American presence in Chile. He was president of the Burlington branch of the Bank of the United States from 1830 to 1836, and then practiced law again in Highgate, Franklin County, Vermont. Died April 7, 1852, in Highgate, Vermont. *References*: *BDAC; DAB;* and Myra Himelhoch, "Herman Allen's Mission to Chile, 1823–1827," *Vermont History* 42 (1974): 55–69.

ALLEN, HENRY WATKINS (1820–1866). Army officer, born April 29, 1820, in Prince Edward County, Virginia, and grew up in Kay (later Lafayette) County, Missouri. Allen attended Marion College (Ely, Mo.). He was a teacher in Grand Gulf, Mississippi; joined the Texas Army in 1842; and established a plantation in Claiborne County, Mississippi, and later in Tensas Parish, Louisiana, and then West Baton Rouge. He served in the Louisiana legislature. He served in the Confederate Army during the Civil War and was governor of Louisiana from 1863 to 1865. He went to Mexico in 1865, where he established and edited the Mexican *Times*, an English-language newspaper in Mexico City, which was subsidized by the government of the Emperor Maximilian. Died April 22, 1866, in Mexico City. *References*: *ACAB*; Vincent H. Cassidy and Amos E. Simpson, *Henry Watkins Allen of Louisiana* (Baton Rouge, La., 1964); *DAB; NCAB* 10:78; and *WWWA*.

ALLEN, JAMES (1824– ?). Balloonist, born September 11, 1824, in Bristol, Rhode Island, and grew up in Providence, Rhode Island. He worked in cotton mills, was a farm laborer and merchant seaman, and became involved in the printing trade from 1841 to 1846 and then in the jewelry business. He made his first ascension in a balloon in 1857 and made public ascents and exhibitions in most New England states from 1857 to 1861. He attempted to introduce balloons in the Union Army in 1861 but failed because of inferior equipment. With his brother **EZRA S. ALLEN**, he joined Thaddeus S. C. Lowe's balloon corps in 1862 and served until 1863. In 1867, he was appointed captain of engineers in the Brazilian Army (and Ezra was appointed assistant aeronaut). He served as a balloonist in the Paraguayan War in 1867. He made his first ascent in that war on June 24, 1867, collecting topographical information. *Reference*: F. Stainsbury Hayden, "Documents Relating to the First Military Balloon Corps Organized in South America: The Aeronautic Corps of the Brazilian Army, 1867–1868," *HAHR* 19 (1939): 504–17.

ALLIANCE FOR PROGRESS. A program to vitalize the social and economic development of Latin America, initiated in 1961 by President John F. Kennedy. Its goals were to strengthen economic institutions, accelerate economic and social development, provide decent homes for the Latin American people, encourage agrarian reform programs, ensure fair wages and satisfactory working conditions for all workers, wipe out illiteracy, reform tax laws, stimulate private enterprise in order to encourage economic development, and accelerate the economic integration of Latin America. The results of the alliance were disappointing, and there was a growing belief that its various goals might have been incompatible. By 1970, the enthusiasm for the alliance had waned in both the United States and Latin America. *References*: *DADH*; *ELA*; Joan M. C. Grace, "The Alliance for Progress: A Means to What End?" Ph.D. diss., Arizona State University, 1980; Jerome Levinson and Juan de Onis, *The Alliance That Lost Its Way: A Critical Report on the Alliance for Progress* (Chicago, 1970); Harvey Perloff, *Alliance for Progress: A Social Intervention in the Making* (Baltimore, 1969); William D. Rogers, *The Twilight Struggle: The Alliance for Progress and the Politics of Development* (New York, 1967); and L. Ronald Scheman, ed., *The Alliance for Progress: A Retrospective* (New York, 1988).

ALSOP AND COMPANY. Established in Valparaiso, Chile, in 1824, and in Lima, Peru, in 1828, the company dealt in guano, hides, and minerals. It lost its substantial holdings in Bolivian mining when the Chileans occupied the Bolivian silver mines in Caracoles in 1879. The company made claims against Peru, Bolivia, and Chile. While Bolivia and Peru settled with the company, the dispute with Chile was only settled through arbitration in 1912. *Reference*: U.S. and Chilean Claims Commission, *The Alsop Claim* (Washington, D.C., 1910).

ALUMINUM COMPANY OF AMERICA. *See* ALCOA

AMERICAN AND FOREIGN POWER COMPANY. Organized in 1923 by Electric Bond and Share Company, a subsidiary of General Electric Company, to acquire utilities in Latin America. It obtained properties in Panama, Guatemala, and Cuba (acquired previously by Electric Bond and Share) and then expanded. It began major property acquisitions in Ecuador in 1925; in Colombia, Brazil, and Venezuela in 1927; in Costa Rica, Chile, and Mexico in 1928; and in Argentina in 1929. Conflicts between the company and host governments were numerous. Expropriations of its properties began in Colombia in 1947, and its subsidiaries were expropriated in Argentina in 1958, in Brazil in 1959 and 1962, in Cuba in 1960, and in Mexico in 1962.

AMERICAN ATLANTIC AND PACIFIC SHIP CANAL COMPANY. Formed in 1849 by Commodore Cornelius Vanderbilt, it received from the Nicaraguan government a contract for a canal. In 1851, it paved a macadam road and established a carriage-steamboat route across Nicaragua. Its rights were transferred to the Accessory Transit Company* in 1851. *References*: *DADH*; and David I. Folkman, Jr., *The Nicaragua Route* (Salt Lake City, Utah, 1972).

AMERICAN BAPTIST HOME MISSION SOCIETY: DIVISION OF LATIN AMERICA. Founded in 1832, it began missionary work in Mexico in 1870, in Cuba and Puerto Rico in 1899, in El Salvador in 1911, in Nicaragua in 1917, and in Haiti in 1923. It later became the International Ministries of the American Baptist Churches in the U.S.A. *References*: American Baptist Home Mission Society Archives, American Baptist Historical Society, Rochester, N.Y.; George Pitt Beers, *Ministry to Turbulent America: A History of the American Baptist Home Mission Society, Covering the Fifth Quarter Century, 1932–1957* (Philadelphia, 1957); Alejandro Treviño, *Historia de los Trabajos Bautistas en Mexico* (El Paso, Tex., 1939); and Charles C. White, *A Century of Faith* (Philadelphia, 1932).

AMERICAN BIBLE SOCIETY. A nondenominational, specialized agency, founded in 1816 to translate, produce, publish, and distribute the Bible and to prepare literacy materials for religious and secular use. Spanish Bibles were supplied in 1820 to an American businessman going to Trinidad and Chile. The first overseas agent for Latin America was appointed in 1833. Over the years, agencies were set up in various areas in Latin America. *References*: American Bible Society Archives, New York City; Henry O. Dwight, *The Centennial History of the American Bible Society* (New York, 1916); *EMCM*; John M. Gibson, *Soldiers of the Word: The Story of the American Bible Society* (New York, 1958); and Creighton Lacy, *The Word-Carrying Giant: The Growth of the American Bible Society (1816–1966)* (Pasadena, Calif., 1977).

AMERICAN CHICLE COMPANY. Formed in 1899 in a consolidation of six companies, it later expanded and absorbed additional firms. It owned the American Chicle Company of Mexico and a large interest in the Chicle Development Company which controlled, through concessions from the governments of Guatemala, Mexico, and British Honduras, over five million acres of chicle producing lands. In 1962, it merged with Warner-Lambert Pharmaceutical.

AMERICAN INSTITUTE FOR FREE LABOR DEVELOPMENT(AIFLD). Organized by the AFL-CIO in 1962 to develop support for U.S.-style trade unionism, increase U.S. presence in Latin America, and combat communist influence in Latin American trade unions, by conducting training programs for trade union leadership, providing technical advice, and supporting social development projects. *References*: American Institute for Free Labor Development, *Twenty-Five Years of Solidarity with Latin American Workers* (Washington, D.C., 1987); Gerald M. Greenfield and Sheldon L. Markam, eds., *Latin American Labor Organizations* (New York, 1987); Jack Scott, *Yankee Unions, Go Home: How the AFL Helped the U.S. Build an Empire in Latin America* (Vancouver, 1978), ch. 17; and Al Weinrub and William Bollinger, *The AFL-CIO in Central America: A Look at the American Institute for Free Labor Development* (Oakland, Calif., 1987).

AMERICAN LEGION OF HONOR. A corps of former U.S. soldiers who went in various contingents to Mexico in 1866–1867, where their officers were commissioned by President Benito Juárez. There were more than one hundred officers, commanded by Colonel George Mason Green.* The legion participated in the battle of Zacatecas and in the siege of Querétaro and Mexico City in 1867. The legion officers were present at the surrender and execution of Emperor Maximilian. Most of the legionnaires returned to the United States in 1868. *References*: Robert R. Miller, "The American Legion of Honor in Mexico," *PHR* 30 (1961): 229–41; and Robert R. Miller, *Arms across the Border: United States Aid to Juares during the French Intervention in Mexico* (Philadelphia, 1963), ch. 6.

AMERICAN SMELTING AND REFINING COMPANY (ASARCO). Incorporated in 1899, it acquired in 1901 the Mexican smelters of the Guggenheim Brothers, who then gained control of the company. It established the Northern Peru Mining and Smelting Company in 1921 and organized the Southern Peru Copper Company in 1953. It sold a majority interest in its Mexican properties to local investors in 1965. Its name was changed in 1975 to the acronym Asarco. *Reference*: Isaac Marcossen, *Metal Magic: The Story of American Smelting and Refining Company* (New York, 1949).

AMMEN, DANIEL (1820–1898). Naval officer, born May 15, 1820, in Brown County, Ohio. Ammen was appointed midshipman in the U.S. Navy in 1836. He was second in command of the expedition to explore and study the Rio de la Plata and its tributaries from 1853 to 1856. He served in the Union Navy during the Civil War. He was chief of the Bureau of Yards and Docks from 1869 to 1871 and of the Bureau of Navigation from 1871 to 1878. He was secretary of the Isthmian Canal Company from 1872 to 1876, and an active proponent of an isthmian canal through Nicaragua, and wrote *The American Interoceanic Ship Canal Question* (Philadelphia, 1880), *The Errors and Fallacies of the Interoceanic Canal Question* (New York, 1886), and *The Old Navy and the New* (Philadelphia, 1891). He retired with the rank of rear admiral in 1878. Died July 11, 1898, near Washington, D.C. *References*: *ACAB*; *DACB*; and *NCAB* 4:393.

ANACONDA COPPER COMPANY. Founded in 1882, it was later renamed Anaconda Company. It purchased the Chile Copper Company from the Guggenheims in 1923 and later expanded its Chilean copper operations. Its mine at Chuquicamata in northern Chile was the most productive copper mine in the world. Its copper mines in Chile were nationalized by the Chilean government in 1971. It was sold in 1977 to the Atlantic Richfield Oil Company. *References*: E. N. Baklanoff, "The Expropriation of Anaconda in Chile: A Perspective on an Export Enclave," *SECOLAS* 4 (March 1973): 16–38; Norman Girvan, *Copper in Chile: A Study in Conflict between Corporate and National Economy* (Kingston, Jamaica, 1972); Isaac Marcosson, *Anaconda* (New York, 1957); Thomas O'Hanlon, "The Perilous Prosperity of Anaconda," *Fortune* 73 (May 1966): 117–21, 235–36; and A. B. Parsons, *The Porphyry Coppers* (New York, 1933), ch. 15.

ANDERSON, RICHARD CLOUGH (1788–1826). Diplomat, born August 4, 1788, in Louisville, Kentucky. Anderson graduated from William and Mary College and studied law. He practiced law in Louisville and served in the state house of representatives in 1812, 1814, and 1815, in the U.S. House of Representatives from 1817 to 1821, and again in the state house of representatives in 1821 and 1822. He was U.S. minister to Colombia from 1823 until his death. In 1824, he negotiated the first treaty the United States ever made with a South American republic. He was appointed in 1826 as one of the American delegates to the Panama Congress. Died July 24, 1826, in Turbaco, Colombia, on his way to Cartagena. *References*: Richard Clough Anderson, *Diary and Journal, 1814–1826*, ed. Alfred Tischendorf and E. Taylor Parks (Durham, N.C., 1964); E. Taylor Parks and Alfred Tischendorf, "Cartagena to Bogota, 1825–1826: The Diary of Richard Clough Anderson, Jr.," *HAHR* 42 (1962): 217–30; *DAB; DADH; NCAB* 6:115; and *WWWA*.

ANDERSON, WILLIAM MARSHALL (1807–1881). Surveyor, born June 24, 1807, near Louisville, Kentucky. Anderson attended Transylvania University (Lexington), studied law, and was admitted to the bar in 1832. In 1834–1835, he made a journey to the Rocky Mountains, joining a fur-trading party. He lived in Chillicothe, Ohio, from 1835 to 1853, practicing law, surveying and managing two farms, and, after 1853, in Circleville, Ohio. He went to Mexico in 1865–1866, ostensibly on a visit to the archaeological ruins of southern Mexico, but spent some time assisting in the establishment of a Confederate colony in Carlota* and was commissioned by Emperor Maximilian to survey lands in northwestern Mexico for possible colonization by the Confederates. Died January 7, 1881, in Circleville, Ohio. *References*: *An American in Maximilian's Mexico, 1865–1866: The Diaries of William Marshall Anderson*, ed. Ramon E. Ruiz (San Marino, Calif., 1959); and Dale L. Morgan and Eleanor T. Harris, "Biography of William Marshall Anderson," in *The Rocky Mountain Journals of William Marshall Anderson: The West in 1834*, ed. Dale L. Morgan and Eleanor T. Harris (San Marino, Calif., 1967), pp. 45–66.

ANDREWS, CHRISTOPHER COLUMBUS (1829–1922). Lawyer and diplomat, born October 27, 1829, in Ipswich, Massachusetts. Andrews studied law at Harvard Law School and was admitted to the bar in 1850. He practiced law in Newton, Massachusetts, and Boston. He was a clerk in the Treasury Department in Washington, D.C., in 1855–1856; practiced law in St. Cloud, Minnesota, after 1857; and was a member of the state senate in 1859–1860. He served in the Union Army during the Civil War. He was U.S. minister to Sweden and Norway from 1869 to 1877 and consul general in Rio de Janeiro from 1882 to 1885. He wrote *Brazil: Its Conditions and Prospects* (New York, 1887). He was chief warden and forest commissioner of Minnesota from 1895 to 1911 and secretary of the state forestry board from 1911 until his death. Died September 21, 1922, in St. Paul, Minnesota. His autobiography, *Christopher C. Andrews, Pioneer in Forestry Conservation in the United States; for Sixty Years a Dominant Influence in the Public Affairs of Minnesota: Lawyer: Editor: Diplomat: General in the Civil War: Recollections: 1820–1922*, ed. Alice E. Andrews (Cleveland, 1928) was published posthumously. *References*: C. C. Andrews Papers, Minnesota Historical Society, St. Paul, Minn.; *ACAB; DAB;* H. H. Kalso, "Christopher C. Andrews," Ph.D. diss., University of Minnesota, 1954; *NCAB* 11:393; and *WWWA*.

ANDREWS, E(DWARD) WYLLYS, IV (1916–1971). Archaeologist, born December 11, 1916, in Chicago. Andrews attended the University of Chicago and graduated from Harvard University. He carried out archaeological reconnaissance in southwestern Campeche for Carnegie Institution and in Mérida, Mexico, in 1941. He served in the Office of Strategic Services during World War II and later in the Central Intelligence Agency. He farmed near Woodstock, Maryland, and then moved to Mérida and carried out fieldwork in Dzibilchaltun in 1956–1957. He was research associate of the Middle American Research Institute of Tulane University and then director of the program of research on the Yucatán Peninsula for the institute. Died July 3, 1971, in New Orleans. *Reference*: *AmAntiq* 37 (1972): 394–403.

ANDREWS, R(AYMA) L(AURENCE) ("ANDY") (1889–   ). Aviator, born October 31, 1889, in Geneva, Indiana. Andrews taught himself to fly in 1910. In 1911, he went on an airplane-selling junket to South America, and in Ecuador demonstrated the airplane's military potential by dropping explosives from the Curtiss biplane. He had a long association with combat aviation as well as with military leaders in Mexico and Latin America. He served with the British Royal Air Force during World War I and with the U.S. Army Air Corps after 1923. He was commander of the Mexican Air Force in 1924, and again commanded the Mexican federal air force detachment, under contract to the Mexican government, during the revolution in 1929. *References*: R. L. Andrews Oral History, East Texas State University Library, Commerce, Tex.; and Jessie Peterson and Thelma Cox Knoles, eds., *Pancho Villa: Intimate Recollections by People Who Knew Him* (New York, 1977), pp. 242–48.

ANGEL, JAMES CRAWFORD ("JIMMIE") (1899–1956). Aviator, born in Springfield, Missouri. Angel ran away from home in 1913, and learned to fly in 1914. He served in the British Royal Flying Corps and then in the U.S. Army

Air Force during World War I. After the war, he flew in Mexico, barnstormed in the United States, and did stunt flying for Hollywood movies. He spent much of later life flying in South America. He flew to the Venezuela jungle in 1926, returned to Venezuela in 1933, and discovered Angel Falls—the world's highest waterfall—in southeastern Venezuela. He later flew missions for oil and mining companies and for Latin American governments. He returned to the United States in 1954. Died December 8, 1956, in Balboa, Panama Canal Zone. *References*: John R. Holl, "Angel on Silver Wings," *Americas* 32 (August 1980): 53–57; and *NYT*, December 9, 1956.

ARCHER, WILLLIAM ANDREW (1894–1973). Botanist, born in Torreon, Mexico, to American parents, and grew up in New Mexico. Archer graduated from New Mexico State College and the University of Michigan. He served in the U.S. Army during World War I. He was a botanist in the Division of Plant Exploration and Introduction of the U.S. Department of Agriculture in Beltsville, Maryland, and a botanist in the Office of Foreign Agriculture Relations, stationed in the Brazilian Research Institute in Belém, Brazil. He was a plant taxonomist and curator in the National Arboretum; organized a botanical laboratory and initiated a botanical garden and herbarium in Medellín, Colombia, from 1929 to 1931; and organized and directed the Indian drug plant project in Nevada from 1937 to 1942. He explored Latin America in search of insecticidal plants, wild and cultivated peanuts, tobacco varieties, vegetables, and ornamentals. He retired in 1964. Died May 7, 1973, in Washington, D.C. *Reference*: *Taxon* 23 (1974): 755–58.

ARMOUR, NORMAN (1887–1982). Diplomat, born October 14, 1887, in Brighton, England. Armour graduated from Princeton and Harvard universities and was admitted to the bar in 1914. He entered the foreign service in 1915 and served in Paris, St. Petersburg, Brussels, the Hague, and Montevideo until 1921. He was first secretary in Italy in 1924–1925 and counselor of embassy in Japan from 1925 to 1928 and in France from 1928 to 1932. He was U.S. minister to Haiti from 1932 to 1935, negotiating the agreements under which U.S. occupation forces were withdrawn. He was minister to Canada from 1935 to 1938, ambassador to Chile in 1938–1939, and ambassador to Argentina from 1939 to 1945. He was involved in the efforts to bring Argentina into World War II on the side of the Allies. He was ambassador to Spain from 1944 to 1946, assistant secretary of state in 1947–1948, ambassador to Venezuela in 1950–1951, and ambassador to Guatemala in 1954–1955. He retired in 1955. Died September 27, 1982, in New York City. *References*: *CA; CB* 1945; *DADH; NYT*, September 29, 1982; *PolProf: Eisenhower; PolProf: Truman; NCAB* G:178; and *WWWA*.

ARMSTRONG, CLARA (JEANETTE) (1847–1917). Educator, born January 22, 1847, in West Alden, near Buffalo, New York. Armstrong graduated from Normal School (Oswego, N.Y.). She was a teacher at Fredonia, New York,

Haddonfield, New Jersey, and Winona, Minnesota; principal of high school in Buffalo; and head of teachers training school in Indianapolis. She taught in Argentina from 1877 until 1896. She was the first woman to found a normal school in South America and served as the first director of the Escuela Normal de Maestra de Catamarca in Catamarca (later named Escuela Normal de Clara J. Armstrong) from 1878 until 1888. In 1888–1889, she helped her sister **FRANCES ARMSTRONG** (1860–1928) set up a normal school at San Nicolás de los Arroyos and later founded a private school in Buenos Aires. She opened a Cuban annex to the normal school in New Paltz, New York, from 1901 to 1905, and was principal of a high school for girls in Los Angeles after 1905. Died September 13, 1917, in Los Angeles. *References*: *Cutolo; Luiggi*; and *Udaondo*.

ARNOLD, RALPH (1875–1961). Petroleum geologist, born April 14, 1875, in Marshalltown, Iowa, and grew up in Pasadena, California. Arnold graduated from Stanford University. He was a field assistant with the U.S. Geological Survey from 1900 to 1903, paleontologist from 1903 to 1908, and geologist in 1908–1909. He also organized the Petroleum Branch of the U.S. Bureau of Mines. From 1911 to 1916, he organized and was director of an economic survey of the oil resources of Trinidad and Venezuela for the Caribbean Petroleum Company, a subsidiary of General Asphalt Company. He later described this job (along with George A. Macready* and Thomas W. Barrington) in *The First Big Oil Hunt—Venezuela, 1911–1916* (New York, 1960). He was a member of the U.S. Income and Excess Profits Tax Board in 1918. He helped organize the Snowolone Oil Company in 1923 and was its vice president until his death. Died April 30, 1961, in Santa Barbara, California. *References*: *BAAPG* 45 (1961): 1897–1900; and *WWWA*.

ASHFORD, BAILEY KELLY (1873–1934). Physician, born September 18, 1873, in Washington, D.C. Ashford graduated from Georgetown University. He entered the medical service of the U.S. Army in 1897. He served in the Spanish-American War in Puerto Rico. He began the investigation of the prevalent disease of tropical anemia among agricultural laborers in the coffee and sugar plantations which resulted in the discovery that the disease was caused by an intestinal infestation by a worm. He was instrumental in the creation of the Puerto Rico Anemia Commission, of which he was a member, and which carried on an extended field campaign in which 300,000 persons were treated. He served in the San Juan military garrison and later participated in the organization of the Institute of Tropical Medicine and Hygiene, and he remained devoted to this institution for the rest of his life. He also practiced medicine in San Juan. When Columbia University took control of the institution in 1926, he became professor of mycology and tropical medicine. He was also head of the medical service of the University Hospital in San Juan. He served as surgeon in the American Expeditionary Force in France during World War I. He wrote *A Soldier in*

Science: The Autobiography of Bailey K. Ashford (New York, 1934). Died November 1, 1934, in San Juan, Puerto Rico. *References: DAB S1; DAMB 84; NYT*, November 2, 1934; and *WWWA*.

ASHMEAD, PERCY [PERCIVAL] H(ERBERT) (1867–1919). Engineer, born in Philadelphia. Ashmead attended Lehigh University (Pa.). He planned railroads for the Chinese government and was in charge of the construction of railroads in the Philippines. He was chief engineer of the Madeira-Mamoré Railway from 1908 to 1910. He was chief engineer of J. G. White and Company of New York City. He served in the Corps of Engineers during World War I. He was head of the Costa Rica-Nicaragua boundary dispute arbitration commission in 1919 and made a survey of that area. Died November 11, 1919, in New York City. *Reference: NYT*, November 12, 1919.

ASSEMBLIES OF GOD, GENERAL COUNCIL: FOREIGN MISSIONS DEPARTMENT. Officially organized in 1914, but missionaries had already gone to Argentina in 1909 and to Brazil in 1911. Missionaries were sent to Chile in 1916, to Puerto Rico in 1918, to Peru in 1919, to Cuba in 1920, to Mexico in 1921, to Nicaragua in 1926, to El Salvador in 1929, to Colombia in 1932, to the Dominican Republic in 1933, to Guatemala and Jamaica in 1937, to Honduras in 1939, to Costa Rica in 1942, to Uruguay in 1944, to Paraguay and Haiti in 1945, to British Honduras in 1946, to Guyana in 1953, and also to the Bahamas. The department was later renamed the Division of Foreign Missions. *References*: Assemblies of God Archives, Springfield, Mo.; Joyce W. Booze, *Into All the World: A History of Assemblies of God Foreign Missions* (Springfield, Mo., 1980); *EMCM*; Cristobal Ramirez, *Les Asambleas de Dios en El Salvador* (Santa Ana, 1971); and Elizabeth A. G. Wilson, *Making Many Rich* (Springfield, Mo., 1955).

ASSOCIATE REFORMED PRESBYTERIAN CHURCH, GENERAL SYNOD: BOARD OF FOREIGN MISSIONS. Organized in 1839, it began missionary work in Mexico in 1878. *References*: W. A. Kennedy, ed., *The Sesquicentennial History of the Associate Reformed Presbyterian Church, 1905–1951* (Clinton, S.C., 1951); James E. Mitchell, *The Emergence of a Mexican Church: The Associate Reformed Presbyterian Church of Mexico* (South Pasadena, Calif., 1970); and Lowry Ware and James W. Gettys, *The Second Century: A History of the Associate Reformed Presbyterians, 1882–1982* (Greensville, S.C., 1983).

ATKINS, EDWIN F(ARNSWORTH) (1850–1926). Manufacturer, born January 13, 1850, in Boston. Atkins began his business career in the Boston office of his father, who was a merchant and banker, under the firm of E. Atkins and Company, in 1867, and became partner in 1870. He spent much of his early life in Cuba, where he devoted himself to the development of sugar planting and manufacturing. He became the owner of the Soledad estate at Cienfuegos and personally managed its large interests, both as a producer on Cuban soil and as a shipper. He was president of Bay State Sugar Refining Company of Boston from 1878 to 1888. He established a botanical garden at Colonia Limones, which he later turned over to Harvard University. He wrote *Sixty Years in Cuba, Reminiscences of Edwin F. Atkins* (Cambridge, Mass., 1926). Died May 20, 1926, in Belmont, Massachusetts. *References: NCAB* 16:52; and *WWWA*.

AULTMAN, OTIS (1874–1943). Photographer, born August 27, 1874, in Holden, Missouri. Aultman worked on architectural, archaeological, and historical finds from 1923 until the end of his career. He was a pioneer in motion picture work under contract with Francisco (Pancho) Villa and Alvaro Obregón in 1916–1917. He worked with the International News Service and later with Pathé News during the Mexican revolution. He was the official photographer of the Juárez Race Track. In 1909, he worked in El Paso. He covered extensively the events of the Mexican revolution, including Pancho Villa's 1916 raid in Columbus, New Mexico. Died March 5, 1943, in El Paso, Texas. *References*: Otis Aultman Archives, El Paso Public Library, El Paso, Tex.; Turner Browne and Elaine Partnow, *Macmillan Biographical Encyclopedia of Photographic Artists and Innovators* (New York, 1983); and William H. Neezley, "Shooting the Mexican Revolution," *Americas* 28 (November-December 1976): 17–19.

B

BACH, T(HOMAS) J(OHANNES) (1881–1963). Missionary, born in Dorf-Flauenskjold, Denmark. Bach attended an engineering school in Copenhagen. He came to the United States in 1899 and was employed in a machine shop in Chicago. He attended the Swedish Institute of the Chicago Theological Seminary. He was a missionary under the Scandinavian Mission Alliance of North America in Venezuela and Colombia from 1906 until 1928, founding the mission in Maracaibo, Venezuela. He also edited *La Estrella del la Mañana*, its monthly magazine, after 1907. He was general director of the society (later the Evangelical Alliance Mission*) from 1928 to 1946. Died June 12, 1963, in Yucaipa, California. *Reference*: Tom Watson, Jr., *Little General: The Story of T. J. Bach, Missionary Statesman* (Grand Rapids, Mich., 1969).

BAGBY, WILLIAM BUCK (1855–1939). Missionary, born November 5, 1855, in Coryell County, Texas. Bagby graduated from Waco University and was ordained in 1879. He was a missionary under the Foreign Mission Board of the Southern Baptist Convention* in Brazil from 1881 until his death. He established the first Brazilian Baptist Church in Rio de Janeiro in 1882, lived there until 1901, and then moved to São Paulo. Died August 5, 1939, in Porto Allegre, Brazil. *References*: *ESB*; and Helen B. Harrison, *The Bagbys of Brazil* (Nashville, Tenn., 1954).

BAGLEY, MELVILLE SEWELL (1838–1880). Manufacturer, born July 10, 1838, in Bangor, Maine. Bagley came to Argentina in 1862 and joined a drug company. He founded his own company in 1864, producing a tonic made from orange rinds, which became very popular, and organizing an extensive advertising campaign. He was active in the establishment of the Office of Patents and Trade Marks in Argentina (and his tonic was the first registered product). Died July 14, 1880, in Buenos Aires. *References*: *Cutolo*; and *Udaondo*.

BAILEY, SOLON IRVING (1854–1931). Astronomer, born December 29, 1854, in Lisbon, New Hampshire, and grew up in Concord, New Hampshire. Bailey graduated from Boston University and studied at Harvard University. He was assistant professor of astronomy at Harvard University from 1893 to 1898, associate professor from 1898 to 1912, and professor from 1912 until his retirement in 1925. In 1888, he went on a tour of South America to select sites for astronomical observatories which led to the establishment of an observatory at Arequipa, Peru. In 1893, he established a meteorological station on the summit of El Misti Mountain in Peru. He wrote *Peruvian Meteorology* (Cambridge, Mass., 1899–1930). He later established an observatory near Hanover, Cape Province, South Africa. Died June 5, 1931, in Lisbon, New Hampshire. *References: ACAB; DAB S1; DSB; NCAB* 28–411; *NYT* June 6, 1931; and *WWWA*.

BAILLY-BLANCHARD, ARTHUR (1855–1925). Journalist and diplomat, born October 1, 1855, in New Orleans. Bailly-Blanchard attended the University of Louisiana Law school. He was assistant editor of *La Petit Journal* (New Orleans). He was U.S. minister to Haiti from 1914 to 1921. He tried unsuccessfully to interest different revolutionary governments in a convention to establish a U.S. customs receivership before the intervention of U.S. Marines in the summer of 1915, but played only a minor role during the occupation. Died August 22, 1925, in Montreal. *References: DADH; NYT*, August 25, 1925; and *WWWA*.

BAKER, LORENZO DOW (1840–1908). Sea captain, planter and merchant, born March 15, 1840, in Wellfleet, Massachusetts. Baker became a sailor boy in 1850 and master of a ship in 1861. In 1870, he was owner and master of a schooner, and he brought the first shipment of bananas from Jamaica to Boston. He then made several voyages a year to Jamaica and back. In 1879, he became the Jamaican agent of a steamship line, and as the banana trade became important, he encouraged people in Jamaica to cultivate the fruit. In 1885 he was involved in the organization of the Boston Fruit Company, and he served as its president until 1899. In 1899, he was involved in the formation of the United Fruit Company* and was managing director of its Jamaica division. Died June 21, 1908, in Boston. *References*: Wilson R. Bartlett, Jr., "Lorenzo Dow Baker and the Development of the Banana Trade between Jamaica and the United States, 1881–1890," Ph.D. diss., American University, 1977; *DAB; NCAB* 14:350; and *NYT*, June 22, 1908.

BALDWIN, WILLIAM (1779–1819). Physician and botanist, born March 29, 1779, in Newlin, Chester County, Pennsylvania. Baldwin graduated from the University of Pennsylvania. He served as surgeon on a merchant ship in 1805–1806, practiced medicine in Wilmington, Delaware, from 1807 to 1811, and was commissioned surgeon in the U.S. Navy in 1812. He was ship's surgeon on the USS *Congress*, with the U.S. South American Commission in 1817–1818, and made botanical explorations during the journey to South America. He was surgeon and botanist with Stephen H. Long's expedition to the Rocky Mountains. Died August 31, 1819, in Franklin, Missouri. *References*: *DAB*; and Harry B. Humphrey, *Makers of North American Botany* (New York, 1961), pp. 15–16.

BALTIMORE **AFFAIR** (1891–1892). An incident in which a group of sailors from the USS *Baltimore* was attacked by a mob in Valparaiso, Chile. Two sailors were killed and sixteen were injured. The United States demanded reparations from Chile and threatened the use of force. Chile paid an indemnity, but for a long time after the incident, relations between the two countries remained strained. *References*: *DADH; ELA*; and Joyce S. Goldberg, *The Baltimore Affair* (Lincoln, Neb., 1986).

"BANANA WARS." The name by which U.S. Marines referred to the U.S. military interventions in the Caribbean and Central America between 1900 and 1934. *References*: Lester D. Langley, *The Banana Wars: An Inner History of the American Empire, 1900–1934* (Lexington, Ky., 1983); and *Musicant*.

BANDELIER, ADOLPH FRANCIS ALPHONSE (1840–1914). Archaeologist, born August 6, 1840, in Berne, Switzerland, and brought to the United States in 1848. Bandelier studied geology in Berne. He joined his father in banking and mining enterprises, and traveled to Mexico and Central America in 1877. He went to New Mexico in 1880–1881 for the Archaeological Institute of America. He explored Cholula and Mitla, Tlacolula and Monte Alban in Mexico from 1881 to 1883, and New Mexico, southern Arizona and Chihuahua, Mexico, from 1883 to 1886, visiting hundreds of ruins and mapping many of them. He was the historiographer of the Hemenway Southwestern archaeological expedition from 1886 to 1889 and in charge of the Henry Villard scientific expedition to Peru and Bolivia in 1892, exploring the islands of Titicaca and Koati. He returned to the United States in 1903, was connected with the American Museum of Natural History from 1903 to 1906, and worked with the Hispanic Society of America after 1906. He was a research associate with the Carnegie Institution of Washington after 1911 in Mexico City, transcribing documents and later in Seville, Spain. He wrote *Report of an Archaeological Tour in Mexico, in 1881* (Boston, 1885), and *The Islands of Titicaca and Koati* (New York, 1910). Died March 18, 1914, in Seville, Spain. *References: A Scientist on the Trail: Travel Letters of A. F. Bandelier, 1880–1881*, ed. George P. Hammond and Edgar F. Goad (Berkeley, Calif., 1949); *ACAB; DAB*; Clarissa P. Fuller, "A Reexamination of Bandelier's Studies of Ancient Mexico." Ph.D. diss., University of North Carolina, 1950; Carroll L. Riley, "Adolph Bandelier: The Mexican Years," *America Indigena* 28 (1968): 425–36; *NCAB* 26:240; *NYT*, March 21, 1914; Jack Schaefer, *Adolphe Francis Alphonse Bandelier* (Santa Fe, N.M., 1966); and *WWWA*.

BANDY, MARK CHANCE (1900–1963). Mineralogist, born July 22, 1900, in Redfield, Iowa. Bandy graduated from Drake, Columbia, and Harvard universities. He entered the employ of the Huasteca Petroleum Company in Tampico, Mexico, in 1926. He later explored various aspects of mining geology in South America and was employed by Bethlehem Steel Corporation in Venezuela from 1927 to 1929 and by the Chile Exploration Company in Chile from 1929 to 1934. He collected minerals for Harvard University and the Smithsonian Institution from 1934 to 1936 and was chief geologist and chief engineer with the Patino Mines and Enterprises in Bolivia from 1936 to 1947 and manager of the Bolivian Tin and Tungsten Company in Huanuni. He returned to the United States in 1947, worked for the Economic Cooperation Administration from 1948 to 1951, and was later a consultant to various corporations. Died June 3, 1963, in Phoenix, Arizona. *References: BGSA* 77: S (February 1966): 13–16; and *NCAB* 51:500.

BARBOUR, THOMAS (1884–1946). Naturalist, born August 19, 1884, on Martha's Vineyard, Massachusetts. Barbour graduated from Harvard University. He was associate curator of reptiles at the Museum of Comparative Zoology of Harvard University after 1910. He was later curator and was director from 1927 until his death. He developed the Atkins Botanical Garden in Soledad, near Cienfuegos, Cuba, and the Barro Colorado tropical station in the Panama Canal Zone. He wrote *Naturalist at Large* (Boston, 1943), *A Naturalist in Cuba* (Boston, 1945), and *A Naturalist's Scrapbook* (Boston, 1946), which was published posthumously. Died January 8, 1946, in Boston. *References: DAB* S4; A. V. Kidder, "Thomas Barbour," in *Saturday Club: A Century Completed, 1920–1956*, ed. Edw. W. Forbes and John H. Finley, Jr. (Boston, 1958), pp. 307–17; and *WWWA*.

BARD, HARRY (ERWIN) (1867–1955). Educator, born August 22, 1867, in Crawfordsville, Indiana. Bard graduated from Columbia University. He was instructor and then principal of the Adams Collegiate Institute (New York City) from 1894 to 1898 and divisional superintendent of schools in the Philippines from 1901 to 1906. He was member of an educational commission to Peru in 1909 and consultant to the Ministry of Instruction in Lima, Peru, from 1909 to 1912. He assisted in preparing the organic school law of Peru from 1910 to 1912. He was secretary of the Pan American Society of the U.S. from 1915 to 1919. He was again adviser to the Ministry of Instruction in Lima after 1919, and introduced and established American methods of education in Peru. He was organizing director of the Pan American division of the American Association of International Conciliation from 1913 to 1915, director general of public instruction in Peru in 1920, and in charge of the reorganization of the public school system under a new school law. He wrote *Intellectual and Cultural Relations between the United States and Other Republics of America* (Washington, D.C., 1914), and *South America* (Boston, 1916). Died July 12, 1955, in Ridgefield, Connecticut. *References: IAB; NYT*, July 13, 1955; and *WWWA*.

BARDWELL, HARRY BROWN (1879–1956). Missionary educator, born March 21, 1879, in Talbotton, Georgia. Bardwell graduated from Emory College. He held a pastorate in Macon, Georgia, from 1899 to 1903. He was a missionary under the Board of Foreign Missions of the Methodist Episcopal Church, South,* in Cuba from 1903 until 1949. He served in Guantánamo until 1908 and then in Havana. In 1909, he founded Candler College in Havana, a boys' school, and headed it until his retirement in 1949 (although he became blind in 1934). Died November 4, 1956, in Havana, Cuba. *References*: *EWM*; and *NYT*, November 7, 1956.

BARNARD, JOHN G(ROSS) (1815–1882). Soldier, born May 19, 1815, in Sheffield, Massachusetts. Barnard graduated from the U.S. Military Academy in 1833, and was commissioned second lieutenant in the corps of engineers. He was involved in the construction of coast artillery defenses and in the improvement of rivers and harbors in Portland, New York, Mobile, and San Francisco. He served during the Mexican War. He was superintendent of the U.S. Military Academy in 1855–1856. He was chief engineer of the Tehuantepec Railroad Company of New Orleans from 1850 to 1852 and made a preliminary survey for a railroad across the Tehuantepec Isthmus. He served in the Union Army during the Civil War. He retired with the rank of brigadier general in 1881. Died May 14, 1882, in Detroit. *References*: *ACAB; DAB; NCAB* 4:183; *NYT*, May 15, 1882; and *WWWA*.

BARNSLEY, GEORGE S(CARBOROUGH) (1837–1918). Physician, born in Woodlands Plantation, Cass County, Georgia. Barnsley attended Oglethorpe University. He served in the Confederate Army during the Civil War. He emigrated to Brazil in 1866, as part of the group under the leadership of Frank McMullan.* He practiced medicine in São Paulo, Brazil, until his death. *Reference*: George S. Barnsley Papers, University of North Carolina Library, Chapel Hill.

BARRETT, JOHN (1866–1938). Diplomat, born November 28, 1866, in Grafton, Vermont. Barrett graduated from Dartmouth College. He worked for several Pacific coast newspapers from 1889 to 1894 and was U.S. minister to Siam from 1894 to 1898. He was war correspondent in Manila during the Spanish-American War and served as adviser to Admiral George Dewey. He was U.S. minister to Argentina in 1903–1904, minister to Panama in 1904–1905, and minister to Colombia in 1905–1906. He was director general of the Pan-American Union from 1907 until 1920. Died October 17, 1938, in Bellows Falls, Vermont. *References*: John Barrett Papers, Manuscript Division, Library of Congress; *DAB S2; DADH*; G. B. Lane, Jr., "The Role of John Barrett in the Development of the Pan American Union, 1907–1920," Ph.D. diss. American University, 1963; *NYT*, October 8, 1938; Salvator Prisco III, *John Barrett, Progressive Era Diplomat: A Study of a Commercial Expansionist, 1887–1920* (University, Ala.,

1973); Salvatore Prisco, "John Barrett's Plan to Mediate the Mexican Revolution," *TA* 27 (1971): 413–25; and *WWWA*.

BARRON, GEORGE DAVIS (1860–1947). Mining engineer, born January 20, 1860, in St. Louis. Barron became a purchasing agent at the Cheltenham works of the St. Louis Smelting and Refining Company after 1880, was purchasing agent for his company in Mexico after 1884, selecting, purchasing, and shipping to the United States precious metal–bearing ores, as well as lead and copper. He then became superintendent of the construction of numerous large Mexican smelting plants for the company. He was then commissioned by the Guggenheim Brothers to make extensive field investigations of metal-bearing deposits in Mexico and was general manager of all Guggenheim enterprises in Mexico. He built the Great National Mexican Smelting Company in Monterrey, Nuevo Leon, in 1890. In 1896, he discovered the mining property near Teziutlán, state of Puebla, received a grant from the Mexican government, and began to develop the La Aurora mining property. He erected a town, Aurora, and smelting and converting plants, as well as a power plant. He relinquished active management in 1901 and settled in New York City. Died April 1, 1947, in Rye, New York. *References*: *NCAB* 36:538; *NYT*, April 2, 1947; and *WWWA*.

BARTON, SETH (1795–1854). Lawyer and diplomat, born December 5, 1795, in Baltimore. Barton studied law and was admitted to the bar. He practiced law in Alabama and later in New Orleans. He was solicitor of the U.S. Treasury from 1845 to 1847. He was U.S. chargé d'affaires in Chile in 1848–1849. He started a new conflict with Chile regarding the *Macedonian* affair,* and entered into a quarrel with the archbishop of Santiago over his marriage with a Chilean woman. Died December 29, 1854, in New Orleans. *Reference*: Thomas R. Shurbutt, "The Mission of Colonel Seth Barton, United States Chargé d'Affaires to Chile, 1847–1849," M.A. thesis, University of Georgia, 1967.

BASSETT, EBENEZER DON CARLOS (1833–1908). Educator and diplomat, born October 16, 1833, in Litchfield, Connecticut. Bassett graduated from Connecticut State Normal School and studied at Yale University. He taught school from 1853 to 1857 in New Haven and was teacher and principal of the Institute for Colored Youth in Philadelphia from 1857 to 1869. He was U.S. minister to Haiti from 1869 to 1877, was involved in trying to assure Haitian neutrality and nonintervention while the administration of President Ulysses S. Grant tried to annex the Dominican Republic, and also dealt with numerous American claims against Haiti, ultimately settling some forty of them. He was consul general for Haiti in New York from 1879 to 1888, and then served as secretary and interpreter to Frederick Douglass,* U.S. minister to Haiti, from 1889 to 1891. In the 1890s, he was again employed by the consul general of Haiti in New York. Died in Philadelphia. *References: DADH; DANB;* Charles

E. Wynes, "Ebenezer Don Carlos Bassett, America's First Black Diplomat," *Pennsylvania History* 51 (1984): 232–40; and *WWWA*.

BASSLER, HARVEY (1883–1950). Geologist, born April 21, 1883, in Myerstown, Pennsylvania. Bassler graduated from Albright College and Lehigh and Johns Hopkins universities. He was chief geologist for Standard Oil Company of New Jersey in Peru from 1921 to 1932, with headquarters in Iquitos. He traversed and mapped some previously unexplored regions of the Amazon Basin and collected more than 10,000 specimens of amphibians and reptiles. He later acquired a large library on jungle flora and fauna. He was in Peru during World War II, building a rubber supply for the U.S. government. He was later on the staff of Franklin and Marshall College (Lancaster, Pa.). Died March 14, 1950, in Downingtown, Pennsylvania. *References*: Harvey Bassler Papers, Lehigh University Library, Bethlehem, Pa.; and Lee Edson, "The Collector," *The Lamp* 64 (Winter 1982): 13–15.

BATES, MARSTON (1906–1974). Zoologist, born July 23, 1906, in Grand Rapids, Michigan. Bates graduated from the University of Florida and Harvard University. He was entomologist and later director of Servicio Tecnico de Cooperacion Agricola of the United Fruit Company* in Honduras and Guatemala from 1928 to 1931. He was a staff member of the International Health Division of the Rockefeller Foundation, serving in Albania, Egypt, and Colombia from 1937 to 1950, special assistant to the president from 1950 to 1952, professor of zoology at the University of Michigan from 1952 to 1972, and director of research at the University of Puerto Rico in 1956–1957. He wrote *Where Winter Never Comes* (New York, 1952), and *The Land and Wildlife of South America* (New York, 1964). Died April 3, 1974, in Ann Arbor, Michigan. *References*: Marston Bates Papers, Bentley Historical Library, University of Michigan, Ann Arbor; *CA*; *CB* 1956; *NYT*, April 5, 1974; and *WWWA*.

BATTY, JOSEPH H. (1847–1906). Taxidermist, born in Springfield, Massachusetts. Batty was in business as a taxidermist in New York City, and later engaged in plume hunting, visiting, for this purpose, western Mexico, Central America, and northern South America, which he crossed from ocean to ocean. He collected natural history specimens for the American Museum of Natural History in the province of Chiriquí, Panama, the Cauca region of Colombia, and in the states of Durango, Sinaloa, Jalisco, and Chiapas in Mexico from 1898 until his death. Killed in an accident on May 26, 1906, near Pijijiapam, state of Chiapas, Mexico. *Reference*: *Auk* 23 (1906): 256–57.

BAY OF PIGS INVASION (1961). United States–sponsored invasion of Cuba by Cuban exiles. The invasion was organized, financed, and led by the U.S. Central Intelligence Agency (CIA) to overthrow the revolutionary regime of Fidel Castro in Cuba, and was a complete disaster. All the invaders were killed or taken prisoner. *References*: *ELA*; Trumbull Higgins, *The Perfect Failure: Kennedy, Eisenhower, and the CIA at the Bay of Pigs* (New York, 1987); Paul L. Kesaris, ed., *Operation ZAPATA: The "Ultrasensitive" Report and Testimony of the Board of Inquiry on the Bay of Pigs* (Frederick, Md., 1981); and Peter Weyden, *The Bay of Pigs: The Untold Story* (New York, 1979).

BAYLIES, FRANCIS (1783–1852). Public official and diplomat, born October 16, 1783, in Boston. Baylies studied law, was admitted to the bar in 1810, and practiced law in Taunton, Massachusetts. He was register of probate for Bristol County, Massachusetts, from 1812 to 1820, member of the U.S. House of Representatives from 1821 to 1827, and member of the state house of representatives from 1827 to 1832. He was U.S. chargé d'affaires to Buenos Aires with full power to negotiate a treaty in 1832. Denying the Argentine right to prohibit fishing around the Falkland islands, the government of Buenos Aires refused to negotiate with him, and he left in that year. He served again in the state house of representatives after 1835. Died October 28, 1852, in Taunton, Massachusetts. *References*: Francis Baylies Papers, Manuscript Division, Library of Congress; Francis Baylies Papers, Old Colony Historical Society, Taunton, Mass.; *BDAC; DAB; DADH*; Samuel Rezneck, ed., "An American Diplomat Writes about Latin America in 1832," *TA* 28 (1971): 206–11.

BEACH, EDWARD L(ATIMER) (1867–1943). Naval officer, born June 30, 1867, in Toledo, Ohio. Beach graduated from the U.S. Naval Academy in 1888, and was commissioned assistant engineer in the U.S. Navy in 1890. He served in the Spanish-American War and was one of Admiral George Dewey's officers at the Battle of Manila Bay and at the capture of Manila in 1898. He then served during the Philippine-American War. He was engineering officer in the Boston Navy Yard in 1910. He commanded the USS *Vestal* during American occupation of Veracruz, Mexico, in 1914, and was commandant of Fortress San Juan de Ulloa. He was chief of staff to Admiral William B. Caperton* and in command of USS *Washington* during the pacification of Haiti and Santo Domingo in 1915. He was Admiral Caperton's chief of staff and his closest adviser in Haiti. He served during World War I and was commandant of the Mare Island Navy Yard, California. He retired with the rank of captain in 1921. He wrote "Admiral Caperton in Haiti" (Ms. in the National Archives). Died December 20, 1943, in Palo Alto, California. *References*: *NYT*, December 21, 1943; *OAB*; and *WWWA*.

BEACH, MOSES Y(ALE) (1800–1868). Journalist, born January 1, 1800, in Wallingford, Connecticut. Beach was first apprenticed to a cabinetmaker, and then was in the cabinetmaking business in Northampton, Massachusetts. He was engaged in the paper mill business in Saugerties on the Hudson, New York, from 1821 to 1835, and then became proprietor of the New York *Sun*. He went to Mexico in 1847 with Jane Maria Eliza Storms Cazneau,* as confidential agent to engage in the preliminary negotiations in preparation for a peace treaty between Mexico and the United States. He gave up his business in 1848 because of ill health. Died January 19, 1868, in Wallingford, Connecticut. *References*: *NCAB* 1:307; and Anna K. Nelson, "Mission to Mexico—Moses Y. Beach, Secret Agent," *New York Historical Society Quarterly* 59 (1975): 227–45.

BEADLE, ELIAS R(OOT) (1878–1946). Marine Corps officer, born November 1, 1878, in Alexandria, Virginia. Beadle enlisted in the U.S. Marine Corps in 1899 and was appointed second lieutenant in 1903. He served in the Philippines and Cuba. He served in the Marine Corps recruit Depot in Parris Island, Virginia, from 1912 to 1921. He was inspector of the First Brigade in Haiti from 1921 to 1923 and served in the headquarters of the Marine Corps in Washington, D.C., from 1923 to 1926. He served in Nicaragua from 1927 to 1929. He organized the Guardia Nacional de Nicaragua in 1927 and was its director with the local rank of brigadier general until 1929. He supervised the general elections in Nicaragua in 1928. He retired in 1930 with the rank of lieutenant colonel. Died November 18, 1946, in Miami, Florida. *Reference*: *NYT*, November 19, 1946.

BEALS, CARLETON (1893–1979). Journalist, brother of Ralph Leon Beals, born November 13, 1893, in Medicine Lodge, Kansas. Beals graduated from the University of California and Columbia University, and studied at the universities of Madrid, Rome, and Mexico. He was principal of the American High School in Mexico City in 1919–1920 and was instructor of the personal staff of President Venustiano Carranza in 1920. He covered numerous revolutions and rebellions in Latin America and was called "the dean of correspondents in Latin America." He was correspondent in Spain and Italy for *The Nation* and *Current History* from 1921 to 1923, member of expeditions to the Indian regions of Mexico in 1926 and 1930–1931, and correspondent in Central America for *The Nation* in 1926–1927. He traveled in Cuba from 1933 to 1935, in 1957, and in 1960–1961; in South America in 1934, 1946, and 1961; in Mexico in 1937, 1946, and 1961; and in Haiti in 1959. He was also a lecturer and writer. He wrote *Mexico: An Interpretation* (New York, 1923), *Brimstone and Chili: A Book of Personal Experiences in the Southwest and in Mexico* (New York, 1927), *Mexican Maze* (Philadelphia, 1931), *Banana Gold* (Lippincott, 1932), *Porfirio Diaz: Dictator of Mexico* (Philadelphia, 1932), *The Crime of Cuba* (Philadelphia, 1933), *Black River* (Philadelphia, 1934), *The Coming Struggle for Latin America* (Philadelphia, 1938), *Glass Houses: Ten Years of Free-Lancing* (Philadelphia, 1938), *The Great Circle: Further Adventures in Free-Lancing* (Philadelphia, 1940), *Rio Grande to Cape Horn* (Boston, 1940), *Down Over the Amazon* (New York, 1943), *House in Mexico* (New York, 1958), *Nomads and Empire: Native Peoples and Cultures of South America* (Philadelphia, 1961), and *Eagles of the Andes: South American Struggle for Independence* (Philadelphia, 1963). Died June 26, 1979, in Middletown, Connecticut. *References*: John A. Britton, *Car-*

leton Beals: A Radical Journalist in Latin America (Albuquerque, N.M., 1987); *CA*; *NCAB* D:442; *NYT*, June 28, 1979; and *WWWA*.

BEALS, RALPH L(EON) (1901–1985). Anthropologist, brother of Carleton Beals, born July 19, 1901, in Pasadena, California. Beals graduated from the University of California at Berkeley. He was assistant professor of anthropology at the University of California in Los Angeles from 1937 to 1941, associate professor from 1941 to 1947, and professor from 1947 to 1969. He was also director of Latin American ethnic studies at the Smithsonian Institution in 1942–1943 and collaborator of the Institute of Social Anthropology from 1944 to 1951. He carried out fieldwork in Mexico from 1930 to 1932, in 1940–1941, and from 1964 to 1967, made an extensive trip through Latin America in 1948–1949, carried out fieldwork in Ecuador, and traveled again in Latin America in 1962–1963. He wrote *The Acaxee, a Mountain Tribe of Durango and Sinaloa* (Berkeley, Calif., 1943), *Ethnology of Nisenan* (Berkeley, Calif., 1933), *The Aboriginal Culture of the Cahita Indians* (Berkeley, Calif., 1943), *The Contemporary Culture of the Cahita Indians* (Washington, D.C., 1945), *Cheran: A Sierran Tarascan Village* (Washington, D.C., 1946), *Community in Transition: Navon, Ecuador* (Los Angeles, 1966), and *The Peasant Marketing System of Oaxaca, Mexico* (Berkeley, Calif., 1975), and was coauthor of *Houses and House Use of the Sierra Tarascans* (Washington, D.C., 1944). Died February 24, 1985, in Los Angeles. *References*: *AA* 88 (1986): 947–53; *AMWS*; *CA*; Ralph Leon Beals, "Anthropologist and Educator" (Los Angeles, 1977); Walter Goldschmidt and Harry Hoijer, eds., *The Social Anthropology of Latin America: Essays in Honor of Ralph Leon Beals* (Los Angeles, 1970); and *WWWA*.

BEAN, ELLIS P(ETER) (1783–1846). Soldier, born in Tennessee. Bean was apprenticed in the shoemaking trade. He went to Natchez in 1799. In 1800, he joined Captain Philip Nolan's expedition to San Antonio, Texas, as second in command. He was captured by the Spanish in 1801, and was imprisoned in Nacogdoches. He was later held prisoner in San Luis Potosí, in Chihuahua until 1807, and then in Acapulco. At the outbreak of the Mexican revolution he was freed on the condition that he fight for the loyalists, but in 1811 he escaped and joined General José María Morelos y Pavón, the rebel leader. He was commissioned colonel, participated in various skirmishes and in guerilla warfare, and then manufactured powder for the rebel troops. In 1812, he captured Acapulco and then marched to Huacaca, where he erected a powder mill and manufactured ammunition. He was sent to the United States in 1814 to enlist aid for the Republican cause. He returned to Mexico in 1815 with fresh stores and ammunition. In 1818, he settled in White County, Texas, and later in Kansas, and in Mount Prairie, Texas, where he received a grant of land from the Mexican government. He was commissioned a colonel in the permanent Mexican forces, and remained in Mexican service, fighting mostly the Indians in East Texas, until his death. Died October 3, 1846, in Jalapa, Mexico. *References*: *Memoir* *of Col. Ellis P. Bean, Written by Himself, about the Year 1816*, ed., W. P. Yoakum (Houston, 1930); Bennett Lay, *The Lives of Ellis P. Bean* (Austin, Tex., 1960); *NCAB* 21:229; and Walter P. Webb, ed., *The Handbook of Texas* (Austin, Tex., 1952).

BEARSS, HIRAM IDDINGS (1875–1938). Marine Corps officer, born April 13, 1875, in Peru, Indiana. Bearss attended the universities of Notre Dame and Purdue as well as DePauw and Norwich universities. He was commissioned second lieutenant in the Marine Corps in 1898, served in the Spanish-American and Philippines-American wars and in the Panama Canal Zone, and commanded the marine barracks in Guantánamo, Cuba, from 1910 to 1920. In 1914, he landed in Veracruz, Mexico, several days before the American forces took over the city and was able to aid in its seizure through the knowledge he had obtained by his personal reconnoitering. He was later in charge of the marines in Santo Domingo, involved in quelling the rebellion of the Juan Calcanos. He penetrated the stronghold of Calcanos in the mountains and captured him single-handedly. He served in France during World War I and retired with the rank of colonel in 1919. In 1925 he organized the New York Federal Reserve Bank's force of guards and watchmen and headed it until 1935. Killed in a car accident, August 27, 1938, near Columbia City, Indiana. *Reference*: *NCAB* 29:27.

BEAULAC, WILLARD LEON (1899–1990). Diplomat, born July 25, 1899, in Pawtucket, Rhode Island. Beaulac attended Brown University and graduated from the School of Foreign Service at Georgetown University. He served in the U.S. Navy during World War I. He entered the foreign service in 1921, served in Tampico, Mexico, Puerto Castilla, and Arica, Chile. He was third secretary in Haiti in 1927–1928, second secretary in Nicaragua from 1928 to 1933, assistant chief of the Division of Latin American Affairs from 1934 to 1937, first secretary of embassy in Cuba from 1937 to 1940, and counselor of embassy in Cuba in 1940–1941 and in Spain from 1941 to 1944. He was U.S. ambassador to Paraguay from 1944 to 1947, ambassador to Colombia from 1947 to 1951, ambassador to Cuba from 1951 to 1953, ambassador to Chile from 1953 to 1956, and ambassador to Argentina from 1956 to 1960. He wrote the partially autobiographical *Career Ambassador* (New York, 1957), and *A Diplomat Looks at Aid to Latin America* (Carbondale, Ill., 1970). He later taught at Southern Illinois and Ball State universities. Died August 25, 1990, in Washington, D.C. *References*: *CB* 1958; *DADH*; and *NYT*, August 28, 1990.

BEAUPRÉ, ARTHUR MATTHIAS (1853–1919). Diplomat, born July 29, 1853, in Oswego Township, Kendall County, Illinois, and grew up in DeKalb, Illinois. Beaupré studied law, and was admitted to the bar. He practiced law in Aurora, Illinois and served as city clerk of Aurora and as clerk of Kane County, Illinois, from 1886 to 1894. He was U.S. consul general and secretary of legation in Guatemala and Honduras from 1897 to 1899, and mediated a dispute between

Great Britain and Honduras. He was consul general and secretary of legation in Colombia from 1899 to 1903 and U.S. minister to Colombia in 1903, where he was involved in obtaining ratification of the Hay-Herren Treaty by the Colombian Congress. He was U.S. minister to Argentina from 1904 to 1908, minister to the Netherlands and Luxembourg from 1908 to 1911, and minister to Cuba from 1911 to 1913. Died September 13, 1919, in Chicago. *References*: *DAB*; *DADH*; *NCAB* 14:381; and *NYT*, September 15, 1919.

BECK, FRANK S(PURGEON) (1888–1969). Medical missionary, born in Canton, South Dakota. Beck was a commercial teacher in the Cochabamba American Institute in Bolivia after 1912 and then in Colegio Ward in Buenos Aires. He later became director of the American Institute in Cochabamba and then of the American Institute in La Paz, Bolivia. He returned to the United States in 1923, graduated from the medical school of Northwestern University, and was back in Bolivia in 1930 as a medical missionary. He served the Altiplano villages. He volunteered his services with the Bolivian forces during the Chaco War from 1931 to 1934. He founded the American Clinic in La Paz and the first nursing school in Bolivia, and in 1956 he started a clinic in Ancoraimes. Died December 17, 1969, in Alta Loma, California. *References*: Natalie Barber, *Dr. and Mrs. Fix-It: The Story of Frank and Bessie Beck* (New York, 1970); and *EWM*.

BEEBE, (CHARLES) WILLIAM (1877–1962). Naturalist, born July 29, 1877, in Brooklyn, New York, and grew up in East Orange, New Jersey. Beebe attended Columbia University. He was assistant curator of ornithology at the New York Zoological Garden from 1899 until 1916. He undertook trips to Trinidad and Venezuela in 1908, and to British Guiana in 1909. He was in South and Southeast Asia from 1909 to 1911, and in Pará, Brazil, in 1915. He established the first field station of the New York Zoological Society's Department of Tropical Research in Kalacoon, British Guiana, in 1916 (later removed to Kartabo), and was its director. He was honorary curator of birds at the New York Zoological Park after 1916. He visited the Galapagos Islands in 1923 and in 1925, conducted oceanographic work centering on Bermuda from 1928 to 1939, and made an expedition to Baja California in 1936 and to the western coast of Central America in 1937–1938. He conducted jungle studies at Caripito, Venezuela, in 1942, and forest studies at Rancho Grande, Venezuela, in 1945–1946 and from 1948 to 1950. He established the Tropical Research Station at Simla, Arima Valley, Trinidad, West Indies, in 1950, and was its director until his retirement in 1952. He wrote *Two Bird Lovers in Mexico* (Boston, 1905), *The Long of the Sun* (New York, 1906), *Jungle Peace* (New York, 1918), *Edge of the Jungle* (New York, 1921), *Galapagos: World's End* (New York, 1924), *Jungle Days* (New York, 1925), *The Arcutrus Adventure* (New York, 1926), *Beneath Tropical Seas* (New York, 1928), *Half Mile Down* (New York, 1934), *Zaca Venture* (New York, 1938), and *High Jungle* (New York, 1949), and was coauthor of *Our Search for a Wilderness* (New York, 1910), and *Tropical Wild Life in British Guiana* (New York, 1917). Died June 4, 1962, in Simla, Trinidad. *References*: *Auk* 81 (1964): 36–41; and Robert H. Welker, *Natural Man: The Life of William Beebe* (Bloomington, Ind., 1975).

BEHRHORST, CARROLL D(EAN) H(ENRY) (1922–1990). Medical missionary, born July 23, 1922, in Brazilton, Kansas. Behrhorst graduated from St. John College (Winfield, Kan.) and Washington University (St. Louis). He served in the U.S. Navy during World War II. He practiced medicine in Winfield, Kansas, from 1951 to 1958. In 1962, he founded the Behrhorst Clinic in Chimaltenango, Guatemala, providing health care to people in Guatemala's highlands. The clinic became an internationally recognized model for rural health care. He also established a foundation that provided training programs to enable people in the highlands to run health, agriculture, and water projects. Died May 7, 1990, in Chimaltenango, Guatemala. *References*: Edwin Barton, *Physician to the Mayas: The Story of Dr. Carroll Behrhorst* (Philadelphia, 1970); and *St. John's Alumni Association Reporter* [Winfield, Kans.], June 6, 1990.

BELCHER, TAYLOR GARRISON (1920–1990). Diplomat, born July 1, 1920, in Staten Island, New York. Belcher graduated from Brown University. He served in the U.S. Navy during World War II. He entered the foreign service in 1947 and served in Mexico City, Glasgow, Nicosia, and Ottawa. He was deputy director for West Coast Affairs in the Bureau of Inter-American Affairs in the U.S. State Department from 1961 to 1964. He was U.S. ambassador to Cyprus from 1964 to 1969 and ambassador to Peru from 1969 until his retirement in 1974. He was involved in relief operations following the earthquake of 1970. Died August 6, 1990, in Peekskill, New York. *References*: *DADH*; and *NYT*, August 8, 1990.

BELUCHE, RENATO (1780–1860). Privateer and naval officer, born December 15, 1780, in New Orleans. Beluche was a pilot's mate in 1802 and a shipmaster after 1804. He was a privateer in the French and U.S. service and was associated with Jean Laffite and his brothers. He was a privateer in the Cartagenan navy from 1812 to 1814. He served during the Battle of New Orleans in 1814–1815. He went again to Cartagena in 1815, and entered the service of Simón Bolívar, serving as a privateer and a commodore in the Colombian Navy. He was in command of the navy in Puerto Cabello in 1828 and sailed the *Colombia* from Puerto Cabello around Cape Horn to Guayaquil in 1829. He retired in 1833 and later became a citizen of Venezuela. In 1836, he participated in a reformist insurrection, and lived in exile, probably in New Orleans, from 1836 until 1845. Died October 4, 1860, in Puerto Cabello, Venezuela. *References*: Jane L. De Grummond, *Renato Beluche, Smuggler, Privateer, and Patriot, 1780–1860* (Baton Rouge, La., 1983); Isidro A. Beluche Mora, *Abor-*

dajes, Biografía Esquemática de Renato Beluche (Caracas, 1960); and Francisco A. Vargas, *Nuestros Próceres Navales* (Caracas, 1964).

BENDER, ROBERT H(ERMANN) (1870–1934). Missionary, born April 17, 1870, in Troy, New York. Bender was trained in a missionary training institute and was a missionary in New York City, Albany, and Troy, New York, until 1897. He was a missionary under the Central American Mission* in El Salvador from 1897 to 1914. He then carried out Spanish missionary work in southern California. He returned to El Salvador in 1927 and served there until his death. Died May 23, 1934, in San Salvador, El Salvador. *Reference*: *Central American Bulletin*, July/September 1934.

BENEDUM, M(ICHAEL) L(ATE) (1869–1959). Petroleum producer, born July 16, 1869, in Bridgeport, West Virginia. Benedum was assistant general manager of the land department of the South Penn Oil Company from 1889 to 1900. He was president of Benedum Trees Oil Company, independent oil operators, from 1900 to 1913 and president of Benedum Trees Company after 1913. He was said to have discovered more oil than any other single man in the industry. He opened rich fields in Illinois, northern Louisiana, Texas, and Rumania. He developed the Tampico fields on Mexico's coast and the DeMares concession pool in Colombia. Died July 30, 1959, in Pittsburgh, Pennsylvania. *References*: Sam T. Mallison, *Great Wildcatter* (Charleston, W.Va., 1953); *NYT*, July 31, 1959; and *WWWA*.

BENNETT, ROBERT ROOT (1865–1933). Archaeologist and explorer, born December 12, 1865, in Toledo, Ohio. Bennett graduated from Columbia (later George Washington) University, was admitted to the bar in 1904, and practiced law in Washington, D.C. He organized a trip of investigation to Quiriga, Honduras, in 1890, and explored Uxmal, Yucatán, and visited Mérida, Campeche, Tekax, and Ticul in 1891. He was a special agent for the U.S. Department of Justice during World War I and confidential agent for the War Department and then served in the intelligence section of the general staff. He was sent on a confidential mission to Central America in 1919. He excavated in Omoa, Honduras, in 1919 and explored Tuloom, Yucatán, and the islands of Mugeres and Cozumel in 1925, the Isthmus of Darien in 1926, and the west coast of Cuba in 1932. Died December 12, 1933, in Washington, D.C. *References*: *NCAB* 24:119; and *WWWA*.

BENNETT, WENDELL C(LARK) (1905–1953). Archaeologist, born August 17, 1905, in Marion, Indiana, and grew up in Oak Park, Illinois. Bennett graduated from the University of Chicago. In 1931, he studied the Tarahumara Indians in northern Mexico, and wrote *The Tarahura, An Indian Tribe of Northern Mexico* (Chicago, 1935). He was assistant curator of anthropology at the American Museum of Natural History from 1931 to 1938, associate professor of anthropology at the University of Wisconsin from 1938 to 1940 and at Yale University from 1940 to 1945, and professor at Yale University from 1945 until his death. He was also a research associate in the Peabody Museum of Yale University. He made field trips to Bolivia and Peru in 1932, 1933–1934, 1936, and 1938, and excavated in Venezuela in 1932. For the Peabody Museum, he made a ceramic survey of Colombia in 1941, excavated in the Cuenca region of highland Ecuador in 1944, participated in the Virú Valley program in Peru in 1946 and excavated in Wari, Peru, in 1950. He wrote *Excavations at Tiahuanaco* (New York, 1934), *Excavations in Bolivia* (New York, 1936), *Excavations at La Mata, Maracay, Venezuela* (New York, 1937), *Archaeology of the North Coast of Peru* (New York, 1939), *Archaeological Regions of Colombia: A Ceramic Survey* (New Haven, Conn., 1944), *The North Highlands of Peru: Excavations in the Callejon de Huaylas and at Chavin de Huantar* (New York, 1944), *Excavations in the Cuenca Region Ecuador* (New Haven, Conn., 1946), *The Gallinazo Group, Virú Valley, Peru* (New Haven, Conn., 1950), and *Excavations at Wari, Ayacucho, Peru* (New Haven, Conn., 1953), and was coauthor of *The Tarahumara: An Indian Tribe of Northern Mexico* (Chicago, 1935), *Northwest Argentine Archaeology* (New Haven, Conn., 1948), and *Andean Culture History* (New York, 1949). Died September 6, 1953, in Martha's Vineyard, Massachusetts. *References*: *AA* 56 (1954): 269–73; *AmAntiq* 19 (1954): 265–70; *IAB; NYT*, September 7, 1953; *Willey*, ch. 6; and *WWWA*.

BENNETT, W(ILLIAM) TAPLEY, JR. (1917–   ). Diplomat, born April 1, 1917, in Griffin, Georgia. Bennett graduated from the University of Georgia and George Washington University, and studied at the University of Freiburg (Germany). He served in the U.S. Army during World War II. He entered the State Department in 1944. He was officer in charge of Central America and Panama affairs from 1949 to 1951, Caribbean affairs in 1951, deputy director of the Office of South American Affairs from 1951 to 1954, special assistant to the undersecretary of state from 1955 to 1957, and counselor of embassy in Austria from 1957 to 1961, in Italy in 1961, and in Greece from 1961 to 1964. He was U.S. ambassador to the Dominican Republic from 1964 to 1966. He was U.S. ambassador to Portugal from 1966 to 1969, deputy U.S. representative to the United Nations and its Security Council from 1971 to 1977, U.S. representative to the Trusteeship Council from 1917 to 1974, and ambassador to the North Atlantic Treaty Organization (NATO) from 1977 to 1984. *References*: *DADH*; and *WWA*.

BERLE, ADOLF AUGUSTUS (1895–1971). Lawyer and diplomat, born January 29, 1895, in Boston. Berle graduated from Harvard University and Harvard Law School. He practiced law in Boston in 1916–1917, and served in the U.S. Army during World War I. He resumed law practice in New York City from 1919 until his death, specializing in Latin American affairs and corporation law. He was a member of Franklin D. Roosevelt's "Brain Trust" during the 1930s, and was assistant secretary of state from 1938 to 1944. He was U.S. ambassador to Brazil in 1945–1946 and was accused of intervention in Brazil's internal affairs. He was chairman of the President's Task Force on Latin America in 1960–1961. He wrote *Latin America: Diplomacy and Reality* (New York, 1962). Died February 17, 1971, in New York City. His wife, **BEATRICE BISHOP BERLE** (1902–   ), wrote *Life in Two Worlds: The Autobiography of Beatrice Bishop Berle* (New York, 1983). *References*: Adolf A. Berle Papers, Roosevelt Library, Hyde Park, N.Y.; *Navigating the Rapids, 1918–1971: From the Papers of Adolf A. Berle*, ed. Beatrice B. Berle and Travis B. Jacobs (New York, 1973); *CB* 1961; *DADH*; *NCAB* 56:137; *NYT*, February 19, 1971; *PolProf: Kennedy; PolProf: Truman*; C. Neale Robbing, "Adolf Berle in Brazil, 1945–46," in *Ambassadors in Foreign Policy: The Influence of Individuals on U.S.–Latin American Policy*, ed. C. Neale Robbing and Albert P. Vannucci (New York, 1987), pp. 74–94; Jordan A. Schwarz, *Liberal: Adolf A. Berle and the Vision of an American Era* (New York, 1987); and *WWWA*.

BIDDLE, CHARLES (1787–1836). Merchant, born in Philadelphia. Biddle was engaged in business in Philadelphia until he failed in 1826, moved to Nashville, Tennessee, studied law, and was admitted to the bar in 1827. He practiced law and established the *Tennessee Reporter* in 1832. He was sent by President Andrew Jackson to Central America and New Granada to investigate the possibility of a trans-Isthmian canal in 1835–1836. He traversed the Isthmus via the Chagres River to the City of Panama. He obtained a concession for the Atlantic and Pacific Transportation Company, a private company, of the right to build and maintain a road to Panama, and exclusive right to steam navigation on the Magdalena River. Died December 21, 1836, in Washington, D.C. *References*: Charles Biddle Letterbook, New York Historical Society, New York City; and John M. Belohlavek, "The Philadelphian and the Canal: The Charles Biddle Mission to Panama, 1835–1836," *Pennsylvania Magazine of History and Biography* 104 (1980): 450–61.

BIDLACK, BENJAMIN ALDEN (1804–1849). Diplomat, born September 8, 1804, in Paris, Oneida County, New York. Bidlack studied law, and was admitted to the bar. He was deputy attorney for Luzerne County, established and edited the *Northern Eagle*, and served in the Pennsylvania state legislature in 1835–1836 and in the U.S. House of Representatives from 1841 to 1845. He was U.S. chargé d'affaires in New Granada from 1845, and successfully negotiated the claims of American citizens. In 1846 he concluded a treaty of peace, friendship, commerce, and navigation between the United States and New Granada that guaranteed the United States the exclusive right of transit across the Isthmus of Panama. Died February 6, 1849, in Bogota, New Granada. *References*: *BDAC*; *DAB*; *DADH*; and *NCAB* 13:415.

BIESANZ, JOHN BERRY (1913–   ). Sociologist and anthropologist, born August 24, 1913, in Winona, Michigan. Biesanz graduated from the universities of Chicago and Iowa. He was associate professor of sociology and anthropology at the University of Pittsburgh in 1947–1948, associate professor of sociology and Middle America research associate at Tulane University from 1948 to 1950, associate professor of sociology at Wayne State University from 1950 to 1955, and professor of sociology and anthropology from 1955 until his retirement in 1972. With his wife, **MAVIS HILTUNEN BIESANZ** (1919–   ), he wrote *Costa Rican Life* (New York, 1944) and *The People of Panama* (New York, 1955). *References*: *AMWS*; and *CA*.

BIGELOW, FRANK HAGER (1851–1924). Meteorologist, born August 28, 1851, in Watertown, Massachusetts. Bigelow graduated from Harvard University. He was assistant astronomer at the Córdoba Observatory from 1873 to 1876. He graduated from Episcopal Theological School (Cambridge, Mass.) and held a pastorate in Natick, Massachusetts, until 1881. He returned to Argentina from 1881 to 1883 and was chief of the climatological division of the U.S. Weather Bureau from 1906 to 1910, and editor of the *Monthly Weather Review* in 1909–1910. He was professor of solar physics at George Washington University from 1894 to 1910 and professor of meteorology at the Oficina Meteorologica in Córdoba from 1910 to 1921. He took part in several eclipse expeditions. Died March 2, 1924, in Vienna, Austria. *References*: *ACAB*; *DAB*; *NCAB* 10:410; and *WWWA*.

BILLINGS, ASA WHITE KENNEY (1876–1949). Engineer, born February 8, 1876, in Omaha, Nebraska. Billings graduated from Harvard University. He was employed in street railway and steam power plant construction in Pittsburgh from 1896 to 1899. In 1899, he was assigned to electrify a streetcar system in Havana and continued to be involved with Cuban electric transit and steam power construction until 1909. He was with F. S. Pearson, consulting engineers, after 1909, and supervised irrigation projects in Texas and Spain until 1916. He served in the U.S. Navy Corps of Civil Engineers during World War II. He was involved in a Mexican power project, and with the Brazilian Traction, Light and Power Company after 1922, he was also involved in developing hydroelectric power in Brazil. He completed the power plant at Ilho dos Pambos in 1924 and the Serra project in 1937, which significantly enlarged the Rio de Janeiro electric system. He was vice president of the company from 1924 to 1944 and president from 1944 to 1946. Died November 3, 1949, in La Jolla, California. *Reference*: *DAB S4*.

BINGHAM, HIRAM (1875–1956). Explorer, born November 19, 1875, in Honolulu, Hawaii. Bingham graduated from the University of California and Harvard University. In 1906–1907, he followed the 1819 march of Simón Bolívar across the northern coast of South America from Caracas to Bogota. He was a lecturer in South American history and geography at Yale University from 1907 to 1910, assistant professor of Latin American history from 1910 to 1915, and professor from 1915 to 1924. In 1908–1909, he retraced the old Spanish trade route from Buenos Aires to Lima. He organized and directed the Yale Peruvian expedition in 1911, and discovered Machu Picchu, Vitcos, and Vilcambamba. He directed another Peruvian expedition in 1912 under the auspices of Yale University and the National Geographic Society, and a third Peruvian expedition under the same auspices in 1914–1915. He served with the U.S. Army Air Service during World War I. He was lieutenant governor of Connecticut from 1922 to 1924 and U.S. senator from 1925 to 1933. He was chairman of the Federal Loyalty Review Board in 1952–1953. He wrote *Journal of an Expedition across Venezuela and Colombia* (New Haven, 1909), *Across South America* (Boston, 1911), *The Monroe Doctrine: An Obsolete Shibboleth* (New Haven, 1913), *Inca Land: Explorations in the Highlands of Peru* (Boston, 1922), *Machu Picchu, a Citadel of the Incas* (New Haven, 1930), and *Lost City of the Incas: The Story of Machu Picchu and Its Builders* (New York, 1948). Died June 6, 1956, in Washington, D.C. *References*: Bingham Family Papers, Yale University Library, New Haven, Conn.; *BDAC*; Alfred M. Bingham, *Portrait of an Explorer: Hiram Bingham, Discoverer of Machu Picchu* (Ames, Iowa, 1989); *DAB S6*; Charles Miller, *Fathers and Sons: The Bingham Family and the American Mission* (Philadelphia, 1982), chs. 5–6; *NCAB* A:28; Bruce Norman, *Footsteps: Nine Archaeological Journeys of Romance and Discovery* (London, 1987), ch. 8; *NYT*, June 7, 1956; and *WWWA*.

BIRBECK, SAMUEL BRADFORD (? –1867). Surveyor, born in Illinois. Birbeck was in Mexico from 1827 to 1860. He was initially in Mexico City, and later in Zacatecas, in the province of Atecas, central Mexico. He served British silver-mining companies and traveled throughout Mexico, examining lands and mines. He left in 1860 for Australia. *References*: Samuel Bradford Birbeck Diaries and Commonplace Book, University of Sydney Library, Sydney, New South Wales, Australia; and David S. Macmillan and Brian Plomley, "An American Surveyor in Mexico, 1837–1860," *New Mexico Historical Quarterly* 34 (1959): 1–8.

BIRD, JUNIUS B(OUTON) (1907–1982). Archaeologist, born September 21, 1907, in Rye, New York. Bird attended Columbia University. He was field assistant at the American Museum of Natural History from 1931 to 1937, assistant curator from 1937 to 1947, associate curator from 1947 to 1957, and curator of South American archaeology after 1957. He organized numerous expeditions to South America. He excavated in Chile during the 1930s, working with what were then the oldest known human remains. He wrote *Excavations in Northern Chile* (New York, 1943) and was coauthor of *Andean Culture History* (New York, 1949) and *The Preceramic Excavations at Huaca Prieta, Chicama Valley, Peru* (New York, 1985). Died April 2, 1982, in New York City. His diaries were published in *Travels and Archaeology in South Chile*, ed. John Hyslop (Iowa City, Ia., 1988). *References*: *AMWS*; *CA*; John Hyslop, "Portrait of an Archeologist," *Natural History* 98 (February 1989): 84–89; *NYT*, April 4, 1982; *Willey*, ch. 7; and Gordon R. Willey, "Junius Bouton Bird and American Archaeology," in *Early Ceremonial Architecture in the Andes*, ed. C. B. Donnan (Washington, D.C., 1985), pp. 7–28.

BISHOP, ALBERT EDWARD (1861–1947). Missionary, born October 8, 1861, and moved to Abilene, Kansas, in 1879. Bishop entered the general merchandise business. He was the first missionary under the Central American Mission* in Honduras from 1896 to 1899, stationed at Santa Rosa de Copán, and in Guatemala from 1899 until 1943. Died December 1, 1947, in Los Angeles. *References*: *Central American Bulletin*, January 1948; Wilkins B. Winn, "Albert Edward Bishop and the Establishment of the Central American Mission in Guatemala, 1899–1922," in *Militarists, Merchants and Missionaries: United States Expansion in Middle America*, ed. Eugene R. Huck and Edward H. Moseley (University, Ala., 1970), pp. 93–106; and Wilkins B. Winn, *Pioneer Protestant Missionaries in Honduras: A. E. Bishop and J. G. Cassel and the Establishment of the Central American Mission in Western Honduras, 1896–1901* (Cuernavaca, Mexico, 1973).

BISHOP, JOSEPH BUCKLIN (1847–1928). Journalist and government official, born September 5, 1847, in Seekons, Massachusetts (later East Providence, Rhode Island). Bishop graduated from Brown University. He was on the editorial staff of the New York *Tribune* from 1870 to 1883, editorial writer with the New York *Evening Post* from 1883 to 1900, and chief of the editorial staff of the New York *Globe* from 1900 to 1905. He was secretary of the Isthmian Canal Commission from 1905 to 1914. He wrote *The Panama Gateway* (New York, 1914) and *Notes and Anecdotes of Many Years* (New York, 1925) and was coauthor of a biography of George Washington Goethals.* Died December 13, 1928, in New York City. *References*: *NYT*, December 14, 1928; and *WWWA*.

BLACK, WILLIAM MURRAY (1855–1933). Army officer, born December 8, 1855, in Lancaster, Pennsylvania. Black graduated from the U.S. Military Academy in 1877 and was commissioned a second lieutenant. He was an instructor at the U.S. Military Academy from 1882 to 1886, district engineer of the Florida military district from 1886 to 1891, and instructor in the engineering school in Willet's Point, New York, from 1891 to 1895. He served in the Office of the Chief of Engineers from 1895 to 1897. He served during the Spanish-American War in Puerto Rico and Cuba, was chief engineer of the Department of Havana in 1899–1900, organized a new department of public works, and established sanitary conditions. He was chief engineer of Cuba in 1900–1901, commanding officer of the engineering school from 1901 to 1903, and observer of the Panama Canal in 1903–1904. He was adviser to the Department of Public

Works of the provisional government of Cuba from 1906 to 1909, devising and starting construction of a comprehensive system of highways for Cuba. He was chief of engineers for the New York District from 1909 to 1916 and chief of engineers for the U.S. Army from 1916 to 1919. He retired with a rank of major general in 1919. Died September 24, 1933, in Washington, D.C. *References*: *DAB S1;* and *NCAB* 44:51.

BLACKFORD, ALEXANDER LATIMER (1829–1890). Missionary, born January 6, 1829, in Jefferson County, Ohio. Blackford graduated from Washington and Jefferson College and Western Theological Seminary (Allegheny, Pa.). He was a missionary under the Board of Foreign Missions of the Presbyterian Church in the U.S.A.* in Brazil from 1860 to 1890, serving in São Paulo from 1863 to 1867 and Rio de Janeiro after 1867. He was also an agent of the American Bible Society* in Brazil from 1877 to 1880. He returned to the United States in 1890. Died May 14, 1890, in Atlanta, Georgia.

BLAND, THEODORICK (1776–1846). Public official and diplomat, born December 6, 1776, in Dinwiddie County, Virginia. Bland practiced law in Virginia, Tennessee, and Kentucky. He settled in Baltimore about 1800, served in the Maryland House of Delegates from 1809 to 1812, and was associate judge of the Maryland sixth judicial district from 1812 to 1818. He was a member of the South American Commission* in 1817–1818. He was judge of Maryland District County from 1819 to 1824 and chancellor of the state of Maryland from 1824 until his death. *References*: Theodorick Bland Papers, Maryland Historical Society, Baltimore; *NCAB* 7:133; and Eugenio Pereira Salas, "La Mision Bland en Chile," *RCHG* 78 (1935): 80–103.

BLENK, JAMES HUBERT (1856–1917). Clergyman, born July 28, 1856, in Neustadt, Bavaria, and came to the United States when he was a baby. Blenk was a teacher at Jefferson College (Convent, La.). He then joined the Marist order and studied in France and Ireland; he was ordained in 1885. He was president of Jefferson College from 1891 to 1897 and later in charge of Holy Name Church in Algiers, Louisiana. He was auditor and secretary to the apostolic delegate to Cuba and Puerto Rico after the Spanish-American War and the first bishop of Puerto Rico from 1899 to 1906. He Americanized the Catholics, provided for education, and adjusted the affairs of church and state. He was archbishop of New Orleans from 1906 until his death. Died April 20, 1917, in New Orleans. *References*: *DAB*; *DACB*; *NCAB* 14:237; and Miriam T. O'Brien, "Puerto Rico's First American Bishop," *Records of the American Catholic Historical Society of Philadelphia* 91 (1980): 3–37.

BLISS, PORTER CORNELIUS (1838–1885). Journalist, born December 28, 1838, in Cattaraugas Reservation of the Senecas in New York State. Bliss attended Yale University and graduated from Hamilton College. He was private secretary to James Watson Webb, U.S. minister to Brazil in 1861–1862. He then went to Buenos Aires and explored the Grand Chaco on a commission from the Argentine government. He edited *River Plate Magazine* in Buenos Aires. He was private secretary to Charles A. Washburn,* U.S. minister to Paraguay from 1866 to 1868. He was appointed in 1866 by President Francisco Solano López to write a history of Paraguay, but the Paraguayan War brought the project to an early end. He was arrested by the Paraguayan police who held him in prison for three months and subjected him to severe torture to force him to admit a conspiracy against López. He returned to the United States and was translator in the State Department. He was secretary of legation in Mexico from 1870 to 1874. He was one of the editors of *Johnson's New Universal Cyclopaedia* in New York City from 1874 to 1877, editor of *Library Table* in 1877, and one of the editors of the *New York Herald* after 1878. He visited South America again as a correspondent of that newspaper from 1879 to 1881. He went later to Mexico on a gold-hunting expedition. Died February 2, 1885, in New York City. *References*: Porter Cornelius Bliss Papers, Tulane University, New Orleans; *DAB*; and *NYT*, January 5, 1885.

BLOM, FRANS FERDINAND (1893–1963). Archaeologist, born August 8, 1893, in Copenhagen, Denmark. Blom was trained in the Museum of Applied Art in Copenhagen. He went to Mexico in 1919 as a member of an oil survey group, working for the Campania Petrolera El Aguila in Chiapas and Tabasco. He became involved in archaeology and was one of the first archaeologists to work in Palenque for the Mexican government in the early 1920s, and for the Carnegie Institution of Washington at Uaxactún and other sites. In 1924, he joined the Department of Middle American Research and was later its director. He participated in the Tulane University expedition to Tuxtla Mountains and Tres Zapotes, in the John Geddings Gray Memorial Expedition in 1928, and in an expedition to Uxmal in 1930. He was coauthor of *Tribes and Temples* (New Orleans, 1926). He resigned and went to Mexico, worked in the state of Chiapas, led in 1948 an expedition to the Lancandón jungle, and worked among the Lancandón Indians. He settled in San Cristóbal de Las Casas, state of Chiapas, in 1950, and became citizen of Chiapas. Died June 23, 1963, in San Cristóbal de Las Casas. *References*: Frans Blom Papers, Tulane University, New Orleans; *AmAntiq* 31 (1966): 406–7; Robert L. Brunhouse, *Frans Blom: Maya Explorer* (Albuquerque, N.M., 1976); Robert L. Brunhouse, *Pursuit of the Ancient Maya: Some Archaeologists of Yesterday* (Albuquerque, N.M., 1975), chs. 6–7; *NYT*, June 24, 1963; and *WWLA*.

BLOW, HENRY TAYLOR (1817–1875). Businessman and diplomat, born July 15, 1817, in Southampton County, Virginia, and grew up in St. Louis. Blow graduated from St. Louis University. He entered business and was a pioneer in the lead and lead products business. He was also president of Iron Mountain Railroad. He served in the Missouri state senate. He was U.S. minister to

Venezuela in 1861–1862. He served in the U.S. House of Representatives from 1862 to 1866. He was U.S. minister to Brazil from 1869 to 1871, and did much to further closer relations between the United States and Brazil. Died September 11, 1875, in Saratoga, New York. *References*: *BDAC; DAB; DADH; NCAB* 4:291; *NYT*, September 12–13, 1875; Norman T. Strauss, "Brazil in the 1870's as Seen by American Diplomats," Ph.D. diss., New York University, 1971; and *WWWA*.

BLUEFIELDS. Colony created in the early 1880s in the Mosquito Reservation on the east coast of Nicaragua. Colonists arrived in increasing numbers, bought tracts of land along the Escondido River, and planted banana plantations. The colony had, for a time, an English-language daily and frequent steamship service to the Gulf ports. Business deteriorated after 1894, and the colony became moribund by the early 1920s. *Reference*: Craig L. Dozier, *Nicaragua's Mosquito Shore: The Years of British and American Presence* (University, Ala., 1985), ch. 7.

BOAL, PIERRE DE LAGARDE (1895–1966). Diplomat, born September 29, 1895, in Thonons-les-Barnes, France, to American parents. Boal served with the French army cavalry, the Lafayette Flying Corps, and the U.S. Air Service during World War I. He entered the foreign service in 1919, and served in Mexico City, Belgrade, Warsaw, Berne, and Lima until 1928. He was secretary of the International Conference of the American States on Conciliation and Arbitration in Washington, D.C., in 1928–1929 and acting secretary general of the Commission of Inquiry and Conciliation of Bolivia and Paraguay in Washington, D.C., in 1929. He was assistant chief of the division of Western European Affairs in the State Department in 1930–1931 and its chief in 1931–1932. He served in Canada from 1932 to 1936 and was counselor of embassy in Mexico City from 1936 to 1941. He was U.S. minister to Nicaragua in 1941–1942 and to Bolivia from 1942 to 1944. He retired in 1947. Died May 24, 1966, in Washington, D.C. *References*: *DADH; NYT*, May 25, 1966; and *WWWA*.

BOGGS, STANLEY HARDING (1914–   ). Archaeologist and anthropologist, born August 8, 1914, in Warsaw, Indiana. Boggs graduated from Northwestern University and the University of Arizona and studied at Harvard University. He was an assistant in the Copán project of the Carnegie Institution of Washington in 1939, archaeologist in the Dimick-El Salvador expedition of Tulane University–Carnegie Institution of Washington in 1940–1941, archaeologist in the El Salvador project of the Institute of Andean Research in 1942, director of the Tazumal excavations for the National Museum of El Salvador from 1943 to 1946, archaeologist in the Zacaleu project of the United Fruit Company in Guatemala in 1946–1947, chief of the department of archaeological investigations of the government of El Salvador from 1947 to 1954, professor at the University of El Salvador from 1963 to 1968, and private archaeological consultant and researcher after 1968. *Reference: AMWS.*

BOND, JAMES (1900–1989). Ornithologist, born January 4, 1900, in Philadelphia. Bond graduated from Cambridge University. He conducted an expedition to the lower Amazon in 1925, an ornithological survey of the West Indies after 1927, and taxonomic studies of birds in Peru and Bolivia after 1940. He was research associate at the Academy of Natural Sciences of Philadelphia from 1933 to 1938, associate curator of birds of the Americas from 1939 to 1962, and curator from 1967 until his retirement in 1972. He wrote *Birds of the West Indies* (Philadelphia, 1936), *Field Guide to Birds of the West Indies* (New York, 1947), and *Check-List of Birds of the West Indies* (Philadelphia, 1950), and was coauthor of *Birds of Bolivia* (Philadelphia, 1942–1943). Died February 14, 1989, in Philadelphia. *References: AMWS; Auk* 106 (1989): 718–20; Mary W. Bond, *To James Bond with Love* (Lititz, Pa., 1980); and *NYT*, February 17, 1989.

BONSAL, PHILIP W(ILSON) (1903–   ). Diplomat, born May 22, 1903, in New York City. Bonsal graduated from Yale University. He worked for American Telephone and Telegraph in Cuba, Spain, and Chile from 1926 to 1935, and for the U.S. Federal Communications Commission from 1935 to 1937. He entered the diplomatic service in 1938, and served in Havana, the U.S. State Department, and Madrid. He was first secretary in the Netherlands in 1947–1948 and was attached to the embassy in Paris from 1948 to 1952. He was U.S. ambassador to Colombia from 1955 to 1957, ambassador to Bolivia from 1957 to 1959, and ambassador to Cuba in 1959–1960, serving as the last U.S. ambassador before the relations with Fidel Castro's regime were broken. He wrote *Cuba, Castro and the United States* (Pittsburgh, 1970). He was ambassador to Morocco in 1961–1962. He retired in 1965. *References: CB* 1959; *DADH*; and *WWA.*

BORLAND, SOLON (1808–1864). Public official and diplomat, born September 21, 1808, near Suffolk, Virginia. Borland studied medicine and practiced in Little Rock, Arkansas. He served during the Mexican War. He served in the U.S. Senate from 1848 to 1853. He was U.S. minister to Central America in 1853–1854. In 1854, he caused an international incident which led to the shelling of Greytown in Nicaragua by the USS *Cyane*, and the town's destruction by fire. He resumed the practice of medicine in Little Rock, and served in the Confederate Army during the Civil War. Died January 1 or 31, 1864, in or near Houston, Texas. *References: DAB; DADH; NCAB* 4:386; and James M. Wood, "Expansionism as Diplomacy: The Career of Solon Borland in Central America 1853–1854," *TA* 40 (1984): 399–416.

BORLAUG, NELSON E(RNEST) (1914–   ). Plant pathologist, born March 25, 1914, near Cresco, Iowa. Borlaug graduated from the University of Minnesota. He was plant pathologist with E. I. du Pont de Nemours and Company from 1941 to 1944. He was a member of a team of agricultural scientists sent out under the auspices of the Rockefeller Foundation to export the United States agricultural revolution to Mexico, and settled in Mexico City. He developed high-yield, highly adaptable dwarf wheat plants and received the Nobel Peace Prize in 1970, for his leadership in the "Green Revolution." *References*: *AMWS*; Lennard Bickel, *Facing Starvation: Norman Borlaug and the Fight Against Hunger* (New York, 1974); *CB* 1971; Don Pearlberg, *Norman Borlaug, Hunger Fighter* (Washington, D.C., 1970); S. Seeger and K. Seeger, "Father of the Green Revolution," *Reader's Digest* 98 (March 1971): 134–38; and *WWA*.

BORTON, FRANCIS (1862–1929). Clergyman and archaeologist, born April 27, 1862, in Oxford Township, McDonough County, Illinois, and grew up in New Orleans. Borton graduated from the University of Southern California, attended the divinity school of Boston University, and was ordained in 1890. He held a pastorate in Newton Highland, Massachusetts. He was a missionary under the Board of Foreign Missions of the Methodist Episcopal Church* in Mexico from 1891 until 1910. He was pastor of the English-speaking Methodist congregation in Mexico City from 1891 to 1895, and principal of the theological department of the Methodist Mexican Institute in Puebla from 1895 to 1910. He carried out archaeological research in Mitla and Monte Alban in the state of Oaxaca and in Tlaxcala. He returned to the United States in 1910 and was curator of the Mission Inn in Riverside, California, from 1910 until his death. Died June 9, 1929, in Long Beach, California. *Reference*: *NCAB* 22:84.

BOWEN, HERBERT WOLCOTT (1856–1927). Diplomat, born February 29, 1856, in Brooklyn, New York. Bowen graduated from Yale and Columbia universities and was admitted to the bar. He practiced law in New York City until 1890. He was U.S. consul in Barcelona from 1890 to 1895, consul general from 1895 to 1899, and U.S. minister to Persia from 1899 to 1901. He was U.S. minister to Venezuela from 1901 to 1905. During the Venezuelan crisis of 1902, he succeeded in obtaining the release of all the foreigners held in Venezuela. Tense relations between Bowen and President Theodore Roosevelt led to the former's dismissal from the foreign service in 1905. He retired in 1905 and wrote his memoirs, *Recollections, Diplomatic and Undiplomatic* (New York, 1926). Died May 29, 1927, near Woodstock, Connecticut. *References*: *DAB; DADH; NCAB* 20:46; *NYT*, May 30, 1927; and *WWWA*.

BOWERS, CLAUDE GERNADE (1878–1958). Journalist and diplomat, born November 20, 1878, in Westfield, Indiana, and grew up in Whitestown, Lebanon, and Indianapolis, Indiana. Bowers was editorial writer on the Indianapolis *Sentinel* from 1899 to 1903, reporter on the Terre Haute *Gazette* and then the Terre Haute *Star* from 1903 to 1911, secretary to U.S. Senator John W. Kern from 1911 to 1917, editor of the Fort Wayne *Journal-Gazette* from 1917 to 1923, editorial writer on the New York *Evening World* from 1923 to 1931, and political columnist for the New York *Journal* and other Hearst newspapers from 1931 to 1933. He was U.S. ambassador to Spain from 1933 to 1939 and ambassador to Chile from 1939 to 1953. He worked to induce Chile to sever relations with the Axis powers and in fostering improved economic and defense cooperation between Chile and the United States. He also worked to counter post–World War II Soviet influences in Chile. He wrote *Chile through Embassy Windows, 1939–1953* (New York, 1958). *My Life: The Memoirs of Claude Bowers* (New York, 1962) was published posthumously. Died January 21, 1958, in New York City. *References*: Claude Bowers Papers, Indiana University Library, Bloomington; *DAB S6; DADH; DLB; NCAB* 44:86; *NYT*, January 22, 1958; and *WWWA*.

BOWLIN, JAMES BUTLER (1804–1874). Lawyer and diplomat, born in Spottsylvania County, Virginia. Bowlin was apprenticed to a mechanic at an early age and then became a teacher. He studied law and was admitted to the bar in 1827. He practiced law in St. Louis and published the *Farmers' and Mechanics' Advocate*. He was chief clerk of the state house of representatives from 1834 to 1835, member of the state legislature from 1835 to 1837, district attorney for St. Louis in 1837, and attorney for the Bank of St. Louis and judge of the criminal court from 1839 to 1843. He served in the U.S. House of Representatives from 1843 to 1851. He was U.S. minister to Colombia from 1854 to 1857 and commissioner to Paraguay in 1858–1859. He then resumed the practice of law in St. Louis. Died July 19, 1874, in St. Louis. *References*: *DADH; NCAB* 5:528; and *WWWA*.

BOWMAN, ISAIAH (1878–1950). Geographer, born December 26, 1878, in Waterloo, Ontario, Canada, and grew up near Brown City. Bowman attended State Normal College (Ypsilanti, Mich.) and Harvard and Yale universities. He was an instructor in geography at Yale University from 1905 to 1909 and assistant professor there from 1909 to 1915. He was leader of the Yale South American expedition of 1907 to the Andes of Peru and the borderlands of Bolivia, geographer and geologist on the Yale Peruvian expedition of 1911, and leader of an expedition to Peru in 1913. He wrote *South America: A Geography Reader* (Chicago, 1915), *The Andes of Southern Peru: Geographical Reconnaissance along the Seventy-Third Meridian* (New York, 1916), and *Desert Trails of Atacamba* (New York, 1924). He was director of the American Geographical Society from 1915 to 1935. At his proposal, the society undertook the major research program leading to the compilation of a map of Hispanic America on a scale of 1:1,000,000 (completed in 1946). During World War I, he worked on the Inquiry, which conducted studies on the problems of peacemaking, and was chief territorial specialist for the American delegation at the Peace Conference in Paris. He was president of Johns Hopkins University from 1935 until his retirement in 1948. Died January 6, 1950, in Baltimore. *References*: Isaiah Bowman Papers, American Geographical Society, Milwaukee; *DAB; Geogra-*

phers: Biobibliographical Studies 1 (1977): 9–18; Geoffrey J. Martin, *The Life and Thought of Isaiah Bowman* (Hamden, Conn., 1980); *NCAB* 40:484; and E. V. Niemeyer, Jr., "Three North Americans in Chile," *Athenea. Revista de Ciencieas, Letras y Artes* [Concepcion, Chile], no. 433 (1976): 61–68.

BOYD, SARAH M. (1843–1919). Educator, born January 1, 1843, in Antrim, New Hampshire, and grew up in Waldboro, New Hampshire. Boyd graduated from Mount Holyoke Seminary. She came to Argentina in 1877 as tutor to the children of Benjamin Apthorp Gould* in Cordoba. She later opened a model grade school in Tucuman and organized a model grade school in Concepción del Uruguay in 1877–1878 and a normal school in Mendoza from 1878 to 1880. She returned to the United States in 1880 and taught in Boston and in Winona, Minnesota, until 1883. Died March 28, 1919, in Winsted, Connecticut. *References: Cutolo*; and *Luiggi*.

BRACKENRIDGE, HENRY MARIE (1786–1871). Lawyer and public official, born May 11, 1786, in Pittsburgh, Pennsylvania. Brackenridge studied law and was admitted to the bar in 1806. He practiced law in Somerset, Pennsylvania, and St. Louis until 1811 and in New Orleans from 1811 to 1814. He served as deputy attorney general and district judge in Louisiana. He was secretary to the U.S. commission to study the political situation in the Spanish provinces of South America in 1817–1818. He wrote *Voyage to South America, Performed by Order of the American Government, in the Years 1817 and 1818, in the Frigate Congress* (Baltimore, 1819). He was secretary and translator and then a judge in Florida from 1821 to 1832. He served in the U.S. House of Representatives in 1840–1841. Died January 18, 1871, near Pittsburgh, Pennsylvania. *References: DAB*; William F. Keller, *Nation's Advocate: Henry Marie Brackenridge and Young America* (Pittsburgh, 1956); *NCAB* 9:468; and A. Curtis Wilgus, "Nineteenth Century Travelers: Henry Marie Brackenridge," *Americas* 24 (April 1972): 31–36.

BRADEN, SPRUILLE (1894–1978). Diplomat, born March 13, 1894, in Elkhorn, Montana. Braden graduated from Yale University. He was involved in various business ventures in Chile from 1914 to 1920, including copper mining and bond negotiations for Westinghouse and the Chilean national army. He was involved with the Monmouth Rag Company of New Jersey from 1925 to 1932, and then reorganized the Rehabilitation Corporation. He led the U.S. delegation to the Chaco Peace Conference in Buenos Aires from 1935 to 1938 and was U.S. ambassador to Colombia from 1939 to 1942, ambassador to Cuba from 1942 to 1945, ambassador to Argentina in 1945, and assistant secretary of state for American republics affairs from 1945 to 1947. He was in private business after 1947, and wrote his memoirs, *Diplomats and Demagogues* (New Rochelle, N.Y., 1971). Died January 10, 1978, in Los Angeles. *References*: Spruille Braden Papers, Columbia University Library, New York City; *DADH*; *ELA*; Gary Frank, *Juan Pe-*

rón vs. Spruille Braden: The Story behind the Blue Book (Lanham, Md., 1980); John C. Kesler, "Spruille Braden," Ph.D. diss., Kent State University, 1985; *NCAB* F:532; *NYT*, January 11, 1978; Shirley N. Rawls, "Spruille Braden: A Political Biography," Ph.D. diss., University of New Mexico, 1977; Miguel Angel Sccenna, *Braden y Peron* (Buenos Aires, 1974); Roger R. Trask, "Spruille Braden versus George Messersmith, World War II, the Cold War and Argentine Policy, 1945–1947," *JISWA* 26 (1984): 69–95; and Albert P. Vannucci, "Elected by Providence: Spruille Braden in Argentina in 1945," in *Ambassadors in Foreign Policy: The Influence of Individuals on U.S.–Latin American Policy*, ed. C. Neale Robbing and Albert P. Vannucci (New York, 1987), pp. 49–73.

BRADEN, WILLIAM (1871–1942). Mining engineer, born March 24, 1871, in Indianapolis. Braden attended Massachusetts Institute of Technology. He was assistant to the chief engineer of the Montana Company at Marysville, Montana; surveyor for the Elkhorn Mining Company and the Anaconda Company; chemist, assayer, and assistant superintendent of the Arkansas Valley Smelter at Leadville, Colorado; and engineer and representative in British Columbia for the Omaha and Grant Smelting and Refining Company, also examining mines for that company in North and South America from 1893 to 1898. He was founder of the Braden Copper Company* in Chile, conducted mine examinations in the United States and Mexico, and was general manager of the Velardena Mines in Mexico and the Bruce Mines in Ontario from 1901 to 1903. He bought Rancagua copper mine in north central Chile in 1904 and was organizer and general manager of the Braden Copper Company in Chile. He was forced to sell the mine to the Guggenheims in 1908. He directed operations of the Andes Exploration Company in South America from 1913 to 1918. He was a consultant, involved in mine examinations from 1919 to 1930 and then in mining explorations in North and South America from 1931 to 1939. Died July 18, 1942, in Reno, Nevada. *References*: *NYT*, July 19, 1942; and *WWWA*.

BRADEN COPPER COMPANY. Organized by William Braden in 1904 to mine the Rancagua copper mine in north central Chile. It was sold to the Guggenheims in 1908, who transferred control of the company to Kennecott Copper Company* in 1915. *References*: Louis Hiriat, *Braden: Historia de una Mina* (Santiago, 1964); and A. B. Parsons, *Porphyry Coppers* (New York, 1933), ch. 7.

BRAGG, EDWARD S(TUYVESANT) (1827–1912). Public official and diplomat, born February 20, 1827, in Unadilla, Otsego County, New York. Bragg graduated from Geneva (later Hobart) College, studied law, and was admitted to the bar in 1848. He practiced law in Unadilla and then in Fond du Lac, Wisconsin. He was elected district attorney in 1853. He served in the Union Army during the Civil War. He served in the state senate in 1868–1869 and in the U.S. House of Representatives from 1877 to 1883 and from 1885 to 1887.

He was U.S. minister to Mexico in 1888–1889 and consul general in Havana, Cuba, in 1902 and in Hong Kong from 1902 to 1906. Died June 20, 1912, in Fond du Lac, Wisconsin. *References*: *ACAB*; *BDAC*; *DAB*; Kenneth J. Grieb, "A Badger General's Foray into Diplomacy: General Edward S. Bragg in Mexico," *Wisconsin Magazine of History* 53 (1969): 21–32; *NCAB* 10:16; and *WWWA*.

BRAINERD, GEORGE WALTON (1909–1956). Archaeologist, born July 9, 1909, in Blacksburg, Virginia, and grew up in Martins Ferry, Ohio. Brainerd graduated from Lafayette College and Ohio State University. He taught at the American Boys' (later Elborz) College in Teheran, Iran, from 1930 to 1933. He was archaeologist to the Division of Historical Studies of the Carnegie Institution from 1939 to 1943. He carried out archaeological investigations in Yucatán in 1940, served in the Special Services Division of U.S. Naval Intelligence during World War II, and directed excavations in the Valley of Mexico in 1946 and in Campeche and other sites in Yucatán in 1949. He was assistant professor of anthropology at the University of California in Los Angeles from 1946 to 1950, and associate professor from 1950 until his death, and staff archaeologist in the Southwest Museum (Los Angeles) from 1946 to 1955. He wrote *The Archaeological Ceramics of Yucatán* (Berkeley, Calif., 1958). Died February 14, 1956, in Pasadena, California. *References*: *AA* 58 (1956): 908–12; *AmAntiq* 22 (1956): 165–68; *NCAB* 46:86; and *NYT*, March 10, 1956.

BRAND, DONALD D(ILWORTH) (1905–   ). Geographer, born March 6, 1905, in Chiclayo, Peru, to American parents. Brand graduated from the University of California. He was assistant professor of anthropological geography at the University of New Mexico in 1934–1935, associate professor from 1935 to 1939, and professor from 1939 to 1947. He was cultural geographer with the Smithsonian Institution in Mexico from 1944 to 1946 and professor of geography at the University of Michigan from 1947 to 1949 and at the University of Texas at Austin from 1949 until his retirement in 1975. He wrote *Quiroga: A Mexican Municipio* (Washington, D.C., 1951) and *Coastal Study of Southwest Mexico* (Austin, Tex., 1957–1958). *Reference*: *WWA*.

BRANDEGEE, TOWNSHEND STITH (1843–1925). Botanist, born February 16, 1843, in Berlin, Connecticut. Brandegee graduated from the Sheffield Scientific School of Yale University. He was city engineer of Cannon City, Colorado. He was botanical collector and topographical assistant to the Hayden Expedition to southwestern Colorado and adjoining parts of Utah and was engineer to the Royal Gorge and Santa Fe surveys and to the northern Transcontinental Survey. He studied the flora of Santa Cruz Island, California, after 1886 and conducted botanical explorations of Baja California, Mexico, after 1889 for the California Academy of Sciences. He later made intermittent visits to Baja California and to the Mexican states of Sonora, Sinaloa, Veracruz, and Puebla.

He became recognized as an authority on the flora of Baja California and the islands of the Gulf of California. He wrote *Plantae Mexicanae Purpusianae* (Berkeley, Calif., 1909–1924). Died April 7, 1925. *References*: Harry B. Humphrey, *Makers of North American Botany* (New York, 1960), pp. 37–38; and W. A. Setchell, "Townshend Stith Brandegee," *University of California Publications in Botany* 13 (1926): 155–78.

BRANIFF, OSCAR (? – ?) and **BRANIFF, THOMAS** (? – ?). Businessmen, from Oklahoma. The Braniff brothers entered Mexico in the early 1880s. By 1902, they owned a farm and milling operation in Guanajuato and operated Braniff and Company in Mexico City. They entered the electric power and street car business in 1906, receiving a concession to form the Puebla Tramway, Light and Power Company, and they constructed four hydroelectric plants which furnished power for Puebla and surrounding towns. Died sometime during the Mexican revolution. *Reference*: Hanrahan, ch. 9.

BRANNER, JOHN CASPER (1850–1922). Geologist, born July 4, 1850, in New Market, Jefferson County, Tennessee. Branner attended Maryville College (near Knoxville, Tenn.) and graduated from Cornell University. He accompanied Charles Frederick Hartt* on an expedition to Brazil from 1874 to 1880. He served as assistant director of the Commissao Geologico do Imperio do Brazil from 1874 to 1877, when the organization was discontinued. He was involved in operating gold mines in the state of Minas Gerais until 1880. He returned to the United States in 1880 but was back in Brazil in that year in the employ of Thomas A. Edison, searching for a vegetable fiber of a quality suitable for incandescent lights until 1881. He was commissioned by the U.S. Department of Agriculture to study the question of cotton culture in Brazil from 1882 to 1884 and was topographer on the Geological Survey of Pennsylvania in 1884–1885. He was professor of geology at Indiana University from 1885 to 1887, state geologist of Arkansas from 1887 to 1891, professor of geology at Stanford University from 1891 to 1916, vice president of the university from 1889 to 1913, and president from 1913 until his retirement in 1916. He studied the ocean reefs lying off the coast of Pernamabuco in 1899, the black diamond areas of Bahía and the geology of the states of Alagoas and Sergipe in 1907, and again the Brazilian coast in 1911. Died March 1, 1922, in Stanford, California. *References*: *DAB*; and *WWWA*.

BRAZIL SQUADRON. Created by the U.S. Navy in 1825, it was for many years one of the busiest in the navy, protecting American trade. Its headquarters were in Rio de Janeiro. It was disbanded in 1861. *Reference*: Donald W. Giffin, "The American Navy at Work on the Brazil Station, 1827–1860," *AN* 19 (1959): 239–56.

BRENNER, ANITA (1905–1974). Journalist and author, born August 13, 1905, in Aguascalientes, Mexico, to American parents. Brenner attended the University of Texas and the National University of Mexico and graduated from Columbia University. She was a freelance correspondent for the *New York Times* and for the North American Newspaper Alliance, Latin American editor of *The Nation* during the 1920s, special correspondent for the *New York Times* from 1933 to 1938, and art editor of the *Brooklyn Daily Eagle* in 1935–1936. She was special correspondent in Mexico for *Fortune* magazine in 1938 and editor and publisher of *Mexico This Month* from 1955 to 1971. She wrote *Idols behind Altars* (New York, 1929), *The Influence of Technique on the Decorative Style in the Domestic Pottery of Culhuacan* (New York, 1931), *Your Mexican Holiday: A Modern Guide Book* (New York, 1932), and *The Wind That Swept Mexico: The History of the Mexican Revolution, 1910–1942* (New York, 1943). Killed December 1, 1974, in a car accident 300 miles north of Mexico City. *References*: *CA*; and *NYT*, December 3, 1974.

BRENT, WILLIAM, JR. (1783–1848). Diplomat, born January 13, 1783, in Richland, Virginia. Brent was a member of the Virginia House of Delegates in 1810–1811. He was a U.S. chargé d'affaires in Buenos Aires from 1844 to 1846. He tried to mediate between Argentina and England and France, and between Argentina and Paraguay, but was unsuccessful, because the U.S. government did not support his efforts. Died May 13, 1848. *Reference*: *NCAB* 5:528.

BRETHREN CHURCH: FOREIGN MISSIONARY SOCIETY OF THE.
Founded in 1900, it began missionary work in Argentina in 1909 and in Brazil in 1949, and also worked in Mexico and Puerto Rico. The name was changed to the National Fellowship of Brethren Churches and later to the Fellowship of Grace Brethren Churches. *References*: *BE*; and Homer A. Kent, Jr., *Conquering Frontiers: A History of the Brethren Church (The National Fellowship of Brethren Churches)* (Winona Lake, Ind., 1972).

BRIGGS, ELLIS ORMSBEE (1899–1976). Diplomat, born December 1, 1899, in Watertown, Massachusetts. Briggs graduated from Dartmouth College. He entered the diplomatic service in 1924 and served in Callao, Lima, Havana, and Santiago. He was assistant chief of the Division of the American Republics in the State Department from 1937 to 1940, counselor of embassy in Cuba from 1942 to 1944, and chief of the division of Central American affairs in the U.S. State Department in 1944. He was U.S. ambassador to the Dominican Republic in 1944–1945, minister-counselor in Chungking, China, in 1945, director of the Office of American Republic Affairs in the State Department from 1945 to 1947, U.S. ambassador to Uruguay from 1947 to 1949, ambassador to Czechoslovakia from 1949 to 1952, ambassador to Korea from 1952 to 1955, ambassador to Peru in 1955–1956, and ambassador to Brazil from 1956 to 1959, where he negotiated for the acquisition of a missile-tracking station on a Brazilian-owned island in the Atlantic Ocean. He was ambassador to Greece from 1959 to 1962. He wrote *Farewell to Foggy Bottom: The Recollections of a Career Diplomat* (New York, 1964). Died February 21, 1976, in Gainesville, Georgia. *References*: *CB* 1965; *DADH; NYT*, February 23, 1976; and *WWWA*.

BRIGHAM, JOHN C(LARK) (1794–1862). Missionary, born February 28, 1794, in New Marlboro, Massachusetts. Brigham graduated from Williams College and Andover Theological Seminary, and was ordained in 1832. He was a missionary under the American Board of Commissioners for Foreign Missions and an agent of the American Bible Society* in South America from 1823 to 1826. With Theophilus Parvin,* he was in Buenos Aires in 1823. He then went to Chile, Lima, and Guayaquil, and later to Mexico from 1824 to 1826. He returned to the United States in 1826. He was an agent of the American Bible Society in New York City in 1826–1827 and its corresponding secretary from 1827 until his death. Died August 10, 1862, in Brooklyn, New York. *References*: William Adams, *Life and Service of Rev. John C. Brigham* (New York, 1863); and J. Orin Olpihant, ''The Parvin-Brigham Mission to Spanish America 1823–1826,'' *Church History* 14 (1945): 85–103.

BRITTON, NATHANIEL LORD (1859–1934). Botanist, born January 15, 1859, in New Dorp, Staten Island, New York. Britton graduated from the School of Mines of Columbia University. He was an instructor of botany at Columbia University from 1886 to 1890, adjunct professor there in 1890–1891, and professor from 1891 to 1896. He was director of the New York Botanical Garden from 1896 until his retirement in 1929. He visited the West Indies more than thirty times. At his recommendation, the government of Puerto Rico established a forest preserve and instituted a reforestation project. He was coauthor of *The Bahama Flora* (New York, 1920) and *The Botany of Porto Rico and the Virgin Islands* (New York, 1923–1925). Died June 25, 1934, in New York City. *References*: *BMNAS* 19 (1938): 147–202; Harry B. Humphrey, *Makers of North American Botany* (New York, 1961), pp. 40–42; *Journal of the New York Botanical Garden* 35 (1934): 169–80; and *Science* 80 (1934): 108–11.

BROOKE, JOHN R(UTTER) (1838–1926). Army officer, born July 21, 1838, in Montgomery County, Pennsylvania. Brooke served in the Union Army during the Civil War. He was appointed lieutenant colonel in the regular army in 1866. He served in the Spanish-American War, participating in the campaign in Puerto Rico. He was the first military governor of Puerto Rico in 1898 and was military governor of Cuba in 1899–1900. He returned to the U.S. in 1900 and was commanding officer of the Department of the East until his retirement in 1902. Died September 5, 1926, in Philadelphia. *References*: John R. Brooke Papers, Historical Society of Pennsylvania, Philadelphia; *ACAB; DAB; NCAB* 9:24; and *WWWA*.

BROWN, EDWARD NORPHELT (1862–1956). Railroad builder, born March 25, 1862, in Barbour County, Alabama. Brown graduated from the Agricultural and Mechanical College (later Alabama Polytechnic Institute, Auburn). He did surveying and construction work on the Athens and Northeastern Railway of Georgia and the Richmond and Danville Railroad in North Carolina and Georgia until 1883 and was engineer of maintenance and assistant chief engineer of the Central Railroad of Georgia from 1883 to 1887. He went to Mexico in 1887 as assistant chief engineer in charge of construction for the National Railroad of Mexico and built the section from Saltillo to San Miguel, opening up a through route from American borders to Mexico City. He was chief engineer in 1889–1890, general superintendent from 1890 to 1900, third vice president and general manager in 1900–1901, first vice president and general manager from 1901 to 1903, president of the National Railroad of Mexico and Mexico International Railway from 1903 to 1908, and president of the National Railways of Mexico from 1908 to 1914. He was chairman of the board of St. Louis–San Francisco Railway Company from 1919 to 1948. Died May 2, 1956, in New York City. *References*: *NCAB* 42:559; *NYT*, May 3, 1956; and *WWWA*.

BRUCE, JAMES (1892–1980). Businessman and diplomat, born December 23, 1892, in Baltimore. Bruce graduated from Princeton University and the University of Maryland. He served in the U.S. Army during World War I. He was vice president of Chase National Bank from 1926 to 1931, president of the Baltimore Trust Company from 1931 to 1933, financial adviser to the board of directors of the Home Owners Loan Corporation in Washington, D.C., 1933–1934, and vice president of National Dairy Products Company from 1935 to 1947. He was U.S. ambassador to Argentina 1947 to 1949. He was the first director of the Mutual Defense Assistant Program in 1949–1950. He wrote *Those Perplexing Argentines* (New York, 1953) and his *Memoirs* (Baltimore, 1975). Died July 17, 1980, in New York City. *References*: *CB* 1949; and *WWWA*.

BRUMBAUGH, MARTIN G(ROVE) (1862–1930). Educator, born April 14, 1862, in Huntington County, Pennsylvania. Brumbaugh graduated from Juniata College (Huntington, Pa.) and the University of Pennsylvania. He was superintendent of school of Huntington County from 1884 to 1890, first professor of pedagogy at the University of Pennsylvania from 1894 to 1900, and president of Juniata College from 1895 to 1907 and again from 1924 to 1930. He was first commissioner of education in Puerto Rico from 1900 to 1902. He organized a public school system in which both teachers and students were bilingual. He also established a normal school and a free public library. He was superintendent of schools of Philadelphia from 1906 to 1915. Died March 14, 1930, in Pinehurst, North Carolina. *References*: *BDAE*; Salvatore M. Messina, "Martin Grove Brumbaugh, Educator," Ph.D. diss., University of Pennsylvania, 1965; *NCAB* 15:409; Aida Negron de Montilla, *Americanization in Puerto Rico and the Public*

School System 1900–1930 (San Juan, P.R., 1975), ch. 3; *NYT*, March 15, 1930; and *WWWA*.

BUCARELI CONFERENCE (1923). A series of meetings held in a building on Bucareli Avenue, Mexico City, in 1923, between representatives of the United States and Mexico to discuss the differences between the two nations stemming from Mexico's agrarian and petroleum policies. It resulted in two treaties and an "extraofficial pact." *References*: *DADH*; D. D. Di Piazza, "The Bucareli Conference and United States-Mexican Relations," Ph.D. diss., University of Missouri, 1966; and *ELA*.

BUCHANAN, WILLIAM INSCO (1852–1909). Diplomat, born September 10, 1852, near Covington, Ohio. Buchanan settled in Sioux City, Iowa, where he was an edge-tool maker, commercial traveler, crockery wholesaler, and theater manager. He helped direct the Iowa exhibit at the Columbian Exposition of 1893. He was U.S. minister to Argentina from 1894 to 1899. He successfully arbitrated an Argentine-Chilean boundary dispute. He was the first U.S. minister to Panama in 1903–1904. He was delegate to the second (1901) and third (1906) international conferences of American states, organized the Central American Peace Conference in 1907, and was a member of several other committees and conferences. Died October 16, 1909, in London, England. *References*: *DAB; DADH; NCAB* 2:271; and Harold F. Peterson, *Diplomat of the Americas: A Biography of William I. Buchanan* (Albany, N.Y., 1977).

BUCK, CHARLES WILLIAM (1849–1930). Lawyer, born March 17, 1849, in Vicksburg, Mississippi. Buck graduated from Georgetown (Ky.) College and University of Kentucky, and was admitted to the bar in 1871. He practiced law in Mississippi until 1874 and in Kentucky after 1874. He was U.S. minister to Peru from 1885 to 1889. He then resumed the practice of law in Louisville, Kentucky. He wrote *Under the Sun: Or, the Passing of the Incas: A Story of Old Peru* (Louisville, 1902). Died November 30, 1930, in Louisville, Kentucky. *References*: James B. Lloyd, ed., *Lives of Mississippi Authors, 1817–1967* (Jackson, Miss., 1981); and *WWWA*.

BUCKLEY, WILLIAM F(RANK), SR. (1881–1958). Petroleum executive, born July 11, 1881, in Washington, Texas. Buckley graduated from the University of Texas. He went to Mexico in 1908 and established a law office in Mexico City in 1909. In 1911, he established a law office in Tampico, Mexico. In 1913, he founded the Mexican Investment Company, for real estate and oil operations, and was its president until 1915. In 1915, he founded, with his brother **EDMUND L. BUCKLEY** (1888–1951), the Pantepec Oil Company, C.A., of Mexico, but was forced to withdraw from Mexico in 1917. He formed the American Association of Mexico for the purpose of opposing the Mexican regime. In 1924, the brothers formed the Pantepec Oil Company, C.A., of

Venezuela. He served as its president until 1943. In 1938, he entered into a contract with the Standard Oil Company of Venezuela to explore and develop certain of Pantepec properties, which led to the discovery of the Mulata and El Roble oil fields in Venezuela, and in 1944, he entered into a contract with the Atlantic Refining Company for the exploration of other Pantepec concessions, resulting in discoveries in Tucupido, Ruiz, Aguasay, and Pirital. He then expanded his operations into other countries and formed Magellan Petroleum Corporation, operating in Guatemala and Ecuador, Pancoastal Petroleum Company, operating in Venezuela and Guatemala, and Pantepec Oil Company, operating in Venezuela. Died October 5, 1958, in New York City. *References*: William F. Buckley Papers, University of Texas Library, Austin; Priscilla L. and William Buckley, Jr., *W.F.B.–An Appreciation* (New York, 1959); *Hanrahan*, ch. 4; Charles L. Markmann, *The Buckleys: A Family Examined* (New York, 1973); *NCAB* 43:110; and *NYT*, October 6, 1958.

BULL, CHARLES LIVINGSTON (1874–1932). Taxidermist and naturalist, born in Oradell, New Jersey. Bull studied at the Philadelphia Art School. He was a taxidermist for Ward's Museum in Rochester, New York, and for the National Museum in Washington, D.C. He made numerous field trips into Mexico and Central and South America where he studied wildlife. He wrote *Under the Roof of the Jungle: A Book of Animal Life in the Guiana Wilds* (Boston, 1911). Died March 22, 1932, in Oradell, New Jersey. *References*: D. L. Tuttle, "Charles Livingston Bull," *Conservationist* 32 (July 1977): 8–13; and *WWWA*.

BULL, JAMES H(UNTER) (1817–1904). Lawyer and traveler, born March 16, 1817, in Warwick Township, Chester County, Pennsylvania. Bull attended Bristol College (Ohio) and Carlisle Law School and was admitted to the bar in 1840. He traveled in Baja California, Mexico, in 1843–1844 and prepared the first known narrative of a crossing of Baja California undertaken by an American. He practiced law in Chester County after 1845 and was special provost marshal for the county during the Civil War and county district attorney from 1875 to 1878. Died May 4, 1904, in West Chester, Pennsylvania. *Reference*: *Journey of James H. Bull, Baja California, October 1843 to January 1844*, ed. Doyce B. Nunis, Jr. (Los Angeles, 1965).

BULLARD, WILLIAM R(OTCH), JR. (1926–1972). Archaeologist, born June 4, 1926, in Boston. Bullard graduated from Harvard University. He served during World War II. He was a field assistant in excavations in Yucatán and British Honduras and field director of the British Honduras archaeological project of the Royal Ontario Museum from 1961 to 1963. He was assistant director of the Peabody Museum of Harvard from 1963 to 1968 and associate curator of the Florida State Museum of the University of Florida (Gainesville, Fla.) from 1968 until his death. He excavated Barta Ramie in the Belize Valley from 1954 to 1956 and later explored Macanché in the Petén. He wrote *Late Classic Finds* *at Baking Pot, British Honduras* (Toronto, 1965) and *Stratigraphic Excavations at San Estevan, British Honduras* (Toronto, 1965); and edited *Monographs and Papers in Maya Archaeology* (Cambridge, Mass., 1970). Died May 21, 1972, in South Dartmouth, Massachusetts. *References*: *AmAntiq* 38 (1973): 80–83; and *Willey*, ch. 14.

BURGESS, PAUL (1886–1958). Missionary, born May 30, 1886, in Lisle, New York. Burgess graduated from Colorado College (Colorado Springs) and McCormick Theological Seminary and was ordained in 1911. He was a missionary under the Board of Foreign Missions of the Presbyterian Church in the U.S.A.* in Guatemala from 1912 to 1945. He served in Quezaltenango from 1912 to 1932 and was a missionary to the Quiche Indians after 1932. He retired in 1956. Died December 28, 1958, in Chichicastenango, Guatemala. *References*: Burgess Family Papers, Presbyterian Historical Society, Philadelphia; and Anna M. Dahlquist, *Burgess of Guatemala* (Langley, B.C., 1985).

BURKE, EDWARD A. (1840?–1928). Businessman who arrived in Louisiana in the late 1860s. He became involved in Louisiana politics and helped negotiate the Compromise of 1877, which ended Reconstruction. He was state treasurer of Louisiana from 1878 until 1888, publisher and editor of the New Orleans *Times-Democrat*, and director general of the World's Industrial and Cotton Centennial Exposition in New Orleans in 1884–1885. In 1886 he received two mining concessions in Honduras along the Jalan and Guayape rivers, and he visited Honduras in 1886 and 1888. While in London in 1889, trying to interest British capital in Honduran mineral lands, he was indicted on the charge of embezzling Louisiana state funds. He did not return to Louisiana to stand trial but went instead to Honduras, residing in Tegucigalpa until 1897, in Puerto Cortés from 1897 until 1926, and again in Tegucigalpa until his death. He formed Olancho Exploration Company Limited, but the mines were not successful. He was assistant superintendent and auditor of the Honduras Interoceanic Railway from 1904 to 1906 and of El Ferrocarril Nacional de Honduras from 1912 to 1926. Died September 25, 1928, in Tegucigalpa, Honduras. *References*: *NYT*, October 22, 1928; David C. Roller and Robert W. Twyman, ed., *Encyclopedia of Southern History* (Baton Rouge, La., 1979); and James F. Vivian, "Major E. A. Burke: The Honduras Exile, 1889–1928," *Louisiana History* 15 (1974): 75–94.

BURKHARDT, JACQUES (1808–1867). Artist, born in Hasle-bei-Burgdorf, Switzerland. Burkhardt studied painting and drawing in Munich and Rome. He worked under Jean Louis Rudolphe Agassiz* at Neuchâtel from 1839 to 1845. He then joined a Belgian expedition to Guatemala, came to the United States, settled in Boston, and worked as an illustrator. He accompanied Agassiz to Brazil in 1865–1866 as official artist of the Thayer expedition and made hundreds of drawings. Died February 20, 1867, in Cambridge, Massachusetts. *References*: *Manthorne*; and *NYT*, February 23, 1867.

BURNS, DANIEL MONROE (1845–1927). Businessman and mine owner, born August 15, 1845, in Ripley, Mississippi, and grew up in Sacramento, California. Burns studied law but never practiced it. He served in the Union Army during the Civil War. He was one of the organizers of the First National Bank and the Home Savings Bank of Woodland, California. In 1883, he paid his first visit to Mexico and during the next thirty-eight years he divided his time between that country and California. He acquired an important group of mines as well as large timber holdings in the states of Durango and Sinaloa, founded the Candelaria Consolidated Mexican Mining Company and a commercial enterprise, Escobosa Burns y Cia., and engaged in the sale of supplies to the general population of the mining districts. The hydroelectric plants that supplied the power to operate his mines and mills were models of engineering and were long in use, as were the series of trails surveyed by him which were necessary for the development of his various mines. He had large holdings in Mendocino County and in the delta of the San Joaquin River, California. He was county clerk of Yolo County from 1876 to 1880 and secretary of state of California from 1880 to 1883. Died May 30, 1927, in Palo Alto, California. *References*: *NCAB* 26:134; and *WWWA*.

BUSH, IRA (JEFFERSON) (1865–1939). Physician, born July 1865 in southern Mississippi. Bush graduated from Louisville Medical College. He practiced medicine in Alto, Louisiana, in 1890–1891 and then moved to Texas and practiced in Fort Davis from 1891 to 1893, in Pecos from 1893 to 1899, and in El Paso from 1899 until his death. In the early years of the twentieth century, he worked for mining companies in Mexico, and during the Mexican revolution he worked as a surgeon in that country. He was chief surgeon in the Mexican revolutionary army under Francisco (Pancho) Villa. He wrote of his adventures during the revolution in *Gringo Doctor* (Caldwell, Idaho, 1939). Died March 10, 1939, in El Paso, Texas. *References*: James B. Lloyd, ed., *Lives of Mississippi Authors, 1817–1967* (Jackson, Miss., 1981); and *NYT*, March 11, 1939.

BUSH, NORTON (1834–1894). Painter, born February 22, 1834, in Rochester, New York. Bush studied art in Rochester and, after 1851, in New York City. He went to the Pacific coast in 1853. He made his first visit to South America in 1853 and devoted himself to painting tropical scenery. He opened a studio in San Francisco in 1868. He visited the Isthmus of Panama in 1868, and again in 1875 and also Ecuador and Peru, and twice crossed the Andes. *References*: *Manthorne*; Dwight C. Miller, *California Landscape Painting, 1860–1885: Artists around Keith and Hill* (Stanford, 1975); *NCAB* 12:338; *NYHSD*; and R. L. Wilson, "Painters of California's Silver Era," *American Art Journal* 16 (Autumn 1984): 71–94.

BUTLER, ANTHONY (WAYNE) (? – ?). Diplomat, born in South Carolina and grew up in Russelville, Kentucky. Butler served in the War of 1812. He then moved to Mississippi, served in the Mississippi state legislature, and later moved to Texas. He was U.S. chargé d'affaires in Mexico from 1829 to 1835. He bungled his mission, trying unsuccessfully to transfer Texas from Mexican ownership to U.S. possession, and played a significant role in the disintegration of Mexican-U.S. diplomatic relations in the 1830s. *References*: Anthony Butler Papers, University of Texas Library, Austin; Joe Gibson, "A. Butler: What a Scamp!" *Journal of the West* 11 (1972): 235–47; Quinton C. Lamar, "A Diplomatic Disaster: The Mexican Mission of Anthony Butler, 1829–1834," *TA* 45 (1988): 1–14; and Richard Sternberg, "President Jackson and Anthony Butler," *Southwest Review* 22 (1937): 391–404.

BUTLER, JOHN WESLEY (1851–1918). Missionary, son of William Butler,* born October 13, 1851, in Shelburne Falls, Massachusetts, and grew up in Wilton, Connecticut, and Chelsea, Massachusetts. Butler attended Boston University School of Theology and was ordained in 1873. He was a missionary under the Board of Foreign Missions of the Methodist Episcopal Church* in Mexico from 1874 until his death. He was the pastor of Trinity Church in Mexico City from 1874 to 1888, publishing agent from 1886 to 1890 and again in 1898, and overseer of schools and acting president of the Mexico Methodist Theological School in 1897. He was editor of *El Abogado Cristiano* and other religious publications from 1892 to 1907 and district superintendent of Mexico from 1889 to 1918. He wrote *Sketches of Mexico* (New York, 1894), *Mexico Coming into Light* (Cincinnati, 1907), and *History of the Methodist Episcopal Church in Mexico. Personal Reminiscences, Present Conditions and Future Outlook* (New York, 1918). Died March 17, 1918, in Mexico City, Mexico. *References*: *DAB*; Richard Millett, "John Wesley Butler and the Mexican Revolution, 1910–1911," in *Dependency Unbends: Case Studies in Inter-American Relations*, ed. Robert H. Claxton (Carrollton, Ga., 1978), pp. 73–87; and *WWWA*.

BUTLER, SMEDLEY D(ARLINGTON) (1881–1940). Marine Corps officer, born July 30, 1881, in West Chester, Pennsylvania. Butler enlisted in the Marine Corps as second lieutenant in 1898. He served in the Philippines in 1899–1900 and in the Boxer Rebellion in China in 1900. He served in Honduras and Panama in 1903–1904, in the Philippines from 1905 to 1907, commanded the Panama Mobile battalion, which was based in the Panama Canal Zone from 1909 to 1914, served in Nicaragua in 1909–1910 and in Haiti from 1915 to 1918. He established the Garde d'Haiti and served as its first commandant. He commanded the major embarkation camp in Europe at Brest, France, during World War I, was commander of the marine base at Quantico from 1920 to 1924, was director of public safety in Pennsylvania from 1924 to 1926, and commanded the marine expedition to China and the marine brigade in Tientsin from 1927 to 1929. He retired in 1931. Died June 21, 1940, in Philadelphia. *References*: Smedley D. Butler Papers, United States Marine Corps Historical Center, Washington, D.C.; Robert T. Cochran, "Smedley Butler, a Marine for All Seasons," *Smithsonian* 15 (June 1984): 137–56; *DAB S2*; *DAMIB; NCAB* 38:536; *NYT*, June 22, 1940;

Hans Schmidt, *Maverick Marine: General Smedley D. Butler and the Contradictions of American Military History* (Lexington, Ky., 1987); Anne C. Venzon, "The Papers of General Smedley Darlington Butler, USMC, 1915–1918," Ph.D. diss., Princeton University, 1982; and *WWWA*.

BUTLER, WILLIAM (1818–1899). Missionary, born January 30, 1818, in Dublin, Ireland, and came to the United States in 1850. Butler graduated from Hardwich Street Mission Seminary (Dublin) and Didsbury College (Manchester). He held pastorates in Williamsburg, Shelburne Falls, and Westfield, New York, and Lynn, Massachusetts. He was founder of the India mission under the Board of Foreign Missions of the Methodist Episcopal Church* from 1857 to 1864. He returned to the United States in 1864 because of ill health. He held pastorates in Chelsea, Melrose, and Boston, Massachusetts, and was secretary of the American and Foreign Christian Union in New York City. He started a mission in Mexico City in 1873 and later expanded missionary activities in Mexico. He was recalled by the Board of Foreign Missions in 1878 and resigned. He was superintendent of a Methodist mission in Mexico City from 1873 to 1879. He held a pastorate in Melrose, Massachusetts, from 1880 to 1883. He visited Mexico again in 1887. He wrote *Mexico in Transition: From the Power of Political Romanism to Civil and Religious Liberty* (New York, 1892). Died August 18, 1899, in Old Orchard, Maine. *References*: *ACAB; DAB; EM; EWM; NCAB* 12:61; and *WWWA*.

BUTT, WALTER RALEIGH (1839–1885). Naval officer, born December 10, 1839, in Portsmouth, Virginia, and grew up in Vancouver, Washington Territory. Butt graduated from the U.S. Naval Academy in 1859. He served in the Confederate Navy during the Civil War. He served in the Peruvian Navy in 1866–1867 and wrote of his experiences in the July 1882 issue of *Californian*. He was a member of the Hydrographic Commission of the Amazon from 1867 to 1874 and led several of its expeditions. He went to California in 1875, served on *City of San Francisco* for the Pacific Mail Steamship Company, and was manager of a ranch near Bakersfield, California. Died April 26, 1885, in San Francisco.

BUTTERFIELD, CARLOS (? –1880). Military and civil engineer, born in upstate New York. Butterfield served as an engineer with the rank of captain in the Civil Engineer Corps of the Spanish Army in Cuba in the early 1840s and was involved in the construction of railroads. He came to Mexico in the mid–1840s, was commissioned as colonel, and served as aide to General Antonio Lopez Santa Anna. He was also engineer in chief and constructor general of the Mexican Navy. Released from this service during the Mexican War, he was appointed alcalde of Veracruz by the American forces. He then remained in Mexico and resumed his military career. He accepted several diplomatic and financial assignments and served as adviser and courier for U.S. ministers to

Mexico. He acquired partnership and interest in an import-export firm. He acquired Mexican citizenship in 1854 and supplied arms to the Ayutla rebels in that year. Died February 14, 1880, in Washington, D.C. *Reference*: William H. Shaw, *General Carlos Butterfield and His Labors in Behalf of International Prosperity on the American Continent* (Berryville, Va., 1897?).

BUYERS, PAUL EUGENE (1878–1960). Missionary, born near Newman, Georgia. Buyers attended Young Harris College (Georgia) and graduated from Vanderbilt University. He was a missionary under the Board of Foreign Missions of the Methodist Episcopal Church, South* in Brazil from 1910 until his retirement in 1949. He was head of Institute Granbery and of its theological seminary and was superintendent at various times of the Instituto Anna Gonzaga and the Instituto Central do Povo. He wrote *Historia de Metodismo* (São Paulo, 1945), and his autobiography, *Autobiografia* (São Paulo, 1952). Died January 5, 1960, in Florida. *Reference*: EWM.

BYRNE, EDWIN V(INCENT) (1891–1963). Clergyman, born August 9, 1891, in Philadelphia. Byrne graduated from St. Charles Seminary (Overbrook, Pa.), and was ordained in 1915. He was a chaplain in the U.S. Navy during World War I. He was a vicar general of Jaro Diocese in the Philippines from 1923 to 1925, first bishop of Ponce, Puerto Rico, from 1925 to 1929, and bishop of San Juan, Puerto Rico, from 1929 to 1943. He was assistant at the Papal Throne from 1940 to 1943 and archbishop of Santa Fe, New Mexico, from 1943 until his death. Died July 25, 1963, in Santa Fe, New Mexico. *References*: Sister Miriam Therese, "Rainbow with Ragged Edges: Archbishop Edwin V. Byrne," *Records of the American Catholic Historical Society of Philadelphia* 94 (1983): 61–79; *NYT*, July 27, 1963; and *WWWA*.

C

CAFFERY, JEFFERSON (1886–1974). Diplomat, born December 1, 1886, in Lafayette, Louisiana. Caffery graduated from Tulane University, studied law, and was admitted to the bar in 1909. He practiced law from 1909 to 1911. He entered the diplomatic service in 1911, served in Caracas, Stockholm, Teheran, Madrid, and Athens, and was counselor of embassy in Tokyo from 1923 to 1925 and in Berlin in 1925–1926. He was U.S. minister to El Salvador from 1926 to 1928 and U.S. minister to Colombia from 1928 to 1933. He allegedly promoted the granting of a concession to the Mellon oil interests, and when the concession was subsequently cancelled, National City Bank cut off credit to the Colombia government, also with his alleged involvement. He was ambassador to Cuba from 1934 to 1937, to Brazil from 1937 to 1944, to France from 1944 to 1949, and to Egypt from 1949 to 1955. *References*: *DADH*; Philip F. Dur, "Jefferson Caffery of Louisiana: Highlights of His Career," *Louisiana History* 15 (1974): 5–34, 367–402; *NCAB* F:534; and *NYT*, April 15, 1974.

CALDERÓN DE LA BARCA, FRANCES ERSKINE (INGLIS) (1804–1882). Author, born December 23, 1804, in Edinburgh, Scotland. She came with her family to the United States in 1831, settled in Boston, and established a school there. In 1837, she moved to New Brighton, Staten Island. In 1838, she married Angel Calderón de la Barca, Spanish minister to the United States. She went to Mexico in 1839, when he became first Spanish envoy to Mexico and remained until 1842. She wrote *Life in Mexico, during a Residence of Two Years in That Country* (New York, 1843). She lived in Washington, D.C., from 1844 to 1853, and later in Spain and Europe. Died September 6, 1882, in Madrid, Spain. *Reference*: *Life in Mexico: The Letters of Fanny Calderón de la Barca; with New Material from the Author's Private Journals*, ed. and annotated Howard T. Fisher and Marion Hall Fisher (Garden City, N.Y., 1966).

CALVERT, PHILIP POWELL (1871–1961). Entomologist, born January 29, 1871, in Philadelphia. Calvert graduated from the University of Pennsylvania and studied at the universities of Berlin and Jena. He was assistant professor of zoology at the University of Pennsylvania from 1907 to 1912 and professor from 1897 until his retirement in 1939. He studied the natural history of Costa Rica in 1909–1910 and wrote *A Year of Costa Rican Natural History* (New York, 1917). Died August 23, 1961. *References: Entomological News* 73 (1963): 113–21; Arnold Mallis, *American Entomologists* (New Brunswick, N.J., 1971), pp. 178–80; *NCAB* 12:335; and *WWWA*.

CAMPBELL, ALLAN (1815–1894). Civil engineer, born October 11, 1815, in Albany, New York. Campbell became involved in engineering work in 1832 and served as an engineer in the construction of railroads in Georgia and as chief engineer of the Harlem Railroad. He went to Chile in 1850, to start the survey and construction of the Copiapó-to-Caldera route. He twice crossed the Andes to Argentina. He returned to the United States in 1856 where he worked again with the Harlem Railroad, and later became president of the Consolidation Coal Company. He was commissioner of public works in New York City from 1876 to 1880. Died March 18, 1894, in New York City. *References: DAB*; *NCAB* 9:154; *NYT*, March 20, 1894; and *WWWA*.

CAMPBELL, LEWIS DAVIS (1811–1882). Lawyer, born August 9, 1811, in Franklin, Ohio. Campbell was editor of the Hamilton (Ohio) *Intelligencer* from 1831 to 1835. He studied law and was admitted to the bar in 1835. He served in the U.S. House of Representatives from 1849 to 1859 and in the Union Army during the Civil War. He was U.S. minister to Mexico in 1866–1867. He was instructed to go with General William T. Sherman into northern Mexico and make contact with the exiled government of Benito Juárez. He failed to reach Juárez and instead returned to the United States and set up an office in New Orleans. He was forced to resign in 1867. He served again in the U.S. House of Representatives from 1871 to 1873. He later farmed near Hamilton, Ohio. Died November 26, 1882, in Hamilton. *References: ACAB*; *DAB*; *DADH*; Martin H. Hall, "The Campbell-Sherman Diplomatic Mission to Mexico," *Bulletin of the Historical and Philosophical Society of Ohio* 13 (1955): 254–70; *NCAB* 13:278; and *WWWA*.

CANANEA CONSOLIDATED COPPER COMPANY (THE "FOUR Cs"). In 1896, William C. Greene* obtained a lease on copper mines in Cananea, Sonora, Mexico. In 1899, he incorporated the Cananea Consolidated Copper Company, S.A., as the operating company. A holding company in the United States, the Greene Consolidated Copper Company was incorporated in 1900. A major strike occurred in 1906, which presaged the Mexican revolution. Greene lost control of the company in 1907. It went into receivership in 1908 and into bankruptcy in 1909. *References*: M. J. Aguirre, *Cananea: Las Garras del Im-*

perialismo en las Entrañas de Mexico (Mexico, 1959); Marvin D. Bernstein, "Colonel William C. Greene and the Cananea Copper Bubble," *Bulletin of the Business Historical Society* 26 (1952): 179–98; Herbert O. Brayer, "The Cananea Incident," *New Mexico Historical Review* 3 (1938): 387–415; Mike Casillas, "The Cananea Strike of 1906," *Southwest Economy and Society* 2 (Winter 1977/78): 18–32; Keon Díaz Cárdenas, *Cananea, Primer Brote del Syndicalismo en Mexico* (Mexico, 1956); and Francisco Medina Hoyos, *Cananea: Cuna de la Revolución Mexicana* (Mexico, 1956).

CANFIELD, C(HARLES) A(DELBERT) (1848–1913). Businessman and petroleum producer, born May 15, 1848, near Buffalo, New York, and grew up in Minnesota. Canfield left home in 1867 and was engaged in mining in Colorado, Nevada, and New Mexico. He moved to Los Angeles in 1887. He made a fortune in the oil fields of southern California and Mexico. With Edward L. Doheny* as his partner, he drilled the first oil well in the Los Angeles district in 1895. In 1896, he discovered Coalinga, which became the most prosperous oil district in California. Then he went to Mexico with Doheny to develop the oil deposits near Tampico. They secured title by purchase to hundreds of thousands of acres of oil lands and founded Mexican Petroleum Company. He had extensive other business enterprises in southern California. Died August 15, 1913, in Los Angeles. *References*: *NCAB* 16:439; and Caspar Whitney, *Charles Adelbert Canfield* (New York, 1930).

CANOVA, LEON J(OSEPH) (1866– ?). Journalist, born February 22, 1866, in St. Augustine, Florida. Orphaned at an early age, Canova moved about Florida working at various jobs. He entered newspaper work in 1894, and was later Associated Press representative for southern Florida. He was aboard the tugboat *Dauntless* during the Spanish-American War. He remained in Cuba as correspondent for the New York *World*. He was managing editor of the *Herald* and *La Lucha*, two of Havana's leading newspapers, from 1906 to 1911. He was also head of the Cuban government official bureau of information from 1909 to 1913. He wrote *Cuba's New Government: Its Platforms, Its Personnel, the Confidence It Inspires* (Havana, 1909), *Cuba* (Havana, 1910), and *Chivor-Somondoco Emerald Mines of Colombia* (New York, 1921). He was special agent of the U.S. State Department in Mexico in 1914–1915 and chief of the Division of Mexican affairs from 1915 to 1918. *References*: *Hill*; and *WWWA*.

CAPERTON, WILLIAM B(ANKS) (1855–1941). Naval officer, born June 30, 1855, in Spring Hill, Tennessee. Caperton graduated from the U.S. Naval Academy in 1875. He was on duty with the U.S. Coast and Geodetic Survey from 1880 to 1883 and on the China station from 1884 to 1887. He served during the Spanish-American War, was inspector of the fifteenth lighthouse district from 1904 to 1907, commanded the USS *Denver* and the USS *Maine*, and was commander in chief of the U.S. Atlantic reserve fleet in 1913–1914. He sailed to Haiti in 1915 and was actively employed with part of his squadron during a revolution. In 1915, he landed forces to restore order and protect life and property in Port-au-Prince and remained in charge of the pacification of Haiti. In 1916, after a revolution broke out in Šanto Domingo, he went there and assumed command of all U.S. forces on the island and in Dominican waters, landing forces and instituting a military occupation until 1916. He was commander in chief of the U.S. Pacific fleet from 1916 until 1919. He retired with the rank of rear admiral in 1919. Died December 21, 1941, in Newport, Rhode Island. *References*: William B. Caperton Papers, Manuscript Division, Library of Congress; "History of U.S. Naval Operations under Command of Rear Admiral W. B. Caperton, USN, Commencing January 5, 1915, Ending April 30, 1919," Naval Records Collection of the Office of Naval Records and Library, National Archives; Edward L. Beach, "Admiral Caperton in Haiti," Ms., Naval Records Collection of the Office of Naval Records and Library, National Archives; David Healy, "Admiral William B. Caperton and United States Naval Diplomacy in South America, 1917–1919," *JLAS* 8 (1976): 297–313; *NCAB* 36:30; *NYT*, December 22, 1941; and *WWWA*.

CARIBBEAN BASIN INITIATIVE (CBI). Approved by the U.S. Congress in 1983, it was designed to strengthen the troubled Caribbean islands' economies and draw the region further into the U.S. orbit. The program allowed for the duty-free import of many Caribbean products and, through investment and tax incentives, encouraged American firms to establish operations in the basin. *References*: *The Caribbean Basin Initiative: Genuine or Deceptive? An Early Assessment*, ed. Glenn O. Phillips and Talbert O. Shaw (Baltimore, 1987); Carmen D. Deere et al., *In the Shadows of the Sun: Caribbean Development Alternatives and U.S. Policy* (Boulder, Colo., 1990), ch. 6; Richard E. Feinberg and Richard Newfarmer, "The Caribbean Basin Initiative: Bold Plan or Empty Promise?" in *From Gunboats to Diplomacy: New U.S. Policies for Latin America*, ed. Richard Newfarmer (Baltimore, 1984), pp. 210–27; and David F. Ross, "The Caribbean Basin Initiative: Threat or Promise?" in *The Central American Crisis: Sources of Conflict and the Failure of U.S. Policy*, ed. Kenneth M. Coleman and George C. Herring (Wilmington, Del., 1985), pp. 137–55.

CARLETON, GEORGE WASHINGTON (1832–1901). Artist and publisher, born in New York City. Carleton worked as a clerk for an importer and commission house. He did caricatures for *The Lantern* and the *Picayune*, and was a partner in a publishing firm after 1857. He traveled in Cuba in 1864–1865 and wrote *Our Artist in Cuba. Fifty Drawings on Wood: Leaves from the Sketchbook of a Traveller, during the Winter of 1864–5* (New York, 1865). He traveled in Peru in 1865–1866, and wrote *Our Artist in Peru: Leaves from the Sketch-Book of a Traveller, during the Winter of 1865–6* (New York, 1866). *References*: Madeline B. Stern, *Books and Book People in 19th-Century America* (New York, 1978), pp. 258–72; and Madeline B. Stern, "G. W. Carleton, His Mark," in

Madeline B. Stern, *Imprints in History: Book Publishers and American Frontiers* (Bloomington, Ind., 1956), pp. 191–205.

CARLOTA. A colony of Confederate exiles established in the Valley of Acon-cinga, seventy miles west of Veracruz, Mexico, in 1865. It was named after the Empress Carlota. Sterling Price* acted as the leader of the colony. In 1866, members began to return to the United States, and the colony broke up in 1867. *References*: Carl C. Rister, "Carlota, a Confederate Colony in Mexico," *Journal of Southern History* 11 (1945): 33–50; and Andrew F. Rolle, *The Lost Colony: The Confederate Exodus to Mexico* (Norman, Okla., 1965), ch. 9.

CAROTHERS, GEORGE C. (1875–1939). Businessman and consul, born in San Antonio, Texas. Carothers was taken in 1899 by his parents to Saltillo, Coahuila, Mexico, and later to Salinas, Mexico, where his father was in business. He spent most of his life in Mexico engaged in the merchandising and mining businesses in Torreón. He was also U.S. consul in Torreón from 1900 to 1913. He was reputed to be on friendly terms with Francisco (Pancho) Villa. He was a special representative of President Woodrow Wilson to Villa from 1913 to 1915 and accompanied Villa during his campaigns. He later represented an American concern in Mexico City. He came to New York City in 1929 where he was secretary of the Home Owners Institute until 1936 and editor of *El Arte Tipografico* from 1936 until his death. Died August 4, 1939, in Lake Hiawatha, New Jersey. *References*: *Hill*; and *NYT*, August 5, 1939.

CARR, ARCHIE FAIRLY (1909–   ). Biologist, born June 16, 1909, in Mobile, Alabama. Carr graduated from the University of Florida. He was a member of the faculty of the University of Florida after 1937, professor of biology at Escuela Agricola Panamericana in Honduras from 1945 to 1949, research associate at the American Museum of Natural History after 1951, technical director of the Caribbean Conservation Corporation in 1961, and its executive vice president and technical director after 1968. He conducted various expeditions to Panama, Costa Rica, and Trinidad in 1953, to Central America in 1955, to Brazil in 1956, to Argentina and Chile in 1958, and to the Caribbean yearly after 1960. He wrote *High Jungles and Low* (Gainesville, Fla., 1953), and *The Windward Road: Adventures of a Naturalist on Remote Caribbean Shores* (New York, 1956), and was coauthor of *The Ecology and Migrations of the Sea Turtles: The Green Turtle in the Caribbean Sea* (New York, 1960). *References*: *American Zoologist* 20 (1980): 487–88; *AMWS*; and *WWA*.

CARRIKER, MELBOURNE A(RMSTRONG), JR. (1879–1965). Ornithologist, born February 14, 1879, in Sullivan, Illinois, and grew up in Nebraska City, Nebraska. Carriker attended the University of Nebraska. He participated in a University of Nebraska expedition to Costa Rica in 1902 to collect birds for the Carnegie Museum and mammals for the American Museum of Natural

History. After 1902, he spent most of his life in the American tropics collecting birds. He collected extensively in Costa Rica, Trinidad, Venezuela, Colombia, Bolivia, Peru, and Mexico. He was a collector for the Carnegie Museum from 1901 to 1922, assistant in the department of ornithology and mammalogy in 1908–1909, collector of mammals for the American Museum of Natural History from 1909 to 1911, field representative and associate curator of birds and in charge of tropical American birds for the Academy of Natural Sciences of Philadelphia, and field representative of the U.S. National Museum of the Smithsonian Institution from 1941 until his death. He wrote *An Annotated List of the Birds of Costa Rica, Including Cocos Island* (Pittsburgh, 1910) and was coauthor of *The Birds of the Santa Marta Region of Colombia: A Study in Altitudinal Distribution* (Pittsburgh, 1922). *Carriker on Mallophaga: Posthumous Papers*, ed. K. C. Emerson (Washington, D.C., 1967), and *Experiences of an Ornithologist along the Highways and Byways of Bolivia: Land of Magnificent Isolation* (n.p., 1977) were published posthumously. Died July 27, 1965, in Bucaramanga, Colombia. *Reference*: *AMWS*.

CARSON, HENRY ROBERTS (1869–1948). Clergyman, born December 8, 1869, in Norristown, Montgomery County, Pennsylvania. Carson attended the University of the South (Sewanee, Tenn.), and was ordained in 1896. He was a general missionary in the diocese of Louisiana of the Protestant Episcopal Church of the USA from 1895 to 1898 and chaplain during the Spanish-American War and then held pastorates in Franklin and Monroe, Louisiana, from 1899 to 1910 and was archdeacon of northern Louisiana from 1910 to 1912. He was archdeacon of Panama and chaplain at Ancon Hospital in the Panama Canal Zone from 1913 to 1922 and was the first missionary bishop of Haiti from 1923 until his death. He was also bishop in charge of the Dominican Republic from 1928 to 1943. Died July 13, 1948, in Port au Prince, Haiti. *Reference*: *WWWA*.

CARTER, HENRY ROSE (1852–1925). Sanitarian and epidemiologist, born August 25, 1852, in Clifton Plantation, Carolina County, Virginia. Carter graduated from the University of Virginia and the University of Maryland School of Medicine. He served with the Marine Hospital Service (later U.S. Public Health Service) from 1879 until 1919. He organized Cuban quarantine service in 1899–1900, inaugurated quarantine service and was director of hospitals in Panama from 1904 to 1908, and directed the malaria eradication program in the South from 1913 to 1919. As a member of the Yellow Fever Council of the International Health Board of the Rockefeller Foundation he was active in campaigns against yellow fever in Central and South America. Died September 14, 1925, in Washington, D.C. *References*: *DAB*; *DAMB 84*; *NCAB* 25:346; *NYT*, September 15, 1925; and *WWWA*.

CASE, ALDEN BUEL (1851–1932). Missionary, born July 25, 1851, in Gustavus, Trumbull County, Ohio. Case graduated from Tabor College and Yale Divinity School and was ordained in 1881. He held pastorates in Madison and

Howard, South Dakota, from 1881 to 1884 and was a missionary under the American Board of Commissioners for Foreign Missions in Parral, Chihuahua, Mexico, from 1894 to 1896, general secretary of the California Spanish Missionary Society from 1896 to 1904, and again a missionary in Mexico from 1904 to 1914. He then resided in California until his retirement in 1925. He wrote *Thirty Years with the Mexicans: In Peace and Revolution* (New York, 1917). Died October 27, 1932, in Pomona, California. *Reference: OAB.*

CATLIN, GEORGE (1796–1872). Painter, born July 26, 1796, in Wilkes-Barre, Pennsylvania. Catlin studied law and then practiced law in Luzerne, Pennsylvania, until 1823. In 1823, he set himself up as miniature and portrait painter in Philadelphia, resided and painted in Washington, D.C., from 1824 to 1829, and then moved to Roanoke, Virginia. In 1830, he made his first visit to the West and began his major life work, the portrayal of American Indians from 1830 to 1838. He took his collection of Indian paintings to Europe. He traveled in Latin America in 1839 and in South America from 1852 to 1857. He wrote *Last Rambles amongst the Indians of the Rocky Mountains and the Andes* (New York, 1867). Died December 23, 1872, in Jersey City, New Jersey. *References*: George Catlin Papers, Archives of American Art, Washington, D.C.; George Catlin, *Episodes from Life among the Indians and Last Rambles*, ed. Marvin C. Ross (Norman, Okla., 1979); *ACAB*; *DAB*; Brian W. Dippie, *Catlin and His Contemporaries: The Politics of Patronage* (Lincoln, Nebr., 1990); Lloyd Haberly, *Pursuit of the Horizon; A Life of George Catlin, Painter Recorder of the American Indian* (New York, 1948); Edgardo C. Krebs, "George Catlin and South America: A Look at His 'Lost' Years and His Paintings of Northeastern Argentina," *American Art Journal* 22, no. 4 (1990): 4–39; *Manthorne*; *NCAB* 3:270; *NYHSD*; William H. Truettner, *The Natural Man Observed: A Study of Catlin's Indian Gallery* (Washington, D.C., 1979).

CAZNEAU, WILLIAM L(ESLEY) (? –1876) and **CAZNEAU, JANE MARIA ELIZA (MCMANUS) STORMS** (1807–1878). Adventurers. William was born in Fort Hill, Boston. He went to Texas and participated in the struggle against Mexico until 1853. Jane was born April 6, 1807, near Troy, New York. She was in Texas in 1832–1833, where she was involved in an unsuccessful effort to establish a colony. She settled in Manhattan, New York, and wrote for the New York *Sun*. In 1846, she accompanied Moses Y. Beach* in his secret peace mission to Mexico City. She was then a lobbyist for Mexican annexation in Washington, D.C. She visited Cuba, and became a backer of Narciso López and his filibustering expeditions to Cuba, and was editor of *La Veradad*, a pro-López paper in New York City. The Cazneaus were married in the late 1840s, and moved to Eagle Pass, Texas, in 1850. They went to Santo Domingo in 1853 and established an estate "Estancia Esmeralda" near Santo Domingo City. He was a special agent of the U.S. government, was involved in the unsuccessful schemes to annex the islands by the United States, and was behind the failed effort to establish a U.S. naval base on Samaná Bay in the Dominican Republic in 1854. His appointment as special agent was renewed in 1859 but his efforts to secure a naval station at Samaná Bay failed. With Joseph W. Fabens,* he organized American West Indian Company in 1862 to promote North American colonization in the Dominican Republic, and she wrote *Our Winter Eden: Pen Pictures of the Tropics* (New York, 1878). The enterprise collapsed in 1865, when they were driven from Santo Domingo by an uprising and took refuge in Jamaica. They later returned to Santo Domingo. He resumed his efforts on behalf of annexation and secured mineral and land rights. She wrote *The Prince of Kashna: A West Indian Story* (New York, 1866), and letters and articles to various newspapers. They later lived near Spanish Town, Jamaica. He died January 1876, in Keith Hall, near Spanish Town, Jamaica. She died December 12, 1878, when the ship she was on, *Emily B. Souder*, sank off Cape Hatteras, on her way from New York to Jamaica. *References*: Robert E. May, "Lobbyists for Commercial Empire: Jane Cazneau, William Cazneau, and U.S. Caribbean Policy, 1846–1878," *PHR* 48 (1979): 383–412; Robert E. May, " 'Plenipotentiary in Petticoats': Jane M. Cazneau and American Foreign Policy in the Mid-Nineteenth Century," in *Women and American Foreign Policy: Lobbyists, Critics, and Insiders*, ed. Edward P. Crapol (Westport, Conn., 1987), pp. 19–44; and *NAW*.

CENTRAL AMERICAN MISSION. Nondenominational agency founded in 1890. It began missionary work in Costa Rica in 1891, in Honduras in 1896, in El Salvador in 1896, in Guatemala in 1899, in Nicaragua in 1900, in Panama in 1944, and in Mexico in 1956. It established elementary schools, theological schools, radio stations, and book stores, and translated the Bible into several Indian dialects. The name later changed to CAM International. *References*: Archives of the Central American Mission, Dallas, Tex.; *EMCM*; Mildred W. Spain, *"And in Samaria": A Story of More than Sixty Years' Missionary Witness in Central America, 1890–1954* (Dallas, 1954); Wilkins B. Winn, "Albert Edward Bishop and the Establishment of the Central American Mission in Guatemala, 1899–1922," in *Militarists, Merchants and Missionaries: United States Expansion in Middle America*, ed. Eugene R. Huck and Edward H. Moslet (University, Ala., 1970), pp. 93–106; Wilkins B. Winn, "A History of the Central American Mission as Seen in the Work of Albert Edward Bishop, 1896–1922," Ph.D. diss., University of Alabama, 1964; and Wilkins B. Winn, *Pioneer Protestant Missionaries in Honduras: A. E. Bishop and J. G. Cassel and the Establishment of the Central American Mission in Western Honduras, 1896–1901* (Cuernavaca, Mexico, 1973).

CERRO DE PASCO COPPER CORPORATION. Founded in 1901 as the Cerro de Pasco Investment Corporation. It constructed its first copper smelter in 1906. It reorganized itself as the Cerro de Pasco Copper Corporation in 1915, later renamed the Cerro Corporation. It was involved in mining copper, silver, lead, gold, and other minerals in Cerro de Pasco, in the Peruvian Andes. It became Peru's largest copper producer, largest private employer, and largest landowner. It was expropriated in 1974 by the Peruvian government and was bought out and merged with the Marmion Group in 1976. *References*: David G. Becker, *The New Bourgeoisie and the Limits of Dependency: Mining, Class and Power in "Revolutionary" Peru* (Princeton, N.J., 1983), ch. 6; Charles H. McArver, Jr., "Mining and Diplomacy: United States Interests at Cerro de Pasco, Peru, 1876–1930," Ph.D. diss., University of North Carolina at Chapel Hill, 1977; and Ann Sediman, ed., *Natural Resources and National Welfare* (New York, 1975), pt. 3.

CHAGNON, NAPOLEON A(LPHONSEAU) (1938–   ). Anthropologist, born August 27, 1938, in Port Austin, Michigan. Chagnon attended Michigan College of Mining and Technology (Sault Ste. Marie, Mich.; later Lake Superior State College) and graduated from the University of Michigan. He was a research associate in human genetics at the Medical School and assistant professor of anthropology at the University of Michigan from 1967 to 1972, associate professor of anthropology, and then professor, at Pennsylvania State University from 1972 to 1981, and professor of anthropology at Northwestern University after 1981. He carried out field studies among the Yanomano Indians in Venezuela and Brazil between 1966 and 1972 and returned several times between 1974 and 1976. He wrote *Yąnomano: The Fierce People* (New York, 1968), and *Studying the Yąnomano* (New York, 1974). *Reference*: AMWS.

CHAMBERLAIN, GEORGE W(HITEHILL) (1839–1902). Missionary, born August 13, 1839, in Waterford, Pennsylvania. Chamberlain attended the University of Delaware and Union and Princeton theological seminaries and was ordained in 1866. He was missionary under the Board of Foreign Missions of the Presbyterian Church in the U.S.A.* in Brazil from 1866 until his death, serving in Rio de Janeiro in 1868–1869, and in São Paulo from 1869 to 1887. Died July 31, 1902, in Rio Vermelho, Bahia, Brazil. *References*: *EM*; and *PrincetonTS*.

CHAMIZAL DISPUTE, EL. A dispute concerning a tract of land on the Rio Grande border between El Paso, Texas, and Ciudad Juárez, Chihuahua, Mexico. At one time, the land was on the Mexican side of the Rio Grande River but subsequent diversions in the course of the river eventually placed this portion of Mexican territory on the U.S. side of the border. The dispute was settled in 1963, when Mexican sovereignty was recognized by the United States. *References*: Alan C. Lamborn and Stephen P. Mumme, *Statecraft, Domestic Politics*, and *Foreign Policy Making: The El Chamizal Dispute* (Boulder, Colo., 1988); and Sheldon B. Liss, *A Century of Disagreement: The Chamizal Conflict 1864–1964* (Washington, D.C., 1965).

CHAPMAN, CONRAD WISE (1842–1910). Painter, born February 14, 1842, in Washington, D.C., and grew up in Rome, Italy. Chapman studied art under his father. He returned to the United States in 1861 and served in the Confederate Army during the Civil War. He went to Mexico after the war, was in Monterrey, and painted the Valley of Mexico. He then went to explore and paint La Huastaca. He returned to Europe in 1866, and after 1874 he lived in Paris. He was again in Mexico City from 1883 until 1889 and 1892 until 1898, depending on painting for his livelihood. He lived in Richmond from 1898 to 1901 and in New York City from 1901 to 1904 and was back in Mexico from 1904 to 1909. Died December 10, 1910, in Hampton, Virginia. *References*: Ben Bassham, "Conrad Wise Chapman: Artist-soldier of the Orphan Brigade," *Southern Quarterly* 25 (1986): 40–56; and Valentine Museum, *Conrad Wise Chapman, 1842–1910: An Exhibition of His Works in the Valentine Museum* (Richmond, 1962).

CHAPMAN, FRANK M(ICHLER) (1864–1945). Ornithologist, born June 12, 1864, in Englewood, New Jersey. Chapman was employed by the American Exchange National Bank in New York City from 1880 to 1886. He was assistant curator in the Department of Mammals and Birds of the American Museum of Natural History from 1888 to 1901, associate curator from 1901 to 1908, curator in charge of birds from 1908 to 1920, and curator of the Department of Birds from 1920 until his retirement in 1942. He wrote *The Distribution of Bird Life in Colombia* (New York, 1917), *Distribution of Bird Life in Ecuador* (New York, 1926), *My Tropical Air Castle* (New York, 1929), *The Autobiography of a Bird Lover* (New York, 1933), and *Life in an Air Castle: Nature Studies in the Tropics* (New York, 1938). He was a special commissioner of the Red Cross to Latin America during World War I. Died November 15, 1945, in New York City. *References*: *American Naturalist* 80 (1946): 476–81; *AMWS*; *Audubon Magazine* 48 (1946): 49–52; *BMNAS* 25 (1949): 11–45; *DAB S3*; *NCAB* 9:327; and *Science* 104 (1946): 152–53.

CHASTAIN, JAMES GARVIN (1853–1955). Missionary, born December 18, 1853, in Rara Avis, Itawamba County, Mississippi. Chastain was ordained in 1875 and graduated from Mississippi College and Southern Baptist Theological Seminary (Louisville, Ky.). He was missionary under the Foreign Mission Board of the Southern Baptist Convention in Mexico from 1888 until 1913. He left Mexico because of the revolution and served under the Home Mission Board in Cuba and Florida from 1913 to 1923. He wrote *Thirty Years in Mexico* (El Paso, Tex., 1927). Died February 20, 1955, in Richton, Mississippi. *References*: *ESB*; and James B. Lloyd, ed., *Lives of Mississippi Authors, 1817–1967* (Jackson, Miss., 1981).

CHAYTER, JAMES (1767– ?). Sea captain, born in Baltimore. Chayter participated in the Venezuelan war of independence until 1814, when the re-volutionaries were defeated. He then came to Rio de la Plata and participated in the Argentina revolutionary war. From 1816 to 1824, he commanded a privateer flying the Buenos Aires flag. He returned to the United States in 1824 but later entered the service of Colombia. Died in Colombia. *References*: *Cutolo*; and *Udaondo*.

CHEAVANS, JOHN S(ELF) (1868–1921). Missionary, born February 4, 1868, in Calloway County, Missouri. Cheavens graduated from William Jewell College and Southern Baptist Theological Seminary and was ordained in 1893. He was a missionary under the Foreign Mission Board of the Southern Baptist Convention* in Mexico from 1898 until 1915. He established a mission and school in Saltillo, Mexico. He left Mexico in 1915, settled in Eagle Pass, Texas, until 1921, and then in El Paso, Texas, where he was superintendent of the Mexican Baptist Publishing House. Died January 23, 1921, in El Paso, Texas. *Reference*: W. Thoburn Clark, *Outriders for the King* (Nashville, 1931), ch. 4.

CHERRIE, GEO(RGE) K(RUCK) (1865–1948). Explorer and naturalist, born August 22, 1865, in Knoxville, Iowa. Cherrie attended Iowa State College. He was assistant taxidermist at the U.S. National Museum and then with the American Museum of Natural History until 1889. He was taxidermist and curator of birds, mammals, and reptiles for the National Museum of Costa Rica from 1889 to 1894, and assistant curator of ornithology at the Field Museum of Natural History in Chicago from 1894 to 1897. He conducted explorations in the Valley of the Orinoco in Venezuela for Lord Rotschild from 1897 to 1899 and in French Guiana for the Tring Museum in 1902–1903 and then explored the Valley of the Orinoco and Trinidad for the Brooklyn Institute of Arts and Sciences. He was curator of ornithology and mammalogy at the Brooklyn Institute of Arts and Sciences from 1899 to 1914; member of the American Museum of Natural History expedition to Colombia, the Valley of the Magdalena River, and the high interior in 1913; represented the museum in the Roosevelt expedition to South America in 1914; was naturalist on the Collins-Roosevelt South American expedition in 1914–1915; and was director of the Cherrie-Roosevelt South American expedition for the American Museum of Natural History in 1916–1917. He served in the U.S. Bureau of Naval Intelligence in 1918–1919. He conducted two expeditions to Ecuador for the American Museum of Natural History in 1920–1921, was leader of an expedition to the Mazaruni River diamond fields in British Guiana in 1922, led an expedition to central Brazil in 1924, and again went to Brazil on the Marshall Field expedition. He wrote *A Contribution to the Ornithology of the Orinoco Region* (Brooklyn, N.Y., 1916), and *Dark Trails, Adventures of a Naturalist* (New York, 1930), a record of his adventures. Died January 20, 1948, in Newfane, Vermont. *References*: *Auk* 68 (1951): 260–61; and *NCAB* 36:397.

CHICAGO EXPLORATION COMPANY. Founded about 1909 to mine silver-copper ore in the Sahuaripa district of eastern Sonora, Mexico. Its subsidiary, Mina Mexico Company, controlled the actual operating unit in Mexico. It withdrew its American employees in 1915 and was dissolved in 1920. *Reference*: David M. Pletcher, "An American Mining Company in the Mexican Revolution of 1911–1920," *Journal of Modern History* 20 (1949): 19–26.

CHILDS, ORVILLE W(HITMORE) (1803–1870). Engineer, born in Saratoga Springs, New York. Childs became a chainman for an engineer in 1820 and was engaged in the construction of the Champlain and Oswego canals and in the construction of the Erie Canal enlargement. He was chief engineer of the New York state public works from 1840 to 1847. In 1850, he was hired by Cornelius Vanderbilt to survey the route for the ship canal in Nicaragua and wrote *Report of the Survey and Estimates of the Cost of Constructing the Interoceanic Ship Canal* (New York, 1852). After 1861, he was engaged in building sleeping cars in Philadelphia and was president of the Central Transportation Railway Company. Died September 6, 1870, in East Philadelphia. *Reference*: NCAB 3:79.

CHILE EXPLORATION COMPANY. Organized in 1912 by the Chile Copper Company, a holding company in which the Guggenheims held a majority interest, to take over and operate the Chuquicamata mine in northern Chile. It was sold to Anaconda in 1923. *Reference*: A. B. Parsons, *The Porphyry Coppers* (New York, 1933), ch. 12.

CHRISTIAN AND MISSIONARY ALLIANCE: FOREIGN DEPART-MENT. Formed in 1897 by the union of the Christian Alliance and the International Missionary Alliance, both of which were established in 1887. It began missionary work in Argentina and Ecuador in 1897, in Chile in 1898, in Colombia in 1923, in Peru in 1926, and in Brazil in 1962. *References*: Christian and Missionary Alliance Records, A. B. Simpson Memorial Historical Library, Nyack College, Nyack, N.Y.; Raymond B. Clark, *Under the Southern Cross: the Story of Alliance Missions in South America* (Harrisburg, Pa., 1938); Robert B. Ekvall et al., *After Fifty Years: A Record of God's Working through the Christian and Missionary Alliance* (Harrisburg, Pa., 1939); *EMCM*; and James H. Hunter, *Besides All Waters; The Story of Seventy Five Years of World-wide Ministry of the Christian and Missionary Alliance* (Harrisburg, Pa., 1964).

CHRISTIANCY, ISAAC PECKHAM (1812–1890). Lawyer and diplomat, born March 12, 1812, in Johnstown, New York. Christiancy studied law and was admitted to the bar in 1835. He was prosecuting attorney for Monroe County, Michigan, from 1841 to 1845, served in the Michigan State Senate, edited the Monroe *Commercial* from 1856 to 1858, and served as justice of the state supreme court from 1856 to 1874. He was a U.S. senator from 1874 to 1879. He was U.S. minister to Peru from 1879 to 1881, serving during the War of the Pacific. His call for U.S. intervention in the war and his quarrel with the U.S. ministers to Chile and Bolivia damaged U.S. attempts to settle the conflict. Died September

8, 1890, in Lansing, Michigan. *References*: *BDAC*; *DAB*; *DADH*; and *NCAB* 23:348.

CHRISTMAS, LEE (1863–1924). Soldier of fortune, born February 22, 1863, near Baton Rouge, Louisiana. He was employed as a pilot on tug boats on Lake Pontchartrain from 1878 to 1880, was a brakeman on the Illinois Central Railroad and a member of a construction crew, and later was baggage master, fireman, and engineer on the Louisville, New Orleans, and Texas Railroad. He went to Honduras in 1894 as a railway engineer, and when his train was captured by revolutionaries, he was drafted at gunpoint into the rebel army. He later took part in several other revolutions in Central America, always on the side of the revolutionaries. In 1910–1911, he headed the revolution that culminated in the overthrow of President Miguel R. Dávila in Honduras in 1910–1911 and reinstated President Manuel Bonilla. He later fled to Nicaragua but was invited back to Honduras to head the federal police. He also served in Nicaragua, El Salvador, and Guatemala, and is credited with having been instrumental in placing five presidents in power in Central America through revolutions. He then had a coconut plantation in Honduras. His U.S. citizenship was canceled but it was restored after he served in U.S. military intelligence during World War I. He was later involved in oil drilling and mining in Honduras. Died January 21, 1924, in New Orleans. *References*: Hermann B. Deutsch, *The Incredible Yankee: The Career of Lee Christmas* (London, 1931); *NCAB* 6:380; and *NYT*, January 22, 1924.

CHURCH, FREDERICK EDWIN (1826–1900). Painter, born May 4, 1826, in Hartford, Connecticut. Church studied painting with Thomas Cole in Catskill, New York. He sketched in New York and New England from 1847 to 1852. He made trips to South America in 1853 and in 1857. His famous painting *Heart of the Andes* (1859) was exhibited in New York City in 1859 and later in other American cities and in England. He made trips to the cost of Newfoundland and Labrador in 1859, to Jamaica in 1865, and to Europe and the Middle East from 1867 to 1869. He had a studio in New York City and then lived in Olana in the Hudson Valley. Died April 7, 1900, in New York City. *References*: Frederick Edwin Church Manuscripts, Archives of American Art, Washington, D.C.; Frederick Edwin Church Letters, Diaries, and Papers, Olana State Historical Site, Hudson, N.Y.; Frederick Edwin Church Correspondence from South America, 1853, Henry Francis du Pont Wintherthur Museum Library, Delaware; *ACAB*; Kevin J. Avery, "*The Heart of the Andes* Exhibition: Frederick E. Church's Window on the Equatorial World," *American Art Journal* 18, no. 1 (1986): 52–72; *DAB*; David C. Huntington, "Frederick Edwin Church, 1826–1900: Painter of the Adamic New World Myth," Ph.D. diss., Yale University, 1960; David C. Huntington, "Landscapes and Diaries: The South American Trips of F. E. Church," *The Brooklyn Museum Annual* 5 (1963–1964): 65–98; Franklin Kelly, "Frederick Church in the Tropics," *Arts in Virginia* 27 (1987): 16–33; Franklin

Kelly, *Frederick Edwin Church and the National Landscape* (Washington, D.C., 1988); Katherine Manthorne, *Creation & Renewal: Views of Cotopaxi by Frederick Edwin Church* (Washington, D.C., 1985); *NCAB* 20:291; and Theodore E. Stebbins, Jr., *Close Observation: Selected Oil Sketches by Frederick E. Church* (Washington, D.C., 1978).

CHURCH, GEORGE EARL (1835–1910). Civil engineer and explorer, born December 7, 1835, in New Bedford, Massachusetts, and grew up in Rhode Island. Church was assistant engineer on the Hoosac Tunnel, and in the construction of railways in Iowa. He went to Buenos Aires in 1857 to serve as chief engineer on a railway project for the Argentine Republic. The work was postponed and he was appointed a member of a scientific commission which was to explore Argentina's southwestern border and report on a system of defense against the Indians of the slopes of the Andes. He was chief assistant engineer on the construction of the Great Northern Railway of Buenos Aires in 1860–1861 which he had previously surveyed and located. He returned to the United States and served in the Union Army during the Civil War. He went after the war to Mexico as special correspondent for the *New York Herald* and attached himself to the army of President Benito Juárez until 1867. He went back to South America in 1868 and was involved with the Madeira and Mamoré Railway. For ten years, at the request of the Bolivian government, he was engaged in the task of opening Bolivia to trade by way of the Amazon River and its tributaries. He obtained from Brazil a concession to construct a railway in order to avoid the falls of the Madeira River, not only conducting the negotiations with the Brazilian government but also persuading European capitalists to finance the undertaking. The enterprise eventually had to be abandoned. In 1880, he was appointed U.S. commissioner to report on the political, financial, and trade conditions of Ecuador. He then settled in London and was concerned with various Argentine railway undertakings. He wrote *Ecuador in 1881* (Washington, D.C., 1883), and *Aborigines of South America* (London, 1912), which was published posthumously. Died January 5, 1910, in London, England. *References: DAB*; Lewis Hanke, "A Note on the Life and Publications of Colonel George Earl Church," *Books at Brown* 20 (1965): 131–63; *NCAB* 13:250; and *NYT*, January 6, 1910.

CHURCH OF GOD (CLEVELAND, TENN.): WORLD MISSION BOARD.
Organized in 1886, it began missionary work in the Bahamas in 1909, in Jamaica in 1924, in Mexico in 1932, in Haiti in 1933, in Guatemala in 1934, in Costa Rica and Panama in 1935, in Barbados, and Windward and Leeward Islands in 1936, in Bermuda in 1939, in Argentina, El Salvador, and the Dominican Republic in 1940, in Cuba in 1942, in Puerto Rico, British Honduras, and Honduras in 1944, in Uruguay in 1945, in the Virgin Islands in 1946, in Peru in 1947, in Nicaragua in 1950, in Brazil in 1951, in Dominica in 1953, in Chile, Paraguay, and Colombia in 1954, in Trinidad and British Guiana in 1957, and in Grenada in 1958. *References: The Church of God in the Americas* (Cleveland, Tenn.,

1954); Charles W. Conn, *Like a Mighty Army: A History of the Church of God, 1886–1976* (Cleveland, Tenn., 1977); Charles W. Conn, *Where the Saints Have Trod: A History of Church of God Missions* (Cleveland, Tenn., 1959); *EMCM*; and Horace McCracken, ed. *History of Church of God Missions* (Cleveland, Tenn., 1943).

CHURCH OF JESUS CHRIST OF LATTER-DAY SAINTS. The first Mormon missionary went to Chile in 1851 to open a South American mission, but the mission was short-lived. An expedition to explore and proselytize Mexico took place in 1875–1876. The mission was opened in Mexico in 1879 but was closed from 1889 to 1901. The mission in South America was reopened in Buenos Aires in 1925, and later in other countries in Latin America. (*See also* Mormon Colonies in Mexico.) *References*: Records, Church of Jesus Christ of Latter-Day Saints, Church Library Archives, Salt Lake City, Utah; F. LaMond Tullis, "The Church Moves Outside the United States: Some Observations on Latin America," in *Mormonism after One Hundred and Fifty Years*, ed. Thomas Alexander (Salt Lake City, 1983), pp. 149–69; F. LaMond Tullis, "Early Mormon Exploration and Missionary Activities in Mexico," *Brigham Young University Studies* 22 (1982): 289–301; and F. LaMond Tullis, "Reopening the Mexican Mission in 1901," *Brigham Young University Studies* 22 (1982): 441–53.

CHURCH OF THE NAZARENE: DEPARTMENT OF FOREIGN MISSIONS. Organized in 1907 as an outgrowth of previous mission boards elected by the individual holiness groups that united in 1907–1908 to form the Church of the Nazarene. It began missionary work in Mexico in 1903, in Guatemala in 1904, in Peru in 1917, in Argentina in 1919, in Barbados and in Trinidad and Tobago in 1926, in British Honduras in 1934, in Puerto Rico in 1943, in Bolivia in 1945, in British Guiana in 1946, in Uruguay in 1949, in Haiti in 1950, in Panama in 1955, in Brazil in 1958, in Nicaragua and the American Virgin Islands in 1961, in Chile in 1962, in El Salvador in 1964, in Jamaica in 1966, in the Bahamas in 1971, in Ecuador in 1972, and in Costa Rica. The name was later changed to the World Mission Division. *References*: Department of Foreign Missions Records, Church of the Nazarene Archives, Kansas City, Mo.; and Mendell Taylor and R. DeLong, *Fifty Years of Nazarene Missions*, vol. 2 (Kansas City, Mo., 1958).

CHURCHWELL, WILLIAM M(ONTGOMERY) (1826–1862). Public official, born February 20, 1826, near Knoxville, Tennessee. Churchwell attended Emory and Henry College (Emory, Va.), studied law, and was admitted to the bar. He practiced law in Knoxville and was one of the judges for Knox County. He served in the U.S. House of Representatives from 1851 to 1855. He was provost marshal for the district of east Tennessee. He was sent on a secret mission to Mexico in 1858–1859 to survey the situation and evaluate the con-

tending factions and, on his return, recommended recognition of the Benito
Juárez government. He served in the Confederate Army during the Civil War.
Died August 18, 1862, in Knoxville, Tennessee. *References*: *BDAC*; Paul Mur-
ray, *Tres Norteamericanos y su Participacion en el Desarrollo del Tratado
McLane-Ocampo, 1856–1860* (Guadalajara, Mexico, 1946); and *WWWA*.

CLARK, EDWARD HARDY (1864–1945). Mining executive, born November
19, 1864, in St. Louis, Missouri. Clark went to California in 1895. He was
business manager of the George Hearst estate from 1896 to 1919, president of
Homestake Mining Company of California from 1914 to 1944, and chairman of
the board from 1944 until his death. He was vice president of Cerro de Pasco
Copper Corporation from 1901 to 1929 and president from 1929 to 1942, and
later chairman of the board. Died December 16, 1945, in San Francisco. *References*: *NCAB* 37:554; and *WWWA*.

CLARK, HERBERT CHARLES (1877–1960). Pathologist, born November
11, 1877, in Economy, Indiana. Clark graduated from Earlham College and the
University of Pennsylvania. He was a pathologist in the U.S. Board of Health
laboratory of the Panama Canal Zone from 1909 to 1922 and served in the U.S.
Army Medical Corps during World War I. He was director of laboratories and
preventive medicine for the United Fruit Company* from 1922 to 1928, re-
searching poisonous snakes and the effects of their bites, and was director of
the Gorgas Memorial Laboratory in Panama from 1929 until his retirement in
1954. Died November 8, 1960, in Allentown, Pennsylvania. *References*: *Journal
of Parasitology* 48 (1962): 173; *Journal of the American Medical Association*
175 (March 4, 1961): 815; and H. H. Martin, "Jungle Doctor," *Saturday Evening Post* 225 (October 4, 1952): 19–21, 111–12.

CLARK, J(OSHUA) REUBEN, JR. (1871–1961). Public official and diplomat, born September 1, 1871, near Grantsville, Utah. Clark graduated from the
University of Utah and Columbia University Law School. He was assistant
solicitor of the U.S. State Department from 1906 to 1910 and solicitor from
1910 to 1913. He practiced law in Washington, D.C., after 1913, and served
in the U.S. Army judge advocate general's staff during World War I. He was
undersecretary of state in 1928–1929 and helped draw the "Clark Memorandum"*; and he was also aide to Dwight W. Morrow.* He was U.S. ambassador
to Mexico from 1930 to 1933. He was second counselor to the president of the
Church of Jesus Christ of Latter-Day Saints* in 1933–1934, first counselor after
1934, and an apostle from 1934 until his death. Died October 6, 1961, in Salt
Lake City. *References*: Joshua Reuben Clark, Jr., Papers, Brigham Young University Library, Provo, Utah; *DAB S7*; *DADH*; Frank W. Fox, *J. Reuben Clark,
Jr., The Public Years* (Provo, Utah, 1980); Ray C. Hillman, ed., *J. Reuben
Clark, Jr., Diplomat and Statesman* (Provo, Utah, 1973); *NCAB* D:290; *NYT*,
October 7, 1961; and *WWWA*.

CLARK MEMORANDUM. Written by J. Reuben Clark, Jr.,* undersecretary of state, in 1928, to clarify the status of the Monroe Doctrine.* It was made public in 1930. It stated that the Roosevelt Corollary* was unjustified in terms of the Monroe Doctrine. It considered the United States no longer responsible for the internal conditions of Latin American countries. *References*: *ELA*; and G. A. Sessions, "Clark Memorandum Myth," *TA* 34 (July 1977): 40–59.

CLARKE, GEORGE W. (fl. 1859–1867). Journalist. Clarke resided in Van Buren, Arkansas, and was editor of the *Arkansas Intelligencer*. In 1859, he was purser in the U.S. Navy and participated in an expedition to Paraguay. He served in the Confederate Army during the Civil War. He went to Mexico in 1865, in connection with Matthew Fontaine Maury's* colonization scheme. He published and edited a newspaper, *The Two Republics*, in Mexico City after 1867, first as a weekly, and later as a semiweekly. It was a continuous and going concern for many years. He also made his way into the good graces of the higher circles of Mexican government. *Reference*: Frank A. Knapp, Jr., "A New Source on the Confederate Exodus to Mexico: *The Two Republics*," *Journal of Southern History* 19 (153): 364–73.

CLAY, JOHN RANDOLPH (1808–1885). Diplomat, born September 29, 1808, in Philadelphia, and grew up in Roanoke, Virginia. Clay studied law, and was admitted to the bar in 1828. He was secretary of legation in Russia from 1830 to 1837, in Austria from 1838 to 1845, and again in Russia from 1845 to 1847. He was U.S. chargé d'affaires in Peru from 1847 to 1853 and minister to Peru from 1853 to 1860. He collected the amount due to the United States under the claims treaty, negotiated a treaty of commerce, was involved in settling the Lobos Islands controversy, and tried, unsuccessfully, to secure the opening of the headwaters of the Amazon River to navigation by all nations. Died August 15, 1885, in Philadelphia. *References*: *NCAB* 12:80; and George I. Oeste, *John Randolph Clay: America's First Career Diplomat* (Philadelphia, 1966).

CLAYTON, HENRY HELM (1861–1946). Meteorologist, born March 12, 1861, in Murfreesboro, Tennessee. Clayton was assistant in the astronomical observatory in Ann Arbor, Michigan, in the Harvard Astronomical Observatory, and at the Blue Hill Meteorological Observatory in Milton, Massachusetts, until 1891. He was a meteorologist in the Blue Hill Meteorological Observatory from 1894 to 1909. He was employed by Oficina Meteorologica Argentina to study methods of weather forecasting in the Argentine Republic and to inaugurate in 1910, near Córdoba, a station for exploring the upper air by means of kites. He was forecasting official at the Oficina Meteorologica Argentina in Buenos Aires from 1913 to 1922, where he inaugurated a new system of weather forecasting. He then conducted research on the relation of weather to solar radiation. He conducted a private weather bureau and was a consulting meteorologist for business organizations from 1925 to 1944. Died October 27, 1946, in Norwood, Massachusetts. *References*: *ACAB*; *NYT*, October 28, 1946; and *WWWA*.

CLAYTON, POWELL (1833–1914). Public official and diplomat, born August 7, 1833, in Bethel County, Pennsylvania. Clayton studied in an engineering school in Wilmington, Delaware. He moved to Kansas in 1855, was involved in civil engineering, and was city engineer of Leavenworth, Kansas. He served in the Union Army during the Civil War. He was governor of Arkansas from 1868 to 1871 and served in the U.S. Senate from 1871 to 1877. He was then involved in business in Little Rock, and later in Eureka Springs, Arkansas. He was U.S. minister to Mexico in 1897–1898 and first U.S. ambassador to Mexico from 1898 until 1905. Died August 25, 1914, in Washington, D.C. *References*: *ACAB*; William H. Burnside, "Powell Clayton: Ambassador to Mexico, 1897–1905," *Arkansas Historical Quarterly* 38 (1979): 328–44; William H. Burnside, "Powell Clayton: Politician and Diplomat, 1897–1905," Ph.D. diss., University of Arkansas, 1978; *DAB*; *NCAB* 16:262; and *WWWA*.

COAN, TITUS (1801–1882). Missionary, born February 1, 1801, in Killingworth, Connecticut. Coan was a missionary under the American Board of Commissioners for Foreign Missions after 1833. He went on a mission of exploration to Patagonia in 1833–1834. He set ashore among the inhabitants of Gregory Bay, on the eastern coast of Patagonia, and lived with them for several months. When the inhabitants became suspicious of his motives, he escaped. He later wrote *Adventures in Patagonia*; *A Missionary's Exploring Trip* (New York, 1880). He was a missionary in Hawaii from 1835 until his death. Died December 1, 1882, in Hilo, Hawaii. *References*: *ACAB*; *DAB*; *EM*; *NCAB* 2:339; and *WWWA*.

COE, JOHN HALSTED (1806–1864). Naval officer, born in Springfield, Massachusetts, and grew up in San Francisco. Coe took a trip to the Pacific in 1824, joined the squadron of Admiral Thomas Cochrane, and served in the siege of Callao. He was appointed lieutenant in the Peruvian Navy by Simón Bolívar in 1825 and joined the Argentine Navy in 1826. He served in the war against Brazil as commander of a frigate under Admiral William Brown and was imprisoned by the Brazilians in 1826–1827. He managed to escape and rejoined the Argentine Navy. He served in the battle of Monte Santiago and was later captured again by the Brazilians. He was discharged from the navy in 1835 and emigrated to Montevideo. He was commander in chief of the Uruguayan Navy after 1841 and organized the fleet of General Fructaso Rivera. He fought the Argentine fleet, commanded by Admiral Brown, near Montevideo in 1841, and forced Brown to retreat. After controlling Rio de la Plata estuaries, he fought two other battles with Brown. He was commanding chief of the Confederation naval forces and established a blockade of Buenos Aires. He then abandoned the cause of General Justo José de Urquiza and founded a refuge in Montevideo. He later returned to Buenos Aires. Died October 30, 1864, in Buenos Aires. *References*: *Cutolo*; Guillermo Gallardo, "La Caída de Rosas y la Traición de Coe en el Relato de un Testigo," *Historia* [Buenos Aires] no. 18 (January-February 1960): 264–89; Jorge Larroca, "La Traicion de Llamaba Coe," *Todo es Historia* [Buenos Aires] no. 4 (1967): 88–93; and *Udaondo*.

COE, MICHAEL D(OUGLAS) (1929–   ). Anthropologist, born May 14, 1929, in New York City. Coe graduated from Harvard University. He was assistant professor of anthropology at the University of Tennessee (Knoxville) from 1958 to 1960, member of the faculty and professor of anthropology at Yale University after 1968. He carried out field work in San Lorenzo Tenochtitlan. He wrote *La Victoria, an Early Site on the Pacific Coast of Guatemala* (Cambridge, Mass., 1961), *Mexico* (New York, 1962), *The Jaguar's Children: Pre-Classic Central Mexico* (New York, 1965), *The Maya* (New York, 1966), and America's *First Civilization: Discovering the Olmec* (New York, 1968), and was coauthor of *Early Cultures and Human Ecology in South Coastal Guatemala* (Washington, D.C., 1967), and *In the Land of the Olmec* (Austin, Tex., 1980). *References*: *CA*; and *WWA*.

COLE, ELI K(ELLEY) (1867–1929). Marine Corps Officer, born September 1, 1867, in Carmel, New York. Cole graduated from the U.S. Naval Academy in 1888 and was appointed second lieutenant in the marine corps in 1890. He was stationed at various posts until 1901, served in the Philippines from 1901 to 1903 and again in 1905 and 1907, and was chief of staff to the marine corps commandant in Washington, D.C. He was commander of the first regiment of marines and was sent to Haiti in 1915. In 1916, as chief of the American occupation, he was given command of the first provisional brigade comprising all American units in Haiti. He cooperated with the Haitian government in its efforts to improve the educational and social conditions of the Haitians. He served with the American Expeditionary Force in France during World War I, and commanded, successively, the Parris Island, Virginia, post; the marine barracks in Quantico, Virginia; and the marine corps department of the Pacific, in San Francisco. Died July 4, 1929, in San Francisco. *References*: *NCAB* 24:309; and *WWWA*.

COLEGIO AMERICANO. School for girls in Rosario, Argentina, founded in 1875 by the Woman's Foreign Missionary Society of the Methodist Episcopal Church.* It was the first Methodist school in all of Latin America. *Reference*: *EWM*.

COLLINS, THOMAS PATRICK (1915–1973). Missionary, born January 13, 1915, in San Francisco. Collins joined Maryknoll Fathers, graduated from Maryknoll Seminary (Ossining, N.Y.), and was ordained in 1942. He was a missionary in Bolivia from 1942 until his retirement in 1969. He was named vicar apostolic of Pando and Bolivia and titular bishop of Sufetula from 1916 to 1969. Died December 7, 1973, in Maryknoll, New York. *Reference*: *DACB*.

COLORADO RIVER LAND COMPANY. Established in 1902, the company was owned by Los Angeles–based entrepreneurs. It held extensive landholdings in northern Baja California. It developed commercially Mexico's Colorado River delta and protected Mexico's right to a fair share of the Colorado River water. Most developed portions of the property were expropriated by the Mexican government in 1937. *Reference*: Dorothy P. Kerig, "Yankee Enclave: The Colorado River Land Company and Mexican Agrarian Reform in Baja California, 1902–1944," Ph.D. diss., University of California at Irvine, 1988.

COLTON, GEORGE R(ADCLIFFE) (1865–1916). Government official, born April 10, 1865, in Galesburg, Illinois. Colton worked on a cattle ranch in New Mexico from 1882 to 1887 and then settled in David City, Nebraska, where he was cashier and manager and later vice president of the Central Nebraska National Bank. He was national bank examiner for the district of Nebraska in 1897 and member of the state legislature in 1889–1890. He served during the Spanish-American War in the Philippines and was military deputy collector of customs of the port of Manila until 1901 and collector of customs in Iloilo until 1905. He went to Santo Domingo in 1905 to assist the government of that island in organizing its customs receivership and was then comptroller and general receiver of Dominican customs. He organized the customs service and was in charge of it until 1907. He was insular collector of customs in the Philippines from 1907 to 1909. He was governor of Puerto Rico from 1909 to 1913 and reorganized the entire Puerto Rican administrative system. He returned to the United States in 1913 and was involved in banking. Died April 6, 1916, in Washington, D.C. *References*: *DAB*; *NCAB* 25:179; *NYT*, April 8, 1916; and *WWWA*.

COMPAÑÍA MEXICANA DE AVIACIÓN, S.A. (CMA). Organized by George L. Rihl* in 1924, as the second airline in Mexico. It purchased the assets of Compañía Mexicana de Transportación, S.A., in 1924. It began to carry mail between Mexico City and Tampico in 1926, and between Mexico City and Merida, Yucatán, in 1928. It was bought by Pan American Airways in 1929.

COMPAÑÍA MEXICANA DE TRANSPORTACIÓN, S.A. (CMTA). The pioneer airline in Mexico which flew the first Mexican air route. It was founded in 1921 in Mexico City by L. A. Winship and Harry J. Lawson, U.S. citizens residing in Mexico. The airline was awarded concession number one to carry passengers, mails, and freight. It was the first Mexican air route. Its assets were purchased in 1924 by the Compañía Mexicana de Aviación, S.A.

CONFEDERATE COLONIES IN LATIN AMERICA. In the first few years after the Civil War, roughly 9,000 ex-Confederates fled to Brazil (5,000 southerners), Mexico (2,500), British Honduras (1,000), and Venezuela (500), settled there, and established colonies. Most settlers (probably 80 percent), had returned to the United States by the early 1870s. *References*: William C. Douglas, "Confederate Exiles," *American History Illustrated* 5 (June 1970): 30–43; Douglas A. Grier, "Confederate Emigration to Brazil, 1865–1879," Ph.D. diss., University of Michigan, 1968; William C. Griggs, *The Elusive Eden: Frank McMullan's Confederate Colony in Brazil* (Austin, Tex., 1987); Alfred J. Hanna and Kathryn A. Hanna, *Confederate Exiles in Venezuela* (Tuscaloos, Ala., 1960); Eugene C. Harter, *The Last Colony of the Confederacy* (Jackson, Miss., 1985); Lawrence F. Hill, "Confederate Exodus to Latin America," *Southwestern Historical Quarterly* 39 (1936): 100–134, 161–99, 309–26; Judith M. Jones, *Soldado Descansa!* (São Paulo, 1967); Andrew F. Role, *The Lost Cause: The Confederate Exodus to Mexico* (Norman, Okla., 1965); Charles W. Simmons, "Racist Americans in a Multi-Racial Society: Confederate Exiles in Brazil," *Journal of Negro History* 57 (1982): 34–39; Daniel F. Sutherland, "Exiles, Emigrants, and Sojourners: The Post-Civil War Confederate Exodus in Perspective," *Civil War History* 31 (1985): 237–56; Blanche H. C. Waever, "Confederate Immigrants and Evangelical Churches in Brazil," *Journal of Southern History* 18 (1952): 446–68; and Bell I. Wiley, "Confederate Exiles in Brazil," *Civil War Times Illustrated* 15 (January 1977): 22–32.

CONVERSE, GEORGE M(ARQUIS) (1870–1962). Physician, graduated from Cooper Medical College (San Francisco). He was acting assistant surgeon in the Public Health and Marine Hospital Service. He was in Peru from 1912 to 1914, at the request of the Peruvian government, and served in the Iquitos region of the Amazon River, engaging in sanitation work and directing the campaign against yellow fever. He served in France with the U.S. Public Health Service during World War I and was in charge of public health work for the army. He helped establish the American Hospital in Paris in 1926 and was a director until 1941. Died May 15, 1962, in Washington, D.C. *Reference: NYT*, May 17, 1962.

CONWAY, MARY E(LIZABETH) (1844–1903). Educator, born in Ballina, Tyrawley, Ireland, and grew up in Rochester and Watkins Glen, New York. Conway came to Argentina in 1877 and served in Tucumán and Buenos Aires. She then opened the American School in Buenos Aires. Died August 3, 1903, in Buenos Aires. *References: Cutolo; Luiggi; NYT*, September 10, 1903; and *Udaondo*.

COOK, FREDERICK C. (1853– ?). Businessman, born September 17, 1853, in New York City, and came with his parents to the Argentine Republic in 1864. Cook served as apprentice in one of the leading British commercial houses until

1870 and then entered the employment of J. Coghlan, civil engineer and promoter of the waterworks of Buenos Aires. In 1872, he established the firm of C. S. Roberts and Company (after 1903, F. C. Cook and Company), import and export merchants doing business with the United States. He was also one of the founders of La Blanca Freezing Company, a packing house. *References*: *Cutolo*; and *Drees*.

COOPER, PRENTICE (WILLIAM), JR. (1895–1969). Public official and diplomat, born September 28, 1895, in Bedford County, Tennessee. Cooper attended Vanderbilt University, graduated from Princeton and Harvard universities, and was admitted to the bar in 1922. He practiced law in Shelbyville and served in the Tennessee state legislature from 1923 to 1925 and the state senate in 1937–1938. He was governor of Tennessee from 1939 to 1945 and the U.S. ambassador to Peru from 1946 to 1948. He successfully negotiated all treaties desired and arranged for the settlement of the debt owned to U.S. bondholders by Peru. He organized and led the relief expedition into the Andes, following the 1946 earthquake. He resumed law practice in Shelbyville and had various business interests in Bedford County, Tennessee, and Henderson County, Kentucky. Died May 18, 1969, in Rochester, Minnesota. *References*: William P. Cooper, "Ambassador Prentice Cooper, 1946–1948," *Tennessee Historical Quarterly* 45 (1986): 41–55, 169–81; *NCAB* 55:199; *NYT*, May 19, 1969; and *WWWA*.

COORDINATOR OF INTER-AMERICAN AFFAIRS. *See* OFFICE OF INTER-AMERICAN AFFAIRS

CORBITT, DUVON C(LOUGH) (1901–   ). Educator, born July 4, 1901, near Pearson, Georgia. Corbitt attended Meridian College, and graduated from Asbury College (Wilmore, Ky.), Emory University, and the University of North Carolina. He was head of the department of English in Candler College in Havana, Cuba, from 1927 to 1929, 1931 to 1943, and 1945–1946. He was chairman of the history department at Columbia (S.C.) College from 1943 to 1945 and professor of history at Asbury College from 1946 to 1975. He wrote *A Study of the Chinese in Cuba, 1847–1947* (Wilmore, Ky., 1971). *References*: *DAS*; Thomas O. Ott, "The Corbitts, the *HAHR*, the United States-Cuban Intellectual Relations," *HAHR* 59 (1979): 108–119; and *WSSW*.

CORNING, FREDERICK GLEASON (1857–1937). Mining engineer, born March 27, 1857, in Brooklyn, New York. Corning graduated from the Royal School of Mines in Freiberg (Germany). He practiced as mining engineer and metallurgist in the United States and Canada, and in Central and South America. He wrote *Papers from the Notes of an Engineer* (New York, 1889). After 1897, he was head of companies operating gold and silver mines in Mexico, South America, and Canada, and was president of the Exploration Company of New

York. Died July 12, 1937, in New York City. *References*: *NYT*, July 13, 1937; and *WWWA*.

CORRIGAN, FRANK [FRANCIS] PATRICK (1881–1968). Surgeon and diplomat, born July 14, 1881, in Cleveland. Corrigan graduated from Western Reserve University and studied at the University of Vienna. He was assistant surgeon at the St. Alexis Hospital in Cleveland from 1910 to 1917 and chief surgeon and medical director of the hospital of the Chile Copper Company in Chuquicamata, Chile, from 1917 to 1919. He practiced surgery in Cleveland after 1919. He was U.S. minister to El Salvador from 1934 to 1937 and negotiated a reciprocal trade treaty between the United States and El Salvador. He was minister to Panama from 1937 to 1939 and was instrumental in averting the so-called postage stamp war between Nicaragua and Honduras. He was the first U.S. ambassador to Venezuela from 1939 to 1947 and negotiated a reciprocal trade agreement between the United States and that country. He was a political adviser on Latin America to the U.S. mission to the United Nations from 1947 until his retirement. Died January 21, 1968, in Trumbull, Connecticut. *References*: K. Jones, "Right-Way Corrigan," *Saturday Evening Post* 218 (January 26, 1946): 41; and *NCAB* 54:330.

CORTHELL, ELMER LAWRENCE (1840–1916). Civil engineer, born September 30, 1840, in Abington (later Whitman), Massachusetts. Corthell graduated from Brown University. He served in the Union Army during the Civil War. He was involved in civil engineering in Providence after 1867, served on railway surveys and construction in Illinois and Missouri, and was chief engineer of bridges over the Mississippi River. He was chief engineer of the Atlantic and Pacific Ship Railway to build a ship railway over the Isthmus of Tehuantepec, Mexico. He was chief construction engineer of the New York, West Shore, and Buffalo Railway; construction engineer in building railways into Chicago; associate chief engineer of several large bridges over the Missouri, Ohio, and other rivers; and chief engineer-bridge in St. Louis, the Brazos River jetties in Texas, and the Tampico Harbor Works in Mexico. He was consulting engineer to the National Public Works of the Argentine Government from 1900 to 1902 and chief engineer of the Port of Para, Brazil, and Rio Grande do Sol. Died May 16, 1916. *Reference*: *WWWA*.

CORWIN, THOMAS (1794–1865). Public official and diplomat, born July 29, 1794, in Borboun County, Kentucky. Corwin studied law, and was admitted to the bar. He served in the Kentucky house of representatives in 1822 and 1829, and in the U.S. House of Representatives from 1831 to 1840. He was governor of Kentucky from 1840 to 1842, served in the U.S. Senate from 1845 to 1850, was secretary of the treasury from 1850 to 1853, and served again in the U.S. House of Representatives from 1859 to 1861. He was U.S. minister to Mexico from 1861 to 1864. He later practiced law in Washington, D.C. Died December

18, 1865, in Washington, D.C. *References*: J. Jeffery Auer, "Lincoln's Minister to Mexico," *Ohio State Archaeological and Historical Quarterly* 59 (1956): 115–28; *BDAC*; *DAB*; and *DADH*.

CORY, CHARLES B(ARNEY) (1857–1921). Ornithologist, born January 31, 1857, in Boston. Cory attended Lawrence Scientific School of Harvard University. He devoted his life, after 1877, to travel and collecting ornithological specimens. He visited the Bahamas in 1878, and Hispaniola in 1881 and 1882–1883. He wrote *Birds of the Bahama Islands* (Boston, 1880), *The Birds of Haiti and San Domingo* (Boston, 1885), *The Birds of the West Indies* (Boston, 1889), *Catalogue of West Indian Birds* (Boston, 1892), and *The Birds of the Leeward Islands* (Chicago, 1909). Died July 29, 1921, in Ashland, Wisconsin. *References*: *DAB*; *NCAB* 13:225; and *WWWA*.

CRABB, HENRY A(LEXANDER) (? –1857). Filibuster, born in Nashville, Tennessee. Crabb studied law and was admitted to the bar. He came to California in 1849, settled in Stockton, practiced law, and served in the state assembly from 1851 to 1853 and in the state senate in 1853–1854. He edited the Stockton (Calif.) *Argus* in 1855–1856. He established the Arizona Colonization Society and went to Sonora, Mexico, in 1857, leading a group intending to colonize part of northern Sonora. He fought a battle with the Mexicans in Caborca. Although willing to surrender, he was shot on April 7, 1857, near Caborca, Sonora, Mexico. *References*: Joseph Y. Ainsa, *History of the Crabb Expedition into North Sonora* (Phoenix, 1951); H. D. Barrows, *Crabb's Filibusters* (Los Angeles, 1911); Robert H. Forbes, *Crabb's Filibustering Expedition into North Sonora, 1857* (Tucson, 1952); J. A. Ruibal Corella, *Y Caborca se Cubrió de Gloria: La Expedición Filbustera de Henry Alexander Crabb a Sonora* (Mexico, 1976); J. A. Stout, "Henry A. Crabb: Filibuster or Colonizer? The Story of an Ill-starred *Gringo Entrada*," *American West* 8 (May 1971): 4–9; Joseph A. Stout, Jr., *The Liberators: Filibustering Expeditions into Mexico 1848–1862 and the Last Trust of Manifest Destiny* (Los Angeles, 1973), ch. 9; and Rufus K. Wyllys, "Henry A. Crabb—A Tragedy of the Sonora Frontier," *PHR* 9 (1940): 183–94.

CRAIG, NEVILLE B(URGOYNE) (1847–1926). Civil engineer, born December 1, 1847, in Pittsburgh. Craig graduated from Yale University and Sheffield Scientific School. He was a topographer with the U.S. Coast Survey from 1873 to 1875, and an inspector of improvements from 1875 to 1877. He was involved in construction of the Madeira and Mamoré Railroad in Brazil and Bolivia from 1877 to 1879, the first effort of U.S. engineers to build a railroad in the Amazon. He was initially chief draftsman of the expedition and then served as assistant and acting principal assistant engineer. He later wrote *Recollections of an Ill-Fated Expedition, Part First: The Origin of the Expedition and Voyage of the "Mercedita"* (Philadelphia, 1904). From 1880 to 1882, he was assistant engineer on the Mexican National Railway, resident engineer in charge of constructing the railroad between Morelia and Pátzcuaro, and also assistant engineer in charge of surveys between Veracruz and Rinconada. He was assistant engineer under the Mississippi River Commission from 1882 to 1885, conducting various surveys from 1885 to 1890, chief engineer of the Antioquia Railway in Colombia in 1890–1891, and principal assistant for surveys in the Department of Public Works of Philadelphia from 1891 to 1899. Died August 8, 1926, in Germantown, Pennsylvania.

CRAIGE, JOHN H(OUSTON) (1886–1954). Marine Corps officer, born July 24, 1886, in Philadelphia. Craige attended the University of Pennsylvania. He traveled to Alaska as a prospector, was a member of the United States Olympic wrestling team in 1908, soldier of fortune in Mexico, professional boxer, and wrestling coach at the University of Pennsylvania. He was commissioned second lieutenant in the U.S. Marine Corps in 1917, served during World War I, and was aide to the commandant of the corps from 1920 to 1925. He served in Haiti from 1925 to 1929, first as an officer with the *Gendarmerie d'Haiti* and later as chief of police of Port-au-Prince. He was later an instructor in topography in the Marine Corps schools in Quantico, Virginia, and editor of *Marine Corps Gazette*. He retired in 1935 because of injuries and became a military analyst for International News Service. He wrote his personal reminiscences, *Black Bagdad* (New York, 1933) and *Cannibal Cousins* (New York, 1934). Died August 14, 1954, in Philadelphia. *Reference*: *NYT*, August 17, 1954.

CRAMER, LAWRENCE W(ILLIAM) (1897–   ). Colonial administrator, born December 26, 1897, in New Orleans, and grew up in Milwaukee. Cramer graduated from the University of Wisconsin and Columbia University. He served in the U.S. Army during World War I. He was an instructor in government at Columbia University. He was lieutenant governor of St. Croix, Virgin Islands, from 1931 to 1935 and governor from 1935 to 1941, where he signed and implemented the Organic Act of 1936. He was secretary general of the Caribbean Commission from 1946 to 1951. *Reference*: *NYT*, July 24, 1935.

CREOLE PETROLEUM COMPANY. Creole Syndicate was incorporated in 1920, with leases in Venezuela, Panama, Colombia, and Santo Domingo. Standard Oil Company of Venezuela was organized in 1921. Standard Oil Company of New Jersey acquired control of Creole Syndicate in 1928 and used it as a holding company until 1943. Standard Oil Company of Venezuela became a subsidiary of Creole, which was renamed Creole Petroleum Company in 1943 and became Standard Oil Company of New Jersey's operating arm in Venezuela. It merged with Lago Petroleum Corporation, which had a concession underlying Lake Maracaibo. Standard Oil Company of Venezuela was then liquidated and its assets transferred to Creole Petroleum Company. In 1961, it was the largest business in Venezuela. It was taken over by the Venezuelan government in 1976 and became Lagoven, a government company. *References*: "Creole Petroleum: Business Embassy," *Fortune* 39 (February 1949): 91–97, 176–83; and Wayne C. Taylor and John Lindmann, *The Creole Petroleum Corporation in Venezuela* (New York, 1955).

CRITTENDEN, THOMAS THEODORE (1832–1909). Public official and consul, born January 1, 1832, near Shelbyville, Shelby County, Kentucky. Crittenden graduated from Centre College (Danville, Ky.), studied law, and was admitted to the bar in 1856. He practiced law in Lexington, Lafayette County, Missouri, after 1857. He served in the Union Army during the Civil War. He served in the U.S. House of Representatives from 1872 to 1874 and from 1876 to 1880 and was governor of Missouri from 1880 to 1884. He was U.S. consul general in Mexico City from 1893 to 1897. He later served on the U.S. district court. Died May 29, 1909, in Kansas City. *References*: Thomas T. Crittenden Papers, University of Missouri Library, St. Louis; *ACAB*; *BDAC*; *DAB*; *NCAB* 12:307; Walter W. Scholes, "Mexico in 1896 as Viewed by an American Consul," *HAHR* 30 (1950): 250–57; and *WWWA*.

CRITTENDEN, WILLIAM LOGAN (1823–1851). Soldier, born May 30, 1823, in Shelby County, Kentucky. Crittenden graduated from the U.S. Military Academy in 1845 and served in the Mexican War. He resigned from the U.S. Army in 1851 and joined the second filibustering expedition of Narciso López to Cuba. When the expedition landed, López divided his forces, leaving about 100 of them behind with Colonel Crittenden in command, while the others marched into the interior. López was deceived in expecting the assistance of the Cubans. Instead, he was attacked by a heavy force of Spaniards, having been betrayed by a native guide, and captured. Crittenden made a forced march in López's assistance, but was intercepted by a large body of Spaniards. He was driven back to the coast and, on attempting to sail to the United States, was captured by a Spanish war vessel and taken to Havana. After a quick trial, he was shot along with the surviving members of his command, on August 15, 1851, in Havana. *Reference*: *NCAB* 4:500.

CRONE, FRANK LINDEN (1875–1960). Educator, born July 19, 1875, in Kendallville, Indiana. Crone graduated from Indiana University. He was a high school teacher until 1901, a teacher in the public schools of the Philippines from 1901 to 1909, an assistant director of education in the Philippines from 1909 to 1913, and director of education from 1913 to 1916. He was in charge of the educational department of General Brokerage Company in Grand Forks, North Dakota, in 1917–1918, and representative of the Bureau of War Trade Intelligence in San Francisco in 1918–1919. He was director of schoolhouse construction for the Peruvian government from 1921 to 1924, regional director of instruction in Peru in 1921–1922, and director general of instruction from 1922 to 1924. He was with D.C. Heath and Company after 1925. Died May 22, 1960, in Richmond, Virginia. *Reference*: *WWWA*.

CROSBY, ELISHA O(SCAR) (1818–1895). Lawyer and diplomat, born July 18, 1818, in Groton, New York. Crosby studied law and was admitted to the bar in 1841. He practiced law in New York City from 1843 to 1849. He came to California in 1849, and practiced law in San Francisco. He was U.S. minister to Guatemala from 1861 to 1864. He was involved in trying to establish a colony of emancipated blacks in Guatemala, an idea that was unacceptable to that country. Crosby won Union sympathizers in Guatemala. He later settled in Alameda, California, and, after 1878, was justice of the peace, judge of the police court, and city recorder. Died in California. *References*: *Memoirs of Elisha O. Crosby, Reminiscences of California and Guatemala from 1848–1864*, ed. Charles A. Barker (San Marino, Calif., 1945); Mary P. Chapman, "Mission of Elisha O. Crosby to Guatemala, 1861–1864," *PHR* 24 (1955): 275–86; and *San Francisco Call*, June 24, 1895.

CROWDER, ENOCH HERBERT (1859–1932). Army officer and colonial administrator, born April 11, 1859, in Edinburgh, Missouri. Crowder graduated from the U.S. Military Academy in 1881 and from the University of Missouri. He was minister of state and justice in Cuba from 1906 to 1909, bringing about economic, legal, and administrative reforms. He was presidential representative to Cuba in 1919 and again from 1921 to 1923, mandated to observe the elections and the political scene in Cuba, and the first U.S. ambassador to Cuba from 1923 to 1927. He later practiced law in Chicago until 1931. Died May 7, 1932, in Washington, D.C. *References*: Enoch H. Crowder Papers, University of Missouri Library, Columbia; *DAB S1*; *DADH*; David A. Lockmiller, *Enoch H. Crowder: Soldier, Lawyer, Statesman* (Columbia, Mo., 1955); *NCAB* A:455; and *NYT*, May 8, 1932.

CUBA, MILITARY OCCUPATION OF (1899–1902). Following the capture of Cuba during the Spanish-American War, U.S. forces occupied Cuba from 1899 until 1902, even after having granted Cuba nominal independence. In 1901, the Cuban Constitutional Convention adopted the Platt Amendment.* The U.S. occupation paid particular attention to health and education. *References*: Graham A. Cosmas, "Securing the Fruits of Victory: The United States Army Occupies Cuba, 1898–1899," *Military Affairs* 38 (1974): 85–91; Howard Gillette, Jr., "The Military Occupation of Cuba, 1899–1902: Workshop for American Progressivism," *American Quarterly* 25 (1973): 410–25; David F. Healy, *The United States in Cuba, 1898–1902* (Madison, Wis., 1963); James H. Hitchman, *Leonard Wood and Cuban Independence, 1898–1902* (The Hague, 1971); Jack C. Lane, "Instrument for Empire: The American Military Government in Cuba, 1899–1902," *Science and Society* 36 (1972): 314–30; *Musicant*, ch. 2; and Louis

A. Pérez, Jr., "Supervision of a Protectorate: The United States and the Cuban Army, 1898–1903," *HAHR* 52 (1972): 250–71.

CUBA, MILITARY OCCUPATION OF (1906–1909). U.S. Marines occupied Cuba in 1906 at the invitation of President Estrada Palma of Cuba to offset the revolt that was preventing his reelection to a second term in office. The occupation carried out an extensive program of public works, organized a modern army, and enacted fair legislation to prevent civil wars. U.S. forces withdrew in 1909. *References*: David A. Lockmiller, *Magooon in Cuba: A History of the Second Intervention, 1906–1909* (Chapel Hill, N.C., 1938); Allan R. Millett, *The Politics of Intervention: The Military Occupation of Cuba, 1906–1909* (Columbus, Ohio, 1968); Ralph E. Minger, "William Howard Taft and the United States Intervention in Cuba in 1906," *HAHR* 41 (1961): 75–89: *Musicant*, ch. 2; and Teresita Yglesias Martínez, *Cuba: Primera República, Segunda Ocupación* (Havana, 1976).

CUBAN MISSILE CRISIS (1962). The United States discovered in 1962 that the Soviet Union was placing nuclear missiles in Cuba. The discovery led to a quarantine of Cuba and the demand that the missiles already in Cuba will be removed, to which the Soviets acquiesced. *References*: G. T. Allison, *Essence of Decision: Explaining the Cuban Missile Crisis* (Boston, 1971); Robert Divine, ed., *The Cuban Missile Crisis* (New York, 1971); Herbert S. Dinerstein, *The Making of a Missile Crisis: October, 1962* (Baltimore, 1976); J. H. Kahan and A. K. Long, "The Cuban Missile Crisis: A Study of Its Strategic Context," *Political Science Quarterly* 87 (1972): 564–90; and Robert F. Kennedy, *Thirteen Days: A Memoir of the Cuban Missile Crisis* (New York, 1969).

CULBERTSON, WILLIAM S(MITH) (1884–1966). Lawyer and diplomat, born August 5, 1884, in Greensburg, Pennsylvania, and grew up in Kansas. Culbertson graduated from the College of Emporia and Yale University, studied at the universities of Berlin and Leipzig, and was admitted to the bar in 1912. He was an examiner for the U.S. Tariff Board in Washington, D.C., from 1910 to 1912, practiced law in Washington from 1912 to 1916, and was a member of the staff of the U.S. Federal Trade Commission in 1916–1917 and a member of the U.S. Tariff Commission from 1917 until 1925. He was U.S. minister to Romania from 1925 to 1928 and ambassador to Chile from 1928 until 1932. He then practiced law in Washington, D.C., until his death. Died August 12, 1966, in Washington, D.C. *References*: William S. Culbertson Papers, Manuscript Division, Library of Congress; *NCAB* 54:101; John R. Snyder, "William S. Culbertson in Chile: Opening the Door to a Good Neighbor, 1928–1933," *IAEA* 26 (Summer 1972): 81–98; and John R. Snyder, *William S. Culbertson: In Search of a Rendezvous* (Washington, D.C., 1980).

CUMBERLAND, WILLIAM WILSON (1890–1955). Economist, born January 2, 1890, in La Verne, California. Cumberland graduated from Occidental College (Los Angeles) and Columbia and Princeton universities. He was assistant professor of agricultural economics at the University of Minnesota from 1916 to 1919, trade expert for the War Trade Board in Washington in 1918, economic expert for the American Commission to Negotiate the Peace in 1919, and financial adviser to the American Military Mission to Armenia (Harbord Mission) from 1919 to 1922. He was foreign trade adviser to the U.S. State Department from 1920 and advised on the reorganization of the finances of Peru from 1921 to 1923; he was later governor of Peru's reserve bank. He helped to organize the finances of Haiti from 1924 to 1927 and of Nicaragua in 1928. He was partner of Wellington and Company from 1928 to 1945 and a partner of Ladenburg, Thalman and Company after 1945. He wrote *Nicaragua: An Economic and Financial Survey* (Washington, D.C., 1928). Died February 20, 1955, in Englewood, New Jersey. *References*: *NYT*, February 21, 1955; and *WWWA*.

CURRIE, LAUCHLIN (BERNARD) (1902–   ). Economist, born October 8, 1902, in West Dublin, Nova Scotia, Canada. He came to the United States in 1925 and was naturalized in 1934. Currie attended St. Francis Xavier University (Antigonish, Nova Scotia), and graduated from the London School of Economics and Political Science and Harvard University. He was assistant director of research and statistics for the Board of Governors of the Federal Reserve System in Washington, D.C., from 1934 to 1939, and administrative assistant in the office of President Franklin D. Roosevelt from 1939 to 1945. He was a member of the International Bank mission to Colombia in 1949–1950. As a consultant to Colombia government agencies from 1951 to 1967, he was involved with the Magdalena Valley Mission from 1954 to 1960, was director of Fundacio para el Colombia in Bogotá from 1961 to 1967, and was involved with Operation Colombia from 1960 to 1967. He became a naturalized citizen of Colombia in 1958. He was a professor at Simon Fraser University (Burnaby, British Columbia) from 1967 to 1971, economic consultant to the government of Colombia from 1971 to 1981, and professor at the Universidad de los Andes (Bogotá) after 1981. He wrote *The Basis of a Development Program for Colombia* (Washington, D.C., 1950), *Operation Colombia: A National Economic and Social Program* (Bogotá, 1961), and *The Role of Economic Advisers in Developing Countries* (Westport, Conn., 1981). *References*: *CA*; and Roger J. Sandeland, *The Life and Political Economy of Lauchlin Currie, New Dealer, Presidential Adviser, and Development Economist* (Durham, N.C., 1990).

CURRIER, CHARLES WARREN (1857–1918). Clergyman, born March 22, 1857, in St. Thomas, West Indies. Currier was taken to the Netherlands in 1871, studied in the Province of Limburg, and was ordained in 1881. He was a missionary in Surinam in 1881–1882 and was transferred to the United States in 1882. He served in the order of the Redemptorists until 1894 and then was attached to the Diocese of Baltimore, where he served as priest and diocesan missionary until 1907 and in the Bureau of Catholic Indian Missions from 1907 to 1910. He traveled through South America .in 1910 and wrote *Lands of the Southern Cross: A Visit to South America* (Washington, D.C., 1911). He was bishop of Matanzas, Cuba, from 1913 until 1915. Died September 23, 1918, on the way from Waldorf, in southern Maryland, to Baltimore. *References*: *DAB*; and *WWWA*.

CURTIS, WILLIAM ELROY (1850–1911). Journalist and traveler, born November 5, 1850, in Akron, Ohio. Curtis graduated from Western Reserve College (later Case Western University). He was a reporter for the *Chicago Inter-Ocean* and then the Washington reporter for the *Chicago Record*. He was special commissioner from the United States to the Republics of Central and South America. He visited many of these countries and wrote *The Capitals of Spanish America* (New York, 1888) and *Trade and Transactions between the United States and Spanish America* (Washington, D.C., 1889). He was the first director of the Bureau of American Republics (later the Pan American Union) from 1889 until 1893 and then became a traveling correspondent for the *Chicago Record*. He wrote *Between the Andes and the Ocean: An Account of an Interesting Journey down the West Coast of South America from the Isthmus of Panama to the Straits of Magellan* (Chicago, 1900). Died October 5, 1911, in Chicago. *References*: *DAB*; *NCAB* 5:43; and *WWWA*.

CUTTER, VICTOR M(ACOMBER) (1881–1952). Business executive, born September 2, 1881, in Dracut, Massachusetts. Cutter graduated from Dartmouth College and Tuck School of Administration and Finance. He joined the United Fruit Company* in 1904. He was sent to one of the plantations in Costa Rica as a timekeeper and soon became the overseer of the plantation. There he started an agricultural experiment station in order to develop better banana plants and fruit. He was superintendent of the Zent division of the company in Costa Rica from 1906 to 1913 and engaged in developing new plantations. He was transferred to Guatemala in 1913 and then to Honduras until 1917, when he returned to the United States. He was vice president in charge of the company's tropic division from 1917 to 1924 and president of the United Fruit Company from 1924 until his retirement in 1933. He was also president of the Revere Sugar Refinery in Boston. Died December 25, 1952, in Falls Church, Virginia. *References*: *NCAB* 46:398; and *WWWA*.

D

DALE, JAMES G(ARY) (1870– ?) and **DALE, KATHERINE (NEEL)** (1872–1941). Missionaries. James G. Dale was born in Oak Hill, Alabama. He graduated from Erskine College (Due West, S.C.) and United Presbyterian Theological Seminary (Pittsburgh). He was a missionary under the Foreign Mission Board of the Associate Reformed Presbyterian Church in Mexico from 1899 to 1913 and from 1919 to 1945. He was principal of the seminary in Rio Verde after 1901. He wrote *Mexico and Our Mission* (Lebanon, Pa., 1910). Katherine Neel Dale was born August 17, 1872, near Troy, South Carolina. She graduated from Due West (S.C.) Female College (later Erskine College) and the Woman's Medical College of Philadelphia. She was a medical missionary under the Foreign Mission Board of the Associate Reformed Presbyterian Church in Mexico from 1899 to 1913 and from 1919 until her death. She served in Ciudad del Maiz, San Luis Potosi, from 1898 to 1900 and at Rio Verde from 1900 to 1914; she built a hospital there in 1905. She served in Tampico from 1919 until 1934. They were forced to leave Mexico during the revolution and returned in 1919 to Tampico. After 1934, they served with the Mexican Indian Mission at Tamazunchale and established a hospital there. She died May 28, 1941, in San Antonio, Texas. *References*: James G. Dale, *Katherine Neel Dale: Medical Missionary* (Grand Rapids, Mich., 1943); and Olive B. Floyd, *Doctora in Mexico; the Life of Dr. Katherine Neel Dale* (New York, 1944).

DANEHY, THOMAS JOSEPH (1914–1959). Missionary, born May 19, 1914, in Fort Wayne, Indiana. Daheny attended Sacred Heart Seminary (Detroit), St. Joseph College (Rensselaer, Ind.), and St. Gregory's Seminary (Cincinnati). He joined the Maryknoll Fathers in 1934 and was ordained in 1939. He taught at Clarks Summit, Pennsylvania, and was then assigned to the Gold Coast. He was one of the first Maryknoll priests sent as missionaries to Bolivia and spent the rest of his life among the Aymara Indians at the headwaters of the Amazon River. Often called "the jungle priest," he was apostolic administrator of the vicariate of Pando from 1948 to 1953 and titular bishop of Bita after 1953. Died October 9, 1959, in Lima, Peru. *Reference*: *DACB*.

DANELLS [or DANELS], JOHN DANIEL (1786–1856). Soldier, born in Baltimore. Danells became a captain in the Colombian Navy in 1818 and served the revolutionary cause in South America as commander of a squadron and by fitting out vessels. When the Republic of Colombia was established, he returned to the United States and gave up his claims for money due for his services, supplies provided by him for the revolution of 1818, expenses incurred by his three ships in the blockade of Puerto Cabello and in guarding La Guaya, and the expenses of a journey to the United States to raise funds for the sloop-of-war *Bolivar*. In 1822, he was acting agent for the Colombian government in the United States. Died in Baltimore. *References*: *ACAB*; and Francisco A. Vargas, *Nuestros Próceres Navales* (Caracas, 1964), pp. 307–13.

DANIELS, JOSEPHUS (1862–1948). Editor and diplomat, born May 18, 1862, in Washington, North Carolina. Daniels studied law and was admitted to the bar in 1885. He was involved in journalism and formed the Raleigh *News and Observer* in 1894 and published it until his death. He was secretary of the navy from 1913 to 1921. He was U.S. ambassador to Mexico from 1933 to 1941. He supported the social and economic goals of the Mexican Revolution, succeeded in improving the diplomatic relations between the United States and Mexico (even after the Mexican government expropriated American oil holdings), which led to the settlement of all major Mexican-American differences and assured a friendly Mexico during World War II. He wrote *Shirt-Sleeve Diplomat* (Chapel Hill, N.C., 1947). Died January 15, 1948, in Raleigh, North Carolina. *References*: Josephus Daniels Papers, Manuscript Division, Library of Congress; Josephus Daniels Papers, Library, University of North Carolina, Chapel Hill; *Roosevelt and Daniels: A Friendship in Politics*, ed. with an introd. by Carroll Kilpatrick (Chapel Hill, N.C., 1952); *DAB S4*; *DADH*; *DLB*; *EWM*; Joseph L. Morrison, *Josephus Daniels, the Small-d Democrat* (Chapel Hill, N.C., 1966); *NCAB* 39:593; *NYT*, January 16, 1948; and *WWWA*.

DANISH WEST INDIES, PURCHASE OF (1917). The Danish islands of St. Croix, St. Thomas, and St. John in the Caribbean Sea were purchased by the United States from Denmark in 1917 in an attempt to forestall possible German efforts to establish a military base in the Caribbean (*see* Virgin Islands). *References*: *DADH*; and Charles C. Tansill, *The Purchase of the Danish West Indies* (Baltimore, 1932).

DASCOMB, MARY P(ARKER) (1842–1917). Educator, born in Providence, Rhode Island, and grew up in Oberlin, Ohio. Dascomb graduated from Oberlin College. She taught in Joliet, Illinois, and in Elyria and Canton, Ohio. She came to Brazil in 1869 and was the tutor of the family of U.S. consul. With Ella

Kuhl,* she taught in the American School in São Paulo after 1877 and then in Batucato. She settled to Curitiba in 1892 and founded an American School there. Died October 10, 1917, in Curitiba, Brazil. *References*: Frank Goldman, "Três Educadores Norte-americanos no Brasil: 1860–1917," *Anhembi* 7 (1957): 450–58; Herculano de Gouvêa, *Homenagem a Miss Mary P. Dascomb* (Curitiba, 1920); and *NYT*, November 20, 1917.

DAVIS, ARTHUR POWELL (1861–1933). Civil engineer, born February 9, 1861, in Decatur, Illinois. Davis graduated from the State Normal School (Emporia, Kan.) and Columbian (later George Washington) University. He was topographer with the U.S. Geological Survey from 1884 to 1894, conducting surveys and explorations in Arizona, New Mexico, and California, hydrographer in charge of all government stream measurements from 1895 to 1897, hydrographer in charge of hydrographic examination of Nicaragua and Panama canal routes from 1898 to 1901, and chief engineer of the U.S. Reclamation Service from 1906 to 1914 and its director from 1914 to 1923. He was consulting engineer in the construction of the Panama Canal in 1909 and examined and reported on irrigation in Puerto Rico in 1909. He was consulting engineer in Russian Turkestan, China, and Russia, and chief engineer and general manager of East Bay Municipal Utility District in Oakland, California, from 1923 to 1929. He wrote *Hydrography of Nicaragua* (Washington, D.C., 1900) and *Hydrography of the American Isthmus* (Washington, D.C., 1902). Died August 7, 1933, in Oakland, California. *References*: *NCAB* 24:116; and *WWWA*.

DAVIS, GEORGE WHITEFIELD (1839–1918). Soldier and engineer, born July 26, 1839, in Thompson, Windham County, Connecticut. Davis served in the Union Army during the Civil War. In 1867, he was commissioned captain in the regular army and served in the Southwest. He was assistant engineer in the construction of the Washington Monument. On a leave of absence, he was engineer for the Niagara Canal Construction Company and its vice president and general manager from 1890 to 1893. He served during the Spanish-American War in Cuba and was military governor of Puerto Rico in 1899–1900. He served in the Philippines from 1901 to 1903 and retired with the rank of brigadier general in 1903. He was a member of the Isthmian Canal Commission after 1904, chairman of its board of engineers, and the first governor of the Panama Canal Zone in 1904–1905. He went twice on special missions to Guatemala. Died July 12, 1918, in Washington, D.C. *References*: *ACAB*; *DAB*; *NCAB* 13:368; and *WWWA*.

DAVIS, JONES EDGAR (1873–1944). Missionary, born March 22, 1873, in Lone Jack, Missouri. Davis graduated from William Jewell College. He held pastorates in Missouri from 1899 to 1904. He was a missionary under the Foreign Mission Board of the Southern Baptist Convention* in Mexico from 1904 until 1943. He established a printery in Toluca, Mexico, in 1905 and founded the

Baptist Spanish Publishing House in León in 1906. When the revolution led to removal of the publishing house to El Paso, Texas, he continued as its manager until his retirement in 1943. He was also editor of *El Expositor Biblico* from 1907 to 1944. Died June 4, 1944, in Independence, Missouri. *Reference*: *ESB*.

DAVIS, NATHANIEL (1925–   ). Diplomat, born April 12, 1925, in Boston. Davis graduated from Brown University and Fletcher School of Law and Diplomacy. He entered the foreign service in 1946 and served in Prague, Florence, Rome, and Moscow until 1956. He was Soviet Union desk officer in the U.S. State Department from 1956 to 1960, first secretary in Venezuela from 1960 to 1962, special assistant to the director of the Peace Corps in 1962–1963, deputy associate director of the Peace Corps from 1963 to 1965, U.S. minister to Bulgaria in 1965–1966, and senior staff member of the National Security Council from 1966 to 1968. He was U.S. ambassador to Guatemala from 1968 to 1971 and ambassador to Chile from 1971 to 1973. He was director general of the foreign service from 1973 to 1975, assistant secretary of state for African affairs in 1975, ambassador to Switzerland from 1975 to 1977, State Department adviser and professor at the Naval War College from 1977 to 1983, and professor of humanities at Harvey Mudd College (Claremont, Calif.) after 1983. He wrote *The Last Two Years of Salvador Allende* (Ithaca, N.Y., 1985). *Reference*: *WWA*.

DAVIS, RICHARD HARDING (1864–1916). Journalist, born April 18, 1864, in Philadelphia. Davis attended Lehigh and Johns Hopkins universities. He entered a journalist career in 1886 and was reporter for the Philadelphia *Press* and then the *Telegraph*. He joined the staff of the New York *Sun* in 1889–1890 and was managing editor of *Harper's Weekly* after 1890. He traveled extensively. He reported on the conditions in the regions bordering on the Canal Zone and wrote *Three Gringos in Venezuela and Central America* (New York, 1896). He reported on the war in Cuba and later on the Spanish-American War, and wrote *Cuba in War Time* (New York, 1897) and *The Cuban and Porto Rican Campaign* (New York, 1898). He also wrote popular fiction, including *Soldiers of Fortune* (New York, 1897). Died April 11, 1916, in Mount Kisco, New York. *References*: *DAB*; *DADH*; *NCAB* 8:176; *NYT*, April 13, 1916; and *WWWA*.

DAVIS, ROY TASCO (1889–1975). Diplomat, born June 24, 1889, in Ewing, Missouri. Davis graduated from LaGrange College (Mo.) and Brown University. He was a clerk in the Missouri legislature, secretary of the Missouri State Capitol Commission, and secretary and business manager of Stephens College until 1921. He was U.S. minister to Costa Rica from 1922 to 1929 and minister to Panama from 1929 to 1933. He chaired the Honduras–Guatemala boundary commission in 1929 and acted as unofficial mediator during the Panama revolution of 1931. He was assistant to the president of Stephens College from 1933 to 1937 and president of National Park Seminary from 1937 to 1942 and filled various international education posts from 1942 to 1953. He was U.S. ambassador to Haiti from 1953 until his retirement in 1957. Died December 27, 1975, in Chevy Chase, Maryland. *References*: *DADH*; *NCAB* E:409; and *WWWA*.

DAVIS, WALTER G(OULD) (1851–1919). Meteorologist, born in Danville, Vermont. Davis was employed by the engineering department of the Portland and Ogdensburg railroad from 1868 to 1876. He went to Argentina in 1876 and was assistant to Benjamin Apthorp Gould* in the astronomical observatory and the meteorological service of Argentina in Córdoba until 1885. He was director of the Argentine Meteorological Office in Córdoba from 1885 to 1901 and in Buenos Aires from 1901 until his retirement in 1915. He established a hydrometric section in 1902 and forecasting and magnetic sections in 1904. He returned to the United States in 1915. Died April 30, 1919, in Danville, Vermont. *References*: *NCAB* 2:171; and *Science* 50 (July 4, 1919): 11–13.

DAWSON, THOMAS CLELAND (1865–1912). Diplomat, born July 30, 1865, in Hudson, Wisconsin. Dawson graduated from Hanover College (Ind.), attended Harvard University, and graduated from Cincinnati Law School. He practiced law in Des Moines and in Council Bluffs, Iowa, from 1886 to 1897 and was assistant attorney general of Iowa from 1891 to 1894. He was secretary of legation in Brazil from 1897 to 1904. He wrote *The South American Republics* (New York, 1903–1904). He was U.S. minister in the Dominican Republic from 1904 to 1907. Because the government of the Dominican Republic was practically bankrupt and European creditors were pressing for payment, he negotiated a convention providing that the United States would conduct the customs of the Dominican Republic, administer its finances, and settle its financial obligations, but this was not ratified. He later negotiated another convention giving legal status to the collection of revenue by a receiver of customs appointed by the United States. He was U.S. minister to Colombia from 1907 to 1909, minister to Chile in 1909–1910, and minister to Panama in 1910. In 1910, he negotiated a political agreement with Nicaragua to settle the differences between the United States and Nicaragua. He was resident diplomatic officer in the State Department in 1911–1912. Died May 1, 1912, in Washington, D.C. *References*: *DAB*; *DADH*; G. J. Kist, "The Role of Thomas C. Dawson in United States—Latin American Diplomatic Relations, 1897–1912," Ph.D. diss., Loyola University, 1971; *NCAB* 13:512; *NYT*, May 2, 1912; and *WWWA*.

DAWSON, WILLIAM, JR. (1885–1972). Diplomat, born August 11, 1885, in St. Paul, Minnesota. Dawson graduated from the University of Minnesota and studied at the Ecole des Sciences Politiques (Paris). He entered the diplomatic service in 1908 and served in St. Petersburg, Barcelona, and Frankfurt. He was consul in Rosario, Argentina, and Montevideo, Uruguay; consul at large from 1922 to 1925; and inspector of consular offices in South and Central America and chief instructor at the Foreign Service School in Washington, D.C. from 1925 to 1928. He was U.S. consul general in Mexico City from 1928 to 1930, minister to Ecuador from 1930 to 1935, minister to Colombia from 1935 to 1937, minister to Uruguay from 1937 to 1939, the first U.S. ambassador to Panama from 1939 to 1941, and the first U.S. ambassador to Uruguay from 1941 until his retirement in 1946. He returned from retirement in 1946 as the first permanent representative on the governing body of the Pan American Union and then served on the Organization of American States until 1948. Died July 3, 1972, in Blue Hill, Maine. *References*: *CB* 1941; *DADH*; *NYT*, July 5, 1972; and *WWWA*.

DE BOOY, THEODOOR (HENDRICK NIKOLAS) (1882–1919). Archaeologist and explorer, born December 5, 1882, in Hellevoetsluis, the Netherlands. De Booy attended the Royal Naval Institute (Holland). He came to the United States in 1906 and became a naturalized citizen in 1916. He went to the Bahama Islands in 1911–1912 and explored the antiquities of the Caicos Islands. He was a member of the staff of the Heye Museum in New York City from 1912 to 1918 and served as its field explorer in the West Indies. He made an expedition to Jamaica in 1913 and in Santo Domingo in 1913 and 1914. He made explorations and excavations on the island of Margarita, Venezuela, in 1915, and later on southeastern Trinidad; made a third expedition to Santo Domingo in 1916; and went to Puerto Rico and Martinique (where he excavated) and to the Virgin Islands in 1916–1917. In 1918, he explored the Sierra de Perijá range of Venezuela for the American Geographical Society and the University Museum of the University of Pennsylvania, and investigated the Macoa and Matilone Indians. He then served as Latin American expert for the Inquiry, an organization set by the U.S. government in 1917 to conduct studies of the problems of peacemaking following World War I, until his death. He was coauthor of *The Virgin Islands, Our New Possessions, and the British Islands* (Philadelphia, 1918). Died February 18, 1919, in Yonkers, New York. *Reference*: *NCAB* 17:313.

DE FOREST, DAVID CURTIS (1774–1825). Merchant, born January 10, 1774, in Huntington, Connecticut. As a boy De Forest ran away to sea and remained there until 1795. He was involved with business in Bridgeport, Connecticut, in 1795–1796 and served in the U.S. Army in 1799–1800. An officer on a vessel in 1800–1801, he quitted it on the coast of Patagonia in 1801, went to Brazil, returned to the Río de la Plata, and settled in Buenos Aires. He established the first permanent American commercial house in Buenos Aires. He was exiled to the United States from 1809 to 1812 but was back in Buenos Aires in 1812 and reopened his establishment, and received much business from the Argentine government. During the Argentine revolutionary war, he received letters of marque for privateers against Spanish shipping, which he gave to American shipowners. He returned to the United States in 1818, settled in New Haven, Connecticut, and was consul general of the Argentine Republic until 1822. Died February 22, 1825, in New Haven, Connecticut. *References*: David

Curtis DeForest Papers, Yale University Library, New Haven, Conn.; *Cutolo*; *DAB*; and Benjamin Keen, *David Curtis DeForest and the Revolution of Buenos Aires* (New Haven, Conn., 1947).

DE KAY, GEORGE COLMAN (1802–1849). Naval officer, born March 5, 1802, in or near New York City. De Kay was shipped to sea as a boy and became a captain of a ship in 1822. He arrived in Buenos Aires in 1826 during a dispute between Argentina and Brazil, offered his services to the Argentine Navy, and was made captain. Commanding the brig *Brandzen*, he ran the Brazilian blockade on the Rio de la Plata, engaging two Brazilian men-of-war and capturing one. In 1827, he captured three Brazilian ships off Pernambuco. In 1828, when the *Brandzen* was surrounded and overpowered by Brazilian ships in the Rio de la Plata, he scuttled the ship and proceeded with his crew, on foot, to Buenos Aires. He later became lieutenant colonel, and after peace came, returned to the United States. He was associated with Henry Eckford, a shipbuilder, and sailed a sloop-of-war to Turkey in 1831. Died January 31, 1849, in Washington, D.C. *References*: *Cutolo*; *DAB*; *NCAB* 9:205; *Udaondo*; Phyllis D. Wheelock, "An American Commander in the Argentine Navy," *AN* 6 (1946): 5–18; and *WWWA*.

DE ROULET, VINCENT W(ILLIAM) (1925–1975). Businessman and diplomat, born September 16, 1925, in California. De Roulet graduated from Claremont Men's College. He served in the U.S. Army Air Force during World War II. He was real estate property manager from 1950 to 1955, chairman of the board of Towne-Oiler Associates, a marketing company, from 1955 to 1957, and investment company from 1958 to 1975, and was mayor of North Hill, Long Island, New York. He was U.S. ambassador to Jamaica from 1969 until 1973. He became involved in Jamaican politics, was declared persona non grata in 1973, and resigned. Died August 9, 1975, in Falmouth Foreside, Maine. *References*: George Crile, "Our Man in Jamaica," *Harper's Magazine* 249 (October 1974): 80–90; *NYT*, August 11, 1975; and *WWWA*.

DEGOLYER, EVERETTE LEE (1886–1956). Petroleum geologist, born October 9, 1886, in Greensburg, Kansas. DeGolyer graduated from the University of Oklahoma. He was a geologist with the La Compania Mexicana de Petroleo de Aguila S. A. (Mexican Eagle Oil Company) from 1909 to 1911, its chief geologist from 1911 to 1914, chief of its land department from 1912 to 1914, and a consulting engineer until 1916. He found oil at Potrero del Plano, an area which became known as "the Golden Lane." He established a consulting office from 1916 to 1919 following a geological reconnaissance of western Cuba in 1915. He organized Amerada Petroleum Corporation and Rycade Oil Company in 1918. He was vice president and general manager of Amerada Petroleum Corporation from 1919 to 1926, its president and general manager from 1926 to 1929, and chairman of the board from 1929 to 1932. He was vice president and general manager of Rycade Oil Company from 1923 to 1926 and its president and general manager from 1926 to 1941. He established Core Laboratories, Incorporated, in Dallas in 1932; founded Atlatl Royalty Corporation and was its president until 1950; and ran DeGolyer and MacNaughton consulting practice from 1936 until his death. Died December 14, 1956, in Dallas, Texas. *References*: *BAAPG* 41 (1957): 969–74; *BMNAS* 33 (1959): 65–86; *BDABL*; *NCAB* 43:12; Lon Tinkle, *Mr. De: A Biography of Everette Lee DeGolyer* (Boston, 1970); and *WWWA*.

DEL VALLE, REGINALDO FRANCISCO (1854–1938). Public official, born December 15, 1854, in Los Angeles. Del Valle graduated from Santa Clara University and was admitted to the bar in 1877. He served in the California state house of representatives and in the state senate and was a member of the Los Angeles Public Service Commission (later the Board of Water and Power Commissioners). In 1913, he went to Mexico as a special agent to observe conditions in that country, investigate its land tenure system, collect information regarding the origins of the rebellion against Victoriano Huerta, evaluate its chief, Venustiano Carranza, assess conditions, and report personal observations. He retired in 1929. Died September 21, 1938, in Los Angeles. *References*: Kenneth J. Grieb, "Reginald del Valle: A California Diplomat Sojourning in Mexico," *California Historical Society Quarterly* 47 (1968): 315–28; *Hill*; and *Los Angeles Times*, September 22, 1938.

DELANO, PAUL (1775–1842). Sea captain, born June 15, 1775, in Fairhaven, Massachusetts. Delano was captain of *Curiacio* and came to Chile in 1819. He joined the Chilean Navy and was commissioned a captain. He was given charge of the troop transports in a naval expedition to Peru in 1829. He was captain of the port of Valparaiso after 1822 and designed and directed the building of the first wharf in that port as well as the first lighthouse, which was constructed at Playa Ancha in 1837. He became the second commanding general of the department of Valparaiso in 1824. Died February 4, 1842, in Talcahuano, Chile. *References*: *Figueroa*; and Virgilio Figueroa, *Diccionario Histórico Biográfico y Bibliografico de Chile* (Santiago de Chile, 1925), 2:553–55.

DEMPSTER, JOHN (1794–1863). Missionary, born January 2, 1794, in Florida, New York. Dempster held pastorates from 1818 to 1832 in lower Canada, was presiding elder of the Cayuga District of the Methodist Church, and was president of the Genesee Wesleyan Seminary (Lima, N.Y.) from 1832 to 1835. He was a missionary under the Missionary Society of the Methodist Episcopal Church* in Argentina from 1836 until 1841. Serving in Buenos Aires and organizing a congregation, he began the first Methodist church building in South America. He helped to found Methodist work in Uruguay in 1838. He also worked in Brazil in 1839–1840, where he organized a church and established a school. He returned to the United States in 1841, was president of the Methodist

a missionary under the Board of Foreign Missions of the Methodist Episcopal Church* in Bolivia after 1943, teacher in the American Institute in Cochabamba after 1943, and the institute's director from 1951 to 1953 and in 1955–1956. He was director of the La Paz American Institute in 1957, served as pastor of the Methodist church in Cochabamba, and was superintendent of the central district of Bolivia for several years. He was executive secretary of the Latin American Mission Board of the Methodist Church in 1960–1961. Killed December 16, 1961, in an automobile accident, on the road to Carnavi, Bolivia. *References*: *EWM*; and Jim Palmer, *Red Poncho and Big Boots: The Life of Murray Dickson* (Nashville, Tenn., 1969).

DILLINGHAM, ALBERT CALDWELL (1848–1925). Naval officer, born June 3, 1848, in Philadelphia. Dillingham graduated from the U.S. Naval Academy in 1870 and was commissioned ensign in the U.S. Navy in 1871. He served during the Spanish-American War. In 1904, he commanded the cruiser *Detroit* and was in charge of U.S. affairs in Santo Domingan waters. He became one of the chief U.S Dominican policymakers, landed troops, stopped a revolution in that republic, and established a stable government. In 1905, he was again sent to Santo Domingo on a special diplomatic mission, and with the U.S. minister, effected an agreement that secured uninterrupted commerce, safety for the lives and properties of the foreign residents, and a guarantee that the debt of the republic would be paid. The agreement placed the customs of the republic under American control. Dillingham retired with rank of rear admiral in 1910. He was recalled to service during World War I. Died December 6, 1925, in Norfolk, Virginia. *References*: *ACAB*; Richard H. Collin, "The 1904 *Detroit* Compact: U.S. Naval Diplomacy and Dominican Revolution," *Historian* 52 (1990): 432–52; *NCAB* 20:383; and *WWWA*.

DIMITRY, ALEXANDER (1805–1883). Educator and diplomat, born February 7, 1805, in New Orleans. Dimitry graduated from Georgetown University. He was editor of the New Orleans *Bee* from 1830 to 1834 and post office clerk in Washington, D.C. from 1834 to 1842. He established a school in St. Charles Parish, Louisiana, in 1842, and directed it until 1847. He was the first state superintendent of schools in Louisiana from 1847 to 1851. He was a translator in the U.S. State Department from 1854 to 1859 and U.S. minister to Costa Rica from 1859 to 1861. He hindered the efforts to settle the Mosquito coast conflict between Britain and Nicaragua. He was assistant postmaster general of the Confederacy and was later involved in education in New Orleans. Died January 30, 1883, in New Orleans. *References*: *BDAE*; *DAB*; *DADH*; *NCAB* 10:176; *NYT*, January 31, 1883; and Clayton Rand, *Stars in Their Eyes: Dreamers and Builders in Louisiana* (Gulfport, Miss., 1953), 108–9.

DITMARS, RAYMOND LEE (1876–1942). Herpetologist, born June 20, 1876, in Newark, New Jersey. Ditmars was an assistant in the entomological department of the American Museum of Natural History from 1893 to 1897, a reporter for the *New York Times* from 1897 to 1899, assistant curator of reptiles at the New York Zoological Park from 1899 to 1910, and curator in chief of reptiles and mammals from 1910 until 1942. He conducted zoological explorations to Central and South America and the West Indies. He wrote accounts of his experiences in *Confessions of a Scientist* (New York, 1934) and *The Making of a Scientist* (New York, 1937). Died May 12, 1942, in New York City. *References*: *CB* 1940; *DAB S3*; *NCAB* 10:452; *NYT*, May 13, 1942; and *WWWA*.

DOHENY, EDWARD L(AWRENCE) (1856–1935). Petroleum producer, born August 10, 1856, in Fond du Lac, Wisconsin. Doheny was involved in surveying in Indian Territory and Mexico and then in gold prospecting in Arizona and New Mexico. He studied law, was admitted to the bar, and practiced in New Mexico, but he soon returned to gold prospecting. He became an oil producer in Los Angeles in 1892, in Fullerton, California, in 1897, and in the Kern River valley in 1899. In 1900, with C. A. Canfield,* he made a pioneering trip to Mexico, acquired property in Tampico, obtained rights in areas along the Tamesi River, and formed the Mexican Petroleum Company of California in 1900 to develop these lands. He made the first major oil strike on the Cerro de la Paz, Mexico, in 1901, and was the first person to produce oil in Mexico on a commercial scale. He acquired additional lands in the Huastaca district in 1905–1906, and formed the Huastaca Petroleum Company. He also constructed a refinery in Tampico. In 1911, he acquired Calorie Company, which distributed petroleum and its products in South America. He disposed of his interests in Mexico to the Standard Oil Company of Indiana in 1925. Died September 8, 1935, in Los Angeles. *References*: *BDABL*; *DAB S1*; *DACB*; Fritz L. Hoffman, "Edward L. Doheny and the Beginnings of Petroleum Development in Mexico," *Mid-America* 24 (1941): 94–108; *Hanrahan*, ch. 1; Walter W. Jenning, *Dozen Captains of American Industry* (New York, 1954), pp. 201–18; Don La Botz, *Edward L. Doheny: Petroleum, Power, and Politics in the United States and Mexico* (New York, 1991); Gabriel Antonio Menédez, *Doheny el Cruel: Episodios de la Sangrienta Lucha por el Petróleo Mexicana* (Mexico City, 1958); *NCAB* 29:238; and *WWWA*.

DOLLAR DIPLOMACY. A phrase used by critics to describe the policy whereby the United States government encouraged American bankers to make loans to Central American and Caribbean governments to improve their financial and political stability and to forestall intervention by European governments. American creditors would be guaranteed a satisfactory return on their investments through U.S. collection of customs in the countries involved and by resorting to force to protect their properties. *References*: *DADH*; *ELA*; P. E. Mulhollan, "Philander C. Knox and Dollar Diplomacy, 1909–1913," Ph.D. diss., University of Texas, 1966; Dana G. Munro, "Dollar Diplomacy in Nicaragua, 1909–1913," *HAHR* 38 (1958): 209–34; Dana G. Munro, *Intervention and Dollar*

Biblical Institute (Newberry, Vt.) from 1844 to 1853, and founded Garrett Biblical Institute (Evanston, Ill.) in 1853. He was Garrett's president until 1861. Died in California. *Reference*: *EWM*.

DENNIS, LAWRENCE (1893–1977). Diplomat, born December 25, 1893, in Atlanta. Dennis graduated from Harvard University. He served in the U.S. Army during World War I and in the U.S. diplomatic service from 1920 to 1927 in Port-au-Prince, Haiti; Bucharest, Rumania; Managua, Nicaragua; and Tegucigalpa, Honduras. He was U.S. commissioner during the first phase of the American intervention in Nicaragua in 1926–1927. It was said that he manipulated Nicaraguan politics to make it possible for Adolfo Diaz to resume the presidency. He resigned in 1927 to enter banking and later the brokerage business. He was the proprietor, editor, and publisher of *The Weekly Foreign Letter* in New York City from 1939 to 1943, and of *Appeal to Reason* after 1946. He was tried by the federal government in 1944 on charges of sedition, but a mistrial was declared and the charges were later dismissed. Died August 20, 1977, in Spring Valley, New York. *References*: *NYT*, August 21, 1977; Ronald Radosh, *Prophets on the Right* (New York, 1975), pp. 275–322; and *WWWA*.

DENNY, HAROLD NORMAN [HOBBS] (1889–1945). Journalist, born March 11, 1889, in Des Moines, Iowa. Denny attended Drake University. He was a reporter and copy editor on the *Des Moines Register* and later on the St. Paul (Minn.) *Pioneer Press*, the *Minneapolis News*, and the *Minneapolis Tribune*. He served in the U.S. Army during World War I. He later worked on the *Chicago Herald Examiner*, the *New York American*, and the *New York Herald Tribune*, and on the staff of the *New York Times* from 1922 until his death. He covered Charles A. Lindbergh's South American flight in 1928, the Nicaraguan crisis in 1928, the Forbes Commission to Haiti* in 1930, and the Cuban crisis in 1930–1931. He wrote *Dollars for Bullets* (New York, 1929). Died July 3, 1945, in Des Moines, Iowa. *References*: *NCAB* 34:300; and *WWWA*.

DERBY, ORVILLE A(DELBERT) (1851–1915). Geologist, born July 23, 1851, in Niles, Cayuga County, New York. Derby graduated from Cornell University. He made two trips to the Amazon valley in 1870–1871. He returned to Brazil in 1875, as assistant to Charles Frederick Hartt.* He was an assistant in the imperial geological commission of Brazil from 1875 until it was abolished in 1877. He was curator of the geological and mineralogical department of the National Museum in Rio de Janeiro from 1880 to 1891 and served as a geologist for a hydrographic survey of the São Francisco and Rio Das Velhas rivers. In 1886, he organized the geological survey of the state of São Paulo and served as state geologist from 1886 to 1904. He was chief of the new federal geological survey of Brazil from 1907 until his death. Committed suicide November 27, 1915, in Rio de Janeiro, Brazil. *References*: *Orville A. Derby's Studies on the Paleontology of Brazil: Selection and Coordination of Some of This Geologist's*

Out of Print and Rare Works, ed. Alpheu Diniz Gonssalves (Rio de Janeiro, 1952); *ACAB*; *BGSA* 27 (1916): 15–21; *NCAB* 10:460; and *WWWA*.

DEVEREUX, JOHN (fl. 1816–1817). Merchant. Devereux went to Buenos Aires in 1816. He was also appointed U.S. commercial agent to Buenos Aires to survey and report on political and economic conditions in Buenos Aires. He tried, without authorization and unsuccessfully, to secure loans for the government of Buenos Aires in the United States in 1816–1817.

DEXTER, EDWIN G(RANT) (1868–1938). Educator, born July 21, 1868, in Calais, Maine, and grew up in Templeton, Massachusetts. Dexter graduated from Brown and Columbia universities. He was a high school science teacher in Colorado Springs, Colorado, from 1892 to 1895, taught psychology at Colorado State Normal School (later University of Northern Colorado in Greely, Colo.) from 1895 to 1900, and was professor of education at the University of Illinois from 1900 to 1907. He was commissioner of education for Puerto Rico from 1907 to 1912. He also served as chancellor of the University of Puerto Rico and president of the Insular Library Board, and he sat in the upper house of the state legislature. He was president of the National Institute of Panama from 1912 to 1918 and served with the American Red Cross during and after World War I. He was president of the U.S. Veterans' Bureau Vocational School at Camp Sheridan, Ohio, from 1922 to 1924, chief of the vocational unit of the U.S. Veteran's Bureau in 1924–1925, chief of its policy subdivision from 1925 to 1930, and its historian from 1930 to 1938. Died December 5, 1938, in Linthicum Heights, Maryland. *References*: *BDAE*; *NCAB* 36:367; Aida Negron de Montilla, *Americanization in Puerto Rico and the Public School System, 1900–1930* (San Juan, P.R., 1975), ch. 6; and *WWWA*.

DICKERSON, ROY E(RNEST) (1877–1944). Petroleum geologist, born August 8, 1877, in Monticello, Illinois, and grew up in San Jose, California. Dickerson graduated from the University of California at Berkeley. He was a science teacher in the California school system, and later was high school principal from 1900 to 1918. He was petroleum geologist for the Stanford Oil Company of California from 1918 to 1926, becoming geological superintendent for the Philippines. He was a geologist with the Atlantic Refining Company from 1926 to 1936, working first at Maracaibo, Venezuela, and later in other parts of Central America, South America, Cuba and Haiti. He was chief geologist of foreign production operations from 1936 until 1942, and chief of the technical section of the Petroleum Division of the U.S. Foreign Economic Administration from 1942 until his death. Died February 24, 1944, in New York City. *References*: *BAAPG* 28 (1944): 888–89; and *NYT*, February 25, 1944.

DICKSON, MURRAY (1915–1961). Missionary, born in Hillsboro, Texas. Dickson graduated from Southern Methodist University and attended Columbia University. He was director of the Wesley Foundation in Austin, Texas. He was

William S. McFeely, *Frederick Douglass* (New York, 1991); *NCAB* 22:309; Merline Pitre, "Frederick Douglass and American Diplomacy in the Caribbean," *Journal of Black Studies* 13 (1983): 457–76; Merline Pitre, "Frederick Douglass and the Annexation of Santo Domingo," *Journal of Negro History* 62 (1977): 390–400; Benjamin Quarles, "Frederick Douglass: Letters from the Haitian Legation," *Caribbean Quarterly* 4 (January 1955): 75–81; and L. M. Sears, "Frederick Douglass and the Mission to Haiti, 1889–1891," *HAHR* 21 (1941): 222–38.

DOWNING, THOMAS G. (1895–1976). Economist, born October 1895, in Philadelphia. Downing graduated from the University of Pennsylvania. He served in the U.S. Army during World War I. He was administrator of customs at El Bluff, Nicaragua, in 1927, assistant general customs collector for the Atlantic coast, and customs administrator and commander of the port of Puerto Cabezas, Nicaragua, from 1928 to 1935. He was assistant general customs collector and auditor for the Servicio Aduanero de Nicaragua after 1942, president of the Junta de Control de Precios y Comercio and a major in the Guardia Nacional de Nicaragua after 1942, and also chief of the Servicio Secreto of the Servicio Aduanero de Nicaragua. Died October 31, 1976, in Scranton, Pennsylvania. *Reference*: *WWLA*.

DREBEN, SAM (1878–1925). Soldier of fortune, born in Russia, and came to the United States in 1898. Dreben enlisted in the regular army and served in the Philippine-American War, and in the defense of Peking during the Boxer Rebellion. He joined General Lee Christmas* in Honduras, took part in the Francisco Madero revolt against Porfirio Díaz in Mexico, and afterward became a follower of Francisco Villa. Died March 15, 1925, in Hollywood, California. *References*: Mac Davis, *Jews at a Glance* (New York, 1956); *Encyclopaedia Judaica* (Jersualem, 1971): 11:1573; and *NYT*, March 16, 1925.

DREES, CHARLES W(ILLIAM) (1851–1926). Missionary, born September 13, 1851, in Xenia, Ohio. Drees graduated from Ohio Wesleyan University and Boston University School of Theology and was ordained in 1874. He was a missionary under the Board of Foreign Missions of the Methodist Episcopal Church* to Mexico from 1874 until 1886. He built up a congregation, organized a boys' orphanage, and founded a seminary. He was superintendent of the Mexican mission from 1878 to 1885 and district superintendent in 1885–1886. He was superintendent of the South American Mission in Buenos Aires from 1886 to 1896 and treasurer and legal representative of the Board of Foreign Missions in South America until 1900. He founded Methodist work in Puerto Rico from 1900 to 1904. He returned to Buenos Aires in 1904 and was superintendent of the District of Buenos Aires, and he went to Spain in 1912 to help in the revision of the Spanish New Testament. He retired in 1924. Died August 30, 1926, in Buenos Aires, Argentina. *References*: *Thirteen Years in Mexico* (*from Letters of Charles W. Drees*), ed. Ada M. C. Drees (New York, 1915); *Drees*; *EWM*; *OAB*; and *WWWA*.

DREXEL, FRANCIS MARTIN (1792–1863). Painter, born April 7, 1792, in Dornbirn, the Austrian Tyrol, near the Lake of Constance, and grew up in Milan, Italy. Drexel studied art there and in other parts of Europe. He came to the United States in 1817 and settled in Philadelphia, where he painted portraits and gave lessons in drawing. He went to South America from 1826 to 1830, traveling extensively, painting portraits, collecting curios, and accumulating considerable wealth. He also made a trip to Mexico from 1835 to 1837. In 1837, he abandoned art and opened brokerage offices in Louisville, Kentucky, and in Philadelphia in 1838; the latter became Drexel and Company. Struck by a train on June 5, 1863, and died in Philadelphia. *References*: Francis Martin Drexel, "Journal of a Trip to South America" (Ms.), Archives of Drexel and Company, Philadelphia; *ACAB*; *DAB*; *Francis Martin Drexel, 1792–1863: An Artist Turned Banker* (Philadelphia, 1976); *Manthorne*; *NYHSD*; Joaquin H. Ugarte y Ugarte, *El Pintor Austriaco Francis Martin Drexel (1792–1863) en la Iconografía Bolivariana* (Lima, 1973); and *WWWA*.

DULLES, JOHN W(ATSON) F(OSTER) (1913–   ). Business executive and author, born May 20, 1913, in Auburn, New York. Dulles graduated from Princeton and Harvard universities and the University of Arizona. He was assistant manager of Compañia Metalurgica Penoles, S.A., in Monterrey, Nuevo Leon, Mexico, from 1946 to 1948, and manager of its ore department from 1948 to 1952. He was director of the commercial division of Compañia Minera de Penoles, S.A. in Monterrey, from 1952 to 1954, assistant general manager from 1954 to 1959, and executive vice president in 1959. He was executive vice president of Compañia de Mineracao Novalimense in Rio de Janeiro, Brazil, in 1959, and vice president from 1960 to 1962. He was professor of Latin American studies at the University of Texas (Austin) after 1962. He wrote *Yesterday in Mexico: A Chronicle of the Revolution, 1919–1936* (Austin, 1967), *Vargas of Brazil: A Political Biography* (Austin, Tex., 1967), *Unrest in Brazil: Political-Military Crises, 1955–1964* (Austin, Tex., 1970), *Anarchists and Communists in Brazil, 1900–1935* (Austin, Tex., 1973), and *Castello Branco: The Making of a Brazilian President* (College Park, Tex., 1978). *References*: *CA*; and *DAS*.

DUNN, BALLARD S(MITH) (1829–1897). Clergyman and colony promoter. Dunn was the Episcopalian preacher and rector of St. Phillips Church in New Orleans. He served as chaplain and ordnance officer in the Confederate Army during the Civil War. He went to Brazil in 1865 in acquired land on the Juquia River, near Iguape, in São Paulo Province. He returned to the United States and wrote *Brazil: The Home for Southerners, or, A Practical Account of What the Author, and Others, Who Visited that Country for the Same Objects, Saw and Did while in that Empire* (New York, 1866) in order to promote his colony in

Diplomacy in the Caribbean, 1900–1921 (Princeton, N.J., 1964); Robert F. Smith, "Cuba: Laboratory for Dollar Diplomacy, 1898–1917," *Historian* 28 (1966): 586–609; and J. S. Tulchin, "Dollar Diplomacy and Non-Intervention: The Latin American Policy of the United States," Ph.D. diss., Harvard University, 1965.

DOLPHIN INCIDENT (1914). Sailors from the USS *Dolphin* landed in Tampico, Mexico, in 1914, and were arrested by Mexican authorities. When Mexico refused to apologize, the U.S. Navy carried out a naval demonstration in Tampico's waters, the U.S. later broke diplomatic relations with Mexico, and U.S. forces occupied Veracruz (*see* Veracruz Affair).

DOMINICAN CRISIS (1965). Following a revolution in the Dominican Republic against a military junta in 1965, U.S. military forces invaded the republic to prevent the establishment of what the U.S. government feared would be a Cuban-style government. U.S. forces were later replaced by an Inter-American peace-keeping force. *References*: *DADH*; Quinten A. Kelso, "The Dominican Crisis of 1965. A New Appraisal," Ph.D. diss., University of Colorado at Boulder, 1982; Piero Gleijeses, *The Dominican Crisis: The 1965 Constitutionist Revolt and the American Intervention* (Baltimore, 1978); Abraham Lowenthal, *The Dominican Intervention* (Cambridge, Mass., 1972); *Musicant*, ch. 8; Bruce Palmer, Jr., *Intervention in the Caribbean: The Dominican Crisis of 1965* (Lexington, Ky., 1989); Herbert G. Schoonmaker, *Military Crisis Management: U.S. Intervention in the Dominican Republic* (Westport, Conn., 1965); and Jerome Slater, *Intervention and Negotiation: The United States and the Dominican Revolution* (New York, 1970).

DOMINICAN REPUBLIC, ATTEMPT TO ANNEX THE (1869–1870). In 1869, a treaty for the annexation of the Dominican Republic to the United States was negotiated between the two countries. Although President Ulysses S. Grant used his influence to see that the treaty was ratified, the U.S. Senate did not do so. *References*: William J. Nelson, *Almost a Territory: America's Attempt to Annex the Dominican Republic* (Newark, Del., 1990); and H. T. Pinkett, "Efforts to Annex the Dominican Republic to the United States 1866–1871," *Journal of Negro History* 26 (1941): 12–45.

DOMINICAN REPUBLIC, INTERVENTION IN (1916–1924). In order to avert complete financial collapse and political anarchy, U.S. Marines landed in Santo Domingo in 1916 to control events in the Dominican Republic. The U.S. administered the country directly by martial law from 1916 to 1922. The marines carried out extensive public works programs, established the Guardia Nacional Dominicana,* and promoted education and public health. The withdrawal of the troops began in 1922 and was completed in 1924. *References*: Bruce J. Calder, "Caudilos and 'Gavilleros' Versus the United States Marines: Guerilla Insurgency During the Dominican Intervention, 1916–1924," *HAHR* 58 (1978): 649–75; Bruce J. Calder, *The Impact of Intervention: The Dominican Republic during the U.S. Occupation of 1916–1924* (Austin, 1984); Bruce J. Calder, "Varieties of Resistance to the United States Occupation of the Dominican Republic, 1916–1924," *SECOLAS Annals* 11 (1980): 103–19; Stephen M. Fuller and Graham A. Cosmas, *Marines in the Dominican Republic, 1916–1924* (Washington, D.C., 1974); *Langley*, chs. 10–12; Richard Millett with G. Dale Gaddy, "Administering the Protectorates: The U.S. Occupation of Haiti and the Dominican Republic," *Revista/Review Interamericana* 6 (1976): 383–402; Kenneth Grieb, "Warren G. Harding and the Dominican Republic: U.S. Withdrawal, 1921–1923," *JIAS* 11 (1969): 425–40; Joseph R. Juarez, "United States Withdrawal from Santo Domingo," *HAHR* 42 (1962): 152–90; and *Musicant*, ch. 6.

DOUGLAS, JAMES (1837–1918). Mining engineer, born November 4, 1837, in Quebec, Canada. Douglas attended the University of Edinburgh and graduated from Queen's University (Kingston, Canada). He was a professor of chemistry in Morrin College (Quebec). He came to the United States in 1875 and was in charge of a copper extraction plant in Phoenixville, Pennsylvania. He was then employed by Phelps, Dodge and Company of New York. He examined copper mines in Bisbee, Arizona, and became president of Copper Queen Consolidated Mining Company, which was involved in mining, smelting, and railroading in Arizona and Sonora, Mexico. He was president of Phelps Dodge Corporation from 1909 to 1916, and chairman of the board in 1917–1918. Died June 25, 1918, in New York City. *References*: Robert G. Clelland, *A History of Phelps Dodge 1834–1950* (New York, 1952), chs. 6–7; *DAB*; Hugh H. Langton, *James Douglas: A Memoir* (Toronto, 1940); and *WWWA*.

DOUGLASS, FREDERICK [AUGUSTUS WASHINGTON BAILY] (1817?–1895). Journalist and diplomat, born a slave, probably in February 1817, in Tuckahoe, Maryland. Douglass went north in 1838 and was involved in various abolitionist and other reform movements. He founded the newspaper *North Star*. In 1871, he was secretary of a commission sent to Santo Domingo to investigate possibilities for annexation. He was U.S. minister and consul general to Haiti and chargé d'affaires for the Dominican Republic from 1889 to 1891. He supported the United States offer of a naval lease at Môle St. Nicholas, which Haiti rejected, although supporters of the project made Douglass the scapegoat. He wrote an autobiography, *Life and Times of Frederick Douglass, Written by Himself* (Boston, 1892). Died February 20, 1895, in Washington, D.C. *References*: *The Frederick Douglass Papers*, ed. John W. Blassingame (New Haven, Conn., 1979–); *A Black Diplomat in Haiti: The Diplomatic Correspondence of U.S. Minister Frederick Douglass from Haiti, 1889–1891*, ed. with introduction by Norma Brown (Salisbury, N.C., 1977); Daniel Brantley, "Black Diplomacy and Frederick Douglass, Caribbean Experiences, 1871 and 1889–1891: The Untold Story," *Phylon* 45 (1984): 197–209; *DAB*; *DADH*; *DANB*;

E

EARLE, FRANKLIN SUMNER (1856–1929). Botanist and agriculturist, born September 4, 1856, in Dwight, Illinois. Earle attended the University of Illinois. He was connected with Mississippi Agricultural Experiment Station in 1894–1895, was assistant pathologist in charge of the mycological herbarium with the U.S. Department of Agriculture in 1895–1896, professor of biology at the Alabama Polytechnic Institute from 1896 to 1901, and then assistant curator in charge of the mycological collection at the New York Botanical Gardens. He was sent by the New York Botanical Gardens to Jamaica and Cuba and by the U.S. Department of Agriculture to Puerto Rico in 1903 to make scientific investigations. He was director of the Estacion Central Agronómica of Cuba, the first agricultural experiment station in that country, from 1904 to 1906. He turned to fruit and vegetable growing in Herradura, Cuba, from 1906 until his death. He was also consulting agriculturist to the Cuban-American Sugar Company from 1908 to 1911 and president of the Cuba Fruit Exchange from 1911 until his death. He was sent by the U.S. Department of Agriculture to Puerto Rico in 1918 to investigate sugar cane disease and served as an expert in sugar cane disease to the government of Puerto Rico from 1919 to 1921, consulting agriculturist to Aguire Sugar Company, director of agriculture to the General Sugar Company in Havana, Cuba, in 1923–1924, and sugar cane technologist to the Tropical Plant Research Foundation, in charge of work with sugar cane varieties, in Cuba after 1924. Died January 31, 1929, in Herradura, Cuba. *References*: *ACAB*; *Mycologia* 21 (1929): 301–3; *NCAB* 41:283; *Phytopathology* 20 (1930): 923–29; and *WWWA*.

EASLEY, GEORGE A(LBERT) (1884–1964). Mining engineer, born August 28, 1884, in Missouri. Easley graduated from the Missouri School of Mines. He was engaged in mining gold and tungsten in Bolivia, was superintendent of Pan American Tin Corporation in 1909–1910, and was general manager of the Olla de Ora mine for the Gold Mines Limited from 1910 to 1914. He acquired mines in Bolivia and was called "the tungsten king" of that nation. He was president of the Bolivian Red Cross. He served on the U.S. War Trades Board during World War I. He then sold his interests in Bolivia and established offices in New York City. He continued to operate various mining interests in Central and South America and had extensive oil interests in Venezuela. He was vice president of the International Mining Corporation after 1929 and also vice president of the Bolivian International Mining Corporation and Tidewater Oil Corporation. He was involved in banking in Morristown, New Jersey, after 1943. Died October 1, 1964, in Morristown. *Reference*: *NYT*, October 3, 1964.

EATON, JAMES DEMAREST (1848–1928). Missionary, born March 18, 1848, in Lancaster, Wisconsin. Eaton graduated from Beloit (Wis.) College, studied at the Chicago Theological Seminary and Yale University, and graduated from Andover Theological Seminary. He held pastorates in Portland, Oregon, and Bound Brook, New Jersey. He was a missionary under the American Board of Commissioners for Foreign Missions in Chihuahua, Mexico, from 1882 until 1912. He returned to the United States in 1912 because of ill health. He was secretary and treasurer of the Ministerial Union of Congregational Ministers in Los Angeles from 1912 to 1922. He wrote an autobiography, *Life under Two Flags* (New York, 1922). Died December 9, 1928, in Los Angeles. *References*: *AndoverTs*; and *NCAB* 21:195.

EBERHARDT, CHARLES CHRISTOPHER (1871–1965). Consul, born July 27, 1871, in Salina, Kansas. Eberhardt attended Kansas Wesleyan University. He entered the lumber business in Salinas in 1891, moved to Springfield, Massachusetts, in 1894, and was involved with the Massachusetts Life Insurance Company until 1903 and with the Waters-Pierce Oil Corporation in Mexico City in 1903–1904. He entered the consular service in 1906 and was consul at Iquitos, Peru, from 1906 to 1908. He prepared a report titled *Concerning the Alleged Existence of Slavery in Peru* (Washington, D.C., 1913). He was consul at Barranquila from 1908 to 1910 and consul general at large in South Central America from 1910 to 1919, in East Asia from 1919 to 1922, and in East Europe from 1922 to 1924. He was U.S. minister to Nicaragua from 1925 to 1930 and minister to Costa Rica from 1930 to 1933. Died February 22, 1965, in Salinas, Kansas. *References*: *DADH*; and *WWWA*.

ECCLESTON, SARAH (EMILY) (CHAMBERLAIN) ("SALLY") (1840–1916). Educator, born April 8, 1840, in Lewisburg, Pennsylvania. Eccleston graduated from the female institute that was allied to Bucknell University. She served with the U.S. Sanitary Commission during the Civil War in hospitals in Nashville, Tennessee. In 1880, she opened a kindergarten in a teacher-training school in Winona, Minnesota. She went to Argentina in 1883 and founded public kindergartens in Paraná in 1884, in Concepcion del Uruguay in 1887, in Buenos Aires in 1897, and in Mendoza in 1910. She also opened two private schools of her own in Buenos Aires after 1903. She was known as the "grandmother

Brazil. The colony was settled in 1867, but ceased to exist in 1868 after he mortgaged the land and returned to the United States.

DUNN, WILLIAM EDWARD (1888–1966). Diplomat, born March 2, 1888, in Sulphur Springs, Texas. Dunn graduated from the University of Texas and from Stanford and Columbia universities. He was associate professor of history at the University of Texas after 1917. He served in U.S. Naval Intelligence during World War I, was assistant chief of the Latin American Division of the U.S. Department of Commerce in 1919, assistant export manager of Simons Hardware Company of St. Louis from 1920 to 1921, trade commissioner and acting commercial attaché in the U.S. embassy in Lima, Peru, from 1921 to 1924, adviser on higher commercial education for the Republic of Peru in 1921, director general of internal revenues in the Republic of Haiti from 1924 to 1927, and manager of the foreign department of Foreman-State Corporation from 1927 to 1930. He was also manager of the Latin American department of Redmond and Company, investment bankers of New York City. He was secretary general of the Kemmerer financial mission to Colombia in 1930; financial adviser and special emergency agent to the Dominican government from 1931 to 1933; assistant director of the U.S. Bureau of Foreign and Domestic Commerce in Washington, D.C., from 1934 to 1937; commercial attaché in the U.S. embassy in Buenos Aires from 1937 to 1939 and in Guatemala City from 1940 to 1942; adviser on Iberian Peninsula affairs to the Division of Defense Materials in the State Department in Washington, D.C., in 1942–1943; counselor for economic affairs to the U.S. embassies in Bogotá, Colombia, from 1943 to 1945 and in Santiago, Chile, from 1945 to 1947; and chief of the coordination staff in the Office of Intelligence Research in the State Department from 1947 to 1949. He was a private consultant on Latin American matters after 1949, a member of the Julius Klein Financial and Economic mission to Peru from 1950 to 1952, and director of the Inter-American Schools Service of the American Council on Education in Washington, D.C., from 1953 until 1959. He wrote *Peru: Commercial and Industrial Handbook* (Washington, D.C., 1925). Died November 18, 1966, in Dallas, Texas. *References*: *NCAB* 54:218; and *WWWA*.

DUNPHY, CHARLES (1878–1933). Mine owner, born September 12, 1878, in Chicago. Dunphy attended Stanford University. In 1899, he became associated with the Home Life Insurance Company of New York. He was involved with various mining developments in Mexico after 1910. He was appointed secretary of the San Dimas Company in 1914, and was president of that company and of Mexican Candelaria Company, S.A., operating gold and silver mines in the states of Sinaloa and Durango, Mexico, from 1921 until his death. He was involved in planning and building a system of roads and developing hydroelectric power installations in both states. In 1923 he formed the Sierra Madre Power Company. He later farmed extensively in California and Mexico. Died September 23, 1933, in San Francisco. *Reference*: *NCAB* 26:135.

DURHAM, JOHN STEPHENS (1861–1919). Journalist and diplomat, born July 18, 1861, in Philadelphia. Durham graduated from Towne Scientific College of the University of Pennsylvania, studied law, and was admitted to the bar in 1893. He was a reporter on the staff of the *Philadelphia Bulletin* and later was its assistant editor. He was U.S. consul in the Dominican Republic in 1890–1891 and U.S. minister and consul general to Haiti and chargé d'affaires to the Dominican Republic from 1891 to 1893. In 1891–1892, he negotiated with the president of the Dominican Republic for the leasing of Samaná Bay to the United States. He later managed a sugar refinery at San Pedro de Macorís in the Dominican Republic, and was assistant attorney with the Spanish Treaty Claims Commission to Cuba from 1902 to 1905. He was involved in the evaluation of the damage caused by the eruption of Mount Pelée in Martinique and was coauthor of *The Martinique Horror and St. Vincent Calamity, Containing Full and Complete Account of the Most Appalling Disaster of Modern Times* (Philadelphia, 1902). Died October 16, 1919, in London. *References*: *DANB*; *NCAB* 4:408; and *WWWA*.

South America, including Colombia, Panama, and the Pacific Slopes of Ecuador and Peru (Pittsburgh, 1922), and *The Fresh-Water Fishes of Chile* (Washington, D.C., 1927). Died April 24, 1927, in Chula Vista, California. *References: DAB*; *DSB*; *NCAB* 21:47; and *WWWA*.

EKHOLM, GORDON FREDERICK (1909–1987). Anthropologist, born November 25, 1909, in St. Paul, Minnesota. Ekholm graduated from the University of Minnesota and Harvard University. He was a special field assistant for the American Museum of Natural History from 1937 to 1941, assistant curator of anthropology from 1942 to 1947, associate curator from 1947 to 1957, and curator of Mexican archaeology from 1957 until his retirement in 1974. He was also a lecturer in anthropology at Columbia University after 1945. He organized the permanent installation of the Hall of Mexico and Central America in the museum in 1970. He participated in and headed many digging expeditions in Mexico, Guatemala, Honduras, and British Honduras. Died December 17, 1987, in Tarrytown, New York. *References: AMWS*; and *NYT*, December 19, 1987.

ELLIOTT, GEORGE FRANK (1846–1931). Marine Corps officer, born November 30, 1846, in Alabama. Elliott attended the U.S. Military Academy and was commissioned second lieutenant in the Marine Corps in 1870. He was fleet marine officer on the Asiatic station and served in Cuba during the Spanish-American War and in the Philippines during the Philippines-American War. He was commandant of the Marine Corps from 1903 until his retirement. He commanded the marine expeditionary force on the Isthmus of Panama in 1903–1904, following the Panamanian revolt against Colombia. He retired with the rank of major general in 1910. Died November 4, 1931, in Washington, D.C. *Reference: WWWA*.

ELLIOTT, JOHN HENRY (1809–ca. 1870). Explorer. Elliott served in the U.S. Navy and then in the Brazilian Navy. He was captured in the Cisplatine campaign of 1827, escaped after two years, and settled in Curitiba, Paraná. He accompanied the president of Paraná, Barão de Antonina, inland in 1845 to explore the Ivaí, Paranapanema, and Paraná rivers. He went with Antonina on another expedition to the Ivaí and Tibagi rivers in 1847. He wrote descriptions of these expeditions in the *Revista do Instituto Histórico e Geographico Brasileiro* (Rio de Janeiro). He lived in Curitaba until at least the late 1860s.

ELLIS, POWHATAN (1790–1863). Diplomat, born January 17, 1790, in "Red Hill," Amherst County, Virginia. Ellis attended Washington College (later Washington and Lee University), graduated from Dickinson College and the College of William and Mary, and was admitted to the bar in 1813. He fought in the War of 1812. He settled in Winchester, Mississippi, in 1817 and practiced law. He was judge on the supreme court of Mississippi from 1818 to 1825, served in the U.S. Senate from 1827 to 1832, and was federal judge of the

Mississippi district from 1832 to 1836. He was U.S. chargé d'affaires in Mexico from 1836 to 1839 and minister to Mexico from 1839 to 1842. He strove successfully to secure the good will of Mexico. He returned to Mississippi, but later in life went back to Richmond, Virginia. Died March 18, 1863, in Richmond. *References: BDAC; DAB; NCAB* 11:53; L. C. Pitchford, Jr., "The Diplomatic Representatives from the United States to Mexico from 1836 to 1848," Ph.D. diss., University of Colorado, 1965; and *WWWA*.

ELLSWORTH, LUTHER T(HOMAS) (1854–1914). Consul, born in Cleveland. Ellsworth graduated from a business school in Cleveland. He was majority stockholder and director of operations of a gold mining company in Colombia from 1873 to 1878, coal station foreman in Indiana from 1882 to 1887, and an assistant to a master carpenter in Cleveland from 1887 to 1898. He entered the consular service in 1898, was U.S. consul in Puerto Cabello, Venezuela, from 1898 to 1904, consul at Cartagena from 1904 to 1907, consul at Chihuahua City, Mexico, in 1907, and consul at Ciudad Porfirio (later Piedras Negras) from 1907 to 1913. He was also special representative of the U.S. Department of Justice in matters of neutrality from 1909 to 1911. He resigned in 1913. Died July 2, 1914, in San Antonio, Texas. *Reference*: Dorothy P. Kerig, *Luther T. Ellsworth, U.S. Consul on the Border during the Mexican Revolution* (El Paso, 1975).

EMERY (H. C.) CLAIM (1908–1909). *See* H. C. EMERY CLAIM

EVANGELICAL ALLIANCE MISSION, THE (TEAM). Founded in 1890 as the Scandinavian Alliance Mission of North America, it began missionary work in Venezuela in 1906, in Colombia in 1923, in the Netherlands Antilles in 1931, in Peru in 1962, and in Trinidad and Tobago in 1964. *References*: Thomas J. Bach, *Pioneer Missionaries for Christ and His Church* (Wheaton, Ill., 1955); *EMCM*; and J. W. Swanson, comp. and ed., *Three Score Years . . . and Then: Sixty Years of Worldwide Missionary Advance* (Chicago, 1951?).

EVANS, CLIFFORD (1920–   ). Archaeologist, born June 13, 1920 in Dallas. Evans graduated from the University of Southern California and Columbia University. He served in the U.S. Army Air Force during World War II. He was an instructor in anthropology at the University of Virginia from 1949 to 1951, associate curator in the division of archaeology of the U.S. National Museum in Washington, D.C., from 1951 to 1962, curator from 1962 to 1969, chairman of the department of anthropology from 1969 to 1975, and curator of South American archaeology after 1975. He carried out archaeological fieldwork in Brazil, Ecuador, Peru, Venezuela, British Guiana, and Dominica in the Lesser Antilles. He carried out archaeological excavations at the mouth of the Amazon, in lowland Ecuador, and in British Guiana. He was co-author of *Cultural Stratigraphy in the Viru Valley, Northern Peru; the Formative and Florescent Epochs* of Argentine kindergarten.'' Died October 10, 1916, in Buenos Aires. *References*: *Cutolo*; and *Luiggi*.

EDER, GEORGE JACKSON (1900–   ). Economist, born September 5, 1900, in New York City. Eder attended Columbia University and graduated from National University (Washington, D.C.). He served in the U.S. Army during World War I. He was assistant manager of the foreign department of Battery Park National Bank of New York City from 1920 to 1923, manager of Three Mountain Coffee Corporation in San José, Costa Rica, in 1926, chief of the Latin American Section of the U.S. Bureau of Foreign and Domestic Commerce from 1926 to 1932, manager of International Securities Division of Standard Statistics Corporation (later Standard and Poor's) Company in New York City from 1932 to 1937, manager of Pan American Management Corporation in Buenos Aires in 1937–1938, South American attorney for the International Telephone and Telegraph Corporation (I.T.T.) in New York City from 1938 to 1946, and assistant general attorney for I.T.T. from 1938 to 1961. He practiced law in Washington, D.C., from 1968 to 1976. He was also economist and legal adviser to the governments of Cuba in 1930, Colombia in 1931, Chile from 1935 to 1937, Argentina in 1946–1947, and Bolivia in 1956–1957. He was founder and executive director of the National Monetary Stabilization Council of Bolivia in 1956–1957. He was coauthor of *International Competition in the Trade of Argentina* (Worcester, Mass., 1931) and *Taxation in Colombia* (Chicago, 1964), and wrote *Inflation and Development in Latin America: A Case History of Inflation and Stabilization in Bolivia* (Ann Arbor, Mich., 1968) as well as romantic novels under the nom de plume Jackson Reed. *References*: *CA*; and *WWA*.

EDWARDS, CHARLES LINCOLN (1863–1937). Naturalist, born December 8, 1863, in Oquawka, Illinois. Edwards graduated from Lombard and Johns Hopkins universities and the University of Leipzig. He was assistant professor of biology at the University of Texas in 1892–1893 and associate professor there in 1893–1894. He was professor of biology at the University of Cincinnati from 1894 to 1900 and professor of natural history at Trinity College (Conn.) from 1900 to 1912; he was director of the department of nature study of the Los Angeles schools after 1912. He conducted zoological investigations in the Bahama islands in 1888, 1891, and 1893, and wrote *Bahama Songs and Stories* (Boston, 1895). Died May 6, 1937, in Los Angeles. *References*: *NCAB* 13:440; *NYT*, May 7, 1937; and *WWWA*.

EDWARDS, JAMES HORTON (1877–1952). Economist, born in Centralia, Illinois. Edwards served during the Spanish-American War. He was a financial adviser to the governor of Puerto Rico and a financial attaché in the embassy in Cuba. He directed customs administration in Nicaragua from 1918 to 1927 and was comptroller of Colombia and first comptroller general of Ecuador. He was chief of the Division of International Economy in the Bureau of Foreign and Domestic Commerce in the U.S. Department of Commerce from 1941 until his retirement in 1949. Died May 18, 1952, in Fort Lauderdale, Florida. *References*: *Fort Lauderdale Daily News*, May 19, 1952; and *NYT*, May 20, 1952.

EDWARDS, WILLIAM HENRY (1822–1909). Entomologist, born March 15, 1822, in Hunter, Greene County, New York. Edwards graduated from Williams College, studied law in New York City, and was admitted to the bar in 1847. He made a journey up the Amazon River in 1846, collecting birds and butterflies, and wrote *A Voyage up the Amazon, Including a Residence at Pará* (New York, 1847). He settled in Coalburg, West Virginia, and was president of Ohio and Kanawha Coal Company. He was an extensive landowner, and was involved in opening coal mines and building railroads. He studied butterflies and prepared *The Butterflies of North America* (Philadelphia, 1868–1897). Died April 4, 1909, in Coalburg, West Virginia. *References*: *DAB*; Arnold Mallis, *American Entomologists* (New Brunswick, N.J., 1971), pp. 288–92; and *WWWA*.

EGAN, PATRICK (1841–1919). Diplomat, born August 18, 1841, in Ballymahon, County Longford, Ireland; came to the United States in 1883 and settled in Lincoln, Nebraska. He was involved in the grain and milling business. He became a citizen in 1888. He was U.S. minister to Chile from 1889 to 1893. He became involved in internal Chilean politics, negotiated an arbitration treaty, and handled the *Baltimore* affair.* He settled in New York City in 1893. Died September 30, 1919, in New York City. *References*: *DAB*; *DADH*; Joyce S. Goldberg, "Patrick Egan: Irish-American Minister to Chile, 1889–93," *Eire-Ireland* 14 (Fall 1979): 883–95; Osgood Hardy, "Was Patrick Egan a 'Blundering Minister'?" *HAHR* 8 (1921): 65–81; and *NCAB* 5:399.

EIGENMANN, CARL H. (1863–1927). Zoologist, born March 9, 1863, in Flehingen, Germany. He was sent to the United States in 1877 and grew up in Rockport, Indiana. Eigenmann graduated from Indiana University. In 1889, he established a small biological station in San Diego and studied the fishes of the region until 1891. He was a professor of zoology at Indiana University from 1891 until his death. He founded the university's biological station at Turkey (later Winona) Lake in 1895 and was its director until 1920. He was curator of fishes at the Carnegie Museum of Pittsburgh from 1909 until 1918. He conducted explorations in Cuba in 1902–1904, in British Guiana in 1908, in Colombia in 1911–1912, in Peru and Bolivia in 1918, and in Chile in 1919. He studied the fish fauna of the Amazon and of other Brazilian rivers, and wrote *The Fresh Water Fishes of Patagonia and an Examination of the Archiplata-archelenis Theory* (Princeton, N.J., 1909–1910), *The Freshwater Fishes of British Guiana, Including a Study of the Ecological Grouping of Species and the Relation of the Fauna of the Plateau to that of the Lowlands* (Pittsburgh, 1912), *The Fishes of Northwestern South America: Part I. The Fresh-Water Fishes of Northwestern*

F

FABENS, JOSEPH W(ARREN) (1821–1875). Consul, born July 23, 1821, in Salem, Massachusetts. Fabens attended Harvard University and Andover Theological Seminary. He was U.S. consul in Cayenne, French Guiana, from 1844 to 1853; commercial agent in San Juan del Norte, Nicaragua, from 1853 to 1855; and special diplomatic agent in Managua, Nicaragua, in 1854–1855. In 1859, he visited Santo Domingo and began to take an interest in the welfare of its inhabitants. He was impressed with the natural resources of the island and became a strenuous advocate of its annexation to the United States. He was special diplomatic agent to Santo Domingo in 1869. In 1874, he visited the island again and developed business ventures there. Died March 13, 1875, in New York City. *References: NCAB* 7:178; and *WWWA*.

FALKLAND ISLANDS CRISIS (1831–1832). A dispute with Argentina over ownership of the Falkland Islands, which began when Argentine forces seized three U.S. sealing vessels for fishing in Argentine waters. The USS *Lexington*, which was commanded by Silas Duncan, raided the islands, looted them, and brought most of the Argentine settlers as prisoners to Montevideo. Diplomatic relations between the United States and Argentina were broken. The problem became moot in 1832 when Great Britain took control of the islands. *References*: John M. Belohlavek, *"Let the Eagle Soar!" The Foreign Policy of Andrew Jackson* (Lincoln, Nebr., 1985), 162–73; P. D. Dickens, "The Falkland Islands Dispute between the United States and Argentina," *HAHR* 9 (1929): 471–87; and Craig E. Klafter, "United States Involvement in the Falkland Islands Crisis of 1831–1833," *Journal of the Early Republic* 4 (1984): 395–420.

FARABEE, WILLIAM CURTIS (1865–1925). Anthropologist, born February 7, 1865, in Washington, Pennsylvania. Farabee graduated from Waynesburg College (Pa.) and Harvard University. He was an instructor in anthropology at Harvard University from 1903 to 1913 and curator of the section of American anthropology in the University Museum of the University of Pennsylvania after

1913. He was leader of the DeMilhan-Harvard South American expedition to Peru east of the Andes and along the Andean Plateau from 1906 to 1909 and in charge of two South American expeditions of the University of Pennsylvania, one to study the Indian tribes of the Amazon basin, from 1913 to 1916, and one to explore southern British Guiana and study the Arawak and Carib tribes of northern Brazil and British Guiana, from 1921 to 1923. He wrote *The Central Arawak* (Philadelphia, 1918) and *Indian Tribes of Eastern Peru* (Cambridge, Mass., 1922). Died June 24, 1925, in Philadelphia. *References: DAB; NCAB* 24:207; and *WWWA.*

FARLAND, JOSEPH S(IMPSON) (1914–   ). Diplomat, born August 11, 1914, in Clarksburg, West Virginia. Farland graduated from West Virginia University. He practiced law in West Virginia from 1938 to 1942, was an agent of the U.S. Federal Bureau of Investigation from 1942 to 1944, and served in the U.S. Navy during World War II. He then resumed his law practice. He was a State Department consultant for the mutual security program in Latin America in 1956–1957. He was U.S. ambassador to the Dominican Republic from 1957 to 1960 and ambassador to Panama from 1960 to 1963. He was unable to deal with the dictator Rafael Trujillo of the Dominican Republic, was an opponent of American foreign aid programs in Panama, and supported increased Panamanian control of the Canal Zone. He was U.S. ambassador to Pakistan from 1969 to 1972 and ambassador to Iran in 1972–1973. He retired in 1973. *References: PolProf: Eisenhower;* and *WWA.*

FARNHAM, ROGER L(ESLIE) (1864–1951). Banker, born in Washington, D.C. Farnham was a journalist and then a public relations agent for the Panama Railroad and later the National City Bank of New York. He was vice president of the National City Bank and its agent in Haiti from 1911 to 1922. He was also president of the National Railway of Haiti from 1911 to 1914. He played a leading role in the financial machination in Haiti, and his name was synonymous with U.S. financial interests in Haiti. He left the National City Bank in 1924. He settled in Miami Beach, Florida, in 1934. Died June 5, 1951, in Miami Beach. *Reference: NYT,* June 6, 1951.

FARON, LOUIS C. (1923–   ). Anthropologist, born July 16, 1923, in New York City. Faron graduated from Columbia University. He served in the U.S. Army during World War II. He was an assistant professor of anthropology at Los Angeles State College (later California State College at Los Angeles) from 1959 to 1962, associate professor of anthropology at the University of Pittsburgh from 1962 to 1964, and professor of anthropology at the State University of New York at Stony Brook (Long Island) from 1964 to 1971. He carried out fieldwork among the Mapuche Indians of Chile from 1952 to 1954, in the central coast of Peru from 1957 to 1959, among the Choco of Panama in 1960, and among the Otomi of Mexico in 1961, 1962, and 1963–1964. He wrote *Mapuche*

(New York, 1952), and with his wife, Betty J. Meggers,* wrote *Archaeological Investigations in British Guiana* (Washington, D.C., 1960), *Archaeological Investigations at the Mouth of the Amazon* (Washington, D.C., 1957), *Early Formative Period of Coastal Ecuador: The Valdivia and Machalilla Phases* (Washington, D.C., 1965), and *Archaeological Investigations on the Rio Napo, Eastern Ecuador* (Washington, D.C., 1968). *References: AMWS*; and *WWA*.

EVANS, JOHN (1812–1861). Geologist, born February 14, 1812, in Portsmouth, New Hampshire. Evans graduated from the St. Louis medical college. He served on geological surveys in the Northwestern states. He carried out geological surveys of the territories of Oregon and Washington. He was the geologist of the Chiriqui commission in Central America. Died April 13, 1861, in Washington, D.C.

EWBANK, THOMAS (1792–1870). Author, born March 11, 1792, in Durham, England. Ewbank was apprentice to the trade of sheet-metal working, and was tinsmith in London from 1812 until 1817. He came to the United States in 1819 and settled in New York. He was involved in the manufacturing of copper, lead, and tin tubing, a business that he sold in 1836. He traveled in South America from 1845 to 1848, studying its natural phenomena and its industrial arts, and wrote *Life in Brazil, or A Journal of a Visit to the Land of the Cocoa and the Palm* (New York, 1856). He was U.S. commissioner of patents from 1849 to 1852. Died September 16, 1870, in New York City. *References: ACAB; DAB; NCAB* 7:559; and *WWWA*.

the Second Brigade of the U.S. Marines in Santo Domingo in 1919–1920 and was commander of the U.S. land forces in Nicaragua from 1927 to 1929. Died July 17, 1936, in Columbus, Ohio. *References*: *NYT*, July 18, 1936; and *WWWA*.

FERGUSON, HENRY AUGUSTUS (1845–1911). Artist, was born January 14, 1845, in Glens Falls, New York. Ferguson received art training in Albany in the 1860s. He crossed the Andes mountains six times, and his South American paintings were the first to bring his name into prominence. He later established a studio in New York City. Died March 22, 1911, in New York City. *References*: *NCAB* 25:184; *NYT*, March 23, 1911; and *WWWA*.

FEUILLE, FRANK (1860–1954). Lawyer, born September 10, 1860, in Havana, Cuba. Feuille graduated from the University of Texas and was admitted to the bar in 1886. He practiced law at Eagle Pass, Texas, and later at Brownsville, Texas; was city attorney of Brownsville from 1890 to 1894; and then practiced law in Corpus Christi and San Diego, Texas. He was a special judge and later attorney general of Puerto Rico from 1902 to 1907. He was a member of the executive council of the upper house of the legislative assembly of Puerto Rico and was instrumental in securing the law that United States citizenship be extended to Puerto Ricans. He was a legal assistant to the supervisor of the Departments of State and Justice in Cuba from 1907 to 1909 and drafted a revision of the administrative laws of Cuba. He returned to the United States in 1909 and practiced law in Austin, Texas, until 1910. He was counsel to George Washington Goethals* and attorney for the Panama Railroad, and he represented the United States before the Panama Canal Commission. He served as adviser to the U.S. legation in Panama and assisted the government of Panama in the preparation of some of its laws. He retired from his work in Panama in 1920. He was engaged by Standard Oil Company of California as counsel in matters relating to Latin America until his retirement in 1945. Died October 8, 1954, in El Paso, Texas. *Reference*: *NCAB* 44:218.

FIALA, ANTHONY (1869–1950). Explorer, born September 19, 1869, in Hudson City (later part of Jersey City), New Jersey. Fiala attended Cooper Union and the National Academy of Design Art School in New York City. He was a stone artist and lithograph designer in New York City and then a cartoonist and art director of *Grit*, a newspaper in Williamsport, Pennsylvania, from 1892 to 1894, and with the *Brooklyn Daily Eagle* from 1894 to 1898. He served during the Spanish-American War. He was official photographer and scientific assistant with the Baldwin-Ziegler Polar Expedition in 1901–1902 and leader of the second Baldwin-Ziegler expedition from 1903 to 1905. He was the leader of one of the three sections of Theodore Roosevelt's exploring expedition to Brazil in 1913–1914. He surveyed, mapped, and made motion pictures in the almost unknown regions of central Brazil and explored the course of the Papagaio, Juruena, and Tapajós rivers. In 1917 he served on the Mexican border. He headed Fiala Arms and Equipment Company in New Haven, Connecticut; he founded Fiala Outfits, Incorporated, in 1922 and was its president until his death. Died April 8, 1950, in Brooklyn, New York. *References*: *ACAB*; *NCAB* 38:53; *NYT*, April 9, 1950; and *WWWA*.

FILIBUSTERS. American adventurers about the middle of the nineteenth century who engaged in private armed expeditions against weak nations in the Caribbean and Central America, which offered a tempting field for adventure and exploitation. *References*: Charles H. Brown, *Agents of Manifest Destiny: The Lives and Times of the Filibusters* (Chapel Hill, N.C., 1980); William O. Scroggs, *Filibusters and Financiers: The Story of William Walker and His Associates* (New York, 1916); Joseph A. Stout, *The Liberators: Filibustering Expeditions into Mexico, 1848–1862 and the Last Thrust of Manifest Destiny* (Los Angeles, 1973); and Harris G. Warren, *The Sword Was Their Passport: A History of American Filibustering in the Mexican Revolution* (Baton Rouge, La., 1943).

FINERTY, JOHN FREDERICK (1846–1908). Journalist, born September 10, 1846, in Galway, Ireland, and came to the United States in 1864. Finerty served in the Union Army during the Civil War. He was a correspondent for the *Chicago Times* in the Sioux wars of 1876 and 1879 and the Apache campaign of 1881, and a newspaper correspondent in Washington, D.C., from 1879 to 1881. He traveled in Mexico in 1879. He established the *Citizen*, a weekly newspaper, in Chicago in 1882, and was a member of the U.S. House of Representatives from 1883 to 1885. Died June 10, 1908, in Chicago. *References*: *BDAC*; *NCAB* 13:324; Wilbert H. Timmons, ed., *John F. Finerty Reports: Porfirian Mexico, 1879* (El Paso, Tex., 1974); and *WWWA*.

FLACK, JOSEPH (1894–1955). Diplomat, born December 5, 1894, in Grenoble, Pennsylvania. Flack graduated from the University of Pennsylvania. He entered the consular service in 1916 and served in Liverpool, Paris, La Paz, Santo Domingo, Vienna, Santiago, Chile, Warsaw, Madrid, and Berlin. He was U.S. consul general in Madrid from 1937 to 1940, counselor of embassy in Spain in 1940–1941, counselor of embassy in Venezuela from 1941 to 1945, and division chief in the American republics section in the State Department in 1945–1946. He was U.S. ambassador to Bolivia from 1946 to 1949 and Costa Rica in 1949–1950. He was U.S. ambassador to Poland from 1950 until 1955. Died May 8, 1955, aboard the liner *United States*, on his way to the United States. *References*: *BRDS*; *NYT*, May 9, 1955; and *WWWA*.

FLANAGAN, JAMES W(AINWRIGHT) (1872–1950). Engineer, born October 26, 1872, in Henderson, Texas. Flanagan worked on various railroads and mining projects in the United States, Cuba, and Mexico from 1882 to 1912. He served as a lieutenant colonel in the Cuban army in 1896–1897 and in the U.S.

Social Structure: Institutional Reintegration in a Patrilineal Society of Central Chile (Urbana, Ill., 1956), *Hawks of the Sun: Mapuche Morality and Its Ritual Attributes* (Pittsburgh, 1964), and *The Mapuche Indians of Chile* (New York, 1968), and was coauthor of *The Native People of South America* (New York, 1959). *References*: *AMWS*; *CA*; and *WWA*.

FARQUHAR, PERCIVAL (1864–1953). Entrepreneur, born October 19, 1864, in York, Pennsylvania. Farquhar graduated from Yale University, studied law in New York City, and was admitted to the bar in 1885. He became an executive of an electric railways company and served in the New York state assembly in the early 1890s. In 1898, he went to Havana. He was involved there in the electrification of Havana's system of horsecars. He was also involved in the building of the railroad from Santa Clara to Santiago in Cuba from 1899 to 1902. From 1904 to 1907, he was in Brazil, where he was involved in the founding of the Rio de Janeiro Tramway, Light and Power Company. In 1906, he acquired an Amazon navigation company, installed new boats, built port works in Belém, Pará, and established Brazil Railway, a holding company. He also bought the concession to build the Madeira-Mamoré Railroad. He founded the town of Porto Velho at the head of navigation on the Madeira River. The railroad and the port were completed in 1912 but proved to be a losing proposition. He bought, consolidated, and extended the railways of southern Brazil; acquired lines in Uruguay, northeastern Argentina, and Paraguay; and created several subsidiaries, including Brazil's largest sawmill, its first meat-packing plant, and what was briefly the world's largest cattle company. By 1912, he had become the most powerful foreigner in Brazil. His South American empire collapsed into receivership after the outbreak of World War I. He returned to Brazil in 1919, attempting to develop the iron ore deposits around Itabira, in Minas Gerais state, with little success. Died August 4, 1953, in New York City. *References*: Percival Farquhar Papers, Yale University Library; *ACAB*; *DAB S5*; Barry Machado, "Farquhar and Ford in Brazil: Studies in Business Expansion and Foreign Policy," Ph.D. diss., Northwestern University, 1975; D. B. McKibbin, "Percival Farquhar: American Promoter in Latin America, 1900–1914," Ph.D. diss., University of Chicago, 1950; *NCAB* 45:503; and *NYT*, August 5, 1953.

FARRELL, JAMES AMBROSE (1886–1960). Lawyer, born April 11, 1886, in Albany, New York. Farrell graduated from the City College of New York and New York University, and was admitted to the bar in 1909. He practiced law in New York City after 1909. He served in the U.S. Army during World War I. As one of the organizers and vice president of Brightman and Company, Incorporated, a financial agency, until 1927, he did exploratory and development work for U.S. business interests in Brazil, investigating sites for port facilities, streets, railways, water works, and other utility enterprises. He also led a party in the exploration of previously undeveloped areas in northern Brazil. Died November 15, 1960, in New Haven, Connecticut. *Reference*: *NCAB* 47:223.

FASSIG, OLIVER LANARD (1860–1936). Meteorologist, born April 5, 1860, in Columbus, Ohio. Fassig graduated from Ohio State and Johns Hopkins universities and studied at Yale University and the University of Berlin. He was connected with the U.S. Weather Bureau from 1883 to 1932 and was a research associate at Harvard University after 1932. He was the leader of one of the relief parties of the Ziegler Arctic expedition in 1905. He organized the climatological service of the U.S. Weather Bureau in the West Indies and was chief of the Climatological Division of the U.S. Weather Bureau after 1930. He wrote *Hurricanes of the West Indies* (Washington, D.C., 1913) and *Rainfall and Temperature of Cuba* (Washington, D.C., 1925). Died December 6, 1936. *Reference*: *WWWA*.

FAUCETT, ELMER J. ("SLIM") (1891–1960). Aviation executive, born in Savona, New York. Faucett worked as an aircraft mechanic at the Hammondsport, New York, headquarters of Glenn H. Curtiss. He was chief mechanic of the Curtiss Flying School in Miami, Florida, during World War I, and chief mechanic in Roosevelt Field in Long Island. He came to Lima, Peru, in 1920, in charge of the maintenance of a Curtiss airplane that the Peruvian government had bought. In 1922, he made a pioneering flight from Lima to Iquitos, the first to cross the Andes from Lima to Amazonia. He then went into the charter flying business. He remained in Peru throughout most of his life, founded the Faucett Aviation Company in 1928 (later renamed Faucett Airlines). It received an air mail and passenger contract and he started regular service between Lima and Arequipa, gradually expanding his airline's operations. Died April 10, 1960, in Lima, Peru. *References*: Malcolm K. Burke and Michael Scully, "Pay Load over the Andes," *Americas* 5 (May 1953): 17–20; and *NYT*, April 11, 1960.

FEELEY, EDWARD F(RANCIS) (1880–1964). Government official and diplomat, born March 6, 1880, in Rochester, New York. Feeley attended Rochester University. He was in the export business, principally in Latin America, from 1902 to 1918. He was trade commissioner in Mexico for the Department of Commerce in 1918–1919 and commercial attaché in the embassy in Mexico City in 1919–1920 and in Buenos Aires, Argentina, from 1920 to 1926. He was a member of the American Commission of Financial Experts in Ecuador and Bolivia from 1927 to 1930. He was U.S. ambassador to Bolivia from 1930 to 1933. He was with the International Nickel Company in New York from 1933 until 1956. Died August 28, 1964, in Rochester, New York. *References*: *NYT*, August 31, 1964; and *WWWA*.

FELAND, LOGAN (1869–1936). Marine Corps officer, born August 18, 1869, in Hopkinsville, Kentucky. Feland was appointed a first lieutenant in the U.S. Marine Corps in 1899. He served in the Spanish-American War. He commanded

Manuscript Division, Library of Congress; John Murray Forbes, *Once Años en Buenos Aires, 1820–1831* (Buenos Aires, 1956); *DAB*; *NCAB* 13:374; Watt Stewart, "The Diplomatic Service of John M. Forbes at Buenos Aires," *HAHR* 14 (1934): 202–18; and *WWWA*.

FORBES COMMISSION TO HAITI (1930). A commission, headed by W. Cameron Forbes (1870–1959), and sent by President Herbert Hoover to Haiti in 1930 to assess the occupation and determine the steps by which it might be rapidly liquidated and whether the thirty-year policy of intervention in the Caribbean had served valid purposes for both the United States and the countries concerned. The report was published as *Report of Commission for the Study and Review of Conditions in Haiti* (Washington, D.C., 1930). *References*: W. Cameron Forbes Journal, Houghton Library, Harvard University, Cambridge, Mass.; Robert M. Spector, *W. Cameron Forbes and the Hoover Commissions to Haiti (1930)* (Lanham, Md., 1985); and Robert M. Spector, "W. Cameron Forbes in Haiti: Additional Light on the Genesis of the 'Good Neighbor Policy,' " *Caribbean Studies* 6 (July 1966): 28–45.

FORDLANDIA. Ford Motor Company developed a major rubber plantation on the Tapajós River in the Amazon drainage in the state of Pará, Brazil, between 1927 and 1945. In 1934, it moved the operation to Belterra, further up the Tapajós River. Despite the large investment, it failed to produce any rubber for large-scale commercial use. The plantation was sold to the Brazilian government in 1945. *References*: Ford R. Bryan, *Beyond the Model T: The Other Ventures of Henry Ford* (Detroit, 1990), ch. 16; John Galey, "Industrialist in the Wilderness: Henry Ford's Amazon Venture," *JISWA* 21 (1979): 261–89; and Barry Machado, "Farquhar and Ford in Brazil: Studies in Business Expansion and Foreign Policy," Ph.D. diss., Northwestern University, 1975.

FORSYTH, JOHN (1812–1879). Editor and diplomat, born October 31, 1812, in Augusta, Georgia. Forsyth graduated from Princeton University and was admitted to the bar in 1834. He practiced law in Alabama and was U.S. attorney for the southern district of Alabama. He edited the Columbus (Ga.) *Times* in the 1840s and served in the Mexican War. He edited the Mobile *Register* after 1853. He was U.S. minister to Mexico from 1856 to 1858, served in the Alabama legislature in 1858–1859, and was mayor of Mobile from 1860 to 1866. Died May 2, 1879, in Mobile Alabama. *References*: *BDC*; Paul Murray, *Tres Norteamericanos y su Participacion en el Desarrollo del Tratado McLane-Ocampo, 1856–1860* (Guadalajara, Mexico, 1946); and James M. Southerland, "John Forsyth and the Frustrated 1857 Mexican Loan and Land Grab," *West Georgia College Studies in the Social Sciences* 11 (1972): 18–25.

FORSYTH, SAMUEL D(OUGLAS) (ca. 1778–1842). Physician and merchant, born probably in Virginia. Forsyth was surgeon's mate in the U.S. Army in 1807–1808, although he received no formal training in medicine. From 1808 to 1813, he was an active participant in filibustering activity on the Texas border. He came to Cartagena, Colombia, in 1815, was aide to Simón Bolívar in 1815, and doctor in the revolutionary armies. He retired in 1824 with the rank of lieutenant colonel. In 1818, he settled in Angostura, Venezuela, and established a commercial house. He was sent by Simón Bolívar to the United States in 1820 to obtain arms and ammunition and was special diplomatic agent to Bogotá in 1820–1821. He later settled in Caracas, where he was involved in commission business and in real estate. Died in the fall of 1842. *Reference*: William C. Olson, "Early North Americans in Venezuelan Commerce, 1810–1830," Ph.D. diss., University of North Carolina at Chapel Hill, 1974, ch. 3.

FORT MISSIONS. A commission headed by John Franklin Fort (1852–1920), sent by President Woodrow Wilson to the Dominican Republic in 1914 to coerce that government to accept President Wilson's condition to avert U.S. military intervention, including holding elections and establishing a new constitutional government, and to Haiti in 1915, to prepare for the establishment of the American custom receivership. *Reference*: *DADH*.

FOSHAG, WILLIAM FREDERICK (1894–1956). Geologist, born March 17, 1894, in Sag Harbor, New York, and grew up in Pomona, California. Foshag graduated from the University of California at Berkeley. He was assistant curator of mineralogy at the U.S. National Museum in Washington, D.C., from 1919 to 1929, curator from 1929 to 1948, and head curator of the department of geology from 1948 until his death. He made a systematic survey of the minerals of Mexico in 1926–1927, 1929, and 1931, under the auspices of the Mexican government, the Smithsonian Institution, and the Harvard Mineralogical Museum. He also studied the silver mines of Guanajuato and the volcano Paricutín, near Mexico City, from its eruption in 1943 to its extinction in 1952. He was coauthor of *Birth and Development of Paricutín Volcano, Mexico* (Washington, D.C., 1956). In 1947, he made a study for the Guatemalan government of ancient jade objects found in Central America. Died May 21, 1956, in Westmoreland, Maryland. *References*: *DAB S6*; *NCAB* 44:108; and *NYT*, May 23, 1956.

FOSTER, GEORGE M(CCLELAND), JR. (1913–   ). Anthropologist, born October 9, 1913, in Sioux Falls, South Dakota. Foster graduated from Northwestern University and the University of California at Berkeley. He was head of the Mexican Center of the Institute of Social Anthropology of the Smithsonian Institution from 1944 to 1946, director of the institute from 1946 to 1952, and professor of anthropology at the University of California at Berkeley after 1955. He carried out fieldwork in Mexico from 1944 to 1946 and from 1958 to 1975. He wrote *Empire's Children: The People of Tzintzuntzan* (Washington, D.C., 1948), *Tzintzuntzan: Mexican Peasants in a Changing World* (Boston, 1967), and *Studies in Middle American Anthropology* (New Orleans, 1976), and an account of his fieldwork in "Field work in Tzintzuntzan: The

Army during the Spanish-American War. He was associated with the Royal Bank of Canada from 1913 to 1919 and closely identified with several large engineering projects in Central and South America, among them the construction of an oil pipeline across Colombia for the Andian National Corporation of Toronto, of which he was vice president and general manager (and later president) from 1923 to 1942. He was special assistant to the executive officer of the U.S. Petroleum for War, serving Puerto Rico, Cuba, and the West Indies from 1942 to 1944. Died July 24, 1950, in Houston, Texas. *References*: *NYT*, July 25, 1950; and *WWWA*.

FLANDRAU, CHARLES MACOMB (1871–1938). Author and traveler, born December 9, 1871, in St. Paul, Minnesota. Flandrau graduated from Harvard University. He began to write and publish stories in 1897. He lived in Mexico and wrote *Viva Mexico!* (New York, 1908), an unorthodox account of that country's life and character as seen from his brother Blair's coffee plantation. He was later the music and dramatic critic of the *St. Paul Pioneer Press* and conducted a daily column for the *St. Paul Dispatch* from 1915 to 1920. Died March 28, 1938, in St. Paul, Minnesota. *References*: Charles Flandrau, *Viva Mexico!* ed. C. Harvey Gardiner (Urbana, Ill., 1964); *ACAB*; *DAB S2*; *NCAB* 22:80; and *NYT*, March 31, 1938.

FLETCHER, FRANK FRIDAY (1855–1928). Naval officer, born November 23, 1855, in Oskaloosa, Iowa. Fletcher graduated from the U.S. Naval Academy in 1876 and was appointed ensign in the U.S. Navy that same year. He served on various vessels until 1882 and with the U.S. Hydrographic Office from 1882 to 1884. He was sent to the Pacific and to Central America and South America to determine the longitude of principal seaports for telegraphic purposes. He was on duty with the bureau of ordnance from 1887 to 1893 and in command of the torpedo boat *Cushing* from 1893 to 1896. He served during the Spanish-American War, commanding the survey ship *Eagle* from 1898 to 1901 and the Newport torpedo station from 1901 to 1904. He was chief of staff of the Asiatic fleet and commanded, successively, the three divisions of the Atlantic fleet from 1911 to 1913. He was chief of naval forces on the east coast of Mexico in 1913 and commanded the naval forces that occupied Veracruz in 1914. He was commander in chief of the Atlantic fleet from 1914 to 1916 and served during World War I. He retired with the rank of admiral in 1919. Died November 28, 1928, in New York City. *References*: William S. Coker, "Naval Diplomacy during the Mexican Revolution: An Episode in the Career of Admiral Frank Friday Fletcher," *North Dakota Quarterly* 40 (1972): 51–64; *NCAB* 36:286; *NYT*, November 29, 1928; and *WWWA*.

FLETCHER, HENRY P(RATHER) (1873–1959). Diplomat, born April 10, 1873, in Greencastle, Pennsylvania. Fletcher studied law and was admitted to the bar in 1894. He practiced law in Chambersburg, Pennsylvania, after 1894.

He served during the Spanish-American War. He served in the legation in Cuba, China, and Portugal from 1902 to 1910. He was U.S. minister to Chile from 1910 to 1914. He succeeded in mitigating the ill will toward the United States caused by the Alsop claims award and other incidents, and established cordial relations with Chile. He was the first U.S. ambassador to Chile from 1914 to 1916 and ambassador to Mexico from 1916 to 1920. He resigned in 1920 but was recalled in 1921. He was ambassador to Belgium from 1922 to 1924 and ambassador to Italy from 1924 to 1929. In 1930 he was a member of the Forbes Commission to Haiti* to investigate conditions there. He was chairman of the U.S. Tariff Commission in 1930–1931. Died July 10, 1959, in Newport, Rhode Island. *References*: *DADH*; Olivia M. Frederick, ''Henry P. Fletcher and United States–Latin American Policy, 1910–1930,'' Ph.D. diss., University of Kentucky, 1977; Mark T. Gilderhus, ''Henry P. Fletcher in Mexico, 1917–1920: An Ambassador's Response to Revolution,'' *Rocky Mountain Social Science Journal* 10 (October 1973): 61–70; *NCAB* 43:80; *NYT*, July 11, 1959; and *WWWA*.

FLETCHER, JAMES COOLEY (1823–1901). Missionary, born April 15, 1823, in Indianapolis, Indiana. Fletcher graduated from Brown University, attended Princeton Theological Seminary, studied in Paris, France, and Geneva, Switzerland, and was ordained in 1851. He was a missionary under the American and Foreign Christian Union and chaplain of the Seaman's Friend Society in Brazil from 1851 to 1854. He was an agent for the American Bible Society* in Brazil in 1855–1856. He returned to the United States in 1856. With Daniel P. Kidder,* he wrote *Brazil and the Brazilians* (New York, 1857). He was an agent of the American Sunday School Union in Brazil in 1862–1863, made a journey of 2,000 miles up the Amazon to the borders of Peru, gathering natural history specimens for Jean Louis Rudolphe Agassiz,* and was an agent of the American Tract Society in Brazil in 1868–1869. He was U.S. consul in Oporto, Portugal, from 1869 to 1873 and resided in Napoli, Italy, from 1873 to 1890, where he engaged in voluntary missionary work. He returned to the United States in 1890 and resided in Los Angeles. Died April 23, 1901, in Los Angeles. *References*: *DAB*; *IAB*; *NCAB* 13:130; and *WWWA*.

FORBES, JOHN MURRAY (1771–1831). Lawyer and diplomat, born August 13, 1771, in St. Augustine, Florida, and grew up in Massachusetts. Forbes graduated from Harvard University and studied law. He practiced law in Boston from 1794 to 1796. He abandoned law and went to Paris in 1796. He was U.S. consul in Hamburg and Copenhagen from 1801 to 1819. He was U.S. agent for commerce and seamen in Buenos Aires from 1820 to 1823, secretary of legation there in 1823–1824, and chargé d'affaires there from 1824 until his death. In 1821, he obtained an alteration of the policy of Buenos Aires in regard to privateering and in 1822, a modification of its ordinance of maritime police. Died June 14, 1831, in Buenos Aires. *References*: John Murray Forbes Papers,

Allies. He was a professor of international relations at the American Institute for Foreign Trade (Phoenix, Ariz.) from 1947 to.1951. Died January 9, 1968, in Winter Park, Florida. *References*: Wesley Frost Papers, Oberlin College Archives, Oberlin, Ohio; *NCAB* 55:168; and *WWWA*.

FRY, JOSEPH (ca. 1828–1873). Sea captain, born in Louisiana. Fry entered the U.S. Navy as a midshipman in 1841. He served in the Confederate Navy during the Civil War. He later settled in Albany, New York. In 1873, he assumed command of the filibustering steamer *Virginius* (*see Virginius* affair) which was blockade running to Cuban rebels during the Ten Years' War in Cuba. The vessel was captured by a Spanish warship. He was shot as a filibuster, November 7, 1873, in Santiago de Cuba. *References*: Jim D. Hill, "Captain Joseph Fry of S.S. *Virginius*," *AN* 36 (1976): 88–100; and *NCAB* 12:64.

FRYE, A(LEXIS) E(VERETT) (1859–1936). Educator, born November 2, 1859, in North Haven, Maine. Frye attended a teacher training class in Boston and graduated from Harvard University. He was engaged in making relief maps in Hyde Park, Massachusetts, from 1880 to 1883, taught in the Cook County Normal School (Chicago) from 1883 to 1886, and was admitted to the bar in 1890, but never practiced law. He was superintendent of schools at San Bernardino, California, from 1891 to 1893, and then wrote school books for Ginn and Company of Boston. He was superintendent of public schools in Cuba from 1899 to 1901. He wrote Cuba's first national school law and organized its first public school system, supervising the employment of teachers and the selection of school books and making arrangements for the opening of schools in every part of the island. He was later involved in writing new and revising old textbooks in geography and growing oranges in San Bernardino Valley, California. Died July 1, 1936, in Loma Linda, California. *References*: *BDAE*; Edward D. Fitchen, "The U.S. Military Government: A. E. Frye and Cuban Education," *Revista/ Review Interamericana* 2 (1972): 123–49; *NCAB* 40:518; and *WWWA*.

FUERTES, LOUIS AGASSIZ (1874–1927). Artist, born February 7, 1874, in Ithaca, New York. Fuertes graduated from Cornell University. He began a series of expeditions in which he studied and painted birds. He participated in expeditions under the American Museum of Natural History to the Bahamas in 1902, to Yucatán in 1910, and to Colombia in 1911 and 1913. Died August 22, 1927, in Ithaca, New York. *References*: Louis Agassiz Fuertes Papers, Cornell University Library, Ithaca, N.Y.; Robert M. Back, *A Celebration of Birds: The Life and Art of Louis Fuertes* (New York, 1982); Mary E. Boyton, ed., *Louis Agassiz Fuertes: His Life Briefly Told and His Correspondence* (New York, 1956); *DAB*; Frederick G. Marcham, *Louis Agassiz Fuertes and the Singular Beauty of Birds* (New York, 1971); and *NCAB* 21:69.

FULLER, PAUL [FRANCISCO] (1847–1915). Lawyer, born January 26, 1847, at sea, and grew up in Vermont. Fuller studied law and was admitted to the bar in 1868. He practiced law in New York City, specializing in international law. He was dean of Fordham Law School from 1905 to 1913. He was adviser to President Woodrow Wilson's administration in Mexico and, as special agent of the U.S. State Department, traveled throughout Mexico to confer with various Latin American leaders. Died November 30, 1915, in New York City. *References*: *Hill*; and *NCAB* 16:380.

FUNSTON, FREDERICK (1865–1917). Army officer, born November 9, 1865, in New Carlisle, Ohio, and grew up in Iola, Kansas. Funston attended Kansas State University (Lawrence). He was botanical explorer for the U.S. Department of Agriculture from 1891 to 1895 in the Dakotas, Death Valley, California, and Alaska. He volunteered for service in the Cuban insurrection in 1896, as artillery commander for the Cuban guerilla forces under Maximo Gomez and Calixto Garcia, participated in twenty-two engagements, was wounded several times, and rose to the rank of lieutenant colonel. He was captured by the Spaniards in 1897 and was condemned to death but escaped and returned to the United States. He served in the Philippine-American War in 1898–1899 and succeeded in capturing Emilio Aguinaldo, Philippine leader, in 1901. He was commissioned brigadier general in the regular army in 1901 and returned to the United States. He commanded the departments of the Colorado, the Columbia, and the Lakes, the Southwestern Division and the Department of California. He served in the Philippines again from 1911 to 1913 and in Hawaii in 1913–1914. He commanded the army troops in the expedition to Veracruz, Mexico, in 1914, and was commander and military commander of the city. He was commander of the Southern Department in 1915. He wrote *Memories of Two Wars: Cuban and Philippines Experiences* (New York, 1911). Died February 19, 1917, in San Antonio, Texas. *References*: Frederick Funston Papers, Kansas State Historical Society, Topeka, Kan.; *ACAB*; Thomas W. Crouch, "The Making of a Soldier: The Career of Frederick Funston, 1865–1902," Ph.D. diss., University of Texas at Austin, 1969; Thomas W. Crouch, *A Yankee Guerriller: Frederick Funston and the Cuban Insurrection 1896–1897* (Memphis, 1975); *DAB*; *NCAB* 11:40; *NYT*, February 24, 1917; John B. B. Trussell, Jr., "Frederick Funston: The Man Destiny Just Missed," *Military Review* 53 (June 1973): 59–73; and *WWWA*.

FURLONG, CHARLES WELLINGTON (1874–1967). Explorer, born December 13, 1874, in Cambridge, Massachusetts. Furlong attended the Art Institute of Chicago, the Massachusetts Normal Art School (Boston), and Harvard and Cornell universities, and studied art in Paris. In 1904, he began a career of exploration. He made an expedition into Tripolitanian Sahara in 1904, and then led other expeditions to Africa, Central and South America, Caribbean and West African islands, the Mediterranean, the Balkans, and the Middle East. He led a

First Thirty Years,'' in *Long-Term Field Research in Social Anthropology*, ed. George M. Foster et al. (New York, 1979). *References*: *AMWS*; and *WWA*.

FOSTER, JOHN WATSON (1836–1917). Public official and diplomat, born March 2, 1836, in Pike County, Indiana. Foster graduated from Indiana University, attended Harvard Law School, and was admitted to the bar in 1857. He served in the Union Army during the Civil War. He was editor of the Evansville *Daily Journal* from 1865 to 1869 and postmaster of Evansville from 1869 to 1873. He was U.S. minister to Mexico from 1873 to 1880, working harmoniously with the Mexican government. He was U.S. minister to Russia in 1880–1881, minister to Spain from 1883 to 1885, and secretary of state in 1892–1893. He wrote an autobiography, *Diplomatic Memories* (Boston, 1909). Died November 15, 1917, in Washington, D.C. *References*: *DAB*; *DADH*; Michael J. Devine, *John W. Foster: Politics and Diplomacy in the Imperial Era, 1873–1917* (Athens, Ohio, 1981); *IAB*; Chester C. Kaiser, ''John W. Foster: United States Minister to Mexico, 1873–1880,'' Ph.D. diss., American University, 1954; *NCAB* 3:268; *NYT*, November 16, 1917; Francis M. Philipps, ''John Watson Foster, 1836–1917,'' Ph.D. diss., University of New Mexico, 1956; and *WWWA*.

FOX, WILLIAMS CARLTON (1855–1924). Diplomat, born May 20, 1855, in St. Louis. Fox attended Washington University (St. Louis). He was U.S. consul in Brunswick, Germany; vice consul general in Teheran, Persia; and secretary of legation in Greece until 1894. He established the *Diplomatic and Consular Review* in 1894. He was chief clerk of the International Bureau of American Republics in Washington, D.C., from 1898 to 1905 and director of the bureau from 1905 to 1907. He was U.S. minister to Ecuador from 1907 to 1911. He arbitrated the controversy between the government of Ecuador and the Guayaquil and Quito Railway Company in 1907. Died January 20, 1924, in New York City. *References*: *NCAB* 14:114; *NYT*, January 21, 1924; and *WWWA*.

FRANCK, HARRY (ALVERSON) (1881–1962). Traveler and author, born June 29, 1881, in Munger, Michigan. Franck graduated from the University of Michigan and studied at Harvard and Columbia universities. He was a teacher of modern languages in Detroit, Bellefonte, Pennsylvania, New York City, and Springfield, Massachusetts. He served in the U.S. Army during World War I. After 1911, he devoted his time to traveling, writing, and lecturing. He wrote *Tramping through Mexico, Guatemala and Honduras: Being the Random Notes of an Incurable Vagabond* (New York, 1916), *Vagabonding Down the Andes: Being the Narrative of a Journey, Chiefly Afoot, from Panama to Buenos Aires* (New York, 1917), *Roaming through the West Indies* (New York, 1920), *Working North from Patagonia; Being the Narrative of a Journey, Earned on the Way, through Southern and Eastern South America* (New York, 1921), and *Rediscovering South America* (New York, 1943), which included many of his photographs. He served in the U.S. Army Air Force during World War II. Died

April 17, 1962, in Langhorne, Pennsylvania. *References*: *CA*; *NCAB* 52:404; and *NYT*, April 19, 1962.

FREDERICKS, CHARLES DE FOREST (1823–1894). Photographer, born December 11, 1823, in New York City. Fredericks was one of the earliest daguerrotypists to travel from the United States to Latin America. In 1843, he went to Venezuela and began to photograph in Angastura and then in the islands of Tobago and St. Vincent. He also went up the Orinoco and down the Amazon. He returned to the United States because of ill health. He was back in Belém, state of Pará, in 1844, and opened a studio there. Until 1853 he traveled down the east coast of South America to Buenos Aires. (None of his South American works survived.) He returned to the United States in 1853, and established himself as photographer in New York City, and after 1856, was a partner in New York's leading daguerrotype studio. Died May 25, 1894, in Newark, New Jersey. *References*: Lisa Bloom, "Charles De Forest Fredericks; 19th Century Entrepreneur in the Photography Industry," Master's thesis, Visual Studies Workshop, New York, 1983; and *NCAB* 2:398.

FRIENDS UNITED MEETING BOARD OF MISSIONS. Organized in 1894 as the American Friends Board of Foreign Mission. Missionary work began in Mexico in 1871 under the New York Yearly Meeting, in Jamaica in 1881 and in Cuba in 1901, by the Iowa Yearly Meeting, and in Guatemala in 1902 and in Honduras in 1914, by the California Yearly Meeting. Work in Bolivia began in 1920, and was adopted by the Oregon Yearly Meeting in 1930. *References*: Phyllis Cammack, *Missionary Moments* (Newberg, Oreg., 1977); Ellen Davis, *Friends in Jamaica* (Richmond, Ind., 1943); Paul Enyart, *Friends in Central America* (South Pasadena, Calif., 1970); Marie Haines, *Friends in Aymara Land 1930–1955* (Portland, Oreg., 1955?); Hiram H. Hilty, *Friends in Cuba* (Richmond, Ind., 1977); Christina H. Jones, *American Friends in World Missions* (Richmond, Ind., 1946); Quentin Nordyke, *Animastic Aymaras and Church Growth* (Newberg, Oreg., 1972); and *Society of Friends in Jamaica* (Richmond, Ind., 1962).

FROST, WESLEY (1884–1968). Diplomat, born June 17, 1884, in Oberlin, Ohio. Frost graduated from Oberlin College and George Washington University. He entered the U.S. State Department in 1909 and was its first economic officer. He was U.S. consul in Charlottetown, Prince Edward Island, Canada, and then consul general in Queenstown, Ireland, until 1917. He then studied law, and was admitted to the bar in 1917. He was chief of the State Department economic work from 1919 to 1921, consul and consul general in Marseilles and Montreal from 1921 to 1929, and counselor of embassy in Brazil in 1935–1936 and in Chile from 1936 to 1941. He was U.S. minister to Paraguay in 1941–1942 and the country's first ambassador from 1942 until his retirement in 1944. He induced Paraguay to break with the Axis powers during World War II and to support the

scientific expedition to Tierra del Fuego in 1907–1908, explored the Fuegian Archipelago and Patagonian channels, and investigated the Yahgan and Ona Indians of that area in three separate expeditions. In 1910, he made an investigation and exposé of the Devil's Island penal colony in French Guiana, and explored, by canoe, the jungle waterways of Suriname and the Orinoco and Apure rivers. He did intelligence work for the U.S. Army in 1915 and served in it during World War I. He went treasure hunting in Bolivia in 1926 and made other journeys in Central and South America during the 1930s and 1940s. He was later a consultant to the Stefansson Collection in the Baker Library of Dartmouth College (Hanover, N.H.). Died October 9, 1967, in Hanover, New Hampshire. *References*: *Cutolo*; *NCAB* 54:292; E. V. Niemeyer, Jr., "Three North Americans in Chile," *Atenea. Revista de Ciencies, Letras y Artes* (Concepcion, Chile), no. 433 (1976): 61–68; *NYT*, October 11, 1967; and *WWWA*.

FURNISS, HENRY W(ATSON) (1868–1955). Physician and diplomat, born February 14, 1868, in Brooklyn, New York. Furniss attended the Medical Department of the University of Indianapolis and graduated from Howard University Medical College and from the College of Pharmacy of Howard University. He practiced medicine in Indianapolis in 1896–1897. He was U.S. consul in Bahia, Brazil, from 1897 to 1905, and U.S. minister to Haiti from 1905 until 1913, where he opposed U.S. receivership for Haiti. He resumed the practice of medicine in Brooklyn, in other places in New York State, and in Hartford, Connecticut, from 1917 until his retirement in 1952. Died December 20, 1955, in Bristol, Connecticut. *References*: *DANB*; and *NCAB* 14:443.

G

GABB, WILLIAM M(ORE) (1839–1878). Paleontologist, born January 20, 1839, in Philadelphia, Gabb studied with James Hall in Albany. He was paleontologist of the state geological survey of California from 1862 to 1867. He traveled in Lower California in 1867 and later crossed it ten times and prepared the first geological map of that peninsula. He conducted a topographic and geologic survey of Santo Domingo for the Santo Domingo Land and Mining Company from 1869 to 1872 and wrote *On the Topography and Geology of Santo Domingo* (Philadelphia, 1873). In 1873 he went to Costa Rica under an appointment from the government of that country, to make a topographical and geological survey. He also made ethnological and natural history collections for the Smithsonian Institution. He made a survey of the province of Talamanca in Costa Rica from 1873 to 1876 and wrote *On the Indian Tribes and Languages of Costa Rica* (Philadelphia, 1875). Died May 30, 1878, in Philadelphia. *References*: *ACAB*; *DAB*; *DSB*; Luis Ferrero, *William M. Gabb, Talamanca: El Espacio y los Hombres* (San Jose, Costa Rica, 1978); *NCAB* 4:376; and *WWWA*.

GADSDEN, JAMES (1788–1858). Diplomat, born May 15, 1788, in Charleston, South Carolina. Gadsden graduated from Yale University. He served in the U.S. Army during the War of 1812 and the Seminole War. He lived in Florida from 1821 to 1839 and was a commissioner to effect the removal of the Seminoles to reservations, a member of the territorial legislative council of Florida, and president of the Louisville, Cincinnati and Charleston Railroad (after 1842, the South Carolina Railroad Company) from 1840 to 1850. He was U.S. minister to Mexico from 1853 to 1856. He purchased from Mexico a small strip of territory for the construction of a railway to the Gulf of Mexico; this was known as the Gadsden Purchase. Died December 26, 1858, in Charleston, South Carolina. *References*: *ACAB*; *DAB*; *DADH*; *NCAB* 12:68; and *WWWA*.

GAILLARD, DAVID DUBOSE (1859–1913). Engineer, born September 4, 1859, in Fulton, Sumter County, South Carolina. Gaillard graduated from the U.S. Military Academy in 1884 and was commissioned second lieutenant of engineers. He was on engineering duty in Florida from 1887 to 1891 and served as a member of the International Boundry Commission to establish the line between Mexico and the United States from 1891 to 1895. He served in the Spanish-American War. He served later in the District of Columbia and the Department of Columbia, and, in 1907, was placed in charge of the department of dredging and excavation in the Panama Canal. He organized the Chagres division and was in charge of the central division from 1908 to 1913. He broke down under the strain and never recovered. Died December 5, 1913, in Baltimore. *References*: *DAB*; *NCAB* 15:318; and *WWWA*.

GALT, FRANCIS LAND (1833–1915). Physician, born December 13, 1833, in Norfolk, Virginia. Galt studied medicine in New York and then at the University of Pennsylvania. He was commissioned assistant surgeon in the U.S. Navy in 1855. He served in the Confederate Navy during the Civil War. He later practiced medicine in Norfolk. He was a member of the Hydrographic Commission of the Amazon in Peru from 1869 to 1872, exploring the headwaters of the Amazon River. He wrote the chapter on popular medicine in James Orton's *The Andes and the Amazon* (3rd ed., Boston, 1876). He practiced medicine in Lynchburg, Virginia, and then in Upperville, Loudon County, Virginia, from 1876, until his retirement in 1909. Died November 17, 1915, in Upperville, Virginia. *References*: Francis Land Galt, "Diary of a Trip to the Headwaters of the Amazon; 1870–73, 1874" (Ms.), National Anthropological Archives, Smithsonian Institution, Washington, D.C.; and *NYT*, November 19, 1915.

GAMMON, SAMUEL R(HEA) (1865–1928). Missionary, born March 30, 1865, in Bristol, Virginia. Gammon graduated from King College (Bristol, Tenn.) and Union Theological Seminary of Virginia, and was ordained in 1889. He was a missionary under the Board of Foreign Missions of the Presbyterian Church in the United States* in Brazil from 1889 until his death. He was president of the Evangelical Institute in Lavras, Brazil, and professor of history, Greek, and Bible there. He wrote *The Evangelical Invasion of Brazil: or, A Half Century of Evangelical Missions in the Land of the Southern Cross* (Richmond, Va., 1910). Died July 4, 1928, in Rio de Janeiro. *References*: Clara G. M. Gammon, "So Shines the Light: A Biography of Samuel Rhea Gammon, 1865–1928" (Ms.), Board of World Missions, Presbyterian Church in the United States, Atlanta, Ga.; and *MDPC*.

GAMMON INSTITUTE. Founded in 1869 as the International School in Campinas, Brazil, by the Board of Foreign Missions of the Presbyterian Church in the United States.* It was moved in 1892 to Lavras, Minas Gerais. A school of agriculture was founded in 1908.

GARDE D'HAITI. The Haitian gendarmerie, renamed Garde d'Haiti in 1928, that was established in 1915, under command of officers of the U.S. Marines, and whose functions included urban and rural police, prison administration, fire protection, and the coast guard. *Reference*: James H. McCrocklin, *Garde d'Haiti: Twenty Years of Organization and Training by the United States Marine Corps, 1915–1934* (Annapolis, Md., 1957).

GARDNER, ARTHUR (1889–1967). Businessman and diplomat, born February 21, 1889, in Omaha. Gardner graduated from Yale University. He was with Equitable Trust Company in New York City from 1910 to 1912, served in the U.S. Army during World War I, was a partner in Anderson and Gardner in Detroit from 1926 to 1931, first vice president of Bundy Tubing Company from 1929 to 1953, and president of Detroit Macoid Company from 1934 to 1953. He was special assistant to the secretary of the treasury in 1947–1948. He was U.S. ambassador to Cuba from 1953 to 1957. He was an admirer and friend of President Fulgencio Batista, whom he supported during Fidel Castro's campaign to overthrow him. Died April 11, 1967, in Palm Beach, Florida. *References*: *CB* 1956; *NCAB* I:266; *NYT*, April 12, 1967, and *WWWA*.

GARRISON, CORNELIUS KINGSLAND (1809–1885). Financier, born March 1, 1809, in Fort Montgomery, Orange County, New York. He became a cabin boy on a Hudson River sloop in 1822, went to New York City in 1825, and studied architecture and engineering. He was employed by the Upper Canada Company from 1828 to 1833 and then settled in St. Louis. He was engaged in designing, building, and running steamboats and organizing regular freight services to New Orleans and other ports. He went to Panama in 1849, where he established a commercial and banking house. He was manager of the Pacific agency of the Nicaragua Steamship Company in San Francisco from 1853 to 1859, served as mayor of San Francisco, and established the banking house of Garrison and Fretz in that city. He returned to New York City in 1859, established a steamship service between New York and Brazil, and promoted extensive trading operations with the countries of South America. Died May 1, 1885, in New York City. *References*: *ACAB*; *DAB*; *NCAB* 7:262; and *WWWA*.

GASTON, JAMES MCFADDEN (1824–1903). Physician and colony promoter, born December 27, 1824, near Chester, South Carolina. Gaston graduated from the University of South Carolina, studied at the University of Pennsylvania, and graduated from the Medical College of South Carolina. He practiced medicine in Chester County from 1846 until 1852 and in Columbia, South Carolina, after 1852. He served as a surgeon in the Confederate Army during the Civil War. He went to Brazil in 1865 to select a home for his family and to report on the country as a possible site for a colony for emigrants from South Carolina. His report, *Hunting a Home in Brazil* (Philadelphia, 1867), led to a migration of many Carolina planter families to Brazil. He first settled in São Paulo, and in 1873 moved to Campinas, where he practiced medicine. The emperor of Brazil offered him the surgical command of the army, which he declined. He returned to the United States in 1883, and practiced medicine in Atlanta, Georgia. He was a professor of the principles and practice of medicine in the Southern Medical College in Atlanta after 1884. Died November 15, 1903, in Atlanta. *References*: *DAB*; *NCAB* 12:290; and *WWWA*.

GATES, WILLIAM E(DMOND) (1863–1940). Archaeologist, born in Atlanta, Georgia. Gates graduated from Johns Hopkins University and studied law. He opened a typewriter selling agency in Cleveland, Ohio; made a business of printing briefs and appeals to the Ohio Supreme Court; and published the daily *Court Record Journal*. He retired in 1905 and moved to southern California. He made his first trip to Mexico in 1918 and traveled to Guatemala in 1921, 1922, and 1923. He organized the Maya Society in 1921 and served as its president. In 1925, he participated in the Tulane University expedition to Honduras and explored Mayan ruins in Central America. He was director of archaeology for the government of Guatemala and director of the Guatemalan Museum from 1922 to 1924. He was director of the department of Middle American Research of Tulane University after 1924 and was at Johns Hopkins University until 1938. After he resigned, he wrote *An Outline Dictionary of Maya Glyphs, with a Concordance and Analysis of Their Relationships* (Baltimore, 1931). Died April 24, 1940, in Baltimore. *References*: William E. Gates Papers, Tulane University Library, New Orleans; Robert L. Brunhouse, *Pursuit of the Ancient Maya: Some Archaeologists of Yesterday* (Albuquerque, N.M., 1975), ch. 6; Alfred L. Bush, "William E. Gates, 1863–1940," *Manuscripts* 15 (Spring 1963): 42–46; *NCAB* D:254; and *NYT*, April 25, 1940.

GAUL, (WILLIAM) GILBERT (1855–1919). Painter, born March 31, 1855, in Jersey City, New Jersey. Gaul studied painting in the National Academy of Design (New York City) and the Art Students' League of New York. He traveled widely in Mexico, the West Indies, Jamaica, Panama, and Nicaragua in quest of subject matter. He wrote an account of his travels in Jamaica in the March 1893 issue of *Century Magazine*. He was later an illustrator for that publication. Died December 21, 1919, in New York City. *References*: *DAB*; *NCAB* 12:366; *NYT*, December 22, 1919; and James F. Reeves, *Gilbert Gaul* (Nashville, Tenn., 1975).

GAUMER, GEORGE F(RANKLIN) (1850–1929). Naturalist, born September 10, 1850, in Monroe Township, Carroll County, Indiana. Gaumer moved with his family to Lawrence, Kansas, in 1868. He graduated from the University of Kansas. He was in Cuba in 1878, and in Yucatán from 1878 to 1881, collecting birds for the British Museum (Natural History). He was professor of natural history at the University of New Mexico from 1882 to 1884, and was then licensed to practice medicine in New Mexico. He resided in Yucatán from 1884 until his death, collecting plants in Yucatán, and also in Cozumel in 1885–1886 and in the bay islands of Honduras from 1886 to 1888. He wrote *Monografia de los Mamiferos de Yucatán* (Mexico, 1917). Died September 2, 1929, in Izamal, Yucatán, Mexico. *Reference*: *Science*, 70 (1929): 321.

GAVIN, JOHN (1928–   ). Actor and diplomat, born John Anthony Golenor, April 8, 1928, in Los Angeles. Gavin graduated from Stanford University, and served in the U.S. Navy. He appeared in several films. In the 1960s, he developed business interests in Latin America, and he was president of Gamma Services Corporation after 1968. He was U.S. ambassador to Mexico from 1981 to 1986. He aroused a good deal of friction with the Mexican government and society by exerting pressure and taking action on issues that the Mexicans considered purely domestic concerns. *References*: *CB* 1962; and *WWA*.

GENTRY, IRMA ELLENDER (1900–   ). Government official, born November 15, 1900, in Pawnee County, Oklahoma. Gentry graduated from Oklahoma A and M University and studied at the National University of Mexico. She was a clerk in the U.S. legation in Guatemala from 1928 to 1937. She was private secretary to President Jorge Ubico of Guatemala and his wife from 1937 to 1944. She returned to the United States in 1944 and worked for the Southwestern Power Administration until her retirement in 1971. *Reference*: Ivie E. Cadenhead, Jr., "An Oklahoman in Guatemala," *Red River Valley Historical Review* 5, no. 3 (1980): 14–21.

GIBSON, ADDISON H(OWARD) (1860–1936). Petroleum producer, born November 30, 1860, in Elderton, Armstrong County, Pennsylvania. Gibson was employed by Pew and Emerson, a gas and oil firm of Pittsburgh, and then was associated with Peoples Natural Gas Company. He later established his own business, purchasing and developing oil and gas leases in western Pennsylvania, West Virginia, Ohio, and Illinois. In 1911, he became interested in the oil developments in Mexico, formed Gibson and Zahniser in 1915 to develop Mexican oil properties, obtained oil land leased in the state of Veracruz in 1916, and organized Compania Petrolera de Tepetate, of which he was president. He also developed oil wells in Amatlan, Mexico. He later drilled wells and developed oil properties in Oklahoma, Illinois, Kansas, and Texas. Died April 18, 1936, in Tulsa, Oklahoma. *Reference*: *NCAB* 28:345.

GIESECKE, ALBERT A(NTHONY) (1883–1970). Educator, born November 30, 1883, in Philadelphia. Giesecke graduated from the University of Pennsylvania and Cornell University, and studied at the universities of Berlin, Paris, and Lausanne. He was special expert in commercial education for the government of Peru in 1909, rector of the San Antonio Abad University in Cuzco, Peru, from 1910 to 1924, director general of public education of Peru from 1924 to 1930, and technical adviser to the Peruvian minister of education after 1930.

He was a member of the Peruvian delegation to the plebiscitary commission of Tacna-Arica in 1925 and special assistant to the U.S. ambassador to Peru after 1954. Died in Lima, Peru. *References*: "Reminiscences of Albert A. Giesecke," Columbia University Library, New York City; Dorothy Walworth, "He's Our One-Man Goodwill Mission," *Reader's Digest* 51 (October 1947): 5–12; and *WWWA*.

GILL, RICHARD C(OCHRAN) (1901–1958). Explorer and author, born November 22, 1901, in Washington, D.C. Gill graduated from Cornell University and attended Columbia and New York universities. He was a field manager in Ecuador, Peru, and Bolivia for the B. F. Goodrich Rubber Corporation from 1928 to 1930. He was president of Gill, Miller Company, ranching in Ecuador during the 1930s, and then president of Gill, Dundas and Company, and Cugil Laboratories in Palo Alto, California. He was leader of the Gill-Merrill expedition and other South American expeditions to the upper Amazon. He was involved in ethnobotany and tropical American pharmacognosy, and in manufacturing curare and other tropical drugs. He was a lecturer after 1937. He wrote *White Water and Black Magic* (New York, 1940) and several works of fiction: *Manga, an Amazon Jungle Indian* (New York, 1937), *Volcano of Gold; a Manga Story* (New York, 1938), and *Flying Death, a Manga Story* (New York, 1942). Died July 7, 1958, in Palo Alto, California. *Reference*: *WWWA*.

GILLIN, JOHN (PHILIP) (1907–1973). Anthropologist, born August 1, 1907, in Waterloo, Iowa. Gillin graduated from the University of Wisconsin and Harvard University and attended the London School of Economics and Political Science. He conducted an expedition to the tropical forest of South America to study the Carib Indians of British Guiana in 1932–1933 under the department of anthropology of Harvard University, was in charge of the work of the Peabody Museum of Archaeology and Ethnology and Peru and Ecuador in 1934–1935, conducted a survey of the inhabitants and cultures of Imbabura province, Ecuador, in 1934, went to Guatemala in 1940 and 1942, carried out fieldwork in the Pueblo of Moche near Trujillo in Peru in 1944–1945 under the Institute of Social Anthropology of the Smithsonian Institution, was in Colombia in 1946 and again in Guatemala in 1948, and was in Cuba in 1949 and 1952. He was a member of the Board of Economic Warfare at the U.S. Embassy in Peru in 1943–1944 and field representative of the Smithsonian Institution in Peru in 1944–1945. He was associate professor of anthropology at Ohio State University from 1937 to 1941, associate professor of anthropology at Duke University from 1941 to 1946, and professor of anthropology at the University of North Carolina at Chapel Hill from 1946 until 1959. He was dean of the social sciences at the University of Pittsburgh from 1959 to 1962 and research professor there until his retirement in 1972. He wrote *The Barama River Caribs of British Guiana* (Cambridge, Mass., 1936), *The Quichua-Speaking Indians of the Province of*

Imbabura (Ecuador) and Their Anthropometric Relations with the Living Population of the Andea Area (Washington, D.C., 1941), *Moche: A Peruvian Coastal Community* (Washington, D.C., 1945), and *The Culture of Security in San Carlos: A Study of a Guatemalan Community of Indians and Ladinos* (New Orleans, 1951), and coauthored *Social Change in Latin America Today: Its Implications for United States Policy* (New York, 1960). Died August 4, 1973, in Chapel Hill, North Carolina. *References*: *NCAB* 58:429; *NYT*, August 5, 1973; and *WWA*.

GILLISS, JAMES MELVILLE (1811–1865). Naval officer and astronomer, born September 6, 1811, in Georgetown, D.C. Gilliss entered the U.S. Navy as a midshipman in 1826. He later attended the University of Virginia and studied in Paris. He was in charge of the Department of Charts and Instruments of the Navy in 1837 and prepared plans for building the new naval observatory in Washington, D.C. He was the leader of an expedition to South America to observe Venus and Mars for the purpose of a new determination of the solar parallax, located the southern station for that expedition in Santiago, Chile, from 1849 to 1852, and observed Venus and Mars. The expedition resulted in the establishment of permanent observatory in Santiago, Chile. He wrote *The U.S. Naval Astronomical Expedition to the Southern Hemisphere During the Years 1849–'50–'51–'52* (Washington, D.C., 1855), *Origin and Operation of the U.S. Naval Astronomical Expedition* (Washington, D.C., 1858), and *Chile: Its Geography, Climate, Earthquakes, Government, Social Conditions, Mineral and Agricultural Resources, Commerce, etc.* (Washington, D.C., 1855). In 1858, he went again to South America and crossed the Peruvian desert to Olmas. He was in charge of the Confederate naval observatory during the Civil War. Died February 9, 1865, in Washington, D.C. *References*: *ACAB*; *DAB*; *NCAB* 9:99; Vincent Ponko, Jr., *Ships, Seas, and Scientists: U.S. Naval Exploration and Discovery in the Nineteenth Century* (Annapolis, Md., 1974), ch. 6; Wayne D. Rasmussen, ''The United States Astronomical Expedition to Chile, 1849–1852,'' *HAHR* 34 (1954): 102–13; and *WWWA*.

GLORIA CITY COLONY. Established in 1899 by the Cuban Land and Steamship Company in the Valley of Cubitas, the first of thirty-seven settlements of North Americans in different parts of Cuba. It reached its peak growth in 1914, with some 3,000 North Americans living in the Valley of Cubitas, but then experienced a gradual decline. *References*: James M. Adams, *Pioneering in Cuba: A Narrative of the Settlement of La Gloria, the First American Colony in Cuba, and the Early Experiences of the Pioneers* (Concord, N.H., 1901); and Enrique Cirules, *The Last American* (Havana, Cuba, 1987).

GOETHALS, GEORGE WASHINGTON (1858–1928). Army officer and engineer, born June 29, 1858, in Brooklyn, New York. Goethals attended the College of the City of New York, graduated from the U.S. Military Academy in 1880, and was commissioned second lieutenant in the Engineers. Goethals was employed on various river works projects and taught at the U.S. Military Academy from 1885 to 1889 and from 1898 to 1900. He served in the Spanish-American War and was attached to the general staff from 1903 to 1907. He was chief engineer and chairman of the Isthmian Canal Commission from 1907, with full authority and complete responsibility for the construction of the Panama Canal. He was first governor of the Panama Canal Zone from 1914 to 1917. He retired with the rank of major general in 1916 but was recalled to active duty during World War I. He then headed his own engineering consulting firm in New York City. Died January 21, 1928, in New York City. *References*: *DAB*; *ELA*; Walt Griffin, "George W. Goethals and the Panama Canal," Ph.D. diss., University of Cincinnati, 1988; *NCAB* 24:6; and *WWWA*.

GOLDMAN, EDWARD ALPHONSO (1873–1946). Zoologist, born July 7, 1873, in Mount Carroll, Illinois, and grew up in Falls City, Nebraska, and Tulare County, California. He was assistant field agent for the U.S. Bureau of Biological Survey after 1892, traveling, collecting, and studying Mexican fauna from 1892 to 1896. He made a faunal survey of the Panama Canal during the construction of the canal under the auspices of the Smithsonian Institution and the U.S. departments of War and Agriculture. He participated in the Nelson-Goldman expedition to Baja California in 1905–1906. He wrote *Mammals of Panama* (Washington, D.C., 1920). He was in charge of the U.S. Bureau of Biological Survey's division of biological investigations and later in charge of the big game and bird reservations. He served in the U.S. Army during World War I. He was senior biologist from 1928 until his retirement in 1944. *Biological Investigations in Mexico* (Washington, D.C., 1951) was published posthumously. Died September 2, 1946, in Washington, D.C. *References*: *AMWS*; *Auk* 64 (1947): 503; *Journal of Mammalogy* 28 (1947): 91–114; *Journal of the Washington Academy of Science* 37 (1947): 35–36; and Keir Sterling, "Naturalists of the Southwest at the Turn of the Century," *Environmental Review* 3 (1978): 20–33.

GOLDMAN, IRVING (1911–   ). Anthropologist, born September 2, 1911, in New York City. Goldman graduated from Brooklyn College and Columbia University. He served in the U.S. Army and the Office of Strategic Services during World War II and was research analyst in the Office of the Coordinator of Inter-American Affairs in 1944–1945 and chief of the Latin American branch of the Office of Research and Analysis of the State Department from 1945 to 1947. He was a professor of anthropology at Sarah Lawrence College after 1947. He carried out fieldwork in the South American tropical forest, the Andes, and the Mexican highlands, and wrote *The Cubeo Indians of the Northwest Amazon* (Urbana, Ill., 1963). *References*: *AMWS*; *CA*; and *WWA*.

GONZALES, WILLIAM ELLIOTT (1866–1937). Editor, publisher, and diplomat, born April 24, 1866, in Charleston, South Carolina. Gonzales attended the Citadel (Charleston). He worked as a reporter for the Columbia (S.C.) bureau of the Charleston *News and Courier*, was secretary to the governor of South Carolina from 1888 to 1890, worked for *The State* after 1891, and was editor in chief of *The State* after 1903. He served in the Spanish-American War. He was U.S. minister to Cuba from 1913 to 1919 and minister to Peru from 1919 to 1921. After he questioned the role of Standard Oil Company of New Jersey in Peru, his assignment was cut short and he was replaced. He resumed the position of editor in chief of *The State* until his death. Died October 20, 1937, in Columbia, South Carolina. *References*: William E. Gonzales Papers, University of South Carolina Library, Columbia; Lewis P. Jones, "Carolinians and Cubans: The Elliots and Gonzales, Their Work and Their Writings," Ph.D. diss., University of North Carolina, 1952; Samuel L. Latimer, Jr., *The Story of The State, 1891–1969, and the Gonzales Brothers* (Columbia, S.C., 1970); *NCAB* 28:277; *NYT*, October 21, 1937; and *WWWA*.

GOOD NEIGHBOR POLICY. Policy initiated by President Franklin D. Roosevelt's administration in 1933, which aimed at establishing friendly relations, and economic as well as cultural cooperation between the United States and Latin American countries. *References*: *ELA*; Irwin F. Fellman, *Good Neighbor Diplomacy: United States Policies in Latin America 1933–1945* (Baltimore, 1980); David Green, *The Containment of Latin America: A History of the Myth and Realities of the Good Neighbor Policy* (Chicago, 1971); Edward O. Guerrant, *Roosevelt's Good Neighbor Policy* (Albuquerque, N.M., 1950); Robert F. Smith, "The Good Neighbor Policy: The Liberal Paradox in United States Relations with Latin America," in *Watershed of Empire: Essays on New Deal Foreign Policy*, ed. Leonard P. Liggio and James J. Martin (Colorado Springs, Colo., 1976), pp. 65–94; Paul A. Varg, "The Economic Side of the Good Neighbor Policy: The Reciprocal Trade Program and South America," *PHR* 45 (1976): 47–71; Bryce Wood, *The Dismantling of the Good Neighbor Policy* (Austin, Tex., 1985); and Bryce Wood, *The Making of the Good Neighbor Policy* (New York, 1961).

GOODFELLOW, WILLIAM (1820–1898). Missionary, born in Ohio. Goodfellow taught at McKendre College, Illinois Wesleyan University, and Garrett Biblical Institute. He was a missionary under the Board of Foreign Missions of the Methodist Episcopal Church* in Buenos Aires, Argentina, after 1857. He expanded Methodist Work and was a pastor in Buenos Aires and a superintendent of the mission from 1857 to 1869. He helped Domingo F. Sarmiento in establishing Argentina's educational system. *Reference*: *EWM*.

GOODSPEED, T(HOMAS) HARPER (1887–1966). Botanist, born May 17, 1887, in Springfield, Massachusetts. Goodspeed graduated from Brown University and the University of California. He was a member of the faculty of the University of California after 1909, and professor after 1928. He was curator of the University of California Botanical Garden from 1926 to 1934 and its director after 1934. He toured many parts of South America in search of unknown varieties of the plant of the genus *nicotiana* (of which the tobacco plant is one species). He traveled up and down the Andes regions and discovered numerous new kinds of *nicotiana*. He wrote *Plant Hunters of the Andes* (New York, 1941) and was coauthor of *The University of California Botanical Garden Expedition to the Andes (1935–1952)* (Berkeley, Calif., 1955). He retired in 1957. Died May 16, 1966, in Berkeley, California. *References*: *NYT*, May 19, 1966; and *WWWA*.

GORDON, GEORGE BYRON (1870–1927). Anthropologist, born August 4, 1870, in New Perth, Prince Edward Island, Canada. Gordon attended the University of South Carolina and graduated from Harvard University. He was chief of Harvard University archaeological expedition to Copán, Honduras, from 1894 to 1900. He was assistant curator in the department of anthropology of the University Museum of the University of Pennsylvania in Philadelphia in 1903–1904, curator from 1904 to 1910, and director of the museum from 1910 to 1927. He was also assistant professor of anthropology at the University of Pennsylvania from 1907 to 1915. He wrote *Researches in the Uloa Valley, Honduras* (Cambridge, Mass., 1898), *The Hieroglyphic Stairway: The Ruins of Copán* (Cambridge, Mass., 1902), and *The Book of Chilam Balam of Chumayel* (Philadelphia, 1913). Died January 30, 1927, in Philadelphia. *References*: *DAB*; and *WWWA*.

GORDON, [ABRAHAM] LINCOLN (1913–   ). Government official and diplomat, born September 10, 1913, in New York City. Gordon graduated from Harvard and Oxford universities. He served with the War Production Board during World War II. He was a professor of government and administration at Harvard University from 1947 to 1950, minister for economic affairs and director of the aid mission at the U.S. embassy in London from 1952 to 1955, and professor of international economic relations at Harvard University from 1955 to 1961. He was U.S. ambassador to Brazil from 1961 to 1966. He supported the military conspiracy against President Joao Goulart, established intimate relationship with President Humbert Castelo Branco, and became a defender of the latter's government. He was assistant secretary of state for inter-American affairs in 1966–1967. He was president of Johns Hopkins University from 1967 to 1971, fellow of the Woodrow Wilson International center for Scholars from 1972 to 1975, and senior fellow of Resources for the Future in Washington, D.C., from 1975 to 1980. *References*: Jan K. Black, "Lincoln Gordon and Brazil's Military Counterrevolution," in *Ambassadors in Foreign Policy: The Influence of Individuals on U.S.–Latin American Policy*, ed. C. Neale Ronning and Albert P. Vannucci (New York, 1987), pp. 95–113; *CA*; *CB* 1962; *PolProf:Johnson*; *PolProf:Kennedy*; and *WWA*.

GORDON, SAMUEL GEORGE (1897–1952). Mineralogist, born June 21, 1897, in Philadelphia. Gordon was assistant curator and then associate curator in the Department of Mineralogy of the Academy of Natural Sciences of Philadelphia. He conducted mineralogical expeditions to the Andes of Ecuador, Peru, Bolivia, and Chile in 1921, to the Andes of Bolivia and Chile in 1925, to South America in 1929–1930, and to Chile in 1930. He served in the U.S. War Department during World War II. Died May 17, 1952, in Cincinnati, Ohio. *References*: *AMWS*; and *NYT*, May 18, 1952.

GORGAS, WILLIAM CRAWFORD (1854–1920). Sanitarian, born October 3, 1854, in Toulminville, near Mobile, Alabama, and grew up in Richmond, Virginia, and Brierfield, Alabama. Gorgas graduated from the University of the South (Sewanee, Tenn.) and Bellevue Hospital Medical College of New York University. He was appointed to the Medical Corps of the U.S. Army in 1880. He was chief sanitary officer in Havana, Cuba, from 1898 to 1902 and chief sanitary officer of the Panama Canal Zone from 1904 to 1913. He directed the program of mosquito control, which decreased the ravages of yellow fever and malaria, and initiated a sanitary campaign which rid Havana of yellow fever. He undertook a similar program in the Panama Canal Zone, which eradicated yellow fever and brought malaria under control, enabling the United States to complete the building of the Panama Canal. He was surgeon general of the U.S. Army from 1914 until 1919 and director of the yellow fever control program of the International Health Board of the Rockefeller Foundation in 1919–1920. He wrote *Sanitation in Panama* (New York, 1915). Died July 3, 1920, in London, England. *References*: *DAB*; *DAMB 84*; John M. Gibson, *Physician to the World: The Life of General William C. Gorgas* (Durham, N.C., 1950); *NCAB* 32; 4; and *WWWA*.

GOSPEL MISSIONARY UNION. Founded in 1892 as the World's Gospel Union, it changed its name in 1901. It began missionary work in Ecuador in 1895, in Colombia in 1908, in Panama in 1953, in British Honduras in 1955, and in Mexico and the Bahamas in 1956. *References*: C. P. Chapman, *With the Bible among the Andes* (Kansas City, Mo., 194?); Frank and Marie Drown, *Mission to the Head-Hunters* (New York, 1961); and *EMCM*.

GOTTSCHALK, LOUIS MOREAU (1829–1869). Composer and pianist, born May 8, 1829, in New Orleans. Gottschalk studied music in Paris, France, and made his formal debut as a professional pianist there in 1849. He returned to the United States in 1853 and toured the country until 1856. He performed in Cuba in 1854 and went there again in 1857, touring the Caribbean and South America. He settled in Basse-Terre, Guadeloupe, in 1859–1860. He was in Cuba again from 1860 to 1862, in the United States from 1862 to 1865, and toured South America from 1865 until his death. Died December 18, 1869, in Tijuca, Brazil. *References*: *DAB*; *The New Grove Dictionary of Music and Musicians*, ed. Stanley Sadie (London, 1980), 7:570–74; F. C. Lange, *Vida y Muerte de Louis Moreau Gottschalk en Rio de Janeiro (1869)* (Mendoza, Argentina, 1951); V. Loggins, *Where the Word Ends: The Life of Louis Moreau Gottschalk* (Baton Rouge, La., 1958); L. A. Rubin, "Gottschalk in Cuba," Ph.D. diss., Columbia University, 1974; Robert Stevenson, "Gottschalk en Buenos Aires," *Inter-American Music Bulletin*, No. 74 (1969): 3–12; and Robert Stevenson, "Gottschalk en el Oester Sudamericano," *Inter-American Music Bulletin*, no. 74 (1969): 13–28.

GOULD, BENJAMIN APTHORP (1824–1896). Astronomer, born September 27, 1824, in Boston. Gould graduated from Harvard University and studied in Berlin and Gottingen. From 1849 until 1861, he published, at his own expense, the *Astronomical Journal*. He organized the Dudley Observatory in Albany, New York, from 1855 to 1858. He came to Argentina in 1871, built the national observatory of the Argentine Republic in Córdoba and was its director until 1885. Studying the southern skies, he prepared *Uranometria Argentina: Brightness and Position of Every Fixed Star, down to the Seventh Magnitude within One Hundred Degrees of the South Pole* (Buenos Aires, 1879), and *Córdoba Photographs. Photographic Observations of Star-Clusters from Impressions Made at the Argentine National Observatory* (Lynn, Mass., 1897). He also organized the national meteorological office and established a chain of meteorological stations throughout Argentina. He returned to the United States in 1885. Died November 26, 1896, in Cambridge, Massachusetts. *References*: Alice Bache Gould Papers, Massachusetts Historical Society Library, Boston; *DAB*; *Drees*; *NCAB* 3:108; and J. E. Hodge, "Benjamin Apthorp Gould and the Founding of the Argentine National Observatory," *TA* 28 (1971): 152–75.

GRAHAM, (NORA) AGNES (1888–1947). Missionary educator, born February 22, 1888, in Yoakum, Texas. Graham was a missionary under the Foreign Mission Board of the Southern Baptist Convention* in Chile from 1920 until her death. She was involved in building and directing Colegio Bautista in Temuco, a Baptist school patronized by many Catholic families. She wrote *Pioneering with Christ in Chile* (Nashville, Tenn., 1942). Died January 15, 1947, in Concepcion, Chile. *References*: *ESB*; and Robert C. Moore, *Agnes Graham of Chile* (Nashville, Tenn., 1954).

GRAHAM, JOHN (1774–1820). Diplomat, born in Dumfries, Prince William County, Virginia. Graham graduated from Columbia College. He then moved to Mason County, Kentucky, and served in the state legislature in 1800–1801. He was secretary of legation and later U.S. chargé d'affaires in Madrid from 1801 to 1803, secretary of the Territory of Orleans (Louisiana) from 1804 to 1807, and chief clerk in the State Department from 1807 to 1817. With Caesar Augustus Rodney* and Theodorick Bland,* he was a member of a special commission to obtain information on the condition and political prospects of the

Spanish provinces in South America that were contending for independence, and indeed he prepared the report. He was U.S. minister to Portugal, resident in Brazil, in 1819–1820. Died August 6, 1820, in Washington, D.C. *References*: *DAB*; *DADH*; and *NCAB* 11:307.

GRAHAM, MARY (OLSTINE) (1842–1902). Educator, born August 13, 1842, in St. Louis, Missouri. Graham graduated from Winona normal school. She taught in St. Louis. She went to Argentina in 1879, taught in normal schools in Paraná and San Juan, and was head of the normal school in La Plata from 1884 until her death. Died March 10, 1902, in La Plata, Argentina. *References*: *Cutolo*; *Luiggi*; and *Udaondo*.

GRAYBILL, ANTHONY (THOMAS) (1841–1905). Missionary, born February 24, 1841, in Botetourt County, Virginia. Graybill graduated from Roanoke College and the Union Theological Seminary of Virginia and was ordained in 1873. He served in the Confederate Army during the Civil War. He was a missionary under the Board of Foreign Missions of the Presbyterian Church in the United States* in Mexico from 1874 until his death, serving in Matamoros from 1874 to 1888 and in Linares from 1888 until 1905. Died January 21, 1905, in Linares, Mexico. *Reference*: *MDPC*.

GREBLE, EDWIN ST. JOHN (1859–1931). Army officer, born June 24, 1859, in West Point, New York. Greble graduated from the U.S. Military Academy in 1881 and was commissioned second lieutenant in the artillery. He served in the Spanish-American War. He was superintendent of public buildings and charities in Havana and administered the department of corrections and charities in the Secretario del Governacion of Cuba from 1906 to 1908, during the second United States intervention. He was a member of the U.S. Army general staff from 1910 to 1914 and served on the Mexican border from 1914 to 1917 and during World War I. He retired in 1918 with the rank of brigadier general. Died September 30, 1931, in West Orange, New Jersey. *References*: *NCAB* 23:198; *NYT*, October 1, 1931; and *WWWA*.

GREEN, BENJAMIN EDWARDS (1822–1907). Diplomat, born February 5, 1822, in Elkton, Kentucky. Green graduated from Georgetown College and studied at the University of Virginia. He practiced law in New Orleans. He was secretary of legation in Mexico from 1843 to 1845, serving as chargé d'affaires ad interim in 1844. He practiced law in Washington, D.C., from 1845 to 1849. He was sent by President Zachary Taylor on an unsuccessful special mission to the West Indies in 1849, in an attempt to purchase Cuba and to arrange for a naval station at Samaná Bay in the Dominican Republic. He was later involved in industrial endeavors in Georgia. Died May 12, 1907, in Dalton, Georgia.

References: *DAB*; *DADH*; and *NCAB* 5:531.

GREEN, GEORGE MASON (1836–1912). Soldier, born in New Brunswick in 1836. Green went to California in 1852, was an itinerant photographer in Mexico, joined the Mexican Army in 1858, and served in it until 1867. He was chief of staff to General Gaspar Sanchez Ochoa. He became commander of the American Legion of Honor* in 1867. He resided in Mexico for the rest of his life. *References*: George Mason Green, "Statement of His Recollections of Life in Mexico, 1853–1855" (Ms.), Bancroft Library, University of California at Berkeley; *Daily Mexican and Mining Press* [Mexico City], January 16, 1912.

GREENE, WILLIAM C(ORNELL) (1851–1911). Entrepreneur, born in Chappaqua, Westchester County, New York. Greene was a government contractor in Kansas and Colorado, a cowboy in Arizona, and later a miner in Tombstone, Arizona. He obtained possession of a tract of land known as La Cananea in the state of Sonora, Mexico, in the 1890s. In 1899, he formed the Cananea Consolidated Copper Company and copper ore was discovered in 1903. He bought large sections of Sonora for ranching and organized several other companies, even building a railroad to his Cananea holdings. He lost control of the company in 1906 and most of his fortune in 1907, except for the Mexican cattle ranches, which he managed until his death. Died August 5, 1911, in Cananea, Sonora, Mexico. *References*: *BDABL*; Marvin D. Bernstein, "Colonel William C. Greene and the Cananea Copper Bubble," *Bulletin of the Business Historical Society* 26 (1952): 179–98; *DAB*; A. Frederick Mignone, "A Fief for Mexico: Colonel Greene's Empire Ends," *Southwest Review* 44 (1959): 332–39; *NYT*, August 6, 1911; *Pletcher*, ch. 7; C. L. Sonnichsen, *Colonel Greene and the Copper Skyrocket: The Spectacular Rise and Fall of William Cornell Greene: Copper King, Cattle Baron, and Promoter Extraordinary in Mexico, the American Southwest, and the New York Financial District* (Tucson, Ariz., 1974); and C. L. Sonnichsen, "Colonel William C. Greene and the Strike at Cananea, Sonora, 1906," *Arizona and the West* 13 (1971): 343–68.

GRENADA, INVASION OF (1983). With support from most island nations of the Caribbean, the United States landed forces in Grenada in 1983 to overthrow a communist regime supported by Cuba. *References*: Mark Adkin, *Urgent Fury: The Battle for Grenada* (Lexington, Mass., 1989); Peter M. Dunn and Bruce W. Watson, eds., *American Intervention in Grenada: The Implications of Operation "Urgent Fury"* (Boulder, Colo., 1985); William Gilmore, *The Grenada Intervention: Analysis and Documentation* (London, 1984); *Musicant*, ch. 9; Hugh O'Shaughnessy, *Grenada: Revolution, Invasion and Aftermath* (London, 1984); Gregory Sanford and Richard Vigilante, *Grenada: The Untold Story* (Lanham, Md., 1984); and Ronald H. Spector, *U.S. Marines in Grenada 1983* (Washington, D.C., 1987).

GREVSTAD, NICOLAY ANDREAS (1851–1940). Journalist and diplomat, born June 2, 1851, in the parish of Sykkelven, Sondmore, Norway. Grevstad studied at the University of Oslo (Norway), practiced law in Oslo, and was editor in chief of the Christiana *Dagbladet*. He came to the United States in 1883, was editorial writer for the *Nordvesten* in St. Paul, Minnesota, from 1883 to 1886, resumed editorial charge of the Christiana *Dagbladet* in 1886–1887, and was the assistant editorial writer for the Minneapolis *Tribune*. He was that paper's leading editorial writer until 1890, editor and publisher of the Minneapolis *Times* from 1890 to 1892, and editor of the Chicago *Daily Skandinaven* from 1892 to 1911. He was U.S. minister to Paraguay and Uruguay from 1912 to 1914 and minister to Uruguay in 1914–1915. He concluded an extradition treaty with Paraguay. He was director of the Republican national committee for foreign language newspapers from 1919 to 1925, representative of a Chicago financial syndicate at Montevideo, Uruguay, in 1926–1927, and again editor of the Chicago *Daily Skandinaven* from 1930 until his death. Died February 20, 1940, in Chicago. *References*: *NCAB* 29:127; and *WWWA*.

GRISCOM, LUDLOW (1890–1959). Ornithologist, born June 17, 1890, in New York City. Griscom graduated from Columbia and Cornell universities. He was an assistant in the Department of Ornithology in the American Museum of Natural History from 1917 to 1921, served in army intelligence during World War I, and was assistant curator of ornithology at the museum from 1921 to 1927. He participated in expeditions to Nicaragua in 1917, to Panama in 1924 and 1927, and to Yucatán in 1926. He was a research curator in zoology at the Museum of Comparative Zoology at Harvard University after 1927. He directed a Harvard University expedition to Guatemala in 1930. He wrote *The Distribution of Bird Life in Guatemala* (New York, 1932), *The Ornithology of the Caribbean Coast of Extreme Eastern Panama* (Cambridge, Mass., 1934), *Ornithology of Guerrero, Mexico* (Cambridge, Mass., 1934), *The Ornithology of the Republic of Panama* (Cambridge, Mass., 1935), and *Distribution and Origin of the Birds of Mexico* (Cambridge, Mass., 1950), and was coauthor of *Birds of Lower Amazon* (Cambridge, Mass., 1941). Died May 28, 1959, in Cambridge, Massachusetts. *References*: *ACAB*; *DAB S6*; *NCAB* 61:189; *NYT*, May 29, 1959; and *WWWA*.

GROVES, WALLACE (1901–1988). Financier, born March 20, 1901, in Norfolk, Virginia. Groves graduated from Georgetown University and was admitted to the bar in 1925. He practiced law and then engaged in the reorganization and management of industrial and financial concerns in New York City. He was a successful investor and was involved in several businesses. His Wall Street career ended in 1941, when he was convicted for mail fraud; he spent two years in federal prison. Late in the 1940s, he became interested in Grand Bahama Island and bought 114,000 acres there. In 1955 he negotiated an agreement with the Bahamian government. He received a wide range of tax concessions as the president of the Grand Bahama Port Authority Limited, in return for attracting and developing industrial and commercial enterprises. He was also responsible for developing utilities, schools, roads, and hospitals. One of his companies, Bahamas Amusement Limited, had the exclusive gambling license for Freeport. He was a major stockholder and chairman of the board of Grand Bahama Port Authority, Limited, and founder of the city of Freeport in Grand Bahama Island, developing it into a major resort and gambling area. He lived in Freeport but also owned a private island, Little Whale Clay, south of Grand Bahama until 1985. Died January 30, 1988, in Miami, Florida. *References*: *NYT*, February 2, 1988; and *WWA*.

GROW, HAROLD B(ARTLEY) (1891–1981). Aviator, born July 5, 1891, in Greenville, Michigan. Grow graduated from the U.S. Naval Academy in 1912. He served on the staff of Northern Bombing Group in France during World War I, was on the staff of aircraft squadrons of the U.S. Battle Fleet from 1920 to 1922, commanding officer of the U.S. Naval Flying School in 1923, and aviation member of the U.S. naval mission to Peru in 1923. He remained in Peru from 1924 to 1930, serving under President August B. Leguía. He created and became first director of the Peruvian naval air service and later was inspector general of the Peruvian air forces. In 1928, he instituted the first true domestic airline in Peru, and was eventually director general of Peruvian sea and land aviation. He was imprisoned in Arequipa, Peru, as the result of Sanchez Cerro's successful revolt but was later released. He then organized, and was president and manager of, Barkeley-Grow Aircraft Corporation from 1936 to 1938. He served in the U.S. Navy during World War II. Died January 28, 1981, in Pensacola, Florida. *References*: *Who's Who in Aviation 1942–43* (Chicago, 1983).

GRUENING, ERNEST (HENRY) (1887–1974). Journalist and public official, born February 6, 1887, in New York City. Gruening graduated from Harvard University and Harvard Medical School but never practiced medicine. He was a journalist in Boston from 1911 to 1917. He served in the U.S. Army during World War I. He was general manager of *La Prensa* in 1919–1920 and managing editor of *The Nation* from 1920 to 1923 and wrote *Mexico and Its Heritage* (New York, 1928). He was founding editor of the Portland (Me.) *Evening News* from 1927 to 1932, director of the Division of Territories and Island Possessions in the U.S. Department of the Interior from 1934 to 1939, territorial governor of Alaska from 1939 to 1953, and U.S. senator from 1958 to 1968. He wrote *Many Battles: The Autobiography of Ernest Gruening* (New York, 1973). Died June 26, 1974, in Washington, D.C. *References*: Ernest Gruening Papers, University of Alaska Library, Fairbanks; *CB* 1966; Thomas A. McMullin and David Walker, *Biographical Directory of American Territorial Governors* (Westport, Ct., 1984); Eugenia W. de Meyer, *Ernest Gruening: Experiencias y Commentarios sobre el Mexico Post-revolucionario* (Mexico, 1970); *NCAB* J:386; *NYT*, June 27, 1974; *Polprof:Eisenhower*; *Polprof:Johnson*; Polprof:Kennedy; *Pol-*

prof:Truman; and Sherwood Ross, *Gruening of Alaska: The Dynamic Career of a Remarkable U.S. Senator* (New York, 1968).

GUANTANAMO BAY, CUBA. U.S. naval base, established in 1898 at the southeastern tip of the island, after it was taken over during the Spanish-American War. It was officially granted in 1901 and transferred in 1903. In 1934, a treaty granted Guantanamo to the United States in perpetuity. *References*: Rigoberto Cruz Diax, *Guantanamo Bay* (Santiago de Chile, 1977); Marion Murphy, *The History of Guantanamo Bay, Cuba* (Guantanamo Bay, Cuba, 1964); Bradley M. Reynolds, "Guantanamo Bay, Cuba: The History of an American Naval Base and Its Relationship to the Formulation of United States Foreign Policy and Military Strategy toward the Caribbean, 1895–1910," Ph.D. diss., University of Southern California, 1982; and Martin J. Scheina, "The U.S. Presence in Guantanamo," *Strategic Review* 4 (Spring 1976): 81–88.

GUARDIA NACIONAL DOMINICANA. A constabulary, created by U.S. authorities in 1917 to replace all other armed forces in the Dominican Republic and to function, under U.S. guidance, as a police force to keep order and to supplement U.S. Marine efforts to combat insurgents. It was staffed and trained by U.S. officers until 1924. By 1927 it had become the Dominican Army. *Reference*: Marvin Goldwert, *The Constabulary in the Dominican Republic and Nicaragua: Progeny and Legacy of United States Intervention* (Gainesville, Fla., 1962).

GUARDIA NACIONAL DE NICARAGUA. A nonpartisan national guard created by the United States in Nicaragua in 1925 and commanded by U.S. officers. The United States hoped that it would serve to perpetuate constitutional government in Nicaragua; instead, it became a powerful armed force after the U.S. Marines departed and was used by Anastasio Somoza to seize political power in Nicaragua and to guarantee his "dynasty" until 1979. *References*: Marvin Goldwert, *The Constabulary in the Dominican Republic and Nicaragua: Progeny and Legacy of United States Intervention* (Gainesville, Fla., 1962), and Richard Millett, *Guardians of the Dynasty: A History of the U.S.-Created Guardia Nacional de Nicaragua and the Somoza Family* (Maryknoll, N.Y., 1977).

GUATEMALAN CRISIS (1954). The United States government, on behalf of United Fruit Company,* conspired to overthrow the government of Jacobo Arbenz in Guatemala after it expropriated land owned by United Fruit. In Operation *Success*, the U.S. Central Intelligence Agency (CIA) instigated an invasion of Guatemala leading to a coup that ousted Arbenz, put in power a government more compatible with United Fruit, and returned the land to that company. *References*: Richard B. Chardkoff, "Communist Toehold in the Americas: A History of Official United States Involvement in the Guatemalan Crisis, 1954," Ph.D. diss., Florida State University, 1967; Richard H. Immerman, *The CIA in*

Guatemala: The Forgotten Policy of Intervention (Austin, Tex., 1982); Stephen Schlessinger and Stephen Kinzer, *Bitter Fruit: The Untold Story of the American Coup in Guatemala* (Garden City, N.Y., 1982); and J. M. Aybar de Soto, *Dependence and Intervention: the Case of Guatemala in 1954* (Boulder, Colo., 1978).

GUAYAQUIL-QUITO RAILWAY. Construction of the railroad from Guayaquil to Quito in Ecuador was authorized in 1865, and the line connecting Durán to Chimbo was completed in 1887. In 1897, Archer Harman* was authorized by the Ecuadorian government to form the Guayaquil and Quito Railway Company. New construction under the direction of the American John Harmer began in 1899 and was completed in 1908. *Reference*: Dawn A. Wiles, "Land Transportation within Ecuador," Ph.D. diss., Louisiana State University, 1971.

GUGGENHEIM, HARRY F(RANK) (1890–1971). Businessman, born August 23, 1890, in West End, New Jersey. Guggenheim attended Sheffield Scientific School of Yale University and graduated from Cambridge University. After 1918, he worked on developing mining properties for American Smelting and Refining Company* (ASARCO). From 1916 to 1923, he played a leading role in the operation of the Latin American interests of Guggenheim Brothers. He left the business in 1926, and was president of the Daniel Guggenheim Foundation for the Promotion of Aeronautics. He was U.S. ambassador to Cuba from 1929 to 1933. He devoted his time to prevail on dictator General Gerardo Machado y Morales to not murder his political enemies. He wrote *The United States and Cuba: A Study in International Relations* (New York, 1934). After 1939, he was owner of *Newsday*. Died January 22, 1971, in Sands Point, Long Island, New York. *References*: *BDABL*; *CB* 1956; *DADH*; *NCAB* 57:127; and *NYT*, January 23, 1971.

GUGGENHEIM ENTERPRISES. M. Guggenheim and Sons was created in 1875. It became involved in mining in 1879 and in smelting in 1888. It opened a smelter in Monterey, California, in 1892, and in Aguascalientes, Mexico, in 1894. It assumed control in :900 of the American Smelting and Refining Company* (ASARCO). It acquired the Braden Copper Company in 1908 (transferred control to Kennecott Copper Company in 1915). It bought Chuquicamata mine in northern Chile and formed Chile Copper Company (sold to the Anaconda Corporation in 1923). It became involved in nitrates in Chile in 1924, and formed the Compañía de Salitre de Chile (Cosach) in 1931. *References*: John H. Davis, *The Guggenheims: An American Epic* (New York, 1978); Edwin P. Hoyt, Jr., *The Guggenheims and the American Dream* (New York, 1967); Milton Lomask, *Seed Money: The Guggenheim Story* (New York, 1964); Thomas F. O'Brien, " 'Rich beyond the Dreams of Avarice': The Guggenheims in Chile," *Business History Review* 63 (1989): 122–59; and Harvey O'Connor, *The Guggenheims* (New York, 1937).

GULF AND WESTERN. Conglomerate that entered the Caribbean in 1967 when it bought the South Puerto Rican Sugar Company and became the largest private landowner in the Dominican Republic as well as the largest taxpayer and employer. In 1984, it had twenty-six subsidiaries in manufacturing and agriculture in the Caribbean. After 1967, when Gulf and Western acquired the South Puerto Rico Sugar Company, it invested over two hundred million dollars in some ninety businesses in the Dominican Republic. It was involved in sugar, tourism, cattle ranching, real estate, and other small businesses. Its chairman, Charles Bluhdorn, became personally interested in the Dominican Republic. In 1985, after Bluhdorn's death, its holdings in the Dominican republic were sold to a Miami-based group. *Reference*: Hank Frundt, *Gulf & Western in the Dominican Republic: An Evaluation* (New York, 1980).

GULICK, JOHN W(ILEY) (1874–1939). Army officer, born November 8, 1874, in Goldsboro, North Carolina. He joined the North Carolina Infantry in 1894, served in the Spanish-American War in Cuba and in the Philippine-American War until 1901. He entered the regular army in 1901. He was U.S. military attaché in Santiago, Chile, in 1911–1912. He was instructor of coast artillery in Chile's military school after 1912 and adviser on coast defense with the Chilean government with the rank of major. He established and conducted a gunnery school for training Chilean coast artillery troops and carried out a program for the reorganization and rearmament of the coast defense of that country. He served during World War I and with the War Plans division of the General Staff in Washington, D.C., from 1920 to 1924. He was chief of coast artillery from 1930 to 1934. He retired with the rank of brigadier general in 1938. Died August 18, 1939, in Portland, Maine. *References*: *NCAB* 31:314; and *WWWA*.

H

H. C. EMERY CLAIM (1908–1909). John D. Emery Company of Boston, a large wood product company, established itself in the Mosquito Reservation on the east coast of Nicaragua in 1884 to cut mahogany. In 1908, the Nicaraguan government canceled the concession of the company. In 1909, the U.S. government forced Nicaragua to pay Emery for its interest. The actions of the Nicaraguan government in this affair contributed to the U.S. decision to support a revolution that overthrew that government. *Reference*: *DADH*.

HAITI, INTERVENTION IN (1915–1934). Following violence and bloodshed and the failure of the Haitians to produce a government able to maintain order, U.S. Marines landed in Port-au-Prince, Haiti, in 1915 to protect American financial interests in that country. The U.S. forces restored order, crushed overt resistance, build roads with forced labor, and tried to improve the economic, educational, and health conditions in Haiti. The Haitian government remained dominated by heavy U.S. control and a U.S. high commissioner headed the combined military and civilian structure from 1922 to 1929. U.S. forces withdrew from Haiti in 1934. *References*: Donald B. Cooper, "The Withdrawal of the United States from Haiti, 1928–1934," *JIAS* 5 (1963): 83–101; David F. Healy, *Gunboat Diplomacy in the Wilson Era: The U.S. Navy in Haiti, 1915–1916* (Madison, Wis., 1976); *Langley*, chs. 10–12; Richard Millett with G. Dale Gaddy, "Administering the Protectorates: The U.S. Occupation of Haiti and the Dominican Republic," *Revista/Review Interamericana* 6 (1976): 383–402; D. G. Munro, "The American Withdrawal from Haiti, 1929–1934," *HAHR* 49 (1969): 1–26; *Musicant*, ch. 5; Walter H. Posner, "American Marines in Haiti, 1915–1922," *TA* 20 (1964): 231–66; and Hans Schmidt, *The United States Occupation of Haiti, 1915–1934* (New Brunswick, N.J., 1971).

HALE, ALBERT (BARLOW) (1860–1929). Traveler, born June 5, 1860, in Jonesville, Michigan. Hale graduated from the University of Michigan and the Chicago Medical College and studied at the University of Strassburg, Germany.

He was associate clinical professor of opthalmology at Rush Medical College in Chicago from 1901 to 1903 but withdrew from active professional life in 1905 to travel in South America. He was employed by the Pan-American Union in Washington from 1908 to 1914 and was commercial attaché for the U.S. Department of Commerce to Argentina, Uruguay, and Paraguay after 1914. He wrote *The South Americans: the Story of the South American Republics, Their Characteristics, Progress and Tendencies* (Indianapolis, 1907) and *Practical Guide to Latin America, including Mexico, Central America, the West Indies and South America* (Boston, 1909). Died April 30, 1929, in San Juan, Puerto Rico. *Reference: WWWA.*

HALE, EDWARD J(OSEPH) (1839–1922). Editor and diplomat, born December 25, 1839, in Fayetteville, North Carolina. Hale graduated from the University of North Carolina. He served in the Confederate Army during the Civil War. He then worked for the Fayetteville *Observer* and was its editor from 1882 to 1913. He was U.S. consul in Manchester, England, from 1885 to 1889, and commissioner for the North of England Trust Company in India in 1889–1890. He was U.S. minister to Costa Rica from 1913 to 1919 and kept the Germans from getting a concession for a wireless station in Costa Rica. Died February 15, 1922, in Fayetteville, North Carolina. *References: DAB; DADH; NCAB* 19:200; *NYT*, February 16, 1922; and *WWWA.*

HALE, SAMUEL B(ROWN) (1804–1888). Businessman, born March 13, 1804, in Boston. Hale graduated from Harvard University. He first came to Argentina as a supercargo in 1830. In 1833, he founded Samuel B. Hale and Company, the principal American importing and exporting house in Buenos Aires. He later established a banking firm and was involved in floating loans for Argentina national and provincial governments. In 1888, he contracted to construct the Buenos Aires water and sewage works and played a leading role in the construction of Western Railway in Argentina. He was a member of the municipality of Buenos Aires. Died September 11, 1888, in Buenos Aires. *References: Cutolo;* and *Drees.*

HALE, WILLIAM BAYARD (1869–1924). Author, born April 6, 1869, in Richmond, Virginia. Hale attended Boston and Harvard universities. He became a writer and lecturer, writing for various magazines, and was a correspondent of the *New York Times* in Paris in 1907. He was a special agent of President Woodrow Wilson to Mexico in 1913 and recommended not recognizing the Victoriano Huerta regime, a policy adopted by the president. He worked for the German information service during World War I, distributing pro-German propaganda in the United States. He went to Germany after the war. Died April 10, 1924, in Munich, Germany. *References: DAB; DADH; Hill; IAB; NCAB* 15:182; and George J. Rausch, Jr., "Poison-Pen Diplomacy: Mexico, 1913," *TA* 24 (1968): 272–80.

HALL, HENRY C(OOK) (1820?–1901). Diplomat, from New York. Hall was deputy consul in Matanzas, Cuba, in 1863–1864, consul from 1864 to 1873, and consul general in Havana from 1873 to 1882. He was U.S. minister to Costa Rica, El Salvador, Guatemala, Honduras, and Nicaragua from 1882 to 1889. In 1884, he initiated treaty negotiations with Nicaragua concerning an Isthmian canal treaty. *References*: *DADH*; and *NCAB* 5:551.

HALLET, STEPHEN ("DON ESTEBAN") (fl. 1821–1870). Publisher, born in the southern United States. Hallet lived in Buenos Aires from 1821 to 1852. He published books and a chain of newspapers and magazines. He published *El Museum Argentino* from 1835 to 1837, the first illustrated magazine in South America. In 1837 he brought modern printing presses from the United States and became the owner of the most modern publishing plants in South America. He was awarded the printing contracts of the Argentine government from 1829 to 1852. He contributed much to the development of the Argentine printing and graphic art industry. He returned to the United States in 1852 and continued to publish in New York City, mostly in Spanish, until his retirement in 1870. *Reference*: *Cutolo*.

HALLIWELL, LEO B(LAIR) (1891–1967). Medical missionary, born October 15, 1891, in Odessa, Nebraska. Halliwell graduated from the College of Medical Evangelists (Loma Linda, Calif.). He was a medical missionary under the Mission Board of the Seventh-Day Adventists in Brazil from 1921 until 1959. He served in the state of Bahia from 1921 to 1928 and later in east and north Brazil. After 1930, he had an aquatic clinic, on the boat *Luzeiro*, which served people along the Amazon River, between Belém and Manaus. In 1942 he opened a clinic in Belém, which became a hospital by 1957. In 1956 he became supervisor of the work of Adventist medical launches in South America. He wrote *Light in the Jungle; the Thirty Years' Mission of Leo and Jessie Halliwell along the Amazon*, ed. Will Oursler (New York, 1959). Died April 19, 1967, in Vista, California. *Reference*: *SDAE*.

HALLOCK, JAMES C. (1869–1918). Engineer, born December 8, 1869, in Treasure City, Nevada. Hallock graduated from Rensselaer Polytechnic Institute (Troy, N.Y.). He went to South America in 1891 and was engineer of the state of Esmeraldas from 1894 to 1903 and director general of public works of that state from 1903 to 1906, when a revolution in Ecuador threw him out of office and he returned to the United States. He was assistant to the chief engineer, and later deputy chief engineer, of Newark, New Jersey. He returned to Ecuador in 1918 to become engineer to that republic, with the task of curbing the annual floods in the River Jubones. Died November 2, 1918, in Ecuador. *References*: Newark (N.J.) *News*, November 13, 1918; and *NYT*, November 14, 1918.

HALSEY, THOMAS LLOYD (ca. 1776–1855). Businessman and consul, born in Providence, Rhode Island. Halsey graduated from the College of Rhode Island (later Brown University). He entered private business. By 1807, he was engaged in commercial activities in Buenos Aires. He is said to have introduced the first merino sheep into Argentina in 1813. He was U.S. consul in Buenos Aires from 1812 to 1819. He furthered commercial ties between Rio de la Plata and the United States, took an active part in local politics, and supplied U.S. arms and munitions to the armies of General José de San Martin. He also commissioned, illegally, privateers against Spain. His recall was requested in 1818 and he was ordered to leave the United Provinces of the Plate River. However, he remained in business in Buenos Aires and amassed a considerable fortune. In the 1830s, he returned to Providence and was director of the Providence National Bank. Died February 2, 1855, in Providence, Rhode Island. *References*: Charles L. Chandler, "The First Yankee Consul in Buenos Aires: Interesting Activities of Thomas Lloyd Halsey from 1813 to 1818," *Comments on Argentine Trade* 1 (July 1922): 1–7; *Cutolo*; *DAB*; *DADH*; William Dusenberry, "Halsey's Claim against the Government of Buenos Aires, 1818–1859," *IAEA* 13 (Spring 1960): 95–107; and *WWWA*.

HAM, CLIFFORD DUDLEY (1861–1950). Government official, born January 2, 1861, in Detroit. Ham graduated from Yale University. He was secretary to the governor of Iowa and then in newspaper work in Dubuque, Iowa. He served during the Spanish-American War. He was editor of the *Dubuque Herald* until 1903. He served in the customs service in the Philippines from 1903 to 1911 and was collector of customs at Iloilo and surveyor of the port in Manila. He was collector general of customs for the republic of Nicaragua by appointment of the president of Nicaragua and fiscal agent for bonded foreign loans of Nicaragua from 1911 until his retirement in 1928. Died January 10, 1950, in Akron, Ohio. *References*: *NYT*, January 12, 1950; and *WWWA*.

HAMILTON, CHARLES W(ALTER) (1890–1972). Petroleum geologist and executive, born April 8, 1890, in Ithaca, Michigan. Hamilton attended Alma College and graduated from the University of Oklahoma. He was field geologist for the Cia Mexicana del Petrolo (Eagle Oil Company) in El Aguila, Mexico, from 1912 to 1915. He was chief geologist of the Mexican Gulf Oil Company in Tampico in 1916–1917 and general agent in Mexico from 1917 to 1922. He was assistant to the vice president of Gulf Oil Companies in New York City from 1923 to 1940, vice president of Gulf Oil Corporation from 1940 to 1957, and chairman of Gulf Eastern Company from 1954 until his retirement in 1957. He wrote *Early Day Oil Tales of Mexico* (Houston, 1966). Died December 9, 1972, in Montclair, New Jersey. *References*: *Montclair Times*, December 14, 1972; and *WWWA*.

HAMILTON, HIRAM P(HILETUS) (1851–1905). Clergyman, born November 28, 1851, in Shekomeko, New York. Hamilton graduated from Princeton University and Union Theological Seminary and was ordained in 1879. He was the first resident agent of the American Bible Society* in Mexico from 1879 until his death. Died April 20, 1905, in Mexico City. *Reference: Alumni Catalogue of the Union Theological Seminary in the City of New York* (New York, 1927).

HANNA, BAYLISS W. (1830–1891). Lawyer and diplomat, born March 14, 1830, in Troy, Ohio, and grew up in Crawfordsville, Indiana. Hanna graduated from Wabash College and was admitted to the bar in 1855. He practiced law in Crawfordsville in 1855–1856 and in Terre Haute, Indiana, after 1857. He was a member of the Indiana legislature from 1862 to 1864 and of the Indiana Senate in 1864, and attorney general of Indiana 1870 to 1872. He was U.S. minister to Argentina from 1885 to 1888. Died August 2, 1891, in Crawfordsville, Indiana. *Reference: NCAB* 12:118.

HANNA, MATTHEW ELTING (1873–1936). Diplomat, born March 9, 1873, in Gillespieville, Ohio. Hanna graduated from the U.S. Military Academy in 1897. He served during the Spanish-American War. He was aide-de-camp to Major General Leonard Wood from 1898 to 1902, as well as commissioner of public schools, and he was a military attaché in Cuba from 1902 to 1904. He resigned from the army in 1913 and was employed by a chemical manufacturing firm until 1917. He was third secretary in the embassy in Mexico 1917 to 1921, chief of the division of Mexican affairs in the State Department from 1921 to 1924, first secretary of embassy in Germany in 1924–1925, and diplomatic inspector for Latin America in 1925–1926 and for Europe in 1927. He was counselor of embassy in Peru in 1927 to 1929 and U.S. minister to Nicaragua from 1929 to 1933. His service coincided with the occupation of Nicaragua by U.S. Marines and he assisted in formulating a program for the withdrawal of the Marines by 1933. As chairman of the central relief committee he was involved in the relief activities following the earthquake and fire in Managua in 1931. He was U.S. minister to Guatemala from 1933 until his death. Died February 19, 1936, in Tucson, Arizona. *References: NCAB* 27:459; and *WWWA*.

HANSON, EARL PARKER (1899–1978). Geographer, born March 16, 1899, in Berlin, Germany, to American parents, and returned to the United States in 1911. Hanson graduated from the University of Wisconsin and studied at Columbia University and the University of Chicago. He conducted an expedition to the Amazon and Orinoco basins for the Carnegie Institution of Washington from 1931 to 1933 to study the fluctuation of the magnetic field, was planning consultant for the Puerto Rico Reconstruction Administration in San Juan in 1935–1936, and served with U.S. Coordinator of Inter-American Affairs in 1941–1942. He served in the U.S. Army during World War II. He studied navigation possibilities in the Amazon basin in 1943 with U.S. Army Engineers expedition and conducted an expedition to Monagas, Venezuela, in 1954–1955, for Creole Petroleum Company. He was professor of geography at the University of Delaware from 1949 to 1955 and consultant to the Department of State of the Commonwealth of Puerto Rico in San Juan from 1955 to 1969. He wrote *Journey to Manaos* (New York, 1938), *Chile: Land of Progress* (New York, 1941), *The Amazon: A New Frontier?* (New York, 1944), *Transformation: The Story of Modern Puerto Rico* (New York, 1955), *Puerto Rico: Land of Wonders* (New York, 1960), and *Puerto Rico: Ally for Progress* (Princeton, N.J., 1962), and edited *South from the Spanish Main; South America Seen through the Eyes of Its Discoverers* (New York, 1967). Died July 19, 1978. *References*: *AMWS*; *CA*; and *WWWA*.

HANSON, HENRY (1877–1954). Public health official, born July 4, 1877, in Glenwood Township, South Dakota. Hanson graduated from Johns Hopkins University School of Medicine. He was assistant superintendent and pathologist at the Milwaukee County Hospital from 1908 to 1910, and director of the Florida State Board of Health bacteriological laboratories from 1909 to 1916, and served in the U.S. Army Medical Corps during World War I. He was chief sanitary inspector for the Panama Canal Zone in 1918–1919, assistant chief health officer for the Panama Canal Health Department after 1919, and later director of yellow fever control for the national health department of Peru. He was instrumental in the survey of Lima which led to the eradication of yellow fever and the reduction of malaria in Peru's Pacific areas. He was a member of the special field staff of Rockefeller Foundation from 1923 to 1927, field medical officer for the Florida State Board of Health in 1928–1929, and state health officer of Florida from 1929 to 1936 and again from 1942 to his retirement in 1945. Died February 13, 1954, in Jacksonville, Florida. *Reference*: *Journal of the American Medical Association* 155 (May 29, 1954): 503.

HARDENBURG, WALTER ERNEST (1886–1956). Traveler, born in Illinois and grew up in Youngville, New York. Hardenburg traveled in South America from 1907 to 1909 and went down the Putumayo River. He narrated his adventures in *The Putumayo, the Devil's Paradise: Travels in the Peruvian Amazon Region and an Account of the Atrocities Committed upon the Indians Therein* (London, 1912), which led to the creation of a British commission to investigate the situation. He emigrated to Canada in 1910 and settled in Red Deer, Alberta, in 1911. *Reference*: Anthony Smith, *Explorers of the Amazon* (New York, 1989), ch. 9.

HARMAN, ARCHER (1860–1911). Engineer, born in Staunton, Virginia. Harman left home at an early age and worked for contractors who built railroads. He then obtained a contract for building the Colorado Midland Railroad. A close and intimate friend of President Eloy Alfaro y Arosmena of Ecuador, in 1897 he received a contract for building a railroad from Guayaquil to Quito. He directed the actual construction, was president of the Guayaquil and Quito Railroad Company, and was vice president of Harman Company. He returned to the United States in 1910. Died October 9, 1911, in Hot Springs, Virginia. *References*: Albert F. Kunze, *Who's Who on the Postage Stamps of Ecuador* (Washington, D.C., 1953), pp. 23–33; and *NYT*, October 10, 1911.

HARNER, MICHAEL J(AMES) (1929–   ). Anthropologist, born April 27, 1929, in Washington, D.C. Harner graduated from the University of California at Berkeley. He was assistant professor at Arizona State University from 1958 to 1961, senior museum anthropologist at the Lowie Museum of the University of California and then associate research anthropologist and assistant director from 1961 to 1967, and associate professor and then professor at the New School of Social Research (New York City) after 1970. He carried out research in the upper Amazon basin in 1956–1957, 1960–1961, 1964, 1969, and 1973, and wrote *The Jivaro: People of the Sacred Waterfalls* (New York, 1972). He was founder and director of the Center for Shamanic Studies in Norwalk, Connecticut. *References*: AMWS; CA; and WWA.

HARRAH, CHARLES JEFFERSON (1817–1890). Railroad builder, born January 1, 1817, in Philadelphia. Harrah was apprenticed to a shipbuilder 1832, and worked in that trade in Philadelphia; Erie, Pennsylvania; and New York City. In 1843, he obtained a contract to build a large steamship in Rio Grande do Sul, Brazil. He conducted a shipyard at Rio Grande do Sul from 1843 to 1852 and in Rio de Janeiro from 1852 to 1857. In 1858, he obtained the contract to construct the mountainous section of the Dom Pedro railroad in Brazil, which he completed in 1863 and which ruined him financially. He was engaged in a mercantile business in Rio de Janeiro from 1863 to 1871 and in 1868 became involved with the Botanical Garden Railroad Company, which built and operated the first street railway in Rio de Janeiro. He organized the Leopoldina Railroad Company in Minas Geraes in 1872. He built the first telegraph line in Brazil in 1869 and served as its president. He helped organize the Brazilian Navigation Company in 1870 and was one of the promoters of the first Brazilian public school in Rio de Janeiro in that year. He returned to the United States in 1873 and was president of the Peoples Passenger Railway Company in Philadelphia and president of the Midvale Steel Company after 1887. Died February 18, 1890, in Philadelphia. *References*: NCAB 24:251; and WWWA.

HARRAR, J(ACOB) GEORGE (1906–1982). Botanist and association official, born December 2, 1906, in Painesville, Ohio. Harrar graduated from Oberlin College, Iowa State College, and the University of Minnesota. He was professor of botany at the College of Agriculture of the University of Puerto Rico in 1929–1930, and chairman of the department from 1930 to 1933, professor of biology at Virginia Polytechnic Institute from 1935 to 1941, and chairman of the department of plant pathology at Washington State College from 1941 to 1943. He was director of the Mexican Agriculture Program from 1943 to 1951, field director for agriculture of the Rockefeller Foundation in New York City from 1952 to 1955, the foundation's director for agriculture from 1955 to 1959, its vice president from 1959 to 1961, and its president from 1961 until his retirement in 1972. He is credited with the development of research programs to produce disease-resistant strains in native wheat and corn varieties that increased production of these food crops in Mexico. Died April 18, 1982, in Scarsdale, New York. *References*: *AMWS*; *CA*; *CB* 1964; *NYT*, April 20, 1982; and *WWWA*.

HARRIET **INCIDENT** (1831). The American fishing schooner *Harriet* was fishing in the area of Falkland Islands when it was seized by Argentine authorities and taken to Buenos Aires. This incident led to the Falkland Islands crisis.* The issue became moot after the islands were occupied by Great Britain in 1833. *Reference*: *DADH*.

HARRINGTON, FRANCIS MARION (1865–1908). Missionary, born in Iowa. Harrington graduated from the law department of the State University of Iowa. He went to Chile in 1895 to work in the Methodist Church and Iquique English College. He returned to the United States in 1904 because of ill health but was back in Iquique in 1905. He went to La Paz, Bolivia, in 1906, was the founder of Methodist work in Bolivia, and organized the first Methodist church there. He established the American Institute in La Paz (later Colegio Evangelico Metodisto) in 1907. Died February 21, 1908, in La Paz. His wife, **MARY R. HARRINGTON** wrote (with Vivian W. Perry), *Adventuring with God* (Stockton, Calif., 1962). *Reference*: *EWM*.

HARRINGTON, GEORGE LEAVITT ("MR. HARRY") (1883–1972). Petroleum geologist, born December 21, 1883, in Hastings, Minnesota. Harrington graduated from the Minnesota School of Mines. He was assistant geologist for the U.S. Geological Survey from 1913 to 1920 and a member of an expedition for the Bolivia-Argentine Exploration Corporation in Colombia in 1920–1921. He was employed by Standard Oil of Argentina and Standard Oil of Bolivia, subsidiaries of Standard Oil Company of New Jersey, from 1921 until his retirement in 1943, and was chief geologist of Standard Oil of Argentina from 1938 to 1943. He was a research associate in geology at Stanford University from 1947 until his death. Died May 25, 1972, in Palo Alto, California. *Reference*: *BAAPG* 56 (1972): 2089–90.

HARRIS, JOHN WILL(IAM) (1876–1956). Missionary, born January 12, 1876, in Dripping Spring, Texas. Harris graduated from Park College (Parkville, Mo.) and Princeton Theological Seminary and was ordained in 1905. He was a missionary under the Board of Home Missions of the Presbyterian Church in the U.S.A.* in Puerto Rico from 1906 until 1937. He founded the Polytechnic

Institute of Porto Rico in San Germán in 1912, which became a college in 1921 (and was renamed the Inter American University of Puerto Rico in 1956), and was its president from 1912 until his retirement in 1937. He returned to the United States in 1937 and settled in Dilley, Texas. Died June 14, 1956, from injuries suffered in an auto accident, in Texas. *References: Riding & Roping: The Memoirs of J. Will Harris*, ed. C. Virginia Matters (San Juan, Puerto Rico, 1977); and *PrincetonTS*.

HARRIS, WILLIAM A(LEXANDER) (1805–1864). Editor and diplomat, born August 8, 1805, in Fauquier County, Virginia. Harris studied law and was admitted to the bar in 1827. He practiced law and served in the legislature of Virginia and in the U.S. House of Representatives from 1841 to 1843. He was editor of the Spectator and subsequently the *Constitution* in Washington, D.C. He was U.S. chargé d'affaires in Buenos Aires from 1846 to 1851. He served as a conciliator between the governments of Buenos Aires and of France and England during the foreign intervention in the Rio de la Plata, aided in the negotiations, and effected a peaceful settlement between the parties. He also tried to promote cordial relations between the Juan Manuel de Rosas regime and Paraguay. He was later editor and proprietor of the *Washington Union*, served as printer for the U.S. Senate from 1852 to 1854, and then moved to Missouri. Died March 28, 1864, in Pike County, Missouri. *References*: *BDAC*; W. Dusenberry, "The Service of William A. Harris at Buenos Aires, 1846–1851," *TA* 16 (1960): 251–70; and *NCAB* 12:529.

HARRISON, WILLIAM HENRY (1773–1841). Public official, born February 9, 1773, in Charles City County, Virginia. Harrison attended Hampden-Sydney College and the College of Physicians and Surgeons (Philadelphia). He joined the army from 1791 to 1798 and was secretary of the Northwest Territory in 1798–1799 and governor of Indiana Territory from 1800 to 1812. He served during the War of 1812. He served in the U.S. House of Representatives from 1816 to 1819, in the Ohio legislature from 1819 to 1821, and in the U.S. Senate from 1825 to 1828. He was U.S. minister to Colombia in 1829 and provoked considerable controversy by his connection with revolutionaries in that country. He was elected president of the United States in 1840. Died April 4, 1841, in Washington, D.C. *References*: *ACAB*; *DAB*; James A. Green, *William Henry Harrison: His Life and Times (Richmond, Va., 1941)*; Randall O. Hudson, American Diplomacy in Action: *William Henry Harrison in Colombia* (Wichita, Kans., 1973); and *WWWA*.

HART, FRANCIS RUSSELL (1868–1938). Engineer, born January 16, 1868, in New Bedford, Massachusetts. Hart graduated from Massachusetts Institute of Technology. He was general manager of the Cartagena-Magdalena Railway in Colombia from 1889 to 1891, vice president and general manager from 1891 to 1893, and president from 1893 to 1906. He was U.S. vice consul, and then consul, in Colombia from 1908 to 1919. He was vice chairman of the board of the Old Colony Trust Company of Boston, and he was president of United Fruit Company* from 1933 until his death. Died January 18, 1938, in Boston. *References*: *NYT*, January 19, 1938; and *WWWA*.

HART, GEORGE OVERBURY ("POP") (1868–1933). Artist, born May 10, 1868, in Cairo, Illinois. Hart began working as sign painter in Chicago in 1892 and attended the school of the Art Institute of Chicago. He traveled in Cuba, Central America, and Mexico from 1900 to 1903. He was in the sign painting business in New Jersey from 1907 to 1912 and designed and painted stage sets for World Pictures film studio from 1912 to 1920. In 1912 he began to travel to the West Indies, visiting Trinidad, Dominica, Santo Domingo, and Mexico until 1931. Died September 9, 1933, in New York City. *References*: George O. Hart Papers, Rutgers, State University of New Jersey Library, New Brunswick, N.J.; *DAB S1*; Gregory Gilbert, *George Overbury "Pop" Hart: His Life and Art* (New Brunswick, N.J., 1986); *NYT*, September 10, 1933; and *WWWA*.

HART, JEANNETTE (1794–1861). Traveler, born in Saybrook, Connecticut. Hart accompanied Commodore Isaac Hull, her brother-in-law, and his family to South America in 1826, and met Simón Bolívar in Lima, Peru. Bolívar courted Jeannette and later proposed marriage to her. She returned to the United States in 1827. She wrote *Letters from the Bahama Island. Written in 1823–4* (Philadelphia, 1827), which was published anonymously. Died August 1861, in Saybrook, Connecticut. *References*: Marion H. Grant, *The Hart Dynasty of Saybrook* (West Hartford, Conn., 1981); and Enrique Naranjo Martínez, "Bolívar y la Bella Norteamericana Jeannette Hart," *Boletín de Historia y Antigüedades* 31 (1944): 1106–33.

HART, JOSEPH LANCASTER (1879–1966). Missionary, born November 26, 1879, in Essex County, Virginia. Hart graduated from Richmond College and Southern Baptist Theological Seminary. He held pastorates in Virginia and Kentucky. He was a missionary under the Foreign Mission Board of the Southern Baptist Convention* in Argentina from 1903 to 1921 and in Chile from 1921 to 1947. He organized ten churches in Rosario and Sante Fe provinces and worked in northern Chile from 1937 to 1947. He wrote *Gospel Triumphs in Argentina and Chile* (Richmond, Va., 1925). Died September 8, 1966, in Dallas, Texas. *Reference*: *ESB S*.

HARTLEY, G(EORGE) INNESS (1887–1949). Ornithologist and painter, born May 21, 1887, in Montclair, New Jersey. Hartley graduated from Cornell University. He was manager of a farm in Middleburg, Virginia, from 1910 to 1914. In 1914, he became a research associate for William Beebe* and accompanied him on expeditions to Brazil and British Guiana to obtain bird specimens for the New York Zoological Society. He served in the U.S. Army during World

War I. After 1919, he traveled extensively and studied art. He worked with Beebe at the Tropical Research Institute in British Guiana from 1919 to 1921. After 1921, he settled in Southampton, New York, and did landscape painting and writing. He was coauthor of *Tropical Wild Life in British Guiana* (New York, 1917), and wrote *The Boy Hunters in Demerrara* (New York, 1921). He also engaged in the real estate business from 1926 to 1932. Died February 11, 1949, in Southampton, Long Island, New York. *References*: *NCAB* 38:212; and *NYT*, February 12, 1949.

HARTT, CHARLES FREDERICK (1840–1878). Geologist and paleontologist, born August 23, 1840, in Fredericton, New Brunswick, Canada. Hartt graduated from Acadia College and studied at the Museum of Comparative Zoology in Cambridge, Massachusetts. He was a geologist on the Thayer expedition to Brazil in 1865–1866 and then went back in 1867 and studied the geology of the Bahia region. He was a professor of natural history at Vassar College in 1867–1868 and professor of geology and physical geography at Cornell University from 1868 to 1875. In 1870, he went on a large expedition to Brazil. On this and a subsequent expedition he worked in the Amazonas. At the invitation of the Brazilian government, he was chief of the Geological Commission of the Empire of Brazil from 1875 until his death. He directed expeditions working in many parts of the country and set up a museum to house all the scientific specimens that were collected. He wrote *The Geology and Physical Geography of Brazil* (Boston, 1870), *Contributions to the Geology and Physical Geography of the Lower Amazon* (Buffalo, N.Y., 1874), and *Amazonian Tortoise Myths* (Rio de Janeiro, 1875). Died March 18, 1878, in Rio de Janeiro. *References*: *ACAB*; *Dictionary of Canadian Biography* (Toronto, 1972), 10:338; *NCAB* 11:260; and *WWWA*.

HASSAUREK, FREDERICK [FRIEDRICH] (1831–1885). Journalist and diplomat, born October 8, 1831, in Vienna, Austria. Hassaurek participated in the revolution of 1848 and, after its failure, fled to Cincinnati, Ohio, in 1849. He was assistant editor of *Ohio Staatszeitung* and then established the weekly *Hochwaechter*, and was member of the Cincinnati city council from 1852 to 1858. He then studied law. He was U.S. minister to Ecuador from 1861 until 1865. He arranged a mixed U.S.–Ecuadorian commission to settle claims between the two countries. He was editor and part owner of *Tagliches Cincinnatier Volkblatt* from 1865 to 1876 and again from 1877 to 1882. He wrote *Four Years among the Spanish Americans* (New York, 1867) and a novel, *The Secret of the Andes: A Romance* (Cincinnati, 1879). Died October 3, 1885, in Paris. *References*: *ACAB*; *DAB*; C. Harvey Gardiner, ed., *Four Years among the Ecuadorians* (Carbondale, Ill., 1967); *NCAB* 11:279; *OAB*; and *WWWA*.

HASTINGS, LANSFORD WARREN (1819–1870). Author, lawyer, and colony promoter, born in Ohio. Hastings was one of the leaders of the first planned overland wagon migration to Oregon in 1842 and then was a land claims lawyer and surveyor of Oregon City. He moved to California in 1843 and led the first California emigrants across the Salt Desert in 1846. He served in the California Battalion, was delegate to the state constitutional convention in 1849, and then practiced law in northern California. He moved to Arizona City (later Yuma) in the late 1850s. He supported the Confederacy and after the war went to Brazil, where he secured permission to colonize Americans on the Amazon River. He published a guidebook to the Amazon region, *The Emigrants' Guide to Brazil* (New York, 1865). In 1868, he established a colony near present-day Santarém, Brazil. Died on the return voyage to Alabama to seek additional emigrants. *References*: T. F. Andrews, "Ambitions of Lansford W. Hastings: a Study in Western Myth-Making," *PHR* 39 (1970): 473–91; Charles H. Carey, ed., *The Emigrants' Guide to Oregon and California* (Princeton, N.J., 1932), pp. vii-xxiv; T. E. Griffin, "Confederates on the Amazon," *Americas* 33 (February 1981): 13–17; William J. Hunsaker, "Lansford Warren Hastings, Empire Dreamer and California Pioneer," *Grizzly Bear* 47 (May 1930): 14–15, 68–71; and *OAB*.

HATCHER, JOHN BELL (1861–1904). Paleontologist, born October 11, 1861, in Cooperstown, Illinois. Hatcher graduated from Sheffield Scientific School of Yale University. He collected vertebrate fossils in Kansas, Nebraska, Texas, North Carolina, Virginia, and the District of Columbia. He was curator of vertebrate paleontology and an assistant in geology at Princeton University from 1893 to 1900. He carried out explorations in Utah, Wyoming, and South Dakota from 1893 to 1895. He led three expeditions to Patagonia and Tierra del Fuego from 1896 to 1899, exploring regions never before invaded by whites. He prepared *Reports of the Princeton University Expeditions to Patagonia, 1896–1899* (Princeton, N.J., 1901–1903) and wrote his own story in *Narrative and Geography* (Princeton, N.J., 1903). He was curator of paleontology and osteology at the Carnegie Institute in Pittsburgh from 1900 until his death. Died July 3, 1904, in Pittsburgh, Pennsylvania. *References*: John Bell Hatcher, *Bone Hunters in Patagonia: Narrative of the Expedition* (Woodbridge, Conn., 1985); Leonard Krishtalka, *Dinosaur Plots & Other Intrigues in National History* (New York, 1989), ch. 13; *NCAB* 21:212; and *Simpson*, ch. 7.

HATFIELD, WILLIS CHARLES ("LUKE") (1898–1970). Petroleum geologist, born November 23, 1898, in Ipswich, Massachusetts. Hatfield graduated from Wesleyan and Columbia universities. He carried out mineral exploration work in northern Rhodesia from 1928 to 1932. He was an instructor in geology at Hunter College from 1935 to 1937. He was a geologist for the Texas Petroleum Company in Bogotá, Colombia, from 1937 to 1940 and chief geologist of the Colombian division from 1940 until his retirement in 1957. He initiated a long-range project of mapping the jungle country east of the Andes. Died March 10, 1970, in Freedom, New Hampshire. *Reference*: *BAAPG* 54 (1970): 1951–53.

HAUPT, LEWIS M(UHLENBERG) (1844–1937). Civil engineer, born March 21, 1844, in Gettysburg, Pennsylvania. Haupt graduated from the U.S. Military Academy in 1867 and was commissioned second lieutenant of engineers. He was a professor of civil engineering at the University of Pennsylvania from 1875 to 1892. He was a member of the Nicaragua Canal Commission from 1897 to 1899 and of the Isthmian Canal Commission from 1899 to 1902. He was later a consulting engineer until his death. Died March 10, 1937, in Cynwyd, Pennsylvania. *References*: *ACAB*; *NCAB* 13:233; *NYT*, March 11, 1937; and *WWWA*.

HAVENS, VERNE LEROY (1881–1944). Engineer, born June 17, 1881, in Atlantic, Iowa. Havens attended the University of Nebraska. He went to Mexico in 1906 and served as assistant engineer of the Mexican Light Power Company and field engineer on the Necaxa Dam. He was engineer in charge of the construction of street railways in San Francisco and Havana, Cuba, in 1906–1907; chief civil engineer of the Mexico tramways and chief engineer of the Pachuca Power and Irrigation Company from 1907 to 1911. He was consulting engineer to the president of Guatemala on public works, ports, and railroads, consulting engineer to Brazilian railways, and location and construction engineer on railroads in Uruguay from 1911 to 1914. He was U.S. commercial attaché in Chile from 1914 to 1917 and wrote *Markets for American Hardware in Chile and Bolivia* (Washington, D.C., 1916). He founded and was editor of *Ingenieria Ferrocarriles* from 1918 to 1922, was employed by the Equitable Life Assurance Society from 1922 to 1925, headed his own development company, Obras Corporation, in New York City, and was representative in South America of New York bankers from 1925 to 1933. He was employed by the Public Works Administration from 1933 until his retirement in 1939. Died August 12, 1944, in New York City. *References*: *NCAB* 34:103; and *NYT*, August 14, 1944.

HAWLEY, ROBERT B(RADLEY) (1849–1921). Businessman, born October 25, 1849, in Memphis, Tennessee. He moved to Galveston, Texas, in 1875 and was a merchant, importer, and manufacturer until 1895. He was president of Galveston Board of Education from 1889 to 1893 and served in the U.S. House of Representatives from 1897 to 1901. He organized the Cuban American Sugar Company in 1900 and was its president until his death. Died November 28, 1921, in New York City. *References*: *BDAC*; and *NYT*, November 29, 1921.

HAY, CLARENCE LEONARD (1884–1969). Archaeologist, born December 19, 1884, in Cleveland, Ohio. Hay graduated from Harvard University. He served in U.S. Army Intelligence during World War I. He undertook archaeological expeditions to southern Mexico under the auspices of the Peabody Museum of Archaeology and Ethnology of Harvard University to Central America in 1911–1912, to Quintana Roo, Yucatán, in 1912, and to Mexico in 1914. He was a research associate in anthropology at the American Museum of Natural History from 1920 to 1924 and secretary of the board of the museum from 1931 to 1960. Died June 4, 1969, in Paris, France. *References*: *NCAB* 54:554; and *WWWA*.

HAYES, CHARLES WILLARD (1858–1916). Geologist, born October 8, 1858, in Granville, Ohio, and grew up in Hanover, Ohio. Hayes graduated from Oberlin College and Johns Hopkins University. He served with the Appalachian division of the U.S. Geological Survey from 1887 to 1897, was in charge of the section of nonmetalliferous resources from 1899 to 1902, and had administrative charge of all the geological work of the survey from 1902 to 1910. He was a geologist with the Nicaragua Canal Commission in 1910 and with the Panama Canal Zone in 1910–1911. He was a geologist with the Aguila Oil Company in Mexico from 1911 until he was forced to leave Mexico during the Mexican Revolution. Died February 8, 1916, in Washington, D.C. *References*: *DAB*; *NYT*, February 10, 1916; and *WWWA*.

HAYMAKER, EDWARD M(CILWAIN) (1859–1948). Missionary, born August 21, 1859, in Murrysville, Pennsylvania. Haymaker graduated from Lafayette College and Princeton Theological Seminary and was ordained in 1884. He was a missionary under the Board of Foreign Missions of the Presbyterian Church in the U.S.A.* in Mexico from 1884 to 1887 and in Guatemala from 1887 to 1903 and from 1912 to 1936. He wrote *Footnotes on the Beginnings of the Evangelical Movement in Guatemala* (El Rancho, El Progreso, Guatemala, 1946). Died January 30, 1948, in Warrenburg, Missouri. *Reference*: *PrincetonTS*.

HAZARD, SAMUEL (1834–1876). Publisher, born March 1, 1834, in Philadelphia. Hazard was in the publishing business and served in the Union Army during the Civil War. He later continued in his business. He visited Cuba twice and wrote *Cuba with Pen and Pencil* (Hartford, Conn., 1871), which he illustrated himself, and *Santo Domingo: Past and Present, with a Glance at Hayti* (New York, 1873). Died January 10, 1876, in Philadelphia.

HCJB, THE VOICE OF THE ANDES. Christian radio station, established in Quito, Ecuador, in 1931 with 250-watt transmitter, which was later increased to 50,000 watts. It became a portion of the World Radio Missionary Fellowship, Inc.* *References*: Frank S. Cook, *Seeds in the Wind: The Story of the Voice of the Andes, Radio Station HCJB, Quito, Ecuador* (Opa Locka, Fla., 1976); and Lois Neely, *Come Up to This Mountain: The Miracle of Clarence W. Jones & HCJB* (Wheaton, Ill., 1980).

HEADE, MARTIN JOHNSON (1819–1904). Painter, born August 11, 1819, in Lumberville, Pennsylvania. Heade began to study painting in 1838, studied in Italy, France, and England from 1837 to 1840, and began exhibiting in 1841. He worked as a portrait and landscape painter in various cities in the United

States. He traveled and painted in Brazil in 1863–1864, in Nicaragua and Colombia in 1866–1867, and in Colombia, Jamaica, and Panama in 1870. He had a studio in New York City from 1866 to 1881 and settled in St. Augustine, Florida, in 1885. Died September 4, 1904, in St. Augustine. *References*: *DAB*; *Manthorne*; Robert G. McIntyre, *Martin Johnson Heade, 1819–1904* (New York, 1848); and Theodore E. Stebbins, Jr., *The Life and Works of Martin Johnson Heade* (New Haven, Conn., 1975).

HEATH, EDWIN R. (1839–1932). Physician and explorer, born July 11, 1839, in Janesville, Wisconsin, and grew up in Sacramento, California. Heath graduated from a New York medical school. He practiced medicine in Wyandotte County, Kansas. He was secretary of legation in Chile after 1869. He explored, navigated, and mapped the entire length of the Beni River in Bolivia in 1880–1881, and his report appeared in the *Bulletin of the American Geographical Society* in 1882. He later practiced medicine in Kansas City. Died October 27, 1932, in Kansas City, Missouri. *Reference*: *NYT*, October 28, 1932.

HEDBERG, HOLLIS D(OW) (1903–1988). Petroleum geologist, born May 29, 1903, in Falun, Kansas. Hedberg graduated from the University of Kansas and Cornell and Stanford universities. He was a petrographer with the Lago Petroleum Corporation in Venezuela from 1926 to 1928, stratigrapher and director of the geological laboratory of Mene Grande Oil Company in Venezuela from 1928 to 1939, and assistant chief geologist there from 1939 to 1946. He was chief geologist for the foreign production division of Gulf Oil Corporation from 1946 to 1951, exploration manager in 1951–1952, chief geologist in 1952–1953, exploration coordinator from 1953 to 1957, vice president from 1957 to 1964, and exploration adviser from 1964 to 1968. He was a professor of geology at Princeton University from 1959 until his retirement in 1971. Died August 14, 1988, in Princeton, New Jersey. *References*: *AMWS*; *NYT*, August 16, 1988; and *WWWA*.

HEDGES, DAYTON (1885–1957). Industrialist, born in Wainscot, near Bridgehampton, Long Island, New York, and grew up in Patchogue, Long Island. He worked as a clerk in hotel and served in the Coast Guard lifesaving station in Blue Point, Long Island. He was supervisor of the Brookhaven Township, Suffolk County, Long Island, and superintendent of marine fisheries there. He went to Cuba in 1919, and was manager of Old Colony Trust Company's Cuba Hydroelectric Company, involved in farming, and, after 1930, in textiles. He built a cotton mill in Bauta, and, in 1948, a rayon factory in Matanzas. He was also involved in growing cotton and raising beef cattle in Cuba. Died June 8, 1957, in New York City. *References*: "Compaña Taxtilera Ariguanabo, S.A.: Mr. Dayton Hedges' Cotton Textile Mill," *Fortune* 23 (June 1941): 84–87; J. P. McEvoy, "Go South, Young Man," *Reader's Digest* 43 (July 1943): 39–42; and *NYT*, June 8, 1957.

HEGEN, EDMUND EDUARD (1920–   ). Geographer, born October 15, 1920, in Doernsdorf, Bohemia. Hegen graduated from the German University of Prague and the University of Florida. He was assistant professor at the University of Florida from 1962 to 1969, associate professor there from 1969 to 1971, and professor of geography at Western Kentucky University (Bowling Green) after 1971. He was field researcher in the upper Amazon Basin in 1964–1965 and wrote *Highways into the Upper Amazon Basin: Pioneer Lands in Southern Colombia, Ecuador, and Northern Peru* (Gainesville, Fla., 1966). *Reference*: AMWS.

HELM, CHARLES JOHN (1817–1868). Consul, born June 21, 1817, in Harnellsville, New York, and grew up in Newport, Kentucky. Helm studied law and was admitted to the bar in 1842: he practiced law in Newport, Kentucky, after that. He served during the Mexican War and in the Kentucky state legislature from 1851 to 1853. He was U.S. commercial agent in St. Thomas, Virgin Islands, from 1853 to 1858, and consul general in Havana from 1858 to 1861. He resigned at the outbreak of the Civil War. He became a Confederate special agent in Cuba, was able to buy arms and administer blockade-running activities without interference, and provided intelligence on Union blockade activities. After the war, he retired to Toronto, Canada. Died February 1868, in Toronto. *References*: *DAB*; *DADH*; and *WWWA*.

HELPER, HINTON ROWAN (1829–1909). Author, born December 27, 1829, in Rowan (later Davie) County, North Carolina. Helper went to New York City in 1850 and was in California from 1850 to 1853. He began publishing, including *The Impending Crisis of the South. How to Meet It* (New York, 1857), an attack on slavery. He was U.S. consul in Buenos Aires from 1861 to 1866 and tried to establish closer relations with South America. He acted as attorney to U.S. citizens seeking to collect their claims against South American governments. He wrote *Oddments of Andean Diplomacy; and Other Oddments* (St. Louis, 1879). He was involved in plans to promote a railway from the Hudson Bay to the Strait of Magellan. He wrote *The Three Americas Railway* (St. Louis, 1881) and visited South America several times in the interests of his plan. Committed suicide March 8, 1909, in Washington, D.C. *References*: Hugh C. Bailey, *Hinton Rowan Helper: Abolitionist-Racist* (Tuscaloosa, Ala., 1965); *DAB*; and *WWWA*.

HEMENWAY, AUGUSTUS (1805–1876). Businessman, born April 25, 1805, in Salem, Massachusetts. Hemenway was employed by various stores in Boston after 1818, and began his own merchandising activities in Boston in 1824. He went to Chile in 1829, established A. Hemenway and Company in Valparaiso, and was the leading merchant in the trade between the United States and the West Coast of South America. He started a smelting establishment at Calderon and copper mines at Cárrizalillo, Chile. He returned to the United States in 1840 and was hospitalized in a sanitarium from 1860 to 1874. Died June 1876, in

Santa Ana, Cuba. *Reference*: Frederic A. Eustis, *Augustus Hemenway 1805–1876: Builder of the United States Trade with the West Coast of South America* (Salem, Mass., 1955).

HENNINGSEN, CHARLES FREDERICK (1815–1877). Soldier, born February 21, 1815, probably in Belgium, and grew up in England. Henningsen was in the service of the Carlists in Spain from 1834 to 1836 and campaigned with the revolutionary Schamyl in the Caucasus and with the Hungarians during the revolution of 1848. He came to the United States in 1851, serving as private secretary to Lajos Kossuth, the Hungarian revolutionary leader. In 1856, he joined the expedition of William Walker to Nicaragua. He was appointed brigadier general in charge of the artillery, and for a time, second in command to Walker. He served until the end of the war. He then settled in Georgia and served in the Confederate Army during the Civil War. Died June 14, 1877, in Washington, D.C. *References*: *ACAB*; *DAB*; *NCAB* 9:236; *NYT*, June 15, 1877; and *WWWA*.

HENRY, JULES (1904–1969). Anthropologist, born November 29, 1904, in New York City. Henry graduated from the College of the City of New York and Columbia University. He carried out research among the Kaingang Indians of southwestern Brazil from 1932 to 1934 and among the Pilaga Indians of northern Argentina in 1936–1937. He was in Mexico from 1939 to 1941, at the invitation of that government, helping to record and alphabetize Indian languages and devising strategies for achieving literacy among those people. He served with the Office of Inter-American Affairs from 1942 to 1947. He was associate professor of anthropology and sociology, and later full professor, at Washington University from 1947 until his death. He wrote *Jungle People: A Kaingang Tribe of the Highland of Brazil* (New York, 1941) and *Doll Play of Pilaga Indian Children* (New York, 1944). Died September 23, 1969, in St. Louis. *References*: *AA* 73 (1971): 788–97; *CA*; and *NYT*, September 26, 1969.

HERNDON, WILLIAM LEWIS (1813–1857). Naval officer, born October 25, 1813, in Fredericksburg, Virginia. Herndon entered the U.S. Navy as a midshipman in 1828, was commissioned lieutenant in 1841, and served during the Mexican War. He was attached to the Naval Observatory in Washington, D.C., in 1848. He was detached in 1851 to make, with Lieutenant Lardner Gibbon, an exploring expedition to the Amazon River. He started from Peru and made a very complete survey of the main branch of the Amazon system during 1851–1852. He wrote *Exploration of the Valley of the Amazon* (Washington, D.C., 1853–1854). He was given leave from the navy in 1855 and was in command of a steamer for the Pacific Mail Steamship Company. Went down with his ship on September 12, 1857, off Cape Hatteras, North Carolina. *References*: *ACAB*; Hamilton Basso, ed., *Exploration of the Valley of the Amazon by William Lewis Herndon* (New York, 1952); Whitfield J. Bell, Jr., ''The

Relation of Herndon and Gibbon's Exploration of the Amazon to North American Slavery, 1850–1855,'' *HAHR* 19 (1943): 494–504; *DAB*; Donald M. Dozer, "Matthew Fontaine Maury's Letter of Instructions to William Lewis Herndon," *HAHR* 28 (1948): 212–28; Donald Dozer, "Pathfinder of the Amazon," *Virginia Quarterly Review* 23 (1947): 554–67; *NCAB* 4:201; Vincent Ponko, Jr., *Ships, Seas, and Scientists: U.S. Naval Exploration and Discovery in the Nineteenth Century* (Annapolis, Md., 1974), ch. 5; and *WWWA*.

HERSKOVITZ, MELVILLE J(EAN) (1895–1963). Anthropologist, born September 10, 1895, in Bellefontaine, Ohio, and grew up in El Paso, Texas, and Erie, Pennsylvania. Herskovitz attended Hebrew Union College and the University of Cincinnati, served in the U.S. Army during World War I, and graduated from the University of Chicago and Columbia University. He became an assistant professor of anthropology at Northwestern University in 1927 and professor in 1935. He carried out fieldwork in Dutch Guiana in 1928–1929, in Haiti in 1934, in Trinidad in 1939, and in Brazil in 1941–1942. With his wife, **FRANCES S(HAPIRO) HERSKOVITZ** (1897–1972), he wrote *Suriname Folklore* (New York, 1936), *Rebel Destiny: Among the Bush Negroes of Dutch Guiana* (New York, 1934), *Life in a Haitian Village* (New York, 1937), and *Trinidad Village* (New York, 1947). He later carried out fieldwork in West Africa. Died February 25, 1963, in Evanston, Illinois. *References*: Melville J. Herskovitz Papers, Northwestern University Library, Evanston, Ill.; *AA* 66 (1964): 83–109; *American Sociological Review* 29 (1964): 278–29; *BMNAS* 42 (1971): 65–93; *CA*; *CB* 1948; *NYT*, February 27, 1963; and *WWWA*.

HEWETT, D(ONNEL) FOSTER (1881–1971). Mining engineer, born June 24, 1881, in Irwin, Pennsylvania. Hewett graduated from Lehigh and Yale universities. He was in mining practice from 1903 to 1909, examining mines for private concerns. He discovered the world's largest deposit of vanadium in Mina Raggare, central Peru, in 1905. He was a geologist with the U.S. Geological Survey from 1911 to 1971, was in charge of metalliferous deposits from 1935 to 1944, and was a research geologist after 1963. Died February 5, 1971, in Palo Alto, California. *References*: *American Mineralogist* 58 (1973): 367–69; *BMNAS* 44 (1974): 111–26; *McGraw-Hill Modern Scientists and Engineers* (New York, 1980); and *WWWA*.

HEYL, JAMES B(ELL) (1826–1905). Pharmacist and photographer, born in New Orleans. Heyl studied pharmacy at Charity Hospital in New Orleans. He came to Bermuda in 1848, established a pharmacy in Hamilton in 1848, and was involved with it until his retirement in 1901. He began to photograph Bermuda in 1868 and is believed to have taken the first photographs of some Bermuda scenes. He became a naturalized British subject but nonetheless served as U.S. vice consul in Hamilton from 1879 to 1903. Died in Hamilton, Bermuda. *References*: Norman H. Franke, "James Bell Heyl: Bermuda's Pharmacist-

Photographer," *Pharmacy in History* 24 (1982): 117–19; and Edith S. G. Hely, comp., *Bermuda through the Camera of James B. Heyl, 1868–1897* (Hamilton, Bermuda, 1951).

HICKEY, JAMES (1800–1866). Missionary, born September 23, 1800, in Siglo, County Cork, Ireland, and came to the United States in 1830. He came as a missionary in Mexico in 1853. He returned to Brownsville, Texas, but was back in Mexico in 1861. He served in Matamoros in 1861–1862 and in Monterrey after 1862. He was also an agent of the American Bible Society* after 1863. In 1864, he organized the first Baptist church in Monterrey. Died December 10, 1866, in Matamoros, Mexico. *Reference*: Walter S. Stewart, *Later Baptist Missionaries and Pioneers* (Philadelphia, 1929), 2:37–61.

HILL, HENRY (1795–1892). Merchant, born January 10, 1795, in Newburgh, New York, and grew up in Catskill-on-the-Hudson, New York. Hill established the first North American business firm in Valparaiso, Chile, was a representative of several agencies and owners of U.S. shipping vessels, and sold supplies and weapons to the Chileans during the War for Independence from 1817 to 1820. He was U.S. vice consul in Santiago and Valparaiso. He returned to the United States in 1821. He wrote *Recollections of an Octogenarian* (Boston, 1884), and *Incidents in Chile, South America, 1817–1821* (Weymouth, Mass., 1895?). Died January 16, 1892, in Cambridge, Massachusetts. *References*: Henry Hill Letterbook, Yale University Library; Eugenio Salas Pereira, "Henry Hill, Commerciant, Vice-consul y Misionero," *RCHG* 87 (1939): 5–30.

HILL, ROBERT C(HARLES) (1917–1978). Government official and diplomat, born September 17, 1917, in Littleton, New Hampshire. Hill graduated from Dartmouth College and attended Boston University Law School. He was employed by W. R. Grace and Company from 1949 to 1953. He was U.S. ambassador to Costa Rica in 1953–1954. He was official observer in the negotiations of a contract between Costa Rica and United Fruit Company,* and helped overthrow the government of Jacobo Arbenz Guzman in Guatemala. He was ambassador to El Salvador in 1954–1955, assistant secretary of state for congressional relations in 1956–1957, and ambassador to Mexico from 1957 to 1961. He was in business from 1961 to 1967 as an executive of the W. R. Grace and Company, and also served in the New Hampshire House of Representatives in 1961–1962. He was U.S. ambassador to Spain from 1967 to 1972, assistant secretary of defense for international security affairs in 1973–1974, and ambassador to Argentina from 1974 to 1977. Died November 28, 1978, in Littleton, New Hampshire. *References*: Robert C. Hill Papers, Dartmouth College Library, Hanover, N.H.; *CB* 1959; *NYT*, November 29, 1978; and *Polprof:Eisenhower*.

HILL, ROBERT T(HOMAS) (1858–1941). Geologist, born August 11, 1858, in Nashville, Tennessee. Hill went to Comanhe, Texas, in 1873 and set type for his brother's weekly newspaper, the *Comanche Chief*, from 1873 to 1880. He graduated from Cornell University. He was a member of the staff of the U.S. Geological Survey from 1886 to 1903, in private consulting practice in New York City from 1903 to 1911, in Los Angeles from 1911 to 1931, and in Dallas, Texas, from 1931 until his death. He conducted a geological reconnaissance of Cuba in 1894 and geological expeditions to Panama and Costa Rica in 1895 and to the West Indies in 1896–1897. He studied the eruption of Mont Pelée on the island of Martinique in 1902. He contributed to the knowledge of the Lesser Antilles, compiled the first systematic descriptions of the geology of Cuba, Jamaica, and Puerto Rico, and wrote *Cuba and Port Rico, with the Other Islands of the West Indies: Their Topography, Climate, Flora, Products, Industries, Cities, People, Political Conditions, etc.* (New York, 1898) and *The Geology and Physical Geography of Jamaica: Study of a Type of Antillean Development* (Cambridge, Mass., 1899). Died July 29, 1941, in Dallas. *References*: Robert T. Hill Collection, Southern Methodist University, Dallas; Nancy Alexander, *Father of Texas Geology, Robert T. Hill* (Dallas, 1976); *NCAB* 40:159; and *NYT*, July 29, 1941.

HILL, ROSCOE R. (1880–1960). Government official, born near Lilly, Illinois. Hill graduated from Eureka College, the University of Chicago and Columbia University. He was a teacher in public schools in Minnesota and Illinois and director of the American School in Matanzas, Cuba. He was engaged in historical research in the Archive of the Indies in Seville, Spain, from 1911 to 1913. He was associate professor of history in the University of New Mexico from 1915 to 1917, president of the Spanish American Normal School of New Mexico from 1917 to 1919, professor at the University of New Mexico in 1919–1920, and regional economist for Latin America in the Office of the Foreign Trade Adviser of the U.S. State Department in 1920. He was U.S. high commissioner in Nicaragua from 1920 to 1928 and chairman of the Nicaraguan Mixed Claims Commission in 1927–1928. He was director for Spain of the Library of Congress's European project, assistant chief of the manuscript division of the Library of Congress from 1933 to 1935, chief of the Classification Division of the National Archives from 1935 to 1941, and chief of the Division of State Department Archives from 1941 until his retirement in 1946. He wrote *Fiscal Intervention in Nicaragua* (New York, 1933) and *The National Archives of Latin America* (Cambridge, Mass., 1945). Died October 26, 1960, in Washington, D.C. *References*: *HAHR* 27 (1947): 170–73; *HAHR* 41 (1961): 337; and *NYT*, October 30, 1960.

HILLIARD, HENRY W(ASHINGTON) (1808–1892). Lawyer and diplomat, born August 4, 1808, in Fayetteville, North Carolina. Hilliard graduated from South Carolina College, studied law, and was admitted to the bar in 1829. He was a professor of English literature at the University of Alabama from 1831 to 1834, practiced law in Montgomery, Alabama, after 1834, served in the state legislature from 1836 to 1838, was chargé d'affaires in Belgium from 1842 to

1844, and served in the U.S. House of Representatives from 1846 to 1851. He served in the Confederate Army during the Civil War and resumed the practice of law in Montgomery and later in Atlanta, Georgia. He was U.S. minister to Brazil from 1877 to 1881. His period of service fell during the time that the emancipation of the slaves was in progress in Brazil and he lent support to those who were agitating a quicker and more drastic method, which attracted wide notice. He then resumed the practice of law. He wrote *Politics and Pen Pictures at Home and Abroad* (New York, 1892). Died December 17, 1892, in Atlanta. *References*: *ACAB*; *BDAC*; *DAB*; *NCAB* 2:114; Norman T. Strauss, "Brazil in the 1870's as Seen by American Diplomats," Ph.D. diss., New York University, 1971; and *WWWA*.

HINE, MARQUIS LAFAYETTE (1823–1867). Consul, born April 1823 in Cairo, New York. Hine came to Costa Rica in 1850 as the first consular representative to Costa Rica and remained in this position until his death, serving first in San Juan del Norte (Greytown) in Nicaragua and later in San José. Died January 1867, in San José. *References*: Norberto de Castro y Tosi, "Genealogía de la Casa de Hine," *Revista de la Academia Costarricense de Ciencias Genealógicas*, nos. 16–17 (1970): 107–14; and Anita G. Murchie, *Imported Spices: A Study of Anglo-American Settlers in Costa Rica 1821–1900* (San José, Costa Rica, 1981).

HISE, ELIJAH (1801–1867). Lawyer and diplomat, born July 4, 1801, in Allegheny County, Pennsylvania, and grew up in Kentucky. Hise graduated from Transylvania University (Lexington, Ky.) and studied law. He practiced law in Russellville, Kentucky, and served in the Kentucky legislature. He was U.S. chargé d'affaires in Guatemala in 1848–1849. He negotiated treaties of friendship with Nicaragua, Honduras, and Guatemala, and, on his own initiative, a canal treaty with Nicaragua in 1849. Because he exceeded his instructions, he was recalled. He resumed the practice of law in Kentucky, served as judge on the Kentucky Court of Appeals from 1851 to 1855, and in the U.S. House of Representatives in 1866–1867. Committed suicide, May 8, 1867, in Russellville, Kentucky. *References*: *BDAC*; *DADH*; *DAB*; *NCAB* 12:54; and *WWWA*.

HODGES, HARRY FOOTE (1860–1929). Military engineer, born February 25, 1860, in Boston. Hodges graduated from the U.S. Military Academy in 1881 and was assigned to the corps of engineers. He was assistant professor of civil and military engineering in the U.S. Military Academy from 1888 to 1892 and then supervised engineering works on the Ohio, Missouri, and Upper Mississippi rivers. He served during the Spanish-American War. He was later engaged in the construction and repair of roads, bridges, reservoirs, refrigerating plants, and defensive works in Puerto Rico in 1898–1899. He was chief engineer for the Department of Cuba in 1901–1902, assistant to chief of engineers in Washington, D.C., from 1902 to 1907, general purchasing officer for the Isthmian Canal Commission in 1907, member of the commission and assistant chief engineer of the Panama Canal, in charge of the design of locks and dams and regulating works from 1908 to 1914, and engineer of maintenance of the canal in 1914–1915. He served during World War I. He retired with the rank of major general in 1921. Died September 24, 1929, in Forest Lake, Illinois. *References*: *DAB*; *NYT*, September 25, 1929; and *WWWA*.

HOEVEL, MATHEW ARNOLD (1773–1819). Publisher and public official, born February 1773, in Gotenburg, Sweden. Hoevel was connected with the revolutionaries who killed King Gustav III, fled to the United States in 1804, and became naturalized in the United States. He became involved in the South American trade. In 1810, he was commissioned by the Chilean government to import into Chile a battery of artillery and a printing press, which arrived from the United States in 1811. It was used to publish the *Aurora de Chile*, Chile's first newspaper. He then accepted Chilean nationality and served as captain of the Chilean militia. With the Spanish reconquest in 1814, he was convicted of being a traitor and was exiled to the Island of Juan Fernández. He returned in 1816 and was intendant of Santiago and national police chief and treasurer of the navy in Valparaiso. Died August 13, 1819, in Valparaiso, Chile. *Reference*: Eugenio Pereira Salas, "Don Mateo Arnoldo Hoevel, 1773–1819," *RCHG* 97 (July–August 1940): 57–93.

HOGAN, JAMES (? –1864). Physician, born in Philadelphia. Hogan graduated from medical school in Philadelphia. He was in California during the gold rush. He came to Costa Rica, and organized and directed Hospital de Sangre in Liberia in Guanacaste. He was the first superintendent of the San Juan de Dios Hospital in San Jose from 1858 until his death. *Reference*: Anita G. Murchie, *Imported Spices: A Study of Anglo-American Settlers in Costa Rica, 1821–1900* (San Jose, 1981).

HOLLANDER, JACOB H(ARRY) (1871–1940). Economist, born July 23, 1871, in Baltimore. Hollander graduated from Johns Hopkins University. He was a member of the faculty of Johns Hopkins University after 1894, associate professor of finance until 1900, associate professor of political economics from 1901 to 1904, and professor after 1904. He was treasurer of Puerto Rico in 1900–1901 and special commissioner to revise its tax laws, devising and introducing a new revenue system. He investigated the public debt of the Dominican Republic in 1905, was confidential agent of the U.S. State Department from 1905 to 1907, and served as financial adviser to the Dominican government from 1907 to 1910. Died July 9, 1940, in Baltimore. *References*: *DAB S2*; *NCAB* 13:372; *NYT*, July 10, 1940; and *WWWA*.

HOLLINS, GEORGE NICHOLS (1799–1878). Naval officer, born September 20, 1799, in Baltimore. Hollins was appointed midshipman in the U.S. Navy in 1814 and served during the War of 1812 and the War with Algeria in 1815.

In 1854, in command of the USS *Cyane*, he bombarded and destroyed the town of San Juan del Norte (Greytown) in retaliation for the harassment of American citizens and property by local authorities. He served in the Confederate Navy during the Civil War. He was later a crier in the city court of Baltimore. Died January 18, 1878, in Baltimore. *References*: *ACAB*; *DAB*; *NCAB* 11:252; and *WWWA*.

HOLLY, JAMES THEODORE (AUGUSTUS) (1829–1911). Missionary, born free in Washington, D.C., and grew up in Brooklyn, New York. In 1850, Holly opened a boot-making shop in Burlington, Vermont, and became involved in the emigration movement of Negroes. He edited *Voice of the Fugitive* in Windsor, Canada, from 1851 to 1854. In 1856, he became a priest of the Protestant Episcopal Church. He traveled to Haiti in 1855 as commissioner of the National Emigration Board to negotiate an emigration treaty and explored the island as a possible site for a mission. He was priest and teacher in New Haven, Connecticut, from 1856 to 1861. In 1860, he worked as recruiting agent of the Haitian government in the United States, and he took his New Haven colony to Haiti in 1861. It disintegrated in 1862, but he remained in Haiti and became a Haitian citizen that same year. He was a missionary under the Board of Missions of the Protestant Episcopal Church in Haiti from 1865 to 1911. He was consecrated a missionary bishop of Haiti in 1874 and became head of the national Episcopal church in Haiti. Died March 13, 1911, in Port-au-Prince, Haiti. *References*: *ACAB*; *DAB*; *DANB*; David M. Dean, *Defender of the Race: James Theodore Holly*, Black Nationalist Bishop (Boston, 1979); J. Carleton Hayden, "James Theodore Holly (1829–1911): First Afro-American Episcopal Bishop: His Legacy to Us Today," *Journal of Religious Thought* 33 (Spring-Summer 1976): 50–62; Hollis R. Lynch, *James Theodore Holly: Ante-Bellum Black Nationalist and Emigrationist* (Los Angeles, 1977); *NCAB* 5:383; and *WWWA*.

HOLMBERG, ALLAN R(ICHARD) (1909–1966). Anthropologist, born October 15, 1909, in Renville, Minnesota. Holmberg graduated from the University of Minnesota and Yale University and attended the University of Chicago. He was an economic analyst at the embassy in La Paz, Bolivia, in 1942, a field technician for the Rubber Development Corporation in Bolivia from 1942 to 1945, and a cultural anthropologist for the Institute of Social Anthropology of the Smithsonian Institution and professor of anthropology at the University of San Marcos in Lima, Peru, from 1946 to 1948. He was assistant professor of anthropology at Cornell University from 1948 to 1951, associate professor from 1951 to 1954, and professor of social sciences after 1954. He was director of the Cornell-Peru Project, which brought the Andean Indians of Vico, Peru, from a sixteenth-century culture to twentieth-century living in a decade. His community development program enabled the Indians to develop land and increase production through modern agricultural methods and to improve health and education facilities. He lived among the Sirino Indians in eastern Bolivia, wrote *Nomads of the Long Bow* (Chicago, 1960), and was coauthor of *Social Change in Latin America Today: Its Implications for United States Policy* (New York, 1960). Died October 13, 1966, in Ithaca, New York. *References: NYT*, October 14, 1966; and *WWWA*.

HOLT, ERNEST G(OLSAN) (1889–   ). Ornithologist, born February 14, 1889, in Barachias, Alabama. Holt attended George Washington University. He was an assistant biologist with the U.S. Biological Survey from 1912 to 1917 and served in the U.S. Army during World War I. He was a field collector for the American Museum of Natural History in Brazil in 1921–1922, assistant ornithologist at the Carnegie Museum from 1924 to 1929, participated in the Carnegie's British Honduras expedition in 1926, explored Argentina, Brazil, Paraguay, and Venezuela in 1926–1927, participated in the National Geographic Society–Carnegie Museum expedition to Venezuela in 1928–1929, and was that expedition's leader from 1929 to 1931. He was a conservation biologist and chief forester for the Soil Conservation Survey of the U.S. Department of Agriculture from 1933 to 1935, head of the wildlife management section from 1935 to 1939, and chief of the biological division from 1939 to 1941. He was leader of a mission to Ecuador for the Office of Foreign Agricultural Relations in 1941–1942 and special representative of the Rubber Development Corporation to Central America and Brazil from 1942 to 1947. He was research specialist for the soil conservation service of the U.S. Department of Agriculture from 1947 to 1949 and chief of a mission for the division of agriculture and natural resources of the Institute of Inter-American Affairs to Honduras from 1950 to 1952. He wrote *An Ornithological Survey of the Serra do Itatiaya, Brazil* (New York, 1928). *Reference: AMWS.*

HOLTON, ISAAC F(ARWELL) (1812–1875). Traveler, born August 30, 1812, near Westminster, Vermont. Holton graduated from Amherst College and Union Theological Seminary, was licensed to preach in 1839, and was ordained in 1860. He was a home missionary in west central Illinois until 1840, taught Greek and natural history at the Mission Institute (Quincy, Il.), and was a professor of botany at New York College of Pharmacy from 1848 to 1852. He traveled in New Granada from 1852 to 1854, conducting a survey of the flora and collecting plants, and wrote an account of his experiences in *New Granada: Twenty Months in the Andes* (New York, 1857). He preached in McHenry County, Illinois, from 1858 to 1863, was a pastor in Hillsgrove, Illinois, from 1863 to 1865, was on the staff of *Boston Recorder* and later the *Congregationalist*, and then became one of the editors of *Daily News*. Died January 25, 1875, in Everett, Massachusetts. *References*: Isaac F. Holton, *New Granada: Twenty Months in the Andes*, ed. with an introduction by C. Harvey Gardiner (Carbondale, Ill., 1967); and *Amherst*.

HOMER, WINSLOW (1836–1910). Painter, born February 24, 1836, in Boston, and grew up in Cambridge. Homer was apprenticed to a lithographer in 1855. He opened his own studio in 1857, worked as an illustrator for various magazines, and illustrated the Civil War for *Harper's Weekly*. He settled in Prouts Neck, near Scarboro, Maine, in 1883. He went on painting trips to the Bahamas and Bermuda in 1884–1885, to the Bahamas in 1898–1899, and to Bermuda from 1899 to 1901. Died September 29, 1910, in Prouts Neck, Maine. *References*: Winslow Homer Archives, Bowdoin College Museum of Art, Brunswick, Me.; Helen A. Cooper, *Winslow Homer Watercolors* (New Haven, Conn., 1986); *DAB*; Lloyd Goodrich, *Winslow Homer* (New York, 1944); Patti Hannaway, *Winslow Homer in the Tropics* (Richmond, Va., 1973); Gordon Hendricks, *The Life and Work of Winslow Homer* (New York, 1979); *NCAB* 11:304; *NYT*, October 1, 1910; and *WWWA*.

HOPKINS, EDWARD A(UGUSTUS) (1822–1891). Entrepreneur, born November 29, 1822, in Pittsburgh, and grew up in Burlington, Vermont. He was a midshipman in the U.S. Navy from 1840 to 1845. He was a special agent of the United States in Asunción, Paraguay, in 1845–1846, sent to report on the recognition of Paraguay, but was soon recalled for exceeding his instructions. He then wrote for the *National Intelligencer and Hunt's Merchants' Magazine*. He visited Paraguay twice. In 1851, he began promoting the United States and Paraguay Navigation Company. He was U.S. consul in Asunción from 1851 to 1854. He bought a large tract of land for his company, erected a sawmill, began to teach Paraguayan workmen to cure tobacco properly and to make a good grade of cigars, and established a cigar factory. Soon he fell out of favor with Cárlos Antonio Lopéz, president of Paraguay (1844–1862), who quickly brought the undertaking to an end. He continued to promote trade between the United States and South America and prepared a report on immigration and public lands in Argentina. He established steam navigation on the Paraná and built a steam railway between Buenos Aires and San Fernando. He was appointed consul general for Argentina in New York from 1864 but the United States refused to recognize him. Died June 10, 1891, in Washington, D.C. *References*: *ACAB*; *DAB*; *ELA*; Victor Johnson, "Edward A. Hopkins and the Development of Argentine Transportation and Communication," *HAHR* 26 (1946): 19–37; Harold F. Peterson, "Edward A. Hopkins: A Pioneer Promoter in Paraguay," *HAHR* 22 (1942): 245–61; Harris G. Warren, "The Hopkins Claim Against Paraguay and "The Case of the Missing Jewels," *IAEA* 22 (1968): 23–44; and *WWWA*.

HOPKINS, EDWIN BUTCHER (1882–1940). Petroleum geologist, born October 25, 1882, in Evans, West Virginia. Hopkins attended West Virginia University and graduated from George Washington University. He served with the U.S. Geological Survey from 1907 to 1909. He went to Mexico in 1909, was field geologist with the Mexican Eagle Petroleum Company from 1909 to 1912, and was assistant to the general manager of the company in 1912. He was manager of the Cuban Oil Company in 1913–1914 and engaged in prospecting for oil in Cuba. He was manager at Tampico, Mexico, for the International Petroleum Company from 1914 to 1916. He located the discovery wells of the Tanhuijo field in Mexico. He was a consulting petroleum geologist in Washington, D.C. after 1916, and later in Houston, Texas, New York City, and Dallas, Texas. He was president of Delta Petroleum Company, vice president and general manager of American Maracaibo Company, and vice president of Drilling and Exploration Company, Incorporated. Died July 5, 1940, in Dallas. *References*: *NCAB* 30:318; and *WWWA*.

HORMAN, CHARLES (EDMUND) (1942–1973). Journalist, born May 15, 1942, in New York City. Horman graduated from Harvard University. He settled temporarily in Chile in 1972 to pursue a career in free-lance writing. Supposedly he stumbled on evidence of U.S. involvement in the military coup against President Salvador Allende and was arrested by Chilean military. In October 1973, his fingerprints were matched with a body in the Santiago, Chile, morgue. His disappearance and the subsequent cover-up were documented in the film *Missing* (1982). *Reference*: Thomas Hauser, *Execution of Charles Horman: An American Sacrifice* (New York, 1978).

HORNE, CHARLES RIDGELY (1800–1884). Merchant, born March 28, 1800, in Baltimore. Horne came to Montevideo in 1820. He was involved in commerce and, in 1828, settled in Buenos Aires and became a shipping agent. He was granted Argentine citizenship in 1828. He was a ship broker after 1831. He was friendly with Juan Manuel de Rosas, dictator of Argentina, and provided financial aid to Rosas after he went into exile in 1851. He was expelled from Buenos Aires in 1853, settled in Montevideo, and represented an English shipping company there. Died March 14, 1884, in Montevideo. *Reference*: *Cutolo*.

HORNER, G(USTAVUS) R(ICHARD) B(ROWN) (1804–1892). Physician, born June 17, 1804, in Warrentown, Virginia. Horner graduated from the University of Pennsylvania Medical School. He served in the U.S. Navy from 1826 to 1871. He was fleet surgeon with the Brazil Squadron during the early 1840s and wrote *The Medical Topography of Brazil and Uruguay with Incidental Remarks* (Philadelphia, 1845). Died August 8, 1892, in Warrentown, Virginia. *Reference*: *Southern Folk Art*, ed. Cynthia E. Rubin (Birmingham, Ala., 1985).

HOWARD, JENNIE E(LIZA) (1845–1933). Educator, born July 24, 1845, in Coldbrook Springs, Massachusetts. Howard graduated from Framingham (Mass.) normal school. She went to Argentina in 1883 and organized and taught in a normal school for girls in Corrientes until 1886, was vice director of normal school in Córdoba from 1886 to 1888, and then was professor of mathematics and education in San Nicolas, Buenos Aires Province, until her retirement in

1903. She wrote her memoirs, *In Distant Climes and Other Years* (n.p., 1931). Died July 29, 1933, in Buenos Aires. *References*: *Cutolo*; and *Luiggi*.

HOWE, ERNEST (1875–1932). Geologist, born September 28, 1875, in New York City. Howe graduated from Yale and Harvard universities. He was assistant geologist with the U.S. Geological Survey from 1900 to 1910, geologist to the first Isthmian Canal Commission in 1906–1907, and consulting geologist there from 1910 to 1926. He was a geologist with the Brazilian expedition in 1916–1917 under the auspices of the Royal Geographical Society of London and reported on the geology of the upper regions of the Amazon. He advised the Mexican geological survey in 1920 and was a member of the Connecticut General Assembly in 1921 and of the state Senate in 1925. He was editor of *American Journal of Science* from 1926 until his death. Died December 18, 1932, in Litchfield, Massachusetts. *References*: *NCAB* 25:246; and *WWWA*.

HOWELL, JOHN BEATTY (1847–1924). Missionary, born March 31, 1847, in Allentown, New Jersey. Howell graduated from the College of New Jersey and Princeton Theological Seminary and was ordained in 1873. He was a city missionary in Wilkes-Barre, Pennsylvania, from 1870 to 1873. He was a missionary under the Board of Foreign Missions of the Presbyterian Church in the U.S.A.* in São Paulo, Brazil, from 1873 to 1890 and from 1894 to 1896. He held pastorates in Burlington, New Jersey, and Philadelphia until 1912. Died January 23, 1924, in Atlantic City, New Jersey. His wife, **ELIZABETH DAY HOWELL**, wrote children's stories about Brazil. *References*: Howell-Day Family Papers, University of New Hampshire, Durham, N.H.; and *PrincetonTS*.

HOWES, PAUL G(RISWOLD) (1892–1984). Naturalist and illustrator, born September 30, 1892, in Stamford, Connecticut. Howes was involved in several scientific expeditions to Central and South America for the American Museum of Natural History and the New York Zoological Society after 1913. In 1916, he was the research assistant and microphotographer on the team that established a permanent tropical research station in British Guiana for the New York Zoological Society. He was assistant curator and taxidermist of the Bruce Museum from 1918 to 1938 and curator-director from 1938 until his retirement in 1965. He was coauthor of *Tropical Wild Life in British Guiana* (New York, 1917) and wrote *Photographer in the Rain-Forests* (Noroton, Conn., 1969). Died June 16, 1984, in Branford, Connecticut. *References*: *CA*; and *NYT*, June 19, 1984.

HOWLAND, EDWARD (1832–1890) and **HOWLAND, MARIE (STEVENS CASE)** (1835–1921). Publicists and authors. Edward was born September 15, 1832, in Charleston, South Carolina. He graduated from Harvard University. He engaged in business and then cofounded the *New York Saturday Press*, a literary journal, in 1858; he was involved with it until 1869. Marie was born in New Hampshire and left home in 1847 to become a mill worker in Lowell,

Massachusetts. She moved to New York City in the early 1850s, graduated from the New York Normal School, and became a school principal. She also was involved in the reform movement. The couple married in 1865, lived in Hammonton, New Jersey, after 1868, and in the 1880s were publicists for Albert Kimsey Owen's* scheme and editors of its journal, *Integral Cooperation*. They went to Topolobampo Bay Colony* in 1885 as colonists and edited *The Credit Foncier of Sinaloa*, the colony's publication, until 1890. Edward died March 25, 1890, in Topolobampo, Sinaloa, Mexico. Marie remained there until 1894, and then moved to the cooperative single-tax colony in Fairhope, Alabama. Died September 1921, in Fairhope, Alabama. *References*: Robert S. Fogarty, *Dictionary of American Communal and Utopian History* (Westport, Conn., 1980); Vicki L. Hill, "Marie Howland," in Lina Mainiero, ed., *American Women Writers* (New York, 1980), 2:245–47; and *NCAB* 4:91.

HUNNICUTT, BENJAMIN HARRIS (1886– ?). Educator, born September 25, 1886, in Turin, Georgia. Hunnicutt graduated from Mississippi Agricultural and Mechanical College and the University of Georgia. He was director of the Lavras Agricultural School in Lavras, Minas Gerais, Brazil, from 1908 to 1926, and professor there from 1927 to 1930. He was president of the Gammon Institute in Lavras in 1933, and president of MacKenzie College in São Paulo, Brazil, after 1934. He wrote *Brazil Looks Forward* (Rio de Janeiro, 1945), and *Brazil, World Frontier* (New York, 1949). *Reference*: WWWA.

HUNT, BENJAMIN PETER (1808–1877). Merchant, born May 18, 1808, in Chelmsford, Massachusetts. Hunt attended Harvard University. He taught for several years in Philadelphia. He was in Jamaica from 1840 to 1842 and in Haiti from 1842 to 1858, where he established a commercial house in Port-au-Prince. He returned to the United States in 1858. He acquired books and manuscripts in Port-au-Prince (now in the Boston Public Library). Died February 2, 1877, in Philadelphia. *Reference*: George W. Cooke, *An Historical and Biographical Introduction to Accompany The Dial* (New York, 1961), 2:176–80.

HUNT, WILLIAM HENRY (1857–1949). Lawyer and colonial administrator, born November 5, 1857, in New Orleans. Hunt attended Yale University, studied law at the University of Louisiana, and was admitted to the bar. He went to Montana Territory in 1882 and practiced law in Helena. He was collector of customs for Montana and Idaho from 1885 to 1887 and attorney general of the territory from 1887 to 1889. He served in the state legislature in 1889, was elected judge of the first judicial district from 1889 to 1894, and was associate justice of the state supreme court from 1894 to 1900. He was first secretary of the civil government of Puerto Rico, president of the executive council of the island in 1900–1901, and governor from 1901 to 1904. He was U.S. district judge for the District of Montana from 1904 to 1910 and associate judge for the U.S. Circuit Court of Appeal in San Francisco from 1911 to 1928. He resumed the practice of law until 1942. Died February 4, 1949, in Charlottesville, Virginia. *References*: *NCAB* 37:249; and *NYT*, February 5, 1949.

HUNTER, WILLIAM, JR. (1774–1849). Public official and diplomat, born November 26, 1774, in Newport, Rhode Island. Hunter graduated from Brown University, studied law in London, and was admitted to the bar in 1820. He practiced law in Rhode Island, was a member of the state house of representatives from 1799 to 1811, member of U.S. Senate from 1811 to 1821, and again a member of the state house of representatives from 1822 to 1826. He then resumed the practice of law. He was U.S. chargé d'affaires to Brazil from 1834 to 1841 and minister there from 1841 to 1844. Died December 3, 1849, in Newport, Rhode Island. *References*: *ACAB*; *BDAC*; *DAB*; *NCAB* 9:269; and *WWWA*.

HURLBUT, STEPHEN AUGUSTUS (1815–1882). Lawyer and diplomat, born November 29, 1815, in Charleston, South Carolina. Hurlbut studied law and was admitted to the bar. He practiced law in Charleston until 1845. He then moved to Illinois and served in the Illinois state legislature. He served in the Union Army during the Civil War. He was U.S. minister to Colombia from 1866 to 1872 and to Peru from 1881 until his death. He became involved in the diplomacy of the War of the Pacific and tried to have the U.S. Navy intervene in the war. He exceeded his instructions by getting Peru to cede to the United States territory for a coaling station. Died March 28, 1882, in Lima Peru. *References*: *ACAB*; *DAB*; *DADH*; Jeffrey N. Lash, "Stephen Augustus Hurlbut: A Military and Diplomatic Politician, 1815–1882," Ph.D. diss., Kent State University, 1980; *NCAB* 4:218; *NYT*, April 3, 1882; and *WWWA*.

HUSK, CHARLES [CARLOS] ELLSWORTH (1872–1916). Physician, born December 19, 1872, in Shabona, DeKalb County, Illinois. Husk graduated from the College of Physicians and Surgeons (Chicago). He was company surgeon for the American Smelting and Refining Company in Mexico from 1898 until his death, first at Tepezala, Aguascalientes, and then in Santa Barbara, Chihuahua. He was also municipal health officer of Santa Barbara. He inaugurated a local vaccination campaign which practically stamped out smallpox. He was surgeon in chief of all the company's interests in Mexico after 1911, involved with a commission organized by Mount Sinai Hospital of New York to investigate typhus fever in Mexico after 1915, and also engaged in a sanitary campaign against the carrier of this disease. Died March 20, 1916, in Laredo, Texas. *References*: *DAB*; and *NYT*, March 21, 1916.

HUTCHINSON, HARRY W(ILLIAM) (1922–   ). Anthropologist, born August 18, 1922, in New York City. Hutchinson graduated from Columbia University. He served in the U.S. Navy during World War II. He carried out fieldwork in Bahia, Brazil, in 1955–1956, and in São Paulo from 1957 to 1959. He was an associate professor of psychiatry and anthropology at the University of Miami from 1961 to 1966 and professor after 1966. He wrote *Village and Plantation Life in Northeastern Brazil* (Seattle, 1957). *Reference*: AMWS.

I

IGLEHART, DAVID STEWART (1873–1946). Businessman, born September 4, 1873, in New Albany, Indiana. Iglehart graduated from Columbia University. He served during the Spanish-American War. He joined W. R. Grace and Company in 1894, was transferred to the Grace office in Lima, Peru, in 1899, and traveled throughout South America. He was resident director in charge of all company activities on the West Coast from 1908, vice president of the company from 1909 to 1929, and its representative in South America from 1901 to 1915, continuing to direct the company's business on the West Coast. He was president of W. R. Grace and Company and president of Grace Line from 1929 until 1946. Died May 14, 1946, in Old Westbury, Long Island, New York. *References*: *NYT*, May 15, 1946; and *WWWA*.

IGLEHART, FANNY (CHAMBERS) GOOCH (1839–1931). Author, born December 9, 1839, in Hillsboro, Mississippi, and grew up in Weatherford and Waco, Texas. She settled with her first husband, G. W. Gooch, in Saltillo, Mexico, probably from 1876 to 1883. She later returned to Mexico and traveled throughout the country. Her sojourn in Mexico led to her first book, *Face to Face with the Mexicans: The Domestic Life, Educational, Social, and Business Ways, Statesmanship and Literature, Legendary and General History of the Mexican People, as Seen and Studied by an American Woman during Seven Years of Intercourse with Them* (New York, 1887). She returned again to Mexico in 1900. She wrote *Tradition of Guadalupe and Mexico: Christmas in Old Mexico* (n.p., 1901), a children's book. Died October 10, 1931, in Austin, Texas. *References*: Fanny Iglehart, *Face to Face with the Mexicans*, ed. C. Harvey Gardiner (Carbondale, Ill., 1966); and James B. Lloyd, ed., *Lives of Mississippi Authors, 1817–1967* (Jackson, Miss., 1981).

ÎLE À VACHE COLONY. A colony for black Americans was established in 1862 on the island, twelve miles offshore from Haiti. The colony continued until 1864. *Reference*: Willis D. Boyd, "The Île à Vache Colonization Venture, 1862–1864," *TA* 16 (1959): 45–62.

ILLICH, IVAN D. (1926–   ). Clergyman and educator, born September 4, 1926, in Vienna, Austria. Illich attended the universities of Florence, Rome, and Munich, graduated from the Gregorian University (Rome) and the University of Salzburg, and was ordained in 1951. He came to the United States in 1951 and later became a U.S. citizen. He was a parish priest in a Puerto Rican community in New York City from 1951 to 1956 and vice rector of the Catholic University of Puerto Rico (Santa Maria, Ponce) from 1956 to 1960. After 1961, he was cofounder and director of the Centro Intercultural de Documentation in Cuernavaca, Mexico, a language school and training station for priests and laymen who want to become Latin American volunteers. He left the priesthood in 1969. *References: CA; CB* 1969; Francine du Plessix Gray, *Divine Disobedience: Profiles in Catholic Radicalism* (New York, 1970); and *WWA.*

INGRAHAM, PRENTISS (1843–1904). Soldier of fortune and author, born December 22, 1843, in Adams County, Mississippi. Ingraham attended Jefferson College (Miss.) and Mobile Medical College. He served in the Confederate Army during the Civil War. He then became a soldier of fortune. He joined the Mexican forces under Benito Juarez in their revolution against the Emperor Maximilian. He subsequently served in the Austrian army in the Austro-Prussian War, in Crete against the Turks, in the Khedive's army in Egypt, and, during Cuba's ten-year revolt from Spain, as a colonel in the Cuban army and a captain in the Cuban navy. He was captured by the Spanish and condemned to death but escaped. He was involved in literary work in London after 1870, and later, in New York, Easton, Maryland, and Chicago. He wrote six hundred novels and four hundred novelettes, which were often derived from his own experience. *The Cuban Conspirator: or, The Island League: A Romance of Cuba and Cuban Waters* (New York, 1874) recounts his adventures in the Cuban revolution. Died August 16, 1904, in Beavoir, Mississippi. *References: ACAB; DAB*; James B. Lloyd, ed., *Lives of Mississippi Authors, 1817–1967* (Jackson, Miss., 1981); and *WWWA.*

INMAN, SAMUEL GUY (1877–1965). Educator, born June 24, 1877, in Trinity, Texas. Inman graduated from Columbia University. He was director of social work at First Church of the Disciples of Christ in New York from 1901 to 1904; a missionary in Monterrey, Mexico, from 1905 to 1907; director of the Peoples' Institute in Piedras Negras, Mexico, from 1907 to 1915; secretary of the Committee on Cooperation with Latin America from 1915 to 1939; and founder and editor of *La Nueva Democracia* from 1920 to 1939. He was a professor at Columbia University from 1919 to 1934 and at the University of Pennsylvania from 1937 to 1942. He wrote *Through Santo Domingo and Haiti: A Cruise with the Marines* (New York, 1919), *Intervention in Mexico* (New York, 1919), *Problems in Pan-Americanism* (New York, 1921), *Building an Inter-American Neighborhood* (New York, 1937), and *Democracy versus the Totalitarian State in Latin America* (Philadelphia, 1938). Died February 19, 1965, in New York City. *References*: Samuel Guy Inman Papers, Manuscript Division, Library of Congress; William J. Castleman, *On This Foundation: A Historical Literary Biography of the Early Life of Samuel Guy Inman . . . Covering the Period 1877– 1904* (St. Louis, 1966); William J. Castleman, *Samuel Guy Inman* (Indianapolis, 1969); Warren F. Kuehl, ed., *Biographical Dictionary of Internationalists* (Westport, Conn., 1983); *NYT*, February 21, 1965; Kenneth F. Woods, "Samuel Guy Inman—His Role in the Evolution of Inter-American Cooperation," Ph.D. diss., American University, 1962; and *WWWA*.

INSTITUTE OF INTER-AMERICAN AFFAIRS (IIAA). An assistance program to Latin America, established in 1942 at the suggestion of Nelson A. Rockefeller.* It aimed at improving health conditions and sanitation in Latin America and improving local agricultural techniques. It established more than 1,500 projects, including hospitals, health centers, and water and sewage projects. It survived until the late 1950s when it was dismantled piecemeal and its projects turned over to local governments. *References*: Claude Erb, "Prelude to Point Four: The Institute of Inter-American Affairs," *DH* 9 (1985): 249–69; and Louis Halle, *The Significance of the Institute of Inter-American Affairs in the Conduct of U.S. Foreign Policy* (Washington, D.C., 1948).

INTER-AMERICAN DEVELOPMENT BANK (IADB). Established in 1959 to facilitate United States loans to Latin American nations and serve as a clearinghouse for development capital from Latin American nations themselves. It was initially funded with a capitalization of one billion dollars. *References*: *DADH*; Sidney S. Dell, *The Inter-American Development Bank: A Study in Development Financing* (New York, 1972); and R. Peter DeWitt, *The Inter-American Development Bank and Political Influence, with Special Reference to Costa Rica* (New York, 1977).

INTER-AMERICAN HIGHWAY. *See* PAN AMERICAN HIGHWAY

INTERNATIONAL BASIC ECONOMY CORPORATION. Founded in 1947 by Nelson A. Rockefeller* to upgrade the basic economies of developing countries by lowering food prices, building sound housing, mobilizing savings, and fostering better distribution of the fruits of economic progress. He founded a number of companies, initially in Venezuela and Brazil and, after 1955, in other countries of Latin America. *Reference*: Wayne G. Broehl, Jr., *The International Basic Economy Corporation* (Washington, D.C., 1968).

INTERNATIONAL PETROLEUM COMPANY (IPC). Organized by Standard Oil Company of New Jersey in 1914 to serve as a holding company for its operations in Peru and, later, Colombia and Ecuador. It bought the London and Pacific Petroleum Company in 1914. It leased the La Brea an Pariñas oilfield in Peru in 1913 and purchased them outright in 1924. In 1957, it obtained control of the Lobitos holdings. Its properties were taken over by the Peruvian government in 1968. *References*: Richard N. Goodwin, "Letter from Peru," *New Yorker* 45 (May 17, 1969): 441–67; Adalberto J. Pinelo, *The Multinational Corporation as a Force in Latin American Politics: A Case Study of the International Petroleum Company in Peru* (New York, 1973); and Kenneth A. Rodman, *Sanctity Versus Sovereignty: The United States and the Nationalization of Natural Resource Investments* (New York, 1988), ch. 7.

INTERNATIONAL TELEPHONE AND TELEGRAPH CORPORATION (I.T.T.). Founded in 1920, it initially merged two telephone companies in Cuba and Puerto Rico. It later expanded its activities to Mexico, southern Brazil, Uruguay, and Argentina, and then to other parts of Latin America. In 1927, it acquired All American Cables, Incorporated.* The company played a crucial role in the attempt to prevent the election of President Salvador Allende of Chile from 1970 to 1973. It supported anti-Allende activities, particularly after the Chilean government outlined in 1971 plans to nationalize I.T.T.'s operations in Chile. Its efforts, directed to create economic chaos in Chile in an attempt to subvert the government, led eventually to Allende's overthrow. *References*: Anthony Sampson, *The Sovereign State of the ITT* (New York, 1973); and Robert Sobel, *I.T.T.: The Management of Opportunity* (New York, 1982).

INTERVENTIONS. *See under name of countries*: CUBA, HAITI, NICARAGUA, PANAMA

IRVINE, BAPTIS (fl. 1818–1824). Journalist and public official, born in Baltimore. Irvine served as a journeyman printer in Philadelphia and edited a newspaper in New York City. He then became one of the editors of the *Whig*, the leading Democratic paper in Baltimore. He was special diplomatic agent to Venezuela in 1818–1819 and was commissioned to seek restitution of United States vessels seized by Simón Bolívar's forces and to report on the progress of the revolution. After his return to the United States, he engaged in various forms of journalistic hack work and was editor of the Washington *City Gazette* in 1821–1822. In 1822, he took part in an expedition against Puerto Rico, led by the Swedish adventurer Ducoudray Holstein, and was taken prisoner by the Dutch colonial authorities in Curaçao. He wrote "Cursory Notes on Venezuela" (Baltimore, 1819, Ms. in the National Archives), and *Traits of Colonial Jurisprudence; or, A Peep at the Trading Inquisition of Curacao* (Baltimore, 1824). *References*: Lewis Hanke, ed. "Baptis Irvine's Report on Simon Bolivar," *HAHR* 16 (1936): 360–73; and John C. Pine, "The Role of United States Special

Agents in the Development of a Spanish American Policy, 1818–1822,'' Ph.D. diss., University of Colorado, 1955, ch. 8.

ISLA DE PINOS [ISLE OF PINES], CUBA. An island southwest of Cuba. After the Spanish-American War, the impression prevailed that the island was to be an American possession. It brought American settlers after 1899, who established an American colony on the northern part of the island. The first American town to be founded was Columbia, at the foot of Mount San Juan. Following the settlement of the question of ownership in 1925, Americans began to leave and American settlement declined. *References*: F. A. Carlson, "American Settlement in the Isla de Pinos, Cuba," *Geographical Review* 32 (1942): 21–35; Janet D. Frost, "Cuba–American Relations Concerning the Isle of Pines," *HAHR* 11 (1931): 336–50; and Filiberto Ramirez Corria, *Excerta de Una Isla Magica: Biografia de un Latifundio* (Mexico, 1959).

ISLAS DEL MAIZ [CORN ISLANDS]. Islands off the coast of Nicaragua. Leased by Nicaragua to the United States from 1916 to 1971, to protect the mouth of the projected Nicaragua canal.

***ITATA* INCIDENT** (1891). The Chilean merchant ship *Itata* carried arms from the United States to Chile in 1891, in the face of U.S. opposition. It was voluntarily handed over by the Chilean authorities to the cruiser USS *Charleston* in order to avoid provoking ill-will. *References*: *DADH*; and Osgood Hardy, "The *Itata* Incident," *HAHR* 5 (1922): 195–226.

IVINS, ANTHONY W(OODWARD) (1852–1934). Mormon leader, born September 16, 1852, in Toms River, Ocean County, New Jersey, and grew up in Salt Lake City and St. George, Utah. Ivins engaged in farming and livestock production, and served as assessor, deputy sheriff, and prosecuting attorney of Washington County and as mayor of St. George. He went on preaching missions to Mexico in 1875–1876 and 1882–1883 and presided over the Mormon colonies in northern Mexico from 1895 to 1908, living in Colonia Juarez. He returned to Salt Lake City in 1908, was appointed one of the twelve apostles in 1909, and was counselor to the president of the Church of Christ of Latter-Day Saints from 1921 until his death. Died September 23, 1934, in Salt Lake City, Utah. *References*: Anthony W. Ivins Papers, Latter-Day Saints Archives, Salt Lake City, Utah; *DAB S1*; and *WWWA*.

J

JACKSON, HENRY G. (1838–1914). Missionary, born in Indiana. Jackson graduated from Indiana Asbury University. He was principal of Stockwell Collegiate Institute (Indiana) and a pastor in New Orleans from 1862 to 1869. He was a pastor in Buenos Aires and superintendent of the South American Mission from 1869 to 1878. He prepared the first hymnal in the Spanish language, *Himnario*, which continued in use for nearly eighty years, going through some seven editions. He returned to the United States in 1878, and held pastorates in Kansas City, Missouri, and Chicago. *Reference*: *EWM*.

JACKSON, HENRY ROOTES (1820–1898). Lawyer and diplomat, born June 24, 1820, in Athens, Georgia. Jackson graduated from Yale University and studied law. He practiced law in Savannah, was a U.S. district attorney from 1843 to 1849, served during the Mexican War, and was a superior court judge from 1849 to 1853. He was chargé d'affaires and later minister in Austria from 1853 to 1858. He was a judge in the Confederate courts in Georgia and later served in the Confederate Army during the Civil War, after which he again practiced law in Georgia. He was U.S. minister to Mexico in 1885–1886 but resigned because of disagreement with his government on the question of *Rebecca*, a schooner seized by Mexico on the charge of smuggling. Died May 23, 1898, in Savannah, Georgia. *References*: *ACAB*; *DAB*; *NCAB* 3:369; and *WWWA*.

JAMES, PRESTON E(VERETT) (1899–1986). Geographer, born February 14, 1899, in Brookline, Massachusetts. James graduated from Harvard and Clark universities. He served in the U.S. Army during World War I. He was assistant professor of geography at the University of Michigan from 1924 to 1928, associate professor from 1928 to 1934, and professor from 1934 to 1945. He was professor of geography at Syracuse University from 1945 until his retirement in 1970. He carried out fieldwork in Latin America in 1921, 1924, 1930, 1938, 1949–1950, 1956, 1959, 1960, 1965, and 1969. He was chief of the Latin

American Division of the U.S. Office of Strategic Service and then head of its
Europe and Africa division during World War II. He wrote *Latin America* (New
York, 1942), *Brazil* (New York, 1946), and *Introduction to Latin America* (New
York, 1964). Died January 5, 1986, in Syracuse, New York. *References*: Preston
E. James Papers, Syracuse University Library, Syracuse, N.Y.; *On Geography:
Selected Writings of Preston E. James*, ed. D. W. Meing (Syracuse, N.Y., 1971);
CA; Journal of Geography 85 (1968): 273–74; David J. Robinson, ed., *Studying
Latin America: Essays in Honor of Preston E. James* (Ann Arbor, Mich., 1980);
and *WWWA*.

JAMES, W(ILLIAM) MC(CULLY) (1874–1942). Physician, born May 29,
1874, in Richmond, Virginia. James graduated from Johns Hopkins University
and the University of Virginia. He came to the Isthmus of Panama in 1906 and
served in the Isthmian Canal Commission medical service until 1916, when he
joined the Panama Hospital staff. He was assistant chief of the medical service
of the Ancon Hospital in the Panama Canal Zone from 1910 to 1914 and chief
of the medical service of Panama Hospital and the Herrick Clinic after 1916.
An authority on tropical medicine, he worked in tropical disease research and
also in the Health Department of the Canal Zone. Died July 10, 1942, in Panama
City, Republic of Panama. *References*: *AMWS*; and *NYT*, July 11, 1942.

JANVIER, THOMAS ALLIBONE (1849–1913). Journalist, born July 16,
1849, in Philadelphia. Janvier did editorial work on the Philadelphia *Press*,
Bulletin, and *Times* from 1870 to 1881, and traveled as a journalist in Colorado,
New Mexico, and Mexico from 1881 to 1884. He later traveled again in Mexico.
He traveled in England and France from 1893 to 1900. He wrote *The Mexican
Guide* (New York, 1886–   ), *The Aztec Treasure House: A Romance of
Contemporaneous Antiquity*, (New York, 1890), *Stories of Old New Spain* (New
York, 1891), and *Legends of the City of Mexico* (New York, 1910). Died June
18, 1913, in New York City. *References*: *ACAB*; *DAB*; *NCAB* 12:460; *NYT*,
June 19, 1913; and *WWWA*.

JAQUES, FRANCIS LEE (1887–1969). Artist and naturalist, born September
28, 1887, in Genesco, Illinois. Jaques attended School of Engineering (Milwaukee). He began as an artist in 1920 and joined the American Museum of
Natural History from 1924 until his retirement in 1942. He participated in expeditions to Panama in 1925, to South America in 1926, to the Bahamas in
1926, and again to South America in 1935. He prepared panoramic background
paintings and murals in the American Museum of Natural History, the Minnesota
Museum of Natural History, the Peabody Museum of Yale University, and the
Boston Museum of Science. Died July 24, 1969, in St. Paul, Minnesota. *References*: *The Art of Francis Lee Jaques* (Minneapolis, 1972); Florence P. Jaques,
Francis Lee Jaques: Artist of the Wilderness World (New York, 1973); Donald

Luce and Laura M. Andrews, *Francis Lee Jaques: Artist-Naturalist* (Minneapolis, 1982); *NYT*, July 25, 1969; and *WWWA*.

JARI PROJECT. Begun in 1967 by Daniel Keith Ludwig on three million acres on the Jari River, in the northern part of the state of Para in Brazil. It was the largest tropical forestry project in the world, in which $750 million were invested. The primary activity was plantations of a fast-growing East India tree to be used for wood fiber. A pulp mill and wood-fired power plant were established in the port of Manguba. The secondary activities were mining, and livestock raising. The project suffered technical setbacks and was unsuccessful. It was sold in 1982 to a consortium of twenty-seven companies backed by the Brazilian government. *References*: Marcos Arruda, "Daniel Keith Ludwig," in Marcos Arruda, Herbert de Souza, and Carlos Afonso, *The Multinational Corporations and Brazil: The Impact of Multinational Corporations in the Contemporary Brazilian Economy* (Toronto, 1975), pp. 130–207; Modesto Da Silveira, *Ludwig: Imperador do Brasil* (Rio de Janeiro, 1981); Norman Gall, "Ludwig's Amazon Empire," *Forbes* 123 (May 14, 1979): 127–44; Gwen Kinkead, "Trouble in D. K. Ludwig's Jungle," *Fortune* 103 (April 20, 1981): 102–117; L. McIntyre, "Jari: A Massive Technology Transplant Takes Root in the Amazon Jungle," *National Geographic Magazine* 157 (May 1980): 698–711; and Jerry Shields, *The Invisible Billionaire: Daniel Ludwig* (Boston, 1986), ch. 18.

JARVIS, HARRY A(YDELOTTE) (1909–1972). Petroleum executive, born May 11, 1909, in Berlin, Maryland. Jarvis graduated from the University of Maryland and attended Harvard University. He joined Compañia Nativa de Petroleo, an affiliate of Standard Oil Company of New Jersey, in Buenos Aires, Argentina, in 1931; was junior engineer at its refinery in Campana from 1931 to 1935; manager of the refinery in Bahia Blanca in 1935–1936; process superintendent of the Campana refinery from 1936 to 1938; assistant superintendent from 1938 to 1941; manager from 1941 to 1945; and president of Compañia Nativa de Petroleo in Buenos Aires and general manager of refining from 1945 to 1947. He was with Creole Petroleum Company after 1947; manager of refinery in Amuay, Venezuela, from 1947 to 1949; manager of the refining department from 1949 to 1954; executive vice president from 1954 to 1961; and president from 1961 until his retirement in 1964. Died October 19, 1972, in Berlin, Maryland. *References*: NCAB 58: 486; and *WWWA*.

JARVIS, THOMAS JORDAN (1836–1915). Public official, born January 18, 1836, in Jarvisburg, North Carolina. Jarvis graduated from Randolph-Macon College. He served in the Confederate Army during the Civil War. He studied law, and was admitted to the bar in 1868. He practiced law, was a member of the state legislature in 1868–1869 and 1870–1871, lieutenant governor of North Carolina from 1877 to 1879, and governor from 1879 to 1885. He was U.S. minister to Brazil from 1885 to 1889. He was a U.S. senator in 1894–1895.

Died June 17, 1915, in Greenville, North Carolina. *References*: *ACAB*; *BDAC*; *DAB*; *NCAB* 4:429; and *WWWA*.

JEFFERS, WILLIAM NICHOLSON (1824–1883). Naval officer, born October 16, 1824, in Swedesboro, New Jersey. Jeffers was appointed a midshipman in 1840 and graduated from the U.S. Naval Academy in 1846. He served in the Mexican War. In 1852–1853 and again in 1857, he was engaged in survey work in Honduras for a proposed interoceanic railway and in 1859–1860 he was hydrographer in surveys for a canal route across the Chiriqui Isthmus. He served in the Brazil squadron from 1853 to 1856. He commanded the USS *Water Witch* in the survey expedition up the Parana and La Plata rivers. The firing on this vessel by the Paraguayan battery led to the naval punitive expedition of 1857. In 1853, he accompanied Dr. Samuel Woodhouse of the Philadelphia Academy of Natural Sciences in his reconnaissance of Nicaragua, reporting favorably on its potential for an interoceanic canal. He served in the Union Navy during the Civil War and was chief of the bureau of ordnance from 1873 to 1881. Died July 23, 1883, in Washington, D.C. *References*: *ACAB*; *DAB*; *NCAB* 4:281; and *WWWA*.

JEFFERSON, BENJAMIN LAFAYETTE (1871–1950). Physician and diplomat, born October 26, 1871, in Columbus, Georgia. Jefferson graduated from the University of Maryland. He practiced medicine in Littleton, Colorado, from 1892 to 1895; Steamboat Springs, Colorado, from 1895 to 1910; and Denver after 1910. He served in the Colorado House of Representatives from 1898 to 1900 and in the state senate from 1900 to 1908. He was U.S. minister to Nicaragua from 1913 to 1921. He took part in the negotiations that resulted in the Bryan-Chamorro Treaty of 1916 by which Nicaragua granted to the United States exclusive rights for a canal route and a naval base. He was superintendent of the Colorado State Home and Training School for Mental Defectives in Grand Junction from 1931 until his death. Died July 21, 1950, in Denver, Colorado. *References*: *NCAB* 40:214; and *WWWA*.

JEFFERSON, MARK (SYLVESTER WILLIAM) (1863–1949). Geographer, born March 1, 1863, in Melrose, Massachusetts. Jefferson graduated from Boston and Harvard universities. He was employed in the National Observatory in Córdoba, Argentina and observed the weather in Córdoba from 1883 to 1887. He was assistant manager and treasurer of La Providencia sugar cane plantation near Tucumán from 1887 to 1889. He was a teacher in Billerica, Turner Falls, and Brockton, superintendent of schools in Lexington, Massachusetts, and a member of the faculty of Michigan State Normal School (later Eastern Michigan University) in Ypsilanti from 1901 to 1939. He was chief cartographer for the American Commission to Negotiate Peace in Paris in 1918–1919. He wrote *The Rainfall of Chile* (New York, 1921), *Recent Colonization in Chile* (New York, 1921), and *Peopling the Argentine Pampas* (New York, 1926). Died August 8,

1949, in Ypsilanti, Michigan. *References*: Mark Jefferson Papers, Eastern Michigan University Library, Ypsilanti; *BDAE*; *DAB S4*; and *WWWA*.

JEWETT, DAVID (1772–1842). Naval officer, born June 17, 1772, in New London, Connecticut. Jewett served in the naval war against France and was commander in the U.S. Navy from 1799 to 1801. In 1815, he entered the service of the United Provinces of the Rio de la Plata (later the Argentine Republic), commanded the bark *Invencible* and captured several Spanish vessels, and then sailed for Port Soledad in the Falkland Islands in command of the armed vessel *Heroina*. He landed there in 1820 in the name of the United Provinces, and set up the claim for legal title that was used in the later international dispute over their ownership. He spent some time on the island and returned to Buenos Aires in 1821. In 1822, he left the employ of the United Provinces, and became captain in the navy of Brazil. He took a prominent and active part under Lord Thomas Cochrane driving the Portuguese fleet out of Bahia, Brazil. He was promoted to chief of division in the Brazilian navy in 1823, and then became admiral and commander in chief of the Brazilian navy. He commanded the naval forces that defeated the Confederation of the Equator at Pernamabuco, and continued in the Brazilian naval service for the rest of his life. He made numerous prolonged visits to the United States on behalf of the Brazilian government, contracted for and superintended the buildings of several ships of war, and contributed a large share to the upbuilding of the strength and tradition of the Brazilian navy. Died July 26, 1842, in Rio de Janeiro. *References*: Cutolo; *DAB; NCAB* 30:80; Mario D. Tesler, "Expedicion de David Jewett a las Islas Malvinas, 1820–1821," *Revista Universidad* [Santa Fe], no. 74 (1968): 105–52; and *WWWA*.

JOHNSON, JAMES WELDON (1871–1938). Author, educator and consul, born June 17, 1871, in Jackson, Florida. Johnson graduated from Atlanta University, studied law, and was admitted to the bar in 1897. He was principal of school in Jacksonville from 1894 to 1901, and then involved in song writing. He was U.S. consul in Puerto Cabello, Venezuela, from 1906 to 1909 and in Corinto, Nicaragua, from 1909 to 1912. He helped maintain peace and order in Corinto and to protect lives and property during the revolution of 1912 in Nicaragua. He stalled attacks by rebel forces on Corinto, which was a stronghold of President Adolfo Diaz and chief entrepot for the American forces, until the arrival of U.S. forces that ended the threat. He was editor of *New York Age* after 1914, and organizer and field secretary for the National Association for the Advancement of Colored People (NAACP) from 1920 to 1931. In 1920, at the urging of the NAACP, he investigated conditions in Haiti and produced a series of articles for *The Nation*. He wrote *Along This Way: The Autobiography of James W. Johnson* (New York, 1933). Died June 26, 1938, in a train accident on the way from Great Barrington to Maine. *References*: *CA*; *DAB S2*; *DANB*; *DLB*; William E. Gibbs, "James Weldon Johnson: A Black Perspective on 'Big Stick,' " *DH* 8 (1984): 329–47; Eugene Levy, *James Weldon Johnson: Black*

Leader, Black Voice (Chicago, 1973); Rayford W. Logan, "James Weldon Johnson and Haiti," *Phylon* 32 (1971): 396–402; *NCAB* C:488; *NYT*, June 28, 1938; and *WWWA*.

JOHNSON, LORENZO M(EDICI) (1843–1904). Financier, born January 22, 1843, in New York City, and grew up in Rochester, Massachusetts. Johnson served in the Union Army during the Civil War. He graduated from Yale University. He was U.S. vice consul in Beirut, Jaffa, Jerusalem, and Damascus from 1867 to 1871. He was engineer, chief engineer, assistant to the general superintendent, and general superintendent of Keokuk and Des Moines Railroad from 1874 to 1877, and its general manager from 1877 to 1880, and general manager of the Cairo and St. Louis Railroad Company from 1881 to 1883. He was general manager of the Mexican International Railroad Company from 1883 to 1902. He was also manager of Alamo, Fuente, Coahuila and Rio Bravo Coal companies, and of the Coahuila and Durango Development Company, and manager of the Mexican Union Railway, the El Carmen Railway, the Aguascalientes Railway, and the Valadena Railway in 1903–1904, with headquarters in Mexico City. Died November 28, 1904, in St. Mary's, Pennsylvania. *References*: *NCAB* 6:402; and *WWWA*.

JOHNSTON, BENJAMIN F(RANCIS) (1867–1937). Manufacturer, born in Virginia. Johnston came to Mexico in 1889. In 1892, he took over land and water rights of the Topolobampo Bay Colony in the Fuerte River Valley. He raised sugar cane in the land around Los Mochis, and constructed there the El Aguila sugar mill. He incorporated the Sinaloa Planting Company (later Sinaloa Sugar Company), and had large sugar plantation interests in the west coast of Mexico, where he had been a successful developer of food producing lands after 1900. He was president of the United Sugar Company. In 1929, the Kansas City, Mexico, and Orient Railway properties in Mexico were transferred to him. Died March 10, 1937, in Hong Kong. *References*: Cuen Fernando, "Benjamin F. Johnston," in Ernest Higuera, comp., *Antología de Prosistas Sinaloenses* (Culiacán, Sinaloa, Mexico, 1959), 1:200–202; Mario Gill, *La Conquista del Valle del Fuerte* (Culiacán, Rosales, Sinaloa, Mexico, 1983), pp. 59–81; and *NYT*, March 11, 1937.

JOHNSTON, SAMUEL B(URR) (fl. 1811–1816). Printer. Johnston came to Chile in 1811 or 1812, under contract to work on a press brought from the United States. He served in the Chilean Navy in the War of Independence, was second in command of the brig *Colt*, bought in 1813 by the Chilean revolutionary government in order to blockade Talcahuano and to prevent the landing of reinforcements and supplies for the royalist army. He fought several engagements in 1813, was captured by the royalist forces and was held prisoner for several months. He wrote *Letters Written during a Residence of Three Years in Chile, Containing an Account of the Most Remarkable Events in the Revolutionary*

Struggles of That Province (Erie, Pa., 1816), the first book about Chile printed in the United States. *References*: Samuel B. Johnston, *Cartas de un Tipógrafo Yanqui en Chile a Peru Durante le Guerra de la Independencia*, traduccion, prologo y notas de Jose Toribio Medina (Buenos Aires, 1967); and Samuel B. Johnston, *Diario de un Tipógrafo Yanqui en Chile y Perú durante la Guerra de la Independencia*, introducion de Armando Donoso (Madrid, 1919).

JONES, CLARENCE F(IELDEN) (1893–1991). Geographer, born August 30, 1893, in Radford, Virginia. Jones graduated from Western Illinois State teachers College (Macomb) and the University of Chicago. He served in the U.S. Army Engineers during World War I. He was assistant professor of geography at Clark University from 1923 to 1926, associate professor from 1926 to 1930, and professor from 1930 to 1942. He carried out field work in Latin America in 1925, 1928, 1931, 1933, 1941, 1948, 1949 to 1955, 1956, and 1959. He wrote *Commerce of South America* (Boston, 1928) and *South America* (New York, 1930), and was coeditor of *Symposium on the Geography of Puerto Rico* (Rio Piedras, 1955). He was chief of the northern South America section of the Board of Economic Warfare and later assistant chief of Europe-African Division of the Office of Strategic Services during World War II. He was professor of geography at Northwestern University from 1945 until his retirement in 1961. Died October 12, 1991, in Galesburg, Illinois. *References*: *Chicago Tribune*, October 17, 1991; Merle C. Prunty, Jr., ed., *Festschrift: Clarence F. Jones*, (Evanston, Ill., 1962).

JONES, CLARENCE W. (1900–   ). Missionary, born December 15, 1900, in Sherrard, Illinois, and grew up in Chicago. Jones played with a Salvation Army band, graduated from Moody Bible Institute, and joined music ministry at the Chicago Gospel Tabernacle until 1931. He went to Ecuador under the Worldwide Christian Couriers, and established radio station HCJB, The Voice of the Andes,* and continued to run it until 1953, when he returned to the United States. *Reference*: Lois Neely, *Come Up to This Mountain: The Miracle of Clarence W. Jones and HCJB* (Wheaton, Ill., 1980).

JONES, ROBERT CUBA (1902–   ). Association official, born May 12, 1902, in Gilbara, Oriente, Cuba, to American parents. Jones graduated from Earlham College and studied at George William College and the University of Chicago. He was director of the Pan American Council of Chicago from 1940 to 1942, associate chief of the division of labor and social affairs of the Pan American Union from 1942 to 1946, and its chief from 1946 to 1949, and senior social affairs officer for the United Nations from 1949 to 1953. He was director of the international cultural center in Mexico from 1953 to 1971. *Reference*: *WSSW*.

JONES, WILLIAM AMBROSE (1865–1921). Clergyman, born July 21, 1865, in Cambridge, New York. Jones graduated from Villanova College (Pa.), joined the Augustinian order, and was ordained in 1890. He held pastorates in Philadelphia and Atlantic City. He was in charge of the first English-speaking Catholic church in Cuba at the beginning of the military occupation by the United States. He was superior of the Augustinian community in Cuba, president of the College of St. Augustine in Havana from 1902 to 1907, and pastor of the Church of Santo Cristo in Havana from 1902 to 1907. He was consecrated bishop of Puerto Rico in 1907. Died February 17, 1921, in Philadelphia. *References: NYT*, February 18, 1921; Miriam T. O'Brien, '' 'El Joven Prelado': Bishop William Ambrose Jones, O.S.A.,'' *Horizontes* [Puerto Rico] 22 (1979): 39–58; and *WWWA*.

JONES, WILLIAM CAREY (1814–1867). Lawyer and diplomat, born in Maine, and grew up in Chillicothe, Ohio. Jones learned the printing trade, and started the *Buckeye*, a weekly newspaper in Chillicothe in 1834. He later studied law, published the *Scioto Gazette* in 1839–1840, went to Louisiana, was admitted to the bar, and was copublisher of the New Orleans *Commercial Review* from 1847 to 1849. He went to California in 1849, and practiced law in San Francisco. He was diplomatic special agent to Costa Rica and Nicaragua in 1857–1858, to report on the situation in these countries. *References: Documentos Diplomaticos de William Carey Jones: Agente Especial de los Estados Unidos ante Costa Rica y Nicaragua, 1857–1858*, traducidos por Orlando Cuadra Downing (Managua, 1974); and *OAB*.

JONESTOWN. A jungle outpost of the People's Temple of the Disciples of Christ, founded by Jim Jones (1931–1978), established in 1974 as an agricultural development community near Port Kaituma, approximately 150 miles northwest of Georgetown, in Guyana's tropical rain forest. The Guyanese government granted the lease of the land in 1976. Jones moved to this retreat in 1977, and was joined by 800 of his followers. All People's Temple members died in mass murder-suicide, November 19, 1978, in Jonestown, Guyana. *References*: David Chidester, *Salvation and Suicide: An Interpretation of Jim Jones, the Peoples Temple, and Jonestown* (Bloomington, Ind., 1988): John R. Hall, *Gone from the Promised Land: Jonestown in American Cultural History* (New Brunswick, N.J., 1987); George Klineman, Sherman Butler, and David Conn, *The Cult That Died: The Tragedy of Jim Jones and the Peoples Temple* (New York, 1980); Tim Reiterman, *Raven: The Untold Story of the Rev. Jim Jones and His People* (New York, 1982); and James Reston, *Our Father Who Art in Hell* (New York, 1981).

JORDAN, THOMAS (1819–1895). Army officer, born September 30, 1819, in Luray, Virginia. Jordan graduated from the U.S. Military Academy in 1840, and was commissioned a lieutenant in the Infantry. He served during the Seminole War, the Mexican War, and second Seminole War, and was stationed on the Pacific coast from 1848 to 1860. He served in the Confederate Army during the Civil War. He was editor of the *Memphis Appeal* from 1866 to 1869. In 1869, he became chief of the general staff and later commander of the Cuban insurgent army, which he organized and drilled, and in 1870, he met and defeated a superior Spanish force at Guaimaro, Cuba. Realizing that the odds were too great to overcome, and with his war supplies becoming exhausted, he resigned his command in 1870, and returned to the United States. He founded and was publisher of the *Financial and Mining Record* (New York) from 1870 until 1892. Died November 27, 1895, in New York City. *References: ACAB; DAB; NCAB* 4:486; *NYT*, November 28, 1895; and *WWWA*.

JORDEN, WILLIAM J(OHN) (1923–   ). Journalist and diplomat, born May 3, 1923, in Bridger, Montana. Jorden graduated from Yale and Columbia universities. He served in the U.S. Army during World War II. He was foreign correspondent for the Associated Press in Japan and Korea from 1948 to 1952, for the *New York Times* from 1952 to 1955, and in the U.S.S.R. from 1956 to 1961. He was member of the Policy Planning Council of the State Department in 1961–1962, special assistant to undersecretary of state for political affairs from 1962 to 1965, deputy assistant secretary of state for public affairs in 1965–1966, and senior member of the staff of the National Security Council from 1966 to 1968 and from 1972 to 1974. He was a member and spokesman of the American delegation to the Vietnam Peace Talks in Paris from 1966 to 1969 and assistant to former president Lyndon B. Johnson from 1969 to 1972. He was U.S. ambassador to Panama from 1974 to 1978. He was scholar in residence at the Lyndon B. Johnson Library (Austin, Tex.) from 1978 to 1980. He wrote *Panama Odyssey* (Austin, Tex., 1984). *Reference*: *WWA*.

JOUETT, JAMES E(DWARD) (1826–1902). Naval officer, born February 7, 1826, near Lexington, Kentucky. Jouett was appointed midshipman in the U.S. Navy in 1841. He served during the Mexican War and in the Union Navy during the Civil War. In 1884, he became commander of the North Atlantic Squadron. In 1885, he commanded the force sent to the Isthmus of Panama to quell a revolt against Colombia, and restored transit across the isthmus. He established free passage for the trains of the Panama Railroad and as a result, the revolt failed. He was president of the Board of Inspection and Survey from 1886 until his retirement, with the rank of rear admiral, in 1890. Died September 30, 1902, in Sandy Spring, Maryland. *References*: *ACAB*; *DAB*; *NCAB* 4:501; and *WWWA*.

JOVA, JOSEPH JOHN (1916–   ). Diplomat, born November 7, 1916, in Newburgh, New York. Jova graduated from Dartmouth College. He was employed by the Guatemala division of the United Fruit Company from 1938 to 1941, served in the U.S. Navy Reserves from 1942 to 1947. He entered the foreign service in 1947, was vice consul in Basra and Tangier, consul in Oporto, and first secretary in Lisbon until 1957. He served in the State Department from 1957 to 1961, was deputy chief of mission in Chile from 1961 to 1965, ambassador to Honduras from 1965 to 1969, ambassador to the Organization of

American States in Washington, D.C. from 1969 to 1974, and ambassador to Mexico from 1974 to 1977. He was president of Meridian House International after 1977. *References*: Matt S. Meier, *Mexican American Biographies: A Historical Dictionary, 1836–1987* (New York, 1987); and *WWA*.

JUAREZ. *See* MORMON COLONIES IN MEXICO

JUDAH, NOBLE BRANDON (1884–1938). Lawyer and diplomat, born April 23, 1884, in Chicago. Judah graduated from Brown University and studied at Northwestern University, and was admitted to the bar in 1907. He practiced law in Chicago after 1907. He served in the U.S. Army on the Mexican border in 1916 and later during World War I. He was a member of the Illinois House of Representatives in 1911–1912. He was U.S. ambassador to Cuba from 1927 to 1929. Died February 26, 1938, in Chicago. *References*: *NCAB* 28:142; *NYT*, February 27, 1938; and *WWWA*.

JUNGLE AVIATION AND RADIO SERVICE. Initiated in 1946 by the Summer Institute of Linguistics in Peru. A separate flight department was organized in 1948. It was incorporated separately in 1963. It operated aircrafts in Peru, Bolivia, Ecuador, Brazil, and Colombia. *References*: Jamie Buckingham, *Into the Glory: The Miracle-Filled Story of the Jungle Aviation and Radio Service* (Plainfield, N.J., 1974); and *EMCM*.

JUST CAUSE, **OPERATION.** *See* PANAMA, INTERVENTION IN (1989)

K

KANSAS CITY, MEXICO AND ORIENT RAILWAY. A railroad linking Kansas City with Topolobampo, Mexico, founded in 1900 by Arthur E. Stilwell,* who built 237 miles of railroad in Mexico before he was replaced in 1912. The Mexican section was transferred in 1929 to Benjamin F. Johnston* and was expropriated in 1937 by the Mexican government, which completed the railroad. It was renamed Ferrocarril de Chihuahua al Pacifico in 1961. *Reference*: John L. Kerr, with Frank Donovan, *Destination Topolobampo: The Kansas City, Mexico & Orient Railway* (San Marino, Calif., 1968).

KEENER, JOHN C(HRISTIAN) (1819–1906). Missionary, born February 7, 1819, in Baltimore. Keener graduated from Wesleyan University. He was in the wholesale drug business in Baltimore from 1835 to 1841 and was ordained in 1841. He held pastorates in Alabama from 1841 to 1853 and in New Orleans from 1853 to 1870. He was superintendent of the Confederate Army chaplains west of the Mississippi during the Civil War. He was elected bishop of the Methodist Episcopal Church, South,* in 1870. He established a mission in Mexico in 1873 and was the first missionary of the Methodist Episcopal Church, South, in Mexico. He retired in 1898. Died January 19, 1906, in New Orleans. *References*: *ACAB*; *EWM*; *NCAB* 13:374; and *WWWA*.

KEITH, MINOR COOPER (1848–1929). Entrepreneur and railroad builder, nephew of Henry Meiggs,* and born January 19, 1848, in Brooklyn, New York. Keith went to Costa Rica in 1871 to help his elder brother Henry, who had received a contract from the Costa Rican government to build a railroad from the Caribbean to San Jose. After his brother's death in 1874, Keith was left in charge of the project. He completed the railroad to the Ríosucio by 1882 and to San Jose in 1890. He experimented with banana plantations near Limón in 1873, and when they prospered, they were expanded and he organized the Tropical Trading and Transport Company in London to take care of the banana interests and their shipment to the United States and to manage a chain of stores that he established along the coast of Costa Rica. He also acquired control of banana plantations in Colombia and Panama. In 1899, he merged his company with the Boston Fruit Company to form the United Fruit Company* and served as its vice president. By 1908 he had completed a railroad from Puerto Barrios on the Caribbean to Guatemala City. He purchased the Western Guatemala Railroad between Guatemala and the Pacific and extended it to the Mexican border in 1911. In 1912, he organized International Railways of Central America and served as its president until 1928. He completed a connecting line between the Guatemalan and Salvadoran railroads in 1929. He also owned a coffee plantation and a cattle ranch in Central America and was president of the Abangarez Gold Fields, Limited, of Costa Rica. He collected Central American antiquities (which he bequeathed to the American Museum of Natural History). Died June 14, 1929, in New York City. *References*: *BDABL*; *DAB*; *DADH*; *ELA*; *NCAB* 22:275; *NYT*, June 15, 1929; Watt Stewart, *Keith and Costa Rica: A Biographical Study of Minor Cooper Keith* (Albuquerque, N.M., 1964); and *WWWA*.

KELLY, ISABEL T(RUESDELL) (1906–1983). Archaeologist, born January 4, 1906, in Santa Cruz, California. Kelly graduated from the University of California at Berkeley. She carried out archaeological investigations in Culiacán, Sinaloa, Mexico, in 1935, and archaeological reconnaissance in west Mexico in 1939. She settled in Mexico in 1940, living in Tlaquepaque from 1941 to 1947 and later in Tepepan, and carried out archaeological investigations in various places in Mexico. She was ethnologist-in-charge of the Smithsonian Institute of Social Anthropology office in Mexico City from 1946 to 1952 and was involved with health care research for the Institute of Inter-American Affairs in El Salvador and Mexico from 1951 to 1960. She wrote *Excavations at Apatzingan Michoacán* (New York, 1947). Died December 1983, in Tepepen, Mexico. *Reference*: Patricia J. Knobloch, "Isabel Trues Dell Kelly (1906–1983)," in *Women Anthropologists: A Biographical Dictionary*, ed. Ute Gacs et al. (Westport, Conn., 1988), pp. 175–80.

KEMMERER, EDWIN W(ALTER) (1875–1945). Economist, born June 29, 1875, in Scranton, Pennsylvania. Kemmerer graduated from Wesleyan and Cornell universities. He served as financial adviser to the U.S. Philippine Commission in 1903 and was chief of the Division of Currency of the Philippines from 1904 to 1906. He was professor of economics and finance at Cornell University from 1906 to 1912 and at Princeton University from 1912 to 1924, and was professor of international finance at Princeton from 1924 until his retirement in 1943. He was counselor to the government of Mexico in 1917 and to the government of Guatemala in 1919 and 1924. He toured seven Latin American countries in 1922, analyzing their economic problems. He headed financial missions to Colombia in 1923 to 1930, to Chile in 1925, to Ecuador in 1926–1927, to Bolivia in 1927, and to Peru in 1931. Died December 16,

1945, in Princeton, New Jersey. *References*: Edwin W. Kemmerer Papers, Princeton University Library; *DAB S3*; Bruce Dalgaard, "E. W. Kemmerer: The Origins and Impact of the 'Money Doctor's' Monetary Economics," in *Variations in Business and Economic History: Essays in Honor of Donald L. Kemmerer*, ed. Bruce Dalgaard and Richard Vedder (Greenwich, Conn., 1982), pp. 31–44; Donald L. Kemmerer and Bruce R. Dalgaard, "Inflation, Intrigue and Monetary Reform in Guatemala 1919–1926," *Historian* 46 (1983): 21–38; *NCAB* E:406; *NYT*, December 17, 1945; and *WWWA*.

KEMMERER MISSIONS. Financial missions to Colombia in 1923 and 1930, to Chile in 1925, to Ecuador in 1926–1927, to Bolivia in 1927, and to Peru in 1931, and headed by Edwin W. Kemmerer.* The missions were intended to stabilize the economies and currencies of countries in South America where American economic interests were rapidly increasing. *References*: Paul W. Drake, *The Money Doctor in the Andes: The Kemmerer Missions, 1923–1933* (Durham, N.C., 1989); and Robert N. Seidel, "American Reformers Abroad: The Kemmerer Missions in South America, 1923–31," *Journal of Economic History* 32 (1972): 520–45.

KENNECOTT COPPER COMPANY. Founded in 1915, the company acquired Braden Copper Company* and El Teniente mine, the world's largest underground copper mine in Chile, in 1915, and ran the mine until 1971, when it was nationalized by the Chilean government. The name was changed to Kennecott Corporation in 1980. *References*: Norman Girvan, *Copper in Chile: A Study in Conflict between Corporate and National Economy* (Kingston, Jamaica, 1972); George Ingram, *Expropriation of U.S. Property in South America* (New York, 1974), pp. 268–90; and John McDonald, "The World of Kennecott," *Fortune* 44 (November 1951): 84–97, 160–76.

KERBEY, JOSEPH ORTON (? –1913). Consul. Kerbey was U.S. consul in Pará, Brazil, in 1890–1891. He visited the area again in 1909. He served later on the staff of the Pan-American Union Bureau. He wrote *The Land of To-Morrow: A Newspaper Exploration up the Amazon and over the Andes to the California of South America* (New York, 1905), and *An American Consul in Amazonia* (New York, 1911).

KIDDER, ALFRED VINCENT (1885–1963). Archaeologist, born October 29, 1885, in Marquette, Michigan, and grew up Cambridge, Massachusetts. Kidder graduated from Harvard University. He served in the U.S. Army during World War I. He was curator of North American archaeology at the Peabody Museum of Harvard University from 1914 to 1926, research associate of the Carnegie Institution of Washington from 1926 until his retirement in 1950, in charge of all archaeological activities of the institution after 1927, and head of the division of historical research after 1929. He was a member of the faculty of Peabody

Museum of Harvard University from 1939 to 1951. He planned and participated in archaeological research in the Maya region of southern Mexico and northern Central America, including fieldwork in the Guatemala highlands, excavating Maya sites, and directing studies in various areas of Mayan cultural history. He was coauthor of *Excavations at Kaminaljuyu, Guatemala* (Washington, D.C., 1940). Died June 11, 1963, in Cambridge, Massachusetts. *References*: *DAB S7*; D. R. Givens, "Alfred Vincent Kidder and the Development of Americanist Archaeology," Ph.D. diss., Washington University, 1986; *NCAB* 50:184; *NYT*, June 15, 1963; and *Willey*, ch. 13.

KIDDER, ALFRED II (1911–1984). Archaeologist, son of Alfred Vincent Kidder,* born August 2, 1911, in Nantucket Island, Massachusetts. Kidder graduated from Harvard University. He served in the U.S. Army Air Force during World War II. He taught at Harvard University from 1937 to 1950 and was associate director of the University Museum of the University of Pennsylvania from 1950 to 1967, curator of the American section from 1967 to 1971, and professor of anthropology of the University of Pennsylvania from 1962 until his retirement in 1971. He carried out survey and excavations in northern Venezuela in 1933–1934, worked in Honduras in 1936 and in Peru in 1937, and carried out excavations at Pucara, Peru, for the Peabody Museum in 1939. He was director of Project 7 of the Institute of Andean Research in the southern highlands of Peru in 1941–1942 and conducted excavations in Lake Titicaca in 1955. He wrote *Some Early Sites in the Northern Lake Titicaca Basin* (Cambridge, Mass., 1943) and *Archaeology of Northwestern Venezuela* (Cambridge, Mass., 1944), and was coauthor of *Preliminary Report on the Smithsonian Institution–Harvard University Archaeological Expedition to Northwestern Honduras, 1936* (Washington, D.C., 1938) and *The Art of the Ancient Maya* (New York, 1959). Died February 2, 1984, in Wayne, Pennsylvania. His wife, **MARY B. KIDDER** (1914–   ) wrote *Leaves from My Diary* (Boston, 1932) and *No Limits But the Sky: The Journal of an Archaeologist's Wife in Peru* (Cambridge, Mass., 1942). *References*: *Boston Sunday Globe*, February 5, 1984; and Karen L. Mohr Chavez, "Alfred Kidder II: 1911–1984," *Expedition* 30, no. 3 (1988): 4–7.

KIDDER, DANIEL P(ARISH) (1815–1891). Missionary, clergyman, and educator, born October 18, 1815, in South Pembroke (later Darien), Genesee County, New York. Kidder attended Hamilton College and graduated from Wesleyan University. He was a missionary under the Board of Foreign Missions of the Methodist Episcopal Church* in Brazil from 1837 until 1840 and established the Methodist mission in that country. From Rio de Janeiro he traveled extensively, distributing the Bible and religious literature and preaching. He returned to the United States in 1840, served in churches in Paterson and Trenton, New Jersey, until 1844, was secretary of his denomination's Sunday School Union and editor of sunday school literature from 1844 until 1856, taught practical theology at Garrett Biblical Institute (Evanston, Ill.) from 1856 to 1871 and at Drew Theological Seminary (Madison, N.J.) from 1871 to 1881, and was secretary of the Board of Education of his church until his retirement in 1887. He wrote *Sketches of Residence and Travel in Brazil, Embracing Historical and Geographical Notices of the Empire and Its Several Provinces* (Philadelphia, 1845), and (with J. G. Fletcher) *Brazil and the Brazilians Portrayed in Historical and Descriptive Sketches* (New York, 1857). Died July 29, 1891, in Evanston, Illinois. *References*: Daniel P. Kidder Papers, Rutgers University Libraries, New Brunswick, N.J.; *ACAB*; *DAB*; *EWM*; and *WWWA*.

KILPATRICK, HUGH JUDSON (1836–1881). Army officer and diplomat, born January 14, 1836, near Deckertown, New Jersey. Kilpatrick graduated from the U.S. Military Academy in 1861 and was commissioned a second lieutenant in the First Artillery. He served in the Union Army during the Civil War. He resigned from the army in 1865 and entered politics. He was U.S. minister to Chile from 1865 to 1868, and was reappointed in 1881. He was involved in a diplomatic controversy with Stephen Augustus Hurlbut,* U.S. minister to Peru, when Chile and Peru were at war. Died December 2, 1881, in Santiago, Chile. *References*: *DAB*; *DADH*; *NCAB* 4:273; *NYT*, December 27, 1881; and *WWWA*.

KIMBALL, WILLIAM W(IRT) (1848–1930). Naval officer, born January 9, 1848, in Paris, Maine. Kimball graduated from the U.S. Naval Academy in 1869. One of the first torpedo officers in the navy, he was on ordnance duty from 1879 to 1882 and from 1886 to 1890 and was engaged in the development of magazines and machine guns. He is said to have designed, constructed, and operated the first armed cars used by U.S. forces. They were used by the landing force that guarded rail transit in Panama in 1885, in which he served. He also prepared a *Special Intelligence Report on the Progress of the Work on the Panama Canal* (Washington, D.C., 1886). He was head of the Office of Naval Intelligence from 1894 to 1897 and commanded the first U.S. torpedo boat flotilla during the Spanish-American War. He was in command of the Nicaragua Expeditionary Squadron in 1909–1910. He retired with the rank of rear admiral in 1910, but was recalled to active duty during World War I. Died January 26, 1930, in Washington, D.C. *References*: *DAB*; *NCAB* 9:461; and *WWWA*.

KING, J(OHN) ANTHONY (1803– ?). Soldier of fortune, born in New York City. King came to Buenos Aires in 1817, enlisted as flag bearer in the Army of the Argentine Republic, rose in service, and attained the rank of colonel. He returned to the United States in 1841 and wrote *Twenty-Four Years in the Argentine Republic; Embracing the Author's Personal Adventures, with the Civil and Military History of the Country, and an Account of Its Political Condition, before and during the Administration of Governor Rosas* (New York, 1846). *Reference*: *Cutolo*.

KINGMAN, LEWIS (1845–1912). Engineer, born February 26, 1845, in Bridgewater, Massachusetts. Kingman studied civil engineering. He was involved in engineering and developing oil wells in Wilkes-Barre and Oil City, Pennsylvania, from 1863 to 1868. He was division engineer for the Atlantic and Pacific Railway from 1868 to 1871, for Maxwell Land Grant and Union Pacific Railway in 1871–1872, for the surveyor general of New Mexico from 1873 to 1876, and for Atcheson, Topeka and Santa Fe Railway from 1884 to 1888, and was chief engineer of Atlantic and Pacific Railway in 1882–1883. He was chief engineer of the northern division of the Mexican Central Railway at Chihuahua, Mexico, in 1883–1884. He was assistant chief engineer of the Atcheson, Topeka and Santa Fe Railway from 1884 to 1888 and city engineer of Topeka from 1889 to 1894. He was chief engineer of the Mexican Central Railway from 1895 to 1909 and then engineer of maintenance of way for the National Railways of Mexico. He wrote *Lewis Kingman to His Children with a Family History* (Mexico City, 1907). Died January 23, 1912. *Reference*: *WWWA*.

KINNEY, HENRY L(AWRENCE) [or LIVINGSTON] (1814–1861). Filibuster, born June 3, 1814, near Shusshequin, Pennsylvania. Kinney went to Illinois in 1830, where he was a farmer and merchant, and served in the Black Hawk War. He came to Texas in 1838, helped found the town of Corpus Christi, and engaged in ranching and trading near it. He fought during the Mexican War. He served in the Texas Senate. He then maintained a small private army in Texas which he employed against both the Indians and the Mexicans. In 1854, he organized the Central American Colonization Company, went to Greytown, Nicaragua, on a filibustering expedition, and established an American colony on the Mosquito coast of Nicaragua. He was chosen civil and military governor of the city and territory of San Juan del Norte and founded a newspaper, *The Central American*. The colony failed and he returned to the United States in 1857. Shot and killed July 1861, in Matamores, Mexico. *References*: James T. Wall, "Henry L. Kinney and the Mosquito Colony," in James T. Wall, ed., *The Landscape of American History: Essays in Memoriam to Richard W. Griffin* (Washington, D.C., 1979), pp. 21–40, and Walter P. Webb, ed., *The Handbook of Texas* (Austin, Tex., 1952).

KINSOLVING, LUCIEN LEE (1862–1929). Clergyman, born May 14, 1862, in Middlebury, Loudon County, Virginia. Kinsolving attended the University of Virginia, graduated from Virginia Theological Seminary, and was ordained in 1889. He was a missionary under the American Church Mission Society (Episcopal) in Porto Alegre, state of Rio Grande do Sul, Brazil, from 1889 to 1898. He was elected missionary bishop for the Brazilian Episcopalian Church in 1898 and was consecrated in 1899. He was elected missionary bishop of southern Brazil in 1907 and served until his retirement in 1928. Died December 18, 1929, in Forest Hills, Long Island, New York. *References*: *ACAB*; A. B. Kinsolving, *Lucien Lee Kinsolving* (Baltimore, 1947); *NCAB* 28:160; *NYT*, December 19, 1929; Anson P. Stokes, Jr., *Lucien Lee Kinsolving of Brazil* (New York, 1956); and *WWWA*.

KIRK, ROBERT C. (1821– ?). Public official, born February 26, 1821, in Mt. Pleasant, Jefferson County, Ohio. Kirk graduated from Franklin College (Athens, Ga.) and studied at the Philadelphia University. He practiced medicine in Fulton County, Illinois, from 1842 to 1844 and engaged in mercantile pursuits in Fulton from 1844 to 1857. He served in the Ohio state senate from 1856 to 1859 and was lieutenant governor of Ohio from 1859 to 1861. He was U.S. minister to Argentina from 1862 to 1866 and from 1869 to 1871 and was minister to Uruguay from 1869 to 1870. He succeeded in settling all the claims due American citizens from Uruguay. He was collector of internal revenues of the 13th Ohio district after 1875. *References*: *Cutolo*; and *NCAB* 12:440.

KLEIN, JULIUS (1886–1961). Government official, born in San Jose, California. Klein attended the University of California and graduated from Harvard University. He was a professor at Harvard University. He was chief of the Latin American division of the Department of Commerce in 1917 to 1919, commercial attaché in Buenos Aires in 1919–1920, director of the Bureau of Foreign and Domestic Commerce from 1921 to 1929, and assistant secretary of commerce from 1929 to 1933. A private economic adviser, he founded the economic consultant firm of Klein-Saks, Incorporated, in Washington, D.C. He was director of economic and financial missions to Peru from 1949 to 1955, to Guatemala in 1955, and to Chile in 1955–1956. Died June 15, 1961, in San Francisco. *References*: *NCAB* C:23; *NYT*, June 16, 1961; Robert N. Seidel, "Progressive Pan Americanism: Development and United States Policy toward South America, 1906–1931," Ph.D. diss., Cornell University, 1973, pp. 151–87; Charles Stevenson, "Private Enterprise Doctor to Underdeveloped Nations," *Reader's Digest* 73 (November 1973): 208–13; and *WWWA*.

KNAPP, HARRY S(HEPARD) (1856–1923). Naval officer, born June 27, 1856, in New Britain, Connecticut. Knapp graduated from the U.S. Naval Academy in 1878 and was commissioned midshipman in 1880. He served on various ships at sea and was chief of staff of the Pacific Fleet in 1907–1908 and member of the General Board of the Navy in 1909–1910 and 1912–1916. He was military governor of Santo Domingo in 1917–1918. He restored order, reformed the judiciary, reorganized the educational system, and improved financial conditions. He was commander of the U.S. Naval Forces in European Waters in 1919–1920. In 1920, he conducted an investigation of the U.S. military occupation of Haiti. He was coauthor of *The Panama Canal, Comprising Its History and Construction, and Its Relation to the Navy, International Law and Commerce* (New York, 1915). He retired with the rank of vice admiral in 1920. Died April 6, 1923, in Hartford, Connecticut. *References*: *NCAB* 20:213; *NYT*, April 7, 1923; and *WWWA*.

KNIGHT, ALBION W(ILLIAMSON) (1859–1936). Clergyman, born August 24, 1859, in White Springs, Florida, and grew up in Savannah, Georgia. Knight graduated from the University of the South (Sewanee, Tenn.), and was ordained in 1883. He did missionary work in Florida, holding pastorates in Palatka, Jacksonville, and Atlanta from 1884 to 1904, and was consecrated bishop in 1904. He was the first Episcopal bishop of Cuba from 1905 to 1913 and was in charge of the Episcopal Church on the Isthmus of Panama from 1908 to 1920. He was vice-chancellor of the University of the South from 1913 to 1922. He wrote *Lending a Hand in Cuba* (Hartford, Conn., 1916). He was bishop coadjutor of New Jersey after 1923. Died June 9, 1936, in Jacksonville, Florida. *References*: *NCAB* 16:212; and *WWWA*.

KORRY, EDWARD M(ALCOLM) (1922–   ). Journalist and diplomat, born January 7, 1922, in New York City. Korry graduated from Washington and Lee University. He was a foreign correspondent for United Press from 1944 to 1954 and European editor for Cowles Magazines and Broadcasting Incorporated from 1954 to 1960. He was assistant to President John F. Kennedy from 1960 to 1962, U.S. ambassador to Ethiopia from 1963 to 1967, and U.S. ambassador to Chile from 1967 to 1971. He did not know of the attempts made by the Central Intelligence Agency to engineer a military takeover and overthrow President Salvador Allende Gossens, and played no role in an aborted coup in 1970. He was president of the Association of American Publishers in 1972–1973 and professor of international relations at Connecticut College after 1979. *References*: "New Evidence Backs Ex-Envoy on His Role in Chile," *NYT*, February 9, 1987; *Newsweek* 89 (January 10, 1977): 25; *Time* 117 (February 23, 1981): 84; and *WWA*.

KUHL, ELLA (1842–1917). Educator, born in Copper Hill, Hunterton County, New Jersey. Kuhl attended Women's College (Bordentown, N.J.) She taught in Copper Hill from 1865 to 1870 and then founded a private school there. She went with Mary P. Dascomb* to Brazil in 1877. They taught in the American School in São Paulo, and then in Botucatu. They settled in Curitiba in 1892 and founded the American School there. Kuhl returned to the United States in 1917. Died October 9, 1917, in New York City. *Reference*: Frank Goldman, "Tres Educadores Norte-americanos no Brasil: 1860–1917," *Anhembi* 7 (1957): 450–58.

L

LA FARGE, OLIVER [HAZARD PERRY] (1901–1963). Author, born December 19, 1901, in New York City. La Farge graduated from Harvard University. He made three archaeological and ethnological expeditions to Mexico and Guatemala. His novel, *Sparks Fly Upward* (Boston, 1931), was based on his second trip to Mexico and his first visit to Guatemala. He lived in New York City from 1929 to 1933, and in Santa Fe, New Mexico, after 1933. He was a historian in the U.S. Army Air Transport Command during World War II. He also wrote *Santa Eulalia: The Religion of a Cuchumatan Indian Town* (Chicago, 1947) and was coauthor of *Tribes and Temples* (New Orleans, 1926–1927) and *The Year Bearer's People* (New Orleans, 1931). Died August 2, 1963, in Albuquerque, New Mexico. *References*: Oliver La Farge Papers, Tulane University Library, New Orleans; *DLB*; Robert A. Hecht, *Oliver La Farge and the American Indian: A Biography* (Metuchen, N.J., 1991); D'Arcy McNickle, *Indian Man: A Life of Oliver La Farge* (Bloomington, Ind., 1971); *NCAB* F:410; *NYT*, August 3, 1963; and Thomas M. Pearce, *Oliver La Farge* (New York, 1972).

LAFETRA, IRA HAYNES (1851–1917). Missionary educator, born March 3, 1851, in Ohio. LaFetra graduated from Wesleyan University of Ohio and Boston University School of Theology. He was a missionary to Chile from 1878 to 1906, serving in Valparaiso and ministering first to seamen in that port city. In 1879, he moved to Santiago, where he reorganized the English-language Union Church and founded the Santiago College in 1880. He was first president of the conference of missionaries that was set up to administer the self-supporting missions that had been established by William Taylor on the west coast of South America. In 1889, he established Imprenta Moderna, publishing books and journals. He also promoted commerce between the United States and Chile. He was coauthor of *Protestant Missions in South America* (New York, 1900). He retired in 1906 because of ill health. *References*: *EWM*; and *Figueroa*.

LAMAR, MIRABEAU BUONAPARTE (1798–1859). Public official, born August 16, 1798, in Warren County, Georgia. Lamar was an unsuccessful merchant in Alabama and then was private secretary to the governor of Alabama from 1823 to 1826. He was editor of the *Columbus [Ga.] Enquirer* from 1826 to 1835. He went to Texas in 1836, participated in the Battle of San Jacinto, and was secretary of war in the provisional cabinet of President David G. Burnet. He was vice president of Texas from 1836 to 1838 and president of the Republic of Texas from 1838 to 1841. He served during the Mexican War and then managed his plantation in Richmond, Texas. He was U.S. minister to Nicaragua and Costa Rica in 1857–1858, but his efforts to establish an American protectorate over Nicaragua were unsuccessful. Died December 18, 1859, in Richmond, Texas. *References*: *ACAB*; *DAB*; Philip Graham, *The Life and Poems and Mirabeau B. Lamar* (Chapel Hill, N.C., 1938); *NCAB* 9:66; Jack C. Ramsay, Jr., *Thunder beyond the Brazos: Mirabeau B. Lamar, A Biography* (Austin, Tex., 1985); Stanley Siegal, *The Poet President of Texas: The Life of Mirabeau B. Lamar, President of the Republic of Texas* (Austin, Tex., 1977); and *WWWA*.

LAMB, DEAN IVAN (1886–1955). Soldier of fortune, born in Canton, Pennsylvania. Lamb became a professional revolutionary, and once estimated that he had served in thirteen armies. A good portion of his military adventures centered in Central and South America. He was credited with having participated in the first aerial combat in 1911 near Nogales, Mexico, and with making the first flight across Central America. He flew for the air force of Honduras in the early postwar years, but after flying against rebel forces, he fell from favor and departed in late 1921 or 1922. He also helped found railroads in the Brazilian interior and mined gold and diamonds in French Guiana. He wrote an autobiography, *The Incurable Filibuster: Adventures of Colonel Dean Ivan Lamb* (New York, 1934), and numerous short stories. He later served in the U.S. Air Force and retired with the rank of colonel. Died November 1, 1955, in Tucson, Arizona. *Reference*: *NYT*, November 3, 1955.

LANE, ARTHUR BLISS (1894–1956). Diplomat, born June 16, 1894, in Bay Ridge, Long Island, New York. Lane graduated from Yale University and studied at the Ecole de L'Isle de France. He entered the diplomatic service in 1917 and served in London, Berne, Warsaw, and Mexico City. He was U.S. minister in Nicaragua from 1933 to 1936. He opposed the military regime headed by the Somoza family which replaced the democratic government created by the United States, but he acquiesced when Washington made clear that it would accept the new government and not intervene in internal Nicaraguan affairs. He was U.S. minister to Estonia, Latvia, and Lithuania in 1936–1937, minister to Yugoslavia from 1937 to 1941, minister to Costa Rica in 1941, ambassador to Colombia from 1942 to 1944, and ambassador to Poland from 1944 to 1947, when he requested his recall. Died August 12, 1956, in New York City. *References*: Arthur Bliss Lane Papers, Yale University Library, New Haven, Conn.; *CB*

1948; *DAB S6*; *DADH*; *NCAB* 45:146; *NYT*, August 14, 1956; Vladimir Petrov, *A Study in Diplomacy: The Story of Arthur Bliss Lane* (Chicago, 1971); *Pol-Prof:Truman*; John A. Sylvester, "Arthur Bliss Lane: American Career Diplomat," Ph.D. diss., University of Wisconsin, 1967; and *WWWA*.

LANE, EDWARD (1837–1892). Missionary, born in Dublin, Ireland. Lane graduated from Oglethorpe University (Ga.) and the Union Theological Seminary of Virginia and was ordained in 1868. He was a missionary under the Board of Foreign Missions of the Presbyterian Church in the United States* in Campinas, south Brazil, from 1869 until his death. He founded a school in Campinas and was editor of *Pulpito Evangelico*. Died March 26, 1892, in Campinas, Brazil. *Reference*: *MDPC*.

LANE, HORACE M(ANLY) (1837–1912). Missionary educator, born July 29, 1837, in Readfield, Maine. He went to Brazil in 1856 to take a commercial position. He became interested in education, returned to the United States, studied medicine, and practiced medicine. He was an educational missionary under the Board of Foreign Missions of the Presbyterian Church in the U.S.A.* in São Paulo, Brazil. He took charge of the Escola Americana and adopted the features of American school practice to Brazilian conditions. In 1891, he established MacKenzie College, an independent, non-sectarian institution of higher education; he was president of both institutions until his death. He was called "the most influential foreigner and educator in Brazil." Died October 27, 1912, in São Paulo, Brazil. *References*: *DAB*; and Frank Goldman, "Tres Educadores Norte-americanos no Brasil: 1860–1917," *Anhembi* 7 (1957): 450–58.

LANGSTON, JOHN MERCER (1829–1897). Educator and diplomat, born in Louisa Court House, Louisa County, Virginia, and grew up in Chillicothe and Cincinnati, Ohio. Langston graduated from Oberlin College, studied law, and was admitted to the bar in 1854. He practiced law in Brownhelm, Ohio, where he served as town clerk and a member of the Oberlin Board of Education. He was inspector general of the Freedmen's Bureau in 1868–1869, dean of the law department of Howard University from 1870 to 1873, and vice president of the university from 1873 to 1875. He was U.S. minister and consul general to Haiti from 1877 to 1885, and chargé d'affaires to the Dominican Republic from 1883 to 1885. He worked to increase American trade and mediated the settlement of a major political dispute that threatened to bring about a revolution. He was president of the Virginia Normal and Collegial Institute (Petersburg, Va.) from 1885 to 1887 and served in the U.S. House of Representatives from 1889 to 1891. He wrote an autobiography, *From the Virginia Plantation to the Nation's Capitol; or, The First and Only Negro Representative in Congress from the Old Dominion* (Hartford, Conn., 1894). Died November 15, 1897, in Washington, D.C. *References*: *BDAC*; William F. Cheek, "Forgotten Prophet: The Life of

John Mercer Langston,'' Ph.D. diss., University of Virginia, 1961; *DAB*; *DADH*; *DANB*; *NCAB* 3:328; and *WWWA*.

LANNING, EDWARD P(UTNAM) (1930–   ). Anthropologist, born September 21, 1930, in Northville, Michigan. Lanning attended the University of Michigan and graduated from the University of California at Berkeley. He was an assistant professor of anthropology at Columbia University from 1963 to 1965, associate professor from 1965 to 1970 there, and professor after 1970. He carried out fieldwork in Peru from 1956 to 1958 and from 1961 to 1963, in Ecuador in 1964, and in Chile from 1966 to 1973. He wrote *A Ceramic Sequence for the Piura and Chira Coast, North Peru* (Berkeley, Calif., 1963), and *Peru before the Incas* (Englewood Cliffs, N.J., 1967). *References*: *AMWS*; and *CA*.

LARUE, CARL (DOWNEY) (1888–1955). Botanist, born April 22, 1888, in Williamsville, Illinois. LaRue graduated from Valparaiso University and the University of Michigan. He was a botanist in Sumatra from 1917 to 1920. He was an assistant professor and then associate professor of botany at the University of Michigan from 1920 to 1944, and professor after 1944; he was a staff member of the Michigan Biological Station from 1925 to 1950. He developed the method for breeding commercial rubber trees, was in charge of South American rubber expedition for the U.S. Department of Agriculture in 1923–1924, and codirected the Ford Motor Company Amazon-Tapajos expedition in 1926–1927 and the rubber investigation expedition to Bolivia, Nicaragua, and Mexico for the U.S. Department of Agriculture in 1940–1941. He wrote *The Hevea Rubber Tree in the Amazon Valley* (Washington, D.C., 1926) and was coauthor of *Cooperative Inter-American Plantation Rubber Development* (Washington, D.C., 1946). Died August 19, 1955, in Ann Arbor, Michigan. *References*: ''The Reminiscences of Carl D. LaRue'' (1955), Henry Ford Museum and Archives, Dearborn, Mich.; *NYT*, August 21, 1955; and *WWWA*.

LATIMER, JULIAN L(ANE) (1868–1939). Naval officer, born October 10, 1868, in Shepherdstown, West Virginia. Latimer graduated from the U.S. Naval Academy in 1890. He served in the Spanish-American War and World War I. He was judge advocate general of the navy from 1921 to 1925 and commander of the Special Service Squadron from 1925 to 1927. He was U.S. Navy commander of all U.S. forces in Nicaragua in 1926–1927, landing U.S. marines to protect the lives and property of U.S. citizens and to maintain order. During a large part of these years, acting as a representative of the U.S. government, he was in virtual control of public affairs in Nicaragua. He was commandant of the Fourth Naval District and the navy yard in Philadelphia from 1927 to 1930. He resigned in 1930 with the rank of rear admiral. Died June 4, 1939, in New York City. *References*: *NCAB* 31:484; *NYT*, June 5, 1939; and *WWWA*.

LATIN AMERICA MISSION (LAM). Founded in 1921 as the Latin American Evangelization Campaign, it launched a large campaign of mass evangelism in the major cities of Latin America. It was the pioneer of the Evangelism in Depth concept and of a Spanish-language school for missionaries, and launched the first Evangelism in Depth campaign, utilizing a mobilized church, in Nicaragua in 1960. It adopted its present name in 1938. *References*: *EMCM*; and R. Kenneth Strachan, ed., *Evangelism in Depth: Experimenting with a New Type of Evangelism* (Chicago, 1961).

LAWRENCE, G(EORGE) O(LIVER) C(ROCKER) (1860–1930). Fruit grower, born May 10, 1860, in South Britain, Connecticut. Lawrence graduated from Amherst College and studied at Gottingen and Berlin universities. He traveled much in Europe and South America. He came to Argentina in 1885 and was involved in the fruit canning business in Tigre, near Buenos Aires. He also ranched on an island in the Paraná River and owned glass works in Buenos Aires. Died November 6, 1930, in Buenos Aires. *References*: *Amherst*; and *Drees*.

LEE, FITZHUGH (1835–1905). Diplomat, born November 19, 1835, in Fairfax County, Virginia. Lee graduated from the U.S. Military Academy in 1856. He served in the Confederate Army during the Civil War. He then farmed in Virginia and was governor of Virginia from 1886 to 1890. He was U.S. consul general in Havana, Cuba, from 1896 to 1898, and played an important role during the Cuban revolution and the events preceding the Spanish-American War. He served in the Spanish-American War and was then in charge of the reestablishment of order in Havana until his retirement, with the rank of brigadier general, in 1901. Died April 28, 1905, in Washington, D.C. *References*: *ACAB*; *DAB*; *DADH*; *DAMIB 84*; G. G. Eggert, "Our Man in Havana: Fitzhugh Lee," *HAHR* 47 (1967): 463–85; *NCAB* 9:1; and *WWWA*.

LEE, HARPER B. (1884–1941). Matador, born James Harper Gillett, September 5, 1884, in Ysleta, Texas, and grew up in Guadalajara, Mexico. Lee became a civil engineer for the Mexican Central Railway but bullfighting fever infected him, and he fought in many cities in Mexico between 1908 and 1911. Beginning in Guadalajara, he appeared in fifty-two corridas, including many times in Mexico City. He was seriously gored several times. He then retired and went to work for a Texas oil company. Died June 26, 1941, in San Antonio, Texas. *Reference*: Marshall Hail, *Knight in the Sun: Harper B. Lee, First Yankee Matador* (Boston, 1962).

LEKIS, LISA CRICHTON (1917–   ). Author, born November 19, 1917, in Vicksburg, Mississippi. Lekis graduated from Stanford University and the University of Florida. She was a publicity representative for the American Export Industries in Mexico from 1940 to 1946 and export manager from 1946 to 1948.

She was dance director and director of Caribbean festivals for the University of Puerto Rico in San Juan from 1949 to 1953, a consultant on rural research for the Division of Agriculture in Ecuador from 1957 to 1959, executive secretary for the Fulbright Commission in Rio de Janeiro from 1959 to 1961, professor of sociology at the University of Bahia from 1961 to 1963, and consultant to the Agency for International Development (AID) in Quito, Ecuador, and Washington, D.C., after 1966. She wrote *Folk Dances of Latin America* (New York, 1954) and *Dancing Gods* (New York, 1960). *References*: *CA*; and James B. Lloyd, ed., *Lives of Mississippi Authors, 1817–1967* (Jackson, Miss., 1981).

LEMLY, HENRY R(OWAN) (1851–1925). Army officer, born January 12, 1851, in Bethania, Forsyth County, North Carolina. Lemly graduated from the U.S. Military Academy in 1872 and was commissioned a second lieutenant in the cavalry in 1874. He served in the western United States. On a leave of absence, he was professor of civil engineering, director of studies, and commandant of cadets in the National Military School in Bogotá, Colombia, with the rank of colonel in the Colombian Army, from 1880 to 1883. He was director of the National Military School in Bogotá from 1890 to 1893 and inspector general of the United States of Colombia Army in 1895–1896. He served in the Puerto Rico campaign in the Spanish-American War. He retired in 1899. He was again in the service of the government of Bogotá, for whom he bought arms and ammunition in New York and served as its agent for manufacturers of munitions in Europe. He served in the U.S. Quartermaster Department during World War I. He wrote *Bolivar, Liberator of Venezuela, Colombia, Ecuador, Peru and Bolivia* (Boston, Mass., 1923). Died October 12, 1925, in Washington, D.C. *References*: *ACAB*; *Annual Report of the Association of the Graduates of the United States Military Academy for 1929*; and *WWWA*.

LE PLONGEON, AUGUSTUS (HENRY JULIUS) (1826–1908) and **LE PLONGEON, ALICE (DIXON)** (1851–1910). Archaeologists. Augustus was born May 4, 1826, on the Island of Jersey. He graduated from Ecole Polytechnique (Paris). He came to San Francisco in 1850, where he was surveyor and engineer. By 1855, he had established a photographic business in San Francisco. He then studied medicine. He had a photographic studio in Lima, Peru, from 1862 to 1870, and also a private medical clinic there. The couple married in London in 1871. They went to Yucatán in 1873, studied the ruins of Chichén Itzá and other sites in Yucatán, and explored the coasts of the Yucatán Peninsula until 1884. They later lived in New York City, lecturing and writing. Augustus wrote *Vestiges of the Mayas* (New York, 1881). Alice wrote *Here and There in Yucatan* (New York, 1886). Augustus died December 13, 1908, in Brooklyn, New York. Alice died June 8, 1910, in New York City. *References*: Robert L. Brunhouse, *In Search of the Maya: The First Archaeologists* (Albuquerque, N.M., 1973), ch. 7; Lawrence G. Desmond and Phyllis M. Messenger, *A Dream* *of Maya: Augustus and Alice Le Plongeon in Nineteenth-Century Yucatan* (Albuquerque, N.M., 1988); and *NYT*, June 10, 1910.

LEPRINCE, JOSEPH ALBERT AUGUSTIN (1875–1956). Public health official, born August 3, 1875, in Leeds, England, and came to the United States in 1887. LePrince graduated from Columbia University. He went to Havana, Cuba, in 1901, and succeeded in eradicating yellow fever in Cuba by eliminating mosquito-producing sources. He was chief sanitary inspector of the Isthmian Canal Commission and a public health officer in Panama from 1904 to 1914, and was a pioneer in the successful fight against malaria and yellow fever during the construction of the Panama Canal. He was a sanitary engineer in the U.S. Public Health Service after 1914 and later was a senior sanitary engineer until his retirement in 1939. He developed malaria control in the oil fields of Mexico in 1923 and assisted the Puerto Rican government to fight a serious malaria outbreak in 1938. He was coauthor of *Mosquito Control in Panama: The Eradication of Malaria and Yellow Fever in Cuba and Panama* (New York, 1916). Died February 10, 1956, in Memphis, Tennessee. *References*: "LePrince, Malaria Fighter," *Public Health Report* 71 (August 1956): 756–58; *NYT*, February 11, 1956; and *WWWA*.

LETGERS, DAVID BRAINERD (1908–   ). Missionary, born on the Sioux and Comanche Reservation in Oklahoma. Letgers graduated from Stetson University, attended Moody Bible Institute (Chicago), graduated from Westminster Theological Seminary (Philadelphia), and was ordained in 1936. He was a missionary under the Board of Foreign Missions of the Presbyterian Church in the U.S.A.,* and later an independent Presbyterian missionary, in Yucatán, Mexico. After 1936, he was stationed in Mérida, Quintana Roo. He translated the Bible into Maya. *Reference*: Laurence Dame, *Maya Mission* (Garden City, N.Y., 1968).

LEWIS, OSCAR (1914–1970). Anthropologist, born December 25, 1914, in New York City, and grew up in Ferndale, New York. Lewis graduated from the City College of New York and Columbia University. He was field director of the Interamerican Indianist Institute in Mexico City in 1943–1944, and carried out fieldwork in Tepoztlan. He was associate professor of anthropology at Washington University from 1946 to 1948 and professor of anthropology at the University of Illinois from 1948 until his death. He carried out fieldwork in San Juan, Puerto Rico, after 1963, and in Cuba from 1968 to 1970. He wrote *Life in a Mexican Village: Tepoztlan Restudied* (Urbana, Ill., 1951), *Five Families: Mexican Case Studies in the Culture of Poverty* (New York, 1959), *The Children of Sánchez: Autobiography of a Mexican Family* (New York, 1961), *Pedro Martinez: A Mexican Peasant and His Family* (New York, 1964), *La Vida: A Puerto Rican Family in the Culture of Poverty—San Juan and New York* (New York, 1966), and *A Death in the Sánchez Family* (New York, 1969). *Living the*

Revolution: An Oral History of Contemporary Cuba (Urbana, Ill., 1977–1978), was completed by his wife, Ruth M. Lewis. Died December 16, 1970, in New York City. *References*: *AA* 74 (1972): 747–57; *CB* 1968; *DAB S8*; *International Encyclopedia of the Social Sciences* (New York, 1979), 18:446–50; and *NYT*, December 18, 1970.

LIDDLE, RALPH ALEXANDER (1896–1963). Geologist, born November 18, 1896, near Argyle, New York. Liddle attended Monmouth College (Ill.) and graduated from Cornell University. He served with the U.S. Engineers during World War I. He was a petroleum geologist with the Standard Oil Company of New Jersey in Venezuela and Trinidad from 1920 to 1926. He crossed Venezuela from one end to another, exploring for oil. He wrote *The Geology of Venezuela and Trinidad* (Fort Worth, Tex., 1927). He was chief geologist of the Texas Producing Division of the Pure Oil Company in Forth Worth from 1926 to 1936, did valuation work for the National City Bank in Chicago from 1936 to 1940, and explored oil concessions in western Venezuela and eastern Ecuador. He went into business for himself in 1946. Died January 16, 1963, in Fort Worth, Texas. *Reference*: *PGSA* 1966 (1968): 285–89.

LIELE [or LISLE], GEORGE (ca. 1750–1820). Preacher, born a slave in Virginia and taken to Burke County, Georgia, prior to 1770. He was manumitted before the American Revolution. He began preaching in 1774, and is said to have been the first ordained Negro preacher. He moved to Savannah in 1778 and preached to black Baptists during the British occupation of Savannah. When the British sailed from Savannah to Jamaica, he accompanied them and came to Kingston, Jamaica, in 1783, as an indentured servant. He obtained his free papers in 1784. He was allowed to preach in Jamaica, and, with Moses Baker, began the Baptist movement in Jamaica and established the first Baptist church there in 1791. *References*: Beverly Brown, "George Lisle: Black Baptist and Pan Americanist, 1750–1826," *Savacau* 11/12 (September 1975): 58–72; and *DANB*.

LIND, JOHN (1854–1930). Lawyer and public official, born March 25, 1854, in Kanna, Smaland, Sweden. He came to the United States with his family in 1868 and grew up in Goodhue, Minnesota. Lind studied law and was admitted to the bar in 1876. He practiced law in New Ulm, Minnesota, and later in Minneapolis. He was superintendent of schools in Brown County, Minnesota, and receiver of the United States land office in Tracy, Lyon County, Minnesota. He was a member of the U.S. House of Representatives from 1887 to 1893 and from 1903 to 1905 and governor of Minnesota from 1899 to 1901. He served during the Spanish-American War. He was an envoy and personal representative of President Woodrow Wilson to Mexico in 1913 to help effect the peaceful overthrow of Victoriano Huerta and the return of a stable government, but was unable to accomplish this objective. He advocated and supported the recognition of Venustiano Carranza. Died September 18, 1930, in Minneapolis. *References*: John Lind Papers, Minnesota State Historical Society, St. Paul, Minn.; *BDAC*; *DAB*; K. J. Grieb, "The Lind Mission to Mexico," *Caribbean Studies* 7 (1968): 25–43; *Hill*; Larry D. Hill, "The Progressive Politician as a Diplomat: The Case of John Lind in Mexico," *TA* 27 (1971): 355–72; *NCAB* 10:69; George M. Stephenson, *John Lind of Minnesota* (Minneapolis, 1935); and *WWWA*.

LINDBERG, ABRAM FRANK (1881–1934). Financial adviser, born March 29, 1881, in Cherokee, Iowa. Lindberg graduated from New York University. He was employed with a firm of certified public accountants from 1905 to 1907. He was assistant auditor of Puerto Rico from 1907 to 1910, financial investigator for the Bureau of Municipal Research in New York City and Philadelphia, auditor for the customs service of Nicaragua, and later, deputy collector general of customs of Nicaragua, from 1911 to 1917. He was a member of the Commission on Public Credit, and later of the High Commission and financial agent of Nicaragua from 1917 to 1920. He was assistant manager of the Mercantile Bank of the Americas from 1920 to 1922, and technical adviser to the Republic of Guatemala in 1924–1925. Died November 30, 1934. *Reference*: *WWWA*.

LINDBERG, IRVING A(UGUSTUS) (1887–1957). Financial adviser, born February 14, 1887, in Cherokee, Iowa. Lindberg attended Iowa State College, graduated from the University of Illinois, and studied at the Washington College of Law and Accounting. He was an economist with President William H. Taft's Economy and Efficiency Commission in Washington, D.C., in 1911–1912; served with the commission to reorganize the fiscal system of Nicaragua in 1912; was collector of customs and captain of the Port of Bluefields, Nicaragua, with the rank of colonel from 1913 to 1941; and was a customs officer of the Atlantic Coast of Nicaragua. He also served in the Nicaragua secret service during World War I with the rank of colonel. He was deputy collector general and auditor of the Custom Service of the Republic of Nicaragua from 1918 to 1951, collector general of customs and American high commissioner to the Republic of Nicaragua after 1928, and president of the board of control of the Nicaragua Foreign Exchange from 1931 until his retirement in 1952. Died April 8, 1957, in Rochester, Minnesota. *References*: *NYT*, April 9, 1957; and *WWWA*.

LINOWITZ, SOL M(YRON) (1913–   ). Lawyer and diplomat, born December 7, 1913, in Trenton, New Jersey. Linowitz graduated from Hamilton College and Cornell University and was admitted to the bar in 1939. He was assistant general counsel of the Office of Price Administration in Washington, D.C., and then served in the U.S. Navy during World War II. He practiced law in Rochester, New York, from 1939 to 1966. He was counsel of the Haloid Company (later the Xerox Company) from 1947 to 1955, its general counsel from 1955 to 1966, and later, chairman of the board of its executive committee until 1966. He was U.S. ambassador of the Organization of American States and U.S. representative on the Inter-American Committee of the Alliance for Progress from 1966 to 1969. In these capacities he traveled extensively throughout Latin America. He resumed the practice of law in 1969. He wrote *The Making of a Public Man: A Memoir* (Boston, 1985). *References*: *CB* 1967; *NCAB* L:160; and *WWA*.

LITCHFIELD, FRANKLIN (1790– ?). Consul, born August 18, 1790. Litchfield graduated from Harvard University, where he trained in medicine. He was U.S. consul at Puerto Cabello, Venezuela, from 1823 until 1841. He was also involved in commercial activities. He resigned in 1841 and remained in Venezuela.

LLOYD, BOLIVAR JONES (1872–1955). Public health official, born May 10, 1872, in Bryan, Texas. Lloyd graduated from the University of Texas School of Medicine (Galveston). He entered the U.S. Public Health Service (USPHS) as assistant surgeon in 1900. He was director and president of the special sanitary commission in Guayaquil, Ecuador, in 1908–1909, when he became special sanitary representative of Panama and Peru and director of health of the Republic of Ecuador. He was physician to the president of Ecuador from 1907 to 1919. He was chief of the division of sanitary reports and statistics from 1922 to 1926. He was associated with the Pan American Sanitary Bureau and was assistant U.S. surgeon general and editor of *Public Health Reports* from 1922 to 1926. He retired in 1938. Died May 28, 1955. *References*: *Journal of the American Medical Association* 158 (July 16, 1955): 962; and *WWWA*.

LOCKEY, JOSEPH B(YRNE) (1877–1946). Historian, born February 2, 1877, in Jackson County, Florida. Lockey graduated from the University of Nashville and Columbia University. He was principal of a public school in Florida from 1902 to 1908. He was a member of the education commission to Peru in 1909 and inspector of public schools in Peru from 1909 until 1914. He served in the U.S. Army during World War I. He was assistant professor of Hispanic-American history at the University of California at Los Angeles from 1922 to 1925, associate professor there from 1925 to 1929 and professor from 1929 until his retirement in 1946. He wrote *Pan-Americanism: Its Beginnings* (New York, 1920), and *Essays in Pan-Americanism* (Berkeley, Calif., 1939). Died September 24, 1946, in Thomasville, Georgia. *References*: *HAHR* 26 (1946): 448–49; *PHR* 15 (1946): 471–72; and *WWWA*.

LOGAN, CORNELIUS AMBROSE (1832–1899). Physician and diplomat, born August 24, 1832, in Deerfield, Massachusetts. Logan graduated from Woodward College (Ohio) and Ohio Medical College. He practiced medicine in Cincinnati and Leavenworth, Kansas, and served as surgeon in the Union Army during the Civil War. He was U.S. minister to Chile from 1873 to 1877. In 1874, he arbitrated the differences between Chile and Peru and was involved in the early stages of the Tacna-Arica dispute. He was U.S. minister to Central America from 1879 to 1882 and again minister to Chile from 1882 until 1885. He played an important role in the negotiations settling the War of the Pacific. A quarrel with the U.S. minister to Peru prevented the United States from playing a more significant role in these negotiations. Died January 30, 1899, in Los Angeles. *References*: *ACAB*; *DAB*; *DADH*; *NCAB* 5:531; *OAB*; and *WWWA*.

LONG, BOAZ WALTON (1876–1962). Diplomat, born September 27, 1876, in Warsaw, Indiana. Long attended St. Michael College (Santa Fe, N.M.) He entered the commission business in 1899, working in San Francisco, Chicago, and Mexico City until 1913. He was U.S. minister to El Salvador from 1914 to 1919 and U.S. minister to Cuba from 1919 to 1922. He aided in earthquake relief in El Salvador in 1917 and mediated the Guatemala–El Salvador boundary dispute in 1918. He arranged commissions for International Telephone and Telegraph in Latin America from 1922 to 1930, headed N. W. Ayer's foreign department from 1930 to 1933, was public relations director for the National Recovery Administration in 1933–1934, and was deputy administrator for Puerto Rico from 1934 to 1936. He was U.S. minister to Nicaragua from 1936 to 1938, minister to Ecuador from 1938 to 1941, ambassador to Ecuador in 1942–1943, and ambassador to Guatemala from 1943 to 1945. He founded the American School in Ecuador in 1940. He retired in 1945 and directed the Museum of New Mexico from 1948 until 1956. Died July 30, 1962, in Santa Fe, New Mexico. *References*: *DADH*; *NCAB* 50:613; *NYT*, July 31, 1962; and *WWWA*.

LONGYEAR, JOHN MUNRO (1914–   ). Anthropologist, born July 30, 1914, in Houghton, Michigan. Longyear graduated from Cornell and Harvard universities. He was a research associate in the Division of History of the Carnegie Institution of Washington from 1938 to 1941, fellow of the Andean Institute in 1941–1942, member of the faculty of Colgate University after 1948, and professor of anthropology there from 1962 until his retirement in 1979. He carried out archaeological fieldwork in Honduras in 1938–1939, in Panama in 1941, and in El Salvador in 1941–1942. He wrote *Archaeological Investigations in El Salvador* (Cambridge, Mass., 1944), and *Copán Ceramics: A Study of Southeastern Maya Pottery* (Cambridge, Mass., 1952). *References*: *AMWS*; and *WWA*.

LOOMIS, FRANCIS BUTLER (1861–1948). Diplomat, born July 27, 1861, in Marietta, Ohio. Loomis graduated from Marietta College. He was member of the staff of the *New York Tribune* in 1884–1885 and of the Philadelphia *Press* in 1885–1886, state librarian of Ohio in 1886–1887, and Washington, D.C., correspondent for the Philadelphia *Express* from 1887 to 1889. He was U.S. consul in Saint Etienne, Grenoble, from 1889 until 1893. He was editor in chief of the *Cincinnati Daily Tribune* until 1896 and then publicity adviser to William McKinley. He was U.S. minister to Venezuela from 1897 to 1901. He arranged for several treaties calculated to expand commerce between the United States and Venezuela and organized scout and information service in Venezuela during the Spanish-American War. He was U.S. minister to Portugal in 1901–1902 and first assistant secretary of state from 1902 to 1914. In 1903, he investigated economic conditions in Santo Domingo. He was later a foreign trade adviser to the Standard Oil Company of California. Died August 5, 1948, in Burlingame, California. *References*: *DADH*; *NCAB* 37:38; *NYT*, August 7, 1948; Stanford University Libraries, *Francis Butler Loomis and the Panama Crisis* (Stanford, Calif., 1965); and *WWWA*.

LOOMIS, FREDERIC B(REWSTER) (1873–1937). Paleontologist, born November 22, 1873, in Brooklyn, New York. Loomis graduated from Amherst College and the University of Munich. He was instructor in biology at Amherst College from 1891 to 1903, associate professor from 1904 to 1908, professor of comparative anatomy from 1908 to 1917, and professor of geology from 1917 until his death. He conducted fossil collecting expeditions in South Dakota and Wyoming. He led the Amherst paleontological expedition to southern Patagonia in 1911–1912. His explorations were related in his *Hunting Extinct Animals in the Patagonian Pampas* (Concord, N.H., 1913) and *The Deseado Formation of Patagonia* (Concord, N.H., 1914). He later collected in Colorado, Nebraska, Florida, and New Mexico. Died July 28, 1937, in Sitka, Alaska. *References*: *NCAB* 30:207; *NYT*, July 31, 1937; and *WWWA*.

LÓPEZ EXPEDITIONS (1849–1851). Narciso López (1798–1851), a Venezuelan, led two filibustering expeditions to Cuba to free it from Spanish rule, with the support of American southerners, who desired the annexation of Cuba to the United States. The first expedition sailed in 1850 from New Orleans with a force of over six hundred men, mostly American veterans of the Mexican War. Reaching Cuba, it found little support from the people there. The troops retreated and escaped to the United States. The second expedition sailed from New Orleans in 1851 with four hundred men, mostly southerners. It reached Cuba but again found little support. The men were defeated by the Spanish army, captured, and executed. *References*: Charles H. Brown, *Agents of Manifest Destiny: The Lives and Times of the Filibusters* (Chapel Hill, N.C., 1980), chs. 3–4; Robert G. Caldwell, *The López Expeditions to Cuba, 1848–1851* (Princeton, N.J., 1915); and H. Portell Vila, *Narciso López y Su Epoca* (Havana, 1930–1958).

LOTHROP, SAMUEL KIRKLAND (1892–1965). Archaeologist, born July 6, 1892, in Milton, Massachusetts. Lothrop graduated from Harvard University. He carried out fieldwork for Harvard University in Puerto Rico, Guatemala, and Honduras from 1915 to 1917; in Panama in 1933, 1940, and 1951; and in Costa Rica in 1948 to 1959. He did fieldwork for the Carnegie Institution of Washington in Guatemala in 1923 and in 1932–1933; for the Museum of the American Indian, Heye Foundation, in Central America in 1924 and 1926; in Tierra del Fuego, Paraná River, Argentina, and Peru in 1924–1925; in Guatemala in 1928; and in

Chile in 1929. He participated in archaeological excavations in the Rio Grande de Cocle in Panama, Tierra del Fuego, San Pablo in Guatemala, and Chichén Itzá in Mexico. He worked in Peru for the Institute of Andean Research from 1941 to 1944. He was curator of Andean archaeology at the Peabody Museum of Harvard University. He wrote *Tulum, an Archaeological Study of the East Coast of Yucatán* (Washington, D.C., 1924), *Pottery of Costa Rica and Nicaragua* (New York, 1926), *Indians of the Paraná Delta, Argentina* (New York, 1932), *Atittlán, an Archaeological Study of Ancient Remains on the Borders of Lake Atittlán, Guatemala* (Washington, D.C., 1933), *Cocle, an Archaeological Study of Central Panama* (Cambridge, Mass., 1937–1942), *Metals from the Cenote of Sacrifice, Chichén Itzá, Yucatán* (Cambridge, Mass., 1952), *Archaeology of the Diquis Delta, Costa Rica* (Cambridge, Mass., 1963), and *Treasures of Ancient America; the Arts of Pre-Columbian Civilizations from Mexico to Peru* (Geneva, 1964), and was coauthor of *A Chancay-Style Grave at Zapallan, Peru* (Cambridge, Mass., 1957). His wife, **ELEANOR (BACHMAN) LOTHROP**, wrote *Throw Me a Bone: What Happens When You Marry an Archaeologist* (New York, 1948). Died January 10, 1965, in Boston. *References*: *AmAntiq* 31 (1965): 256–61; *BMNAS* 48 (1976): 253–72; *NYT*, January 13, 1965; *Willey*, ch. 9; and *WWWA*.

LOWE, D. WARREN (1839–1916). Editor, born September 6, 1839, in New York State and grew up in Massachusetts. Lowe served the Union Army during the Civil War. He came to Argentina in 1877 and was editor of *Buenos Aires Herald* and subsequently its proprietor. Died August 1, 1916, in Buenos Aires. *Reference*: *Drees*.

LOWRY, ROBERT K. (? –1826). Merchant. Lowry was a commercial agent for various Baltimore merchants. He was a U.S. marine and commercial agent in La Guaira, Venezuela, from 1810 to 1812, and consul at La Guaira in 1812– 1813. He returned to La Guaira in 1821 and was again consul there from 1823 until his death as well as principal agent for a consortium that obtained a concession for the Aroa copper mines (the first such mineral concession granted to foreigners in Latin America) from 1824 until his death. Died January 24, 1826, at San Esteban, outside Puerto Cabello, Venezuela. *Reference*: William C. Olson, "Early North Americans in Venezuelan Commerce, 1810–1830," Ph.D. diss., University of North Carolina at Chapel Hill, 1974, ch. 2.

LUDLOW, WILLIAM (1843–1901). Engineer, born November 27, 1843, in Islip, Long Island, New York. Ludlow attended the University of the City of New York (later New York University), graduated from the U.S. Military Academy in 1864, and served in the Union Army during the Civil War. He was assistant to the U.S. Army's chief of engineers from 1867 until 1872, chief of engineers of the Department of Dakota from 1872 to 1876, on duty in Philadelphia from 1876 to 1882 in connection with river and harbor work, chief engineer of

Philadelphia from 1883 to 1886, and engineer commissioner of the District of Columbia from 1886 to 1893. He was military attaché in London from 1893 to 1896. He served during the Spanish-American War. He was military governor of Havana from 1898 to 1900. Died August 30, 1901, in Convent Station, New Jersey. *References*: *ACAB*; *DAB*; *NCAB* 9:23; *NYT*, August 31, 1901; and *WWWA*.

LULL, EDWARD PHELPS (1836–1887). Naval officer, born February 20, 1836, in Windsor, Vermont. Lull graduated from the U.S. Naval Academy in 1855. He served in the Union Navy during the Civil War. He served in the West India Squadron from 1866 to 1869. He was in charge of the USS *Guard* of the Darien Surveying Expedition in 1870–1871 and commanded the Nicaragua Exploring Expedition in 1872–1873. He served on the Interoceanic Ship Canal Commission and commanded the Panama Surveying Expedition from 1873 to 1875. He was hydrographic inspector in the U.S. Coast and Geodetic Survey from 1875 to 1880. In 1882 he visited Nicaragua in the interest of the Provisional Interoceanic Canal Society. He was later commandant of the Pensacola, Florida, Navy Yard. Died March 5, 1887, in Pensacola. *References*: *ACAB*; *DAB*; and *WWWA*.

LUNDELL, CYRUS LONGWORTH (1907–   ). Botanist, born November 5, 1907, in Austin, Texas. Lundell graduated from Southern Methodist University and the University of Michigan and attended Columbia University. He was assistant curator of the herbarium of the University of Michigan from 1935 to 1939 and curator from 1939 to 1943, and research associate at the Carnegie Institution of Washington from 1933 to 1941. He was professor of botany at Southern Methodist University from 1941 to 1948 and director of the university herbarium from 1946 to 1948. He was executive vice president, chief scientist, and head of the Hoblitzelle Agricultural Laboratory of the Texas Research Foundation from 1946 to 1972, director of the plant sciences laboratory at the University of Texas at Dallas after 1972, professor of plant sciences there from 1972 to 1975, and professor of botany and environment sciences from 1975 until his retirement in 1978. He was director and botanist of the University of Michigan and the Carnegie Institution of Washington expeditions to Mexico and Central America from 1933 to 1938. He discovered and explored the Mayan cities of Calakmul in 1931 and Polol in 1933. He wrote *Ruins of Polol and Other Archaeological Discoveries in the Department of Petén, Guatemala* (Washington, D.C., 1934) and *The Vegetation of Petén* (Washington, D.C., 1937). *References*: *AMWS*; and *WWA*.

LUTHERAN CHURCH—MISSOURI SYNOD: BOARD FOR MISSIONS IN NORTH AND SOUTH AMERICA. Organized in 1847, it began missionary work in Brazil in 1901, Argentina in 1905, Paraguay and Uruguay in 1936, Mexico in 1940, Panama in 1942, Guatemala and Cuba in 1947, Venezuela in

1951, El Salvador in 1952, Chile in 1954, and Costa Rica and Honduras in 1964. *References*: Lutheran Church—Missouri Synod Archives, Concordia Historical Institute Collections, St. Louis; E. Theodore Bachmann, *Lutherans in Brazil* (Minneapolis, 1970); William J. Danker, *Two Worlds or None: Rediscovering Missions* (St. Louis, 1964); *EMCM*; and F. Dean Lueking, *Missions in the Making: The Missionary Enterprise among Missouri Synod Lutherans, 1846–1963* (St. Louis, 1964).

LYKES, FREDERICK EUGENE (1877–1951). Shipping executive, born July 2, 1877, in Brooksville, Florida. Lykes graduated from East Florida Seminary (later part of the University of Florida). He managed the family interests in Spring Hill, Florida, until 1899. He then went to Havana, Cuba, and supervised cattle ranches and the importation of beef cattle from Florida until 1901. In 1900 he formed, with his brother, the Lykes Brothers Company in Havana for importing cattle, and served as its president. He acquired extensive ranch property in Cuba and built the first modern packing plant in the island. After 1910, the company became involved in shipping activities in South and Central America and Mexico. In 1922, he formed Lykes Brothers Steamship Company, Incorporated. He retired in 1923 and returned to the United States. Died November 10, 1951, in Brooksville, Florida. *References*: *NCAB* 40:550; and *NYT*, November 11, 1951.

M

MCARTHUR, DONALD (1895–1960). Petroleum geologist, born February 8, 1895, in Claiborne County, Mississippi. McArthur graduated from Mississippi State University and studied at Stanford University. He served in the U.S. Army during World War I. He was employed by Tropical Oil Company to work on the de Mares Concession in Colombia from 1921 to 1925 and worked for Atlantic Refining Company in Colombia and Venezuela from 1927 until 1931. He was a consultant for the Texas Company in Argentina and then in Colombia and Venezuela from 1936 until his retirement in 1950. He helped to organize the Instituto Colombiano de Petroleos in Bogotá. Died August 1, 1960, in Wiggins, Mississippi. *Reference*: *BAAPG* 44 (1960): 1940–41.

MACAULEY, ALEXANDER (? –1813). Soldier, of Baltimore. Macauley served with the Colombian forces from 1811 to 1813, ranked as a colonel, and showed great resource and bravery. In 1811, he led his troops against the royalists at Popayán in New Granada and won an important victory. He took several other places, including Pasto. Marching to join the patriots advancing from Quito, he met with reverses at the hands of the royalist force and was captured. Executed, June 26, 1813, in Pasto, Colombia.

MCBRIDE, GEORGE M(CCUTCHEN) (1876–1971). Geographer, born October 11, 1876, in Benton, Kansas. McBride graduated from Park College (Parkville, Mo.), Auburn Theological Seminary, and Yale University. He taught at the English Institute in Santiago, Chile, from 1901 to 1907. He was its director from 1905 to 1907 and director of the American Institute in La Paz, Bolivia, from 1907 to 1915. He was a member of the faculty of the University of California in Los Angeles from 1922 until his retirement in 1942. He returned to South America in 1929–1930 and 1938–1939, studied land settlement problems in Chile, Bolivia, and Mexico, and wrote *Agrarian Indian Communities of Highland Bolivia* (New York, 1921), *Land Systems of Mexico* (New York, 1923), and *Chile: Land and Society* (New York, 1936). He was a U.S. technical advisor to the Ecuador-Peru Boundary Commission from 1942 to 1948. Died October 7, 1971, in Claremont, California. *References*: *AAAG* 62 (1972): 685–88; *GR* 62 (1972): 428–30; E. V. Niemeyer, Jr., "Three North Americans in Chile," *Atenea. Revista de Ciencies, Letras y Artes*, no. 433 (1976): 61–68; and *WWWA*.

MCBRYDE, F(ELIX) WEBSTER (1908–   ). Geographer, born April 23, 1908, in Lynchburg, Virginia. McBryde graduated from Tulane University and the University of California and attended the University of Colorado and Clark University. He carried out fieldwork in Latin America, especially in the Maya area of Central America, and discovered early pre-Inca petroglyphs in Virú Valley, Peru. He wrote *Cultural and Historical Geography of Southwestern Guatemala* (Washington, D.C., 1947). He served in the Military Intelligence Division of the U.S. War Department during World War II. He was director of the Peruvian office of the Institute of Social Anthropology of the Smithsonian Institution in Lima, Peru, from 1945 to 1947; special representative of the Institute of Andean Research in Lima in 1947–1948; professor of geography at the University of Maryland from 1948 to 1959; chief of the U.S. census mission to Ecuador from 1949 to 1951; president of F. W. McBryde Associates, Incorporated, in Washington, D.C. and Guatemala from 1958 to 1964; field director of the bioenvironmental program of the Atlantic-Pacific Interoceanic Sea-Level Canal studies in Panama and Colombia for the Battelle Memorial Institute from 1965 to 1970; field director of the Andean ecology project in South America from 1967 to 1969; founder of the McBryde Center for Human Ecology, and its director after 1969; and consultant in ecology after 1970. *References*: *AMWS*; and *WWE*.

MCCALL, MOSES NATHANIEL (1874–1947). Missionary, born December 15, 1874, in Screven County, Georgia. McCall graduated from Mercer and Denison universities and Southern Baptist Theological Seminary. He was a missionary under the Home Mission Board of the Southern Baptist Convention* in Cuba from 1905 until 1945. He founded two missions and churches in Havana and in Piñar del Rio, and began a seminary in 1906. He developed the Southern Baptist denomination in Cuba. He wrote *Baptist Generation in Cuba* (Atlanta, Ga., 1942). Died March 8, 1947, in Jacksonville, Florida. *References*: *ESB*; A. L. Munoz, *Apostol Bautista en la Perla Antillana* (Havana, Cuba, 1943); Louie D. Newton, *Amazing Grace: The Life of M. N. McCall, Missionary to Cuba* (Atlanta, 1948); and *NYT*, March 10, 1947.

MCCONNELL, WILLIAM W(ASHINGTON) (1860–1910). Missionary, born July 23, 1860, in Dodge County, Wisconsin. McConnell was the first missionary of the Central American Mission.* He served in Costa Rica from 1891 until 1909. He returned to the United States in 1909 because of ill health. Died August 2, 1910, in Roswell, New Mexico. *Reference*: *Central American Bulletin*, October 1910.

MCCOY MISSION (1927–1928). A mission to Nicaragua in 1927–1928, headed by Major General Frank R. McCoy (1874–1954) to supervise the 1928 Nicaraguan presidential elections and thereby expedite the removal of U.S. military forces from Nicaragua. The mission failed to demonstrate the strength of American domination or to terminate decisively U.S. intervention. *References*: Frank R. McCoy Papers, Manuscript Division, Library of Congress; A. J. Bacevich, "The American Electoral Mission in Nicaragua, 1927–1928," *DH* 4 (1980): 241–61; and A. J. Bacevich, *Diplomat in Khaki: Major General Frank Ross McCoy and American Foreign Policy, 1898–1949* (Lawrence, Kans., 1989).

MACDONNELL, GEORGE N(OWLANDS) (1873–1953). Missionary and physician, born in Savannah, Georgia. MacDonnell graduated from Emory College (Oxford, Ga.) and studied at Vanderbilt University. He later graduated from Atlanta Medical College (later part of Emory University). He served as a surgeon in the Spanish-American War and was the first Methodist missionary in Cuba. He then practiced medicine in Minas Viejas, near Vilaldama, Mexico. He later practiced medicine in Miami, Florida, and was head of the city's health department. Died December 8, 1953, in Miami, Florida. *References*: *EWM*; and *NYT*, December 11, 1953.

MACEDONIAN AFFAIR. Chilean forces in southern Peru under Lord Thomas Cochrane in 1818 seized money from Captain Eliphalet Smith of the U.S. merchant ship *Macedonian*, claiming that it was Spanish property. The affair was finally arbitrated by the king of Belgium in 1863 and Chile was forced to repay the money. *Reference*: Augusto Marambio Cabrera, *La Cuestión del Macedonian: En las Relaciones de Chile Estados Unidos de América y Bélgica (1819–1863)* (Santiago de Chile, 1989).

MACKENZIE, MURDO (1850–1939). Cattleman, born April 24, 1850, near Tain, Ross County, Scotland. Mackenzie graduated from the Royal Academy (Tain, Scotland). He was employed as assistant factor and insurance agent until 1885. He came to the United States in 1885 as the American manager of the Prairie Cattle Company, Limited, in Trinidad, Colorado, and was manager of the Matador Land and Cattle Company in northwestern Texas from 1891 to 1911 and from 1922 to 1937. He was manager of the Brazil Land, Cattle and Packing Company from 1912 to 1918 in São Paulo, Brazil. He undertook the task of acquiring some ten million acres of pasture land and stocking the new ranges with tens of thousands of cattle. Died May 30, 1939, in Denver, Colorado. *References*: *BDABL*; *DAB S2*; *NYT*, May 31, 1939; and *WWWA*.

MCLANE, ROBERT MILLIGAN (1815–1898). Diplomat, born June 23, 1815, in Wilmington, Delaware. McLane graduated from the U.S. Military Academy in 1837. He served in the Seminole War. He studied law and was admitted to the bar in 1840. He served in the Maryland legislature from 1845 to 1847 and the U.S. House of Representatives from 1847 to 1851. He was U.S. commissioner to China in 1853–1854. He was U.S. minister to Mexico in 1859–1860. He signed the McLane-Ocampo treaty, allowing the United States the right to intervene in Mexico and rights to transit routes across the Isthmus of Tehuantepec and in northern Mexico. The treaty was rejected by the U.S. Senate. McLane resumed law practice, served again in the U.S. House of Representatives from 1879 to 1883, and was governor of Maryland from 1883 to 1885 and minister to France from 1885 to 1889. He remained in Paris. Died April 16, 1898, in Paris, France. His *Reminiscences, 1827–1897* (n.p., 1903) was published posthumously. *References*: *BDAC*; *DAB*; *DADH*; Paul Murray, *Tres Norteamericanos y su Participación en el Desarrollo del Tratado McLane-Ocampo, 1856–1860* (Guadalajara, Mexico, 1946); *NCAB* 9:311; and Jerome J. Niosi, "The McLane Mission to Mexico, 1859–1860," Ph.D. diss., New York University, 1954.

MCLAUGHLIN, WILLIAM PATTERSON (1849–1921). Clergyman, born August 27, 1849, in Cincinnati. McLaughlin graduated from Ohio Wesleyan University and Boston University School of Theology and was ordained in 1874. He held pastorates in Lafayette, Bloomingsburg, Frankfort, Westerville, Chillicothe, and Lancaster, Ohio, from 1874 to 1885 and in New Orleans from 1885 to 1892. He was pastor of the First Methodist Episcopal ("American") Church in Buenos Aires from 1892 until his death. Died February 18, 1921, in Buenos Aires. *Reference*: *Drees*.

MACLURE, WILLIAM (1763–1840). Geologist, born October 27, 1763, in Ayr, Scotland. Maclure entered a mercantile house and came to the United States in 1782 and again in 1796, and became a U.S. citizen in 1803. He made the first geologic map of the United States, traveling through the entire region east of the Mississippi River. He founded and was a leader of the Philadelphia Academy of Natural Sciences. He visited the West Indies in 1816–1817, studying the volcanic phases of the country's geology, lived in Spain, and became interested in the New Harmony community in Indiana. He visited Mexico in 1827–1828 and settled there in 1828, hoping to aid in the educational development of Mexico, and lived there until his death. His "Letters from Mexico" were published in *Opinions on Various Subjects, Dedicated to the Industrious Producers* (New Harmony, Ind., 1831–1838). Died March 23, 1840, in the village of St. Angel, near Mexico City, Mexico. *References*: *The European Journals of William Maclure*, ed. John S. Doskey (Philadelphia, 1988); *ACAB*; *DAB*; *DSB*; *NCAB* 13:368; and *WWWA*.

MCMAHON, MARTIN T(HOMAS) (1838–1906). Soldier, born March 21, 1838, in Laprairie County, Quebec, Canada. McMahon came to New York City early in his life. He graduated from St. John's College (Fordham, N.Y.), studied law, and was admitted to the bar in 1860. He served in the Union Army during the Civil War. He was corporation counsel in New York City from 1866 to 1868. He was U.S. minister to Paraguay in 1868–1869. He was receiver of taxes in New York from 1873 to 1885, U.S. marshal for the southern district of New York from 1885 to 1889, member of the New York state assembly in 1890–1891 and the state senate from 1891 to 1895, and judge of the court of general sessions from 1896 until his death. Died April 21, 1906, in New York City. *References*: *Martin T. McMahon: Diplomatico en al Estridor de las Armas*, ed. Arthur H. Davis (Asunción, Paraguay, 1985); *ACAB*; John J. Delany and James E. Tobin, *Dictionary of Catholic Biography* (Garden City, N.Y., 1961); *NCAB* 4:129; *NYT*, April 22, 1906; and *WWWA*.

MCMANUS, JAMES E(DWARD) (1900–1976). Clergyman, born October 10, 1900, in Brooklyn. McManus entered the Congregation of the Most Holy Redeemer in 1922. He graduated from the Redemptorist Seminary of Mount St. Alphonsus (Esopus, N.Y.) and Catholic University of America, and was ordained in 1927. He was a missionary in Caguas, Puerto Rico, from 1929 to 1934; professor of canon law at Mt. St. Alphonsus from 1937 to 1940; and pastor in Aquadilla, Puerto Rico, from 1940 to 1945 and at Mayaguez, Puerto Rico, from 1945 to 1947. He was bishop of Ponce, Puerto Rico, from 1947 to 1963, and led opposition to Puerto Rican Governor Luis Muñoz Marin. He was a pastor in New York City, vicar of Sullivan and Ulster counties, and auxiliary bishop of New York until 1970. Died July 1, 1976, in Long Branch, New Jersey. *References*: *NYT*, July 3, 1976; Miriam Therese, "Bishop McManus and the Catholic University of Puerto Rico," *Horizontes* [Puerto Rico] 31 (1987): 35–46; and *WWWA*.

MCMATH, ROBERT EMMETT (1833–1918). Engineer, born April 28, 1833, in Varick, Seneca County, New York. McMath graduated from Williams College. He moved to St. Louis in 1858 and was deputy county surveyor from 1859 to 1862. He conducted several topographical surveys during the Civil War. In 1865, he was a member of a survey across the Isthmus of Nicaragua for Central American Transit Company from the mouth of the San Juan River at Greytown to its source in Lake Nicaragua. He was later assistant engineer in the survey of the Illinois River and worked on the improvement of the Mississippi River until 1883. He was sewer commissioner of St. Louis from 1883 to 1891. Died May 31, 1918, in Webster Groves, Missouri. *Reference*: *NCAB* 50:40.

MCMILLIN, BENTON (1845–1933). Businessman and diplomat, born September 11, 1845, in Monroe County, Kentucky. McMillin attended Kentucky Agricultural and Mechanical College (Lexington, Ky.) and studied law. He practiced law in Celina, Clay County, Tennessee, after 1871. He served in the Tennessee House of Representatives and in the U.S. House of Representatives from 1879 to 1899, and was governor of Tennessee from 1899 to 1903. He was involved in the insurance business in Nashville from 1903 to 1913. He was U.S. minister to Peru from 1913 to 1919 and minister to Guatemala from 1919 to 1922. He resumed his insurance business in 1922. Died January 8, 1933, Nashville, Tennessee. *References*: *BDAC*; *DAB S1*; *NCAB* 13:79; and *WWWA*.

MCMULLAN, FRANK (1835–1867). Colony promoter, born in Walker County, Georgia, and grew up in Mississippi. McMullan settled in Hill County, Texas, in 1853. He served under William Walker* in Nicaragua in 1857 and then attended McKenzie Institute (Red River County, Texas). He was in Mexico during the Civil War. He went to Brazil in 1865–1866, exploring the possibilities of emigration and searching for land for a colony. He returned to the United States in 1867, organized a group of colonists from Texas, and was back in Brazil in 1867, organizing a colony in the upper São Lourenco River in São Paulo Province. He was naturalized as a Brazilian citizen. Died September 29, 1867, in Iguape, Brazil. *Reference*: William C. Griggs, *The Elusive Eden: Frank McMullan's Confederate Colony in Brazil* (Austin, Tex., 1987).

MACOMB, MONTGOMERY MEIGS ("MONTY") (1852–1924). Soldier, born October 12, 1852, in Detroit. Macomb graduated from the U.S. Military Academy in 1874 and was commissioned second lieutenant in the artillery. He participated in the U.S. Geological Survey West of the 100th Meridian from 1876 to 1883 and was an instructor in mathematics and assistant professor of drawing at the U.S. Military Academy from 1887 to 1891. He served on special duty under the International Railway Commission in charge of surveys and explorations in Central America from 1891 to 1896. He served during the Spanish-American War and was a military attaché with the Russian Army during the Russo-Japanese War from 1903 to 1905, commander of the Hawaiian department of the U.S. Army from 1911 to 1913, and president of the Army War College from 1914 to 1916. He retired in 1916 but was recalled to duty during World War I. Died January 19, 1924, in Washington, D.C. *References*: *NCAB* 20:212; and *WWWA*.

MCRAE, COLIN J(OHN) (1812–1877). Businessman and diplomat, born October 22, 1812, in Sneedsboro, North Carolina, and grew up in Mississippi. McRae attended Catholic College (Biloxi, Miss.). He was a member of the Mississippi legislature in 1838. He moved to Mobile, Alabama in 1840 and operated a cotton commission house. He speculated in lands and promoted railroads. He was a member of the provisional Confederate Congress and then a Confederate financial agent. In the fall of 1867, he was sent to South America to establish a colony of American exiles. He bought a plantation and store at Puerto Cortés, Honduras, where he dealt in cattle, mahogany, and mercantile goods. Died February 1877, in Belize, British Honduras. *References*: *BDC*; and Charles S. Davis, *Colin J. McRae: Confederate Financial Agent* (Tuscaloosa, Ala., 1961).

MACREADY, GEORGE ALEXANDER (1885–1955). Petroleum geologist, born June 17, 1885, in Tacoma, Washington, and grew up in San Diego and Los Angeles. Macready graduated from Throop Polytechnic Institute (later California Institute of Technology) in Pasadena and Stanford University. He was a geologist with the General Asphalt Company in Trinidad and Venezuela from 1911 to 1916, chief geologist for General Asphalt and its subsidiaries, Trinidad Lake Petroleum Company and Caribbean Petroleum Company, from 1916 to 1919, and was involved in the discovery of many important oil fields in Venezuela and Trinidad. He was coauthor (with Ralph Arnold* and Thomas W. Barrington) of *The First Big Oil Hunt, Venezuela, 1911–1916* (New York, 1960). He was employed by Shell Company of California in San Francisco and Los Angeles from 1919 to 1926 and was an independent consultant after 1926. Died November 10, 1955, in Los Angeles. *Reference: BAAPG* 40 (1956): 2040–43.

MADEIRA-MAMORÉ RAILWAY COMPANY. Organized in 1878 by George Earl Church* to construct a railroad in western Brazil. Construction was soon abandoned. The concession was bought by Percival Farquhar* in 1907, and construction began that year. The railroad was completed and opened in 1912. The Brazilian government assumed control of the railroad in 1935 and acquired the company in 1937. The railroad was closed in 1972. *References*: Manoel R. Ferreira, *A Ferrovia do Diabo: Historia de uma Estrada de Ferro na Amazonia* (São Paulo, 1981); and Frank W. Kravigny, *The Jungle Route* (New York, 1940).

MAGOFFIN, JAMES WILEY (1799–1868). Businessman and diplomat, born in Harrodsburg, Mercer County, Kentucky. As early as 1825, Magoffin began trading in northern Mexico, and he served as U.S. consul in Saltillo from 1825 to 1833. He had moved to Chihuahua by 1836, where he entered the Santa Fe trade and gained influence in the social and economic life of the northern provinces of Mexico. He was established in Independence, Missouri, in 1844. He played an important role in the peaceful occupation of New Mexico during the Mexican War. Attempting to do the same thing in Chihuahua, Mexico, he was arrested as a spy and remained nine months in prison. He founded a hacienda and a freighting business in El Paso in 1849. Died September 27, 1868, in San Antonio, Texas. *References: DAB*; Stella M. Drumm, ed., *Down the Santa Fe Trail and into Mexico: The Diary of Susan Shelby Magoffin, 1846–1847* (New Haven, Conn., 1962); Rex W. Strickland, *Six Who Came to El Paso: Pioneers of the 1840's* (El Paso, Tex., 1963); and *WWWA*.

MAGOON, CHARLES E(DWARD) (1861–1920). Lawyer and government official, born December 5, 1861, in Steele County, Minnesota, and grew up in Platte County, Nebraska. Magoon attended the University of Nebraska and studied law. He practiced law in Lincoln, Nebraska, from 1882 to 1889. He was law officer of the Bureau of Insular Affairs in the War Department from 1899 to 1904, specializing in matters growing out of the acquisition by the United States of Cuba, Puerto Rico, and the Philippines. He was general counsel of the Isthmian Canal Commission in 1904–1905, member of the commission in 1905–1906, governor of the Canal Zone and minister to Panama in 1905–1906, and provisional governor of Cuba from 1906 to 1909. Died January 14, 1920, in Washington, D.C. *References*: *DAB*; *DADH*; *ELA*; David A. Lockmiller, *Magoon in Cuba: A History of the Second Intervention, 1906–1909* (Chapel Hill, N.C., 1938); *NCAB* 14:32; *NYT*, January 15, 1920; and *WWWA*.

MAGRUDER, JOHN B(ANKHEAD) (1810–1871). Army officer, born August 15, 1810, in Winchester, Virginia. Magruder graduated from the U.S. Military Academy in 1830 and was commissioned second lieutenant in the infantry and later in the artillery. He served in Texas, and during the Seminole War, and the Mexican War. He served in the Confederate Army during the Civil War. At the end of the war, he went to Mexico and became a major general in the Mexican Imperial Army under the Emperor Maximilian. He returned to the United States after the downfall of the emperor and lectured about his Mexican experience. Died February 18, 1871, in Houston, Texas. *References*: *DAB*; *NCAB* 4:294; Thomas M. Settles, "John Bankhead Magruder," in *Ten Texans in Gray*, ed. W. C. Nunn (Hillsboro, Tex., 1968), pp. 103–21; and Thomas M. Settles, "The Military Career of John Bankhead Magruder," Ph.D. diss., Texas Christian University, 1972.

MAGUIRE, BASSETT (1904–   ). Botanist, born August 4, 1904, in Alabama City, Alabama. Maguire graduated from the University of Georgia and Cornell University and attended the University of Pittsburgh. He was a professor at Utah State University from 1931 to 1943. He was curator and then head curator of the New York Botanical Garden after 1943, assistant director in 1968–1969, director of botany from 1969 to 1971 and from 1973 to 1975, and a senior scientist after 1971. He was also director of botany at the Jardin Botanico Nacional in Santo Domingo, the Dominican Republic, and founder and executive director of the Organization for Flora Neotropica from 1964 to 1975. In 1953 he discovered (with John J. Wurdack) Serrania del la Neblina mountain complex on the Venezuelan-Brazilian frontier. He was a member, leader, and director of numerous expeditions to tropical South America, including to Roraima Mountain and the Amazon basin. He explored the Kaieteur Plateau in British Guiana. *References*: *AMWS*; Olga Reifschneider, *Biographies of Nevada Botanists, 1844–1963* (Reno, 1964); and *WWA*.

MAINE, USS. Explosions occuring in the second-class battleship *Maine*, under the command of Captain Charles D. Sigsbee, while lying moored in Havana harbor in 1898, caused the ship to sink, with a loss of 260 officers and crew. The disaster produced great excitement in the United States and was a major factor in bringing it to a declaration of war against Spain (*see* SPANISH-

AMERICAN WAR). *References*: Louis A. Perez, Jr., "The Meaning of the *Maine*: Causation and the Historiography of the Spanish-American War," *PHR* 58 (1989): 293–322; and Hyman G. Rickover, *How the Battleship "Maine" Was Destroyed* (Washington, D.C., 1976).

MANEY, GEORGE EARL (1826–1901). Lawyer and diplomat, born August 24, 1826, in Franklin, Tennessee. Maney graduated from the University of Nashville. He served during the Mexican War. He was admitted to the bar in 1850 and practiced law in Tennessee. He served in the Confederate Army during the Civil War. He was president of the Tennessee and Pacific Railroad after 1868 and served in the state legislature. He was U.S. minister to Colombia in 1881–1882, minister to Bolivia and consul general in La Paz from 1882 to 1889, and minister to Uruguay and Paraguay from 1889 until 1894. Died February 9, 1901, in Washington, D.C. *Reference*: DAB.

MANGIN, WILLIAM (PATRICK) (1924–). Anthropologist, born June 2, 1924, in Syracuse, New York. Mangin graduated from Syracuse and Yale universities. He was assistant professor of anthropology at Syracuse University in 1956–1957, associate professor from 1959 to 1966, and professor after 1966. He carried out fieldwork in Vicos, Ancash, Peru, in 1951–1953, 1957, 1958, 1959, 1960, 1961, 1962–1967, and 1975. He wrote *The Mayors of Cajamarca: A Participant-Observer's View of a Municipal Development Project in Peru* (Syracuse, N.Y., 1985) and an account of his experiences in "Thoughts on Twenty-Four Years of Work in Peru: The Vicos Project and Me," in George M. Foster et al., *Long-Term Field Research in Social Anthropology* (New York, 1979). *Reference*: AMWS.

MANN, THOMAS C(LIFTON) (1912–). Diplomat, born November 11, 1912, in Laredo, Texas. Mann graduated from Baylor University. He practiced law in Laredo from 1934 to 1942. He entered the foreign service in 1947, was deputy assistant secretary of state for inter-American affairs in 1950–1951, and served in the U.S. embassy in Guatemala in 1955. He was U.S. ambassador to El Salvador from 1955 to 1957, assistant secretary of state for economic affairs from 1957 to 1960, and assistant secretary of state for inter-American affairs in 1960–1961 and again in 1964–1965. He was U.S. ambassador to Mexico from 1961 to 1963 and undersecretary of state for economic affairs in 1965–1966. He retired in 1966. *References*: CB 1964; DADH; ELA; Polprof:Eisenhower; Polprof:Kennedy; Polprof:Johnson; and WWA.

MANTON, BENJAMIN M. (1829–1911). Naval officer and consul, born May 10, 1829, in Providence, Rhode Island. He went to sea in 1846, commanding a vessel trading to Montevideo in 1852. He served in the Union Navy during the Civil War. After the war, he built two steamships which he placed in the South American trade. He was U.S. consul in Colonial, Uruguay, from 1868 until 1907. He installed in Colonial the first dock for repairing vessels ever established on the River Plate and equipped it with American material and machinery. After retirement, he settled in Barbados. Died July 30, 1911, in Barbados. *References*: *Drees*; *NCAB* 8:482; and *NYT*, August 5, 1911.

MARBUT, C(URTIS) F(LETCHER) (1863–1935). Soil scientist, born July 19, 1863, in the Ozark Mountain region of Missouri. Marbut graduated from the University of Missouri and Howard University. He was on the staff of the Missouri Geological Survey from 1890 to 1893. He was an instructor, assistant professor, and professor at the University of Missouri from 1895 to 1910, director of the Soil Survey of Missouri from 1905 to 1910, and a special agent of the U.S. Bureau of Soils in 1909–1910. He became chief of the Division of Soil Survey in the U.S. Department of Agriculture in 1910. He made soil surveys in Central and South America, Cuba, and Puerto Rico, and was a member of a Department of Commerce expedition to study the soil of the Amazon River in 1923–1924. Died August 25, 1935, in Harbin, Manchukuo, East Asia. *References*: *DAB S1*; *PGSA 1936*, pp. 221–24; *NCAB* 33:109; *NYT*, August 26, 1935; and *WWWA*.

MARINES IN HAITI. *See* HAITI, INTERVENTION IN

MARINES IN NICARAGUA. *See* NICARAGUA, INTERVENTION IN

MARINES IN THE DOMINICAN REPUBLIC. *See* DOMINICAN REPUBLIC, INTERVENTION IN

MARITIME CANAL COMPANY OF NICARAGUA. A concession to build a canal was obtained from the Nicaraguan government in 1887, and the company was incorporated in 1889. The construction party went to Nicaragua in 1889 and began work in 1890, but the work stopped in 1893, and the company went into bankruptcy. Its concession was cancelled in 1898.

MARKBREIT, LEOPOLD (1842–1909). Publisher and diplomat, born in Vienna, Austria. He came to the United States in 1848. Markbreit studied law and was admitted to the bar. He served in the Union Army during the Civil War. He held city office in Cincinnati and served on the staff of the governor of Ohio. He was U.S. minister to Bolivia from 1869 to 1873. He went on a business mission to Brazil, Bolivia, Uruguay, Chile, Peru, and Ecuador in 1873–1874. He was president and manager of the Cincinnati Volksblat Company after 1875, assistant treasurer of the U.S. at Cincinnati from 1882 to 1886 and mayor of Cincinnati in 1908–1909. Died July 27, 1909, in Cincinnati. *References*: *NCAB* 12:467; *NYT*, July 28, 1909; and *WWWA*.

MARSH, RICHARD O(GLESBY) (1883–1953). Engineer and explorer, born March 27, 1883, in Washington, D.C. Marsh attended Massachusetts Institute of Technology and the University of Lausanne (Switzerland). He was resident engineer for the Philippine Railroad Company in 1906–1907, assistant chief engineer on the Bolivia National Railroad in 1907–1908, division engineer for the Mississippi River Power Company in Warsaw, Illinois, from 1911 to 1916, owner and president of Port Barre Lumber Company in Louisiana from 1916 to 1922, junior partner in the consulting engineering firm of George W. Goethals in New York City from 1923 to 1927, and president of Richard O. Marsh and Company, Incorporated, engineering consultants, in New York City from 1929 to 1933. He conducted three scientific expeditions in the Darien country in Panama under the auspices of the Smithsonian Institution, the American Museum of Natural History, and the University of Rochester. In his second expedition, in 1924–1925, in search of good lands in Panama for possible rubber plantations, he studied the Cuna Indians of the San Blas Islands and the Darien jungle. He then took the cause of the Cuna Indians against the Panama government, leading their revolt. He wrote *White Indians of Darien* (New York, 1934). He later traveled in other parts of Latin America, including the area between Peru and Bolivia. He was employed by the Public Works Administration, the Department of Agriculture, the National Defense Board, and the Federal Power Commission from 1933 to 1941. He was consulting engineer for the U.S. Rubber Development Corporation and consultant to the War and Navy departments from 1941 until his retirement in 1948. Died September 4, 1953, in Vero Beach, Florida. *References*: Richard Chardkoff, "The Cuna Revolt," *Americas* 22, no. 7 (1970): 14–21; *NCAB* 40:573; and *WWWA*.

MARTIN, F(REDERICK) O(SKAR) (1871–1951). Mining engineer and geologist, born August 20, 1871, in Mittweida, Germany, and came to the United States in 1891. Martin attended George Washington and Harvard universities and Catholic University of America (Washington, D.C.). He was engaged in mining and prospecting work in Alaska, California, Idaho, Washington, and Montana from 1894 to 1900. He was an assistant with the U.S. Bureau of Soils from 1901 to 1905 and assistant engineer in the division of meteorology and river hydraulics on the Panama Canal in 1905–1906. He engaged in engineering and railway construction in Idaho, Montana, and Washington from 1906 to 1909 and was mineral inspector for the U.S. Department of Interior from 1909 to 1919. He was geologist with Union Oil Company of California from 1919 to 1930. He conducted exploratory work in the interior of Colombia from 1920 to 1926, and reported on his explorations in the October 1929 issue of the *Geographical Review*. He was in private practice in Pasadena, California, from 1930 to 1933, mining engineer in the division of investigation of the U.S. Department of Interior from 1933 to 1941, and again in private consulting practice from 1941 until his death. Died June 30, 1951, in South Pasadena, California. *Reference*: *NCAB* 39:410.

MARTIN, HANDEL T(ONGUE) (1862–1931). Paleontologist, born in Nottingham, England. He came to the United States in 1886 and settled in Logan County, Kansas. He began to make fossil collections in 1888 and was connected with the University of Kansas searches for fossils after 1894. He was assistant curator of paleontology at the University of Kansas Museum from 1907 until his death. He led a paleontological expedition to Patagonia in 1903–1904. Died January 15, 1931, in Lawrence, Kansas. *References*: *Kansas City Times*, January 16, 1931; and Larry G. Marshall, "The Handel T. Martin Paleontological Expedition to Patagonia in 1903," *Ameghiniana* 12 (1975): 109–111.

MARTIN, JOHN BARTLOW (1915–1987). Author and diplomat, born August 4, 1915, in Hamilton, Ohio, and grew up in Indianapolis. Martin graduated from De Pauw University. He served in the U.S. Army during World War II. He was a free-lance writer from 1938 to 1962. He was U.S. ambassador to the Dominican Republic from 1962 to 1964. He returned to the Dominican Republic in 1965 as special envoy when the United States dispatched troops there. He then resumed writing and was professor of journalism at Northwestern University from 1970 to 1980. He was also a speech writer in the presidential campaigns of Adlai Stevenson, John F. Kennedy, Lyndon B. Johnson, and Hubert H. Humphrey. He wrote *Overtaken by Events: The Dominican Crisis from the Death of Trujillo to the Civil War* (Garden City, N.Y., 1966), *U.S. Policy in the Caribbean* (Boulder, Colo., 1978), and his memoir, *It Seems Like Only Yesterday: Memoirs of Writing, Presidential Politics, and the Diplomatic Life* (New York, 1986). Died January 3, 1987, in Highland Park, Illinois. *References*: *CA*; J. F. Martin, "John Bartlow Martin," *American Scholar* 59 (1990): 95–100; *NYT*, January 5, 1987; *Polprof:Kennedy*; and *WWWA*.

MARYKNOLL FATHERS. Founded in 1911 under the legal title of the Catholic Foreign Mission Society of America. It began missionary work in Peru, Bolivia, and Chile in 1942, in Ecuador, Guatemala, and Mexico in 1943, and in El Salvador in the 1950s. It later withdrew from Ecuador and Mexico. *References*: Maryknoll Fathers and Brothers Archives, Maryknoll, N.Y.; and Albert Nevins, *The Meaning of Maryknoll* (New York, 1954).

MASON, GREGORY (1889–1968). Anthropologist and author, born July 3, 1889, in New York City. Mason graduated from Williams College, Columbia University, and the University of Southern California. He was a reporter and special writer for the New York *Evening Sun* in 1912–1913, member of the editorial staff of *Outlook* magazine from 1914 to 1920, and its foreign correspondent in Mexico in 1914 and 1916. In 1926, he was coorganizer and coleader of an anthropological and zoological expedition to eastern Yucatán for the Museum of the American Indian and the Museum of Comparative Zoology of Harvard University. He was field leader of an aerial and archaeological expedition to Central America in 1930 for the University Museum of the University of

Pennsylvania and director of anthropological trips for the University Museum and the Museum of the American Indian to Colombia in 1931 and 1936 and to Honduras in 1932. He was assistant professor of journalism at New York University from 1937 to 1942 and professor there from 1942 to 1954. He wrote *Green Gold of Yucatan* (New York, 1926), *Silver Cities of Yucatan* (New York, 1927), *Columbus Came Late* (New York, 1931), and *South of Yesterday* (New York, 1940), and was coauthor of *Mexican Gallop* (New York, 1937). Died November 30, 1968, in Greenwich, Connecticut. *References*: *NCAB* 54:263; and *NYT*, December 1, 1968.

MASON, JOHN ALDEN (1885–1967). Anthropologist, born January 14, 1885, in Germantown, Philadelphia. Mason graduated from the University of Pennsylvania and the University of California at Berkeley. He was in Mexico City from 1911 to 1913 and carried out fieldwork for the Puerto Rican Insular Survey in 1914–1915. He was assistant curator of Mexican and South American Archaeology at the Field Museum of Natural History from 1917 to 1924 and excavated at Santa Maria, Colombia. He was assistant curator of Mexican Archaeology at the American Museum of Natural History from 1924 to 1926, curator of the American section of the University of Pennsylvania Museum from 1926 until his retirement in 1955, and editor and field adviser for the New World Archaeological Foundation after 1955. He wrote *The Ancient Civilizations of Peru* (New York, 1957). Died November 7, 1967, in Bryn Mawr, Pennsylvania. *References*: *AA* 71 (1969): 871–79; *Journal of American Folklore* 82 (1969): 266–67; and *NYT*, November 9, 1967.

MATTHEWS, HERBERT L(IONEL) (1900–1977). Journalist, born January 10, 1900, in New York. Matthews graduated from Columbia University. He served in the U.S. Army during World War I. He was a correspondent with the *New York Times* from 1922 to 1967, including a post as chief of its London bureau from 1945 to 1949, and was a member of its editorial staff from 1949 to 1967. He was frequently credited with introducing Fidel Castro to the English-speaking public following his interviews of Castro in 1957 in the Sierra Maestra in Cuba. He wrote *The Cuban Story* (New York, 1961), *Return to Cuba* (Stanford, Calif., 1964), *Fidel Castro: A Political Biography* (New York, 1969), *A World in Revolution: A Newspaperman's Memoir* (New York, 1972), and *Revolution in Cuba: An Essay in Understanding* (New York, 1975). Died July 30, 1977, in Adelaide, Australia. *References*: Herbert L. Matthews Papers, Columbia University Library, New York City; *CA*; Jerry W. Knudson, *Herbert L. Matthews and the Cuban Story* (Lexington, Ky., 1978); *NYT*, July 31, 1977; Richard E. Welch, Jr., "Herbert L. Matthews and the Cuban Revolution," *Historian* 47 (November 1984): 1–18; and *WWWA*.

MAURY, MATTHEW FONTAINE (1806–1873). Naval officer, born January 14, 1806, in Spotsylvania, Virginia, and grew up in Williamson County, Tennessee. Maury was appointed a midshipman in the U.S. Navy in 1825. He was a superintendent of the Depot of Charts and Instruments of the U.S. Navy after 1842. He served in the Confederate Navy during the Civil War. He was sent on a secret mission to England in 1862 and was involved in purchasing supplies for the Confederate Navy. He went to Mexico in 1865 and was Emperor Maximilian's imperial commissioner of immigration. He attempted, unsuccessfully, to establish in Mexico a Confederate colony. He returned to the United States in 1868 and was professor of physics at the Virginia Military Institute (Lexington) and superintendent of the physical survey of Virginia from 1868 until his death. Died February 1, 1873, in Lexington, Virginia. *References*: *ACAB*; *DAB*; A. J. Hanna, "The Role of Matthew Fontaine Maury in the Mexican Empire," *Virginia Magazine of History and Biography* 55 (1947): 105–25; John Leighly, "Matthew Fontaine Maury (1806–1873)," *Geographers: Biobibliographical Studies* 1 (1978): 59–63; *NCAB* 6:35; Andrew F. Rolle, *The Lost Cause: The Confederate Exodus to Mexico* (Norman, Okla., 1965), ch. 14; Frances L. Williams, *Matthew Fontaine Maury, Scientist of the Sea* (New Brunswick, N.J., 1963); and *WWWA*.

MAYER, BRANTZ (1809–1879). Diplomat, archaeologist, and author, born September 27, 1809, in Baltimore. Mayer graduated from St. Mary's College (Baltimore) and the University of Maryland and was admitted to the bar in 1832. He practiced law until 1841. He was secretary of legation in Mexico from 1841 to 1844. He then lived, traveled, and studied in Mexico, and wrote *Mexico as It Was and as It Is* (New York, 1844) and *Mexico, Aztec, Spanish and Republican: A Historical, Geographical, Political, Statistical and Social Account of That Country from the Period of the Invasion by the Spaniards to the Present Time* (Hartford, Conn., 1851). He resumed the practice of law until 1855 and then devoted himself to writing. He wrote *Observations on Mexican History and Archaeology* (Washington, D.C., 1857) and *Outlines of Mexican Antiquities* (Philadelphia, 1858). He served in the Union Army during the Civil War and later worked in the pay department of the army from 1865 to 1875. Died February 23, 1879, in Baltimore. *References*: *DAB*; and *NCAB* 10:32.

MEANS, PHILIP AINSWORTH (1892–1944). Archaeologist, born April 3, 1892, in Boston. Means graduated from Harvard University. He was a member of the expedition to Peru organized by Yale University and the National Geographic Society in 1914–1915 and returned to Peru in 1917–1918, 1918–1919, 1920–1921, and 1933–1934, working under the sponsorship of the U.S. National Museum, the Smithsonian Institution, and the American Geographical Society. He was director of the Museo Nacional (Sección de Arqueología) of Peru in 1920–1921 and associate in anthropology of the Peabody Museum of Harvard University from 1921 to 1927. He visited Mexico in 1925–1926. He settled in Pomfret, Massachusetts, in 1929. He wrote *Biblioteca Andina* (New Haven, Conn., 1928), *Ancient Civilizations of the Andes* (New York, 1931), *Fall of the Inca Empire and the Spanish Rule in Peru: 1530–1780* (New York, 1932), *The*

Spanish Main (New York, 1935), and *Tupak of the Incas* (New York, 1942). Died November 24, 1944, in Boston. *References*: *AA* 48 (1946): 234–47; and *AmAntiq* 11 (1945): 109–12.

MEGGERS, BETTY J(ANE) (1921–   ). Archaeologist, born December 5, 1921, in Washington, D.C. Meggers graduated from the universities of Pennsylvania and Michigan and from Columbia University. She was a research associate in the Smithsonian Institution after 1954. She carried out archaeological investigations in the Amazon region, Ecuador, and Guiana and did fieldwork in coastal Ecuador, the upper Orinoco in Venezuela, and Dominica. She wrote *Ecuador* (New York, 1966), *Amazonia: Man and Culture in a Counterfeit Paradise* (Chicago, 1971), and *Prehistoric America* (Chicago, 1972), and, with her husband, **CLIFFORD EVANS,*** *Archaeological Investigations at the Mouth of the Amazon* (Washington, D.C., 1957), *Archaeological Investigations in British Guiana* (Washington, D.C., 1960), and *Early Formative Period in Coastal Ecuador* (Washington, D.C., 1965). She was coeditor of *Tropical Forest Ecosystems in Africa and South America: A Comparative Review* (Washington, D.C., 1973). *References*: *AMWS*; *CA*; and *WWAW*.

MEIGGS, HENRY (1811–1877). Railroad builder, born July 7, 1811, in Catskill, New York. Meiggs worked in the lumber trade in Catskill, Boston, and New York, and operated his own lumberyard in Williamsburg, New York, from 1837 to 1842. He went to San Francisco in 1848 and was involved in lumbering. After finding himself in heavy debt (most of which he later repaid), he ran away from San Francisco in 1854 and went to Chile. He became construction superintendent of the San Francisco al Sur Railroad. In 1861, he contracted with the Chilean government to complete the Valparaiso and Santiago line and successfully completed it in 1865. He made surveys for a road across the Andes, planned railroads in Bolivia, dealt in Bolivian guano, and founded a bank in La Paz. After 1868, he secured from the Peruvian government contracts for railroad lines, and the first, from Mollendo to Arequipa, was completed in 1870. It was continued to Puno on Lake Titicaca and a branch was built to Cuzco. He then began constructing the Callao, Lima and Oroya Railroad. He also built parks and boulevards in Lima. Died September 29, 1877, in Lima. *References*: *DAB*; *DADH*; *ELA*; *Figueroa*; *NCAB* 13:138; *NYT*, October 12, 1877; and Watt Stewart, *Henry Meiggs, Yankee Pizarro* (Durham, N.C., 1946).

MEIN, JOHN GORDON (1913–1968). Diplomat, born September 10, 1913, in Cadiz, Kentucky. Mein graduated from Georgetown (Ky.) College and George Washington University Law School. He worked in the U.S. Department of Agriculture from 1936 to 1941. He entered the foreign service in 1941. He served as minister-counselor in the Philippines from 1960 to 1963 and in Brazil from 1963 to 1965. He was U.S. ambassador to Guatemala after 1965. Assassinated August 28, 1968, in Guatemala City, Guatemala, the first American ambassador to be assassinated at his post. *References*: *DADH*; *NCAB* 54:528; and *NYT*, August 29, 1968.

MELLON, WILLIAM LARIMER, JR. (1910–   ). Medical missionary, born June 26, 1910, in Pittsburgh, Pennsylvania. Mellon attended Princeton University and, in 1935, became a rancher in Rimrock, New Mexico. He served with the Office of Strategic Services during World War II. He graduated from Tulane University Medical School. He went to Haiti in 1952 and built a hospital in Deschappeles, in the Artibonite Valley, which was opened in 1956. *References*: *CB* 1965; Peter Michelmore, *Dr. Mellon of Haiti* (New York, 1964); and *Who's Who in the World* (Chicago, 1974).

MENNONITE BOARD OF MISSIONS AND CHARITIES. Founded in 1906, it began missionary work in Argentina in 1917, in Puerto Rico in 1945, in Brazil, Uruguay, and Cuba in 1954, in Jamaica in 1955, and in Mexico in 1958. The mission in Cuba was closed down in 1960. *Reference*: Josephus W. Shank, *The Gospel under the Southern Cross: A History of the Argentine Mennonite Mission of South America, Celebrating Its Twenty-Fifth Anniversary, 1917–1942* (Scottsdale, Pa., 1943).

MENOCAL, ANICETO GARCIA (1836–1908). Civil engineer, born September 1, 1836, in Cuba. Menocal graduated from Rensselaer Polytechnic Institute. He was assistant engineer and later chief engineer in charge of construction at the waterworks of Havana from 1862 to 1870. He served with the Department of Public Works of New York City from 1870 to 1872. He was commissioned chief engineer in the U.S. Navy in 1874. He was chief engineer of all the surveys made in Panama and Nicaragua, mapped Nicaragua from 1872 to 1874 and the Panama Isthmus in 1874–1875, and was chief engineer of the Provisional Interoceanic Canal Society from 1870 to 1887. Under the auspices of the Nicaraguan government, he carried out improvements at Greystown, Nicaragua. He also investigated conditions in Panama. He was chief engineer of the Maritime Canal Company of Nicaragua from 1887 to 1890. He retired from the navy in 1898 with the rank of commander. From 1906 to 1908, he developed an irrigation system for the northern provinces of Cuba. Died July 20, 1908, in New York City. *References*: *DAB*; *NCAB* 14:354; *NYT*, July 21, 1908; and *WWWA*.

MERCER, HENRY CHAPMAN (1856–1930). Archaeologist, born June 24, 1856, in Doylestown, Bucks County, Pennsylvania. Mercer graduated from Harvard University and studied law at the University of Pennsylvania but never practiced. He was involved in antiquarian studies and explored caves in Tennessee, Ohio, and Texas. He was curator of American and prehistoric archaeology at the Free Museum of Science and Arts (later University Museum) of the University of Pennsylvania. He was leader of the Corwith expedition to Yucatán in 1895, visiting twenty-nine caves and excavating thirteen of them. He wrote

The Hill-Caves of Yucatan: A Search for Evidence of Man's Antiquity in the Caverns of Central America (Philadelphia, 1896). He later investigated colonial and early American implements and trades and founded the Moravian Pottery and Tile Works. Died March 9, 1930, in Fonthill, Pennsylvania. *References*: J. A. Mason, "Henry Chapman Mercer, 1856–1930," *Pennsylvania Archaeologist Bulletin* 26 (1956): 152–65; Cleota Reed, *Henry Chapman Mercer and the Moravian Pottery and Tile Works* (Philadelphia, 1987); and J. Eric S. Thompson, "Introduction," in Henry C. Mercer, *The Hill Caves of Yucatán* (Norman, Okla., 1975), pp. vii–xliv.

MERRILL, JOHN LENORD (1866–1949). Businessman, born September 17, 1866, in Orange, New Jersey. Merrill entered the service of the Mexican Telegraph Company and the Central and South American Telegraph Company (later All America Cables, Incorporated) in 1884. He was auditor of the companies from 1902 to 1915, vice president from 1915 to 1918, president from 1918 to 1939, and chairman of the board from 1939 until his retirement in 1947. He traveled throughout the Americas. After the company became part of International Telephone and Telegraph (I.T.T.) Corporation system in 1927, he was vice president of I.T.T. from 1927 to 1944. Died December 18, 1949, in New York City. *References*: *New York Botanical Garden Journal* 51 (1950): 22–23; *NYT*, December 19, 1949; and *WWWA*.

MERRY, WILLIAM LAWRENCE (1842–1911). Sea captain, merchant, and diplomat, born December 27, 1842, in New York City. Merry was a junior officer of a steamship between New York and Central America in 1858, commanded a New York clipper on the Pacific coast in 1862, and visited Lake Nicaragua in that year. He was an agent for the U.S. Mail Steamship Company on the Isthmus of Panama in 1863–1864, commanded a steamer between San Francisco and Nicaragua from 1864 to 1867, and was general agent in charge of Nicaragua transit for the Central American Transit and the North American Steamship companies from 1867 to 1870. He moved to San Francisco in 1874 and was president of the North American Navigation Company and consul general of Nicaragua on the west coast. He was promoter of the Nicaragua canal project from 1890 to 1895 and wrote *The Nicaragua Canal, the Gateway between the Oceans* (San Francisco, 1895). He was U.S. minister to El Salvador from 1897 to 1907, minister to Nicaragua from 1897 to 1908, and minister to Costa Rica from 1897 to 1911. Died December 14, 1911, in Battle Creek, Michigan. *References*: *DAB*; *DADH*; *NCAB* 42:635; *NYT*, December 16, 1911; and *WWWA*.

MESSERSMITH, GEORGE S(TRAUSSER) (1883–1960). Diplomat, born October 3, 1883, in Fleetwood, Pennsylvania. Messersmith graduated from Keystone State Normal School (Kutztown, Pa.) and attended Delaware State College (Newark). He held teaching and administrative positions in the Delaware school system, and entered the foreign service in 1914. He served in consular posts in

Fort Erie, Curaçao, and Antwerp, and was consul general in Antwerp, Buenos Aires, and Berlin until 1934. He was U.S. minister in Austria from 1934 to 1937 and assistant secretary of state for administration from 1937 to 1940. He was U.S. ambassador to Cuba from 1940 to 1942 and ambassador to Mexico from 1942 to 1946, where he supervised the flow of strategic materials to the American war economy and worked to regain access to Mexican oil fields for American companies. He was ambassador to Argentina in 1946–1947. He tried to restore amicable relations between the United States and Argentina and helped to get the Argentine Congress to accept the Act of Chapultepec of 1945. He also worked closely with Argentine President Juan Perón, whom he liked. He resigned in 1947 because of disagreements with U.S. State Department policy. He was chairman of the board of the Mexican Power and Light Company from 1947 until his retirement in 1955. Died January 29, 1960, in Houston, Texas. *References*: George S. Messersmith Papers, University of Delaware Library, Newark; *NCAB* 47:663; *NYT*, January 30, 1960; Jesse H. Stiller, *George S. Messersmith, Diplomat of Democracy* (Chapel Hill, N.C., 1987); and Roger T. Trask, "Spruille Braden versus George Messersmith, World War II, the Cold War and Argentine Policy, 1945–1984," *JISWA* 26 (1984): 69–95.

METHODIST EPISCOPAL CHURCH: BOARD OF FOREIGN MISSIONS. Founded in 1819, it began missionary work in Argentina in 1836, in Brazil from 1836 to 1842 (reopened in 1880, work was transferred to the Methodist Episcopal Church, South* in 1900), in Uruguay from 1839 to 1842 (reopened in 1868), in Mexico in 1873, in Paraguay from 1886 to 1917, in Peru and Chile in 1890, in Ecuador from 1898 to 1910, in Bolivia in 1901, in Panama in 1905, and in Costa Rica in 1917. *References*: Wade C. Barclay, *History of Methodist Missions* (New York, 1949–1973); *1873–1923 Souvenir Book of the Golden Anniversary of Jubilee of the Methodist Episcopal Church in Mexico* (Mexico, 1924); and Thomas B. Neely, *The Methodist Episcopal Church and Its Foreign Missions* (New York, 1923).

METHODIST EPISCOPAL CHURCH, SOUTH: BOARD OF MISSIONS. Founded in 1844 when it broke off from the Methodist Episcopal Church,* it began missionary work in Mexico in 1873, in Brazil in 1875, and in Cuba in 1883. *References*: James Cannon III, *History of Southern Methodist Missions* (Nashville, 1926); and Sterling A. Neblett, *Methodism's First Fifty Years in Cuba* (Wilmire, Ky., 1976).

MEXICAN INTERNATIONAL RAILROAD. The International Construction Company received in 1881 a concession from the Mexican government to build a railroad from Piedras Negras to Mexico City with several branches. The company was reorganized as the Mexican Railroad Company, was acquired in 1901 by the Mexican National Railroad* Company, and merged into the National Railways of Mexico in 1909.

MEXICAN NATIONAL RAILWAY. A concession was granted in 1880 by Mexican President Porfirio Díaz to the William J. Palmer and James Sullivan interests, operating under the name of Mexican National Construction Company, to build a railroad from Mexico City to Laredo and from Mexico City to Manzanillo, with extensions to Guadalupe Hidalgo and El Salto. When sections of the railroad were completed, they were taken over by the operating company, the Mexican National Railway. It was reorganized as the Mexican National Railroad Company in 1887 and merged into the National Railways of Mexico in 1909.

MEXICAN PUNITIVE EXPEDITION (1916–1917). Military expedition under the command of General John J. Pershing* that was sent into Mexico in 1916–1917 in pursuit of the Mexican revolutionary leader Francisco (Pancho) Villa and his followers. After several skirmishes between Mexican and American soldiers, the American troops left Mexico in 1917. *References*: Haldeen Braddy, *Pershing's Mission in Mexico* (El Paso, Tex., 1966); Clarence C. Clendenen, *Blood on the Border* (New York, 1961); Calvin W. Hines, *The Mexican Punitive Expedition of 1916* (San Antonio, Tex., 1962); Herbert M. Mason, Jr., *The Great Pursuit* (New York, 1970); Michael L. Tate, "Pershing's Punitive Expedition: Pursuer of Bandits or Presidential Panacea?" *TA* 32 (1975): 46–72; Robert S. Thomas and Inez V. Allen, *The Mexican Punitive Expedition* (Washington, D.C., 1954); and Vernon Williams, *Lieutenant Patton and the American Army in the Mexican Expedition, 1915–1916* (Austin, Tex., 1983).

MEXICAN TIMES. An English-language newspaper published in Mexico City and edited by Henry Watkins Allen* in 1865–1866 and by John N. Edwards in 1866, at which time the subsidy from the empire was discontinued. Thereafter, it was independent and often critical of the empire. *References*: Alfred J. Hanna, "A Confederate Newspaper in Mexico," *Journal of Southern History* 12 (1946): 67–83; and Andrew F. Rolle, *The Lost Cause: The Confederate Exodus to Mexico* (Norman, Okla., 1965), ch. 16.

MEYERHOFF, HOWARD A(GUSTUS) (1899–1982). Geologist, born May 27, 1899, in New York City. Meyerhoff graduated from the University of Illinois and Columbia University. He was curator of paleontology at Columbia University from 1921 to 1924 and professor of geology at Smith College from 1924 to 1949. He was geologist on the Scientific Survey of Puerto Rico and the Virgin Islands from 1924 to 1943, consulting geologist to the Puerto Rico Bureau of Mines from 1932 to 1943, and consulting geologist to the Dominican Republic in 1937–1938 and from 1942 to 1949. He was executive secretary of the American Association for the Advancement of Science in 1945–1946 and its administrative secretary and editor of *Science* from 1949 until 1953. He was a partner in Geosurveys, mineral consultants, from 1955 to 1973. He wrote *Geology of Puerto Rico* (Rio Piedras, P.R., 1933) and was coauthor of *Geology of the Virgin Islands,*

Culebra and Vieques (New York, 1927). Died March 24, 1982, in Tucson, Arizona. *References*: *CA*; *NCAB* K:510; *Science* 216 (May 7, 1982): 613; and *WWA*.

MICHLER, NATHANIEL (1827–1881). Army officer, born September 13, 1827, in Easton, Pennsylvania. Michler attended Lafayette College and graduated from the U.S. Military Academy in 1848. He served with the topographical engineers, made surveys in Texas and New Mexico, and was engaged in the Mexico Boundary Survey from 1851 to 1857. He was chief topographical engineer in charge of the surveys for a project of a canal extending from the Gulf of Darien to the Pacific Ocean from 1857 to 1860. He served in the Union Army during the Civil War. He was superintendent of public buildings and grounds from 1867 to 1871, on the staff of the Pacific Coast command and lighthouse engineer from 1871 to 1876, superintendent of river and harbor improvement of Lake Erie from 1876 to 1878, and military attaché in Vienna, Austria, in 1879–1880. Died July 17, 1881, in Saratoga Springs, New York. *References*: *ACAB*; *DAB S1*; *NYT*, July 19, 1881; and *WWWA*.

MIGNOT, LOUIS REMY (1831–1870). Painter, born in Charleston, South Carolina. Mignot studied art in Charleston and then in the Hague, Holland. He opened a studio in New York City in 1855. He accompanied Frederick Edwin Church* on a trip to Ecuador in 1857. He lived in London, England, after 1862. Died September 22, 1870, in Brighton, England. *References*: *ACAB*; *DAB*; *Manthorne*; and *NYHSD*.

MILITARY OCCUPATION OF CUBA. *See* CUBA, MILITARY OCCUPATION OF

MILLER, GEORGE A(MOS) (1868–1961). Clergyman, born July 8, 1868, in Mendon, Illinois, and grew up in the Sacramento and the San Joaquin valleys in California. Miller attended the University of Southern California, graduated from Stanford University, and was ordained in 1896. He held pastorates in Hanford and Fresno, California, until 1904; in Manila, the Philippines, from 1905 to 1907; and in San Francisco and San Jose, California, from 1908 to 1916. He was mission superintendent in Panama from 1917 to 1919 and later pioneered Methodist work in Costa Rica. He was executive secretary of mission work in South America for the Methodist Episcopal Church,* serving in Mexico City, Buenos Aires, and Santiago until his retirement in 1934. He was elected bishop in 1924. He then held a pastorate in Lafayette, California. He wrote *Prowling about Panama* (New York, 1919) and *Adventures with Christ in Latin America* (New York, 1927). Died October 12, 1961. *Reference*: *EWM*.

MILLER, LEO EDWARD (1887–1952). Explorer and author, born May 11, 1887, in Huntingburg, Indiana. Miller was a member of the American Museum of Natural History's expedition to Colombia in 1911–1912, became a member of the ornithological staff of the museum, and then headed expeditions for the museum to Venezuela, Bolivia, Brazil, Peru, British Guiana, and Argentina from 1912 to 1917, collecting zoological specimens. He accompanied Theodore Roosevelt's expedition to Brazil in 1914. He served in the Aviation Service of the U.S. Army during World War I. He was employed by Oakley Chemical Company (later Oakite Products, Incorporated) in New York City from 1926 until his death. He wrote *In the Wilds of South America: Six Years of Exploration in Colombia, Venezuela, British Guiana, Peru, Bolivia, Argentina, Paraguay, and Brazil* (New York, 1918), *The Hidden People: The Story of a Search for Incan Treasure* (New York, 1920), and works of fiction, including *Adrift on the Amazon* (New York, 1923) and *Jungle Pirates* (New York, 1925). Died October 6, 1952, in New Haven, Connecticut. *References: IAB; NCAB* 40:320; and *WWWA*.

MILLER, PAUL G(ERARD) (1875–1952). Educator, born January 23, 1875, in Pickett, Wisconsin. Miller graduated from the University of Wisconsin. He served during the Spanish-American War. He was supervisor of the San German school in Puerto Rico from 1899 to 1902, superintendent of the school in San Juan in 1902, and chief of the division of supervision of the Puerto Rico Department of Education and principal of the Insular Normal School from 1903 to 1908. He taught Romance languages at the University of Wisconsin from 1908 to 1910 and 1911 to 1915, was commissioner of education of Puerto Rico from 1915 to 1921, and played an important role in the development of the island's schools. He worked for Rand McNally and Company from 1921 to 1947. Died May 21, 1952, in Winneconne, Wisconsin. *References: BDAE*; Aida Negron de Montilla, *Americanization in Puerto Rico and the Public School System 1900–1930* (San Juan, P.R., 1975), ch. 8; *NYT*, May 22, 1952; and *WWWA*.

MILLS, JAMES E(LLISON) (1834–1901). Mining geologist, born February 13, 1834, in Bangor, Maine. Mills graduated from Lawrence Scientific School of Harvard University and was ordained in 1860. He held a pastorate in Brooklyn, New York, until 1863. He then took up geological work, was a consulting geologist in New York City from 1863 to 1870, and explored in Nova Scotia, Alabama, West Virginia, Pennsylvania, Missouri, and Virginia, examining mines and conducting geological survey work. In 1878, he examined and reported on gold mines in Rio Grande do Sul and in Minas Gerais in Brazil. He was superintendent of Sao Cyrianco Gold Mining Company in Minas Gerais and worked in Mexico after 1895, developing mining property for the San Fernando Mining Company in San Fernando in Durango. Died July 25, 1901, in San Fernando, Durango, Mexico. *Reference: BGSA* 14 (1902): 512–17.

MILLSPAUGH, ARTHUR C(HESTER) (1883–1955). Financial adviser, born March 1, 1883, in Augusta, Michigan. Millspaugh graduated from Albion College, the University of Illinois, and Johns Hopkins University. He served in the

State Department from 1918 to 1922 and headed a financial mission to Persia (Iran) from 1922 to 1927. He was financial adviser and general receiver for Haiti from 1927 to 1929 and wrote *Haiti under American Control, 1915–1930* (Boston, 1931). He was a member of the staff of the Brookings Institution from 1929 to 1942 and again from 1946 to 1948, and headed another mission to Iran in 1943–1944. Died September 24, 1955, in Kalamazoo, Michigan. *References*: *NYT*, September 26, 1955; and *WWWA*.

MILLSPAUGH, CHARLES FREDERICK (1854–1923). Botanist, born June 20, 1854, in Ithaca, New York. Millspaugh attended Cornell University and graduated from the New York Homeopathic Medical College and Hospital. He practiced medicine at Binghamton, New York, from 1881 to 1890, and in Waverly, New York, in 1890–1891. He was professor of botany at the University of West Virginia from 1891 to 1893 and curator of botany at the Field Museum of Natural History in Chicago from 1893 until his death. He made many collecting trips to Mexico, Yucatán, the Bahamas, and the West Indies, and explored in Mexico, the West Indies, and Brazil. He also investigated a number of uninhabited Bahamian islets. He wrote *Contribution to the Coastal and Plain Flora of Yucatán* (Chicago, 1895–1898), and *Plantae Yucatanae* (Chicago, 1903–1904). Died September 15, 1923, in Chicago. *References*: *DAB*; *DAMB 84*; Harry B. Humphrey, *Makers of North American Botany* (New York, 1961), pp. 181–83; *NCAB* 25:120; *NYT*, September 17, 1923; and *WWWA*.

MISSIONARY AVIATION FELLOWSHIP. Founded as the Christian Airmen's Missionary Fellowship in 1944. The name changed to Missionary Aviation Fellowship in 1946 and to the current name in 1973. It began to function in Mexico in 1946, in Ecuador in 1948, in Honduras in 1949, in Brazil in 1956, in Surinam in 1963, in Venezuela in 1965, in Colombia and Haiti in 1971, and in Nicaragua in 1972. *References*: *EMCM*; and *Wings of Praise and Prayer* (Fullerton, Calif., n.d.).

MIZNER, LANSING BOND (1825–1893). Lawyer and diplomat, born December 5, 1825, in Monroe County, Illinois. Mizner attended Shurtleff College (Ill.) and studied law. He served in the U.S. legation in Colombia from 1840 to 1844 and fought during the Mexican War. In 1850, he went to California, was admitted to the bar, and was elected associate justice of the first court of sessions of Solano County. He was appointed collector of customs in 1853 and was elected to the state senate in 1865. He was U.S. minister to the five Central American states in 1889–1890, with residence in Guatemala City. He helped mediate the war between Guatemala and El Salvador in 1890 and was involved in the Barrundia affair of 1890, in which General J. Martin Barrundia of Guatemala was killed on the Pacific Mail steamer *Acapulco*; Mizner was recalled that same year. Died in San Francisco in 1893. *References*: Mary P. Chapman,

"The Mission of Lansing Bond Mizner to Central America," *Historian* 19 (1957): 385–401; and *NCAB* 5:556.

MÔLE ST. NICOLAS, HAITI. A harbor of a bay at the extreme northwestern tip of Haiti, envisioned by some U.S. government officials as the primary U.S. naval station in the Caribbean. An effort to establish a U.S. naval base there in 1891 was thwarted when Haiti refused to lease the area to the United States. *References*: Myra Himelhoch, "Frederick Douglass and Haiti's Môle St. Nicolas," *Journal of Negro History* 56 (1971): 161–80; and William S. McFeely, *Frederick Douglass* (New York, 1991), ch. 26.

MOMSEN, RICHARD P(AUL) (1890–1964). Lawyer, born September 12, 1890, in Milwaukee, Wisconsin. Momsen graduated from George Washington University and the Faculty of Social and Juridical Sciences in Rio de Janeiro, and was admitted to the bar in 1913. He was U.S. deputy consul general in Rio de Janeiro in 1913 and retired as acting consul general in 1919. He established the law firm of Momsen and Freeman and practiced law until his retirement in 1963 as senior partner of Momsen, Freeman and Cardinale, lawyers in New York and Rio de Janeiro. He was said to have been the only American lawyer admitted to the practice of law in Brazil. (Legislation against the admittance of foreigners to the Brazilian bar was passed shortly after he started practice.) As a representative of Rotary International, he worked for the construction of some forty schools in Brazil. Died February 19, 1964, in Cross River, New York. *References*: *NYT*, February 21, 1964; and *WWWA*.

MONROE DOCTRINE. A statement of United States policy made by President James Monroe in 1823, though written largely by secretary of state John Quincy Adams, which indicated that the United States would oppose any attempt by European nations to establish new colonies in the Western Hemisphere and to intervene in the affairs of independent nations in Latin America. *References*: Harry Ammon, "The Monroe Doctrine: Domestic Politics or National Decision?" *DH* 5 (1981): 53–70; Cecil V. Crabb, Jr., *The Doctrines of American Foreign Policy: Their Meaning, Role, and Future* (Baton Rouge, La., 1982), ch. 1; Frank Donovan, *Mr. Monroe's Message: The Story of the Monroe Doctrine* (New York, 1963); Donald M. Dozer, *The Monroe Doctrine: Its Modern Significance* (New York, 1965); *ELA*; Ernest May, *The Making of the Monroe Doctrine* (Cambridge, Mass., 1975); and Dexter Perkins, *A History of the Monroe Doctrine* (Boston, 1967).

MONTEVERDE. American settlement in Costa Rica, established in Monteverde in the Cordillera de Tilaran in 1950 by Quakers from Fairhope, Alabama, who emigrated mainly because of their opposition to the U.S. war economy. The colony's principal commercial product was cheese. It also established the Monteverde Conservation League to purchase pieces of the rain forest. *Refer-*

ences: Donald E. Lundberg, *Adventure in Costa Rica* (Tallahassee, Fla., 1960), ch. 14; and Ulv Nasing, "Foreign Agricultural Colonies in Costa Rica," Ph.D. diss., University of Florida, 1964.

MONTGOMERY, GEORGE WASHINGTON (1804–1841). Diplomat, born in Alicante, Spain, to an American father. Montgomery was a private secretary to the Marquis of Casa Yrujio in Madrid until 1826 and was attached to the U.S. legation in Madrid from 1826 to 1828 as a translator. He was involved in translating American literature into Spanish. He was U.S. consul in San Juan, Puerto Rico, from 1835 to 1838, and in Tampico, Mexico, in 1840–1841. He traveled in Guatemala and wrote *Narrative of a Journey to Guatemala, in Central America, in 1838* (New York, 1839). Died June 5, 1841, in Washington, D.C. *References*: *DAB*; and *NCAB* 18:278.

MOORE, THOMAS PATRICK (1797–1853). Public official and diplomat, born in Charlotte County, Virginia, and grew up in Harrodsburg, Mercer County, Kentucky. Moore attended Transylvania University (Lexington, Ky.). He served in the War of 1812. He was a member of the Kentucky House of Representatives in 1819–1820 and the U.S. House of Representatives from 1823 to 1829. He was U.S. minister to New Granada from 1829 to 1833. He ingratiated himself with Simón Bolívar and obtained important commercial concessions for the United States. After the withdrawal of Ecuador and Venezuela from New Granada, he tried to bring about the reunification of the three states. After his efforts had failed, he asked to be recalled in 1832. He served during the Mexican War. Died July 21, 1853, in Harrodsburg, Kentucky. *References*: *BDAC*; and *DAB*.

MORALES, FRANKLIN E. (1884–1962). Businessman and diplomat, born January 26, 1884, in Philadelphia. Morales graduated from business college (Atlantic City, N.J.). He was involved in the export business and was vice president of International Commercial Corporation from 1916 to 1919. He was a representative of American jewelry manufacturers in Latin America from 1919 to 1921 and a partner of real estate and insurance brokers. He was U.S. minister to Honduras from 1921 to 1925. Died July 19, 1962, in Toms River, New Jersey. *References*: *NYT*, July 21, 1962; and *WWWA*.

MOREHEAD, JOSEPH C. (ca. 1824– ?). Filibuster, born in Kentucky. Morehead served during the Mexican War. He then moved to California, where he served in the state legislature and as state quartermaster general. He absconded with state funds. In 1851, he organized a secret mission to invade Sonora, Mexico, and arrived in Mazatlán with a small party. No further information about him is known. *References*: Joe A. Stout, Jr., "Joseph C. Morehead and Manifest Destiny: A Filibuster in Sonora, 1851," *Pacific Historian* 15 (1971): 62–70; and Joseph A. Stout, Jr., *The Liberators: Filibustering Expeditions into*

Mexico 1848–1862 and the Last Trust of Manifest Destiny (Los Angeles, 1973), ch. 3.

MORGAN, EDWIN VERNON (1865–1934). Diplomat, born February 22, 1865, in Aurora, New York. Morgan graduated from Harvard University and studied at the University of Berlin. He was an instructor in history at Adelbert College (Cleveland) from 1895 to 1898, secretary to the Samoan High Commission in 1899, secretary of legation in Korea in 1900, vice- and deputy consul general in Seoul in 1900–1901, second secretary of embassy in St. Petersburg in 1901–1902, and confidential clerk to the third assistant secretary of state in Washington, D.C., from 1902 to 1905. He was U.S. minister to Cuba from 1905 to 1910, minister to Uruguay and Paraguay in 1910–1911, minister to Portugal in 1911–1912, and ambassador to Brazil from 1912 to 1933. He was instrumental in negotiating the coffee and wheat exchange agreements between Brazil and the United States and was a patron of Brazilian artists. Died April 16, 1934, in Petropolis, Brazil. *References*: Lewis House, "Edwin V. Morgan and Brazilian-American Diplomatic Relations, 1912–1935," Ph.D. diss., New York University, 1969; *NCAB* 39:278; and *WWWA*.

MORGAN, PHILIP H(ICKY) (1825–1900). Lawyer and diplomat, born November 9, 1825, in Baton Rouge, Louisiana. Morgan studied law in Paris and was admitted to the bar. He served during the Mexican War and practiced law in New Orleans after 1852. He served as judge of the second district court of Louisiana from 1852 to 1856, district attorney of Louisiana, a state supreme court judge from 1873 to 1876, and a judge of the international court in Egypt from 1877 to 1880. He was U.S. minister to Mexico from 1880 to 1885. He later resumed the practice of law in New York City. Died August 12, 1900, in New York City. *References*: *ACAB*; *DAB*; *NCAB* 13:596; and *WWWA*.

MORGAN, WILLIAM A(LEXANDER) (1928–1961). Soldier, born in Toledo, Ohio. Morgan served in the U.S. Army until 1950. He came to Cuba in 1957 and joined the Second Front in the Esambray Hills of central Cuba, fighting against the regime of Fulgencio Batista. He then served in Fidel Castro's revolutionary army and was later given command of the city of Cienfuegos by Fidel Castro. In 1959, he posed as a double agent and frustrated a conspiracy against the Castro regime by elements of the former Batista government with the support of the Dominican Republic. His U.S. citizenship was revoked in 1959 and he was granted Cuban citizenship by presidential decree. In 1960, he was accused of aiding rebels against Castro's regime. He was tried by a military court, found guilty, and executed on March 11, 1961, in Havana. *References*: *NYT*, August 15, 1959; and *NYT*, March 10, 1961.

MORISON, GEORGE SHATTUCK (1842–1903). Engineer, born December 19, 1842, in New Bedford, Massachusetts. Morison graduated from Harvard University and was admitted to the bar in 1866. He practiced law in New York

City in 1866–1867 but then entered the engineering profession in 1867. He was assistant to the chief engineer of the Erie Railroad from 1873 to 1875. He organized a bridge contracting firm in New York City from 1875 to 1880 and then was in consulting practice from 1880 to 1884, involved in building a large number of railroad bridges. He was a member of the Isthmian Canal Commission from 1899 to 1901. His powerful advocacy of the Panama route, backed by an exhaustive study of the situation, proved an important factor in bringing about the final decision. Died July 1, 1903, in New York City. *References*: *DAB*; George A. Morison, *George Shattuck Morison, 1842–1903* (Peterborough, N.H., 1940); *NCAB* 10:129; *NYT*, July 3, 1903; and *WWWA*.

MORLAN, ALBERT E(DMUND) (1850–1926). Businessman and diplomat, born February 18, 1850, in Fallston, Beaver County, Pennsylvania. Morlan was obliged to leave school at an early age and earn a living. He was apprenticed in the jewelry business in 1871. He worked in New York and Mobile, Alabama, and then settled in New Orleans. In 1879, he visited Central America and established himself in the jewelry and general mercantile business in Belize, British Honduras. He was U.S. consul in Belize from 1882 until 1889. He opened a commission business in New Orleans with branches in Tegucigalpa, Bocas del Toro, and Belize, which were closed after a short time. He traveled extensively, became well acquainted with Honduras and its population, and wrote *A Hoosier in Honduras* (Indianapolis, 1897). He lived in Indiana after 1894 and was an artist and secretary of Central University, a correspondence school. Died January 10, 1926, in Indianapolis. *References*: *IAB*; and *NCAB* 8:371.

MORLEY, SYLVANUS GRISWOLD (1883–1948). Archaeologist, born June 7, 1883, in Chester, Pennsylvania. Morley graduated from Harvard University. He was a fellow of the School of American Archaeology of the Archaeological Institute of America (later the School of American Research) in Santa Fe, New Mexico, from 1909 to 1914, and research associate in American archaeology at the Carnegie Institution of Washington from 1914 until his death. He conducted an archaeological survey in Yucatán in 1909, the first of forty consecutive seasons in the Maya area. He conducted his first excavation at a Maya site in Quiriguá, Guatemala, in 1910, and made numerous expeditions into the tropical jungles of Central America, examining Maya sites at Copán in Honduras and in the Petén district of northern Guatemala. In 1924, he began extensive excavations at Chichén Itzá in Yucatán and continued them until 1934. He also did preliminary work at Uaxactún, Guatemala. He wrote *An Introduction to the Study of the Maya Hieroglyphs* (Washington, D.C., 1915), *The Inscriptions at Copán* (Washington, D.C., 1920), *The Inscriptions of Petén* (Washington, D.C., 1937–1938), and *The Ancient Mayas* (Stanford, Calif., 1946). Died September 2, 1948, in Santa Fe, New Mexico. References: *DAB S5*; Robert H. Lister and Florence C. Lister, ed., *In Search of Maya Glyphs: From the Archaeological Journals of*

Sylvanus G. Morley (Santa Fe, 1971); *NCAB* 38:19; and *NYT*, September 3, 1948.

MORMON COLONIES IN MEXICO. Mormon colonists trekked to Mexico because of the mounting pressure against polygamy that they were encountering in the United States. The first colony, Colonia Juárez, was established on the Pedras Verdes River in 1885. By 1911, there were nine colonies in the state of Chihuahua and two colonies in the state of Sonora. During the Mexican revolution, nearly all the Mormon colonists were driven out of Mexico and only a few remained in Chihuahua. *References*: Blaine C. Hardy, "The Mormon Colonies in Northern Mexico: A History, 1885–1912," Ph.D. diss., Wayne State University, 1963; Carmon Hardy, "Cultural 'Encystement' as a Cause of the Mormon Exodus from Mexico in 1921," *PHR* 34 (1965): 439–54; Nelle S. Hatch, *Colonia Juarez: An Intimate Account of a Mormon Village* (Salt Lake City, Utah, 1954); Elizabeth H. Mills, "The Mormon Colonies in Chihuahua after the 1912 Exodus," *New Mexico Historical Review* 29 (1954): 165–82, 290–310; Thomas C. Romney, *The Mormon Colonies in Mexico* (Salt Lake City, 1938); Estelle W. Thomas, *Uncertain Sanctuary: A Story of Mormon Pioneering in Mexico* (Salt Lake City, 1980); Karl E. Young, *The Long Hot Summer of 1912: Episodes in the Flight of the Mormon Colonists from Mexico* (Provo, Utah, 1967); and Karl E. Young, *Ordeal in Mexico: Tales of Danger and Hardship Collected from Mormon Colonists* (Salt Lake City, 1968).

MORRISON, DELESSEPS S(TORY) (1912–1964). Public official and diplomat, born January 18, 1912, in New Roads, Louisiana. Morrison graduated from Louisiana State University. He served in the U.S. Army during World War II. He was mayor of New Orleans from 1946 to 1961 and expanded the city's port facilities in an effort to attract trade with Latin America. He met personally with Latin American political leaders and was friendly with many of them. He was U.S. ambassador to the Organization of American States from 1961 to 1963. Died May 22, 1964, in an airplane crash, near Ciudad Victoria, Mexico. His memoir, *Latin American Mission; an Adventure in Hemisphere Diplomacy*, edited and with an introduction by Gerold Frank (New York, 1965), was published posthumously. *Reference*: *Polprof:Kennedy*.

MORROW, DWIGHT W(HITNEY) (1873–1931). Businessman and diplomat, born January 11, 1873, in Huntington, West Virginia. Morrow graduated from Amherst College and Columbia Law School. He practiced law in New Jersey from 1899 to 1914 and was involved with the banking house of J. P. Morgan and Company from 1914 to 1927. He was U.S. minister to Mexico from 1927 to 1930. He succeeded in reestablishing good relations between the United States and Mexico, in settling some of the disputes between the two countries, and in settling, informally, the conflicts between the Mexican government and the Catholic Church. He served in the U.S. Senate in 1931. Died

October 5, 1931, in Englewood, New Jersey. His wife, **ELIZABETH CUTTER MORROW** (1873–1955), wrote *Casa Manana* (Groton Falls, N.Y., 1932) and *The Mexican Years: Leaves from the Diary of Elizabeth Cutter Morrow* (New York, 1953). *References*: Dwight W. Morrow Papers, Amherst College Library, Amherst, Mass.; *DAB*; *ELA*; Richard Melzer, "The Ambassador *Simpatico*: Dwight Morrow in Mexico 1927–30," in *Ambassadors in Foreign Policy: The Influence of Individuals on U.S.–Latin America Policy*, ed. C. Neale Robbing and Albert P. Vannucci (New York, 1987), pp. 1–27; *NCAB* 23:10; *NYT*, October 6, 1931; *NYT*, January 24, 1955; S. R. Ross, "Dwight W. Morrow, Ambassador to Mexico," *Americas* 14 (January 1958): 273–89; Robert F. Smith, "The Morrow Mission and the International Committee of Bankers on Mexico: The Interaction of Finance Diplomacy and the New Mexican Elite," *JLAS* 1 (1969): 149–66; and *WWWA*.

MORTON, JAMES ST. CLAIR (1829–1864). Army officer and engineer, born September 24, 1829, in Philadelphia. Morton graduated from the U.S. Military Academy in 1851 and was commissioned a second lieutenant in the Corps of Engineers. He was involved in engineering works in Charleston harbor, South Carolina; Fort Delaware, Delaware; and Sandy Hook Fort, New Jersey, and then was a lighthouse engineer until 1860. He was an engineer with the expedition to Chiriquí area of Central America in 1860 to explore a possible railroad route across the isthmus of Chiriquí. He served in the Union Army during the Civil War and was killed June 17, 1864, in the assault on Petersburg, Virginia. *References*: *ACAB*; *DAB*; and *WWWA*.

MOTON COMMISSION ON EDUCATION (1930). A presidential commission, headed by Robert Russa Moton (1867–1940), which was sent to Haiti in 1930 by President Herbert Hoover to assess Haitian education. It prepared the *Report of the United States Commission on Education in Haiti* (Washington, D.C., 1930). *Reference*: W. H. Hughes and F. D. Patterson, eds., *Robert Russa Moton of Hamilton and Tuskegee* (Chapel Hill, N.C., 1956).

MOULTON, HENRY DE WITT (1828–1893). Photographer, born November 14, 1828, in Bedford, New Hampshire. Moulton worked as a photographer in New York City. He went to Lima, Peru, in 1859, worked in Benjamin F. Pease's* gallery until 1860, and opened an independent gallery in Lima in 1862. He returned to the United States between mid–1863 and 1865 and was a photographer in Spencer, New York, from 1867 to 1871. Died December 21, 1893, in Concord, Massachusetts. *Reference*: Keith McElroy, "Henry De Witt Moulton: Rays of Sunlight from South America," *History of Photography* 8 (1984): 7–21.

MUNRO, DANA G(ARDNER) (1892–1990). Diplomat and educator, born July 18, 1892, in Providence, Rhode Island. Munro graduated from Brown University and the universities of Wisconsin and Pennsylvania. He was an economic consul in Valparaiso, Chile, in 1920–1921, a member of the staff of the Latin American Division in the State Department from 1921 to 1923, its assistant chief from 1923 to 1925 and chief in 1929–1930, secretary of legation in Panama from 1925 to 1927 and in Nicaragua from 1927 to 1929, and U.S. minister in Haiti from 1930 to 1932. He was professor of Latin American history and affairs in the Wilson School of Public and International Affairs at Princeton University from 1939 to 1958, president of the Foreign Bondholders Protective Council from 1958 to 1967, and chairman of its executive committee from 1967 to 1969. He wrote *The Five Republics of Central America* (New York, 1918), *The United States and the Caribbean Area* (Boston, 1934), *Latin American Republics, a History* (New York, 1942), *Intervention and Dollar Diplomacy in the Caribbean 1900–1921* (Princeton, N.J., 1964), *The United States and the Caribbean Republics, 1921–1933* (Princeton, N.J., 1974), and a memoir, *A Student in Central America, 1914–1916* (New Orleans, 1983). Died June 16, 1990, in Waquoit, Massachusetts. *References*: *DAS*; and *NYT*, June 19, 1990.

MURPHY, ROBERT CUSHMAN (1887–1973). Ornithologist, born April 29, 1887, in Brooklyn, New York, and grew up in Mount Sinai Harbor, Long Island, New York. Murphy graduated from Brown and Columbia universities. He was curator of the Department of Mammals and Birds of Brooklyn Museum from 1911 to 1917 and curator of the Department of Natural Sciences from 1917 to 1920. He was associate curator of birds at the American Museum of Natural History from 1921 to 1924, assistant director there from 1924 to 1926, curator of oceanic birds from 1926 to 1942, chairman of the department of birds from 1942 to 1954, and curator of birds from 1948 until his retirement in 1955. He was a scientist and naturalist on a research cruise from Dominica, West Indies, to South Georgia Island in 1912–1913, and a leader of expeditions to Lower California and Mexico in 1915, to the coasts and islands of Peru under the auspices of Brooklyn Museum, the American Museum of Natural History, and the American Geographical Society to Peru and Ecuador in 1924–1925, to the Pacific coast of Colombia in 1937 and again in 1941, to the Pearl Islands in the Caribbean in 1945, to Bermuda in 1950–1951, to Venezuela and the Caribbean Islands in 1952, to Peru in 1953–1954, and to the Bahama Islands in 1953– 1954. He wrote *Bird Island of Peru: The Record of a Sojourn on the West Coast* (New York, 1925), *Oceanic Birds of South America* (New York, 1936), and *Logbook for Grace: Whaling Brig Daisy, 1912–1913* (New York, 1947), and was coauthor of *Land Birds of America* (New York, 1953). Died March 20, 1973, in Stony Brook, Long Island, New York. His wife, **GRACE E(MLINE) BARSTOW MURPHY**, wrote *There's Always Adventure: The Story of a Naturalist's Wife* (New York, 1951). *References*: *AMWS*; N. Ashby, "Birdman of the Seven Seas," *Audubon Magazine* 63 (March 1961): 96–99; *NYT*, March 21, 1973; and "Time-Line of the Life of R.C.M.," *American Birds* 40 (1986): 372–78.

MURPHY, ROBERT F(RANCIS) (1924–   ). Anthropologist, born March 3, 1924, in Rockaway Beach, New York. Murphy graduated from Columbia University. He was an assistant professor of anthropology at the University of California at Berkeley from 1955 to 1961 and associate professor from 1961 to 1963. He was a professor of anthropology at Columbia University after 1963. He carried out fieldwork among the Mundurucú Indians of Pará and wrote *Mundurucú Religion* (Berkeley, Calif., 1958), *Headhunters' Heritage* (Berkeley, Calif., 1960), *Headhunters' League* (Berkeley, Calif., 1960), and *The Body Silent* (New York, 1987), and was coauthor of *The Trumaí Indians of Central Brazil* (Locust Valley, N.Y., 1955). *References*: *AMWS*; and *WWA*.

MURRAY, WILLIAM H(ENRY) (DAVID) ("ALFALFA BILL") (1869– 1956). Public official and colony promoter, born November 21, 1869, near Collinsville, Grayson County, Texas. He was an editor of newspapers in Dallas and Corsicana, Texas, and engaged in teaching in Limestone and Navarro counties, Texas, until 1890. He studied law, was admitted to the bar in 1895, and practiced law in Fort Worth, Texas. He moved to Tishomingo, Johnston County, Indian Territory (later Oklahoma) in 1898 and was legal adviser to the governor of the Chickasaw Nation from 1898 to 1901. He served as president of Oklahoma's first constitutional convention in 1906. He was a member of the Oklahoma House of Representatives from 1907 to 1909 and of the U.S. House of Representatives from 1913 to 1917. He established a frontier colony for white Americans in the southeastern portion of Bolivia following two abortive ventures, one in Bolivia in 1920 and another in Peru in 1923. He received a land lease from the Bolivian government in 1923 and established an agricultural colony in Bolivia's Chaco region near Aguagrande in 1924. By 1925, however, all the original colonists except his family had departed. He returned to the United States in 1929. He was the governor of Oklahoma from 1931 to 1935. He wrote *Memoirs of Governor Murray and True History of Oklahoma* (Boston, 1945). Died October 14, 1956, in Oklahoma City, Oklahoma. *References*: *DAB S5*; Courtney A. Vaughn, "By Hook or by Crook: Alfalfa Bill Murray, Colonizer in Bolivia," *Journal of the West* 18 (1979): 67–73; *NCAB* 43:530; and *NYT*, October 16, 1956.

MUYBRIDGE, EADWEARD (1830–1904). Photographer, born Edward James Muggeridge, April 9, 1830, in Kingston-upon-Thames, England. Muybridge came to the United States in 1851. He was a commission merchant in New York City from 1851 to 1855 and a bookseller in San Francisco from 1855 to 1860. He returned to England because of ill health but was back in San Francisco in 1867 and became a photographer. He was employed by the U.S. government as director of photographic surveys along the coast of California, participated in a survey of Alaska, and photographed railroads from 1872 to 1877. He was a photographer for the Pacific Mail Steamship Company in Central America and the Isthmus of Panama in 1875–1876. He was later involved in the development of motion pictures. He returned to England·in 1900. Died May 8, 1904, in Kingston-on-Thames, England. *References*: Turner Browne and Elaine Partnow, *Macmillan Biographical Encyclopedia of Photographic Artists and Innovators* (New York, 1963); E. Bradford Burns, *Eadweard Muybridge in Guatemala, 1875: The Photographer as Social Recorder* (Berkeley, Calif., 1986); *DAB*; *Eadweard Muybridge: The Stanford Years, 1872–1882* (Stanford, Calif., 1972); Robert B. Haas, *Muybridge. Man in Motion* (Berkeley, Calif., 1976); Gordon Hendricks, *Eadweard Muybridge: The Father of the Motion Picture* (New York, 1975); Kevin MacDonnell, *Eadweard Muybridge: The Man Who Invented the Moving Picture* (Boston, 1972); *NCAB* 19:152; and *WWWA*.

MYERS, PHILLIP VAN NESS (1846–1937). Educator, born August 10, 1846, in Tribes Hill, New York. Myers graduated from Williams College and attended Yale Law School. With his brother **HENRY MORRIS MYERS** (d. 1872), he participated in a scientific expedition sent out by the Lyceum of Natural History of Williams College in 1867 and in another expedition to Honduras in 1870–1871. The brothers wrote *Life and Nature under the Tropics: or, Sketches of Travels among the Andes, and on the Orinoco, Rio Negro, Amazonas, and in Central America* (New York, 1871). Phillip was later president of Farmers College (Ohio) until 1890, and professor of history and political economy at the University of Cincinnati from 1890 until his retirement in 1919. Died September 20, 1937, in Cincinnati. *References*: *NCAB* 12:149; *NYT*, September 21, 1937; and *WWWA*.

N

NATIONAL CITY BANK. Established in New York City in the nineteenth century, it specialized in commercial banking and the financing of international trade. After 1914, it was the New York bank that devoted the most energy to the conquest of Latin American markets and resources. The first nationally chartered U.S. bank to open a foreign branch, it opened a branch in Buenos Aires in 1914. It then opened other branches throughout the region and, by 1920, had fifty-six branches in Latin America. It also directly promoted major investments in Chilean and Peruvian copper mines and in Cuban sugar plantations and refineries. *References*: Harold van B. Cleveland and Thomas F. Huertas, *Citibank 1812–1970* (Cambridge, Mass., 1985); R. S. Mayer, "The Influence of Frank A. Vanderlip and the National City Bank on American Commerce and Foreign Policy, 1910–1920," Ph.D. diss., Rutgers University, 1968; and Robert Mayer, "The Origins of the American Banking Empire in Latin America: Frank A. Vanderlip and the National City Bank," *JISWA* 15 (1973): 60–76.

NAVASSA. An island, some thirty miles west of Haiti. It was discovered in 1857 to contain guano. American guano diggers took possession of the island in the name of the United States. It led to a confrontation with Haiti and a U.S. naval vessel was sent to protect American diggers. The guano deposit was worked principally by the Navassa Phosphate Company until the first decade of the century, when digging ceased and the island was abandoned. The U.S. government established a lighthouse there in 1917. *Reference*: R. F. Nichols, "Navassa: A Forgotten Acquisition," *American Historical Review* 38 (1933): 505–10.

NEGROPONTE, JOHN D(IMITRY) (1939–   ). Diplomat, born July 21, 1939, in London, England. Negroponte graduated from Yale University. He entered the diplomatic service in 1960. He was vice-consul in Hong Kong, second secretary in South Vietnam until 1968, and served on the staff of the National Security Council from 1970 to 1973. He was a political counselor in the embassy in Ecuador from 1973 to 1975; consul general in Thessaloniki,

Greece, from 1975 to 1977; deputy assistant secretary of state for oceans and fisheries affairs from 1977 to 1979; and deputy assistant secretary of state for East Asian and Pacific affairs in 1980–1981. He was U.S. ambassador to Honduras from 1981 to 1985, serving during·the height of the Contra buildup in the early 1980s, in which he was involved. He was assistant secretary of state for oceans and for international environment and scientific affairs from 1985 to 1987, deputy at the National Security Council from 1987 to 1989, and ambassador to Mexico after 1989. *References*: *Newsweek* 100 (November 8, 1982): 46; *Newsweek* 113 (February 20, 1989): 30; and *WWA*.

NELSON, EDWARD W(ILLIAM) (1855–1934). Naturalist, born May 8, 1855, in Amoskeag, near Manchester, New Hampshire, and grew up in Manchester, New Hampshire; Franklin County, New York; and Chicago. Nelson attended Northwestern University. In 1877, he embarked on his first expedition (for the Smithsonian Institution) to arctic Alaska. In 1892, he was sent by the U.S. Department of Agriculture as its field agent to Mexico to make a biological survey. It was followed by succeeded expeditions until 1916 and covered every section of the country. He was chief of the Bureau of Biological Survey of the Department of Agriculture from 1916 until his retirement in 1927. Died May 19, 1934, in Washington, D.C. *References*: Will C. Barnes, "Edward William Nelson, Naturalist, Explorer, Writer, and Arizona Cattleman," *Arizona Historical Review* 6 (October 1935): 43–49; *DAB S1*; *NCAB* 26:434; P. H. Oehser, "Two Eds: Nelson and Goldman, Scientists of the Old School," *Land* 9 (Spring 1950): 101–7; and *WWWA*.

NELSON, ERIK ALFRED (1862–1939). Missionary, born December 17, 1862, in Orebro, Sweden. Nelson came to the United States in 1869 and grew up in Neosho County, Kansas. He was ordained in 1897. He was a free-lance missionary to the Amazon Valley of Brazil from 1891 until 1898, serving in Belém, Pará. He organized the first Baptist church in Belém in 1897 and in Manaus in 1890. He served under the Foreign Mission Board of the Southern Baptist Convention* after 1898. He resided in Santarem and San Luis and then returned to Manaus. He traveled over the equatorial region, and established churches in the states of Maranhao, Piaui, and Ceara. He returned to the United States in 1936 but was back in Brazil in 1938. Died June 15, 1939, in Manaus, Amazonas, Brazil. *References*: Erik Alfred Nelson Collection, Historical Commission of the Southern Baptist Convention, Nashville, Tenn.; Lewis M. Bratcher, *The Apostle of the Amazon* (Nashville, Tenn., 1951); *ESB*; and John M. Landers, "Eric Alfred Nelson: The First Baptist Missionary on the Amazon, 1891–1939," Ph.D. diss., Texas Christian University, 1982.

NELSON, LOWRY (1893–   ). Sociologist, born April 16, 1893, in Ferron, Utah. Nelson graduated from Utah State College and the University of Wisconsin. He was director of the extension division of Brigham Young University from

1921 to 1935 and professor of rural sociology and economics there from 1929 to 1935. He was assistant director of the rural resettlement division of the Resettlement Administration in 1935–1936 and director of the experimental station of Utah State University in 1936–1937. He was a professor of sociology at the University of Minnesota from 1937 to 1958. He studied rural life in Cuba in 1945–1946 and wrote *Rural Cuba* (Minneapolis, 1950). He also wrote *Cuba: The Measure of a Revolution* (Minneapolis, 1972) and *In the Direction of His Dreams: Memoirs* (New York, 1985). *References*: Lowry Nelson Papers, University of Utah, Salt Lake City; and *AMWS*.

NELSON, THOMAS HENRY (1823–1896). Lawyer and diplomat, born near Maysville, Kentucky. Nelson studied and practiced law in Rockville, Indiana, until 1850, and later in Terre Haute, Indiana. He was U.S. minister to Chile from 1861 to 1866 and U.S. minister to Mexico from 1869 to 1873. In Chile, he exerted his best efforts to win the friendship of that country for the United States and was successful in bringing American claims against Chile to a successful conclusion. In 1865, he tried, unsuccessfully, to bring about a peaceful settlement in the hostilities between Chile and Spain. Died March 14, 1896, in Terre Haute, Indiana. *References*: *DAB*; *NCAB* 11:550; and Carl A. Ross, Jr., "Chile and Its Relations with the United States during the Ministry of Thomas Henry Nelson, 1861–1866," Ph.D. diss., University of Georgia, 1966.

NEW TRIBES MISSION. A nondenominational, independent faith mission founded in 1942 to take the Gospel to unenlightened tribes around the world. It began missionary work in Bolivia in 1942, in Colombia and Mexico in 1944, in Paraguay and Venezuela in 1946, in Brazil in 1949, and in Panama in 1953. *References*: *Early History of the New Tribes Mission and Life and Work of Paul Fleming* (Woodworth, Wis., 1962); Margaret Jank, *Mission Venezuela: Reaching a New Tribe* (Chicago, 1977); Jean D. Johnson, *God Planted Five Seeds* (New York, 1966); and Kenneth J. Johnston, *The Story of New Tribes Mission* (Sanford, Fla., 1985).

NEW YORK AND BERMÚDEZ COMPANY. Organized in 1885 in New York City as a subsidiary of General Asphalt Company of Philadelphia. It was assigned the concession obtained by Horatio B. Hamilton in 1883 for exploitation of asphalt in the state of Bermúdez, Venezuela. It began to extract natural asphalt from the Guanoco Lake in eastern Venezuela in 1887. *References*: Charles E. Carreras, *United States Economic Penetration of Venezuela and Its Effects on Diplomacy, 1895–1906* (New York, 1987), chs. 2–3; John C. Rayburn, "United States Investments in Venezuelan Asphalt," *IAEA* 7 (1953): 20–36; and Orray E. Thurber, *The Venezuelan Question: Castro and the Asphalt Trust* (New York, 1907).

NEW YORK AND HONDURAS ROSARIO MINING COMPANY. Organized in 1880, it obtained a concession from the Honduran government to mine silver. The Rosario mine, near San Juancito, Honduras, had been, by the 1920s, the largest silver mine in Central America. It was closed down in 1954. *References*: Kenneth V. Finney, "Precious Metal Mining and the Modernization of Honduras: In Quest of El Dorado (1880–1900)," Ph.D. diss., Tulane University, 1973; and Kenneth V. Finney, "Rosario and the Election of 1887: The Political Economy of Mining in Honduras," *HAHR* 59 (1979): 81–107.

NEW YORK, RIO, AND BUENOS AIRES AIRWAYS (NYRBA). Established by Ralph A. O'Neill* in 1929 to fly once a week from New York to Buenos Aires. Unable to win a U.S. airmail contract, it was sold to the Pan American World Airways in 1930.

NEWBERY, GEORGE HARKNESS (1856–1935). Explorer, born November 23, 1856, in Brentwood, New York. Newbery graduated from New York College of Dentistry. He came to Argentina in 1877 as a dentist. He explored the Chaco region in 1877 and the Pampa Central in 1878. He founded the Media Luna Ranch in the Pampa. In 1884, he again explored the Pampa Central, crossing the Neuquén Territory into Chile. He was the first pioneer to take up grazing land in the Neuquén lands, and was the first English-speaking person to take part in the cattle trade with Chile, employing the passes through the southern Andes. He explored the Territory of Misiones and southern Brazil in 1891. He also became known for his paintings of Patagonia. Died February 1, 1935, in Buenos Aires. *Pampa Grass: The Argentine Story as Told by an American Pioneer to His Son, Diego Newbery* (Buenos Aires, 1953) was published posthumously. *Reference*: Drees.

NEWHOUSE, EDGAR L. (1865–1937). Mining engineer, born March 28, 1865, in Philadelphia. Newhouse graduated from the School of Mines of Columbia University. He worked with Kansas City Smelting Company and then as an independent assayer in Kansas City. In 1886, he became associated with the Guggenheims, initially in Pueblo, Colorado. He worked as an assayer in Mexico for the Consolidated Kansas City Smelting and Refining Company. He later traveled throughout the reaches of the Mexican mining states and wrote articles for *Engineering and Mining Journal*. As point man for Guggenheim Brothers' Mexican ventures, he was vice president from 1899 to 1920, and later chairman of the board of American Smelting and Refining Company* (ASARCO) from 1920 until his retirement in 1928. He was active in the organization of ASARCO, in building business in Mexico, and in acquiring Mexican properties. He was also instrumental in putting ASARCO in business in South America, notably in Chile. Died July 13, 1937, in New York City. *Reference*: *NYT*, July 14, 1937.

NEWMAN, JUNIUS E. (1819–1895). Missionary, born October 16, 1819, near Point Pleasant, West Virginia. Newman was ordained in 1848 and worked mainly in eastern Mississippi until 1867. He was a missionary under the Methodist Episcopal Church, South,* in Brazil from 1867, initially in Rio de Janeiro and later in the Province of São Paulo. He preached to the Americans who emigrated to Brazil, organized a church in Santa Barbara do Oeste, São Paulo, served as superintendent of the mission until 1879, and was founder of permanent Methodist work in Brazil. He returned to the United States in 1889 because of ill health. Died May 1895, in Point Pleasant, West Virginia. *Reference: EWM.*

NICARAGUA, INTERVENTION IN (1912). The United States supported Adolfo Díaz as president of Nicaragua from 1911 to 1917 and concluded with him arrangements for New York bankers to lend money to Nicaragua and to control Nicaragua's customs collections, national bank, and national railroads until the loans were repaid. When the position of the pro-American Díaz was threatened by a civil war, he requested U.S. intervention, and U.S. Marines landed in Corinto in 1912. A small legation guard of Marines remained until the loans were repaid in 1924. The Marines withdrew in 1925. *References*: J. O. Baylen, ''American Intervention in Nicaragua, 1909–33: An Appraisal of Objectives and Results,'' *Southwestern Social Science Quarterly* 35 (1954): 128–54; *Langley*, chs. 5–6; and *Musicant*, ch. 4.

NICARAGUA, INTERVENTION IN (1927–1934). A civil war in Nicaragua and the possible collapse of the conservative regime brought a landing of U.S. Marines in 1926. They supervised elections in Nicaragua and organized and trained a constabulary. The U.S. Marines fought a protracted and ineffective counterguerilla war on behalf of the Nicaraguan government against the forces by Augusto Cesar Sandino. The U.S. Marines withdrew in 1933. *References*: J. O. Baylen, ''American Intervention in Nicaragua, 1909–33: An Appraisal of Objectives and Results,'' *Southwestern Social Science Quarterly* 35 (1954): 128–54; Lejeune Cummins, *Quijote on a Burro: Sandino and the Marines* (Mexico, 1958); William Kamman, *A Search for Stability: United States Diplomacy toward Nicaragua, 1925–1933* (Notre Dame, 1968); *Langley*, chs. 14–16; *Musicant*, ch. 7; Bernard C. Natly, *The United States Marines in Nicaragua* (Washington, D.C., 1962); and John J. Tierney, Jr., ''The United States and Nicaragua, 1927–1932: Decisions for De-Escalation and Withdrawal,'' Ph.D. diss., University of Pennsylvania, 1969.

NIXON'S GOODWILL MISSION (1958). Goodwill mission of vice president Richard Nixon to South America in 1958, intended to reassure the people of Latin America that the United States had not forgotten them or their concerns. Nixon was received by student riots in Lima, Peru, and mob riots in Caracas, Venezuela. The mission focused attention on U.S.–Latin American relations in an unfavorable way and stimulated the United States to reshape its policies toward

Latin America. *References*: Stephen E. Ambrose, *Nixon: The Education of a Politician, 1913–1962* (New York, 1987); Stephen G. Rabe, *Eisenhower and Latin America: the Foreign Policy of Anti-Communism* (Chapel Hill, N.C., 1988), ch. 6; and Marvin R. Zahniser and W. Michael Weis, "A Diplomatic Pearl Harbor? Richard Nixon's Goodwill Mission to Latin America in 1958," *DH* 13 (1989): 163–90.

NOBLE, ALFRED (1844–1914). Civil engineer, born August 7, 1844, in Livonia, Michigan. Noble served in the Union Army during the Civil War. He graduated from the University of Michigan. He was in charge of improvements of the St. Mary's Falls Canal and St. Mary's River from 1870 to 1882 and general assistant engineer for the Northern Pacific Railroad from 1883 to 1886 and supervised construction of various bridges across the Mississippi River and elsewhere in the United States from 1886 to 1904. He was a member of the Nicaragua Canal Board in 1895 and visited Central America to examine the lines of the Nicaragua and Panama canals. He was a member of the U.S. Board of Engineers on Deep Waterways from 1897 to 1900, member of the Isthmian Canal Commission from 1899 to 1903, and member of the board of consulting engineers of the Panama Canal in 1905. He was later chief engineer of the Pennsylvania Tunnel and Terminal Railroad Company. Died April 19, 1914, in New York City. *References*: *NCAB* 9:44; *NYT*, April 20, 1914; and *WWWA*.

NOBLE, G(LADWYN) KINGSLEY (1894–1940). Biologist, born September 20, 1894, in Yonkers, New York. Noble graduated from Harvard and Columbia universities. He was the leader of the Harvard expedition to Guadeloupe in 1914 and to Newfoundland in 1915 and zoologist on the Harvard expedition to Peru in 1916. He was leader of the American Museum of Natural History expedition to Santo Domingo in 1922. He was curator of herpetology at the American Museum of Natural History after 1919 and curator of its department of experimental biology after 1938. Died December 9, 1940, in Englewood, New Jersey. *References*: *AMWS*; *DAB S2*; *NCAB* 31:396; *NYT*, December 10, 1940; and *WWWA*.

NORMAN, BENJAMIN MOORE (1809–1860). Author and traveler, born December 22, 1809, in Hudson, New York. Norman was a clerk in New York City and, upon his father's death, took charge of the book business in Hudson, New York, making visits to Europe and the West Indies. In 1837, he established a book business in New Orleans and was a printer, binder, bookseller, and publisher. In 1841, he embarked for the Windward Islands, but was turned aside to Yucatán. There he became interested in exploration and the study of antiquities. He wrote *Rambles in Yucatan, or, Notes of Travel Through the Peninsula, including a Visit to the Remarkable Ruins of Chi-Chen, Kabah, Zayi, and Uxmal* (New York, 1842) and *Rambles by Land and Water, or Notes of Travel in Cuba and Mexico; Including a Canoe Voyage up the River Panuco and Researches* *among the Ruins of Tamaulipas* (New York, 1845), illustrated with drawings made by the author. In 1844 he made a journey of exploration to the Tamaulipas country in Mexico. Died February 1, 1860, near Summit, Mississippi. *References: ACAB*; and *NCAB* 18:190.

NORRIS, WILLIAM H. (1801–1878). Missionary, born October 28, 1801, in Prono, Maine. Norris was ordained in 1825. He held several pastorates, in Maine until 1837 and then in Brooklyn, New York. He was a missionary under the Missionary Society of the Methodist Episcopal Church* in Montevideo, Uruguay, from 1839 to 1842, the first permanent Methodist missionary to Uruguay. He was a missionary in Buenos Aires, Argentina, from 1842 to 1847. He was an agent of the American Bible Society* in Mexico during the Mexican War, held several pastorates in New York State, was agent of the American Bible Society in Panama and Central America, and again was a missionary in Buenos Aires in 1864–1865. Died October 19, 1878, in Hamstead, Long Island, New York. *Reference: EWM.*

NORTHCOTT, ELLIOTT (1869–1946). Lawyer and diplomat, born April 26, 1869, in Clarksburg, West Virginia. Northcott studied at the University of Michigan and was admitted to the bar in 1891. He practiced law in Huntington, West Virginia, after 1891, was city attorney of Huntington in 1897–1898, assistant U.S. attorney for the southern district of West Virginia from 1898 to 1905, and U.S. attorney for the same district from 1905 to 1909. He was U.S. minister to Colombia from 1909 to 1911, minister to Nicaragua in 1911, and minister to Venezuela from 1911 to 1913. He resumed law practice in Huntington from 1913 to 1922, was again U.S. attorney for the southern district of West Virginia from 1922 to 1927, and was judge of the U.S. Circuit Court of Appeals from 1927 until his retirement in 1939. Died January 3, 1946, in Arcadia, Florida. *References: NCAB* 47:498; and *NYT*, January 5, 1946.

NUTTAL, ZELIA MARIA MAGDALENA (1857–1933). Archaeologist, born September 6, 1857, in San Francisco. She grew up in Europe. She made her first visit to Mexico in 1884 and developed an interest in early Mexican civilizations. She went to Europe, lived in Dresden, Germany, from 1886 to 1899, and traveled throughout Europe. In 1902, she settled in Casa Alvardo, in Coyoacan, a suburb of Mexico City. She continued her scholarly activity in uncovering the pre-Columbian past of Mexico and Central America. She investigated Isla de Sacrificios in 1910. She left Mexico in 1911 but was back in 1917 and became famous as a hostess. Died April 12, 1933, in Coyoacan, Mexico City. *References: AA* 25 (1933): 475–82; Beverly N. Chiñas, "Zelia Maria Magdalena Nuttall (1857–1933)," in *Women Anthropologists: A Biographical Dictionary*, ed. Ute Gacs et al. (Westport, Conn., 1988), pp. 269–74; *HAHR* 13 (1933): 487–89; *NAW*; and *WWWA.*

NUTTING, CHARLES CLEVELAND (1858–1927). Zoologist, born May 25, 1858, in Jacksonville, Illinois, and grew up in Indianapolis. Nutting graduated from Blackburn University (Carlinville, Ill.). He was commissioned by the Smithsonian Institution to investigate Nicaragua and Costa Rica where, in 1881–1882, he collected birds and antiquities. He was professor of zoology and curator of the museum in the State University of Iowa (Iowa City) after 1886. He made a trip to the Bahamas in 1888 and, in 1893, organized and headed a party that made a cruise for the purpose of studying the natural history of the Bahamas and adjacent seas. He wrote *Narrative and Preliminary Report of Bahama Expedition* (Iowa City, Ia., 1895). He organized and directed a trip to the West Indies in 1918, investigating the shore and literal stations of Barbados and Antigua, and wrote *Barbados-Antigua Expedition: Narrative and Preliminary Report of a Zoological Expedition from the University of Iowa to the Lesser Antilles* (Iowa City, Ia., 1919). Died January 23, 1927, in Iowa City, Iowa. *References*: *AMWS*; *DAB*; *NCAB* 21:467; and *WWWA*.

O

OAKSMITH, APPLETON (1827–1887). Filibuster, born February 14, 1827, in Portland, Maine. Oaksmith was a shipping agent in Panama from 1847 to 1850 and in San Francisco in 1850–1851. He returned to New York in 1852, establishing a shipping firm. In 1855, he became enmeshed in an abortive scheme to supply Cuban revolutionaries with arms and ammunition. He was William Walker's* chief agent, supply agent, recruiter, and financier in the United States. He was successively a magazine editor, railroad speculator, and paper mill owner, and then went back into the shipping business. Died October 29, 1887. *References*: Appleton Oaksmith Papers, Duke University Library, Durham, N.C.; and J. J. TePoske, "Appleton Oaksmith, Filibuster Agent," *North Carolina Historical Review* 35 (1958): 427–47.

OBER, FREDERICK ALBION (1849–1913). Ornithologist, born February 13, 1849, in Beverly, Massachusetts. Ober learned to stuff and mount birds, collected birds in Florida, and explored the Lake Okeechabee region from 1872 to 1874 for *Forest and Stream* and the Smithsonian Institution. He made an ornithological investigation of Lesser Antilles, West Indies, from 1876 to 1878 and in 1880. He traveled in Mexico in 1881, 1883, and 1885 and later in Spain, North Africa, South America, and again in West Indies. He wrote *Camps in the Caribbees: The Adventures of a Naturalist in the Lesser Antilles* (Boston, 1880), *Travels in Mexico and Life among the Mexicans* (Boston, 1883), *Under the Cuban Flag; or, The Caciques Treasure* (Boston, 1897), *Crusoe's Island: A Bird-Hunter's Story* (New York, 1898), *Puerto Rico and Its Resources* (New York, 1899), *The Storied West Indies* (New York, 1900), and *Our West Indian Neighbors* (New York, 1904). Using his knowledge of Mexico and the West Indies, he wrote books of travel and adventure, including *Guide to the West Indies and Bermuda* (New York, 1908) and *Guide to the West Indies, Bermuda and Panama* (New York, 1913). He was involved in real estate in Hackensack, New Jersey, from 1908 until his death. Died June 1, 1913, in Hackensack, New Jersey. *References*: *DAB*; *NCAB*; 54:322; *NYT*, June 2, 1913; and *WWWA*.

O'BRIEN, EDWARD CHARLES (1860–1927). Diplomat, born April 20, 1860, in Fort Edward, New York. O'Brien was engaged in the flour commission business in Plattsburg, New York. He was disbursing clerk of the U.S. House of Representatives from 1889 to 1891, U.S. commissioner of navigation in 1892–1893, commissioner of docks and president of the Board of Docks of the City of New York from 1895 to 1898, and then president of International Express Company and of the Cuban and Pan-American Express Company. He was U.S. minister to Paraguay and Uruguay from 1905 to 1909. He negotiated extradition, naturalization, and arbitration treaties with Paraguay and a naturalization treaty with Uruguay, and helped end the hostilities during a revolution in Paraguay in 1908. After 1909, he promoted trade in and with Latin America and was involved in many enterprises connected with the development of South American ports and internal communications. Died June 21, 1927, in Montevideo, Uruguay, while working on a plan to build a highway between the capitals of Uruguay and Argentina. *References*: *DAB*; *DCB*; *NCAB* 14:492; and *WWWA*.

O'DWYER, WILLIAM (1890–1964). Public official and diplomat, born July 11, 1890, in County Mayo, Ireland. He came to the United States in 1910. O'Dwyer attended the University of Salamanca (Spain) and graduated from Fordham University Law School. He practiced law in New York City after 1923. He was county court judge of Kings County in 1938–1939 and Kings County district attorney from 1939 to 1942. He served in the U.S. Army Air Force during World War II. He was mayor of New York City from 1946 to 1950. He was U.S. ambassador to Mexico from 1950 to 1952. He became well versed in Mexican affairs and, after resigning as ambassador, practiced law in Mexico City until 1960, when he returned to the United States. Died November 24, 1964, in New York City. *References*: *DADH*; *NCAB* G:254; *NYT*, November 25, 1964; and *WWWA*.

OFFICE OF INTER-AMERICAN AFFAIRS (OIAA). Established to promote inter-American trade and counter Nazi propaganda, it launched a propaganda operation, fostered mutual understanding and appreciation, and sponsored a broad variety of cultural programs in order to enhance cultural relations between the United States and Latin America, to build support among Latin American nations for the war aims of the United States, and to ease wartime shortages in food and other essential products through the stimulation of local production. *Reference*: Donald W. Rowland, *History of the Office of the Coordinator of Inter-American Affairs* (Washington, D.C., 1947).

O'HARA, THOMAS (1856–1919). Lawyer and consul, born March 9, 1856, in Le Roy, Genesee County, New York. O'Hara was employed as a cabin boy, steward, and clerk on steamboats on Lake Erie. He studied law, and was admitted to the bar in 1880. He was county clerk of Berrien County, Michigan, from 1882 to 1886 and judge of the second judicial circuit after 1886. He served on a special mission to Nicaragua in 1894 to adjust certain difficulties over the Mosquito coast and was U.S. consul in San Juan del Norte, Nicaragua, from 1894 to 1898. He later practiced law in St. Joseph, Detroit, and Chicago. Died December 30, 1919, in Chicago. *Reference*: NCAB 18:333.

OLCOTT, EBEN(EZER) ERSKINE (1854–1929). Mining engineer, born March 11, 1854, in New York City. Olcott attended the College of the City of New York and graduated from the School of Mines of Columbia University. He was a chemist and, later, superintendent for the Hunt and Douglas process plant in North Carolina and assistant superintendent of the Pennsylvania Lead Company works at Mansfield Valley, Pennsylvania. He was superintendent of a gold mine in Venezuela from 1876 to 1879 and superintendent of St. Helena Mines in Sonora, Mexico, from 1881 to 1885. A consulting engineer in New York City after 1885, he studied copper deposits in Cerro de Pasco, Peru, made two exploring expeditions to Guiana and Colombia, and explored the gold and copper district of eastern Peru in 1890–1891. He was president of the Hudson River Day Line after 1895. Died June 5, 1929, in New York City. *References*: Eben Erskine Olcott Papers, New York Historical Society, New York City; Eben Erskine Olcott Papers, University of Wyoming Library, Laramee; *ACAB*; *DAB*; *NCAB* 5:265; *NYT*, June 6, 1929; and *WWWA*.

OLIVER, JAMES H(ARRISON) (1857–1928). Naval officer, born January 15, 1857, in Houston County, Georgia. Oliver attended Washington and Lee University and graduated from the U.S. Naval Academy in 1877. He was commissioned ensign in the U.S. Navy in 1881 and made nine cruises at sea. He was director of naval intelligence from 1914 to 1917. He was the first U.S. governor of the Virgin Islands and commandant of the naval station there from 1917 to 1919. He was on duty at the Navy Department from 1919 to 1921, when he retired with the rank of rear admiral. Died April 6, 1928, in Shirley, Virginia. *References*: *NYT*, April 7, 1928; and *WWWA*.

OLNEY COROLLARY. A policy announced by Secretary of State Richard Olney in 1895, according to which the United States was entitled to resent and resist any forcible increase by any European power of its territorial possessions in Latin America. *Reference*: George B. Young, "Intervention under the Monroe Doctrine: The Olney Corollary," *Political Science Quarterly* 57 (1942): 247–70.

OLTMAN, ROY E(DWIN) (1911–1977). Hydrologist, born in Minneapolis, Minnesota. Oltman graduated from the University of Minnesota. He served with the U.S. Geological Service after 1934. He served in the U.S. Navy during World War II. He led an expedition that undertook the U.S. Geological Survey's first hydrological exploration of the Amazon River in Brazil in 1962. He then participated in a joint research project with the Brazilian government. His team established for the first time scientific measurements of the width, flow, and physical and chemical characteristics of the world's largest river. He was a senior member of the Interior Department's Office of Water Resources Research from 1965 to 1967 and assistant division chief for research and technical coordination at the U.S. Geological Survey from 1967 until his retirement in 1972. Died March 23, 1977. *References*: *Civil Engineering* 47 (October 1977): 149; *Hydrological Sciences Bulletin* 22 (1977): 325–26.

O'NEIL, CHARLES (1842–1927). Naval officer, born March 15, 1842, in Manchester, England. He was brought to the United States in 1847, and grew up in Boston. O'Neil went to sea at age sixteen. He served in the Union Navy during the Civil War. In 1868 he was appointed lieutenant in the regular navy. While he was serving as first commander of the USS *Marblehead*, that warship was sent to the Nicaraguan coast in 1894, at the time of the final adjustment of the sovereignty of the Mosquito coast. O'Neil was chief of ordnance of the navy from 1897 until his retirement in 1904. Died February 28, 1927, in Boston. *References*: *NCAB* 24:313; *NYT*, March 1, 1927; and *WWWA*.

O'NEILL, RALPH A. (1896–1980). Aviation executive, born December 7, 1896, in San Francisco. O'Neill attended Lehigh University. He served in the U.S. Army during World War I. He organized and commanded the military and civilian aviation service of Mexico from 1920 to 1925, under contract from the Mexican government. In 1924, he commanded an air squadron in the unsuccessful rebellion led by Adolfo de la Huerta. He was an exclusive agent in all Latin American countries for the Boeing Airplane Company and Pratt and Whitney Aircraft Company from 1927 to 1929. He founded New York, Rio & Buenos Aires Line (NYRBA) in 1929 and was its president, but lost it in a merger with Pan American Airways in 1930. In 1932, he formed Bol-Inca Mining Corporation, a gold mining company, in Bolivia. He wrote (with Joseph F. Hood) his memoirs, *A Dream of Eagles* (Boston, 1973). Died October 23, 1980, in Redwood City, California. *Reference*: *NYT*, November 5, 1980.

O'REILLY, EDWARD S(YNNOTT) ("TEX") (1880–1946). Journalist and soldier of fortune, born August 15, 1880, in Denison, Texas. O'Reilly served with the U.S. Army in Cuba and the Philippines during the Spanish-American War and in China during the Boxer Rebellion. He then joined the bodyguard of the emperor of Korea and was a drill instructor with the Chinese Imperial Army in 1901–1902 and with the international police force in Shanghai, China. He served in the military forces of Honduras, Nicaragua, and Mexico. He was an officer in the Mexican Army in 1913–1914 and an officer on the staff of Francisco (Pancho) Villa in 1914. He also participated in a revolution in Venezuela. He wrote *Roving and Fighting: Adventures under Four Flags* (London, 1918). He served in the Texas National Guard from 1918 to 1924, joined the French Foreign Legion in 1924, and fought the Riffs in North Africa. Died December 8, 1946, in Sunmount, New York. *References*: Lowell Thomas, *Born to Raise Hell: The Life Story of Tex O'Reilly, Soldier of Fortune* (Garden City, N.Y., 1936); *NYT*, December 9, 1946; and *WWWA*.

ORGANIZATION OF AMERICAN STATES (OAS). Created in 1948 to provide for hemispheric collective security, it has managed to settle numerous minor Latin American disputes in which the United States has not deemed its vital interests to be deeply involved. The United States has frequently attempted, with only partial success, to manipulate the OAS for its own purposes. *References*: M. Margaret Ball, *The OAS in Transition* (Durham, N.C., 1969); *DADH*; John C. Dreier, *The Organization of American States and the Hemisphere Crisis* (Baltimore, 1962); *ELA*; Jerome Slater, *The OAS and United States Foreign Policy* (Columbus, Ohio, 1967); O. C. Stoetzer, *The Organization of American States: An Introduction* (New York, 1965); and Ann Van Wynen Thomas and A. J. Thomas, Jr., *The Organization of American States* (Dallas, 1963).

ORINOCO NAVIGATION COMPANY. Organized in the state of New York, the company obtained in 1874 a monopoly of coastal and river shipping from La Guaira to Nutrias on the Orinoco River in Venezuela. William Anderson Pile (1829–1889), U.S. minister to Venezuela from 1871 to 1874, resigned to become general manager of the company. It terminated its activities in 1883.

ORINOCO STEAM NAVIGATION COMPANY. Organized in 1859 by Edward A. Turpin, U.S. Minister to Venezuela from 1858 to 1861, and Frederick Anthony Beelen, U.S. consul in Ciudad Bolívar from 1850 to 1853, who received a concession from the Venezuelan government to establish steam navigation on the Orinoco River. In 1859, it began to regularly operate two steamers on the Orinoco. It put together the first steamboat to be constructed on the Orinoco from prepared parts imported from the United States. The last steamer was seized by Venezuelan soldiers and the company was dissolved in 1865. *Reference*: William H. Gray, "Steamboat Transportation on the Orinoco," *HAHR* 25 (1945): 455–69.

ORTON, JAMES (1830–1877). Zoologist and explorer, born April 21, 1830, in Seneca Falls, New York. Orton graduated from Williams College and Andover Theological Seminary and was ordained in 1860. He held pastorates in New York State and Maine until 1866. He was an instructor in natural history at the University of Rochester from 1866 to 1869 and professor of natural history at Vassar College from 1869 until his death. He made three expeditions to South America. He explored the equatorial Andes and the region of the Amazons. In 1867 he traversed the region from Guayaquil to Quito, down the Napo River to Pebas on the Maranon, and from there to Pará by steamer. He wrote *The Andes and the Amazons* (New York, 1870). In 1873, he went from Pará up the Amazons to Yurimaguas and from there over the Andes to Peru. In 1876, he intended to explore the Beni River for the commercial advantage of the Bolivian government. He reached Lake Titicaca and started to sail across it to Puno in Peru. Died September 25, 1877, on Lake Titicaca. *References*: *DAB*; *DSB*; Robert R. Miller, "James Orton: A Yankee Naturalist in South America, 1867–1877," *Proceedings of the American Philosophical Society* 126 (1982): 11–25; *NCAB* 11:280; E. Nunez, "Over the Andes and along the Amazon," *Americas* 12 (March 1960): 27–31; and *NYT*, November 8, 1877.

ORTON, WILLIAM A(LLEN) (1877–1930). Plant pathologist, born February 28, 1877, in North Fairfax, Vermont. Orton graduated from the University of Vermont. He was a plant pathologist with the U.S. Department of Agriculture from 1899 to 1924 and scientific director and general manager of the Tropical Plant Research Foundation from 1924 until his death. He investigated problems in sugar growing in Cuba, conducted a survey of the sugar and cotton industries of Peru, made investigations of chicle production in British Honduras, and did forestry and timber surveys in Cuba and South American countries. Died January 7, 1930, in Takoma Park, Washington, D.C. *References*: *NCAB* 21:60; and *WWWA*.

OSBON, BRADLEY SILLICK (1828–1912). Naval officer, born August 16, 1828, in Rye, Westchester County, New York. Osbon went to sea at ten years of age and served on a New Bedford whaler. He served in the Chinese Navy as commander of a Chinese warship fighting pirates in Hong Kong waters. He was an officer in the Argentine Navy under Commodore John Halsted Coe* and participated in several sea fights. He served in the Union Navy during the Civil War. He then served in the Mexican Navy with the rank of admiral. He later went to Venezuela, and held important positions in the asphalt mines of the New York and Bermudez Company. He was a volunteer naval scout during the Spanish-American War. He was a founder and editor of *The Nautical Gazette*, the first maritime newspaper published in the United States, in 1871. He wrote *A Sailor of Fortune; Personal Memoirs of Captain B. S. Osbon*, by Albert B. Paine (New York, 1906). Died May 6, 1912, in New York City. *References*: *NYT*, May 7, 1912; and *WWWA*.

OSBORN, THOMAS ANDREW (1836–1898). Lawyer and diplomat, born October 26, 1836, in Meadville, Pennsylvania. Osborn was apprenticed to a printer, settled in Kansas in 1857, and practiced law in Elwood, Kansas, after 1858. He was elected attorney of Doniphan County in 1858, and served in the state senate from 1859 to 1862. He was lieutenant governor of Kansas from 1862 to 1864, U.S. marshal from 1864 to 1867, and governor of Kansas from 1873 to 1877. He was U.S. minister to Chile from 1877 to 1881. When Chile became involved in war with Peru and Bolivia, he attempted to effect a peaceful settlement between the countries but was unsuccessful. With Thomas Ogden Osborn,* he was instrumental in settling the long-standing Patagonian boundary dispute between Argentina and Chile. He was U.S. minister to Brazil from 1881 to 1885. He then resumed his business and political interests in Kansas and was state senator from 1889 to 1893. Died February 4, 1898, in Meadville, Pennsylvania. *References*: *DADH*; *NCAB* 8:345; and Homer E. Socolofsky, *Kansas Governors* (Lawrence, Kans., 1990), pp. 99–101.

OSBORN, THOMAS OGDEN (1832–1904). Army officer and diplomat, born 1832 in Jersey, Ohio. Osborn graduated from Ohio State University, studied law, and was admitted to the bar in 1856. He practiced law in Chicago from 1858. He served in the Union Army during the Civil War and then resumed his law practice. He was treasurer of Cook County, Illinois, from 1867 to 1869, and member of the international commission to settle disputed claims between the United States and Mexico in 1873. He was U.S. minister to Argentina from 1874 to 1885. In 1880, he helped to terminate the civil war between the national government and the province of Buenos Aires and in 1881 he helped to negotiate a boundary treaty between Argentina and Chile. He remained in South America and engaged in railway projects. He returned to the United States in 1890 and retired. Died March 27, 1904, in Washington, D.C. *References*: *DADH*; *NCAB* 10:146; and *WWWA*.

O'SHAUGHNESSY, NELSON (JARVIS WATERBURY) (1876–1932). Diplomat, born February 12, 1876, in New York City. O'Shaughnessy attended Georgetown University, graduated from St. John's College, Oxford University, and studied international law at the Inner Temple, London. He entered the diplomatic service in 1904, was secretary of legation in Denmark, third secretary of embassy in Germany, second secretary in Russia, and secretary of legation in Rumania until 1911. He was second secretary in Mexico in 1911–1912, secretary in 1912–1913, and chargé d'affaires in 1913 continuing during the period of nonrecognition by the United States of the government of General Victoriano Huerta. His efforts at reconciliation having failed, he was given his passports by the Huerta government in 1914. He retired from diplomatic service in 1916, was a representative in South America of Western Union Telegraph Company in 1918–1919, and represented American bondholders in Belgrade, Yugoslavia, until 1928. Died July 26, 1932, in Vienna, Austria. His wife, **EDITH LOUISE (COUES) O'SHAUGHNESSY** (1870–1930), recounted her experiences in Mexico in *A Diplomat's Wife in Mexico: Letters from the American Embassy in Mexico City* (New York, 1916), *Diplomatic Days* (New York, 1917), and *Intimate Papers of Mexican History* (New York, 1920). *References*: *DAB*; *DADH*; *DCB*; *NYT*, July 27, 1932; *NYT*, February 19, 1939; and *WWWA*.

OTTERBOURG, MARCUS (1827–1893). Journalist and consul, born in Landau, Rhenish Palatinate, Bavaria. Otterbourg came to the United States and was engaged in journalism in Milwaukee. He was a reporter of the Wisconsin legislature and then a news correspondent in Washington in 1860–1861. He was

U.S. consul in Mexico City from 1861 to 1867. He was later in charge of the legation and minister to Mexico in 1867. He urged the Emperor Maximilian to leave Mexico but was not able to save his life. He later studied law, practiced it in New York City until his death, and was a police justice from 1873 to 1882. Died December 2, 1893, in New York City. *Reference*: R. L. Benjamin, "Marcus Otterbourg, United States Minister to Mexico in 1867," *American Jewish Historical Society Publications*, no. 32 (1931): 65–94.

OWEN, ALBERT KIMSEY (1847–1916). Colony promoter, born May 17, 1847, in Chester, Pennsylvania. Owen graduated from Jefferson College. He was a railroad engineer and town promoter in Chester until 1871. He was in Colorado in 1871, involved in developing the Clear Creek Canyon Railroad and the town of Colorado Springs. He explored Topolobampo Bay, Mexico, in 1872 to survey land for a railroad in Mexico. He spent the next twenty years promoting a railroad scheme that would link the west with the Orient via the harbor at Topolobampo. He was granted concession for a railroad in 1881, organized the Credit Foncier Company for the purpose of establishing colonies along the route including one large city, Pacific City, in Topolobampo. Topolobampo Bay Colony* was established in 1886 and existed until 1893. Owen was later involved with transportation problems. Died July 12, 1916, in New York City. *References*: Mario Gill, *La Conquista del Valle del Fuerte* (Culiacan, Rosales, Sinaloa, Mexico, 1983), pp. 19–55; Juan Antonio Lastras Ramirez, *Topolobampo: Albert Kimsey Owen, Socialista en Mexico* (Los Mochis, Sinaloa, Mexico, 1971); and *Pletcher*, ch. 4.

P

PACIFIC MAIL STEAMSHIP COMPANY. Organized in 1848 by William H. Aspinwall and others to connect Panama with San Francisco and directly, or through subsidiary companies, with Pacific ports of Central America and Mexico and to carry out a federal government contract for passenger and mail service. *References*: David I. Folkman, Jr., *The Nicaragua Route* (Salt Lake City, Utah, 1972); John H. Kemble, "The Genesis of the Pacific Mail Steamship Company," *California Historical Society Quarterly* 13 (1934): 240–54; and John H. Kemble, *The Panama Route, 1848–1969* (Berkeley, Calif., 1943).

PAGE, THOMAS JEFFERSON (1808–1899). Naval officer and explorer, born January 4, 1808, in Matthews County, Virginia. Page was appointed a midshipman in the U.S. Navy in 1827. He worked on coast survey work from 1833 to 1842 and was attached to the U.S. Naval Observatory from 1844 to 1848. He commanded an expedition in the small side-wheeler USS *Water Witch* to survey and explore the River La Plata and its tributaries from 1853 to 1855. He ascended the Paraná and Paraguay rivers, exploring the area. In 1854, the *Water Witch* was excluded from the Paraguayan waters, and it was fired upon in 1855, resulting in a naval expedition against Paraguay in 1857 (*See* WATER WITCH INCIDENT). He resumed explorations in 1859–1860, ascending the Paraguay river to the head of navigation. He wrote *La Plata, the Argentine Confederation, and Paraguay. Being a Narrative of the Exploration of the Tributaries of the River La Plata and Adjacent Countries During the Years 1853, '54, '55, and '56, under the Orders of the United States Government* (New York, 1859). He served with the Confederate Navy during the Civil War. After the Civil War, he went to Argentina, settled on a cattle farm in Entre Ríos, was superintendent of the construction of Argentina ironclads in Europe, and went to Florence, Italy, in 1880. Died October 26, 1899, in Rome, Italy. *References*: "Autobiographical Sketch of Thomas Jefferson Page," *USNIP* 49 (October 1923): 1661–91; *ACAB*; *DAB*; *Drees*; *NCAB* 10:297; Vincent Ponko, Jr., *Ships, Seas, and Scientists:*

U.S. Naval Exploration and Discovery in the Nineteenth Century (Annapolis, Md., 1974), ch. 7; *Udaondo*; and *WWWA*.

PALLISTER, JOHN C(LARE) (1891–1980). Entomologist, born June 12, 1891, in Cleveland, Ohio. Pallister attended Cleveland College and Western Reserve University. He served in the U.S. Army during World War I. He participated in entomological expeditions to the Amazon Valley in 1911, Central and South America in 1930–1931, to Mexico in 1945, to Peru and the headwaters of the Amazon River in 1946–1947, to Yucatán in 1952, and to southern and eastern Mexico and British Honduras in 1964. He was head of the department of entomology and invertebrate zoology at the Cleveland Museum of Natural History from 1918 to 1932, professional lecturer on natural history and travel from 1932 to 1938, and worked on the staff of the department of entomology of the American Museum of Natural History after 1939. Died March 6, 1980, in Cleveland, Ohio. *References*: *CA*; *New Yorker* 23 (September 13, 1947): 24–25; and *New Yorker* 35 (August 15, 1959): 17–18.

PALMER, ROBERT HASTINGS (1882–1948). Petroleum geologist, born December 1, 1882, in Toledo, Ohio. Palmer graduated from Adrian (Mich.) College, University of Chicago Law School, and Stanford University. He practiced law in Pocatello, Idaho, from 1912 to 1917 and served in the U.S. Army during World War I. He was chief stratigrapher and paleontologist with the Instituto Geologico de Mexico from 1921 to 1923. He was employed as a geologist and paleontologist in the state of Washington in 1926–1927, in Colombia for the Gulf Oil Company in 1928, and in Cuba for the Atlantic Refining Company from 1929 to 1931. He was a consultant for oil companies in Havana, Cuba, from 1931 until his death. He traveled widely over the island of Cuba and became an authority on birds of the northern Caribbean islands. Died May 14, 1948, in Bay Pines, Florida. *References*: *BAAPG* 33 (1949): 1313–15; *PGSA* 1949 (1950): 211–12; and *NYT*, May 20, 1948.

PALMER, THOMAS W(AVERLY) (1891–1968). Lawyer, born February 25, 1891, in Tuscaloosa, Florida. Palmer graduated from the University of Alabama and Harvard University and studied in Spain. He practiced law in Birmingham, Alabama, from 1914 to 1917, and served in the field artillery during World War I. He was attorney to the Chile Exploration Company and U.S. consular agent in Chuquicamata, Chile, from 1919 to 1921; counsel for the Standard Oil Company of New Jersey from 1921 to 1926; executive representative and counsel of Tropical Oil Company in Colombia from 1927 to 1929; counsel for Standard Oil Company of New Jersey from 1929 to 1950; and president of Ancon Insurance Company and Balboa-Insurance Company from 1950 to 1956. He was counsel for the Petroleum Supply Committee for Latin America under the Petroleum Administration for War during World War II. He wrote *Gringo Lawyer* (Gainesville, Fla., 1956). Died May 28, 1968, in Bronxville, New York. *References*: *CB* 1949; *NCAB* G:305; *NYT*, May 31, 1968; and *WWWA*.

PALMER, WILLIAM JACKSON (1836–1909). Railroad builder, born September 18, 1836, in Leipsic, Kent County, Delaware, and grew up in Philadelphia. Palmer was rodman on the Hempfield Railroad from 1853 to 1856, served in the Union Army during the Civil War, was treasurer of the eastern division of the United Pacific Railroad, and took charge of its construction in the West. Then he was employed by the Denver and Rio Grande Railroad as its first president from 1870 to 1883. He established the first steel plant in Colorado in 1879 and was engaged in mining development. He also established Utah Fuel Company. He became identified with the building of Mexican railroads in the 1860s and 1880s. In 1880, he received a concession from the Mexican government and was president of the Mexican National Railroad from 1881 to 1888. He sold his Mexican National Railway interests in the late 1890s and retired. Died March 13, 1909, in Colorado Springs, Colorado. *References*: Brit Allan, "William Jackson Palmer: A Biography," Ph.D. diss., University of Kentucky, 1968; George L. Anderson, *He Conquers the Rockies: General Palmer, an Empire Builder* (Colorado Springs, 1938); *BDABL*; *DAB*; John S. Fisher, *A Builder of the West: The Life of General William Jackson Palmer* (Caldwell, Id., 1939); *NCAB* 23:399; *NYT*, September 30, 1909; and *WWWA*.

PAN AMERICAN AND GRACE AIRWAYS (PANAGRA). Formed in 1929 by W. R. Grace and Company and Pan American Airways, it operated on the west coast of South America. It was acquired by Braniff International Airways in 1967. *References*: "The Long Cold War of Panagra," *Fortune* 45 (June 1952): 117–18, 154–56; and Andrew B. Shea, *Panagra: Linking the Americas during 25 Years* (New York, 1954).

PAN AMERICAN HIGHWAY. A system of roads linking the mainland republics of Latin America and the United States. It was originated in 1923 and envisaged as an automobile road extending from the northern boundary of Mexico to the southern part of South America. The road that connects the northern boundary of Guatemala and the Panama Canal Zone is known as the Inter-American Highway. *References*: *ELA*; Louis W. Kemp, "Highway Diplomacy: The United States and the Inter-American Highway, 1923–1955," Ph.D. diss., George Washington University, 1989; J. Fred Rippy, "The Inter-American Highway," *PHR* 24 (1955): 287–98; and Hugo Williams, "The Pan American Highway," in Philip J. Griffiths et al., *Great Journeys* (New York, 1990), pp. 79–117.

PAN AMERICAN RAILWAY. The crusade for an intercontinental railroad began in 1879 by Hinton Rowan Helper,* who continued to publicize it until his death. The Intercontinental Railway Commission was established by President

Benjamin Harrison in 1890 and sent survey parties to ascertain the practicability of connecting the various railway systems of Central and South America. A permanent Pan American Railway Committee was established in 1902 but the project never materialized. *Reference*: John A. Caruso, "Pan American Railway," *HAHR* 31 (1951): 608–39.

PAN AMERICAN UNION. International agency of Western Hemisphere nations, with headquarters in Washington, D.C.; it was founded in 1890 as the International Bureau of the American Republics and renamed the Pan American Union in 1910. Created originally to collect and distribute commercial information, it sought to promote inter-American cooperation. It became the permanent secretariat of the Organization of American States* (OAS) in 1948 and worked to promote economic, social, juridical, and cultural relations among OAS members. *References*: Clifford B. Casey, "The Creation and Development of the Pan American Union," *HAHR* 13 (13): 437–56; and Leo S. Rowe, *The Pan American Union and the Pan American Conferences: The Pan American Union, 1890–1940* (Washington, D.C., 1940).

PAN AMERICAN WORLD AIRWAYS, INCORPORATED. Founded in 1927, it started the first regular airmail service from Key West, Florida, to Havana, Cuba. It expanded to Mexico, the Caribbean islands and Central America. It purchased Compañía Mexicana de Aviación, S.A.,* in 1928, and Sociedad Colombo Alemano de Transport Aereos (SCADTA) in 1929. With W. R. Grace and Company, it organized Pan American and Grace Airways (PANAGRA) in 1929. It acquired New York, Rio, and Buenos Aires Airways* in 1930, and was then flying throughout most of Latin America. It enlarged its business during the 1930s but its share of the Latin American business began to fall during the 1950s and it went into bankruptcy in 1990. *References*: Marglin Bender and Selig Altschul, *The Chosen Instrument* (New York, 1982); Robert Daley, *An American Saga: Juan Trippe and His Pan Am Empire* (New York, 1980); Mathew Josephson, *Empire of the Air: Juan Trippe and the Struggle for World Airways* (New York, 1944); Wesley P. Newton, *The Perilous Sky: U.S. Aviation Diplomacy and Latin America, 1919–1931* (Coral Gables, Fla., 1978); P. St. John Turner, *Pictorial History of Pan American World Airways* (London, 1973); and Iona S. Wright, "The Caribbean: Working Laboratory for Pan Am's Transatlantic Flights," *Secolas Annals* 12 (March 1981): 96–114.

PANAMA, INTERVENTION IN (1885). Rebels in Panama seized control of the Isthmus and of Panama City and attacked the Panama Railroad and U.S. shipping in 1885. The United States sent eight warships and landed marines in Panama to stop the revolt and protect U.S. interests. The U.S. troops occupied Colón and Panama City. The forces withdrew after the collapse of the revolution. *References*: Kenneth J. Hagan, *American Gunboat Diplomacy and the Old Navy 1877–1889* (Westport, Conn., 1973), ch. 9; *Musicant*, ch. 3; Jack Shulimson,

"U.S. Marines in Panama, 1885," in *Assault from the Sea: Essays on the History of Amphibious Warfare*, ed. Merrill L. Bartlett (Annapolis, Md., 1983), pp. 107–20; and Daniel H. Wicks, "Dress Rehearsal: United States Intervention on the Isthmus of Panama, 1885," *PHR* 49 (1980): 581–605.

PANAMA, INTERVENTION IN (1901–1903). After the Colombian legislation refused to ratify the Hay-Herran Treaty authorizing the construction of an interoceanic canal in Panama by the United States, a revolution broke out in Panama, instigated and aided by the United States, in which the revolutionaries proclaimed the Republic of Panama. The USS *Nashville* prevented Colombian forces from reaching Panama, since the U.S. considered itself to have the right to intervene in Panama to maintain freedom of transit across the isthmus. *References*: *Musicant*, ch. 3; John N. Nikol and Francis X. Holbrook, "Naval Operations in the Panama Revolution, 1903," *AN* 37 (1977): 253–61; and Richard W. Turk, "The United States Navy and the 'Taking' of Panama, 1901–1903," *Military Affairs* 38 (1974): 92–96.

PANAMA, INTERVENTION IN (1989). United States forces invaded Panama in 1989 to overthrow the Panamanian regime of General Manuel Antonio Noriega. U.S. forces occupied Panama City and other key areas. Noriega fled but later surrendered and was extradited. *References*: Kevin Buckley, *Panama: The Whole Story* (New York, 1991); *Musicant*, ch. 10; and Bruce W. Watson and Peter G. Tsouras, eds., *Operation Just Cause: The U.S. Intervention in Panama* (Boulder, Colo., 1991).

PANAMA CANAL. The French Panama Canal Company received a concession from Colombia in 1878 to build a canal. The United States bought the assets of the French company in 1902. The Hay-Bunau-Varilla Treaty between the United States and Panama gave the United States exclusive rights to build and control a canal. It was opened in 1914. In 1950, the operation of the canal was transferred to the Panama Canal Company, a U.S. government corporation. The United States agreed in 1978 to effect a transfer of the canal to Panama in the year 2000. *References*: *ELA*; J. Michael Hogan, *The Panama Canal in American Politics: Domestic Advocacy and the Evolution of Policy* (Carbondale, Ill., 1986); David McCullough, *The Path between the Seas: The Creation of the Panama Canal, 1870–1914* (New York, 1977); and Walter LaFeber, *The Panama Canal: The Crisis in Historical Perspective* (New York, 1978).

PANAMA CANAL ZONE. According to the Hay-Bunau-Varilla Treaty of 1903 with the new Republic of Panama, the United States was granted in perpetuity a strip of land five miles wide on either side of the site across the Isthmus of Panama on which to build an interoceanic canal. Since 1914, the administration of the Panama Canal Zone has been in the hands of general officers of the U.S. Army who also serve ex-officio as the president of the Panama Canal Company.

A treaty with Panama that was ratified in 1978 provided that complete control of the canal and the canal zone would be transferred to Panama in the year 2000. *References*: Duncan H. Cameron, "Panama's Unusual Guest: The Canal Zone in United States-Panamanian Relations," Ph.D. diss., Columbia University, 1965; Michael L. Conniff, *Black Labor on a White Canal: Panama, 1904–1981* (Pittsburgh, 1985); and Herbert and Mary Knapp, *Red, White, and Blue Paradise: The American Canal Zone in Panama* (San Diego, 1984).

PANAMA RAILROAD. A railroad crossing the Isthmus of Panama between Colón and Panama City. Construction by an American company began in 1849 as a link to the California gold mines and was completed in 1855. The railroad was acquired by the French Panama Canal Company in 1881 and by the U.S. government in 1902. After 1951, it was operated by the Panama Canal Company. *References*: *ELA*; John H. Kemble, *The Panama Route 1848–1869* (Berkeley, Calif., 1943); Joseph L. Schott, *Rails over Panama: The Story of the Building of the Panama Railroad 1849–1855* (Indianapolis, 1967).

PARKER, FRANK (1872–1947). Army officer, born September 21, 1872, in Georgetown, South Carolina. Parker attended the University of South Carolina and graduated from the U.S. Military Academy in 1894. He was stationed in Puerto Rico from 1898 to 1900, serving part of the time as collector of customs in Arecibo. He was a military attaché in Venezuela and Argentina in 1905–1906. He served with the army of Cuban pacification from 1906 to 1908. He was an adviser for the Cuban Rural Guard from 1909 to 1912. He established a demonstration squadron of mounted troops, organized the Academia de Aplicacion de Caballeria, a military school, and was instructor of the Cuban cavalry. He was known as one of the most influential men in Cuba. He served in France during World War I. He later commanded the Sixth Corps area, the Second Army, the Philippine Department, and the First Division until his retirement in 1936. He was executive director of the Illinois War Council during World War II. Died March 13, 1947, in Chicago. *References*: Frank Parker Papers, University of North Carolina Library, Chapel Hill; *NCAB* 35:481; *NYT*, March 14, 1947; and *WWWA*.

PARSONS, JAMES J(EROME) (1915–   ). Geographer, born November 15, 1915, in Cortland, New York, and grew up in Pasadena, California. Parsons graduated from the University of California at Berkeley. He served in the U.S. Army Air Force during World War II. He was a member of the faculty of the University of California at Berkeley after 1946 and a professor of geography there from 1960 until his retirement in 1986. He carried out fieldwork in Colombia, the Caribbean, Mexico, Nicaragua, Ecuador, and Costa Rica. He wrote *Antioqueno Colonization in Western Colombia* (Berkeley, Calif., 1949), *San Andres and Providencia: English-Speaking Islands in the Western Caribbean* (Berkeley, Calif., 1956), *The Green Turtle and Man* (Gainesville, Fla., 1962), and *Antioquia's Corridor to the Sea: An Historical Geography of the Settlement of Uraba* (Berkeley, Calif., 1967). *References*: *Hispanic Lands and Peoples: Selected Writings of James J. Parsons*, ed. William M. Denevan (Boulder, Colo., 1989); and *WWA*.

PARTRIDGE, JAMES R(UDOLPH) (1823–1884). Diplomat, born in Baltimore. Partridge graduated from Harvard University and Harvard Law School. He practiced law in Baltimore after 1843. He served in the Maryland legislature from 1856 to 1858 and was Maryland secretary of state from 1858 to 1861. He was U.S. minister to Honduras in 1862, minister to El Salvador from 1863 to 1866, and minister to Venezuela in 1869–1870. He convinced Venezuela to meet the payments that had been awarded to U.S. citizens by the U.S.–Venezuelan mixed claims commission. He was U.S. minister to Brazil from 1871 to 1877 and minister to Peru in 1882–1883. He was involved in bringing a peace settlement between Peru and Chile, but he exceeded his instructions and returned to the United States under suspicion. Committed suicide February 24, 1884, in Alicante, Spain. *References*: *DAB*; *DADH*; *NCAB* 7:519; Norman T. Strauss, "Brazil in the 1870's as Seen by American Diplomats," Ph.D. diss., New York University, 1971; and *WWWA*.

PARVIN, THEOPHILUS (1798–1835). Missionary, born in Fairton, New Jersey. Parvin graduated from the University of Pennsylvania and attended Princeton Theological Seminary; he was ordained in 1826. He was a missionary under the American Board of Commissioners for Foreign Missions from 1823 to 1826. With John C. Brigham,* he explored the feasibility of missionary work in Argentina, Chile, Peru, and Mexico. He arrived in Buenos Aires in 1823, taught at the University of Buenos Aires, and later began a girls' school and a boys' school there. He returned to the United States in 1826 and taught in Bridgeton, New Jersey. Died December 15, 1835, in Fairfield, New Jersey. *References*: *Cutolo*; J. Orin Oliphant, "The Parvin-Brigham Mission to Spanish America, 1823–1826," *Church History* 14 (1945): 85–103; and *PrincetonTS*.

PATTERSON, JEFFERSON (1891–1977). Diplomat, born May 14, 1891, in Dayton, Ohio. Patterson graduated from Yale University and was admitted to the bar in 1919. He served in the U.S. Army during World War I. He entered the foreign service in 1921, and served in Peking, Bogota, Istanbul, Wroclaw, Poland, Oslo, and Berlin until 1939. He was deputy chief of mission in Peru from 1941 to 1945, in Belgium in 1945–1946, and in Egypt from 1946 to 1949. He was U.S. representative on the United Nations Special Committee on the Balkans with the personal rank of minister from 1950 to 1952. He was U.S. ambassador to Uruguay from 1956 to 1958. He wrote *Diplomatic Duty and Diversion* (Cambridge, Mass., 1956) and *Diplomatic Terminus: An Experience in Uruquay* (Cambridge, Mass., 1962). Died November 12, 1977, in Washington, D.C. *References*: *CA*; *NCAB* 59:41; *NYT*, November 14, 1977; and *WWWA*.

PAULDING, HIRAM (1797–1878). Naval officer, born December 11, 1797, in Westchester County, New York. Paulding was appointed a midshipman in the U.S. Navy in 1811. He served in the War of 1812. In 1824, he carried dispatches from Commodore Isaac Hull to General Simón Bolívar's headquarters in the Andes. He described the meeting in *Bolivar in His Camp* (New York, 1834). He was later in charge of the Washington Navy Yard. He commanded the Home Squadron from 1855 to 1858, operating mainly in the Caribbean. In 1857, he broke up William Walker's* second expedition to Nicaragua, seizing Walker and about 150 filibusters who had landed at Greytown in Nicaragua, compelling their surrender and returning them to the United States. He was later head of the Bureau of Detail, governor of the U.S. Naval Asylum in Philadelphia, and port admiral in Boston. Died October 20, 1878, near Huntington, Long Island, New York. *References*: *ACAB*; *DAB*; *NCAB* 4:135; *NYT*, October 21, 1878; Frank V. Rigler, "The Forgotten Admiral," *Daughters of the American Revolution Magazine* 111 (April 1977): 318–25; and *WWWA*.

PAULIN, WILLIAM (1812–1871). Balloonist, born April 3, 1812, in Philadelphia. Paulin constructed his first balloon in 1833 and made his first ascent in Philadelphia. In 1841, he sailed for Valparaiso, Chile, and made numerous ascents in South America, and later in Cuba, Haiti, Puerto Rico, and Mexico. He served with the balloon corps of the Army of the Potomac during the Civil War. *Reference*: *ACAB*.

PEACE CORPS. United States government agency, created in 1961, which sent volunteers to many countries, several thousands of whom went to the countries of Latin America. Volunteers have served in Antigua (1967–   ), Barbados (1965–   ), Belize (1962–   ), Bolivia (1962–1972, 1975–1976), Brazil (1962–1980), Carriacou (1967–   ), Chile (1961–   ), Colombia (1961–1981), Costa Rica (1963–   ), Dominica (1967–   ), Dominican Republic (1962–   ), Ecuador (1962–   ), El Salvador (1962–1980), Grenada (1963–   ), Guatemala (1967–   ), Guyana (1967–1971), Honduras (1962–   ), Jamaica (1962–   ), Montserrat (1967–   ), Nicaragua (1969–1979, 1979–1980), Panama (1963–1972), Paraguay (1967–   ), Peru (1962–1974), St. Kitts-Nevis (1967–   ), St. Lucia (1961–   ), St. Vincent (1967–   ), Uruguay (1963–1974), and Venezuela (1962–1977). *References*: Kevin Lowther and C. Payne Lucas, *Keeping Kennedy's Promise: The Peace Corps* (Boulder, Colo., 1978); Gerard T. Rice, *Twenty Years of Peace Corps* (Washington, D.C., 1981); and Robert B. Taxtor, ed., *Cultural Frontiers of the Peace Corps* (Cambridge, Mass., 1966).

PEARSON, FRED(ERICK) STARK (1861–1915). Electrical engineer, born July 3, 1861, in Lowell, Massachusetts. Pearson graduated from Tufts College. He was an instructor in mathematics and applied mechanics at Tufts College from 1883 to 1886, mining engineer in the United States and Brazil from 1886 to 1888, chief engineer of the West End Street Railway in Boston 1889 to 1893, and chief engineer for the Dominion Coal Company in 1893–1894 and the Metropolitan Street Railway Company of New York City from 1894 to 1899. He visited South America in 1898, and was consulting engineer after 1899. He organized and developed the São Paulo Tramway, Light and Power Company and later the Rio de Janeiro Tramway, Light, and Power Company to provide electric power to these cities. These companies were consolidated later with others to form the Brazilian Traction, Light and Power Company, Limited, of which he was president until his death. He organized in 1902 the Mexican Light and Power Company, Limited, and built a hydroelectric power station at the falls of Necaxa River in Mexico, providing power to Mexico City and its suburbs. In 1907, he took over control of the tramways in Mexico City and in 1909, he organized the Mexican Northwestern Railway. Died May 7, 1915, with the sinking of the *Lusitania* by a German submarine in the Atlantic Ocean. *References*: *ACAB*; *DAB*; Duncan McDowall, *The Light: Brazilian Traction, Light and Power Company Limited 1899–1945* (Toronto, 1988); *NCAB* 18:123; *NYT*, May 8, 1915; and *WWWA*.

PEARSON, PAUL MARTIN (1871–1938). Educator and colonial administrator, born October 22, 1871, near Litchfield, Illinois. Pearson graduated from Baker University. He was a teacher in the high school in Cherryvale, Kansas, from 1891 to 1894, and in Northwestern University from 1896 to 1901. He was professor of public speaking at Swarthmore (Pa.) College from 1902 to 1919. He founded the Swarthmore Chautauque Association in 1912, and was its director until 1921 and its president until 1930, when it was forced out of existence. He was the first civil governor of the Virgin Islands, from 1931 to 1935. He succeeded in increasing the responsibility of the islanders for their own affairs and self-support by the local governments, worked to improve the economic, social, educational, health, and sanitary conditions, and assisted in the creation of the Virgin Islands Company. He was assistant director of the housing division of the U.S. Public Works Administration in 1935–1936. Died March 26, 1938, in San Francisco. *References*: *NCAB* 37:319; *NYT*, March 27, 1938; and *WWWA*.

PEASE, BENJAMIN F(RANKLIN) (1822–ca. 1888). Photographer, born November 17, 1822, in Poughkeepsie, New York. Pease was active as wood engraver in New York City between 1845 and 1847 and later worked in a photographic establishment in that city. He went to Lima, Peru, in 1852, established a photographic studio, and was Peru's first permanent photographer, being virtually the only professional daguerrotypist active in Lima from 1854 to 1858. He also opened a shoe factory, which he lost in 1882. He later ran a studio in the port of Callao. Died in Pisco, Peru. *References*: Keith McElroy, "Benjamin Franklin Pease, an American Photographer in Lima, Peru," *History of Photography* 3 (1979): 195–209; and *NYHSD*.

PECK, ANNIE SMITH (1850–1935). Mountain climber, born October 19, 1850, in Providence, Rhode Island. Peck graduated from Rhode Island Normal School and the University of Michigan and studied at Hanover, Germany, and the American School of Classical Studies in Athens, Greece. She taught Latin at Purdue University and Smith College until 1887 and lectured after 1892. She began climbing in Europe in 1885. She climbed the Popocatépetl and Mount Orizaba in Mexico in 1897, the Aconcagua in Argentina in 1900, and Huascarán in Peru in 1908 (the northern peak of Huascarán was later named in her honor). In 1921, she climbed Mount Coropuna in Peru, and in 1929–1930 she made an extensive tour of South America to demonstrate the potential of commercial aviation for the region. She wrote *A Search for the Apex of America: High Mountain Climbing in Peru and Bolivia, Including the Conquest of Huascarán, with Some Observations on the Country and People Below* (New York, 1911), *The South American Tour* (New York, 1913), *Industrial and Commercial South America* (New York, 1922), and *Flying over South America: Twenty Thousand Miles by Air* (Boston, 1932). Died July 18, 1935, in New York City. *References: NAW; NCAB* 15:152; *NYT*, July 19, 1935; Elizabeth F. Olds, *Women of the Four Winds* (Boston, 1985), pp. 5–70; and *WWWA*.

PECK, HENRY EVERARD (1821–1867). Educator and diplomat, born July 27, 1821, in Rochester, New York. Peck graduated from Bowdoin College (Brunswick, Me.), attended Lane and Auburn theological seminaries and Oberlin College, and was ordained. He taught history and belles lettres at Oberlin College after 1852. He was U.S. commissioner to Haiti from 1865 until his death. Died June 9, 1867, in Port-au-Prince, Haiti. *References: ACAB;* Ludwell L. Montague, "Henry Everard Peck: Le Premier Ministre Résident des États-Unis à Port-au-Prince, 1862–1866," *Revue de Societé d'Histoire et de Géographie d'Haiti* 11, no. 35 (1939): 15–19; and *NCAB* 12:115.

PEDRICK, HOWARD A(SHLEY) ("DAD") (1863–1941). Prospector and inventor. Pedrick served as an apprentice in his father's machine shop. He was a prospector and miner in Dutch Guiana and spent some time building a railroad and digging for gold in the swamps of both Dutch and French Guiana. He wrote *Jungle Gold; Dad Pedrick's Story,* ed. Will DeGrouchy and William L. Magil (Indianapolis, 1930). He established his machine shop company in 1914 and is believed to have invented more portable machine tools than anyone else, which brought him more than fifty patents. Died March 5, 1941, in State College, Pennsylvania. *References: NCAB* 37:467; and *NYT*, March 7, 1941.

PENDLETON, JOHN STROTHER (1802–1868). Lawyer and diplomat, born March 1, 1802, in Culpeper County, Virginia. Pendleton studied law and was admitted to the bar in 1824. He practiced law in Culpeper County. He served in the Virginia House of delegates from 1831 to 1833 and from 1836 to 1839. He was U.S. chargé d'affaires in Chile from 1841 to 1844 and induced the

Chilean government to settle the claims of U.S. citizens from Chile. He served in the U.S. House of Representatives from 1845 to 1849. He was U.S. chargé d'affaires to the Argentine Confederation from 1851 to 1854. With Robert C. Schenck,* U.S. minister to Brazil, he concluded with the Argentine Confederation in 1853 a treaty of friendship, commerce, and navigation and a treaty for the free navigation of the Parana and Uruguay rivers. Died November 19, 1868, in Culpeper County, Virginia. *References*: *BDAC*; *Cutolo*; *DAB*; Courtney Letts de Espil, "John Pendleton and His Friendship with Urquiza," *HAHR* 33 (1953): 152–67; and *NCAB* 12:323.

PENDLETON, JOSEPH HENRY (1860–1942). Marine Corps officer, born June 2, 1860, in Rochester, Pennsylvania. Pendleton graduated from the U.S. Naval Academy in 1882 and was commissioned a second lieutenant in the U.S. Marines in 1884. He served during the Spanish-American War. He commanded a marine regiment in the Philippines from 1904 to 1906 and a brigade from 1909 to 1912. He commanded the first provisional regiment of marines in Corinto, Nicaragua, in 1912, to counteract a revolution that had interrupted railway transit across the isthmus. He commanded the Fourth Regiment in Santo Domingo from 1916 to 1918. He served in the provisional military government and commanded the national police force which was established in 1917. He was acting military governor of the Dominican Republic in 1917–1918 and later, commander of the Fifth Marine Brigade. He retired with the rank of major general in 1924. He served as mayor of Coronado, California, from 1928 to 1930. Died February 4, 1942, in Coronado. *References*: *DAMIB*; *NCAB* 46:404; *NYT*, February 5, 1942; and *WWWA*.

PEPPER, CHARLES M(ELVILLE) (1859–1930). Journalist, born November 11, 1859, in Bloomfield, Morrow County, Ohio. Pepper graduated from the University of Wooster (Ohio). He was Washington correspondent for the *Chicago Tribune* from 1886 to 1895 and staff correspondent of the *New York Herald* in 1896–1897. He reported from Cuba to leading American newspapers from 1897 to 1901. He was special commissioner for the Pan-American Railway Commission in 1903, resided in Cuba in 1903–1904, was foreign trade commissioner for the Department of Commerce and Labor from 1906 to 1909, and was foreign trade adviser to the State Department from 1909 to 1913. He was a newspaper correspondent in South America and Mexico from 1913 to 1917 and representative of American companies in Chile from 1917 to 1924. He was chairman of the Pan-American Railway Commission after 1924. He wrote *To-Morrow in Cuba* (New York, 1899) and *Panama to Patagonia: The Isthmian Canal and the West Coast Countries to South America* (Chicago, 1906). Died November 4, 1930, in New York City. *References*: *NYT*, November 5, 1930; and *WWWA*.

PERRET, FRANK ALVORD (1867–1943). Volcanologist, born August 2, 1867, in Hartford, Connecticut. Perret graduated from Brooklyn Polytechnic Institute. He was an assistant in Thomas A. Edison's East Side Laboratory, later inventing an electric motor, and organized the Elektron Manufacturing Company in Brooklyn. After a nervous breakdown, he took up the study of volcanoes in 1904 and investigated by direct research eruptions of various volcanoes between 1906 and 1914. He was summoned by the government of Martinique in 1929 to investigate the possibility that Mount Pelée was resuming activity and lived at the foot of Mount Pelée from 1929 until 1939. He wrote *The Eruption of Mt. Pelée 1929–32* (Washington, D.C., 1932). In 1934–1935, he investigated the volcano in the Soufriere Hills, Montserrat, British West Indies. Died January 12, 1943, in New York City. *References*: *NCAB* 15:334; *NYT*, January 13, 1943; and *WWWA*.

PERRINE, CHARLES D(ILLON) (1867–1951). Astronomer, born July 28, 1867, in Steubenville, Ohio. Perrine was secretary of the Lick Observatory from 1893 to 1895 and assistant astronomer after 1895. He led several eclipse expeditions. He was director of the Argentine National Observatory in Córdoba from 1909 to 1936. His main task was the completion of the *Córdoba Durchmusterung: Brightness and Position of Every Fixed Star Down to the Tenth Magnitude* (Buenos Aires, 1892–1932) for the southern sky. He was responsible for a detailed Córdoba zone catalogue and for the Córdoba section of the *Astrographic Catalogue*. In 1931, he escaped an attempt to assassinate him. He was forced to retire from the directorship of the Córdoba Observatory in 1936. Died June 21, 1951, in Villa General Mitre, Argentina. *References*: *DAB S5*; *DSB*; *NCAB* 13:556; and *WWWA*.

PERRINE, HENRY (1797–1840). Plant explorer, born April 5, 1797, in Cranbury, New Jersey. Perrine studied medicine and practiced in Ripley, Illinois, from 1819 to 1823. He moved to Natchez, Mississippi, in 1823, and practiced there until 1827. He was U.S. consul in Campeche, Mexico, from 1827 to 1837. There he made botanical collections, after which he made persistent and enthusiastic efforts to introduce useful tropical plants into southern Florida. In 1832 he proposed the establishment of a tropical plant introduction station in southern Florida and established a nursery on Indian Key in 1833, which was destroyed in 1835. He introduced the sisal and henequen plants to the United States. Died August 7, 1840, in Indian Key, Florida. *References*: *DAB*; and *WWWA*.

PERRY MISSION (1819). A diplomatic mission to Venezuela undertaken by Oliver Hazard Perry (1785–1819) to try and reach some kind of accord with Simón Bolívar to stem his privateers and to secure compensation for the losses already suffered by captured U.S. vessels. Perry reached Angostura and the Venezuelans agreed to U.S. demands. Perry died on his way back. *References*: Maury Baker, "The Voyage of the United States Schooner *Nonsuch* up the Orinoco: Journal of the Perry Mission of 1819 to South America," *HAHR* 30 (1950): 480–98; Richard Dillon, *We Have Met the Enemy: Oliver Hazard Perry: Wilderness Commodore* (New York, 1978), pp. 213–20; and James F. Vivian,

"The Orinoco River and Angostura, Venezuela, in the Summer of 1819: The Narrative of a Maryland Naval Chaplain," *TA* 24 (1967): 160–66.

PERSHING, JOHN J(OSEPH) (1860–1948). Army officer, born September 13, 1860, in Laclede, Missouri. Pershing graduated from the U.S. Military Academy in 1886 and was commissioned in the cavalry. He served in the West, in Cuba during the Spanish-American War, and in the Philippines from 1899 to 1903 and from 1907 to 1913. In 1915, he was sent to patrol the Mexican border and remained there until 1917. In 1916, he led the Mexican Punitive Expedition into Mexico in pursuit of Francisco (Pancho) Villa but a year later the search ended without success, in large part owing to severe restrictions placed on the Americans' movements. He was commander of the Southern Department in 1917, commander of the American Expeditionary Force in France during World War I, and army chief of staff from 1921 to 1924. He retired with the rank of general of the armies in 1924. In 1925, he served as head of the plebiscitary commission with the task of settling the Tacna-Arica border dispute between Chile and Peru; the commission failed in its mission. Died July 15, 1948, in Washington, D.C. *References*: *DAB S5*; *DAMIB*; Richard Goldhurst, *Pipeclay and Drill: John J. Pershing, the Classic American Soldier* (New York, 1977); *NCAB* 35:1; Donald Smythe, *Guerilla Warrior: The Early Life of John J. Pershing* (New York, 1973); and *WWWA*.

PERSHING PUNITIVE EXPEDITIONS. *See* MEXICAN PUNITIVE EXPEDITION

PETERKIN, GEORGE WILLIAM (1841–1916). Clergyman, born March 21, 1841, in Clear Spring, Washington County, Maryland. Peterkin attended the University of Virginia and graduated from the Theological Seminary in Virginia; he was ordained in 1869. He served in the Confederate Army during the Civil War. He held pastorates in Culpeper County, Virginia, and Baltimore until 1878. He was the first bishop of the Diocese of West Virginia of the Protestant Episcopal Church from 1878 to 1893. He was a missionary under the Board of Missions of the Protestant Episcopal Church in charge of the missionary district in southern Brazil from 1893 to 1899. Died September 22, 1916, in Richmond, Virginia. *References*: *ACAB*; *DAB*; *NCAB* 12:88; and *WWWA*.

PEURIFOY, JOHN EMIL (1907–1955). Diplomat, born August 9, 1907, in Walterboro, South Carolina. Peurifoy attended the U.S. Military Academy. He was an insurance underwriter and a cashier in New York City from 1929 to 1934 and held various positions in the Labor and State departments until 1947. He was assistant secretary of state for administration from 1947 to 1949, deputy under secretary of state for administration in 1949–1950, and U.S. ambassador to Greece from 1950 to 1953. He was U.S. ambassador to Guatemala in 1953–1954 and was instrumental in the overthrow of the regime of Jacobo Arbenz

Guzmán. He was ambassador to Thailand from 1954 until his death. Died August 12, 1955, in an automobile accident, in Bangkok, Thailand. *References*: *CB* 1949; *NCAB* H:325; *NYT*, August 13, 1955; *PolProf:Truman*; and *WWWA*.

PHELPS, SETH LEDYARD (1824–1885). Businessman and diplomat, born January 13, 1824, in Parkman, Ohio. Phelps was commissioned a midshipman in the U.S. Navy in 1841. He served in the Union Navy during the Civil War. He then became vice president of the Pacific Mail Steamship Company. He was cofounder of the Provisional Interoceanic Canal Society, which in 1879 acquired a concession from Nicaragua. He organized the Maritime Canal Company and tried, unsuccessfully, to begin the construction of an isthmian canal through Nicaragua. He was U.S. minister to Peru from 1883 until his death. He was involved in the settlement of the War of the Pacific. Died June 24, 1885, in Lima, Peru. *References*: *DADH*; *NCAB* 12:358; and *NYT*, June 25, 1885.

PHILLIPS, RUBY HART (1902–1985). Journalist, born December 12, 1902, in Okene, Oklahoma. Phillips went to Cuba in 1923 as a Spanish-speaking stenographer and served as an assistant to her husband, James Doyle Phillips, as Cuban correspondent of the *New York Times* from 1931 until his death in 1937. She succeeded her husband as Cuban correspondent of the *New York Times* from 1937 until 1961. She wrote *Cuban Sideshadow* (Havana, Cuba, 1935), *Cuba, Island of Paradox* (New York, 1959), and *The Cuban Dilemma* (New York, 1962). She was the Latin American correspondent of *Newsday* after 1963. Died October 28, 1985, in Cocoa Beach, Florida. *References*: *CA*; *NYT*, October 30, 1985; and *Time*, 73 (January 19, 1959): 86–87.

PICKETT, JAMES CHAMBERLAYNE (1793–1872). Diplomat, born February 6, 1793, in Fauquier County, Virginia, and grew up in Mason County, Kentucky. Pickett served in the U.S. Army from 1813 to 1815 and again from 1818 to 1821. He studied law, practiced law in Maysville, Kentucky, served in the Kentucky state legislature in 1822, and was secretary of state of Kentucky from 1825 to 1828. He was secretary of legation in Colombia from 1829 to 1835 and fourth auditor of the Treasury Department from 1836 to 1838. He was U.S. chargé d'affaires to the Peru-Bolivian Confederation from 1838 to 1844. He concluded a treaty of peace, friendship, navigation, and commerce with Ecuador and a claims convention with Peru. He edited the *Daily Globe* in Washington, D.C., from 1848 to 1853. Died July 10, 1872, in Washington, D.C. *References*: *DAB*; and *NCAB* 13:159.

PICKETT, JOHN T. (1820s–1890s). Diplomat, born probably in the 1820s, in Maysville, Macon County, Kentucky. Pickett attended the U.S. Military Academy and Lexington (Ky.) Law School. He participated in the Narciso López expedition to Cuba in 1850 and commanded at the battle of Cardenas. He served as a general in the Hungarian army. He was U.S. consul in Turks Island in the

West Indies from 1845 to 1849 and in Veracruz, Mexico, from 1853 to 1861. He resigned in 1861, served as secretary of the Confederate peace mission to Washington, D.C. in 1861, was Confederate commissioner to Mexico in 1861–1862, and was Confederate special envoy to Mexico in 1865. He later settled in Washington, D.C., and practiced law. *References*: *BDC*; Edward J. Berbusse, "Two Kentuckians Evaluate the Mexican Scene from Vera Cruz, 1853–1861," *TA* 34 (1975): 501–12; *DADH*; and J. Fuentas Mares, "La Mision de Mr. Pickett," *Historia Mexicana* 11 (April 1962): 487–518.

PIERCE, HENRY CLAY (1849–1927). Businessman, born in St. Lawrence, Jefferson County, New York. Pierce was clerk and cashier in a bank in St. Louis. He was then a seller and distributor of refined oil, and bought a refinery in 1871. In 1873, he founded Water-Pierce Oil Company (later Corporation), and was its president until 1906. In 1880, he extended his operations of oil development to Mexico and had total control of the Mexican oil business until 1896. He also had control of the Mexican Central Railway from 1902 to 1906. He was later president of Pierce Investment Trust Company of St. Louis. Died June 27, 1927, in New York City. *References*: *ACAB*; *Hanrahan*, ch. 3; *NCAB* 12:15; *NYT*, June 28, 1927; and *WWWA*.

PIERSON, DONALD (1900–   ). Sociologist and anthropologist, born September 8, 1900, in Indianapolis. Pierson graduated from the College of Emporia and the University of Chicago. He carried out fieldwork in Bahia, Brazil, from 1935 to 1937. He was a research associate at Fisk University from 1937 to 1939, a professor of sociology and social anthropology at the Escola de Sociologia e Politica of São Paulo, Brazil, from 1939 to 1959, and an anthropologist with the Institute of Social Anthropology of the Smithsonian Institution in charge of its Brazilian program of research and research training in cooperation with the Escola de Sociologia e Politica of São Paulo from 1945 to 1952. He wrote *Negroes in Brazil: A Study of Race Contact in Bahia* (Chicago, 1942) and *Survey of Literature on Brazil of Sociological Significance Published up to 1940* (Cambridge, Mass., 1945) and was coauthor of *Cruz das Almas: A Brazilian Village* (Washington, D.C., 1952). *References*: *AMWS*; *IAB*; and *WWA*.

PIKE, EUNICE V(ICTORIA) (1913–   ). Linguist, born November 6, 1913, in Woodstock, Connecticut. Pike attended Becker Business College and Moody Bible Institute and graduated from Massachusetts General Hospital. She was a Bible translator and linguistics consultant for Wycliffe Bible Translators and Summer Institute of Linguistics (Huntington Beach, Calif.) after 1936 and lecturer at the University of Oklahoma after 1948. She participated in field trips to Mexico, Peru, and Ecuador, and lived among the Mazatec-speaking people of Oaxaca, Mexico. She wrote *Words Wanted* (Huntington Beach, Calif., 1958), *Not Alone* (Chicago, 1964), and *An Uttermost Part* (Chicago, 1971). *References*: *CA*; and *WWAW*.

PILGRIM HOLINESS CHURCH: DEPARTMENT OF WORLD MIS-SION. Founded in 1897, it began missionary work in St. Kitts in 1902, in British Guiana in 1907, in Trinidad in 1912, in Mexico in 1920, in the Virgin Islands in 1924, in Peru in 1946, in Surinam in 1950, in the Netherlands West Indies in 1954, and in Brazil in 1958. *Reference*: Paul W. Thomas and Paul William, *The Days of Our Pilgrimage: The History of the Pilgrim Holiness Church* (Marion, Ind., 1976).

PITKIN, JOHN R(OBERT) G(RAHAM) (1841–1901). Diplomat, born February 12, 1841, in New Orleans. Pitkin graduated from the University of Louisiana and was admitted to the bar in 1861. He was principal of a public high school in New Orleans from 1861 to 1863 and practiced law in New Orleans after 1863. He was register in bankruptcy for Louisiana from 1867 to 1871 and U.S. marshal for Louisiana until 1877 and again from 1882 to 1885; he then practiced law. He was U.S. minister to Argentina from 1888 to 1892. In 1890, he stopped the bombardment of Buenos Aires by a rebel fleet. Died in New Orleans. *Reference*: NCAB 11:553.

PLATT, ROBERT S(WANTON) (1891–1964). Geographer, born December 4, 1891, in Columbus, Ohio. Platt graduated from Yale University and the University of Chicago. He was a member of the faculty of the University of Chicago after 1920 and professor of geography there from 1939 until his retirement in 1957. He carried out fieldwork in Latin America in 1922, 1923, 1928, 1930, 1933, and 1935–1936, studying rural areas in most of the major regions of each of the Latin American countries. He also made field trips to South America in 1947 and 1948. In 1948, he concentrated on the problems of Tierra del Fuego. He wrote *Latin America: Countrysides and United Regions* (New York, 1942). Died March 1, 1964, in Chicago. *Reference*: AAAG 54 (1964): 630–37.

PLATT AMENDMENT. Amendment to the Army Appropriation bill of 1901, to regulate the relations between the United States and Cuba. It authorized U.S. intervention for the preservation of Cuban independence and the maintenance of a government adequate for the protection of life, property, and individual liberty. Cuba also agreed to sign no treaty that might impair its independence and to limit its freedom to contract debts. It was adopted by the Cuban Constituent Assembly as an appendix to the constitution of 1903. It was abrogated in 1934. *References*: Lejune Cummins, "The Formulation of the 'Platt Amendment,' " *TA* 23 (1967): 370–89; *DADH*; *ELA*; James H. Hitchman, "The Platt Amendment Revisited: A Bibliographical Survey," *TA* 33 (1967): 343–69; and Louis A. Perez, Jr., *Cuba under the Platt Amendment, 1902–1934* (Pittsburgh, 1986).

PLUMB, EDWARD LEE (1827–1912). Railroad builder, born July 17, 1827, in Gowanda, New York. Plumb was an apprentice in a mercantile house in Hartford, Connecticut. He went to California in 1849 and to Mexico in 1854.

He was involved in the establishment of the Mexican Pacific Coal and Iron Mining and Land Company in 1855, leading a prospecting expedition to central Mexico in 1856–1857. He was chargé d'affaires ad interim in Mexico from 1866 to 1868 and consul general in Havana in 1869. One of the first Americans to appreciate the economic potentialities of Mexico, he became a railroad promoter in Mexico in 1871, was an agent of the International Railroad Company of Texas, and obtained a charter for the Mexican International Railroad Company to build two main lines of track crossing Mexico. He was vice president of the company from 1881 until his retirement in 1889. Died April 18, 1912, in Washington, D.C. *References*: Edward Lee Plumb Papers, Manuscript Division, Library of Congress; Edward Lee Plumb Collection, Stanford University Library; *ACAB*; David M. Pletcher, "A Prospecting Expedition across Central Mexico, 1856–1857," *PHR* 21 (1952): 21–41; and *Pletcher*, ch. 3.

POINDEXTER, MILES (1868–1946). Public official and diplomat, born April 22, 1868, in Memphis, Tennessee, and grew up near Lexington, Virginia. Poindexter graduated from Washington and Lee University. He settled in Walla Walla, Washington, in 1891. He practiced law there until 1896 and then in Spokane, Washington. He was assistant prosecuting attorney for Spokane County from 1899 to 1904, judge of the superior court from 1904 to 1908, and member of the U.S. House of Representatives from 1908 to 1910 and of the U.S. Senate from 1910 to 1922. He was U.S. ambassador to Peru from 1922 to 1928. As a result of his experiences in Peru, he wrote *Peruvian Pharaohs* (Boston, 1938) and *The Ayar-Incas* (New York, 1930). Died September 21, 1946, in Greenlee, Virginia. *References*: Miles Poindexter Papers, University of Virginia, Charlottesville, Va.; Howard W. Allen, *Poindexter of Washington: A Study in Progressive Politics* (Carbondale, Ill., 1981); *DAB S4*; *NCAB* 15:211; *NYT*, September 22, 1946; and *WWWA*.

POINSETT, JOEL R(OBERTS) (1779–1851). Diplomat, born March 2, 1779, in Charleston, South Carolina. Poinsett studied in a medical school in Edinburgh and at the military academy in Woolwich, England. He was a special diplomatic agent to Buenos Aires and Chile in 1811 and U.S. consul general in Buenos Aires from 1811 to 1815. He sympathized with and helped the revolutionary movements. He served in the South Carolina General Assembly from 1816 to 1820 and in the U.S. House of Representatives from 1821 to 1825. He was special agent to Mexico in 1822. He was the first U.S. minister to Mexico from 1825 to 1829. He was accused of interfering in Mexican politics and was forced to return to the United States in 1829. He was U.S. secretary of war from 1837 to 1841. He introduced the poinsettia flower to the United States. He wrote *Notes on Mexico, Made in the Autumn of 1822* (Philadelphia, 1824). Died December 12, 1851, near Statesburg, South Carolina. *References*: Joel R. Poinsett Papers, Historical Society of Pennsylvania, Philadelphia; Joel R. Poinsett Papers, Manuscript Division, Library of Congress; *DAB*; *DADH*; *ELS*; Jose

Fuentes Mares, *Poinsett, Historia de una Gran Intriga* (Mexico, 1964); Guillermo Gallardo, *Joel Roberts Poinsett, Agente Norteamericano, 1810–1814* (Buenos Aires, 1984); Guillermo Gallardo, "El Viaje de Buenos Aires a Santiago de Chile de Joel Roberts Poinsett," *Revista de Historia Americana y Argentine*, 4, nos. 7–8 (1962–1963): 9–49; F. J. Gaxiola, *Poinsett en Mexico (1822–1828)* (Mexico, 1936); G. A. Hrunemi, "Palmetto Yankee: The Public Life and Times of Joel Roberts Poinsett: 1824–1851," Ph.D. diss., University of California at Santa Barbara, 1972; *NCAB* 6:435; Dorothy M. Parton, *The Diplomatic Career of Joel Roberts Poinsett* (Washington, D.C., 1934); H. E. Putnam, *Joel Roberts Poinsett: A Political Biography* (Washington, D.C., 1935); James F. Rippy, *Joel R. Poinsett, Versatile American* (Durham, N.C., 1935); Victoriano Salado Alvarez, *Poinsett y Algunas de su Discipulas* (Mexico, 1968); Ralph E. Weber, "Joel R. Poinsett's Secret Mexican Dispatch Twenty," *South Carolina Historical Magazine* 75 (1974): 67–76; and *WWWA*.

POLLOCK, HARRY E(VELYN) D(ORR) (1900–1982). Archaeologist, born June 24, 1900, in Salt Lake City, and grew up in Missouri and Pasadena, California. Pollock graduated from Harvard University. He served in the U.S. Army Air Corps during World War II. He carried out excavations and explorations in Guatemala for the Carnegie Institution of Washington in 1928 and 1937 and in Yucatán and Mexico from 1929 to 1932, 1935 to 1937, 1940, 1948, and 1951 and 1955. He was an archaeologist for the Carnegie Institution of Washington from 1931 to 1950, director of its department of archaeology from 1950 to 1958, and research associate from 1958 to 1963. He was curator of Mayan archaeology at Harvard University from 1963 to 1968. He wrote *Round Structures of Aboriginal Middle America* (Washington, D.C., 1936) and *The Puuc: An Architectural Survey of the Hill Country of Yucatán and North Campeche* (Cambridge, Mass., 1980) and was coauthor of *A Preliminary Study of the Ruins of Coba, Quintana Roo, Mexico* (Washington, D.C., 1932) and *Mayapan, Yucatán, Mexico* (Washington, D.C., 1962). Died March 15, 1982, in Boston. *References*: *AmAntiq* 48 (1983): 782–84; *Willey*, ch. 15; and *WWWA*.

POPENOE, F(REDERICK) WILSON (1892–   ). Plant explorer, born March 9, 1892, in Topeka, Kansas. Popenoe attended Pomona College and graduated from the Universidado de San Marcos (Lima, Peru). He was a plant explorer with the U.S. Department of Agriculture from 1913 until 1925. He was in Mexico and Central America from 1913 to 1915, looking for avocado. He searched for new plants in Brazil in 1913–1914, in the West Indies in 1915, in Guatemala in 1916–1917, in Mexico in 1918, in Costa Rica, Colombia, Ecuador, Peru, and Chile from 1919 to 1921, and in Ecuador in 1925. He wrote *The Avocado in Guatemala* (Washington, D.C., 1919) and *Manuel of Tropical and Subtropical Fruits, excluding the Banana, Coconut, Pineapple, Citrus Fruits, Olive, and Fig* (New York, 1920). He coauthored *The Navel Orange of Bahia: With Notes on Some Little-Known Brazilian Fruits* (Washington, D.C., 1917).

He started and directed United Fruit Company's* Lancetilla experiment station near Tela, Honduras, after 1925. He settled in Antigua, Guatemala, in 1930. During World War II, he worked on production of a chichona source of quinine and on rubber in Central America. He founded and directed Escuela Agrícola Panamericana in Zamorano, Honduras, from 1943 until his retirement in 1957. *References*: Louis Adamic, *The House in Antiqua: A Restoration* (New York, 1937); Melvin J. Frost and B. Ira Judd, "Plant Explorer of the Americas," *Economic Botany* 24 (1970): 471–78; Frances L. Jewell and Clare L. Mc-Causland, *Plant Hunters* (Boston, 1958), pp. 140–73; and *WWLA*.

PORTER, DAVID (1780–1843). Naval officer, born February 1, 1780, in Boston. Porter entered the U.S. navy as a midshipman in 1798. He served during the war with Tripoli and the War of 1812. He commanded the USS *Essex* and sailed to the Pacific Ocean in 1812–1813, the first U.S. naval vessel to sail these waters. His vessel was captured by British vessels near Valparaiso, Chile. He wrote *Journal of a Cruise Made to the Pacific Ocean, . . . in the USS Frigate Essex, in the Year 1812, 1813 and 1814 Containing Descriptions of the Cape de Ver Islands, Coasts of Brazil, Patagonia, Chile and Peru, and of the Galapagos Islands* (Philadelphia, 1815). He was commissioner of the Navy board from 1815 to 1823 and commander of the West India Squadron from 1823 to 1825. He resigned from the Navy in 1826, went to Mexico, and was commander in chief of the Mexican Navy from 1826 to 1829. He returned to the United States in 1829, was U.S. chargé d'affaires to Turkey from 1831 to 1839, and was the first U.S. minister to Turkey from 1839 until his death. Died March 3, 1843, in Constantinople, Turkey. *References*: David Porter Papers, Manuscript Division, Library of Congress; *ACAB*; *DAB*; *DAMIB*; E. W. Flaccus, "Commodore David Porter and the Mexican Navy," *HAHR* 34 (1954): 365–73; David F. Long, *Nothing Too Daring: A Biography of Commodore David Porter 1780–1843* (Annapolis, Md., 1970); *NCAB* 2:98; and *WWWA*.

PORTER, KATHERINE ANNE (1890–1980). Author, born Callie Russell Porter, May 15, 1890, in Indian Creek, Texas, and grew up in Kyle, San Antonio, and Victoria, Texas. She was a reporter on the Fort Worth *Critic* in 1917 and on the *Rocky Mountain News* in Denver in 1918–1919. She worked for a motion picture magazine in New York City in 1919–1920, and began publishing stories in 1921. She traveled to Mexico in 1920 and lived in Mexico from 1922 to 1929. She helped to prepare an exhibit of Mexican folk art and wrote *Outline of Mexican Popular Arts and Crafts* (Mexico City, 1922). She returned to Mexico in 1930. She lived in Europe from 1931 to 1936. Died September 18, 1980, in Silver Spring, Maryland. *References*: *CA*; *DLB*; Joan Givner, *Katherine Anne Porter: A Life* (New York, 1982); Willene Hendrick and George Hendrick, *Katherine Anne Porter* (Boston, 1988); *NYT*, September 19, 1980; Darlene H. Unrue, *Truth and Vision in Katherine Anne Porter's Fiction* (Athens, Ga., 1985); and *WWWA*.

PORTER, ROBERT P(ERCIVAL) (1852–1917). Journalist, born June 30, 1852, in Norwich, England, and grew up in California. Porter was a reporter for the Chicago *Daily Inter Ocean*, involved in preparing the Tenth U.S. Census in 1880–1881, and a member of the editorial staff of the *New York Tribune* and the Philadelphia *Press* from 1884 to 1887. He founded and was involved with the *New York Press* from 1887 to 1894, was involved in the administration of the Eleventh Census, and was head of the Census Office from 1889 to 1893. He was sent to Cuba and Puerto Rico in 1898 as a special fiscal and tariff commissioner and wrote *Industrial Cuba; Being a Study of Present Commercial and Industrial Conditions* (New York, 1899). In 1899, he succeeded in inducing General Maximo Goméz to disband the Cuban Army. He served on the staff of London *Times* from 1904 until his death and was its principal correspondent in Washington, D.C., from 1906 to 1909. He later traveled extensively in South America and wrote *The Ten Republics* (London, 1911). Died February 28, 1917, in London, from injuries received in an automobile accident. *References*: *DAB*; *NCAB* 12:216; and *NYT*, March 1, 1917.

POWELL, WILLIAM D(AVID) (1854–1934). Missionary, born July 1, 1854, in Madison, Mississippi. Powell graduated from Union University (Tenn.) and Southern Baptist Theological Seminary and was ordained in 1874. He was a missionary under the Foreign Missionary Board of the Southern Baptist Convention* in Mexico from 1882 to 1898 and under the Home Board in Cuba from 1898 to 1907. He established the Madero Institute in Saltillo, Mexico, and in 1883 organized the first Baptist Church there. He was corresponding secretary and treasurer of the Baptist State Board of Mission in Kentucky from 1906 to 1917 and field secretary of the Foreign Mission Board of the Southern Baptist Convention from 1917 until 1933. Died May 15, 1934, in Opelika, Alabama. *References*: *ESB*; and *WWWA*.

POWELL, WILLIAM FRANK (1848–1920). Educator and diplomat, born June 26, 1848, in Troy, New York. Powell graduated from New Jersey Collegiate Institute. In 1870, he opened perhaps the first state school for Negro children in Alexandria, Virginia. He was principal of a school in Bordentown, New Jersey, from 1875 to 1881, bookkeeper at the fourth auditor's office, U.S. Treasury Department from 1881 to 1884, superintendent of schools in Camden, New Jersey, from 1884 to 1886, and teacher in the Camden high school from 1886 to 1894. He was U.S. minister to Haiti from 1897 to 1905 and chargé d'affaires to Santo Domingo from 1897 to 1904. He was an editorial writer for the *Philadelphia Tribune* after 1909. Died January 23, 1920. *References*: *DANB*; *NCAB* 12:195; and *WWWA*.

PRANCE, GHILLEAN T(OLMIE) (1937–   ). Botanist, born July 13, 1937, in Brandeston, England. Prance graduated from Oxford University. He was a research fellow in tropical botany at the New York Botanical Garden from

1963 to 1966, associate curator there from 1966 to 1968, curator of Amazonian botany from 1968 to 1975, vice president from 1977 to 1981, director of botany after 1975, and senior vice president for research after 1981. He was head of the New York Botanical Garden's Amazon project. He was later director of the Royal Botanical Gardens at Kew, England. He prepared *An Index of Plant Collectors in Brazilian Amazonia* (Belem, n.d.), and was coeditor of *Amazonia* (Oxford, 1985). *References: AMWS*; and *WWE*.

PRATT, HENRY B(ARRINGTON) (1832–1912). Missionary, born May 26, 1832, near Darien, Georgia. Pratt graduated from Oglethorpe University and Princeton Theological Seminary and was ordained in 1855. He was a missionary under the Board of Foreign Missions of the United Presbyterian Church in North America in Colombia from 1856 to 1859. He was a chaplain in the Confederate Army during the Civil War. He held pastorates in Hillsboro and Sugar Creek, North Carolina, from 1861 to 1869. He returned to Colombia as a missionary from 1869 to 1877. He held pastorates in Winnsboro and Lancaster, South Carolina, from 1878 to 1886. He translated the Bible into modern Spanish for the American Bible Society.* He was an evangelist in Mexico, Cuba, and southwestern Texas from 1893 to 1899. He held a pastorate in Brooklyn, New York, from 1900 to 1902. Died December 11, 1912, in Hackensack, New York. *References: NYT*, December 12, 1912; and *PrincetonTS*.

PRATT, PARLEY PARKER (1807–1857). Mormon leader, born April 12, 1807, in Burlington, New York, and grew up in Ohio. Pratt joined the Mormon Church in 1830 and was ordained an elder and, in 1835, one of the twelve apostles. He went on several missions to Canada, New York, and England. He went to Salt Lake City in 1847. He went to Chile in 1851–1852 to open the South American mission of the Mormon Church, but it was short-lived. Killed May 13, 1857, near Fort Gibson, in the Cherokee Indian reservation (later Arkansas). *The Autobiography of Parley Parker Pratt, One of the Twelve Apostles of the Church of Jesus Christ of Latter-Day Saints, Embracing His Life, Ministry and Travels*, ed. Parley P. Pratt, Jr. (New York, 1874) was published posthumously. *References: ACAB*; *DAB*; *NCAB* 16:16; *OAB*; F. LaMond Tullis, "California and Chile in 1851 as Experienced by the Mormon Apostle Parley P. Pratt," *Southern California Historical Quarterly* 67 (1985): 291–307; and *WWWA*.

PRATT, REY L(UCERO) (1878–1931). Mormon leader, grandson of Parley Parker Pratt,* born in Salt Lake City, Utah, and grew up in Colonia Dublan, one of the Mormon colonies in Chihuahua, Mexico. In 1900, he settled in a ranch outside Dublan. He was president of the Mexican mission of the Church of the Latter-Day Saints from 1907 to 1913. He returned to Mexico in 1917. He was sent to Buenos Aires, Argentina, in 1925–1926, as the first Spanish-speaking Mormon missionary to return to South America. Died April 14, 1931, in Salt Lake City. *Reference*: Dale F. Beecher, "Rey L. Pratt and the Mexican Mission," *Brigham Young University Studies* 15 (Spring 1975): 293–307.

PRESBYTERIAN CHURCH IN THE UNITED STATES: BOARD OF FOREIGN MISSIONS. Established in 1861, it began missionary work in Brazil in 1869, in Colombia from 1869 to 1878, in Mexico in 1874, and in Cuba from 1899 to 1923. It shared in the United Andean Indian Mission in Ecuador after 1945. It was later renamed the Board of World Missions and then the Division of International Mission. It merged with the United Presbyterian Church in the U.S.A.* in 1983 to form the Presbyterian Church (U.S.A.). *References*: Board of Foreign Missions Archives, Department of History (Montreat), Presbyterian Church (U.S.A.), Montreat, N.C.; Robert L. McIntire, *Portrait of Half a Century: Fifty Years of Presbyterianism in Brazil (1859–1910)* (Cuernavaca, Mexico, 1969); *Our Church Faces Foreign Missions* (Nashville, Tenn., 1931); William A. Ross, *Sunrise in Aztec Land: Being an Account of the Mission Work that Has Been Carried on in Mexico since 1874 by the Presbyterian Church in the United States* (Richmond, Va., 1922); and James P. Smith, *An Open Door, Being a Brief Survey of the Mission Work Carried on in Brazil since 1869 by the Presbyterian Church in the United States* (Richmond, Va., 1925).

PRESBYTERIAN CHURCH IN THE U.S.A.: BOARD OF FOREIGN MISSIONS. Organized in 1837, it began missionary work in Colombia in 1856, in Brazil in 1859, in Mexico in 1872, in Chile in 1873, in Guatemala in 1882, and in Venezuela in 1897. It also worked in Puerto Rico. It merged with the Presbyterian Church in North America in 1958 to form the United Presbyterian Church in the U.S.A., which merged in 1983 with the Presbyterian Church in the United States to create the Presbyterian Church (U.S.A.). *References*: Board of Foreign Missions Papers, Department of History, Presbyterian Church (U.S.A.), Philadelphia; Arthur J. Brown, *One Hundred Years: A History of the Foreign Missionary Work of the Presbyterian Church in the U.S.A.* (New York, 1929); Charles M. Brown, "A History of the Presbyterian Church, U.S.A. in Brazil," Ph.D. diss., Ohio State University, 1947; Robert L. McIntire, *Portrait of Half a Century: Fifty Years of Presbyterianism in Brazil (1859–1910)* (Cuernavaca, Mexico, 1969); Graeme S. Mount, *Presbyterian Mission to Trinidad and Puerto Rico. The Canadian Presbyterian Mission to Trinidad and the Missions of the Presbyterian Church in the United States of America to Puerto Rico: The Formative Years, 1868–1914* (Hanstport, Nova Scotia, 1983).

PRESSLY, NEILL ERSKINE (1850–1920). Missionary, born September 11, 1850, in Moffaysville, Anderson County, South Carolina. Pressly graduated from Erskine College and Seminary and was ordained in 1878. He was the first missionary under the Foreign Missions Board of the Associate Reformed Presbyterian Church in Mexico from 1879 to 1917. He served in Tampico, state of Tamaulipas, where he also founded a school for girls. He returned to the United

States, because of ill health, in 1917. Died November 1, 1920, in Tampa, Florida. *Reference*: *The Sesquicentennial History of the Associate Reformed Presbyterian Church* (Clinton, S.C., 1951), pp. 630–31.

PRESTON, ANDREW W(OODBURY) (1846–1924). Businessman, born June 29, 1846, in Beverly, Massachusetts. Preston entered the employ of a fruit and produce commission firm in Boston and, in 1870, was the first to sell bananas in Boston. He established a fruit commission business in 1882, and then formed, with Lorenzo Dow Baker,* the Boston Fruit Company, which was incorporated in 1887 to launch a banana-importing enterprise. Preston was the firm's general manager. He merged this company into the United Fruit Company* in 1899, and was its president until his death. Died September 26, 1924, in Swampscott, Massachusetts. *References*: *BDABL*; *NCAB* 26:302; *NYT*, September 27, 1924; and *WWWA*.

PREVOST, JOHN B(ARTOW) (1766–1825). Lawyer and diplomat, born March 9, 1766, in Paramus, New Jersey. Prevost was judge of the supreme court of the Territory of Orleans in New Orleans in 1805–1806 and practiced law in New Orleans after 1806. He was a special diplomatic agent to the Columbia River in 1817. As a representative of the United States, he was sent to repossess the Oregon Territory from Great Britain. He was an agent for commerce and seamen in Peru, Chile, and Buenos Aires after 1817. Died March 5, 1825, probably in Lima. *References*: *Cutolo*; and John C. Pine, "The Role of United States Special Agents in the Development of a Spanish American Policy, 1810–1822," Ph.D. diss., University of Colorado, 1955, ch. 7.

PRICE, HENRY MANROE (ca. 1821– ?). Physician, probably born in Stockport, England. He was brought to the United States about 1823 and grew up in Charlottesville, Virginia. He edited *Southern Medical Reformer* in Forsyth, Georgia, from 1845 to 1847, and then moved the publication to Petersburg, Virginia. He was a member of the Scientific Eclectic Medical Institute, the Botanico Medical Infirmary, and the Botanic Medicine Store there. He served in the Confederate Army during the Civil War. He established the Venezuela Emigration Company and promoted a Confederate colony in Venezuela in 1865, receiving a land grant, the Price Grant,* from the Venezuelan government. He led a group of colonists to Venezuela in 1867 but returned after one year because of ill health. Died after 1901, in Jackson, Tennessee. *References*: Alfred J. Hanna and Kathryn A. Hanna, *Confederate Exiles in Venezuela* (Tuscaloosa, Ala., 1960); and Frank J. Merli, ed., "Alternative to Appomattox: A Virginian's Vision of an Anglo-Confederate Colony on the Amazon, May 1865," *Virginia Magazine of History and Biography* 94 (1986): 210–19.

PRICE, RICHARD (1941–   ). Anthropologist, born November 30, 1941, in New York City. Price graduated from Harvard University and attended the Ecole Pratique des Hautes Etudes (Paris). He was an assistant professor of anthropology at Yale University from 1970 to 1973 and associate professor in 1973–1974. He was a professor of anthropology at Johns Hopkins University from 1974 to 1987. He carried out fieldwork in Peru in 1961, in Martinque in 1962–1963, 1983, 1986, and 1988, in Mexico in 1965–1966, and in Suriname in 1966–1968, 1974, 1975, 1976, 1978, and 1979. He wrote *Saramaka Social Structure: Analysis of a Maroon Society in Surinam* (Rio Piedras, P.R., 1975), *The Guiana Maroons: A Historical and Bibliographical Introduction* (Baltimore, 1976), *First Time: The Historical Vision of an Afro-American People* (Baltimore, 1983), *To Slay the Hydra: Dutch Colonial Perspectives of the Saramaka Wars* (Ann Arbor, Mich., 1983), and *Alabi's World: Conversion, Colonialism, and Resistance on an Afro-American Frontier* (Baltimore, 1989) and edited *Maroon Societies: Rebel Slave Communities in the Americas* (Garden City, N.Y., 1973). With his wife, **SALLY PRICE** (1943–   ), he wrote *Afro-American Arts of the Suriname Rain Forest* (Berkeley, Calif., 1983). *References*: *CA*; and *WWA*.

PRICE, STERLING (1809–1867). Public official and army officer, born September 20, 1809, in Prince Edward County, Virginia. Price attended Hampden-Sydney College and studied law. He settled in Chariton County, Missouri, in 1831. He served in the state legislature from 1836 to 1840 and from 1840 to 1844 and was a member of the U.S. House of Representatives from 1844 to 1846. He served in the Mexican War. He was governor of Missouri from 1852 to 1856. He served in the Confederate Army during the Civil War, after which, he moved to Mexico where he attempted to establish a colony of Confederate loyalists. After the fall of Emperor Maximilian, he returned to Missouri. Died September 29, 1867, in St. Louis. *References*: *DAB*; *NCAB* 12:304; Ralph R. Rea, *Sterling Price: The Lee of the West* (Little Rock, Ark., 1959); and Robert E. Shalhope, *Sterling Price, Portrait of a Southerner* (Columbia, Mo., 1971).

PRICE GRANT. In 1865, the government of Venezuela gave Henry Manroe Price* a land grant of 240,000 square miles. A colony of former Confederates was established in 1866 southeast of the Orinoco River, Venezuela. The grant was abrogated in 1869 and most of the colonists had left Venezuela by 1870. *References*: *American, English, and Venezuelan Trading and Commercial Company, The Emigrant's Vade-Mecum, or Guide to the "Price Grant" in Venezuelan Guyana* (London, 1868); and Alfred J. Hanna and Kathryn A. Hanna, *Confederate Exiles in Venezuela* (Tuscaloosa, Ala., 1960).

PRINGLE, CYRUS GUERNSEY (1838–1911). Plant explorer, born May 6, 1838, in East Charlotte, Vermont. Pringle farmed in East Charlotte and devoted much of his time to the breeding of plants. He also collected plants in Vermont, northern New England, and eastern Canada. He made botanical explorations in the Pacific states from 1880 to 1885 and made many botanical exploration trips in Mexico after 1885. He made a systematic study of Mexican flora and had placed specimens in most of the important herbaria. He built up an herbarium (which was later housed at the University of Vermont). Died May 25, 1911, in Burlington, Vermont. *References*: *DAB*; *Life and Work of Cyrus Guernsey Pringle* (Burlington, Vt., 1936); *NCAB* 23:175; and *WWWA*.

PROSKOURIAKOFF, TATIANA (AVENIVOVNA) (1909–1985). Archaeologist, born January 23, 1909, in Tomsk, Russia, brought to the United States in 1916. Proskouriakoff graduated from Pennsylvania State University. She worked on architectural restoration in Piedras Negras, northwestern Guatemala, from 1934 to 1938 and was in Copán, Honduras, in 1939 and in Yucatán in 1940. She was involved in the deciphering of Mayan hieroglyphs. She wrote *An Album of Maya Architecture* (Washington, D.C., 1946), *A Study of Classic Maya Sculpture* (Washington, D.C., 1950), and *Jades from the Cenote of Sacrifice, Chichén Itzá, Yucatán* (Cambridge, Mass., 1974). Died August 30, 1985, in Watertown, Massachusetts. *References*: *AmAntiq* 55 (1990): 6–11; *CA*; Joyce Marcus, "Tatiana Proskouriakoff (1909–1985)," in Ute Gacs et al., eds., *Women Anthropologists: A Biographical Dictionary* (Westport, Conn., 1988), pp. 297–302; and *NYT*, September 11, 1985.

PROTESTANT EPISCOPAL CHURCH IN THE UNITED STATES OF AMERICA: DOMESTIC AND FOREIGN MISSIONARY SOCIETY. Organized in 1835, it began missionary work in Mexico in 1857, in Haiti in 1861, in Cuba in 1871, in Brazil in 1890, in Puerto Rico in 1899, in Panama in 1906, in the Dominican Republic in 1918, in the Virgin Islands in 1919, in Costa Rica and Nicaragua in 1947, in Colombia in 1952, in Honduras, Guatemala, and El Salvador in 1957, in Ecuador in 1960. *References*: Domestic and Foreign Missionary Society Archives, Church Historical Society, Austin, Texas; Julia C. Emery, *A Century of Endeavor 1821–1921: A Record of the First One Hundred Years of the Domestic and Foreign Missionary Society of the Protestant Episcopal Church in the United States of America* (New York, 1921).

PROUDFIT, ARTHUR (1898–1980). Petroleum executive, born in Los Angeles. Proudfit attended Oregon State Agricultural College. He began his career in the oil business as a drilling tool dresser in Mexico in 1919. He was superintendent of Lago Petroleum Corporation in 1927. He was employed in the oil industry in Venezuela for almost thirty years. He was general manager of Creole Petroleum Company and president from 1945 to 1954 and again from 1959 to 1961. Died February 27, 1980, in New York City. *Reference*: *NYT*, February 29, 1980.

PUERTO RICO. Acquired by the United States in 1898 as a result of the Spanish-American War. The island was under military government until 1901, when it came under civilian rule. In 1947, Puerto Ricans were granted the right to elect their own governor, and in 1952 Puerto Rico became a commonwealth of the United States. *References*: Edward J. Berbusse, *The United States in*

Puerto Rico, 1898–1900 (Chapel Hill, N.C., 1966); Surendra Bhana, *The United States and the Development of the Puerto Rican Status Question, 1936–1968* (Lawrence, Kans., 1975); Raymond Carr, *Puerto Rico, a Colonial Experiment* (New York, 1984); Truman R. Clark, *Puerto Rico and the United States, 1917– 1933* (Pittsburgh, 1975); Jorge Heine, ed., *Time for Decision: The United States and Puerto Rico* (Lanham, Md., 1983); Roberta A. Johnson, *Puerto Rico, Commonwealth or Colony?* (New York, 1980); Gordon K. Lewis, *Puerto Rico: Freedom and Power in the Caribbean* (New York, 1968); Thomas G. Mathews, *Puerto Rican Politics and the New Deal* (Gainesville, Fla., 1960); and Rexford G. Tugwell, *The Stricken Land: the Story of Puerto Rico* (Garden City, N.Y., 1947).

PULLIAM, WILLIAM E(LLIS) (1871–1949). Government official, born December 25, 1871, in Louisville, Kentucky. Pulliam graduated from the University of Oregon. He was deputy collector of customs in Portland, Oregon, from 1893 to 1898, special agent of the Treasury Department from 1898 to 1901, customs expert in Manila, Philippines, from 1901 to 1903, and special duputy collector of customs of the Philippines from 1903 to 1907. He was receiver general of customs for the Dominican Republic from 1907 until his retirement in 1939. Died August 9, 1949, in Monterey, California. *References*: *NYT*, August 10, 1949; and *WWWA*.

PUNITIVE EXPEDITIONS. *See* MEXICAN PUNITIVE EXPEDITION

PURDIE, SAMUEL A(LEXANDER) (1843–1897). Missionary, born March 5, 1843, in Columbus, New York. Purdie was a teacher in Centre and Back Creek, North Carolina, from 1866 to 1871. He was a missionary under the Friends New York Yearly Meeting in Matamoros, Mexico, from 1871 to 1895. He established a printing press, began publishing a monthly, *El Ramo de Olivo*, in 1872, and also published textbooks. He also traveled in Mexico. He wrote *Memoirs of Angela Aguilar de Mascorro, and Sketches of the Friends' Mexican Mission* (Chicago, 1885). He served in the Central American Mission in El Salvador in 1897. Died August 6, 1897, in San Salvador, El Salvador. *References*: *Central American Bulletin*, October 15, 1897; and James P. Knowles, *Samuel A. Purdie, His Life and Letters, His Work as a Missionary and Spanish Writer and Publisher in Mexico and Central America* (Plainfield, Ind., 1908).

R

RAGUET, CONDY (1784–1842). Editor and economist, born January 28, 1784, in Philadelphia. Raguet was trained in a Philadelphia mercantile house and was a supercargo to Santo Domingo in 1804–1805. He then established himself in business. He visited Haiti in 1809 and wrote "Memoirs of Haiti" in the May and June 1809 issues of *Portfolio*. He served during the War of 1812, was admitted to the bar and practiced law, and served in the Pennsylvania Senate. He was U.S. consul to Rio de Janeiro from 1822 to 1827 but was unable to deal with the disputes between Brazil and the United States and returned to the United States in 1827. He then began publishing the *Free Trade Advocate and Journal of Political Economy* and, later, *The Examiner* and the *Journal of Political Economy*. He was also proprietor of the Philadelphia *Gazette*. Died March 21, 1842, in Philadelphia. *References*: *ACAB*; *DAB*; Zelia Sa Viana Camurca, "Condy Raguet: His Life, Work, and Education," Ph.D. diss., University of Pennsylvania, 1988; and *WWWA*.

RAINEY, FROELICH (GLADSTONE) (1907–   ). Archaeologist, born June 18, 1907, in Black River Falls, Wisconsin. Rainey graduated from The University of Chicago and Yale University. He carried out archaeological research in the West Indies under the auspices of the Peabody Museum of Yale University from 1931 to 1935. He was assistant professor at the University of Alaska from 1935 to 1942. He was a member of the Board of Economic Warfare in 1942 and director of the quinine mission to Ecuador in 1943–1944. He was director of the University Museum of the University of Pennsylvania, professor of anthropology at the University of Pennsylvania after 1947, and director of its Applied Science Center for Archaeology after 1960. *References*: *AMWS*; *CB* 1967; and *WWA*.

RAND, CHARLES FREDERICK (1856–1927). Mine owner, born August 17, 1856, in Canaan, Maine. Rand began his business career with the Milwaukee, Lake Shore and Western Railway Company from 1876 to 1886, was later manager of the Aurora Iron Mining Company and in charge of other iron mines in Michigan. He discovered Mayari iron ore deposits in Cuba. He was president of the Spanish-American Iron Company, operating iron ore mines at Daiquiri and Mayari in Cuba from 1893 to 1915. He was also executive officer of the Ponupo Manganese Company, El Cuero Iron Mines, and other Cuban properties from 1906 to 1922. He organized and was president of the Buena Vista Iron Mining Company of Cuba from 1909 to 1915 and was president of Moa Bay Iron Company, which had large iron deposits in Cuba. Died June 21, 1927, in West Orange, New Jersey. *References*: *ACAB*; *NCAB* 21:333; and *WWWA*.

RANKIN, MELINDA (1811–1888). Missionary, born March 21, 1811, in Littleton, New Hampshire. Rankin taught in Kentucky and then in Mississippi from 1840 to 1847. She was a teacher in the Huntsville Male and Female Academy in Huntsville, Texas, in 1847–1848. She established a school in Cincinnati, Texas, in 1848 and administered it until 1852. She opened a school in Brownsville, Texas, in 1852 (which in 1854 became the Rio Grande Female Seminary) and administered it until 1862. She went to Matamoros, Mexico, in 1862–1863, and opened a school there. In 1866, she moved to Monterrey, Mexico, opened the first Protestant mission in Mexico, and was a missionary under the auspices of the American and Foreign Christian Union until 1872. She wrote *Twenty Years among the Mexicans: A Narrative of Missionary Labor* (Cincinnati, 1875). Died December 7, 1888, in Bloomington, Illinois. *References*: Mary M. Rakow, "Melinda Rankin and Magdalen Hayden: Evangelical and Catholic Forms of Nineteenth Century Christian Sprituality," Ph.D. diss., Boston College, 1982; John C. Rayburn, "Introduction," in Melinda Rankin, *Texas in 1850* (Waco, Tex., 1966); and Walter P. Webb, ed. *The Handbook of Texas* (Austin, Tex., 1952).

RANSOM, JOHN J(AMES) (1853–1934). Missionary, born July 8, 1853, in Rutherford County, Tennessee. Ransom graduated from Emory and Henry College (Va.) and was ordained in 1874. He was a missionary under the Board of Missions of the Methodist Episcopal Church, South,* in Brazil from 1876 until 1886. He served in Rio de Janeiro and organized the first Methodist church there. He returned to the United States in 1886 and held pastorates in Franklin, Springfield, Fayetteville, and Shelbyville, Tennessee, after 1890. Died October 18, 1934, in Nashville. *References*: *EWM*; and *Journal of the One Hundred and Twenty-First Session of the Tennessee Annual Conference of the Methodist Church, South* (Nashville, Tenn., 1934), pp. 84–85.

RAWSON, AMAN (1792–1847). Physician, born in Montague, Franklin County, Massachusetts. Rawson studied medicine and became a surgeon in the U.S. Navy in 1814. He came to Buenos Aires in 1818, went to Mendoza and then to San Juan, settled in that province, practiced medicine, and set up a pharmacy. In 1822, he promoted the establishment of a colony in the districts of Caucete and Vienticinco de Mayo, acquired the land from the government, organized a society, and settled the colony with Argentines. He helped General José de San Martin during the War of Independence in Argentina with medical knowledge. He served in the Argentine legislature several times after 1822. He was involved in controlling an outbreak of smallpox with vaccination and served again as physician in San Juan from 1840 to 1846. Died January 11, 1847, in San Juan, Argentina. *References*: *Cutolo*; Chesar H. Guerrero, *Dr. Amán Rawson: Un Apóstol de la Medicina* (San Juan, Argentina, 1971); and *Udaondo*.

REDFIELD, ROBERT (1897–1958). Anthropologist, born December 4, 1897, in Chicago. Redfield graduated from the University of Chicago and was admitted to the bar in 1921. He practiced law from 1921 to 1924. He carried out fieldwork in Tepoztlan, Morelos, Mexico, in 1926. He was assistant professor at the University of Chicago from 1928 to 1930, associate professor from 1930 to 1934, and professor from 1934 until his death. Between 1930 and 1942 he spent much time in Central America, particularly in Yucatán and Guatemala, making a study of the effects of the process of civilization on primitive peoples. He wrote *Tepoztlan, a Mexican Village: A Study of Folk Life* (Chicago, 1930), *Chan Kom, a Maya Village* (Washington, D.C., 1934), *The Folk Culture of Yucatán* (Chicago, 1941), and *A Village That Chose Progress: Chan Kom Revisited* (Chicago, 1950). Died October 16, 1958, in Chicago. *References*: Robert Redfield Papers, University of Chicago Library; Robert A. Rubenstein, ed. with an introduction, *Fieldwork: The Correspondence of Robert Redfield & Sol Tax* (Boulder, Colo., 1991); *AA* 61 (1959): 652–62; *American Sociological Review* 24 (1959): 256–57; *NCAB* 44:76; *NYT*, October 17, 1958; and *Science* 130 (September 11, 1959): 609–10.

REDHEAD, JOSEPH JAMES THOMAS (1767–1847). Physician. Redhead came to Buenos Aires in 1803, commissioned by the British government to study natural sciences in South America. He studied vegetation in Jujuy and Salta and typhus and malaria in Rosario de Lerma. He was medical officer to the army in Tucumán from 1812 to 1820. He was personal physician to Manuel Belgrano and helped him translate George Washington's "Farewell Address" into Spanish. He wrote *Memoria sobre la Dilatacion Progresiva del Aire Atmosferico* (Buenos Aires, 1819). He was physician of Martín Güemes in Salta from 1820 until his death. *References*: *Cutolo*; and Romero Sosa, "Tres Medicos Coloniales en Salta: Miln, Redhead y Castellanos," *Publicaciones de la Catedra de Historia de la Medicina* [Buenos Aires] 8 (1944): 217–33.

REDPATH, JAMES (1833–1891). Journalist and editor, born in Berwick-on-Tweed, Scotland. He came with his family to the United States about 1850 and settled near Kalamazoo, Michigan. Redpath was a printer and writer in Detroit, a correspondent, and, after 1852, staff member and contributor for the *New York Tribune*. He visited Haiti in 1859 and again in 1860, developed a colonization scheme, and edited *A Guide to Hayti* (Boston, 1860). In 1860, he became general agent of emigration in the United States for the Republic of Haiti and set up his headquarters in Boston. Immigrants went to Haiti in 1861 and 1862 but the scheme soon failed. He was a war correspondent during the Civil War. He was later superintendent of education in Charleston, South Carolina, and in 1868 established the Boston Lyceum Bureau, an agency for booking lectures. Died February 10, 1891, after being run over by a streetcar, in New York City. *References*: James Redpath Papers, Manuscript Division, Library of Congress; Willis D. Boyd, "James Redpath and American Negro Colonization in Haiti, 1860–1862," *TA* 12 (1955): 169–82; *DAB*; *NYT*, February 11, 1891; and William Seraille, "Afro-American Emigration to Haiti during the American Civil War," *TA* 35 (1978): 185–200.

REED, ALMA M(ARIE) (SULLIVAN) (1896–1966). Author. Reed graduated from Los Angeles Normal School. She was a newspaper reporter in San Francisco and came to Mexico in 1923. She planned to marry Governor Felipe Carrillo Puerto of Yucatán, who was executed by rebel forces during the Mexican revolution in 1924, twelve days before the scheduled wedding. She remained in Mexico, was a reporter for the *New York Times* and for California and Mexican newspapers, and wrote a weekly column in *The News*, an English-language newspaper in Mexico City. She wrote *The Mexican Muralists* (New York, 1960) and *The Ancient Past of Mexico* (New York, 1966). Died November 20, 1966, in Mexico City. *Reference*: *NYT*, November 21, 1966.

REED, JOHN (1887–1920). Journalist, born October 22, 1887, in Portland, Oregon. Reed graduated from Harvard University. He served on the staff of *American Magazine* from 1910 to 1913 and then on the staff of *The Masses*. He was sent to Mexico by the *Metropolitan Magazine* to report on the Mexican Revolution, and accompanied Francisco (Pancho) Villa's army. His articles were later published in *Insurgent Mexico* (New York, 1914). He reported from Germany and Eastern Europe at the beginning of World War I, went to Russia and reported the Russian Revolution. Died October 19, 1920, in Moscow. *References*: *DAB*; Drewey W. Gunn, "Three Radicals and a Revolution: Reed, London, and Steffens in Mexico," *Southwest Review* 55 (1970): 393–410; Eric Homberger, *John Reed* (Manchester, 1991); *NCAB* 19:292; *NYT*, October 19, 1920; Richard O'Connor and Dale L. Walker, *The Lost Revolutionary: A Biography of John Reed* (New York, 1967); Jim Tuck, *Pancho Villa and John Reed: Two Faces of Romantic Revolution* (Tucson, 1984); and *WWWA*.

REED, WILL EUGENE (1867–1946). Missionary, born March 16, 1867, in Weeping Water, Nebraska. Reed graduated from Dartmouth College, and was ordained in 1892. He held a pastorate in Dallas, Texas, from 1892 to 1896. He was independent missionary under the Evangelical Missionary Union in Guayaquil, Ecuador, teaching English at the Vincente Rocafuerte College of Guayaquil from 1910 to 1920. He was missionary under the Christian and Missionary Alliance after 1922, and superintendent of the Ecuador Christian and Missionary Alliance from 1922 to 1930. Died January 26, 1946, in Guayaquil, Ecuador. *References: The Alliance Weekly*, March 9, 1946; *WWLA*.

REILY, E(MMETT) MONT(GOMERY) (1866–1954). Businessman and colonial administrator, born October 21, 1866, in Sedalia, Pettis County, Missouri, and grew up in Fort Worth, Texas. Reily graduated from Texas Wesleyan University. He was engaged in the real estate and brokerage business and was involved in the mortgage loan business in Kansas City after 1910. He was assistant postmaster of Kansas City from 1904 to 1912. He was governor of Puerto Rico from 1921 to 1923. He advocated the ''Americanization'' of the island and its incorporation as an American state, and his administration was unpopular. Died October 31, 1954, in Kansas City. *References*: E. Mont. Reily Papers, New York Public Library; *NCAB* B:231; and *NYT*, November 1, 1954.

REINKE, JONATHAN (1860–1928). Clergyman, born July 9, 1860, in Brooklyn, New York. Reinke attended the Moravian College and Theological Seminary (Bethlehem, Pa.) and was ordained in 1882. He was a teacher and assistant missionary in Jamaica from 1879 until his death. He served in Carmel from 1881 until 1885 and in Irwin Hill in 1885, and then was in charge of the Moravian church in Kingston from 1885 until his death. He was active in promoting education in Jamaica, serving for twenty-five years as secretary of the government's board of education and for many years as a director of the Mico Training College in Kingston. He rebuilt the Moravian church in Kingston following its destruction in the earthquake of 1907 and was a member of the relief committee following the earthquake. Died July 29, 1928, in Kingston, Jamaica. *Reference*: *NCAB* 22:265.

RÉMY, HENRY (ca. 1811–1867). Editor and author, born in Agen, Department of Lot-en-Garonne, France. Rémy was exiled from France after the revolution of 1830 and came to the United States about 1836. He taught French and Italian in New Orleans, studied law, and was admitted to the bar in 1840. He was involved in publishing a French newspaper. He joined William Walker* in Nicaragua. After Walker's defeat in 1857, he escaped to Santo Domingo. He made a long trip over the island of Hispaniola, crossed to Mexico and finally returned to New Orleans. He published his impressions of Mexico (in French) in *Tierra Caliente: Impressions au Mexique* (St. Jacques, 1859). He left in manuscript a partial autobiography, a long account about Santo Domingo, another of Haiti, and a history of the Walker expedition. Died February 21, 1867, in New Orleans. *References*: *DAB*; and *WWWA*.

RENO, LOREN M(ARION) (1872–1935). Missionary, born June 17, 1872, in New Castle, Pennsylvania. Reno graduated from Bucknell University and Crozier Theological Seminary. He was a missionary under the Foreign Mission

Board of the Southern Baptist Convention* in Brazil from 1904 until his death in 1935. He served in Vitória, state of Espírito Santo, where he established the Colegio Batista. He wrote (with his wife, Alice W. Reno) *Reminiscences: Twenty-Five Years in Victoria, Brazil* (Richmond, Va., 1930). Died in Brazil in 1935.

RENWICK, WILLIAM W. (1890–1950). Financial adviser, born in Marengo, Illinois. Renwick graduated from Beloit College and Columbia University. He went to South America for the National Cash Register Company in 1912 and joined the National City Bank* in 1918. He was named American fiscal representative in control of customs of El Salvador in 1923. In 1925, he served on the Kemmerer mission for the organization of the finances of Chile, was consultant to the government of Guatemala on customs legislation in 1927, worked with the Kemmerer mission on Columbian finances in 1930, and was director of the Social Betterment Corporation of El Salvador from 1943 until his death. Died March 27, 1950, in San Salvador, El Salvador. *Reference*: *NYT*, March 28, 1950.

REVERE, JOSEPH WARREN (1812–1880). Naval officer, born May 17, 1812, in Boston. Revere entered the U.S. Navy as a midshipman in 1828. He served in the Mexican War. He resigned from the navy in 1850, settled on a ranch near Sonoma, California, and made trading voyages down the Mexican coast. He served as a colonel in the Mexican Army in 1851–1852, organizing the artillery branch. He was badly wounded in 1852 during an insurrection in Morelia, state of Michoacán, Mexico. He served in the Union Army during the Civil War. He wrote *Keel and Saddle: A Retrospect of Forty Years of Military and Naval Service* (Boston, 1872). Died April 20, 1880, in Hoboken, New Jersey. *References*: *DAB*; and *NCAB* 4:37.

REYNOLDS, THOMAS C(AUTE) (1821–1887). Lawyer, born October 11, 1821, in Charleston, South Carolina, and grew up in Virginia. Reynolds graduated from the University of Virginia, studied in Heidelberg (Germany), and was admitted to the bar in 1844. He was secretary of legation in Madrid. He moved to St. Louis in 1850 and was U.S. district attorney for Missouri from 1853 to 1857, lieutenant governor of Missouri in 1860–1861, and governor-in-exile from 1862 to 1865. After the war, he fled to Mexico where he was counselor to the Emperor Maximilian and general superintendent of the Mexican Railway Company in 1867. He returned to the United States in 1868, served in the state legislature from 1874 to 1876, and was member of a U.S. Commission to South and Central America in 1886. Committed suicide March 30, 1887, in St. Louis. *References*: Thomas C. Reynolds Papers, Manuscript Division, Library of Congress; and *BDC*.

REYNOLDS METALS COMPANY. Founded in 1919 as the U.S. Foil Company, it was incorporated as the Reynolds Metals Company in 1928. It organized the Reynolds Jamaica Mines, Limited, in 1944, and began production in 1951. It sold 51 percent of its mines and land in Jamaica to the Jamaican government in 1975. It opened a wholly owned extraction subsidiary, the Reynolds Guyana Mines, Limited, in British Guiana in 1952. It was nationalized by Guyana in 1975. It also had mines in Haiti and Brazil. It founded an aluminum company in Venezuela in 1960 and had other subsidiaries in Santo Domingo, Mexico, and Peru. *References*: Monique P. Garrity, "The Multinational Corporation in Extractive Industries: A Case Study of Reynolds Haitian Mines, Inc.," in *Working Papers in Haitian Society and Culture* (New Haven, Conn., 1975), pp. 183–290; "Recycling of Reynolds Metals," *Forbes* 113 (January 15, 1974): 22–24; and Margaret A. Rowles, "Reynolds Metals Company: A Corporate Response to Expropriation of Extraction Industries in Developing Countries," M.A. thesis, University of Virginia, 1982.

RICE, [ALEXANDER] HAMILTON (1875–1956). Explorer and geographer, born August 29, 1875, in Boston. Rice graduated from Harvard University and Harvard Medical School, and attended the School of Geographical Surveying and Field Astronomy of the Royal Geographical Society (London). From 1901 to 1925, he explored and mapped some five hundred thousand square miles of jungle in South America. He organized and led seven expeditions to the vicinity of the Colombia Caqueta, the Brazilian Amazonas, and the Venezuelan Guayana. His early surveys were mostly in Colombia. He later explored the tributaries of the Amazon River, observing and mapping the geography of the northwest Amazon basin. In 1901, he duplicated Francisco de Orellana's voyage down the Amazon. In 1907, he followed Simón Bolívar's route from Caracas to Bogota and then to the sources of the Rio Uaupés, which he followed to the Rio Negro. In 1912, he returned to the Amazon basin to identify the rivers and to ascertain the character of the country. He served as director and surgeon of a base hospital of the American Ambulance Service in France, and then in the U.S. Navy during World War I. In 1919, he made an expedition in an attempt to find the sources of the Orinoco River in the Roraima Mountains and to make further observations of the Rio Negro in the Amazons. In 1917, he went to Rio Negro and began mapping the Rio Casiquiare. In 1919–1920, he again mapped the Rio Casiquiare. In 1924–1925, he surveyed and mapped the Rio Branco and its western affluent, the Rio Uraricuera, following its source in the Sierra Parina, and demonstrated that the Orinoco and the Parima rivers had separate sources. He worked to improve sanitation and bring the first elements of civilization to the Indians of the Amazon basin. He established a community for Indians at Sao Gabriel on the Rio Negro, with an agricultural school, a training and elementary school, a nurses' school, and a hospital. He was instrumental in founding another hospital in Boa Vista on the Rio Branco and a research laboratory at Manaus. He founded the Institute of Geographical Exploration at Harvard University in 1930 and served as its director until 1952. He was a professor of geographical exploration at Harvard University from 1930 to 1952. Died July 23, 1956, in Newport, Rhode Island. *Reference*: *NCAB* 45:404.

RICHARDSON, TRACY (1889–1949). Soldier of fortune, born November 21, 1889, in Broken Bow, Nebraska, and grew up in Lamar, Missouri. Richardson worked for Prairies Gas and Oil Company in Oklahoma and Louisiana until 1909. He joined the Nicaraguan revolutionary army in 1909–1910 and the Venezuelan revolutionaries in 1911. He fought in a revolution in Honduras as a colonel under Lee Christmas* and in Mexico as a colonel under the Porfirio Díaz regime until 1914. He was then brigadier under Francisco Madero and chief of gunnery under Venustiano Carranza. He joined the U.S. troops landing at Veracruz, Mexico, in 1914, serving as a private scout for General Frederick Funston. He served during World War I with the Princess Patricia's Canadian Light Infantry and transferred to the British Royal Naval Air Services and later to the U.S. Air Service. He recounted his experiences in articles in the October through December 1925 issues of *Liberty Magazine*. Between the wars, he held various jobs, exploring mining areas of the Patuca River region of Honduras, conducting an oil survey in Guatemala, surveying the mahogany timber country in Chiapas, Mexico, and managing a gold mine at Ixtapan del Oro, Mexico. He rejoined the U.S. Army Air Corps during World War II. Died April 20, 1949, in Springfield, Missouri. *References*: *NYT*, April 23, 1949; *Time*, May 2, 1949; and Dale L. Walker, *Mavericks: Ten Uncorralled Westerners* (Phoenix, Ariz., 1989), pp. 73–82.

RICKETSON, OLIVER (GARRISON, JR.) (1894–1952). Archaeologist and explorer, born September 19, 1894, in Pittsburgh, and grew up in Cumberland Island, Georgia. Ricketson graduated from Harvard University and Harvard Medical School but did not practice medicine. He served in the U.S. Navy during World War I. He participated in archeological expeditions in Central America from 1921 to 1925, in Yucatán in 1921 and 1922 and Petén in 1923. He also excavated at Uaxactún, Guatemala. In 1929, he flew with Charles A. Lindbergh in an air expedition over unexplored jungles of South America. He lived in Guatemala City from 1929 to 1936 and returned to the United States in 1936. He wrote *Excavations at Baking Pot, British Honduras* (Washington, D.C., 1931) and was coauthor of *Uaxactún, Guatemala: Group E—1926–1931* (Washington, D.C., 1937). Died October 17, 1952, in Bar Harbor, Maine. *References*: *AmAntiq* 19 (1953): 69–72; and *NYT*, October 19, 1952.

RICKETTS, HOWARD TAYLOR (1871–1910). Pathologist, born February 9, 1871, in Findlay, Ohio. Ricketts graduated from University of Nebraska and Northwestern University and studied in London, Berlin, Vienna, and Paris. He was instructor and later, assistant professor, in the department of pathology and bacteriology at the University of Chicago from 1902 to 1910. He investigated

Rocky Mountain spotted fever. He established a laboratory in Mexico City in 1909 to investigate tabardillo, or Mexican typhus fever, and discovered its cause. Died of Mexican typhus fever, May 3, 1910, in Mexico City. *References*: *DAB S1*; *DAMB 84*; and *NCAB* 34:543.

RICKETTS, LOUIS D(AVIDSON) (1859–1940). Mining engineer, born December 19, 1859, in Elkton, Maryland. Ricketts graduated from Princeton University. He was surveyor and superintendent of mines in Colorado from 1883 to 1885 and state geologist from Wyoming from 1887 to 1890. He was consulting engineer for Phelps, Dodge and Company from 1890 to 1906. He was involved in various operations in the Southwest and in northern Sonora, Mexico, until 1905. In 1895, he began extensive investigations in northern Sonora, and upon his advice, the Fortuna and Philares properties at Nacozari were purchased by Phelps, Dodge and Company from the Guggenheims in 1898. He became general manager of the Montezuma mine there. He was a manager of the Old Dominion mine at Golbe, Arizona, from 1903 to 1906, consulting engineer for Cananea Consolidated Copper Company in Cananea, Mexico, and that firm's general manager in 1907. He was later consulting engineer for various other companies with offices in Warren, Arizona, and later in New York City and Pasadena, California. He was president of the Arizona Oil Company from 1914 until his death. He purchased the Erupcion Mining Company and the Ahumada Lead Company in Chihuahua, Mexico, in 1919, and was their president. Died March 4, 1940, in Los Angeles. *References*: Walter R. Bimson, *Louis D. Ricketts (1859–1950)* (Princeton, N.J., 1949); *NCAB* 33:189; and *WWWA*.

RIDDLE, JOHN WALLACE (1864–1941). Diplomat, born July 12, 1864, in Philadelphia. Riddle graduated from Harvard University and Columbia Law School and studied at the Ecole des Sciences Politiques in Paris. He entered the diplomatic service in 1893, was secretary of legation in Turkey from 1893 to 1900, secretary of embassy in Russia from 1901 to 1903, agent and consul general in Egypt from 1903 to 1905, U.S. minister to Romania and Serbia in 1905–1906, and ambassador to Russia from 1906 to 1909. A Republican, he was out of the diplomatic service until 1921. He served in the military intelligence branch at the U.S. War College in Washington, D.C., in 1917–1918. He was U.S. ambassador to Argentina from 1921 until his retirement in 1925 and was involved in efforts to improve trade relations between Argentina and the United States. Died December 8, 1941, in Farmington, Connecticut. *References*: *DADH*; *NCAB* 30:288; and *NYT*, December 9, 1941.

RIDGWAY, ROBERT (1850–1929). Ornithologist, born July 2, 1850, in Mount Carmel, Illinois. Ridgway was a zoologist with the U.S. Geological Exploration of the Fortieth Parallel from 1867 to 1869 and with the Smithsonian Institution after 1869. He was curator of birds at the U.S. National Museum after 1880. He carried out fieldwork in Costa Rica in 1904 and 1908. He wrote

Birds of North and Middle America (Washington, D.C., 1901–1919). Died March 25, 1929, in Olney, Illinois. *References*: *ACAB*; *AMWS*; *DAB*; *DSB*; *NCAB* 8:460; *NYT*, March 26, 1929; and *WWWA*.

RIGGS, ELMER S(AMUEL) (1869–1963). Paleontologist, born January 23, 1869, in Trafalgar, Indiana. Riggs graduated from the University of Kansas and studied at Princeton University. He was assistant curator of paleontology at the Field Museum of Natural History from 1899 to 1921, associate curator from 1921 to 1937, and curator from 1937 until his retirement in 1942. He was a member of paleontological expeditions for the Field Museum of Natural History to Argentina and Bolivia from 1923 to 1925 and in 1926–1927. He wrote on his experiences in the May 1926 issue of *Natural History*. Died March 25, 1963, in Sedan, Kansas. *References*: *AMWS*; *BGSA* 75 (1964): P129–P131; and *Simpson*, ch. 10.

RIHL, GEORGE L(AWRENCE) (1887– ?). Aviator, born July 5, 1887, in Gunnison, Colorado. Rihl graduated from the University of Washington. He was involved in oil well drilling in the early 1920s. In 1924, he joined with William (''Slim'') Mallory to fly payrolls to inaccessible mining camps in the Tampico area. He founded Compañía Mexicana de Aviación, S.A.* in 1924 and was its president until 1928, when it was bought by Pan American Airways. He was vice president of the Pan American Airways System and of Pan American-Grace Airways, Incorporated, from 1929 until his retirement in 1945. He then went back to Mexico. *Reference*: *Who's Who in Aviation* (Chicago, 1942).

RIVER PLATE COLLEGE. Coeducational college, with a secondary section, founded by the Seventh-Day Adventist Church in 1898 in Puiggari, near Diamante, Argentina. It was known as Diamante College from 1901 to 1908. The present name was adopted in 1908. *References*: *SDAE*; and Egil H. Wensell, ''River Plate College: An Historical Study of a Missionary Institution, 1898–1951,'' Ph.D. diss., Andrews University, 1982.

ROBERTS, HENRY B(UCHTEL) (1904–1960). Archaeologist and anthropologist, born April 12, 1904, in Denver, Colorado. Roberts graduated from the University of Denver. He was staff member of the division of historical research and archaeology of the Carnegie Institution of Washington, D.C., after 1930. He headed several archaeological expeditions to Mexico and Central America in the 1930s under the sponsorship of the Peabody Museum of Harvard University and the Carnegie Institution of Washington, and carried on excavations in 1930, 1931, and 1933 in Panama. He was coauthor of *Excavations at the Sitio Conte* (Cambridge, Mass., 1937). He served in the U.S. Army during World War II. He was employed by Prentice-Hall, Incorporated, after 1946. Died April 3, 1960, in New York City. *References*: *AMWS*; and *NYT*, April 5, 1960.

ROBERTS, WILLIAM MILNOR (1810–1881). Civil engineer, born February 12, 1810, in Philadelphia. Roberts studied architectural drafting. He was engaged in the construction of canals and railroads in Pennsylvania from 1825 to 1849 and in building the Bellefontaine and Indiana, the Allegheny Valley, the Atlantic and Mississippi, and the Iron Mountain railroads. He was involved in constructing several midwestern railroads from 1855 to 1857. From 1857 to 1866 he was in Brazil, where he obtained a contract to build the Dom Pedro Segundo Railroad. He returned to the United States in 1866. He was associate chief engineer in the construction of the bridge across the Mississippi in St. Louis and chief engineer of the Northern Pacific Railroad from 1869 to 1879. He went to Brazil again in 1879 as chief engineer of all public works in the country, and was occupied with the examination of rivers, harbors, and waterworks there. Died July 14, 1881, in Soledade, Brazil. *References*: *ACAB*; *DAB*; *NCAB* 29:182; and *WWWA*.

ROBINSON, CHRISTOPHER (1806–1889). Lawyer and diplomat, born May 15, 1806, in Providence, Rhode Island. Robinson graduated from Brown University, studied law, and was admitted to the bar in 1833. He practiced law in Cumberland after 1833. He was attorney general of Rhode Island in 1854–1855 and a member of the U.S. House of Representatives from 1859 to 1861. He was U.S. minister to Peru from 1861 to 1865. He negotiated treaties in the settlement of difficulties that had arisen with that country and settled most of the claims against the Peruvian government by means of a mixed claims commission. Although Peru had many Confederate supporters, he succeeded in swaying the government to the Union side. He was Peruvian general diplomatic agent to Europe in 1865–1866. He resumed his law practice in Woonsocket in 1866. Died October 3, 1889, in Woonsocket, Rhode Island. *References*: *BDAC*; *DAB*; *DADH*; *NCAB* 12:117; and *WWWA*.

ROBINSON, JEREMY (1787–1834). Diplomat, born May 30, 1787, in Boxford, Massachusetts. Robinson was a commercial agent for Massachusetts merchants in Europe from 1808 to 1813 and then settled in western Virginia. He was an agent for commerce and seamen in Chile and Peru from 1818 to 1823, even though his commission was revoked in 1817 at his time of sailing from the United States, and he reported extensively about these countries. He was special diplomatic agent to Havana, Cuba, to receive the Spanish archives of Florida from 1832 to 1834. Died November 11, 1834, in Havana. *References*: Jeremy Robinson Papers, Manuscript Division, Library of Congress; Jeremy Robinson, "Diario Personal, May-June 1818," *RCHG* 85, no. 93 (1938): 99–126; R. W. Gronet, "Early Latin American–United States Contacts: An Analysis of Jeremy Robinson's Communications to the Monroe Administration," Ph.D. diss., Catholic University of America, 1970; A. J. Hanna, "Diplomatic Missions of the United States to Cuba to Secure the Spanish Archives of Florida," in *Hispanic American Essays*, ed. A. Curtis Wilgus (Chapel Hill, N.C., 1942),

pp. 208–33; Eugenio Pereira Salas, "Jeremias Robinson, Agente Norteamericano en Chile (1818–1823)," *RCHG* 82 (1937): 201–36.

ROBINSON, TRACY (1833–1915). Author, born December 22, 1833, in Clar-
endon, New York. Robinson attended Rochester University and Antioch College.
He was superintendent of the Mississippi Central and Tennessee Railroad from
1857 to 1861 and fiscal and shipping agent and assistant superintendent of the
Panama Railroad from 1861 to 1874. He was U.S. vice-consul at Colon from
1863 to 1868 and in 1892 and editor of *Panama Star and Herald* from 1876 to
1878. He wrote *Fifty Years in Panama, 1861–1911* (New York, 1912). Died in
Panama. *Reference*: WWWA.

ROBINSON, WILLIAM DAVIS (1774–1822?). Merchant, born probably in
Georgetown, Maryland (later, Washington, D.C.). Robinson was involved in
business from an early age. He went to Caracas, Venezuela, in 1799 on business
and had business dealings with the Venezuelan government that were unprofit-
able. In 1806, he went to Cartagena, Colombia. In 1816, he went to Mexico,
to collect a large amount of money from the Mexican revolutionary authorities.
He was captured by the Spaniards, was imprisoned at Oaxaca and Veracruz,
and was taken to Spain. He escaped in 1819 and returned to the United States.
He wrote *Memoirs of the Mexico Revolution: Including a Narrative of the Expedition of General Xavier Mina* (Philadelphia, 1820). Died sometime before
1823. *References*: NCAB 18:185; Eduardo E. Ríos, *El Historiador Davis Robinson y su Aventura en Nueva Espana* (Mexico, 1939); and Eduardo E. Ríos,
Robinson y su Aventura en Mexico (Mexico, 1958).

ROCHELLE, JAMES HENRY (1826–1889). Naval officer, born November
1, 1826 in Jerusalem (later Courtland), Southampton County, Virginia. Rochelle
was appointed acting midshipman in the U.S. Navy in 1841, served during the
Mexican War, and graduated from the U.S. Naval Academy in 1848. He served
in the Mediterranean Squadron from 1849 to 1853, with Matthew C. Perry's
expedition to Japan from 1853 to 1855, and with the U.S. Coast Survey from
1855 to 1858. He served on the USS *Southern Star* on the expedition to Paraguay
in 1859. He served in the Confederate Navy during the Civil War. He farmed
in Southampton County, Virginia, until 1870. He served with the Hydrographic
Commission of the Amazon in Iquitos, Peru, from 1870 to 1874 and participated
in the hydrographic survey of the upper Amazon River east of the Andes in Peru
from 1870 to 1874. He was later again involved in farming. He wrote *Life of
Rear Admiral John Randolph Tucker, Commander in the Navy of the United
States . . . with an Appendix Containing Notes on Navigation of the Upper Amazon River and Its Principal Tributaries, and Containing a Biographical Sketch
of the Author* (Washington, D.C., 1903), which was published posthumously.
Died March 31, 1889, near Courtland, Southampton County, Virginia. *Reference*: James Henry Rochelle Papers, Duke University Library, Durham, N.C.

ROCK, MILES (1840–1901). Engineer, born October 10, 1840, in Ephrata, Pennsylvania. Rock attended Franklin and Marshall College and graduated from Lehigh University. He was instructor in mineralogy and geology at Lehigh University. He served in the Union Army during the Civil War. In 1870, he went to Córdoba, Argentina, as an astronomical assistant in the observatory and was engaged in mapping the stars of the southern skies from 1870 to 1873. He was attached to the U.S. Hydrographic Office from 1874 to 1877 and was assistant astronomer of the U.S. Naval Observatory from 1879 to 1883. He was head of the Guatemala Commission to determine the Mexico-Guatemala boundary from 1883 to 1898. Died October 1, 1901, in Guatemala City, Guatemala. *Reference*: *AA* 3 (1901): 208.

ROCKEFELLER, NELSON A(LDRICH) (1908–1979). Public official, born July 8, 1908, in Bar Harbor, Maine, and grew up in New York City. Rockefeller graduated from Dartmouth College. He was involved in banking, international business, and philanthrophy, and served as director of the Creole Petroleum Company from 1935 to 1940. In 1940, he created Campañia de Fomento Venezolano as a development enterprise in Venezuela. He was coordinator of inter-American affairs from 1940 to 1944 and assistant secretary of state for Latin American Affairs in 1944–1945. He founded the International Basic Economy Corporation* in 1947. He was governor of New York from 1958 until 1973. In 1969, he was sent by President Richard Nixon as head of a fact-finding mission to Latin America and prepared *Rockefeller Report on the Americas: The Official Report of a United States Presidential Mission for the Western Hemisphere* (New York, 1969), which portrayed a crisis in Latin America and made numerous recommendations for U.S.–Latin American policy. He was vice president of the United States from 1974 to 1977. Died January 26, 1979, in New York City. *References*: *CB* 1951; Elizabeth A. Cobbs, "Entrepreneurship as Diplomacy: Nelson Rockefeller and the Development of the Brazilian Capital Market," *Business History Review* 63 (1989): 88–121; Peter Collier and David Horowitz, *The Rockefellers: An American Dynasty* (New York, 1976); *DADH*; *ELA*; Claude C. Erb, "Nelson Rockefeller and United States–Latin American Relations, 1940–1945," Ph.D. diss., Clark University, 1982; Joe A. Morris, *Nelson Rockefeller* (New York, 1960); *NCAB* I:196; *NYT*, January 28, 1979; *PolProf:Johnson*; *Polprof:Kennedy*; *PolProf:Nixon/Ford*; *Polprof:Truman*; and *WWWA*.

RODDY, WILLIAM FRANKLIN (1871–1940). Financial adviser, born June 27, 1871, in Larisa, Texas. Roddy studied accountancy. He fought during the Spanish-American War. He served as collector of customs in various ports in the Philippines from 1900 to 1918. He was collector of customs in Corinto, Nicaragua, from 1918 to 1927. He was adviser of customs for the Ecuadorian government in 1927, director general of customs there from 1927 to 1930, and technical adviser of customs in 1930–1931. He was member of the Kemmerer mission to reorganize the finances of Peru in 1931 and technical adviser of customs in Colombia from 1931 to 1933. Died February 5, 1940. *Reference*: *WWWA*.

RODNEY, CAESAR AUGUSTUS (1772–1824). Lawyer and diplomat, born January 4, 1772, in Dover, Delaware, and grew up in Wilmington, Delaware. Rodney graduated from the University of Pennsylvania, studied law, and was admitted to the bar in 1793. He practiced law in Wilmington and New Castle after 1793. He was a member of the Delaware house of representatives from 1796 to 1802, member of the U.S. House of Representatives from 1803 to 1805, and U.S. attorney general from 1807 to 1811. He served in the War of 1812 and was a member of the state senate from 1815 to 1817. He was a member of the special commission to South America in 1817–1818 for the purpose of ascertaining the political status of the newly established republics in that continent. He served in the U.S. House of Representatives from 1821 to 1823 and in the U.S. Senate in 1822–1823. He was the first U.S. minister to the Argentine Republic from 1823 until his death. Died June 10, 1824, in Buenos Aires. His son, **THOMAS MCKEAN RODNEY** (1800–1874), attended the U.S. Military Academy and studied law. He accompanied his father to Buenos Aires in 1823–1824 and was vice-consul in Havana, Cuba, in 1824–1825 and consul in Havana from 1825 to 1829. *References*: Caesar A. Rodney Papers, Manuscript Division, Library of Congress; *ACAB*; *DAB*; Peter T. Dalleo, "Thomas McKean Rodney: U.S. Consul in Cuba: The Havana Years, 1825–1829," *Delaware History* 22 (1987): 204–18; Enrique Loudet, *El Primer Diplomático Norteamericano en la República Argentina* (Buenos Aires, 1938); *NCAB* 3:11; *Udaondo*; and *WWWA*.

ROMUALDI, SERAFINO (1900–1967). Labor official, born November 18, 1900, in Bastia Umbria, Italy. He fled Italy in 1923 and came to the United States. He joined the editorial staff of the International Ladies Garment Workers Union (ILGWU) in 1933. He was an agent of the U.S. Bureau of Latin American Research in South America during World War II. He was Latin American director for the Free Trade Union Committee of the American Federation of Labor after 1945 to 1961, which was intended to provide support for noncommunist labor groups, and director of the American Institute for Free Labor Development (AIFLD) from 1961 to 1965, which worked to counteract the impact of the Cuban revolution on Latin America. He wrote *Presidents and Peons: Recollections of a Labor Ambassador in Latin America* (New York, 1967). Died November 11, 1967, in Mexico City. *References*: Gary M. Fink, ed., *Biographical Dictionary of American Labor* (Westport, Conn., 1984); and *PolProf:Kennedy*.

ROOSEVELT, THEODORE (1858–1919). Public official, born October 27, 1858, in New York City. Roosevelt graduated from Harvard University. He served in the New York State Assembly. He was civil service commissioner from 1889 to 1895, president of New York City's Board of Police Commissioners, and assistant secretary of the Navy. With Leonard Wood,* he organized a volunteer cavalry regiment, known as the "Rough Riders,"* and served during the Spanish-American War in Cuba. He was governor of New York, vice president of the United States in 1900–1901, and president from 1901 to 1909. He participated in the Roosevelt-Rondon expedition in 1913–1914, which descended and mapped the Rio de Duvida ("River of Doubt"), a tributary of the Madeira River. He wrote *Through the Brazilian Wilderness* (New York, 1914). Died January 6, 1919, in Sagamore Hill, near Oyster Bay, Long Island, New York. *References*: Theodore Roosevelt Papers, Manuscript Division, Library of Congress; Paul A. Cutright, *Theodore Roosevelt, the Naturalist* (New York, 1956); *DAB*; and Joseph L. Gardner, *Departing Glory: Theodore Roosevelt as Ex-President* (New York, 1973).

ROOSEVELT COROLLARY. Formulated by President Theodore Roosevelt in 1904, it interpreted the Monroe Doctrine and held that under certain circumstances, the United States might exercise international police power in the Western Hemisphere and was duty-bound to intervene unilaterally in the affairs of the nations of Latin America when their domestic politics or finances were in such disorder as to invite intervention by European powers. This interpretation became the policy mandate for numerous interventions in the Caribbean and Central America. It was repudiated in 1930 and renounced in 1933. *References*: *ELA*; Gerald K. Haines, "The Roosevelt Administration Interprets the Monroe Doctrine," *Australian Journal of Politics and History* 24 (1978): 322–45; and J. Fred Rippy, "The Antecedents of the Roosevelt Corollary of the Monroe Doctrine," *PHR* 9 (1940): 267–79.

ROOT, JOSEPH POMEROY (1826–1885). Physician and diplomat, born April 23, 1826, in Greenwich, Massachusetts. Root graduated from Berkshire Medical College (Pittsfield, Mass.). He practiced medicine in New Hartford, Connecticut, after 1851 and served in the Connecticut legislature in 1855–1856. He emigrated to Kansas in 1856. He was state senator from 1857 to 1859 and lieutenant governor from 1861 to 1863. He served as army surgeon in the Union Army during the Civil War. He was U.S. minister to Chile from 1870 to 1873. He traveled extensively throughout Chile, crossed the Andes into Argentina, and reported on the trip to the State Department in the form of a treatise on the cause of earthquakes. He accompanied the Chilean minister of foreign affairs to southern Chile to investigate the Indians, provided useful medical service during a severe smallpox epidemic in Santiago in 1872, and served on the Santiago Board of Health. He resumed medical practice in Kansas. Died July 20, 1885, in Wyandotte, Kansas. *References*: *DAB*; *DADH*; *NCAB* 13:309; and *WWWA*.

ROPES, HENRY J. (? –1873). Merchant, born in Salem, Massachusetts. Ropes came to Buenos Aires in 1828. He started an import and export business in 1843 in the name of Enrique J. Ropes and Company, which was considered one of the most important American import and export houses in Buenos Aires.

It traded principally in the import of flour, sugar, lumber, and hardware, and in exports of hides, tallow, and guano. Died July 19, 1873, in Buenos Aires. *References*: *Cutolo*; and *Drees*.

ROSENCRANS, WILLIAM S(TARKE) (1819–1898). Army officer, born September 6, 1819, in Delaware County, Ohio. Rosencrans graduated from the U.S. Military Academy in 1842. He was an instructor there until 1847 and then held various other assignments. He left active service in 1854, worked as an engineer and architect in Cincinnati, and managed an oil refinery. He served in the Union Army during the Civil War. He was a U.S. minister to Mexico in 1868–1869. He encouraged railway construction and helped bring about greater political stability. He was later involved in various Mexican railroads and industrial ventures, including the Tehuantepec Isthmian railway project from 1869 to 1881. He was a member of the U.S. House of Representatives from 1881 to 1885 and register of the Treasury Department from 1885 to 1893. Died March 11, 1898, in Redondo Beach, California. *References*: *BDAC*; *DAB*; *DADH*; David M. Pletcher, "General William S. Rosencrans and the Mexican Transcontinental Railroad Project," *Mississippi Valley Historical Review* 38 (1952): 657–78; *Pletcher*, ch. 2; *NCAB* 4:162; *NYT*, March 12, 1898; and *WWWA*.

ROSENTHAL, LOUIS SAMUEL PHILIP (1890–1943). Banker, born November 9, 1890, in St. Louis, Missouri, and grew up in Watertown, New York. Rosenthal attended Cornell University. He was a reporter on the Watertown *Daily Times* and then was employed in railroad construction in Massachusetts and British Columbia. In 1914, he was an assistant engineer on the staff of the Alaska Railroad Commission, constructing the Anchorage Railroad. He served in the U.S. Army during World War I. He was engaged in engineering construction in the Panama Canal Zone. He entered banking in 1919. He was a member of the staff of the National Bank of Nicaragua at Managua after 1920, assistant manager from 1920 to 1924, general manager from 1924 to 1930, and controller of the currency of Nicaragua. He performed intelligence work for the U.S. Marine Corps. He was in charge of the Chase National Bank of New York's branch in Havana in 1930–1931, second vice president and manager of the Havana branch from 1931 until 1940, in charge of the bank's Latin American business in New York City after 1940, and in charge of the foreign interests of the Chase Bank after 1942. Died January 20, 1943, in New Rochelle, New York. *References*: *NYT*, January 21, 1943; and *WWWA*.

ROSS, LOUIS (1859– ?). Mining engineer, born May 25, 1859, in Bangor, Maine. A self-made man, Ross spent a great part of his life in mining and ranching in Mexico. In 1881, he went to Mexico to work in the mines of Cusihuiriachic and Santa Eulalia. He was involved in the building of the Mexican Central Railroad in Chihuahua and was later in charge of various mining properties, some of them as part owner. He was managing director of the San Luis

Company, near Durango, from 1902 to 1906. He examined the copper deposits at Chuquicamata in Chile in 1911, obtained an option, and established the Chile Copper Company. *Reference*: *NCAB* 18:127.

ROSS, RODERICK MALCOLM (1834–1898). Industrialist and businessman, born in New York City. Ross came to Rosario, Argentina, in 1866, as a machinist on a tugboat. In 1867, he acquired an iron and bronze foundry, and manufactured a variety of machinery and equipment. In 1874, he manufactured water pumps which were used to provide water for Rosario, and 1885 he obtained the contract to install the tramway in Rosario, the first section of which was laid by 1886. It was later extended throughout the city. Died May 29, 1898, in Buenos Aires. *Reference*: *Cutolo*.

"ROUGH RIDERS." Formally, the First United States Volunteer Cavalry Regiment, under the command of Leonard Wood. The "Rough Riders" took part in the Spanish-American War, fighting in Cuba. *References*: Charles Herner, *The Arizona Rough Riders* (Tucson, Ariz., 1970); Virgil C. Jones, *Roosevelt's Rough Riders* (Garden City, N.Y., 1971); and Clifford P. Westermeier, *Who Rush to Glory; the Cowboy Volunteers of 1898: Grigsby's Cowboys, Roosevelt's Rough Riders, Torrey's Rocky Mountain Riders* (Caldwell, Idaho, 1958).

ROUSE, IRVING (1913–   ). Archaeologist, born August 29, 1913, in Rochester, New York. Rouse graduated from Yale University. He was assistant curator of anthropology of the Peabody Museum of Natural History at Yale University from 1938 to 1947, associate curator from 1947 to 1954, and research associate in anthropology from 1954 to 1962. He was also assistant professor of anthropology from 1943 to 1948, associate professor from 1948 to 1954, and professor after 1970. He carried out archaeological field trips to Haiti in 1935, to Puerto Rico from 1936 to 1938, to Cuba in 1942, to Trinidad in 1946, and later to Venezuela, Martinique, St. Lucia, Antigua, Guadeloupe, Bahamas, and the Dominican Republic. He wrote *Prehistory in Haiti: A Study in Method* (New Haven, 1939), *Culture of the Ft. Liberte Region, Haiti* (New Haven, 1941), *Archaeology of the Maniabon Hills, Cuba* (New Haven, 1942), *Porto Rican Prehistory: Excavations in the Interior, South and East, Chronological Implications* (New York, 1952), *Porto Rican Prehistory: Introduction—Excavations in the West and North* (New York, 1952), and *Guianas: Indigenous Period* (Mexico, 1953). *References*: *AMWS*; *CA*; and *WWA*.

ROWE, BASIL L(EE) (1896–1973). Aviator, born February 10, 1896, in Shandaken, New York. Rowe learned to fly in Hempstead, New York, from 1916 to 1918. He served in the U.S. Army Air Service during World War I. He was a barnstormer–exhibition flyer in the United States, Mexico, West Indies, and Central America, and operator of Rowe Flyers, a barnstorming and exhibition firm, from 1919 to 1927. In 1927–1928, he established the West Indian Aerial

Express, the first airmail and passenger service in the West Indies, between the Virgin Islands and Santiago, Cuba. He was assigned to fly a new airmail route between Miami and Puerto Rico. His company was absorbed by Pan American Airways in 1928. He was captain for Pan American after 1928 and chief and senior pilot of its Latin-American division until his retirement in 1956. He wrote *Under My Wings* (Indianapolis, 1956). Died October 28, 1973, in Coral Cables, Florida. *References*: Albert A. LeShane, Jr., "Basil Rowe and the West Indian Aerial Express," *American Aviation Historical Society Journal* 26 (1981): 231–42; *NYT*, November 1, 1973; and *Who's Who in Aviation* (Chicago, 1942).

ROWE, JOHN HOWLAND (1918–   ). Anthropologist, born June 10, 1918, in Sorrento, Maine. Rowe graduated from Brown and Harvard universities and studied at the University of Paris. He served in the U.S. Army during World War II. He was a member of the faculty at the University of California at Berkeley after 1948 and professor of anthropology after 1956. He was also curator of South American anthropology at the Museum of Anthropology after 1949. He carried out field research in Guambia and Popayán, Colombia, from 1946 to 1948, and in Peru in 1939, 1941–1943, 1946, 1954, 1958–1959, 1961–1978, and 1980–1987. He wrote *An Introduction to the Archaeology of Cuzco* (Cambridge, Mass., 1944). *Reference*: WWA.

ROWE, LEO STANTON (1871–1946). Educator and diplomat, born September 17, 1871, in McGregor, Iowa, and grew up in Philadelphia. Rowe graduated from the University of Pennsylvania and the University of Halle (Germany) and was admitted to the bar in 1895. He was assistant professor of political science at the University of Pennsylvania from 1896 to 1904 and professor from 1904 until 1917. From 1900 to 1902, he was a member of the commission to revise and compile the laws of Puerto Rico and chairman of the Insular Code Commission. He was secretary of the United States–Mexico Mixed Claims Commission in 1916–1917 and U.S. assistant secretary of the Treasury from 1917 to 1920. He was director general of the Pan American Union from 1920 until his death. He traveled extensively in Latin America, encouraging cultural exchanges, improvement of education, and the establishment of libraries. Killed December 5, 1946, in a car accident, in Washington, D.C. *References*: *CB* 1947; *DAB S4*; *DADH*; *HAHR* 27 (1947): 187–88; "In Memoriam: Leo Stanton Rowe, Citizen of the Americas," *Pan American Union Bulletin* 81 (April 1947): 181–286; *NCAB* 18:316; *NYT*, December 6, 1946; A. Ortiz, "Legacy for Learning," *Americas* 8 (August 1956): 27–31; and Gustav A. Sallas, "Leo S. Rowe: Citizen of the Americas," Ph.D. diss., George Washington University, 1956.

ROYS, RALPH L(OVELAND) (1879–1965). Anthropologist, born February 14, 1879, in Greenville, Michigan. Roys graduated from the University of Michigan. He entered the family lumber business, and lived in Vancouver, British Columbia, from 1911 until 1940. He made the first trip to Mexico in 1906 and to

Yucatán in 1921, and made additional trips to Yucatán in 1933, 1935, 1937, 1942, 1949, and 1952. He was a part-time staff member of the Department of Middle American Research at Tulane University after 1924 and a part-time worker for the Division of Historical Research of the Carnegie Institution of Washington after 1932. He wrote *The Book of Chilam Balam of Chumayel* (Washington, D.C., 1933), *The Indian Background of Colonial Yucatán* (Washington, D.C., 1943), and *The Political Geography of the Yucatán Maya* (Washington, D.C., 1957), and was coauthor of *The Maya Chontal Indians of Acalan-Tixchel: A Contribution to the History and Ethnography of the Yucatán Peninsula* (Washington, D.C., 1948). Died December 12, 1965. *References*: *AmAntiq* 32 (1967): 95–99; and Pierre Ventura, *Maya Ethnohistorian: The Ralph L. Roys Papers* (Nashville, Tenn., 1978).

RUBENS, HORATIO (SEYMOUR) (1869–1941). Lawyer, born June 6, 1869, in New York City. Rubens graduated from the College of the City of New York and Columbia University and studied law. He was a clerk in the office of Elihu Root, later becoming the managing clerk. He was counsel to El Salvador and joined the Cuban junta which was formed in New York in 1895 to agitate for the independence of Cuba from Spain, acting as legal adviser to the Cuban Revolutionary Junta in New York in the 1890s. He divided his time between New York and Havana from 1895 to 1898. He was a close friend of Jose Marti. He was appointed colonel in the Cuban Army of Liberation. He was a member of the American Insular Commission to Puerto Rico in 1900, member of the commission for the division of codes and laws for Cuba and also a member of Cuba's tax, prison, and election law commissions, president of the Consolidated Railroads of Cuba, and president and chairman of the board of the Cuba Northern Railways Company until his death. He returned to the United States during World War I and later headed the United States Industrial Alcohol Company. He wrote *Liberty: The Story of Cuba* (New York, 1932). Died April 3, 1941, in New York. *References*: *NYT*, April 4, 1941; and *WWWA*.

RUPERT, JOSEPH ANTHONY (1916–1972). Plant pathologist, born October 23, 1916, in Eveleth, Minnesota. Rupert graduated from the University of Minnesota, Michigan State University, and West Virginia University. He served in the U.S. Army Medical Corps during World War II. He was field agronomist in the Rockefeller Foundation's agricultural program in Mexico from 1947 to 1950, associate plant pathologist and geneticist in the Cooperative Agricultural Research program of the Colombian government and the Rockefeller Foundation in Colombia from 1950 until 1955, director of the cooperative agricultural research and production program for the Chilean government and the Rockefeller Foundation in Chile from 1955 to 1965, and administrative representative of the Rockefeller Foundation in Chile from 1965 to 1968. He was involved in developing new wheat varieties at the University of California in Davis from 1968 until his death. Died May 16, 1972, in Sacramento, California. *References*: *NCAB* 58:230; and *NYT*, May 18, 1972.

RUPPERT, KARL (1895–1960). Archaeologist, born September 19, 1895, in Phoenix, Arizona. Ruppert graduated from the University of Arizona and George Washington and Harvard universities. He served in the U.S. Army during World War I. He was a member of the staff of the Carnegie Institution of Washington from 1925 until 1956, where he was involved in Maya archaeology. He carried out fieldwork at Chichén Itzá, participating in the exploration and study of Maya cities in the southern area and the east coast of Yucatán as well as in Campeche, Quintana Roo, and Nicaragua, and Guatemala. Died August 14, 1960, in Rochester, Minnesota. *References*: *AMWS*; and *AmAntiq* 27 (1961): 101–03.

RUSBY, HENRY HURD (1855–1940). Botanist, born April 26, 1855, in Franklin, New Jersey. Rusby was professor of materia medica at the Columbia University College of Pharmacy from 1888 to 1930. He also taught at the New York University Medical School and the New York Veterinary College. He conducted botanical explorations to establish new sources of supply for drugs and to search for new drug plants. He made the journey from La Paz to Pará in 1885–1886 to locate supplies of coca leaves and other plants, and to collect cinchona species. He conducted a botanical survey of Venezuela south of the Orinoco in 1896 and investigated rubber-yielding trees in Mexico. He traveled again from La Paz to Pará in 1919. He wrote *Jungle Memories* (New York, 1933). Died November 18, 1940, in Sarasota, Florida. *References*: George A. Bender, "Henry Hurd Rusby: Scientific Explorer, Societal Crusader, Scholastic Innovator," *Pharmacy in History* 23 (1981): 71–85; *DAB S2*; *Garden Journal* 24 (1974): 70–74; *NCAB* A:172; and *Science*, n.ser., 93 (1941): 53–54.

RUSSELL, JOHN HENRY (1872–1947). Marine Corps officer, born November 14, 1872, in Mare Island, California. Russell graduated from the U.S. Naval Academy in 1892 and was assigned to the U.S. Marine Corps in 1894. He served in the Spanish-American War. He was marine commandant at Camp Elliot, Panama Canal Zone, and was attached to the American legation in Peking, China, from 1910 to 1913. He was assigned to the Office of Naval Intelligence from 1913 to 1917 and was then commander of the Third Regiment with headquarters in Santo Domingo, the Dominican Republic. He later was ordered to Haiti to command the marines in that country. He was high commissioner to Haiti from 1922 with the rank of ambassador and remained in that position until 1934, when the United States withdrew its forces from Haiti. He was commanding officer of the Marine base at Quantico, Virginia, until 1933, assistant commandant of the marine corps in 1933–1934, and commandant from 1934 to 1936. He retired with the rank of major general in 1936. Died March 6, 1947, in Coronado, California. *Reference*: *NCAB* 39:379.

RUSSELL, WILLIAM WORTHINGTON (1859–1944). Diplomat, born December 3, 1859, in Washington, D.C. Russell graduated from the U.S. Naval Academy in 1881. As a civil engineer, he helped survey rail routes in South America, including the proposed route for the Tehuantepec ship–railway project in the 1880s. He was secretary of legation in Venezuela from 1895 to 1904; U.S. chargé d'affaires in Panama in 1904, as the first U.S. diplomatic representative there; and minister to Colombia in 1904–1905, where he tried to restore amicable relations between the United States and that country. He was minister to Venezuela from 1905 to 1908 and minister to the Dominican Republic from 1910 to 1913 and 1915 to 1925, serving during the U.S. intervention in that country. He was minister to Siam from 1925 until his retirement in 1927. Died March 11, 1944, in Washington, D.C. *References*: *DADH*; and *NCAB* 15:58.

RYAN, WILLIAM ALBERT CHARLES (1843–1873). Soldier of fortune, born March 28, 1843, in Toronto, Canada. Ryan later came to the United States, served in the Union Army during the Civil War, and was employed in the mining camps of Montana until 1868. He was commissioned colonel in the Cuban Army in 1868, to serve in its struggle against Spain. He was captured by the Spaniards in 1873 on board the *Virginius* (*see* VIRGINIUS AFFAIR). Executed November 4, 1873, in Santiago, Cuba. *References*: *ACAB*; and John G. Ryan, *Life and Adventures of General W.A.C. Ryan, the Cuban Martyr: Captured on the Steamer Virginius and Murdered by the Spaniards at Santiago, Cuba, November 4, 1873* (New York, 1876).

RYDER, JEANETTE (FORD) (1866–1931). Humanitarian, born June 11, 1866, in Wisconsin, and grew up in Iowa, Michigan, and California. She came to Cuba in 1899, where her husband established a medical practice. She founded and was president of Bando de Piedad de la Isla de Cuba, a welfare society, which was devoted to helping the handicapped, wayward women, the poor, and children, and to protect animals. *Reference*: John W. Leonard, ed., *Woman's Who's Who in America, 1914–1915* (New York, 1914).

S

SADLER, EVERIT J(AY) (1879–1947). Engineer, born May 1, 1879, in Brockport, New York, and grew up in Kansas and Oklahoma. Sadler graduated from the U.S. Naval Academy in 1899. He served during the Spanish-American War. He resigned from the Navy in 1902 and entered the oil business. He was a roustabout and operator in the Kansas oil fields and then joined Paine Oil and Gas Company in 1906 as a junior engineer. He was in charge of the properties of Standard Oil Company of New Jersey in Rumania from 1909 until 1916. He served in the U.S. Navy during World War I. He then went to Mexico to increase production of oil there, and supervised Standard Oil's first oil field in Mexico. He was vice president in charge of production for Standard Oil Company of New Jersey from 1930 until his retirement in 1942. Died October 28, 1947, in New Orleans. *Reference*: *NYT*, October 29, 1947.

SAINT PATRICK'S BATTALION. Foreign legion, known also as Batallón de San Patricio, composed mostly of European Catholic immigrants who deserted the U.S. Army during the Mexican War and other foreign residents of Mexico. The name was given by its Irish-American leader, John Riley. Many members were killed in action and some were executed by the U.S. Army following courts-martial. After the war, the unit continued to function for nearly a year, patrolling different areas to protect the populace from highwaymen and hostile indians. It was later involved in the Paredes-Jarauta revolt and was dissolved in budget cuts in 1848. Many of its members remained in Mexico. *References*: Robert R. Miller, *Shamrock and Sword: The Saint Patrick's Battalion in the U.S.-Mexican War* (Norman, Okla., 1989); Dennis J. Wynn, "The San Patricios and the United States–Mexican War of 1846–1848," Ph.D. diss., Loyola University of Chicago, 1982; and Dennis J. Wynn, *The San Patricio Soldiers: Mexico's Foreign Legion* (El Paso, Tex., 1984).

SALM-SALM, AGNES ELISABETH WINONA LECLERCQ JOY, PRIN-CESS (1840–1912). Adventuress, born December 25, 1840, in Franklin County, Vermont, or Philipsburg, Quebec. She went to Washington early in the Civil War and married Felix Constantin Alexander Johann Nepomuk, Prince of Salm-Salm (1828–1870), a German soldier of fortune. She accompanied her husband to Mexico in 1866, when he became Emperor Maximilian's chief aide. She attempted, unsuccessfully, to save the life of the emperor. After her husband's death, she was involved in relief work in camps and field hospitals for the Prussian Army, and settled down in Germany. She wrote *Zehn Jahre aus Meinem Leben* (Stuttgart, 1875) which was translated as *Ten Years of My Life* (London, 1876). Died December 21, 1912, in Karlsruhe, Germany. *References*: *ACAB*; Florence Arms, *Bright Morning* (Boston, 1962); *DAB*; and *NYT*, December 22, 1912.

SAMANÁ BAY (1854). David Dixon Porter (1813–1891), a naval officer, traveled in the Dominican Republic in 1846, and reported the utility of Samaná Bay, an inlet on the northeast coast of that country, as a naval base. Discussions between the Dominican Republic and the United States governments in 1854 nearly resulted in the establishment of a U.S. naval base on Samaná Bay. In 1869, a treaty was signed between the Dominican Republic and the United States for a ninety-nine-year lease of Samaná Bay, but the U.S. Senate refused to ratify the treaty.

SAN DOMINGO IMPROVEMENT COMPANY. In 1892, the company took over the collection of customs in the Dominican Republic and distributed the proceeds to the Dominican Republic and its creditors. It also issued loans and engaged in the building of railroads. In 1901, it was barred from the collection of customs, and it relinquished its interests in the Dominican Republic in 1903. *Reference*: *DADH*.

SANCALA AFFAIR (1844). Captain Philip F. Voorhees (1792–1862), in command of the USS *Congress*, serving on the Brazil Squadron of the U.S. Navy, seized in 1844 the Argentine squadron that was blockading Montevideo, Uruguay, after the Argentine vessel *Sancala*, fired on a U.S. naval vessel. Voorhees also refused to allow the Argentine blockade to be enforced against American vessels. The Argentine ships were later released. Voorhees was court-martialed in 1845 for disobeying orders calling for neutrality. *Reference*: K. Jack Bauer, "The *Sancala* Affair: Captain Voorhees Seizes an Argentine Squadron," *AN* 29 (1969): 174–86.

SANDS, WILLIAM FRANKLIN (1874–1946). Diplomat, born July 29, 1874, in Washington, D.C. Sands graduated from Georgetown University. He entered the diplomatic service in 1896. He was second secretary in the U.S. legation in Japan from 1896 to 1898, first secretary in Korea in 1898–1899, and special adviser to the Korean emperor from 1899 until 1904, when he was expelled from Korea by the Japanese after their invasion. He was U.S. chargé d'affaires in Panama from 1904 to 1906, in Guatemala in 1907, and in Mexico in 1908, and was minister to Guatemala from 1909 until 1911. He left the diplomatic service in 1911 and was involved with several corporations in Washington, D.C., Boston, Philadelphia, and London. He represented the New York banking firm of Speyer and Company in Ecuador in 1911 and the Central Aquirre Sugar Company of Boston in Puerto Rico in 1911–1912, and was manager and secretary of the Pan-American Financial Conference in 1915. He wrote *Our Jungle Diplomacy* (Chapel Hill, N.C., 1944). Died June 17, 1946, in Washington, D.C. *References*: William Franklin Sands Papers, St. Charles Borromeo Seminary Library, Overbrook, Philadelphia; *DACB*; *NCAB* 41:20; *NYT*, June 19, 1946; and *WWWA*.

SANFORD, CHARLES H. (1840–1928). Financier, born April 16, 1840, in Tennent, New Jersey. In 1864, Sanford became connected with the wholesale drug firm of Lanman and Kemp, and he came to Argentina in 1866 as the company's representative. In 1876, he became a partner in the firm of Samuel B. Hale and Company at Buenos Aires. He was involved in the development of the modern port facilities of Buenos Aires and the city's streetcar enterprise. Died December 22, 1928, in London. *References*: *Drees*; and *NYT*, December 25, 1928.

SATTERTHWAITE, LINTON (1897–1978). Archaeologist, born February 8, 1897, in Trenton, New Jersey. Satterthwaite graduated from Yale University and the University of Pennsylvania and was admitted to the bar in 1923. He served in the British Royal Air Force during World War I. He practiced law from 1923 to 1928 and engaged in archaeological research after 1929, principally in the Maya ruins in British Honduras and Guatemala. He was curator of the University Museum of the University of Pennsylvania and professor of anthropology at the university. He was coauthor of *Piedras Negras Archaeology: Architecture* (Philadelphia, 1943) and two works that were published posthumously: *The Monuments and Inscriptions of Caracol, Belize* (Philadelphia, 1981) and *The Monuments and Inscriptions of Tikal* (Philadelphia, 1982). Died February 11, 1978, in West Chester, Pennsylvania. *Reference*: *WWA*.

SAUER, CARL O(RTWIN) (1889–1975). Geographer, born December 24, 1889, in Warrentown, Missouri. Sauer graduated from Central Wesleyan University, attended Northwestern University, and graduated from the University of Chicago. He was a member of the faculty of the University of Michigan from 1915 to 1922 and professor of geography at the University of California in Berkeley from 1923 until his retirement in 1957. He carried out fieldwork in Baja California and northern Mexico, and in the late 1920s and 1930s led field parties into Mexico almost every year. He wrote *The Road to Cíbola* (Berkeley,

Calif., 1932) and was coauthor of *Azatalán, Prehistoric Mexican Frontier on the Pacific Coast* (Berkeley, Calif., 1931). Died July 18, 1975, in Berkeley, California. *References*: Carl O. Sauer Papers, Bancroft Library, University of California at Berkeley; *Andean Reflections: Letters from Carl O. Sauer while on a South American Trip under a Grant from the Rockefeller Foundation, 1942*, ed. Robert C. West (Boulder, Colo., 1982); *Land and Life: A Selection from the Writings of Carl Ortwin Sauer*, ed. John B. Leighly (Berkeley, Calif., 1963); *Selected Essays 1963–1975: Carl O. Sauer*, ed. Bob Callahan (Berkeley, Calif., 1981); *AAAG* 66 (1976): 337–48; *Geographical Review* 66 (1976): 83–89; Martin S. Kenzer, ed., *Carl O. Sauer: A Tribute* (Corvallis, Ore., 1987); J. Leighly, "Carl Ortwin Sauer, 1889–1975," *Geographers: Biobibliographical Studies* 2 (1978): 99–108; *NYT*, July 21, 1975; Robert C. West, *Carl Sauer's Fieldwork in Latin America* (Ann Arbor, Mich., 1979); and Robert C. West, "The Contributions of Carl Sauer to Latin American Geography," in *Geographic Research on Latin America: Benchmark 1980*, ed. T. L. Martinson and G. S. Elbow (Muncie, Ind., 1981), pp. 8–21.

SAVAGE, CHARLES (1785–1840). Merchant and consul, born January 5, 1785, in Barnstable, Massachusetts. Savage came to Boston in 1800, where he was an apprentice in a store. He was in the commission business in Boston until 1817 and then in Lexington and Louisville, Kentucky. He was U.S. consul in Guatemala City from 1824 to 1838. He also traveled in other parts of Central America and in Cuba. Died September 23, 1840, in Matagorda, Texas. *Reference*: Lawrence Park, *Major Thomas Savage of Boston, and His Descendants* (Boston, 1914).

SAVILLE, MARSHALL H(OWARD) (1867–1935). Archaeologist, born June 24, 1867, in Rockport, Massachusetts. Saville was assistant at the Peabody Museum of Archaeology and Ethnology of Harvard University from 1889 to 1894 and assistant curator in anthropology at the American Museum of Natural History in New York City after 1894. He made a collecting trip to Yucatán under the auspices of the Peabody Museum in 1890 and studied the ruined city of Copán in Honduras in 1891–1892. He made a collecting expedition for the American Museum of Natural History to Palenque, Chiapas, Mexico, in 1897 and excavated Mitla and Monte Albán in Oaxaca and Xochicalo, Morelos, Mexico. He was professor of archaeology at Columbia University after 1903 and curator of Mexican and Central American archaeology at the American Museum of Natural History until 1907. He joined the Museum of the American Indian, Heye Foundation, of New York City, and conducted collecting expeditions to Colombia and Ecuador. He wrote *The Antiquities of Manobi, Ecuador: A Preliminary Report* (New York, 1907), *The Antiquities of Manobi, Ecuador: Final Report* (New York, 1910), *The Goldsmith's Art in Ancient Mexico* (New York, 1920), and *The Wood-Carver's Art in Ancient Mexico* (New York, 1925). Died May 7, 1935, in New York City. *References*: *DAB S1*; Donald McViker,

"Prejudice and Context: The Anthropological Archaeologist as Historian," in *Archaeology's Past: The Historiography of Archaeology*, ed. Andrew L. Christiensen (Carbondale, Ill., 1989), 113–26; *NCAB* 28:468; *NYT*, May 9, 1935; and *WWWA*.

SAVOY, GENE (1927–   ). Explorer and author, born May 11, 1927, in Bellingham, Washington. Savoy attended the University of Portland. He served with the Naval Air Service during World War II. He was publisher and editor of a lumberman's trade journal from 1949 until 1956. From 1957 to 1963, he conducted explorations in the jungles east of the Andes in Peru to prove his theory that the high civilizations of Peru may have had their origin in the jungles. He was president and founder of the Andean Explorer Club in Lima, Peru. He explored the ruins of Gran Pajaten in Peru from the air in 1963. He discovered the lost city of the Inca at Vilcabamba, Cuzco, in 1964–1965 and other ancient cities in Amazonia, including Gran Pajaten and Monte Peruvia. He wrote *Antisuyo: The Search for the Lost Cities of the Amazon* (New York, 1970) and *On the Trail of the Feathered Serpent* (Indianapolis, Ind., 1974). He was field director of the Archaeological Society of Amazonas. *References*: Susan Gilbert, "Found in Peru: Lost Cities of the Andes. An Explorer Restakes His Jungle Claims," *Science Digest* 93 (June 1985): 46–53, 83; and *Who's Who in the World* (Chicago, 1974).

SCHENCK, ROBERT C(UMMING) (1809–1890). Diplomat, born October 4, 1809, in Franklin, Ohio. Schenck graduated from Miami University and was admitted to the bar in 1830. He practiced law in Dayton, Ohio. He served in the Ohio House of Representatives from 1841 to 1843 and in the U.S. House of Representatives from 1843 to 1851. He was U.S. minister to Brazil from 1851 to 1853. With John S. Pendleton,* he negotiated commercial treaties with Uruguay and Paraguay and two treaties with Argentina but failed to secure a treaty with Brazil providing for the free navigation of the Amazon. He served in the Union Army during the Civil War. He served again in the U.S. House of Representatives from 1863 to 1870 and was U.S. minister to Great Britain from 1870 to 1876. He then practiced law in Washington, D.C. Died March 23, 1890, in Washington, D.C. *References*: *ACAB*; *DAB*; *NCAB* 3:2061; *NYT*, March 24, 1890; *OAB*; J. R. Therry, "The Life of General Robert Cumming Schenck," Ph.D. diss., Georgetown University, 1968; and *WWWA*.

SCHOENRICH, OTTO (1876–1977). Lawyer, born July 9, 1876, in Baltimore. Schoenrich graduated from Baltimore City College and the University of Maryland. He practiced law in Maryland and New Mexico from 1897 until 1900. He was assistant to the commission to revise and compile the laws of Puerto Rico in 1900–1901; district judge in Arecibo, Puerto Rico, from 1901 to 1904; municipal judge of Mayaguez from 1904 to 1906; secretary to the American special commissioner to investigate the finances of Santo Domingo in 1905–1906; and secretary to the minister of finance of the Dominican Republic in 1906 and to the provisional government of Cuba from 1906 to 1909. He was a member of the law commission that drafted new Cuban laws, district judge of Mayaguez, Puerto Rico, from 1909 to 1911, president of the Nicaraguan Mixed Claims commission from 1911 to 1915, and district judge in Humacao, Puerto Rico, in 1916. He practiced law in New York City from 1916 until his retirement in 1965. He wrote *Reminiscences of an Itinerant Lawyer* (Baltimore, 1967). Died February 8, 1977, in Baltimore. *References*: *NYT*, February 9, 1977; and *WWWA*.

SCHOTT, ARTHUR CARL VICTOR (1814–1875). Geologist, born February 27, 1814, in Stuttgart, Germany. Schott attended the institute of agriculture in Hohenheim, Germany. He was manager of several rural estates in Germany and directed mining property in Hungary. He came to the United States in 1850 and was employed by the U.S. Topographical Engineers in Washington. He was assistant surveyor and collector with the U.S.-Mexico boundary survey from 1853 to 1857, member of the party to survey for an interoceanic canal near the Isthmus of Darien in 1857–1858, and engaged in geological survey of Yucatán from 1864 to 1866, under commission from the governor. He later served in the office of the U.S. Coast Survey. Died July 26, 1875, apparently in Washington, D.C. *Reference*: Clark A. Elliott, *Biographical Dictionary of American Science: Seventeenth through the Nineteenth Centuries* (Westport, Conn., 1979).

SCHULTES, RICHARD EVANS (1915–   ). Botanist, born January 12, 1915, in Boston. Schultes graduated from Harvard University. He was research associate at the Botanical Museum of Harvard University from 1941 to 1953, curator of the orchid herbarium from 1953 to 1958, curator of economic botany after 1958, and executive director of the museum from 1967 to 1970. He was professor of natural sciences from 1973 to 1980 and professor of biology after 1980. He was a member of the Rockefeller Foundation survey of Mexican agriculture in 1941, plant explorer in the Amazon Valley for the National Research Council in 1941–1942 and for the U.S. Department of Agriculture in the Amazon Valley from 1945 to 1953, field agent of the Rubber Development Corporation of the United States in South America in 1943–1944, member of the Alpha-Helix Amazon Expedition in Brazil in 1967, and chief scientist for the Alpha-Helix Amazon Expedition in Peru in 1977. He conducted field studies in Mexico, Costa Rica, Colombia, Trinidad, Cuba, Brazil, Peru, and Argentina. He wrote *A Contribution to Our Knowledge of Rivea Corymbosa: The Narcotic Ololiuqui of the Aztecs* (Cambridge, Mass., 1941), *Native Orchids of Trinidad and Tobago* (New York, 1960), and *Where the Gods Reign: Plants and Peoples of the Colombian Amazon* (Oracle, Ariz., 1988). *References*: *AMWS*; *CA*; *Economic Botany* 33 (1979): 258; and *WWA*.

SCHURZ, WILLIAM L(YTLE) (1886–1962). Economist, born November 25, 1886, in South Lebanon, Ohio. Schurz graduated from the University of California. He was assistant professor of Latin American history and affairs at the

University of Michigan from 1916 to 1918 and adviser on Latin American affairs to Colonel Edward M. House, an aide to President Woodrow Wilson in 1918. He was trade commissioner in the Department of Commerce from 1918 to 1920, commercial attaché in the U.S. embassy in Brazil from 1920 to 1926, chief of field expedition for a crude rubber survey for the U.S. Department of Commerce in 1923–1924, and economic adviser to the government of Cuba in 1926–1927. He was director of the Latin American division of Johnson and Johnson of New Brunswick, New Jersey, from 1928 to 1930; manager for Latin America and the Far East for J. Walter Thompson Advertising Agency in New York City from 1930 to 1932; editorial writer and special writer on Latin American affairs for the *New York Herald Tribune* from 1926 to 1940; deputy administrator of the National Recovery Administration from 1933 to 1935; chief of training for the Social Security board from 1936 to 1941; assistant chief of the division of cultural relations at the U.S. State Department from 1936 to 1944; and director of the department of area studies in the American Institute for Foreign Trade in Phoenix, Arizona, from 1946 to 1949 and its president from 1949 to 1951. He was professor of area studies on international relations after 1951. He wrote *Paraguay: A Commercial Handbook* (Washington, D.C., 1920), *Bolivia, an Industrial Handbook* (Washington, D.C., 1921), *Latin America: Descriptive Survey* (New York, 1941), *This New World: The Civilization of Latin America* (New York, 1954), and *Brazil, the Infinite Country* (New York, 1961), and was coauthor of *Rubber Production in the Amazon Valley* (Washington, D.C., 1925). Died July 26, 1962, in Glendale, Arizona. *References*: *HAHR* 43 (1963): 409–10; *NYT*, July 27, 1962; *OAB*; and *WWWA*.

SCHUYLER, JAMES DIX (1848–1912). Engineer, born May 11, 1848, in Ithaca, New York. Schuyler was a chain man on the construction of the Colorado Railway from 1869 to 1873. In Los Angeles after 1873, he was involved in a variety of engineering work, later specialized in water works and constructing several dams. He was then a consulting hydraulic engineer, engaged in building large power plants as well as reservoirs and flumes for irrigation purposes in Mexico and South America. He was employed by the Mexican Light and Power Company in the construction of four large dams for furnishing power in the Nexcaxa Valley, state of Puebla. Died September 13, 1912, in Santa Monica, California. *References*: *NCAB* 18:317; and *WWWA*.

SCOTT, HUGH LENOX (1853–1934). Army officer, born September 22, 1853, in Danville, Kentucky, and grew up in Princeton, New Jersey. Scott graduated from the U.S. Military Academy in 1876 and was commissioned in the cavalry. He served on the frontier until 1897. He was adjutant general of the Department of Havana, Cuba, in 1899–1900, and adjutant general of the Division of Cuba (later Department of Cuba) from 1900 to 1902. He took an active part in the transfer of the government into Cuban hands. He was military governor of the Sulu Archipelago in the Philippines from 1903 to 1906 and

superintendent of the U.S. Military Academy from 1906 to 1910. He then served
in the U.S. Southwest until 1914. He was chief of staff of the army from 1914
to 1917. He acted in a diplomatic role with Mexican border officials. He retired
with the rank of major general in 1919. He later served on the Board of Indian
Commissioners and the New Jersey State Highway Commission. He wrote *Some
Memories of a Soldier* (New York, 1928). Died April 30, 1934, in Washington,
D.C. *References*: *ACAB*; *DAB S1*; *DAMIB*; J. W. Harper, "Hugh Lenox Scott:
Soldier and Diplomat, 1876–1917," Ph.D. diss., University of Virginia, 1968;
James W. Harper, "Hugh Lenox Scott y la Diplomacia de los Estados Unidos
Hacia la Revolucion Mexicana," *Historia Mexicana* 27 (1978): 427–45; *NYT*,
May 1, 1934; and *WWWA*.

SCOVEL, HENRY SYLVESTER (1869–1905). Journalist, born July 29, 1869,
in Denny Station, Allegheny County, Pennsylvania. Scovel attended the universities of Wooster and Michigan. He worked as an engineer in Tennessee,
Kentucky, and Pennsylvania. He was correspondent for the *Pittsburgh Dispatch*
and the *New York Herald* and covered the revolution in Cuba from 1895 to 1897.
He was arrested by the Spanish authorities in Havana in 1896, escaped, and
became a reporter for the New York *World* in Cuba, living much of the time
with the Cuban insurgents. He was captured again by the Spaniards in 1897 but
they were forced to release him. He also served as a correspondent during the
Spanish-American War until 1899. He was a consulting engineer to the Cuban
customs service of the U.S. military government from 1899 to 1902 and then
engaged in various commercial enterprises in Havana. Died February 11, 1905,
in Havana. *References*: *DAB*; Joyce Milton, *The Yellow Kids: Foreign Correspondents in the Heyday of Yellow Journalism* (New York, 1989); and *WWWA*.

SCOVELL, JOSIAH THOMAS (1841–1915). Scientist, born July 29, 1841,
in Vermontville, Michigan. Scovell attended Olivet (Mich.) College and graduated from Oberlin College and Rush Medical College (Chicago). He served
during the Civil War. He practiced medicine in Central City, Colorado, from
1868 to 1870, was head of the science department of Indiana State Normal
School (Terre Haute) from 1872 to 1881, was involved in the abstract business
from 1881 to 1895, and was head of the science department of Terre Haute High
School from 1895 until his death. He made several trips to Cuba and Mexico
in 1879–1880 and ascended Mount Orizaba (or Citlaltépel) in Mexico in 1892.
He was associated with the U.S. Fish Commission from 1891 to 1913. Died
May 8, 1915, in Terre Haute, Indiana. *References*: *IAB*; and *NCAB* 16:32.

SCRUGGS, WILLIAM LINDSAY (1836–1912). Diplomat, born September
14, 1836, on the French Broad River near Knoxville, Tennessee. Scruggs studied
law and was admitted to the bar in 1861. He edited the Columbus (Ga.) *Daily
Sun* from 1862 to 1865 and the *Atlanta Daily New Era* from 1870 to 1872. He
was U.S. minister to Colombia from 1873 to 1876, served as arbitrator in a

claims case between the British and Colombian governments, and negotiated a successful settlement of the *Montijo*, a long-standing maritime case. He was U.S. consul at Chin-Kiang and then Canton, in China. He was again U.S. minister to Colombia from 1882 to 1885 and was minister to Venezuela from 1889 to 1892. He was involved in the dispute between Venezuela and Great Britain over the British Guiana boundary. In 1894, he was Venezuela's legal adviser and a special agent of Venezuela, and in 1895, he was Venezuela's special agent before the Venezuela and British Guiana boundary commission. He wrote *British Aggressions in Venezuela; or, The Monroe Doctrine on Trial* (Atlanta, 1894), *The Venezuelan Question* (Atlanta, 1896), and *The Colombian and Venezuelan Republics* (Boston, 1900). Died July 18, 1912, in Atlanta, Georgia. *References*: *DAB*; *DADH*; John A. S. Grenville and George B. Young, "The Diplomat as Propagandist: William Lindsay Scruggs, Agent for Venezuela," in John A. S. Grenville and George B. Young, *Politics, Strategy, and American Diplomacy: Studies in Foreign Policy, 1873–1917* (New Haven, Conn., 1966), ch. 5; T. D. Jervey, "William Lindsay Scruggs, a Forgotten Diplomat," *South Atlantic Quarterly* 27 (1928): 292–309; *NCAB* 2:165; W. G. Wolff, "The Diplomatic Career of William L. Scruggs: United States Minister to Colombia and Venezuela and Legal Advisor to Venezuela, 1872–1912," Ph.D. diss., Southern Illinois University, 1975; and *WWWA*.

SCRYMSER, JAMES A(LEXANDER) (1839–1918). Businessman, born July 18, 1839, in New York City. Scrymser served in the Union Army during the Civil War. He became involved in a project involving a telegraph cable connecting the United States with Cuba and other Caribbean islands and was the prime mover in the formation of the International Ocean Telegraph Company in 1865. He received in 1866 an exclusive grant from the U.S. Congress to connect Florida, with Cuba and laid the first cable between Punta Rossa, Florida, and Havana, Cuba, in 1866. He connected other Caribbean islands by cable from 1866 to 1870. In 1878, he became involved in cable communication in Mexico, Central, and South America. In 1879, he established the Mexican Cable Company and received permission to establish cables and lines connecting Mexico City, Veracruz, and Tampico with Galveston, Texas. He organized the Central and South America Telegraph Company, and was president of this company, which was later renamed All America Cables, Incorporated, until his death. He wrote *Personal Reminiscences of James A. Scrymser in Times of Peace and War* (Easton, Pa., 1915). Died April 21, 1918, in New York City. *References*: *DAB*; *NCAB* 18:314; *NYT*, April 22, 1918; and *WWWA*.

SEAGER, D. W. (fl. 1839–1867). Photographer, born probably in England, and then came to the United States. He claimed to have taken the first daguerreotype in the United States in 1839. He later gave up photography and became an adviser on national economy for the Benito Juárez government in Mexico in the 1860s. He wrote *The Resources of Mexico apart from the Precious Metals*

(Mexico City, 1867). He urged agricultural reforms through irrigation, the storage of grain, and the abolishment of local excise taxes on produce. *Reference*: Beaumont Newhall, *The Daguerreotype in America* (New York, 1976).

SELFRIDGE, THOMAS OLIVER (1836–1924). Naval officer, born February 6, 1836, in Charlestown, Massachusetts. Selfridge graduated from the U.S. Naval Academy in 1854. He served in the Union Navy during the Civil War. In 1869, he conducted a survey of the Isthmus of Darien for an interoceanic canal. He explored all the country south of Panama to the headwaters of the Atrato River in Colombia. He wrote *Reports of Explorations and Surveys to Ascertain the Practicability of a Ship-Canal between the Atlantic and Pacific Oceans by the Way of the Isthmus of Darien* (Washington, D.C., 1874). In 1878, he made a survey of the Amazon and Madeira rivers. He was commander of the Naval Torpedo Station in Newport, Rhode Island, after 1881. He retired with the rank of rear admiral in 1898. He wrote *Memoirs of Thomas O. Selfridge, Jr., Rear Admiral, U.S.N.* (New York, 1924). Died February 4, 1924, in Washington, D.C. *References*: *DAB*; *NCAB* 7:552; and *WWWA*.

SHAFTER, WILLIAM R(UFUS) (1835–1906). Army officer, born October 16, 1835, in Kalamazoo County, Michigan. Shafter served in the Union Army during the Civil War. He remained in the regular army after the war and was on frontier duty along the Rio Grande and in west Texas from 1869 to 1879. He then served in the departments of Columbia and California. He served in the Spanish-American War. In command of the expeditionary forces to Cuba in 1898, he launched the main attack on the port city of Santiago. He concluded the terms of surrender of the Spanish forces. He retired with the rank of major general in 1901. Died November 13, 1906, in Bakersfield, California. *References*: William R. Shafter Papers, Stanford University Library, Stanford, Calif.; *ACAB*; Paul H. Carlson, *"Pecos Bill": A Military Biography of William R. Shafter* (College Station, Texas, 1989); *DAB*; *DAMIB*; Stewart H. Holbrook, *Lost Men of American History* (New York, 1946), pp. 283–94; *NCAB* 9:18; *NYT*, November 13, 1906; and *WWWA*.

SHALER, WILLIAM (1773?–1833). Sea captain and consul, born in Bridgeport, Connecticut. Shaler became a sea captain, and from 1797 to 1815 was engaged in trade in South America and the Pacific. He was U.S. consul and agent for commerce and seamen at Havana from 1810 to 1812, official agent to report on filibustering activities of the Mexican revolutionists in Louisiana and Natchitoches from 1812 to 1814, and an observer at the European peace congress in Ghent in 1814. He was consul general to Algiers from 1815 to 1830. He was consul general to Havana from 1830 until his death. Died March 29, 1833, in Havana. *References*: William Shaler Papers, Historical Society of Pennsylvania; *ACAB*; *Cutolo*; *DAB*; *NCAB* 4:532; Roy F. Nichols, *Advance Agents of American Destiny* (Philadelphia, 1956), chs. 3–5; and *WWWA*.

SHANNON, RICHARD C(UTTS) (1839–1920). Lawyer, born February 12, 1839, in New London, Connecticut. Shannon graduated from Waterville (now Colby) College. He served in the Union Army during the Civil War. He was secretary of legation at Rio de Janeiro from 1871 to 1875. In 1876, he took charge of the Botanical Garden Railroad Company in Rio de Janeiro, of which he subsequently became vice president and general manager, and finally president until 1883. He returned to the United States in 1883, graduated from the law department of Columbia University, was admitted to the bar in 1886, and practiced law in New York City. He was U.S. minister to Nicaragua, El Salvador, and Costa Rica from 1891 to 1893. He was a member of the U.S. House of Representatives from 1895 to 1899, and then resumed the practice of law in New York City from 1899 until his retirement in 1903. Died October 5, 1920, in Brockport, Monroe County, New York. *References*: *BDAC*; *NCAB* 12:361; and *WWWA*.

SHANNON, WILSON (1802–1877). Lawyer and diplomat, born February 24, 1802, in Mount Olivet, Belmont County, Ohio Territory. Shannon attended Ohio and Transylvania universities, studied law, and was admitted to the bar in 1830. He practiced law in St. Clairsville, Ohio, after 1830. He was Ohio state's attorney in 1833 and governor of Ohio from 1838 to 1840 and 1842 to 1844. He was U.S. minister to Mexico in 1844–1845 but followed a tactless course; he was recalled in 1845. He resumed the practice of law in Cincinnati and later in Lecompton and Topeka, Kansas. He was a member of the U.S. House of Representatives from 1853 to 1855 and governor of Kansas Territory in 1855–1856. Died August 30, 1877, in Topeka, Kansas. *Reference*: Donald E. Day, "A Life of Wilson Shannon, Governor of Ohio, Diplomat, Territorial Governor of Kansas," Ph.D. diss., Ohio State University, 1978.

SHANTON, GEORGE REYNOLDS (1868–1930). Soldier, born October 28, 1868, in Rome, New York, and grew up in Kansas, Omaha, Nebraska, and Ft. Laramie, Wyoming. He was the original "Laramie Kid" in Buffalo Bill's Wild West Show and then deputy U.S. marshal in Wyoming. He served during the Spanish-American War in the "Rough Riders."* He remained in Cuba, assisting surgeon general William Crawford Gorgas* in his sanitation campaign and helping to organize and train the constabulary until 1904. He was the first commissioner of police in the Panama Canal Zone from 1904 to 1909. He later served as commander of the insular constabulary in Puerto Rico and served as an intelligence officer in Puerto Rico during World War I. He served in the Federal Bureau of Investigation from 1922 to 1924 and was a real estate operator in Florida after 1924. Died September 29, 1930, in New York City. *References*: *NCAB* 25:185; and *NYT*, September 25, 1930.

SHEFFIELD, JAMES ROCKWELL (1864–1938). Diplomat, born August 13, 1864, in Dubuque, Iowa. Sheffield graduated from Yale University and attended Harvard Law School and was admitted to the bar in 1889. He practiced law in New York City after 1889 and was a member of the New York State Legislature in 1894–1895. He was U.S. ambassador to Mexico from 1924 to 1927. He was responsible for the intensification of the friction between Mexico and the United States, advocating a strong-arm policy toward Mexico, and his mission was a failure. Died September 2, 1938, in Upper Saranac Lake, New York. *References*: James Rockwell Sheffield Papers, Yale University Library, New Haven, Conn.; *ACAB*; Israel Carmonas, "Anatomy of a Diplomatic Failure: A Study of the Tenure of Ambassador James Rockwell Sheffield in Mexico, 1923–1927," Ph.D. diss., University of Southern California, 1969; J. J. Horn, "Diplomacy by Ultimatum: Ambassador Sheffield and Mexican-American Relations, 1924–1927," Ph.D. diss., State University of New York, Buffalo, 1969; J. J. Horn, "El Embajador Sheffield Contra el Presidente Calles," *Historia Mexicana* 20 (1970): 265–84; *NCAB* 31:518; *NYT*, September 3, 1938; and *WWWA*.

SHELBY, JOSEPH ORVILLE (1830–1897). Army officer, born December 12, 1830, in Lexington, Kentucky. Shelby attended Transylvania University. He was engaged in rope manufacturing in Lexington and later in Berlin and Waverley, Missouri, where he established a rope factory. He served in the Confederate Army during the Civil War. He urged his men to cross into Mexico, there to join forces with either Benito Juárez or Emperor Maximilian. He crossed the border in 1865. Against Shelby's judgment, his men voted to support Maximilian, but the emperor refused the proffered aid. He gave Shelby some land on which the Carlota colony was formed. He returned to the United States, settled in Bates County, Missouri, and was U.S. marshal for the western district of Missouri from 1893 until his death. Died February 13, 1897, in Adrian, Missouri. *References*: *DAB*; Daniel O'Flaherty, *General Jo Shelby, Undefeated Rebel* (Chapel Hill, N.C., 1954); and *NCAB* 6:524.

SHELTON, CORNELL NEWTON (1908–1965). Aviation executive, born April 16, 1908, in Provo, Utah. Shelton learned to fly in Los Angeles in 1927. He was a private aircraft operator in 1929, an instructor and pilot in Mexico in 1929–1930, and a pilot and adviser to the government of Honduras in 1931. He founded and operated Empreso Nacional de Transportes Aerreos S.A. (ENTA), the first domestic airline in Costa Rica in 1931–1932. He was chief pilot of Empresa Dean in Honduras from 1932 to 1934, vice president of operations and chief pilot of Transportes Aereos Centro-Americanos (TACA) in Central America from 1934 to 1938, captain of Mid-Continent Airlines, Incorporated, from 1938 to 1940, and copilot with Trans World Airlines (TWA) from 1940 to 1946. He founded and operated Transportes Aereos Nacionales (TAN) in Honduras after 1947. He also founded and was involved with Compañia Ecuatoriana de Aviacion (CEA) from 1957 to 1963, and was involved with Aerolineas Peruanas, S.A. (APSA) after 1958. Died March 15, 1965, in Lima, Peru. *References*: Philip

Schleit, *Shelton's Barefoot Airlines* (Annapolis, Md., 1982); and *Who's Who in Aviation* (Chicago, 1942).

SHEPHERD, ALEXANDER R(OBEY) (1835–1902). Entrepreneur, born January 31, 1835, in Washington, D.C. Shepherd was a store boy, carpenter's apprentice, and plumber's assistant. He then opened his own plumbing establishment and was engaged also in real estate and building operations. He entered municipal politics in Washington, D.C., and was owner of the *Evening Star* after 1867. He served on the territorial government for Washington, D.C., and was territorial governor in 1873–1874. He then became interested in a silver mine in Batopilas, Chihuahua, Mexico, moved to Mexico in 1880, and converted the property into a highly valuable one. Died September 1, 1902, in Batopilas. His son, **GRANT SHEPHERD**, wrote *The Silver Magnet* (New York, 1938), an autobiography. *References*: *DAB*; *Hanrahan*, ch. 5; *NCAB* 13:80; *NYT*, September 13, 1902; *Pletcher*, ch. 6; and *WWWA*.

SHOOK, EDWIN MARTIN (1911–   ). Archaeologist, born November 22, 1911, in Newton, North Carolina. Shook graduated from Drexel Institute (Philadelphia), Columbia Institute of Technology (Washington, D.C.), and George Washington and Harvard universities. He was assistant archaeologist in the Division of Historical Research of the Carnegie Institution of Washington from 1933 to 1940 and archaeologist from 1940 to 1958. He was a field agent for the cinchona project of the U.S. government in Guatemala from 1943 to 1946 and archaeological director of the Tikal project for the University Museum of the University of Pennsylvania after 1955. He wrote *Explorations in Orkintok, Yucatán* (Mexico City, 1940) and *Excavations in Kaminaljuyú, Guatemala* (Washington, D.C., 1944).

SHUBRICK, WILLIAM B(RANFORD) (1790–1874). Naval officer, born October 31, 1790, in Bull's Island, South Carolina. Shubrick entered the Navy as a midshipman in 1806. He served in the War of 1812 and the Mexican War and in various routine assignments. He was head of the Philadelphia navy yard and later head of the bureau of construction and repair from 1849 to 1852. He commanded an expedition sent to settle commercial and other difficulties of Paraguay. The fleet arrived in 1859 to Asunción, and Shubrick, with the American commissioner James Butler Bowlin,* secured a treaty settling all points in dispute. He retired in 1861 and was promoted to rear admiral in 1862. Died May 27, 1874, Washington, D.C. *References*: *ACAB*; *Cutolo*; *DAB*; *NCAB* 2:237; and *WWWA*.

SHUNK, WILLIAM F(INDLEY) (1830–1907). Engineer, born September 6, 1830, in Harrisburg, Pennsylvania. Shunk served in the U.S. Navy until 1850. He was an engineer for various railroads until 1876. He supervised the construction of the elevated railroad in Manhattan and Brooklyn. He was in charge of

Intercontinental Railroad surveys from 1890 to 1892 and chief engineer of the Guayaquil and Quito Railroad from 1898 to 1902. Died June 22, 1907, near Harrisburg, Pennsylvania. *References*: *NCAB* 2:288; *NYT*, June 23, 1907; and *WWWA*.

SIBERT, WILLIAM LUTHER (1860–1935). Military engineer, born October 12, 1860, in Gadsden (later in Etowah County), Alabama. Sibert attended the University of Alabama and graduated from the U.S. Military Academy in 1884. He was commissioned second lieutenant in the corps of engineers. He was involved in river and harbor engineering in Ohio, Kentucky, the Great Lakes Region, and Arkansas, and in the Philippines in 1899–1900. He was involved with improving navigation on the Ohio, Allegheny, and Monongahela rivers from 1900 to 1907. He was a member of the Isthmian Canal Commission in 1907–1908 and worked in the locks, dams, and regulating works of the Panama Canal. He was in charge of the Atlantic division from 1908 to 1914, served during World War I, and organized the Chemical Warfare Service for the U.S. Army from 1918 to 1920. He retired with the rank of major general in 1920. Died October 16, 1935, in Bowling Green, Kentucky. *References*: *DAB*; *NCAB* 35:258; *NYT*, October 17, 1935; and *WWWA*.

SILLIMAN, JOHN (REID) (1855–1919). Consul, born December 7, 1855, in Green County, Alabama. Silliman graduated from Princeton University. He was employed by the Texas and St. Louis Railroad Company in Tyler, Texas, from 1879 to 1883 and was then secretary of the Tyler Compress Company until 1892. He was a member of Stone and Silliman, insurance agents, in San Antonio from 1893 to 1897. He went to Mexico in 1897, leasing land near Saltillo, state of Coahuila, and engaged in farming and dairying until 1907. He was vice-consul in Saltillo from 1907 to 1914. He was arrested by the Mexican Federales in 1914 and held incommunicado in prison for several months. A classmate of President Woodrow Wilson and a close friend of Venustiano Carranza, he served as a special agent in 1915–1916. He was consul in Guadalajara from 1916 until his death. Died January 19, 1919, in Guadalajara, Mexico. *References*: *Hill*; and *NYT*, January 19, 1919.

SIMONTON, ASHBEL GREEN (1833–1867). Missionary, born January 20, 1833, in Dauphin County, Pennsylvania. Simonton graduated from the College of New Jersey and Princeton Theological Seminary and was ordained in 1859. He was a missionary in Brazil from 1859 to 1867. He was a pastor in the First Presbyterian Church of Rio de Janeiro from 1862 to 1867. Died December 9, 1867, in São Paulo, Brazil. *References*: "Journal of the Rev. Ashbel Green Simonton, First Presbyterian Missionary in Brazil" (n.d.), (Ms.) Commission on Ecumenical Mission and Relations of the United Presbyterian Church in the U.S.A., New York City; Philip S. Landes, *Ashbel Green Simonton: A Model*

Pioneer Missionary of the Presbyterian Church of Brazil (Fort Worth, Tex., 1956); and *PrincetonTS*.

SIMPSON, GEORGE EATON (1904–   ). Sociologist, born October 4, 1904, in Knoxville, Iowa. Simpson graduated from Coe College and the universities of Missouri and Pennsylvania. He was assistant professor of sociology at Temple University from 1934 to 1939, associate professor of sociology at Pennsylvania State University from 1939 to 1943 and professor from 1943 to 1947, and professor of sociology and anthropology at Oberlin College from 1947 until his retirement in 1971. He carried out fieldwork in Haiti in 1936–1937, studying Voodoo practices and Haiti folklore. He worked in Jamaica in 1953 and in Trinidad in 1960, investigating revivalist cults. He wrote *Jamaica Revivalist Cults* (Jamaica, 1956), *The Shango Cult in Trinidad* (Rio Peidras, P.R., 1965), *Caribbean Papers* (Cuernavaca, 1970), *Religious Cults of the Caribbean: Trinidad, Jamaica and Haiti* (Rio Piedras, 1970), and *Black Religions in the New World* (New York, 1978). *References*: *AMWS*; *CA*; and *WWA*.

SIMPSON, GEORGE GAYLORD (1902–1984). Paleontologist, born June 16, 1902, in Chicago. Simpson attended the University of Colorado and graduated from Yale University. He was assistant curator of vertebrate paleontology at the American Museum of Natural History in 1927, associate curator from 1928 to 1942, and curator of fossil mammals from 1942 to 1959. He served in the U.S. Army during World War II. He was also professor of vertebrate paleontology at Columbia University from 1942 to 1959 and at the Museum of Comparative Zoology from 1959 to 1970, and professor of geosciences at the University of Arizona from 1967 to 1984. He conducted expeditions to collect fossil mammals to the Patagonia region of Argentina and Chile in 1930–1931 and 1933–1934, to Venezuela in 1938–1939, and to Brazil in 1954–1955 and 1956. He wrote *Attending Marvels: A Patagonian Journal* (New York, 1934), *The Beginning of the Age of Mammals in South America* (New York, 1948–1967), *Concession to the Improbable: An Unconventional Autobiography* (New Haven, Conn., 1978), *Splendid Isolation: The Curious History of South American Mammals* (New Haven, Conn., 1980), and *Discoverers of the Lost World: An Account of Some of Those Who Brought Back to Life South American Mammals Long Buried in the Abyss of Time* (New Haven, Conn., 1984). Died October 6, 1984, in Tucson, Arizona. *Simple Curiosity: Letters from George Gaylord Simpson to His Family, 1921–1970*, ed. Leo F. Laporte (Berkeley, Calif., 1987), was published posthumously. *References*: *AMWS*; *CA*; *NYT*, October 8, 1984; and *WWWA*.

SINGLEWALD, JOSEPH T(HEOPHILUS, JR.) (1884–1963). Economic geologist, born September 25, 1884, in Baltimore. Singlewald graduated from Johns Hopkins University and studied in the Bergakademis of Freiberg (Germany). He was assistant professor of economic geology at Johns Hopkins University from 1913 to 1917, associate professor there from 1917 to 1922, and professor from 1922 to 1952. He participated in an exploration trip to Latin America in search for minerals for industrial wartime usage in 1915 and in a tour of geological research in South America in 1919. He was coauthor of *Mineral Deposits of South America* (New York, 1919). He conducted geological exploration in Mexico for the Transcontinental Oil Company in 1921–1922 and participated in the Lincoln Ellsworth expedition up the Amazon in Brazil in 1924 and in oil reconnaissance of the upper Amazon of Peru in 1925, and conducted an extensive survey of Venezuela and Colombia in 1946. He was chief production specialist for the Board of Economic Warfare during World War II. He was also director of the Maryland Department of Geology, Mines and Water Resources from 1943 to 1962. He wrote *Bibliography of Economic Geology of South America* (New York, 1943). Died October 20, 1963, in Baltimore. *References*: *BAAPG* 48 (1964): 732–35; and *Economic Geology* 59 (1964): 195.

SKUTCH, ALEXANDER F(RANK) (1904–   ). Ornithologist, born May 20, 1904, in Baltimore. Skutch graduated from Johns Hopkins University. He conducted research in Panama and Honduras from 1928 to 1931 and was a botanist on a rubber survey in Peru, Ecuador, and Colombia in 1940–1941. He was a naturalist working independently in Guatemala from 1932 to 1934, and in Panama, and Costa Rica in 1935, paying his own way by collecting and selling botanical specimens. He bought a farm in Costa Rica in 1941, settling there to continue his studies. He wrote *Life Histories of Central American Birds* (Berkeley, Calif., 1954–1960), *A Naturalist in Costa Rica* (Gainesville, Fla., 1971), *A Bird Watcher's Adventures in Tropical America* (Austin, Tex., 1977), *The Imperative Call: A Naturalist's Quest in Temperate and Tropical America* (Gainesville, Fla., 1979), *A Naturalist on a Tropical Farm* (Berkeley, Calif., 1980), *Birds of Tropical America* (Austin, Tex., 1983), *Nature through Tropical Windows* (Berkeley, Calif., 1983), and *A Naturalist amid Tropical Splendor* (Iowa City, 1987). *References*: *CA*; and Frank Graham, Jr., "Alexander Skutch and the Appreciative Mind," *Audubon* 81 (March 1979): 82–117.

SLOCUM, HERBERT J(ERMAIN) (1855–1928). Army officer, born April 25, 1855, in Cincinnati. Slocum graduated from the U.S. Military Academy in 1876 and was commissioned a second lieutenant in the U.S. Army. He served in the American West. During the Spanish-American War he served as a military adviser to the commanding general of the Cuban Army. He supervised the provincial rural guards in Cuba from 1899 to 1902, served in the Philippines from 1903 to 1905, and then was inspector general with the army of Cuban pacification. He was chief supervisor of the Cuban Rural Guard from 1906 to 1909. He served on the Mexican border from 1915 to 1917 and during World War I. He retired in 1919. Died March 29, 1928, in Washington, D.C. *References*: *NCAB* 24:237; and *WWWA*.

SMITH, AUGUSTUS LEDYARD (1901–1985). Archaeologist, born October 18, 1901, in Milwaukee. Smith graduated from Harvard University. He was a member of the staff of the Carnegie Institution of Washington, D.C., from 1927 to 1958. He participated in field programs in the late 1920s and throughout 1930s, excavating at Uaxactún; he was later field director there. He carried out a survey and diggings in the Guatemalan highlands until 1950 and in Mayapan, Yucatán, from 1950 until 1958. He was assistant curator of Middle American archaeology at the Peabody Museum of Harvard University from 1958 to 1982 and excavated Altar de Sacrificios and Seibel, Department of Petén, Guatemala. He wrote *Uaxactún, Guatemala: Excavations of 1931–1937* (Washington, D.C., 1950), *Archaeological Reconnaissance in Central America* (Washington, D.C., 1955), *Excavations at Altar de Sacrificios: Architecture, Settlement, Burials, and Caches* (Cambridge, Mass., 1972), and *Excavations at Seibal, Department of Petén, Guatemala: Major Architecture and Caches* (Cambridge, Mass., 1982), and was coauthor of *Explorations in the Motagua Valley, Guatemala* (Washington, D.C., 1943), *Mayapan, Yucatán, Mexico* (Washington, D.C., 1962), *The Ruins of Altar de Sacrificios, Department of Petén, Guatemala: An Introduction* (Cambridge, Mass., 1969), and *Excavations at Seibal, Department of Petén, Guatemala: Introduction: The Site and Its Setting* (Cambridge, Mass., 1975). Died December 5, 1985, in Needham, Massachusetts. *References*: *AmAntiq* 53 (1986): 683–85; W. R. Bullard, ed., *Monographs and Papers in Maya Archaeology* (Cambridge, Mass., 1970); and *Willey*, ch. 16.

SMITH, EARL E(DWARD) T(AILER) (1903–1991). Diplomat, born in Newport, Rhode Island. Smith attended Yale University. He was a stockbroker in New York City, a member of the New York Coffee and Sugar Exchange after 1925, and a member of the New York Stock Exchange after 1926. He served in the U.S. Army and the U.S. Army Air Force during World War II. He was U.S. ambassador to Cuba from 1957 to 1959. He criticized the U.S. State Department sympathies with Fidel Castro's aspirations and wrote *The Fourth Floor: An Account of the Castro Communist Revolution* (New York, 1962). He was mayor of Palm Beach, Florida, from 1971 to 1977, and a member of the Presidential Commission on Broadcasting to Cuba. Died February 15, 1991, in Palm Beach, Florida. *References*: *DADH*; *Palm Beach Post*, February 17, 1991; and *WWA*.

SMITH, EDMOND REUEL (1829–1911). Traveler. Smith attended Georgetown University. He served as a captain's clerk in the U.S. Navy. He worked with James Melville Gilliss* on the U.S. Astronomical Expedition to the Southern Hemisphere in Chile from 1849 to 1852, which was stationed in Santiago. He also collected natural history specimens. He later traveled in south Chile and wrote *The Araucanians; or, Notes of a Tour among the Indian Tribes of Southern Chile* (New York, 1855). Died probably in New York City. *References*: *Manthorne*; and *NYHSD*.

SMITH, HERBERT H(UNTINGTON) (1851–1919). Naturalist, born January 21, 1851, in Manlius, New York. Smith attended Cornell University. A collector of natural history specimens, he traveled to Brazil in 1871, from 1873 to 1877, and from 1881 to 1886 and to Mexico in 1889, for the *Biologia Centrali-Americana*; to the West Indies from 1890 to 1895 for the West Indian Commission of the Royal Society and the British Association for the Advancement of Science; and to Colombia from 1898 to 1901. He was curator at the Carnegie Museum in Pittsburgh from 1896 to 1898 and curator of the Alabama Museum of Natural History after 1910. He wrote *Brazil, the Amazons and the Coast* (New York, 1879). Died March 22, 1919, in University, Alabama. His newspaper articles in the *Gazeta de Notícias* (Rio de Janeiro) in 1886–1887 were later published as *Do Rio de Janeiro a Cuyabá; Notas de um Naturalista*, ed. João Capistrano de Abreu (São Paulo, 1922). *Reference*: WWWA.

SMITH, J(OHN) ROCKWELL (1846–1918). Missionary, born December 29, 1846, in Lexington, Kentucky. Smith attended the University of Virginia, graduated from Union Theological Seminary of Virginia, and was ordained in 1872. He was a missionary under the Board of Foreign Missions of the Presbyterian Church in the United States* in Brazil from 1872 until his death. He served in Pernamabuco from 1872 to 1892 and was professor at the Theological Nova Friburgo from 1892 to 1895, at the Theological Seminary of Brazil Synod in São Paulo from 1895 to 1907, and at the Theological Seminary of Presbyterian Church of Brazil in Campinas from 1907 to 1918. Died April 9, 1918, in Campinas, Brazil. *Reference*: MDPC.

SMITH, JOSIAH (? –1825). Traveler. Smith was the first North American to visit and describe Mexico during the years of Mexican independence. His son, **BUCKINGHAM SMITH** (1810–1871), author, graduated from Harvard University Law School and was secretary of legation in Mexico in 1851–1852. He sent to the United States large numbers of books and documents about Mexican history. Died in New York City.

SMITH, ROBERT (1755–1782). Merchant. Smith served during the Revolutionary War. He was the official representative of the Continental Congress in Havana from 1780 until his death. He performed innumerable services for his fellow citizens doing business in Havana. He was also Robert Morris's agent in Havana. Died in late 1782 in Havana. *Reference*: Robert Morris, *The Papers of Robert Morris: 1781–1784*, ed. E. James Ferguson (Pittsburgh, 1973), 1:167.

SMITH, ROBERT ELIOT (1899–   ). Archaeologist, born May 24, 1899, in Arcachon, France, to American parents. Smith graduated from Harvard University. He was a member of the staff of the Carnegie Institution of Washington from 1930 to 1959, director of excavation for the Instituto Nacional de Antropologia e Historia in Córdoba, Mexico, from 1960 to 1962, and a research associate in Middle American ceramics at the Peabody Museum of Harvard University from 1965 to 1968. He was a special assistant to the U.S. military attaché in Guatemala during World War II. He conducted archaeological studies in Mexico, Guatemala, Honduras, British Honduras, and El Salvador. He wrote *A Study of Structure: A-I Complex at Uaxactun, Petén, Guatemala* (Washington, D.C., 1937), *Pottery from Chipoc Alta Verapaz, Guatemala* (Washington, D.C., 1952), *Ceramic Sequence at Uaxactún, Guatemala* (New Orleans, 1955), and *The Pottery of Mayapan* (Cambridge, Mass., 1971). *References*: AMWS; and CA.

SMITH, WAYNE S. (1932–   ). Diplomat, born August 16, 1932, in Texas. Smith graduated from the Universidad de las Americas and Columbia University. He served in the U.S. Marine Corps. He entered the foreign service in 1958 and served as third secretary in Havana from 1958 to 1961. He was in charge of the Cuban desk in the State Department from 1964 to 1966 and director of Cuban affairs from 1977 to 1979. He was chief of the U.S. Interests Section in Havana from 1979 to 1982. He left service because of serious disagreements with the Ronald Reagan administration's policies on Cuba and Central America. He was an adjunct professor of Latin American studies at Johns Hopkins School of Advanced International Studies (Washington, D.C.). He wrote *The Closest of Enemies: A Personal and Diplomatic Account of U.S.-Cuban Relations since 1957* (New York, 1987). *Reference*: BRDS.

SNOWDEN, THOMAS (1857–1930). Naval officer, born August 12, 1857, in Peekskill, New York. Snowden graduated from the U.S. Naval Academy in 1879. He served during the Spanish-American War. He was later a hydrographer with the Navy Department and commander of a squadron of the battleship force of the Atlantic Fleet during World War I. He was military governor of Santo Domingo and military representative of the United States in Haiti from 1919 to 1921. He retired with the rank of rear admiral in 1921. Died January 27, 1930, in Washington, D.C. *References*: DAB; NYT, January 29, 1930; and WWWA.

SOBIESKY, JOHN (1842–1927). Soldier, born September 10, 1842, in Warsaw, Poland. Sobiesky came to the United States in 1855 and enlisted as a bugler in the U.S. Army. He was in Indian service until 1861 and then served during the Civil War. In 1865, he organized a group of Union veterans to aid Benito Juárez and fight the forces of Emperor Maximilian. He was chief of staff of General Mariano Escobedo and commander of the reserve firing squad at the execution of Maximilian in 1867. He settled in Minnesota, was a member of the state house of representatives in 1868, and was one of the founders of the Prohibition party. He was admitted to the bar in 1870. He wrote *The Life Story and Personal Reminiscences of Col. John Sobiesky* (Los Angeles, 1907) and *Life of President Benito Pablo Juarez* (St. Joseph, Mo., 1919). Died November

12, 1927, in Los Angeles. *References*: Francis Bolek, ed., *Who's Who in Polish America* (New York, 1943); *DCB*; *NYT*, November 13, 1927; and *WWWA*.

SOLDIERS' AND GOSPEL MISSION OF SOUTH AMERICA. Founded in 1924 and began missionary work to soldiers in Tacna, Chile, in 1924. Its work was extended to other parts of Chile and the name was later changed to Gospel Mission of South America. *References*: *EMCM*; and Edith Nanz, *Soldiering for Christ in Chile: The Story of the Soldiers' and Gospel Mission of South America* (Grand Rapids, Mich., 1942).

SONORA RAILWAY COMPANY. Organized by the Atchison, Topeka and Santa Fe Railroad in 1879, it obtained a concession from the Mexican government in 1880 to build and operate a railroad from Guaymas to the Mexican border. The railroad from Guaymas to Nogales was completed in 1882 and was operated until 1898, when the Southern Pacific assumed the operation of the railway. *Reference*: David Pletcher, "The Development of Railroads in Sonora," *IAEA* 1 (1948): 17–20.

SOPER, FRED L(OWE) (1893–1977). Public Health official, born December 13, 1893, in Hutchinson, Kansas. Soper graduated from Kansas University, Rush Medical College (Chicago), and Johns Hopkins University. He fought during World War I. He served with the International Health Board (later International Health Division) of the Rockefeller Foundation from 1920 until 1950, working on hookworm eradication in Brazil from 1920 to 1922 and in Paraguay from 1923 to 1927. He was regional director of the International Health Division of the Rockefeller Foundation, with headquarters in Rio de Janeiro, from 1927 to 1942, directed a Rockefeller Foundation project against yellow fever in 1939–1940, and also directed Brazil's malaria service of the northeast. He was consultant to the U.S. Secretary of War on epidemic diseases from 1942 to 1946 and director of the Pan American Sanitary Bureau (after 1958, the Pan American Health organization) from 1947 to 1959. He was coauthor of *Anopheles Gembiae in Brazil, 1930–1940* (New York, 1943) and wrote *Building the Health Bridge: Selections from the Works of Fred L. Soper*, ed. J. Austin Kerr (Bloomington, Ind., 1970) and *Ventures in the World Health: the Memoirs of Fred Lowe Soper*, ed. John Duffy (Washington, D.C., 1977). Died February 9, 1977, in Wichita, Kansas. *References*: *American Journal of Public Health* 67 (1977): 483–84; *CA*; *NCAB* 60:197; *NYT*, February 11, 1977; M. Waserman, "Fred L. Soper: Ambassador of Good Health," *Americas* 27 (October 1975): 30–37; and *WWWA*.

SOUTH AMERICA INDIAN MISSION (SAIM). An interdenominational missionary society, founded in 1914 to proselytize the unreached Indians in the interior of South America. It was known as the Inland South America Missionary Union from 1919 to 1939. It began missionary work in Brazil in 1914, in Peru in 1921, in Bolivia in 1922, in Colombia in 1934, and in Venezuela in 1972.

Name was changed to South America Mission, Incorporated, in 1970. *References*: *EMCM*; Martha L. Moennich, *Pioneering for Christ in Xingu Jungles: Adventure in the Heart of South America* (Grand Rapids, Mich., 1942); Ethel C. Tylee, *The Challenge of Amazon's Indians: A Story of Missionary Adventures in South America among the Nhambiquara Indians* (Chicago, 1931); and C. Peter Wagner, *Defeat of the Bird God* (Grand Rapids, Mich., 1967).

SOUTH AMERICAN COMMISSION (1817–1818). A commission, sent by President James Monroe in 1817 to southern South America to collect information and learn the progress of the revolution there and the probability of its success as well as the capacity and willingness of the people to establish and maintain an independent government. It was also intended to impress the United Provinces of the Plate River with U.S. interest and friendship for their cause. The members of the commission were Caesar Augustus Rodney,* John Graham,* and Theodorick Bland.* Henry Marie Brackenridge* was its secretary. *References*: John C. Pine, "The Role of United States Special Agents in the Development of a Spanish American Policy, 1810–1822," Ph.D. diss., University of Colorado, 1955, ch. 5; Wayne D. Rasmussen, "Diplomats and Plant Collectors: The South American Commission, 1817–1818," *Agricultural History* 29 (1955): 22–31; and Watt Stewart, "The South American Commission, 1817–1818," *HAHR* 9 (1929): 31–59.

SOUTHERN BAPTIST CONVENTION: FOREIGN MISSION BOARD. Founded in 1845. It began missionary work in Mexico in 1880, in Brazil in 1881, in Argentina in 1903, in Uruguay in 1911, in Chile in 1917, in Colombia in 1941, in Paraguay in 1945, in Guatemala in 1948, in Costa Rica and Venezuela in 1949, in Ecuador and Peru in 1950, in Honduras in 1954, in the French West Indies in 1961, in the Dominican Republic, Guyana, Tobago, and Trinidad in 1962, in Bermuda in 1966, in Surinam in 1971, in Barbados in 1972, in El Salvador, Grenada, and Panama in 1975, in Nicaragua and Tortoloa in 1976, in Belize, Cayman Islands, Martinique, and St. Vincent in 1977, in Haiti in 1978, and in Bolivia and St. Martin in 1979. *References*: Baker J. Cauthen, *Advance: A History of Southern Baptist Foreign Missions* (Nashville, Tenn., 1970); Asa R. Crabtree, *Baptist in Brazil* (Rio de Janeiro, 1953); Harold F. Greer, Jr., "History of Southern Baptist Mission Work in Cuba, 1886–1916," Ph.D. diss., University of Alabama, 1965; Harold F. Greer, Jr., "Southern Baptist in Cuba, 1884–1916," in *Militarists, Merchants and Missionaries: United States Expansion in Middle America*, ed. Eugene R. Huck and Edward H. Moseley (University, Ala., 1970), pp. 63–79; Una R. Lawrence, *Cuba for Christ* (Atlanta, 1926); Una R. Lawrence, *Missionaries of the Home Mission Board* (Atlanta, 1936); Frank W. Patterson, *A Century of Baptist Work in Mexico* (El Paso, Tex., 1979); and Alejandro Trevino, *Historia de los Trabajos Bautistas en Mexico* (El Paso, Tex., 1939).

SOUTHERN PACIFIC RAILROAD OF MEXICO [SP DE MEX]. Incorporated in 1909, it completed construction of a railroad from Nogales to Guadalajara in 1927. It was sold to the Mexican government in 1951 and operated as Ferrocarril del Pacifico. *References*: Robert A. Trennert, "The Southern Pacific Railroad of Mexico," *PHR* 35 (1966): 265–84; and Neill C. Wilson and Frank J. Taylor, *Southern Pacific, the Roaring Story of a Fighting Railroad* (New York, 1952).

SOWELL, SIDNEY MACFARLAND (1871–1954). Missionary, born December 18, 1871, in Hardware, Virginia, and graduated from Richmond College and Southern Baptist Theological Seminary. He was the first missionary under the Foreign Mission Board of the Southern Baptist Convention* in Argentina from 1903 until his death. He was editor of *El Expositor Bautista*, served as pastor of churches in Buenos Aires and Rosario, was president of the River Plate Seminary from 1918 to 1942, and served the River Plate Mission at various times as chairman, secretary, treasurer, vice president, and president. Died March 2, 1954, in Buenos Aires, Argentina. *References*: William L. Cooper, "Sidney MacFarland Sowell: Mighty Man of Faith," *Baptist History and Heritage* 3 (1968): 99–103; *ESB*; Orestes Marotta, *Dr. Sidney MacFarland Sowell* (Buenos Aires, n.d.); and Benjamin L. Sowell, *Pioneer Parson: Life of Sidney MacFarland Sowell, First Southern Baptist Missionary to Argentina* (Silver Spring, Md., n.d.).

SPANISH-AMERICAN WAR (1898). A war between the United States and Spain in 1898, in which the Spanish Navy was destroyed in Manila Bay, the Philippines, and off Santiago, Cuba, and in which United States forces landed in Cuba, Puerto Rico, and the Philippines. Peace was signed that year, with Spain recognizing the independence of Cuba and ceding Puerto Rico, the island of Guam and the Philippines to the United States. *References*: C. H. Brown, *Correspondents' War: Journalists in the Spanish-American War* (New York, 1967); Graham A. Coasmas, *An Army for Empire: The United States Army in the Spanish-American War* (Columbia, Mo., 1971); P. S. Foner, *The Spanish-Cuban-American War and the Birth of American Imperialism, 1895–1902* (New York, 1972); Frank Freidel, *Splendid Little War* (Boston, 1958); Walter LeFeber, "That 'Splendid Little War' in Historical Perspective," *Texas Quarterly* 11 (1968): 89–988; G. F. Linderman, *The Mirror of War: American Society and the Spanish-American War* (Ann Arbor, Mich., 1974); Walter Mills, *The Martial Spirit: A Study of Our War with Spain* (Boston, 1931); H. Wayne Morgan, *America's Road to Empire: The War with Spain and Overseas Expansion* (New York, 1965); and G.J.A. O'Toole, *The Spanish War: An American Epic, 1898* (New York, 1984).

SPAULDING, JUSTIN (1802–1865). Missionary, born in Vermont. Spaulding was ordained in 1825. He held a pastorate in Augusta, Maine. He was a missionary under the Methodist Missionary Society in Brazil from 1836 to 1841, serving in Rio de Janeiro and initiating the Methodist mission in Brazil. In 1836, he opened a school in Rio de Janeiro. He was recalled in 1841 because of the financial straits of the society. He later served in New Hampshire. *Reference*: *EWM*.

SPEARS, WILLIAM O(SCAR) (1885–1966). Naval officer, born September 18, 1885, in Jasper, Tennessee. Spears graduated from the U.S. Naval Academy in 1905 and was commissioned ensign in the U.S. Navy in 1907. He participated in the Veracruz affair* in 1914. He was a member of U.S. naval mission to Brazil from 1917 to 1927, serving as a gunnery instructor. He was a member of another naval mission to Brazil from 1923 to 1926, serving as adviser to the chief of Brazilian naval operations. He was chief of a U.S. naval mission to Peru from 1929 to 1933, serving as commander in chief of the Peruvian Navy. He was in command of the USS *Richmond* in Cuba during the revolution of 1933. He retired with the rank of rear admiral in 1940. He was the first director of the Pan-American Division of the Navy Department from 1940 to 1946. Died May 27, 1966, in Kensington, Maryland. *References*: *NCAB* 54:30; and *WWWA*.

SPECIAL SERVICE SQUADRON. Created by the U.S. Navy in 1920 to show the flag in Latin American ports with a view of fostering good relations at all times, to collect hydrographic and intelligence information, to meet military and other emergencies, to protect American interests. It was abolished in 1940. *Reference*: Richard Millett, ''The State Department's Navy: A History of the Special Service Squadron, 1920–1940,'' *AN* 35 (1975): 118–38.

SPINDEN, HERBERT J(OSEPH) (1879–1967). Anthropologist, born August 16, 1879, in Huron, South Dakota. Spinden graduated from Harvard University. He was assistant curator of anthropology at the American Museum of Natural History from 1909 to 1921, curator of Mexican archaeology and ethnology at Peabody Museum of Harvard University from 1921 to 1929, and concurrently curator of anthropology at the Buffalo Museum of Arts and Sciences from 1926 to 1929. He was curator of American Indian art and primitive cultures at the Brooklyn Museum from 1929 until his retirement in 1951. He explored Petén in 1914 and Copán in 1917, and served as intelligence agent in Central America during World War I. He made extended explorations in Mexico, Guatemala, Honduras, and Nicaragua from 1919 to 1926. He wrote *A Study of Maya Art* (Cambridge, Mass., 1913), *Ancient Civilizations of Mexico and Central America* (New York, 1917), *The Reduction of Maya Dates* (Cambridge, Mass., 1924), and *Maya Dates and What They Reveal* (Brooklyn, N.Y., 1930). Died October 23, 1967, in Beacon, New York. *References*: Robert L. Brunhouse, *Pursuit of the Ancient Maya: Some Archaeologists of Yesterday* (Albuquerque, N.M., 1975); *NCAB* E:73; and *NYT*, October 24, 1967.

SPRATLING, WILLIAM PHILIP (1900–1967). Architect, silversmith, and author, born September 22, 1900, in Sonyea, New York. Spratling attended Beaux Art Institute (New York City) and Alabama Polytechnic Institute (Auburn). He was instructor in architecture at the Alabama Polytechnic Institute from 1917 to 1922 and associate professor of architecture at Tulane University from 1922 to 1927. He came to Mexico in 1927. He was a lecturer at the National University of Mexico from 1927 to 1929. He settled in Taxco, state of Guerrero, where he was proprietor and manager of Spratling y Artesamos, S.A., manufacturer of silver, and, after 1931, a collector of and writer on pre-Hispanic art. He promoted the silver industry and the teaching of new silvercraft techniques and designs, and put the name of the ancient colonial village of Taxco on the map as a leading silvercraft center. He also founded a silvercraft school there. He wrote *Little Mexico* (New York, 1932), *More Human than Divine* (Mexico City, 1960), *A Small Mexican World* (Boston, 1964), and *File on Spratling: An Autobiography* (Boston, 1967). Died in a car accident, August 8, 1967, in Taxco, Mexico. *References*: Ruby N. Castrejón and Jaime Castrejón, *William Spratling* (Taxco, Mexico, n.d.); Robert D. Duncan, "William Spratling's Mexican World," *Texas Quarterly* 9 (Spring 1966): 97–104; J. P. McEvoy, " 'Silver Bill,' Practical Good Neighbor," *Reader's Digest* 47 (September 1945): 19–22; *NYT*, August 9, 1967; *WWLA*; and *WWWA*.

SQUIER, EPHRAIM GEORGE (1821–1888). Journalist, diplomat, and archaeologist, born June 17, 1821, in Bethlehem, New York. He was involved in journalism after 1837, edited the Hartford (Conn.) *Evening Journal*, and published the *Scioto Gazette* (Chillicothe, Ohio). He was a clerk of the Ohio House of Representatives in 1847–1848. He studied the remains of the Mound Builders in Ohio and later in New York. He was appointed U.S. chargé d'affaires to Central America in 1849 but did not proceed to his post. He signed an agreement with Nicaragua for the American construction of an interoceanic canal. In 1853, as secretary of the Honduras Interoceanic Railway Company, he visited Central America to examine the proposed route for the railroad. After 1860, he was chief editor of the publishing house of Frank Leslie. He was U.S. commissioner to Peru from 1863 to 1865 and settled financial claims between the two countries. He was consul general of Honduras in New York City after 1868. He wrote *Nicaragua: Its People, Scenery, Monuments, and the Proposed Interoceanic Canal* (New York, 1851), *The States of Central America* (New York, 1858), *Peru: Incidents of Travel and Exploration in the Land of the Incas* (New York, 1877), and, under the pseudonym of Samuel A. Baord, *Waikna; or, Adventures on the Mosquito Coast* (New York, 1855). Died April 17, 1888, in Brooklyn, New York. *References*: E. George Squier Papers, Tulane University Library, New Orleans; *DAB*; *DADH*, *DCB*; John R. Hebert, "Maps by Ephraim George Squier: Journalist, Scholar, and Diplomat," *Quarterly Journal of the Library of Congress* 29 (January 1972): 14–31; David Lindsey, "Ephraim George Squier: Archaeologist, Diplomat, Editor," *American History Illustrated* 15 (April 1980):

30–35; Keith McElroy, "Ephraim George Squier: Photography and the Illustrations of Peruvian Antiquities," *History of Photography* 10 (1986): 99–129; Mariana Mould de Peaso, "Observaciones a un Observador: Hurgando en el Tintero de Ephraim George Squier," in *Etnografía e Historia del Mundo Andino; Continuidad y Cambia*, ed. Shozo Masuda (Tokyo, 1986), pp. 35–107; *NCAB* 4:79; *NYT*, April 18, 1888; Michael D. Olien, "E. G. Squier and the Miskito: Anthropological Scholarship and Political Propaganda," *Ethnohistory* 32 (1985): 111–133; Charles L. Stansifer, "The Central American Career of E. George Squier," Ph.D. diss., Tulane University, 1959; and Charles L. Stansifer, "E. George Squier and the Honduras Interoceanic Railroad Project," *HAHR* 46 (1966): 1–27.

SQUIERS, HERBERT GOLDSMITH (1859–1911). Army officer and diplomat, born April 20, 1859, in Madoc, Canada, to American parents. Squiers graduated from Minnesota Military Academy (Minneapolis) and was commissioned a second lieutenant in 1877. He was a teacher of military science at St. John's College (Fordham, N.Y.) from 1885 until 1890. He resigned from the army in 1891. He was second secretary of embassy in Germany from 1894 to 1897 and secretary of legation in China from 1898 to 1902. He was U.S. minister to Cuba from 1902 to 1905 and minister to Panama from 1906 to 1910. He retired because of ill health. Died October 20, 1911, in London. *References*: *DAB*; *DADH*; *DCB*; *NCAB* 12:333; and *WWWA*.

STABLER, J(ORDAN) HERBERT (1885–1938). Businessman and diplomat, born October 16, 1885, in Baltimore. Stabler graduated from Johns Hopkins University and studied at the University of Maryland, the Sorbonne, and the College de France. He was secretary of legation in Ecuador 1909 to 1911, chargé d'affaires in Guatemala in 1911–1912, secretary of legation in Sweden in 1912–1913, assistant to the chief of the Division of Latin American Affairs in the U.S. State Department in 1913–1914, second secretary in London from 1914 to 1916, acting chief of the Division of Latin American Affairs in 1916–1917, and its chief of that division from 1917 to 1919. He was adviser to the American Commission to Negotiate Peace in Paris in 1918. He was vice president of All America Cables, Incorporated, from 1919 to 1922, secretary general with the rank of minister of the Conference of Central American Affairs in 1922–1923, secretary general of the Plebiscitary Commission for the Tacna-Arica Arbitration in 1925–1926, and chief of the Division of Latin American Affairs at the State Department in 1926–1927. He was a representative of Venezuela Gulf Oil Corporation in Caracas from 1927 until 1937. He traveled to the Ecuadorean headwaters of the Amazon in 1910, to Haiti in 1913, to Ecuador in 1924, and to Venezuela and Colombia in 1928. Died December 30, 1938, in Paris. *References*: *NYT*, December 31, 1938; and *WWWA*.

STAHL, FERDINAND [FERNANDO] A(NTHONY) (1874–1950). Missionary, born January 3, 1874, in Pentwater, Michigan. Stahl studied nursing at the Battle Creek Sanitarium. He worked as a nurse in Cleveland and Akron. He was a missionary under the Seventh-Day Adventist Church in Bolivia from 1909 to 1911, working among the Indians in and around La Paz. From 1911 to 1921, he worked on the Peruvian side of Lake Titicaca, among the Aymara and the Quechua Indians, and established several mission stations in Peru. In 1921, he established the Metraro mission at the headwaters of the Amazon. He returned to the United States in 1939. He wrote *In the Lands of the Incas* (Mountain View, Calif., 1920). Died November 30, 1950, in Paradise, California. *Reference*: SDAE.

STANDARD FRUIT AND STEAMSHIP COMPANY. Established as the Vacaro Brothers and Company in New Orleans in 1889, it was consolidated into Standard Fruit and Steamship Company in 1923. It was involved in the fruit trade between Central America and New Orleans. It received a concession to develop lands in Honduras, and became the largest single landowner in that country, most of which was devoted to raising bananas. It was acquired in 1964 by Castle and Cooke, Incorporated. *Reference*: Thomas L. Karnes, *Tropical Enterprise: Standard Fruit and Steamship Company in Latin America* (Baton Rouge, La., 1979).

STANDARD OIL COMPANY OF NEW JERSEY. The company established refining plants in Mexico after purchasing a majority interest in the Waters-Pierce Company, its sales affiliate in Mexico until 1911. The International Petroleum Company, a subsidiary of its Canadian affiliate, Imperial Oil Limited, obtained interests in Colombia in 1920 and in Peru in 1924. In 1921, it organized another affiliate, Standard Oil Company of Venezuela, to carry out oil exploration. In 1928, it obtained a major interest in Creole Petroleum Company. In 1932, it acquired ownership of Lago Petroleum Company with wide holdings in Venezuela and a refinery in Aruba, Netherlands Antilles. Most of the interests in Venezuela were consolidated into Creole Petroleum Company in 1943. The firm also had affiliates in Argentina, Brazil, Chile, Uruguay, and all the Caribbean and Central American nations. Its holdings in Bolivia were confiscated in 1937, when the company was accused of fraud, and its properties in Cuba were expropriated in 1960. *References*: Jonathan C. Brown, "Jersey Standard and the Politics of Latin American Oil Production, 1911–30," in *Latin American Oil Companies and the Politics of Energy*, ed. John D. Wirth (Lincoln, Nebr., 1985), pp. 1–50; Kenneth J. Grieb, "Standard Oil and the Financing of the Mexican Revolution," *California Historical Quarterly* 50 (1971): 59–71; Ralph W. Hidy et al., *History of Standard Oil Company (New Jersey)* (New York, 1955–1971); and Bennett H. Wall, *Growth in a Changing Environment: A History of Standard Oil Company (New Jersey) 1950–1972 and Exxon Corporation 1972–1975* (New York, 1988).

STANDLEY, PAUL C(ARPENTER) (1884–1963). Botanist, born March 21, 1884, in Avalon, Missouri. Standley attended Drury College (Springfield, Mo.), and graduated from New Mexico State College (Las Cruces). He was assistant and then associate curator in the division of plants of the U.S. National Museum, Washington, D.C., from 1909 to 1928; associate curator of the herbarium of the Field Museum of Natural History in Chicago from 1929 to 1936; and curator there from 1937 to 1950. He made many expeditions to Mexico and Central America and wrote *Trees and Shrubs of Mexico* (Washington, D.C., 1920–1926), *Flora of the Panama Canal Zone* (Washington, D.C., 1928), *Flora of Yucatan* (Chicago, 1930), and *Flora of Costa Rica* (Chicago, 1937–1938). He was coauthor of *The Forests and Flora of British Honduras* (Chicago, 1936), and *Flora of Guatemala* (Chicago, 1958–1976). He lived in Honduras after 1950 and carried out research at the Escuela Agrícola Panamerica in El Zamorano, until 1957. Died June 2, 1963, in Tegucigalpa, Honduras. *References: AMWS*; *Chicago Natural History Museum Bulletin* 34 (November 1963): 4; *Homage to Standley: Papers in Honor of Paul C. Standley*, ed. Louis O. Williams (Chicago, 1963); and *WWWA*.

STARR, FREDERICK (1858–1933). Anthropologist, born September 2, 1858, in Auburn, New York. Starr graduated from Lafayette College (Easton, Pa.). He was a professor of biology at Coe College (Cedar Rapids, Ia.) from 1883 to 1887, served in the department of ethnology at the American Museum of Natural History from 1889 to 1891, and was professor of geology and anthropology at Pomona College (Claremont, Calif.) in 1891–1892. He was assistant professor of anthropology at the University of Chicago from 1892 to 1895, associate professor there from 1895 to 1923, and curator of anthropology at the Walker Museum of the University of Chicago. He made twelve separate trips to Mexico between 1894 and 1904, studying the ethnography and archaeology of Mexico. He wrote *Notes on Mexican Archaeology* (Chicago, 1894), *Indians of Southern Mexico; an Ethnographic Album* (Chicago, 1899), *Notes upon the Ethnography of Southern Mexico* (Davenport, Ia., 1900–1902), *In Indian Mexico: A Narrative of Travel and Labor* (Chicago, 1908), and *Mexico and the United States; a Story of Revolution, Intervention and War* (Chicago, 1914). Died August 14, 1933, in Tokyo, Japan. *References*: Frederick Starr Papers, University of Chicago Library; *AA* 36 (1945): 271; *DAB*; Donald McViker, "Prejudice and Context: The Anthropological Archaeologist as Historian," in *Archaeology's Past: The Historiography of Archaeology*, ed. Andrew L. Christiensen (Carbondale, Ill., 1989), 113–26; *NCAB* 13:115; *NYT*, August 15, 1933; and *WWWA*.

STEARNS, GEORGE ALBERT (1843–1916). Educator, born March 30, 1843, in Hampton Falls, New Hampshire. Stearns graduated from Harvard University. He went to Argentina in 1870 and set up Argentina's first normal school in Paraná in 1871. He closed the school in 1876 and returned to the United States. He graduated from Columbia University Law School and practiced law in Poughkeepsie, New York, and then in New York City. Died March 16, 1916, in Long Island City, New York. His brother, **(JOHN) WILLIAM STEARNS** (1839–1909), was born August 10, 1839, in Stockbridge, Massachusetts. He came to Argentina in 1874 and opened Argentina's second normal school in Tucumán in 1875. He returned to the United States in 1877, where he was president of the normal school in Whitewater, Wisconsin, until 1885 and head of the department of education at the University of Wisconsin (Madison) from 1885 until his retirement in 1905. Died March 6, 1909, in San Diego, California. *References*: *Cutolo*; and *Luiggi*.

STEFFENS, (JOSEPH) LINCOLN (1866–1936). Journalist, born April 6, 1866, in San Francisco, and grew up in Sacramento, California. Steffens graduated from the University of California. He was later a reporter for the New York *Evening Post*, city editor for the *Commercial Advertiser* from 1897 to 1901, and managing editor of *McClure's Magazine* from 1901 to 1906 and of *American Magazine* in 1906–1907. He was a free-lance journalist after 1907. He traveled with Venustiano Carranza in Mexico in 1914. He wrote *Autobiography of Lincoln Steffens* (New York, 1931). Died August 9, 1936, in Carmel, California. *References*: *DAB*; Drewey W. Gunn, "Three Radicals and a Revolution: Reed, London, and Steffens in Mexico," *Southwest Review* 55 (1970): 393–410; Justin Kaplan, *Lincoln Steffens* (New York, 1974); *NCAB* 14:455; *NYT*, August 10, 1936; Harry H. Stein, "Lincoln Steffens and the Mexican Revolution," *American Journal of Economics and Sociology* 34 (1957): 197–212; and *WWWA*.

STEGGERDA, MORRIS (1900–1950). Anthropologist, born September 1900, in Holland, Michigan. Steggerda graduated from Hope College and the University of Illinois. He carried out fieldwork in Jamaica from 1926 to 1928. He was assistant professor of zoology at Smith College from 1928 to 1930; investigator for the department of genetics of Carnegie Institution of Washington, in Cold Spring Harbor, New York, from 1930 to 1944; and professor of anthropology at the Kennedy School of Mission of Hartford Seminary Foundation from 1944 until his death. He made ten trips to Yucatán, Mexico, and several trips to Guatemala between 1933 and the mid-1940s, and he studied the Maya Indians of Yucatán. He wrote *Anthropometry of Adult Maya Indians* (Washington, D.C., 1932) and *Maya Indians of Yucatán* (Washington, D.C., 1941). Died March 15, 1950, in Hartford, Connecticut. *References*: *NCAB* 38:345; and *NYT*, March 16, 1950.

STEINHART, FRANK (MAXIMILIAN) (1864–1938). Businessman, born May 12, 1864, in Munich, Germany. He came to the United States in 1876. Steinhart enlisted in the U.S. Army in 1882, was clerk and assistant chief clerk from 1889 to 1898, and chief clerk after 1898. He accompanied General John R. Brooke* to Puerto Rico, was chief clerk in the Department of Puerto Rico, and then was transferred to Cuba as chief clerk of the military government until 1902. He was an agent for the War Department with residence in Cuba, in charge of the archives of the military government in 1902–1903, and consul general in Havana from 1903 to 1907. He was in business in Havana after 1907. Often considered one of the most powerful Americans in Cuba, his interests included street railways, electric lighting and gas utilities, and insurance and brewery businesses. He was president and general manager of Havana Electric Railway Company. Died December 9, 1938, in Havana. *References*: *NYT*, December 10, 1938; and *WWWA*.

STEPHENS, JOHN LLOYD (1805–1852). Traveler, archaeologist, and author, born November 28, 1805, in Shrewsbury, New Jersey. Stephens graduated from Columbia University, studied law, and was admitted to the bar. He practiced law in New York City until 1834. He traveled in the Mediterranean, Eastern Europe, and the Near East from 1834 to 1836. In 1839, he was sent on a confidential diplomatic mission to Central America. He was urged to investigate the ancient civilizations of Central America and took with him the English artist Frederick Catherwood. He investigated the ruins in Honduras, Guatemala, and Yucatán, at Copán, Uxmal, Palenque, and elsewhere. He wrote *Incidents of Travel in Central America, Chiapas, and Yucatán* (New York, 1841). He returned in 1841 and wrote *Incidents of Travel in Yucatán* (New York, 1843). He was the first to make Central America generally known in the United States and inaugurated modern studies of the Mayas. He became promoter of the Ocean Steam Navigation Company, and a supporter of the Hudson River Railroad and the Panama Railroad. He was vice president of the Panama Railroad after 1849 and handled the necessary negotiations for the railroad in Bogotá. He was then president of the company, and went to Panama to supervise the surveys and the preliminary work for the railroad. Died October 12, 1852, in New York City. *References*: Robert L. Brunhouse, *In Search of the Maya: The First Archaeologists* (Albuquerque, N.M., 1973), ch. 5; *DAB*; *DADH*; *ELA*; and Victor W. Van Hagen, *Maya Explorer: John Lloyd Stephens and the Lost Cities of Central America and Yucatan* (Norman, Okla., 1947).

STEVENS, JOHN FRANK (1853–1943). Civil engineer, born April 25, 1853, near West Gardiner, Maine. Stevens graduated from the State Normal School (Farmington, Mass.). He was involved in railroading in Minnesota, Texas, New Mexico, Iowa, Manitoba, and British Columbia from 1873 to 1886 and with the Duluth, South Shore and Atlantic Railroad from 1886 to 1893. He was assistant chief engineer of the Great Northern Railway in 1893–1894, chief engineer from 1895 to 1903, and chief engineer of the Chicago Rock Island and Pacific Railway from 1903 to 1906. He was chief engineer of the Isthmian Canal Commission in 1906–1907, with control over the construction and engineering phases of the Panama Canal. He was vice president of the New York, New Haven and Hartford Railroad from 1907 to 1909, president of the Oregon Trunk Railway Company from 1909 to 1911, private consultant from 1911 to 1917, and involved with the Russian railway system in Siberia from 1917 until 1923, when he returned to the United States. He wrote *An Engineer's Recollections* (New York, 1936). Died June 2, 1943, in Southern Pines, North Carolina. *References*: *DAB S3*; David McCullough, *The Path between the Seas: The Creation of the Panama Canal, 1870–1914* (New York, 1977), ch. 17; *NCAB* 32:326; *NYT*, June 3, 1943; and *WWWA*.

STEVENS, JOHN LEAVITT (1820–1895). Journalist and diplomat, born August 1, 1820, in Mt. Vernon, Maine. Stevens attended Maine Wesleyan Seminary. He was one of the owners and an editor of the *Kennebec Journal* from 1855 and its chief editor from 1857. He served in the Maine legislature from 1865 to 1870. He was U.S. minister to Uruguay and Paraguay from 1870 to 1874. He negotiated a commercial treaty with Uruguay and mediated a conflict between Uruguay and Argentina. He was U.S. minister to Norway and Sweden from 1877 to 1883 and minister to Hawaii from 1889 to 1893. Died February 8, 1895, in Augusta, Maine. *References*: *DAB*; *DADH*; and *NCAB* 2:172.

STEVENS, WALTER H(USTED) (1827–1867). Engineer, born August 24, 1827, in Penn Yan, New York. Stevens graduated from the U.S. Military Academy in 1848 and was commissioned in the Corps of Engineers. He served in Louisiana and Texas and in the Confederate Army during the Civil War. He went to Mexico in 1865, where he was chief engineer of the Imperial Mexican Railroad Company and superintendent and constructing engineer of a railroad between Veracruz and Mexico City. Died November 12, 1867, in Veracruz. *References*: *DAB*; and *NCAB* 12:258.

STILWELL, ARTHUR E(DWARD) (1859–1928). Businessman and railroad builder, born October 21, 1859, in Rochester, New York. Stilwell was an officer of the Travelers Insurance Company in Hartford until 1887, after which he settled in Kansas City. He built the Kansas City Sun Belt Railroad, the Kansas City Southern Railway, and several other railroads. He designed and built the city of Port Arthur, Texas, and the Port Arthur Ship Canal. He received a concession from the Mexican government in 1900 to build a railroad from Kansas City to Topolobampo, Mexico, and established the Kansas City, Mexico, and Orient Railway. It went into receivership in 1912 and he retired in 1916. He wrote two memoirs: "I Had a Hunch," (series, with James R. Crowell) in *The Saturday Evening Post*, December 3, 1927, to February 4, 1928; and *Forty Years of Business Life* (New York, 1926?). Died September 26, 1928, in New York City. *References*: Keith L. Bryant, Jr., *Arthur E. Stilwell, Promoter with a Hunch* (Nashville, Tenn., 1971); *NCAB* 14:460; *NYT*, September 27, 1928; *Pletcher*, ch. 8; and *WWWA*.

STIMSON, FREDERIC JESUP (1855–1943). Lawyer and diplomat, born July 20, 1855, in New York City or Dubuque, Iowa. Stimson graduated from Harvard University and Harvard Law School and practiced law in Boston after 1878. He was U.S. ambassador to Argentina from 1914 to 1921. He was credited with helping induce Argentina to sell large quantities of wheat to the Allies during World War I. He wrote *My United States* (New York, 1931). Died November 19, 1943, in Dedham, Massachusetts. *References*: Frederic Jesup Stimson Papers, Massachusetts Historical Society, Boston; *ACAB*; *DAB S3*; *NCAB* 44:84; *NYT*, November 21, 1943; and *WWWA*.

STIRLING, MATTHEW W(ILLIAM) (1896–1975). Anthropologist, born August 18, 1896, in Salinas, California. Stirling graduated from the University of California at Berkeley and George Washington University. He was assistant curator of the Division of Ethnology of the U.S. National Museum in Washington, D.C., from 1921 to 1924. He made a trip to Peru in 1924 to explore the upper Amazon River. He was chief of the Bureau of American Ethnology from 1928 to 1947 and director of the bureau from 1947 until his retirement in 1958. He led thirteen joint Smithsonian Institution–National Geographic Society expeditions to Mexico, Panama, and Ecuador between 1938 and 1957, including a long-term project among Olmec sites of southern Mexico from 1939 to 1946, Tres Zapotes in 1939–1940, Cerro de las Mesas in 1941, La Venta in 1942–1943, and San Lorenzo in 1945–1946. He conducted archaeological excavations in Panama between 1948 and 1952, in the Manabi Province of Ecuador in 1957, and in the Linea Vieja and Bagaces regions of Costa Rica in 1964. He wrote *Archaeological Investigations in the Bay Islands, Spanish Honduras* (Washington, D.C., 1935) and *Paracas, Nazca, and Tiahuanacoid Cultural Relationships in South Coastal Peru* (Washington, D.C., 1957). Died January 23, 1975, in Washington, D.C. *References*: *AA* 78 (1976): 886–88; *AmAntiq* 41 (1976): 67–73; Elizabeth P. Benson, ed., *The Olmecs and Their Neighbors: Essays in Memory of Matthew W. Stirling* (Washington, D.C., 1981); *CA*; *NCAB* 58:307; *NYT*, January 25, 1975; *Willey*, ch. 11; and *WWWA*.

STIRTON, RUBEN ARTHUR (1901–1966). Paleontologist, born August 20, 1901, in Muscatah, Kansas. Stirton graduated from the universities of Kansas and of California at Berkeley. He was a mammalogist with the Donald R. Dickey expeditions to El Salvador in 1925 and 1927. He was curator of fossil mammals at the Museum of Paleontology of the University of California from 1928 to 1949, associate professor of paleontology there from 1946 to 1949, and director of the museum and professor after 1949. He conducted paleontological expeditions to Colombia in 1944–1945, 1946, 1949, and 1951. Died June 14, 1966, in Long Beach, California. *References*: *Journal of Mammalogy* 48 (1967): 298–304; *Simpson*, ch. 11; and *WWWA*.

STONE, CHARLES POMEROY (1824–1887). Army officer, born September 30, 1824, in Greenfield, Massachusetts. Stone graduated from the U.S. Military Academy in 1845. He served during the Mexican War and resigned in 1856. He was chief of an exploring party in the state of Sonora, Mexico, in 1858–1859, intended to survey and map its public lands, and wrote *Notes on the State of Sonora* (Washington, D.C., 1861). He served in the Union Army during the Civil War, was engineer and superintendent for the Dover Mining Company in Goochland County, Virginia, from 1865 to 1869, and was chief of staff and lieutenant-general in the Egyptian Army from 1870 to 1883. He was later the constructing engineer for the foundations of the Statue of Liberty in New York harbor. Died January 24, 1887, in New York City. *References*: *ACAB*; Rodolfo F. Acuna, *Sonoran Strongman: Ignacio Pesqueira and His Times* (Tucson, Ariz., 1974), pp. 56–63; *DAB*; *NCAB* 11:215; and *WWWA*.

STONE, DORIS (ZEMURRAY) (1909–   ). Archaeologist, daughter of Samuel Zemurray,* and born November 19, 1909, in New Orleans. Stone graduated from Radcliffe College. She was an associate archaeologist at the Middle American Research Institute of Tulane University after 1930, research associate at the Peabody Museum of Archaeology and Ethnology of Harvard University from 1954 to 1966, and associate in Central American archaeology and ethnology from 1966 to 1971. She carried out fieldwork in Honduras and Costa Rica. She wrote *Masters in Marbles* (New Orleans, 1932), *Some Spanish Entradas* (New Orleans, 1932), *Archaeology of the North Coast of Honduras* (Cambridge, Mass., 1941), *The Boruca of Costa Rica* (Cambridge, Mass., 1949), *The Archaeology of Central and Southern Honduras* (Cambridge, Mass., 1958), *Introduction to the Archaeology of Costa Rica* (San Jose, Costa Rica, 1958), and *The Talamancan Tribes of Costa Rica* (Cambridge, Mass., 1962). She moved to San Jose, Costa Rica, in 1941. *References*: *AMWS*; W. Wyllys Andrews V, ed., *Research and Reflections in Archaeology and History: Essays in Honor of Doris Stone* (New Orleans, 1986); *CA*; J. Vargas Cato, "Doris and the Indians," *Americas* 5 (January 1953): 9–11, 29; *WWA*; and *WWAW*.

STORK, HARVEY ELMER (1890–1959). Botanist, born March 28, 1890, in Zoar, Indiana. Stork graduated from Indiana State Normal School (Terre Haute) and Indiana and Cornell universities. He was assistant professor of botany at Carleton College (Minnesota) from 1920 to 1926 and professor there from 1926 until his retirement in 1955. He carried out research in Central America in 1920, 1923, 1928, and 1929, participated in a Carleton College expedition to Cuba in 1928. He was second-in-command of the University of California botanical expedition into the Andes in 1938–1939. He collected tropical woods in Costa Rica in 1955–1956. Died September 30, 1959, in Tongaloo, Mississippi. *References*: *American Biology Teacher* 22 (1960): 268–69; and *AMWS*.

STRACHAN, R(OBERT) KENNETH (1910–1965). Missionary, born June 1, 1910, in Tandil, Argentina, and came to the United States in 1917. He went with his family to Costa Rica in 1921 and was back in the United States in 1925. Strachan graduated from Wheaton (Ill.) College and Evangelical Theological College (Dallas). He was a missionary under Latin American Evangelization Campaign (LAEC, after 1939, the Latin America Mission*) in Costa Rica after 1936. He became codirector of the mission in 1948 and its director general after 1951. Died February 24, 1965, in Pasadena, California. *References*: Elizabeth Elliot, *Who Shall Ascend: The Life of R. Kenneth Strachan of Costa Rica* (New York, 1968); *NYT*, February 26, 1965; and W. Dayton Roberts, *Strachan of Costa Rica: Missionary Insights and Strategies* (Grand Rapids, Mich., 1971).

STRAIN, ISAAC G. (1821–1857). Naval officer and explorer, born March 4, 1821, in Roxbury, Pennsylvania. Strain entered the U.S. Navy in 1837 as a midshipman. In 1843–1844, he secured a leave of absence from the navy and conducted an exploring expedition into Brazil under the auspices of the Academy of Natural Sciences of Philadelphia. He served during the Mexican War. He crossed the South American continent from Valparaiso, Chile, to Buenos Aires in 1849 on horseback, and wrote *Cordillera and Pampa, Mountain and Plain: Sketches of a Journey in Chile and the Argentine Provinces in 1849* (New York, 1853). He served on the Mexican Boundary Commission. He conducted an exploration of the Isthmus of Darien, between Caledonia Bay and the Gulf of San Miguel, in 1853, to determine the possibility of a ship canal along this route, and wrote *A Paper on the History and Prospects of Interoceanic Communication by the American Isthmus* (New York, 1856). Died May 14, 1857, in Aspinwall (later-Colón), Panama. *References*: *ACAB*; *Cutolo*; *DAB*; Ralph Z. Kirkpatrick, "Strain's Panamerican Expedition," *USNIP* 61 (August 1935): 1128–35; Vincent Ponko, Jr., *Ships, Seas and Scientists: U.S. Naval Exploration and Discovery in the Nineteenth Century* (Annapolis, Md., 1974), ch. 9; and *WWWA*.

STRAND, PAUL (1890–1976). Photographer, born October 16, 1890, in New York City. Strand studied photography and set himself up as commercial photographer in 1912. He served in the U.S. Army Medical Corps during World War I. He was a free-lance movie cameraman from 1922 to 1932. He was in Mexico from 1932 to 1934, serving as chief of photography and cinematography for the Department of Fine Arts of the Secretariat of Education of Mexico. He photographed and supervised production for the Mexican government of *Redes*, a film about fishermen (released in the United States as *The Wave*). He was president of Frontier Films, a nonprofit educational motion picture production company, from 1937 to 1942. He moved to France in 1950. He produced *Photographs of Mexico* (New York, 1940). During the 1950s, he photographed in Italy, the Outer Hebrides, France, Egypt, Rumania, Morocco, and Ghana. Died March 31, 1976, in Orgeval, France. *References*: *CA* 65; *CB* 1965; Sarah Greenough, *Paul Strand: An American Vision* (Washington, D.C., 1990); *NYT*,

April 2, 1976; *Paul Strand* (Washington, D.C., 1990); *Paul Strand, a Retrospective Monograph* (Millerton, N.Y., 1971); *Paul Strand 1890–1976* (New York, 1987); and *WWWA*.

STROBEL, EDWARD HENRY (1855–1908). Diplomat, born December 7, 1855, in Charleston, South Carolina. Strobel graduated from Harvard University and Harvard Law School and was admitted to the bar in 1883. He practiced law in New York City from 1883 to 1885. He was secretary of legation in Madrid from 1885 to 1890, third assistant secretary of state in 1893–1894, U.S. minister to Ecuador in 1894, and minister to Chile from 1894 to 1897. He prepared a report, *Resumption of Specie Payments in Chile* (Washington, D.C., 1896), and acted as an arbitrator between Chile and France regarding claims. In 1899, he was counsel for Chile before the U.S. and Chilean claims commission in Washington. He was professor of international law at Harvard Law School from 1898 to 1906 and general adviser to the government of Siam after 1903. Died January 15, 1908, in Bangkok, Siam. *References*: *DAB*; *DADH*; *NCAB* 18:140; and *NYT*, January 16, 1908.

STRONG, WILLIAM DUNCAN (1899–1962). Archaeologist, born January 30, 1899, in Portland, Oregon. Strong graduated from the University of California at Berkeley. He served in the U.S. Navy during World War I. He was assistant curator of North American ethnology and archaeology at the Field Museum of Natural History in Chicago from 1926 to 1929, professor of anthropology and director of the Archaeological Survey at the University of Nebraska from 1929 to 1931, anthropologist with the Bureau of American Ethnology from 1931 to 1937, associate professor of anthropology at Columbia University from 1937 to 1942, and professor there from 1942 until his death. He conducted numerous archaeological and ethnological expeditions to Peru, Mexico, and Honduras. He led an anthropological expedition to Honduras for the Smithsonian Institution in 1933 and was leader of the Smithsonian Institution–Harvard University expedition to Honduras in 1936 and to Peru in 1941, 1942, 1946, and 1952. He was coauthor of *Archaeological Studies in Peru, 1941–42* (New York, 1943) and *Cultural Stratigraphy in the Viru Valley, Northern Peru: The Formative and Florescent Epochs* (New York, 1952). Died January 28, 1962, in Kent Cliffs, New York. *References*: *AA* 65 (1963): 1102–1111; *NCAB* 49:385; *NYT*, January 30, 1962; and *Willey*, ch. 4.

STUART, GRANVILLE (1834–1918). Public official and diplomat, born August 27, 1834, in Clarksburg, Virginia, and grew up in Princeton, Illinois, and Black Hawk Purchase (later Muscatine County, Iowa). He prospected for gold in California from 1852 to 1857. In 1858, he came to Deer Lodge Valley (later in Montana) and settled there in 1867. He served in the Territorial Council in 1871 and 1883, and in the Territorial Lower House in 1876 and 1879. In 1879, he became involved in cattle raising on the open range. He was U.S. minister to Paraguay from 1894 to 1898. He was librarian of the Butte City Library after 1904. Died October 2, 1918, in Missoula, Montana. *Forty Years on the Frontier, as Seen in the Journals and Reminiscences of Granville Stuart, Goldminer, Merchant, Rancher, and Politician* (Cleveland, 1925) was published posthumously. *References*: Granville Stuart Manuscripts and Diaries, Yale University Library, New Haven, Conn.; Stuart Collection, Montana Historical Society Library; *DAB*; Victor C. Dahl, "Account of South American Journey, 1898," *TA* 20 (October 1963): 143–47; Victor C. Dahl, "Granville Stuart in Latin America: A Montana Pioneer's Diplomatic Career," *Montana* 21 (July 1971): 18–33; Victor C. Dahl, "A Montana Pioneer Abroad: Granville Stuart in South America," *Journal of the West* 4 (1965): 345–66; and Victor C. Dahl, "Uruguay under Juan Indiarte Borda, an American Diplomat's Observations," *HAHR* 46 (1966): 66–77.

SULLIVAN, JAMES MARK (1873–1920). Diplomat, born January 6, 1873, in Killarney, Ireland, and was brought to the United States when a child. Sullivan graduated from Yale University. He practiced law in Connecticut from 1902 to 1906 and in New York from 1906 to 1913. He was U.S. minister to the Dominican Republic from 1913 to 1915. In 1915, President Woodrow Wilson appointed a special commissioner to investigate allegations that Sullivan had interfered in the politics of Santo Domingo and had obtained public utility concessions for one of his relatives. He was removed as unfit. He went to Ireland and organized the Film Company of Ireland, producing the first motion picture ever made there. He returned to the United States in 1920. Died August 15, 1920, in St. Petersburg, Florida. *References*: *NCAB* 29:362; *NYT*, August 20, 1920; and *WWWA*.

SUMMER INSTITUTE OF LINGUISTICS (SIL). Founded in 1934 by W. Cameron Townsend,* to provide training in descriptive linguistics for missionary translators and incorporated in 1942. It began operations in Mexico in 1935, in Peru in 1946, in Central America in 1952, in Ecuador in 1953, in Bolivia in 1955, in Brazil in 1956, in Colombia and Panama in 1962, and in Surinam in 1967. *References*: Peter Aaby and Soren Hvalkof, eds., *Is God an American? An Anthropological Perspective on the Missionary Work of the Summer Institute of Linguistics* (Copenhagen, 1981); Ruth M. Brend and Kenneth L. Pike, ed., *The Summer Institute of Linguistics: Its Works and Contributions* (The Hague, 1977); and *EMCM*.

SUMTER, THOMAS, JR. (1734–1832). Diplomat. Sumter served as a secretary of legation in France in 1802. He was a gentleman planter in South Carolina from 1803 to 1809, with little success. He was U.S. minister to the Court of Portugal in Brazil, residing at Rio de Janeiro from 1809 to 1819. He did not succeed in negotiating a commercial treaty with the Portuguese. *Reference*: Phil B. Johnson, "Diplomatic Dullard: The Career of Thomas Sumter, Jr. and Diplomatic Relations of the United States with the Portuguese Court in Brazil, 1809–

1821,'' in *Dependency Unbends: Case Studies in Inter-American Relations*, ed.
Robert H. Claxton (Carrollton, Ga., 1978), pp. 21–35.

SUTTON, CHARLES WOOD (1877–1949). Civil engineer and irrigation engineer, born January 26, 1877, near Smyrna, Delaware, and grew up in Seattle, Washington. Sutton graduated from the University of Washington and studied at the University of Pennsylvania. He was employed by the Seattle and International Railway from 1898 to 1902 and was assistant topographer with the U.S. Geological Survey from 1902 to 1904. He conducted a survey of water and mineral resources in Peru from 1904 to 1906 for the Peruvian government and made recommendations on irrigation and conservation policies. He was assistant engineer with the U.S. Bureau of Reclamation from 1906 to 1908. He returned to Peru in 1908 to implement his recommendations, organized the national irrigation service of Peru, and acted as its chief engineer until 1914. He was also consulting engineer to the Peruvian department of agriculture from 1908 to 1914 and to the board of water supply of Lima in 1913–1914. He was consulting engineer in New York City from 1914 to 1919. He returned to Peru in 1919 and was a consulting and construction engineer in the Department of Irrigation Works of the Peruvian government after 1919. Died May 19, 1949, in Lima, Peru. *References*: *NCAB* 18:316; *NYT*, May 20, 1949; and *WWWA*.

SUTTON, GEORGE MIKSCH (1898–1982). Ornithologist, born May 16, 1898, in Bethany, Nebraska. Sutton attended Texas Christian University and graduated from Bethany (W. Va.) College and Cornell University. He was a member of the staff of Carnegie Museum in Pittsburgh from 1919 to 1925, state ornithologist of Pennsylvania from 1925 to 1929, and curator of birds at Cornell University from 1931 to 1945. He conducted several expeditions to Mexico and the Galapagos Islands. He wrote *Birds in the Wilderness: Adventures of an Ornithologist* (New York, 1936), *Mexican Birds: First Impressions* (Norman, Okla., 1951), *At a Bend in a Mexican River* (New York, 1972), *Portraits of Mexican Birds: Fifty Selected Paintings* (Norman, Okla., 1975), and *Bird Student: An Autobiography* (Austin, Tex., 1980), and edited *To a Young Bird Artist: Selected Letters from Louis Agassiz Fuertes to George Miksch Sutton* (Norman, Okla., 1979). Died December 7, 1982, in Norman, Oklahoma. *References*: *AMWS*; *CA*; and *WWA*.

SUTTON, WARNER P(ERRIN) (? –1913). Consul, born in Michigan. Sutton was a teacher and superintendent of schools at Saugatuck, Michigan. He was successively a commercial agent, consul, and consul general in Matamoros, Mexico, from 1878 to 1889, and consul general in Neuvo Laredo, Mexico, from 1889 to 1893. Died May 30, 1913, in Madison, Ohio. *Reference*: David M. Pletcher, ''Consul Warner P. Sutton and American-Mexican Border Trade during the Early Diaz Period,'' *Southwestern Historical Quarterly* 79 (1976): 373–99.

SWAN ISLANDS [ISLAS DEL CISNE]. Two islets in the Caribbean Sea, ninety-seven miles north of Honduras. They were occupied by William Walker* in 1860, and Honduras staked its claim in 1861. They were placed under U.S. sovereignty in 1863 by the Guano Islands Act, and have been prized by guano hunters and turtle fishermen. The islands were turned over to Honduras in 1971. Weather, navigation, and communication stations continue to be operated by the United States in agreement with Honduras. *Reference*: Carlos A. Ferro, *El Caso de las Islas Santanilla* (Tegucigalpa, Honduras, 1972).

T

TABER, SAMUEL WILLIAM (1780–1813). Merchant, born in New York City. Taber was involved in business in New York City and then went to the Rio de la Plata in 1810, planning to establish himself in business there. He went to Buenos Aires, joined the revolutionaries, and submitted a plan for a submarine to the Argentine Junta de Mayo in 1811. It was accepted by the junta, and the construction, for which Taber used his own funds, began that year. He was sent by the junta on a secret mission to Montevideo in 1811, was captured and imprisoned by the Royalists at Montevideo, and was forced to leave the country, but he returned to Buenos Aires and renewed work on his submarine, which was probably never used. In 1812, he was sent on a secret mission to Chile. Died November 8, 1813, near Buenos Aires. *References*: *Cutolo*; Alberto D. Leiva, *Samuel William Taber, 1780–1813. Un Pionero de la Armada Argentina* (Buenos Aires, 1969); Mario Fermio Pensotti, "Samuel Guillermo Taber," *Del Mer* 111 (May–August 1979): 29–42; and *Udaondo*.

TAFFINDER, SHERWOODE AYERST (1884–1965). Naval officer, born March 18, 1884, in Council Bluffs, Iowa. Taffinder graduated from the U.S. Naval Academy in 1906 and was commissioned ensign in the U.S. Navy in that year. He served on the Asiatic, Atlantic, and Pacific stations from 1906 until 1924. He headed a naval mission to Peru from 1924 to 1926 and was in command of the Peruvian Navy. He served in the Canal Zone from 1928 to 1930 and in the Navy Department from 1936 to 1939. He was chief of staff of the U.S. Fleet in 1940–1941, commandant of Puget Sound Navy Yard in Bremerton, Washington, in 1942–1943, commander of the Service Force Atlantic Fleet in 1944, and commandant of the 14th Naval District and Hawaiian Sea Frontier in 1945. He retired with the rank of vice admiral in 1947. Died January 25, 1965, in Newport, Rhode Island. *References*: *NYT*, January 26, 1965; and *WWWA*.

TALCOTT, ANDREW (1797–1883). Engineer, born April 20, 1797, in Glastonbury, Connecticut. Talcott graduated from the U.S. Military Academy in 1818, was commissioned second lieutenant in the corps of engineers, and served until 1836, being involved in engineering work and fortifications in New York, Virginia, Missouri, Rhode Island, and Delaware. He worked as civil engineer in railroad construction, in improving the delta of the Mississippi River, and in other engineering works. He was in Mexico from 1857 to 1867, where he was involved in the construction of a railroad from Veracruz to Mexico City and manager of the Sonora Exploring and Mining Company. He retired in 1867. Died April 23, 1883, in Richmond, Virginia. *References*: *ACAB*; *DAB*; *NCAB* 13:405; and *WWWA*.

TANNENBAUM, FRANK (1893–1969). Journalist and educator, born March 4, 1893, in Austria. He came with his family to the United States in 1905, and grew up in Great Barrington, Massachusetts. Tannenbaum left for New York at age thirteen. He became involved with the Industrial Workers of the World movement, was convicted of disturbing the peace and spent some time in prison on Blackwell's (later Welfare) Island. He graduated from Columbia University, studied at the New School for Social Research, and graduated from Brookings Graduate School of Economic and Political Science (Washington, D.C.). He was a correspondent for *Survey* magazine in Mexico from 1922 to 1924, and traveled extensively throughout South America. He surveyed land and agricultural conditions in Mexico for the Institute of Economics in Washington, D.C., from 1925 to 1927, made a survey of economic and social conditions in Puerto Rico for the Brookings Institution from 1928 to 1930, and studied rural education in Mexico for the Mexican government in 1931. In 1932–1933, he visited every country of South America, making three separate trips down the Amazon River by dugout and canoe. He taught at Cornell University from 1932 to 1935. He was a lecturer of Latin American history at Columbia University from 1935 to 1937, associate professor there from 1937 to 1945, and professor from 1945 until his retirement in 1961. He was also director of Columbia University Seminars from 1961 to 1969. He wrote *The Mexican Agrarian Revolution* (New York, 1929), *Peace by Revolution: An Interpretation of Mexico* (New York, 1933), *Whither Latin America? An Introduction to Its Economic and Social Problems* (New York, 1934), *Mexico, The Struggle for Peace and Bread* (New York, 1950), and *Ten Keys to Latin America* (New York, 1962). Died June 1, 1969, in New York City. *References*: German Arciniegas, "Tannenbaum and Latin America," *Americas* 28 (April 1970): 27–31; *CA*; Helen Delpar, "Frank Tannenbaum: The Making of a Mexicanist, 1914–1933," *TA* 45 (1988): 153–71; *HAHR* 50 (1970): 345–48; and *NYT*, June 2, 1969.

TARBOUX, JOHN WILLIAM (1858–1940). Missionary, born September 13, 1858, in Charleston, South Carolina. Tarboux graduated from Wofford College and was ordained in 1877. He was a missionary under the Board of Foreign

Missions of the Methodist Episcopal Church* in Brazil from 1883 until 1921. He was president of Granbery College in Juiz de Fora, state of Minas Gerais, from 1909 until his retirement in 1921, and founded schools of dentistry, pharmacy, and law. He held a pastorate in Miami from 1921 to 1930. In 1931, he was elected first bishop of the autonomous Methodist Church in Brazil; he served from 1931 to 1939. Died May 2, 1940, in Miami. *Reference*: EWM.

TAYLOE, EDWARD THORNTON (1803–1876). Diplomat, born January 31, 1803, in Washington, D.C. Tayloe graduated from Harvard University. He served as private secretary to Joel R. Poinsett,* U.S. minister to Mexico, from 1825 to 1828, and was secretary of legation in Colombia in 1828–1829. He was later a planter at Powhatan Hill, Virginia. Died November 26, 1876, in Powhatan Hill, Virginia. *References*: Edward Thornton Tayloe Journal, Manuscript Division, Library of Congress; Edward Thornton Tayloe Colombian Journal and Letters, in Tayloe Family Papers, University of Virginia Library, Charlottesville, Va.; and *Mexico, 1825–1828: The Journal and Correspondence of Edward Thornton Tayloe* ed. Gardiner C. Harvey (Chapel Hill, N.C., 1959).

TAYLOR, RICHARD COWLING (1789–1851). Geologist, born January 18, 1789, in Hinton, Suffolk, or Banham, Norfolk, England. Taylor went to London in 1826 and was engaged on the ordnance survey of England. He came to the United States in 1830, where he was involved in the survey of the Blossburg coal region and in the exploration of the coal and iron veins of the Dauphin and Susquehanna Coal Company. He later explored many mineral districts containing gold, silver, lead, copper, coal, asphaltum, and other materials. He explored the copper mines of Cuba and the gold fields of Panama. Died October 27, 1851, in Philadelphia. *References*: DAB; NCAB 9: 265; and WWWA.

TAYLOR, WILLIAM. *See* WILLIAM TAYLOR SELF-SUPPORTING MISSIONS IN SOUTH AMERICA

TAYLOR, ZACHARY CLAY (1851–1919). Missionary, born January 1851 near Jackson, Mississippi. Taylor attended Waco University and graduated from Baylor University and Southern Baptist Theological Seminary. He was ordained in 1879. He was a missionary under the Foreign Mission Board of the Southern Baptist Convention* in Brazil from 1882 until 1909. He served in Bahia, published *The Echo of Truth*, a monthly paper, after 1884, and established a college there in 1898. He returned to the United States in 1909 because of ill health. Drowned in a hurricane, September 14, 1919, in Corpus Christi, Texas. *References*: ESB; and W. S. Stewart, *Later Baptist Missionaries and Pioneers* (Philadelphia, 1929), 2:1–36.

TEE-VAN, JOHN (1897–1967). Ichthyologist, born July 6, 1897, in Brooklyn, New York. Tee-Van attended New York University. He was a member of twenty-three expeditions for zoological oceanographic research in British Guiana, Venezuela, Galapagos Islands, Haiti, Bermuda, and Central America. He was an assistant in the department of tropical research of the New York Zoological Garden from 1917 to 1924, general assistant from 1925 to 1930, general associate from 1931 to 1941, executive secretary of the New York Zoological Society and Aquarium from 1942 to 1952, director from 1952 to 1956, and general director from 1956 until his retirement in 1962. He wrote *Field Book of the Shore Fishes of Bermuda* (New York, 1933). Died November 5, 1967, in Sherman, Connecticut. *References*: E. Iglauer, "Wonderful Zoo in the Bronx," *Harper's* 217 (September 1954): 46–54; *New Yorker* 28 (September 6, 1952): 29–30; *NYT*, November 6, 1967; and *WWWA*.

TEHUANTEPEC RAILROAD COMPANY. Incorporated in 1849 to build a railroad across the Isthmus of Tehuantepec in Mexico. It received a concession from the Mexican government in that year. A survey was made by John G. Barnard* in 1850 but the concession was declared void by the Mexican government in 1851. *References*: Genaro Fernández MacGregor, *El Istmo Tehuantepec y los Estado Unidos* (Mexico City, 1954); Edward B. Glick, *Straddling the Isthmus of Tehuantepec* (Gainesville, Fla., 1959); Edward B. Glick, "The Tehuantepec Railroad: Mexico's White Elephant," *PHR* 22 (1953): 373–82; and M. S. Meier, "History of the Tehuantepec Railroad," Ph.D. diss., University of California, 1954.

TELLES, RAYMOND L., JR. (1915–   ). Diplomat, born September 5, 1915, in El Paso, Texas. Telles attended Texas Western College (later University of Texas, El Paso). He was a cost accountant and administrator in the U.S. Department of Justice from 1934 to 1941, served in the Air Force during World War II, and served as chief of lend-lease to Latin American countries and in the U.S. Army during the Korean War. He was El Paso county clerk from 1948 to 1957 and mayor of El Paso from 1957 to 1961. He was U.S. ambassador to Costa Rica from 1961 to 1967, and was influential in bringing that country into the Central American Common Market. He was in private business until 1971. He was a member of the Equal Employment Opportunity Commission from 1971 to 1976, and again went into private business. *References*: Matt S. Meier, *Mexican American Biographies: A Historical Dictionary, 1836–1987* (New York, 1987); and *WWA*.

TERRELL, ALEXANDER WATKINS (1829–1912). Lawyer and diplomat, born November 3, 1829, in Patrick County, Virginia, and grew up in Missouri. Terrell studied at the University of Missouri and was admitted to the bar in 1849. He practiced law in St. Joseph, Missouri, from 1849 to 1852, and in Austin, Texas, after 1852. He was judge of the second judicial district from 1857 to 1863 and then served in the Confederate Army during the Civil War. He was a major in the Mexican Imperial Army. He wrote *From Texas to Mexico and the Court of Maximilian in 1865* (Dallas, Tex., 1933). He resumed his law practice in Houston but in 1867 retired to his plantation in Robinson County, Texas. He returned to Austin in 1871. He was a member of the Texas State Senate in 1875 and 1879 and U.S. minister to Turkey from 1893 to 1897. *References*: *NCAB* 5:555; and *WWWA*.

TERRY, T(HOMAS) PHILIP (1864–1945). Author, born June 6, 1864, in Georgetown, Kentucky, and grew up in Paris, Kentucky. Terry went to Mexico in 1885, was a correspondent there for various American newspapers, and was on the staff of the *Mexican Financier*. He was manager of the Sonora News Company in Mexico from 1905 to 1910. He returned to the United States in 1912. He wrote *Terry's Guide to Mexico* (Boston, 1909) and *Terry's Guide to Cuba* (Boston, 1926). Died May 21, 1945, in Boston. *Reference*: *WWWA*.

THATCHER, MAURICE HUDSON (1870–1973). Government official, born August 15, 1870, in Chicago. Thatcher attended Bryant and Stratton Business College (Louisville, Ky.). He served as clerk of the circuit court of Butler County, Kentucky, from 1893 to 1896, studied law, and was admitted to the bar in 1898. He was assistant attorney general of Kentucky from 1898 to 1900, practiced law in Louisville in 1900–1901, and was assistant U.S. district attorney for the western district of Kentucky from 1901 to 1906 and state inspector and examiner for Kentucky from 1908 to 1910. He was a member of the Isthmian Canal Commission from 1910 to 1913. As head of its Department of Civil Administration, he functioned as civil governor of the Canal Zone from 1910 until 1913. He reformed the penal system, used prison labor for highway construction, introduced the teaching of Spanish to the public schools, and drafted a vehicular traffic code for the Canal Zone. He was also responsible for relations with the government of Panama. He resumed practice of law in Louisville in 1913, served in the U.S. House of Representatives from 1923 to 1933, and later practiced law in Washington, D.C. He wrote *Autobiography in Poetry* (New York, 1924). Died January 6, 1973, in Washington, D.C. *References*: *BDAC*; *NCAB* 58:439; *NYT*, January 7, 1973; and *WWWA*.

THOMAS, WILLIAM MATTHEW MERRICK (1878–1951). Missionary, born May 3, 1878, in Saint Marys County, Maryland. Thomas graduated from the University of Virginia and Virginia Theological Seminary, and was ordained in 1905. He was a missionary under the Domestic and Foreign Missionary Society of the Protestant Episcopal Church in the U.S.A. in Mexico after 1904 and served in Rio Grande do Sul from 1904 to 1910. He was a professor at the Brazilian Episcopal Theological Seminary, rector of a church, treasurer of the mission, and, from 1911 until his retirement, resided in Porto Alegre. He was consecrated bishop in 1925, suffragan bishop of southern Brazil from 1925 to 1928, and missionary bishop of that district from 1928 until his retirement in 1949. He founded a school for boys in Porto Alegre in 1912 and was its headmaster in 1926, and founded a school for girls in Pelotas in 1932. He was also a professor of canon law, liturgics, and ethics at Porto Alegre Theological Seminary from 1921 to 1925. Died September 18, 1951, in Washington, D.C. *References*: *NCAB* 40:376; *NYT*, September 20, 1951; and *WWWA*.

THOME, JOHN [JUAN] M(ACON) (1843–1908). Astronomer, born August 22, 1843, in Palmyra, Pennsylvania. Thome graduated from Lehigh University. He went to Argentina in 1870 and was assistant to Benjamin Apthorp Gould* at the Córdoba Observatory. He contributed the great bulk of the observations to the *Cordoba Durchmusterung* (Buenos Aires, 1892–1914), a catalogue of the stars of the Southern Hemisphere, which was his principal achievement. He was director of the Córdoba Observatory from 1885 until 1908. He was also U.S. vice-consul in Córdoba from 1877 until 1906. Died March 1908, in Córdoba, Argentina. *References*: John E. Hodge, "Juan M. Thome, Argentine Astronomer from the Quaker State," *JISWA* 13 (1971): 215–29; and *Monthly Notices of the Royal Astronomical Society* 69 (1909): 255–57.

THOMPSON, AMBROSE W(ILLIAM) (1810–1882). Entrepreneur, born in Lewes, Delaware, and grew up in Philadelphia. Thompson was involved in shipbuilding and later established a coastal steamship line which prospered until the Civil War. He moved to New York City in 1857 and was involved in marine underwriting and in the construction and operation of railroads. In 1854, he was granted a concession from the provincial legislature of the Province of Chiriquí, Colombia, to operate a transit road from Bocas del Toro to David. He also hoped to establish a colony of freed U.S. slaves in Chiriquí and to operate it, but the Colombian legislature annulled the agreement. Died May 27, 1882, in Philadelphia. *References*: *Philadelphia Enquirer*, May 30, 1882; Paul J. Scheips, "Ambrose W. Thompson: A Neglected Isthmian Promoter," M.A. thesis, University of Chicago, 1949; and Paul J. Scheips, "Gabriel Lafond and Ambrose W. Thompson: Neglected Isthmian Promoters," *HAHR* 36 (1956): 211–218.

THOMPSON, DAVID EUGENE (1854–1942). Diplomat, born February 28, 1854, in Branch County, Michigan. Thompson learned the watchmaker trade but in 1872 began employment with the Burlington Railway in Nebraska and was its superintendent from 1881 to 1890. He was then involved in the management of various industrial enterprises and became president and owner of the Lincoln *Daily Star* and the Columbia Fire Insurance Company after 1902. He was U.S. minister to Brazil from 1902 to 1905 and ambassador in 1905–1906 and served as ambassador to Mexico from 1906 to 1909. In 1909 he bought the Pan-American Railroad and was involved in its management. *Reference*: *NCAB* 14:166.

THOMPSON, EDWARD H(ERBERT) (1856–1935). Explorer and archaeologist, born September 28, 1856, in Worcester, Massachusetts. Thompson attended Worcester County Free Institute of Industrial Science (later Worcester

Polytechnic Institute). He was engaged in various work until 1885. He was U.S. consul in Merida, Mexico, from 1885 to 1893, and consul at Progreso from 1897 to 1909. He was charged by the American Antiquarian Society to investigate scientifically certain Mayan structures in Yucatán and therefore explored Maya antiquities. He purchased a plantation and explored the Sacred Well in Chichén Itzá. He wrote *People of the Serpent: Life and Adventures among the Mayas* (Boston, 1932). Died May 11, 1935, in Plainfield, New Jersey. *References: AA* 37 (1935): 711–12; Robert L. Brunhouse, *In Search of the Maya: The First Archaeologists* (Albuquerque, N.M., 1973), pp. 166–95; *DAB S1*; *NYT*, May 12, 1935; and *WWWA*.

THOMPSON, J(OHN) ERIC S(IDNEY) (1898–1975). Archaeologist, born December 31, 1898, in London, England. Thompson served in the British Army during World War I. He graduated from Winchester College of Cambridge University. He was assistant curator in charge of Central and South American archaeology and ethnology at the Chicago Natural History Museum from 1926 to 1935, senior archaeologist on the staff of the department of archaeology of the Carnegie Institution of Washington from 1935 to 1958, and a member of the faculty of archaeology and anthropology of Cambridge University from 1958 to 1975. He carried out numerous archaeological trips to Central America and Mexico, conducted excavations in British Honduras and at Chichén Itzá, was a member of the British Museum Expedition to British Honduras in 1927, and worked at Rio Bec and El Palmar in 1936 and again in British Honduras in 1938. He was involved in deciphering Mayan hieroglyphic writing and calculating correlations between the Mayan and Christian calendars. He wrote *The Civilization of the Mayas* (Chicago, 1927), *A Correlation of the Mayan and European Calendars* (Chicago, 1927), *Archaeological Investigations in the Southern Cayo District, British Honduras* (Chicago, 1931), *Ethnology of the Mayas of Southern and Central British Honduras* (Chicago, 1931), *A Preliminary Study of the Ruins of Coba, Quintana Roo, Mexico* (Washington, D.C., 1932), *The Solar Year of the Mayas at Quirigua, Guatemala* (Chicago, 1932), *Mexico before Cortez: An Account of the Daily Life, Religion, and Ritual of the Aztecs and Kindred Peoples* (New York, 1933), *Archaeology of South America* (Chicago, 1936), *Excavations at San Jose, British Honduras* (Washington, D.C., 1939), *Maya Hieroglyphic Writing: An Introduction* (Washington, D.C., 1950), *The Rise and Fall of Maya Civilization* (Norman, Okla., 1954), *Maya History and Religion* (Norman, Okla., 1970), *Maya Hieroglyphics without Tears* (London, 1972), and his autobiography, *Maya Archaeologist* (Norman, Okla., 1963). Died September 9, 1975, in Cambridge, England. *References: AmAntiq* 42 (1977): 180–90; *CA*; Norman Hammond, ed., *Social Process in Maya Prehistory: Studies in Honour of Sir Eric Thompson* (London, 1977); *NYT*, September 11, 1975; and *WWWA*.

THOMPSON, THOMAS LARKIN (1838–1898). Diplomat, born May 31, 1838, in Charleston, Kanawha County, Virginia (later West Virginia), and grew up in California. Thompson became involved in journalism in 1855, established a newspaper in Petaluma, California, in that year, and was editor and publisher of the *Sonoma Democrat* from 1860 until his death. He was secretary of state of California from 1882 to 1886 and a member of U.S. House of Representatives from 1887 to 1889. He was U.S. minister to Brazil from 1893 to 1897. He succeeded in keeping the United States uninvolved during the revolt of the Brazilian Navy of 1893–1894 and later negotiated a treaty of extradition between the United States and Brazil. Died February 1, 1898, in Santa Rosa, California. *References*: *BDAC*; *DAB*; and *NCAB* 8:178.

THOMPSON, WADDY, JR. (1798–1868). Lawyer and diplomat, born September 8, 1798, in Pickensville, South Carolina. Thompson graduated from South Carolina College (later University of South Carolina), studied law, and was admitted to the bar in 1819. He practiced law in Edgefield, South Carolina, from 1819 to 1826 and served in the South Carolina legislature from 1826 to 1830 and in the U.S. House of Representatives from 1835 to 1840. He was U.S. minister to Mexico from 1842 to 1844. He obtained the release of the prisoners captured by the Mexicans during the hostilities between Texas and Mexico, worked out adjustments to claims settlements, persuaded the Mexican government to continue allowing U.S. immigrants into California, and began negotiations for the acquisition of that state. He was popular in Mexico. He wrote *Recollections of Mexico* (New York, 1846). He was later a real estate entrepreneur. Died November 23, 1868, in Tallahassee, Florida. *References*: *BDAC*; *DAB*; *DADH*; and *NCAB* 3:511.

THOMSON, THADDEUS AUSTIN (1853–1927). Diplomat, born January 17, 1853, in Burleson County, Texas. Thomson attended Salado College and Texas Military Institute. He was a planter and ranchman, studied law, and was admitted to the bar in 1881. He practiced law in Austin from 1883 until 1896 and then was involved in the real estate business. He was U.S. minister to Colombia from 1913 to 1916. He negotiated and signed a treaty between the United States and Colombia in 1914, which was known as the Thomson-Urrutia treaty. He resumed his real estate business in Austin in 1916. Died January 18, 1927, in Austin, Texas. *References*: *NCAB* 37:116; and *WWWA*.

THORNE, JOHN (1807–1885). Naval officer, born March 8, 1807, in New York City. Thorne first resided in Brazil and then came to Buenos Aires. He settled there in 1825. He served in the Argentine Navy in the war against Brazil in 1826–1827. As a privateer in 1827, he was taken prisoner by the Brazilians and was a prisoner in Rio de Janeiro until the end of the war. He served in the merchant marine from 1828 to 1831 and then returned to the Argentine Navy. He participated in the expedition to Paraguay in 1831. He navigated up the Rio Colorado to Patagoras in 1833–1834. He held the captaincy of the Port of Buenos Aires in 1835, served in the war against the French in 1838 in the island of Martin Garcia, and was taken prisoner. He later went to Entre Rios where he participated in battles, was commander of a squadron on the Paraná River, and served against Anglo-French forces in 1844. He lost his hearing in Vuelto de Obligado and became known as *El Sordo de Obligado* (The Deaf Man of Obligado). He was in charge of the Argentine Confederation fleet that conducted a blockade of Paraguayan ports in 1855. Died August 10, 1885, in Buenos Aires. *References*: *Cutolo*; Ricardo Piccirilli and Leoncio Gianello, *Biografías Navales* (Buenos Aires, 1963), pp. 293–301; and *Udaondo*.

THRASHER, JOHN S(IDNEY) (1817–1879). Editor and adventurer, born in Portland, Maine, and moved with his parents to Cuba in 1832 or 1833. Thrasher was a clerk in the mercantile house of Tyng and Company, ship brokers and commission merchants, until 1847. He was a revolutionary agitator and propagandist for Narciso López and others from 1848 to 1851 (*see* LÓPEZ EXPEDITIONS). He was coeditor of *El Faro Industrial de la Habana* in 1850–1851, was tried by court martial in 1851 for anti-Spanish activities, and was imprisoned in 1851–1852. He went to New Orleans and aided other Cuban filibusters from 1852 to 1855. He was employed by the *New York Herald* after 1855 and traveled in Mexico and South America until 1859. He was editor of *Beacon of Cuba, and a Preliminary Essay on the Purchase of Cuba* (New York, 1859). Died November 10, 1879, in Galveston, Texas. *References*: *ACAB*; *DAB*; and *WWWA*.

TIERNAN, FRANCES CHRISTINE FISHER (1846–1920). Author, born July 5, 1846, in Salisbury, North Carolina. Tiernan began to write early and her first novel appeared in 1870. In 1888, she went to Mexico with her husband, James Marquis Tiernan, who had mining interests there, and lived in Mexico until his death in 1898, when she returned to the United States. She published under her pseudonym, Christian Reid. Many of her later novels have Mexican settings and characters and make use of Mexican history and legends, including *"The Land of the Sky,"* or, *Adventures in Mountain By-Ways* (New York, 1875) and *The Picture of Las Cruces; a Romance of Mexico* (New York, 1896). Died March 24, 1920, in Salisbury, North Carolina. *References*: *DAB*; and *NCAB* 20:293.

TODD, CHARLES STEWART (1791–1871). Lawyer and diplomat, born January 22, 1791, near Danville, Virginia (later in Kentucky). Todd graduated from the College of William and Mary, studied law, and was admitted to the bar in 1811. He practiced law in Lexington, Kentucky. He served in the army during the War of 1812. He was secretary of state of Kentucky in 1816–1817 and a member of Kentucky State Legislature in 1817–1818. He was U.S. diplomatic agent to Colombia from 1820 to 1832, observing the conditions with a view to guiding the United States government in its recognition policy, pressing for the settlement of American claims against Colombia, and working for the removal of discriminating tariffs. He was U.S. minister to Russia from 1841 to 1846. In

1850, he was appointed a commissioner to treat with Indian tribes on the Mexican border and drew up the final report. He was later editor of the Louisville *Industrial and Commercial Gazette*. Died May 17, 1871, in Baton Rouge, Louisiana. *References*: *DAB*; *NCAB* 6:227; and D. J. Trester, "The Political Career of David Todd," Ph.D. diss., Ohio University, 1950.

TOLEDO. Colony of ex-Confederates, mostly Louisiana sugar planters, who settled in British Honduras about 1867. They bought the cutover timber lands of Young, Toledo and Company of British Honduras and established a community near the town of Punta Gorda in southern British Honduras (in the present Toledo district), in which they raised sugar cane. After 1890, the colony began to decline, and after 1925 its members gradually began to return to the United States, and by 1929, it ceased to exist. *References*: Desmond Holdridge, "Toledo: A Tropical Refugee Settlement in British Honduras," *Geographical Review* 30 (1940): 376–93; and Daniel G. Rosenberger, "An Examination of the Perpetuation of Southern United States Institutions in British Honduras by a Colony of Ex-Confederates," Ed.D. diss., New York University, 1958.

TOOR, FRANCES (1890–1956). Author, born in Plattsburgh, New York. Toor graduated from the University of California. She settled in Mexico, traveled throughout the country, and studied its folkways, especially the fiestas. She served on the faculty of the University of Mexico for twenty-five years. She was a friend of the Mexican artists Diego Maria Rivera, José Clemente Orozoco, David Alfaro Siqueiros, and Carlos Merida, and helped to introduce their work into the United States. She wrote *Frances Toor's Guide to Mexico* (Mexico City, 1933), *Mexican Popular Arts* (Mexico City, 1939), *Frances Toor's New Guide to Mexico* (Mexico City, 1944), *A Treasury of Mexican Folkways* (New York, 1947), and *Three Worlds of Peru* (New York, 1949). Died June 16, 1956, in New York City. *Reference*: *NYT*, June 18, 1956.

TOPOLOBAMPO BAY COLONY. Utopian colony founded by Albert Kimsey Owen* in 1884 in Topolobampo Bay, the state of Sinaloa, on the west coast of Mexico, in 1884, on the terminus of a projected railroad line. It was based on his principles of integral cooperation in which the processes of production and distribution would be located in one place and would be owned by the colonists. The colonists began to leave in 1894 and the colony had disintegrated by 1899. *References*: Credit Foncier of Sinaloa Collection, California State University Library, Fresno, Calif.; Leopold Katscher, "Owen's Topolobampo Colony, Mexico," *American Journal of Sociology* 12 (1906): 145–75; Bennett Lowenthal, "The Topolobampo Colony in the Context of Porfirian Mexico," *Communal Societies* 7 (1987): 47–66; Sergio Ortega Noriega, *El Eden Subvertido: La Colonization de Topolobampo, 1886–1896* (Mexico City, 1978); Ray Reynolds, *Cat's Paw Utopia* (El Cajon, Calif., 1972   ıd Thomas A. Robertson, *A Southwestern Utopia* (Los Angeles, 1964).

TOTTEN, GEORGE MUIRSON (1809–1884). Engineer, born May 28, 1809, in New Haven, Connecticut. Totten graduated from Norwich (Vt.) Military Academy (later Norwich University). He was assistant engineer on the Farmington Canal from 1827 to 1828, on the Juniata Canal in Pennsylvania from 1828 to 1831, and on the Delaware and Raritan Canal in New Jersey from 1831 to 1835. He was employed to assist in the construction of railroad in Pennsylvania, Virginia, and North Carolina from 1835 to 1843. In 1843, he built the Canal del Dique in the harbor in Cartagena in Colombia to connect the harbor with the Magdalena River. In 1850, he was engineer in chief in the construction of the Panama Railroad. He spent some twenty-five years on the isthmus. When Ferdinand de Lesseps became president of the Panama Canal Company in 1879, Totten was asked to remain on the isthmus as chief engineer, and the only American member, of de Lesseps's staff. Later he went to Venezuela on railroad work near Caracas and served as consulting engineer in connection with the first Panama Canal project and on many other canal and railroad works. Died May 17, 1884, in New York City. *References*: *DAB*; *NCAB* 18:109; and *NYT*, May 17, 1884.

TOWNE, ROBERT S(AFFORD) (1858–1916). Mining engineer, born September 17, 1858, in Portsmouth, Scioto County, Ohio. Towne graduated from the Ohio State University. He was active in the development of Mexico, as an officer in many Mexican corporations, establishing ore-buying agencies in northern Mexico, acquiring mines, and erecting smelters. He built the Mexican Northern Railway Company and served as its president and treasurer. He was also president of the Alvarez Land and Timber Company, Presnillo Mining Company, Mexican Lead Company, Potosi and Rio Verde Railway Company, Montezuma Lead Company, Soubrette Mining Company, Compañía Metalingica Mexicana, Teziutlan Copper Mining and Smelting Company, and Minerals Extractor Corporation. Died August 3, 1916, in New York City. *References*: *NYT*, August 4, 1916; and *Ohio State University Monthly*, December 1916.

TOWNER, HORACE M(ANN) (1855–1937). Lawyer, born October 23, 1855, in Belvidere, Illinois. Towner attended the University of Chicago and Union College of Law (Chicago) and graduated from the State University of Iowa. He was admitted to the bar in 1877. He practiced law in Corning, Iowa, from 1880 to 1890, was judge of the third judicial district of Iowa from 1890 to 1910, and served in the U.S. House of Representatives from 1911 to 1923. He was governor of Puerto Rico from 1923 to 1929. He made a serious attempt to understand Puerto Rican aspirations, and believing that Puerto Rico must become a state, he granted a generous measurement of self-government. He then resumed the practice of law in Corning. Died November 23, 1937, in Corning, Iowa. *References*: *BDAC*; *NCAB* B:374; *NYT*, November 24, 1937; and *WWWA*.

TOWNSEND, CHARLES H(ENRY) T(YLER) (1863–1944). Entomologist, born December 5, 1863, in Oberlin, Ohio. Townsend graduated from Columbia (S.C.) College and George Washington University. He taught at the New Mexico College of Agriculture and Mechanical Arts (Las Cruces) from 1891 to 1893, was curator of the Public Museum in Kingston, Jamaica, from 1893 to 1898 and the New Mexico Agricultural Experiment Station (Las Cruces) in 1898– 1899, and taught in the Philippines from 1904 to 1906. He was entomologist and director of the experiment station of Peru from 1909 to 1913 and systematic entomologist with the Bureau of Entomology in Peru and Brazil from 1919 to 1929. Involved in agricultural and medical entomology, he discovered the insect vector of verruga, the cause of a skin disease common in Peru. He later founded his own publishing company in São Paulo, Brazil. Died March 17, 1944, in São Paulo. *References*: Arnold Mallis, *American Entomologists* (New Brunswick, N.J., 1971), pp. 391–93; *NYT*, January 29, 1944; and C. H. Wilson, *Ambassadors in White* (New York, 1942).

TOWNSEND, W(ILLIAM) CAMERON (1896–1982). Missionary and linguist, born July 9, 1896, in Eastvale, California, and grew up in Downey and Compton, California. Townsend attended Occidental College (Los Angeles). He was a Bible salesman in Guatemala in 1917. He then spent twelve years with the Quiche, or Cakchiquel, Indians in the western highlands of Guatemala, and translated the New Testament into the Quiche language. He cofounded the Summer Institute of Linguistics* in 1934 and Wycliffe Bible Translators in 1935 and he headed the Jungle Aviation and Radio Service. He wrote *They Found a Common Language* (New York, 1972) and (with Richard Pittman) *Remember All the Way* (Huntington Beach, Calif., 1975). Died April 23, 1982, in Lancaster, South Carolina. *References*: *CA*; James C. Hefley and Marti Hefley, *Uncle Cam: The Story of William Cameron Townsend, Founder of the Wycliffe Bible Translators and the Summer Institute of Linguistics* (Waco, Tex., 1974); and *NYT*, April 29, 1982.

TOZZER, ALFRED MARSTON (1877–1954). Anthropologist, born July 14, 1877, in Lynn, Massachusetts. Tozzer graduated from Harvard University. He was a member of faculty of Harvard University after 1902 and professor of archaeology and curator of Middle American Archaeology and Ethnology at the Peabody Museum of Harvard University until his retirement in 1949. He carried out fieldwork in Yucatán from 1902 to 1905. He was director of Peabody Museum's expedition to Tikal and Nakum in Guatemala in 1910 and 1911 and of the International School of American Archaeology in Mexico in 1914. He wrote *A Comparative Study of the Mayas and the Lancandones* (New York, 1907) and *Preliminary Study of the Prehistoric Ruins of Tikal, Guatemala* (Cambridge, Mass., 1911). He served in the U.S. Army Air Service during World War I and in the Office of Strategic Service during World War II. Died October 4, 1954, in Cambridge, Massachusetts. *References*: *AA* 57 (1955): 614–18; *AmAntiq* 21

(1955): 72–80; *BMNAS* 30 (1957): 383–97; *NYT*, October 6, 1954; *Willey*, ch. 12; and *WWWA*.

TRAUTWINE, JOHN CRESSON (1810–1883). Engineer, born March 30, 1810, in Philadelphia. Trautwine entered the office of a civil engineer and architect in Philadelphia in 1828 and received technical training. He assisted in the construction of various public buildings and was also involved in railroad construction. He was assistant engineer of the Philadelphia, Wilmington and Baltimore Railroad in 1835–1836 and chief engineer of the Hiwassee Railroad from 1836 to 1843. He went to New Granada in 1844 and worked on construction of Canal de Dique, connecting the Magdalena River with the harbor of Cartagena, from 1844 to 1849. He was in the Isthmus of Panama from 1849 to 1851, making surveys for Panama Railroad, and prepared a map of the isthmus. He was back in Panama in 1852 to search for an interoceanic canal route. He ascended the Atrato River to its source and explored its principal tributaries and descended the San Juan River to the Pacific. He published his report in the March-July and July-November issues of the *Journal of the Franklin Institution*. He surveyed a route for an interoceanic railway in Honduras in 1857, planned systems of docks for Montreal in 1858, and a harbor for Big Glace Bay, Nova Scotia, Canada, in 1864. He was later a consultant on various engineering problems. Died September 14, 1883, in Philadelphia. *References*: *ACAB*; *DAB*; *NCAB* 5:196; *NYT*, September 16, 1883; and *WWWA*.

TRIST, NICHOLAS PHILIP (1800–1874). Diplomat, born June 2, 1800, in Charlottesville, Virginia. Trist attended the U.S. Military Academy. He was a clerk in the U.S. State Department from 1827 to 1833. He was U.S. consul in Havana from 1833 to 1841 and chief clerk of the State Department. In 1847, he was sent as a special agent to Mexico to negotiate a treaty of peace. He was eager to bring his negotiations to a successful and speedy conclusion in order to save Mexico from collapse and anarchy. Although he was recalled in 1847, he remained in Mexico and his negotiations resulted in the Treaty of Guadalupe-Hidalgo in 1848, ending the Mexican War. He then practiced law and served as postmaster in Alexandria, Virginia, from 1870 until his death. Died February 11, 1874, in Alexandria, Virginia. *References*: Nicholas Trist Papers, Manuscript Division, Library of Congress; *ACAB*; Robert A. Brent, "Nicholas Philip Trist: Biography of a Disobedient Diplomat," Ph.D. diss., University of Virginia, 1950; Albert Castel, "The Clerk Who Defied a President: Nicholas Trist's Treaty with Mexico," *Virginia Cavalcade* 34 (Winter 1985): 136–43; *DAB*; *DADH*; T. J. Farnham, "Nicholas Trist and James Freaner and the Mission to Mexico," *Arizona and the West* 11 (1969): 247–60; K. M. Johnson, "Baja California and the Treaty of Guadalupe Hidalgo," *Journal of the West* 11 (1972): 335–47; R. M. Ketchum, "Thankless Task of Nicholas Trist," *American Heritage* 21 (August 1970): 13–15, 86–90; *NCAB* 7:505; Jack Northrup, "The Trist Mission," *Journal of Mexican American History* 3 (1973): 13–31; and *WWWA*.

TRUMBULL, DAVID (1819–1889). Missionary, born November 1, 1819, in Elizabeth, New Jersey. Trumbull graduated from Yale University and Princeton Theological Seminary and was ordained in 1845. He was missionary under the Foreign Evangelical Society (later the American and Foreign Christian Union) from 1845 to 1873, when the mission was transferred to the Board of Foreign Missions of the Presbyterian Church in the U.S.A.,* and he served in Valparaiso, Chile, until his death. In 1869, he established a school in Valparaiso (later renamed Colegio David Trumbull). Died February 1, 1889, in Valparaiso, Chile. *References*: *Figueroa*; H. McKennie Goodpastur, "David Trumbull: Missionary Journalist and Liberty in Chile, 1845–1889," *Journal of Presbyterian History* 56 (1978): 149–65; Irven Paul, *A Yankee Reformer in Chile: The Life and Works of David Trumbull* (South Pasadena, Calif., 1973); and *PrincetonTS*.

TRUSLOW, FRANCIS ADAMS (1906–1951). Lawyer, born May 4, 1906, in Summit, New Jersey. Truslow graduated from Yale University and Harvard Law School and was admitted to the bar in 1932. He practiced law in New York City. From 1942 to 1944, he was in charge of U.S. government operations for the reopening of wild rubber procurement in the upper Amazon region in eastern Peru, as a special representative of the Rubber Reserve Company and the Rubber Development Corporation. He was vice president, and later president, of the Rubber Development Corporation in 1944–1945. He resumed his practice of law and was president of the New York Curb Exchange from 1947 to 1951. Died July 8, 1951, en route to Brazil. *References*: *NCAB* 39:76; *NYT*, July 9, 1951; and "Rubber Man," *New Yorker* 23 (March 29, 1947): 26–27.

TSCHOPIK, HARRY (SCHLESINGER), JR. (1915–1956). Anthropologist, born August 23, 1915, in New Orleans. Tschopik attended Tulane University and graduated from the University of California. He was assistant curator of ethnology at the American Museum of Natural History in New York City from 1946 until his death. From 1940 to 1942, he was engaged in a community study of the Aymara Indians in southern Peru under the auspices of the Peabody Museum and the Division of Anthropology of Harvard University. He was a confidential informant to the office of the legal attaché of the U.S. embassy in Lima, Peru, during World War II. He carried out the reconnaissance of highland communities of central Peru and a Mestizo community study at Sicaya, near Huancayo, Peru, in 1945–1946, under the auspices of the Institute of Social Anthropology of the Smithsonian Institution; a field survey of rural communities in Costa Rica in 1952; and an ethnological reconnaissance of the Ucayali River in Peru in 1953. He wrote *The Aymara of Chucuito, Peru* (New York, 1951). Died November 12, 1956, in Pleasantville, New York. *References*: *AA* 60 (1958): 132–40; *NCAB* 45:264; and *NYT*, November 13, 1956.

TUCKER, HUGH CLARENCE (1857–1956). Missionary, born October 4, 1857, in Nashville, Tennessee. Tucker graduated from Vanderbilt University and was ordained in 1879. He held various pastorates in Tennessee until 1886.

He was a missionary under the Board of Foreign Missions of the Methodist Episcopal Church, South,* in Brazil from 1886 until 1934. He served in Rio de Janeiro, was pastor in an English-speaking church, and then traveled widely in Brazil. He was also agency secretary of the American Bible Society* from 1887 until 1934. He founded Instituto Central do Povo in 1906, a social service project, two hospitals, and the Young Men's Christian Association (YMCA). He started the first public playground for children in Rio de Janeiro. He wrote *The Bible in Brazil: Colporter Experiences* (New York, 1902). He retired in 1934. Died November 4, 1956, in Media, Pennsylvania. *References*: *EWM*; Lula T. Holmes, *Citizen of the Americas: Hugh Clarence Tucker* (New York, 1951); *NYT*, November 6, 1956; and *WWWA*.

TUCKER, JOHN RANDOLPH (1812–1883). Naval officer, born January 31, 1812, in Alexandria, Virginia. Tucker was appointed a midshipman in the U.S. Navy in 1826 and was commissioned lieutenant in 1837. He served in Home Squadron, in the East Indies, in the Mediterranean Squadron, and during the Mexican War. He served in the Confederate Navy during the Civil War. After the Civil War, he was an agent of the Southern Express Company at Raleigh, North Carolina. He was commissioned as rear admiral in the Peruvian Navy. He commanded the combined fleets of Peru and Chile in the war with Spain but the war was concluded in 1869 without an opportunity to engage the Spanish fleet. He was then appointed president of a hydrographical commission to survey the upper waters of the Amazon, which he accomplished in the face of hostile Indians. He was sent to New York to prepare the charts for publication but the financial difficulties of Peru caused the termination of the commission in 1877. Died June 12, 1883, in Petersburg, Virginia. *References*: John Randolph Tucker Papers, Old Dominion University Archives, Norfolk, Va.; *ACAB*; *DAB*; *NCAB* 4:334; David P. Werlich, *Admiral of the Amazon: John Randolph Tucker, His Confederate Colleagues and Peru* (Charlottesville, Va., 1990); and *WWWA*.

TUDOR, WILLIAM (1779–1830). Diplomat, born January 28, 1779, in Boston. Tudor graduated from Harvard University. He entered a Boston counting room and was sent to Paris and Leghorn on business. He then went to develop the ice trade in the West Indies. He served in the Massachusetts legislature. He was founder and first editor of the *North American Review* from 1815 to 1817. He was an agent for commerce and seamen in Lima, Peru, from 1821 to 1823 and the first consul in Lima from 1823 to 1827. He was involved in solving the conflict between Peru and Colombia, and was U.S. chargé d'affaires in Brazil from 1827 until his death. Died March 9, 1830, in Rio de Janeiro, Brazil. *References*: William Tudor Correspondence, Houghton Library, Harvard University, Cambridge, Mass.; *ACAB*; *DAB*; *NCAB* 8:351; *WWWA*.

TUGWELL, REXFORD G(UY) (1891–1979). Government official, born July 10, 1891, in Sinclairville, New York. Tugwell graduated from the University of Pennsylvania. He was an instructor in economics at Columbia University from

1920 to 1922, assistant professor from 1922 to 1926, associate professor from 1926 to 1931, and professor from 1931 to 1937. He was assistant secretary of agriculture in 1933, under secretary from 1934 to 1937, and chairman of the New York City Planning Commission in 1938. In 1940, he investigated enforcement procedures in Puerto Rico regarding corporate land-purchasing limitations. He was chancellor of the University of Puerto Rico in 1941 and governor of Puerto Rico from 1941 to 1946. He established many rectifying programs, formed a budget bureau, and updated the administrative structure. He was a professor of political science and director of the Institute of Planning at the University of Chicago from 1946 until his retirement in 1957. He wrote *Changing the Colonial Climate: The Story, from His Official Messages, of Governor Rexford Guy Tugwell's Efforts to Bring Democracy to an Island Possession Which Serves the United Nations as a Warbase* (San Juan, 1942), *Puerto Rican Public Papers of R. G. Tugwell, Governor of Puerto Rico* (San Jose, 1945), *The Stricken Land: The Story of Puerto Rico* (Garden City, N.Y., 1947), and *To the Lesser Heights of Morningside: A Memoir* (Philadelphia, 1982). Died July 21, 1979, in Santa Barbara, California. *References*: *AMWS*; *CA*; *CB* 1963; Charles T. Goodsell, *Administration of a Revolution: Executive Reform in Puerto Rico under Governor Tugwell, 1941–1946* (Cambridge, Mass., 1965); Michael V. Namorato, *Rexford G. Tugwell: A Biography* (New York, 1988); *NCAB* D:25; *NYT*, July 24, 1979; *Polprof: Truman*; Bernard Sternsher, *Rexford Tugwell and the New Deal* (New Brunswick, N.J., 1964); and *WWWA*.

TURNER, JOHN KENNETH (1879–1948). Journalist, born April 5, 1879, in Portland, Oregon, and grew up in Stockton, California. Turner attended the University of California. He was a reporter on the Los Angeles *Express*. He went on a fact-finding trip to Mexico in 1908–1909, posing as a wealthy American businessman who wanted to invest heavily in Mexican henequen and tobacco, and was sports editor on the *Mexican Herald* in Mexico City in 1909. His articles, which appeared in *American Magazine* and later in *Appeal to Reason* and other magazines, and which were published in *Barbarous Mexico* (Chicago, 1911), were an exposé and indictment of the regime of Porfirio Díaz. He served as confidential agent for the Liberal party junta in Los Angeles in 1910–1911 and was chief adviser to the rebels in Baja California during the first phase of the Mexican revolution. In 1911 he settled in Carmel, California. He was back in Mexico in 1912–1913. Arrested and released, he fled Mexico but returned in 1915, 1916, and, finally, in 1921. Died in Carmel, California. His wife, **ETHEL DUFFY TURNER** (1885–1969), wrote *Revolution in Baja California: Ricardo Flores Magon's High Noon*, ed. Rey Devis (Detroit, 1981) and *Ricardo Flores Magon y el Partido Liberal Mexicano* (Mexico, 1960). *Reference*: Sinclair Snow, "Introduction," in John Kenneth Turner, *Barbarous Mexico* (Austin, Tex., 1969), pp. xi–xxix.

TURNER, ROSS STERLING (1847–1915). Painter, born June 29, 1847, in Westport, New York, and grew up in Williamsport, Pennsylvania. Turner was employed as a mechanical draftsman in the Patent Office in Washington, D.C., until 1876. He then studied art in Paris, Munich, Florence, Rome, and Venice. He settled in Boston in 1882 and in Salem, Massachusetts, in 1884, becoming a popular teacher of watercolor painting. He was also an instructor in the architecture department of the Massachusetts Institute of Technology in 1884–1885 and from 1886 to 1914, and taught in the Massachusetts Normal Art School after 1909. He traveled in search of subject matter to Mexico and the Caribbean, particularly the Bahamas. Died in Nassau, the Bahamas. *References*: *DAB*; and *WWWA*.

TURNER, TIMOTHY ("TIM") G(ILMAN) (1885–1961). Journalist, born July 9, 1885, in Independence, Missouri, and grew up in Grand Rapids, Chicago, St. Joseph, Missouri, and Memphis. He worked as a cowboy in West Texas, Kansas, and Colorado until 1906. He was a reporter on the Grand Rapids (Mich.) *Herald* and the Grand Rapids *Press* and on the El Paso (Tex.) *Herald*, and was correspondent for the *El Diario* of Mexico City. He was Associated Press correspondent in Mexico from 1910 to 1915, reporting on the Mexican Revolution while serving with Francisco (Pancho) Villa's army. He wrote a firsthand account of the revolution in *Bullets, Bottles, and Gardenias* (Dallas, Tex., 1935). He was a reporter and special writer on Latin American affairs for the *New York Herald* from 1915 to 1921, editorial reporter for the *Los Angeles Times* from 1924 to 1929, in public relations from 1929 to 1935, and again a reporter on the *Los Angeles Times* from 1935 until 1954, and public relations director for the Biltmore Hotel from 1954 to 1959. Died April 7, 1961, in Los Angeles. *Reference*: *Los Angeles Times*, April 8, 1961.

TWEDDLE, HERBERT W(ILKIN) C(OLGUHOUN) (1832– ?). Petroleum producer, born in Liverpool, England, and came to the United States in 1853. Tweddle was involved in the refining of oils, soaps, and fats, and the production of cottonseed oil in New York City, Providence, Rhode Island, St. Louis, and New Orleans. He developed a process for the distillation of oils and began to use his method in the distillation of petroleum in Pennsylvania in 1862. In 1886, he pioneered the development of oil fields in Russia. In 1888, he purchased La Brea y Pariñas oil field in Talara, northwestern Peru, and erected a large petroleum refinery to process local crude oil. He established the London and Pacific Petroleum Company, to which he leased the La Brea y Pariñas property. He sold his Peruvian assets in 1890. He later served as adviser and supervisor of oil drilling operations in Egypt. *Reference*: *NCAB* 12:463.

U

UNITED CHRISTIAN MISSIONARY SOCIETY. Organized in 1920, it began missionary work in Jamaica in 1885, in Mexico in 1895, in Puerto Rico in 1899, in Argentina in 1906, in Paraguay in 1917, in Venezuela in 1963, in Brazil in 1968, and in Peru in 1970. It was restructured in 1973 and the name changed to Christian Church, Disciples of Christ: Division of Overseas Mission. *References*: Elma C. Irelan, *Fifty Years with Our Mexican Neighbors* (St. Louis, 1944); J. Dexter Montgomery, *Disciples of Christ in Argentina, 1906–1956: A History of the First Fifty Years of Mission Work* (St. Louis, 1956); Clement M. Morton, *Kingdom Building in Puerto Rico: A Story of Fifty Years of Christian Service* (Indianapolis, Ind., 1949); and Robert G. Nelson, *Disciples of Christ in Jamaica, 1858–1958: A Centennial of Missions in the "Gem of the Caribbean"* (St. Louis, 1958).

UNITED FRUIT COMPANY. Formed in 1899, when the Boston Fruit Company merged with three other banana companies owned by Minor Cooper Keith.* It merged with Samuel Zemurray's* Cuyamel Fruit Company in 1929. The mergers combined extensive growing, shipping, and distribution resources with extensive land holdings in Jamaica, Costa Rica, Nicaragua, and Colombia, and later in other Central American and Caribbean countries. The company developed the land, undertook extensive sanitation projects, built railroads, and operated a shipping line. It was much criticized in the countries of Central America, where it was often called "the Octopus." In 1954 it encouraged the U.S. administration to overthrow the government of Jacobo Arbanez in Guatemala. Its sugar plantations in Cuba were nationalized in 1959. In 1969, it was taken over by the AMK Corporation, a holding company, and it was renamed United Brands Company in 1970. *References*: Sam G. Baggett, "The United Fruit Company and the Caribbean Area," in *The Caribbean: Contemporary International Relations*, ed. A. Curtis Wilgus (Gainesville, Fla., 1963), pp. 155–63; *ELA*; Carlos Cordoba Pineda, *La United Fruit Company en Honduras y Su Influencia Economica Politica* (Mexico City, 1962); Charles D. Kepner, Jr., and Jay H. Soothill,

The Banana Empire: A Case Study of Economic Imperialism (New York, 1935); Richard A. Labarge, *The Impact of the United Fruit Company on the Economic Development of Guatemala* (New Orleans, 1960); Thomas P. McCann, *An American Company: The Tragedy of United Fruit* (New York, 1976); Stacy May and Galo Plaza Lasso, *The United Fruit Company in Latin America* (Washington, D.C., 1958); A. A. Pollan, *The United Fruit Company and Middle America* (New York, 1943); and Charles M. Wilson, *Empire in Green and Gold: The Story of the American Banana Trade* (New York, 1947).

UNITED PRESBYTERIAN CHURCH IN THE U.S.A.: COMMISSION ON ECUMENICAL MISSION AND RELATIONS. Organized in 1837, it began missionary work in Colombia in 1856, in Brazil in 1859, in Mexico in 1872, in Chile in 1873, in Guatemala in 1882, in Venezuela in 1897, and in Ecuador in 1945. *Reference*: Walter N. Jamison, *The United Presbyterian Story: A Centennial Study 1858–1958* (Pittsburgh, 1958).

UNITED STATES AND PARAGUAY NAVIGATION COMPANY. Organized in Rhode Island by Edward A. Hopkins* and his associates. It placed steamers on the Paraguay River to Asunción. Troubles with Carlos Antonio López, the dictator of Paraguay, caused its bankruptcy.

UNITED STATES MAIL STEAMSHIP COMPANY. Organized in 1848 by George Law and his associates to provide mail and passenger service between New York and other Atlantic ports and Aspinwal (later Colón), Panama. *Reference*: John H. Kemble, *The Panama Route, 1848–1869* (Berkeley, Calif., 1943).

***URGENT FURY*, OPERATION.** *See* GRENADA, INVASION OF.

V

VAIL, THEODORE N(EWTON) (1845–1920). Telephone executive, born July 16, 1845, near Minerva, Carroll County, Ohio. Vail became a telegraph operator in 1864. He was assistant superintendent of railway mail service in Washington, D.C., in 1873–1874, assistant general superintendent from 1874 to 1876, and general superintendent from 1876 to 1878. He was general manager of Bell Telephone Company from 1878 to 1885, organized an expanding telephone system, and was the first president of American Telephone and Telegraph Company, from 1885 until 1887. He retired in 1889 and farmed in Vermont until 1894. He became involved in public utility projects in Argentina from 1894 until 1907. He developed the water power project at Córdoba, introduced an American electric street railway system in Buenos Aires, and installed the telephone system in the principal Argentine cities. He then sold his South American interests and returned to the United States in 1907. He was again president of American Telegraph and Telephone Company from 1907 until 1919. Died April 25, 1920, in Baltimore. *References: BDABL; DAB;* Albert B. Paine, *Theodore Vail* (New York, 1929); and *WWWA.*

VAILLANT, GEORGE CLAPP (1901–1945). Archaeologist, born April 5, 1901, in Boston. Vaillant graduated from Harvard University. He was assistant curator at the American Museum of Natural History from 1927 to 1930, associate curator of Mexican archaeology from 1930 to 1941, and director of the University Museum of the University of Pennsylvania from 1941 until his death. He carried out a series of detailed stratigraphic excavations in the Valley of Mexico from 1928 to 1936, including at Zacatenco, Ticoman, El Arbolillo, and Gualupita. He wrote *The Aztecs of Mexico: Origin, Rise and Fall of the Aztec Nation* (Garden City, N.Y., 1941) and was coauthor of *Excavations at Gualupita* (New York, 1934). He was senior cultural relations officer in the U.S. embassy in Lima, Peru, in 1943–1944. Committed suicide, May 13, 1945, in Devon, Pennsylvania. *References: AmAntiq* 11 (1945): 113–16; *DAB S3; NCAB* 34:194; and *Willey,* ch. 5.

VALENTINE, WASHINGTON S(AMUEL) (1859–1920). Entrepreneur, born January 4, 1859, in St. Louis. Valentine began in business with an uncle. He went to Honduras in 1879 and obtained mining and oil concessions leading to the development of the region, for which he acquired the sobriquet "King of Honduras." He formed the New York and Honduras Rosario Mining Company and was its manager until 1881. He was president of the San Pedro Electric Light and Power Company and vice president of the Sinclair Central American Oil Company. Died March 17, 1920, in Atlantic City, New Jersey. *References*: Kenneth V. Finney, "Our Man in Honduras: Washington S. Valentine," in *Dependency Unbends: Case Studies in Inter-American Relations*, ed. Robert H. Claxton (Carrollton, Ga., 1978), pp. 13–20; *NCAB* 18:319; and *NYT*, March 18, 1920.

VAN DEUSEN, WALTER MERRITT (1877–1935). Banker, born February 21, 1877, in Pittsfield, Massachusetts. Van Deusen was employed by the National Bank of New Jersey in New Brunswick, New Jersey, from 1893 to 1896 and by the Newark National Bank from 1896 to 1917. He was employed by the Mercantile Bank of the Americas in New York from 1917 to 1932 and organized a branch in Cuba from 1917 to 1920. He was elected vice president in 1920 and was transferred to Colombia, where he was manager of the Banco Mercantil Americano until 1932. He was financial adviser to the Central Bank of Chile from 1926 to 1932 and a member of the Kemmerer mission to advise the government of Peru. He was financial adviser to various agencies of the state of New Jersey from 1933 to 1935. Died June 20, 1935, in Port-au-Prince, Haiti, while on a cruise in the Caribbean. *Reference*: *Encyclopedia of American Biography* (New York, 1934–1970), 6:304–5.

VAN PATTEN, CHARLES HANSEN (1814–1889). Physician, born in Schenectady, New York. Van Patten graduated from Harvard University. He was a botanist for the Smithsonian Institution, and made a botanical investigation trip to Central America in 1859. He made a scientific investigation of Costa Rica for the Smithsonian Institution from 1860 to 1862. He settled in Costa Rica in 1865. *References*: Charles A. Van Patten, "El Origen de la Familia Van Patten," *Revista de la Academia Costarricense de Ciencias Genealogicas*, no. 16–17 (1970): 133–34; Charles A. Van Patten, "Schenectady Emigré of Costa Rica," *De Halve Maen* 22 (January 1947): 7; and Anita G. Murchie, *Imported Spices: A Study of Anglo-American Settlers in Costa Rica, 1821–1900* (San Jose, Costa Rica, 1981).

VENEZUELAN STEAM TRANSPORTATION COMPANY. Organized in 1866 in New York, the company began a steamboat line on the Orinoco in 1869 which was run by American mechanics and crews. Business was terminated in 1881 because of the seizure of its vessels by government and insurgent troops.

Reference: William H. Gray, "Steamboat Transportation on the Orinoco," *HAHR* 25 (1945): 454–69.

VERACRUZ AFFAIR (1914). United States forces occupied Veracruz in Mexico in 1914 during the Mexican revolution. The U.S. fleet sailed into the Gulf of Mexico after the Mexican government refused to apologize for the *Dolphin* incident.* To prevent war supplies from reaching the forces of Victoriano Huerta, President of Mexico, the United States landed troops in Veracruz, which was captured after hard fighting. The city was evacuated after seven months. *References*: Merlin H. Forster, "U.S. Intervention in Mexico: The 1914 Occupation of Veracruz," *Military Review* 57 (1977): 88–96; *Langley*, chs. 7–9; Andrea Martinez, *La Intervención Norteamericana: Veracruz, 1914* (Mexico, 1982); Robert E. Quirk, *An Affair of Honor: Woodrow Wilson and the Occupation of Veracruz* (New York, 1962); Paul B. Ryan, "Ten Days at Veracruz," *USNIP* 98 (1972): 64–73; and Jack Sweetman, *The Landing at Veracruz: 1914* (Annapolis, Md., 1968).

VERRILL, ADDISON EMERY (1839–1926). Zoologist, born February 9, 1839, in Greenwood, Maine. Verrill graduated from Lawrence Scientific School of Harvard University. He was a professor of zoology at Yale University from 1864 until his retirement in 1907. He also taught geology in the Sheffield Scientific School from 1870 to 1894 and was curator of the Peabody Museum of Yale University from 1867 to 1910. He was in charge of the scientific work of the U.S. Commission of Fish and Fisheries in southern New England. He investigated the invertebrate life of the Gulf Stream, the Pacific coast of Central America, Bermuda, and the West Indies. He wrote *The Bermuda Islands* (New Haven, Conn., 1901–1907), and *Report on the Starfishes of the West Indies, Florida and Brazil* (Iowa City, Ia., 1915). Died December 10, 1926, in Santa Barbara, California. *References*: *DAB*; R. W. Dexter, "Three Young Naturalists Afield: The First Expedition of Hyatt, Shaler, and Verrill," *Scientific Monthly* 79 (July 1954): 45–51; and *WWWA*.

VERRILL, ALPHEUS HYATT (1871–1954). Naturalist, son of Addison Emery Verrill,* and born July 23, 1871, in New Haven, Connecticut. Verrill attended Yale School of Fine Arts. He conducted extensive explorations in Bermuda, the West Indies, Guiana, and Central America from 1889 to 1920. He lived in the British West Indies from 1903 to 1906, in British Guiana from 1913 to 1917, and in Panama from 1917 to 1921. He participated in ethnographic and archaeological expeditions to Panama, Peru, Bolivia, Chile, and Surinam from 1926 to 1928. He discovered and excavated the remains of an unknown prehistoric culture in Panama, made archaeological expeditions in Peru and Bolivia from 1928 to 1932, and attempted to salvage a seventh-century Spanish galleon in the West Indies in 1933–1934. Much of his fieldwork was done for the Museum of the American Indian, Heye Foundation, in New York City. In

1940, he established the Anhiarka Experimental Gardens and Natural Science Museum at the site of the ancient Indian village at which Hernando de Soto made his first settlement in Florida. He later established a shell business in Lake Work, Florida, in 1944. He wrote an autobiography, *Thirty Years in the Jungle* (London, 1929), and *The Real Americans* (New York, 1954). Died November 14, 1954, in Chiefland, Florida. *References*: Alpheus Hyatt Verrill Papers, Museum of the American Indian, Heye Foundation, New York City; *DAB S5*; *NYT*, November 16, 1954; and *WWWA*.

VILLAMIL, JOSEPH [JOSÉ] M. (1789–1866). Soldier, born in Louisiana. Villamil served in the volunteer reserves in 1805. After 1810, he sailed to Maracaibo, Venezuela, and became a revolutionary. He became a permanent resident in Guayaquil in 1815. He defended Punta de Piedra in 1816, was attorney general of the royal government in 1820, was involved in the revolution against the Spanish rule in Guayaquil in that year, and participated in several battles against Spanish troops. In 1830, he declared the Galapagos Islands an integral part of the Republic of Ecuador. He received a grant of Floreana Island and established a colony there. He also served as chief of the military forces of the department of Guayas. He was chief of staff and operations and division general, mayor of Guayaquil, department prefect, and collector of customs at Manabi. He was minister of war of Ecuador in 1852. Died May 12, 1866, in Guayaquil. *References*: Frederic W. Goding, "General Joseph Villamil," *Bulletin of the Pan-American Union* 48 (1918): 24–27; and Albert F. Kunze, *Who's Who on the Postage Stamps of Ecuador* (Washington, D.C., 1953), pp. 51–52.

VINCENT, MORDELO (1870–1934). Businessman, born March 31, 1870, in Tuxpam, Veracruz, to American parents. Vincent began his career selling sewing machines outside Tampico, was a stevedore on Tampico docks, and foreman for a company dredging the waterways around the port. He was involved in sisal growing from 1904 to 1910, and in oil exploration and drilling in the Tampico area after 1910. At first he was involved in lease brokering for the Cortez Oil Company; later, he formed Tepetate Oil Company. He sold his oil production business to Atlantic Gulf Oil Corporation. Died February 1934. *Reference*: *Hanrahan*, ch. 2.

VIRGIN ISLANDS. A group of islands in the Caribbean, comprising the islands of St. Croix, St. Johns, St. Thomas, and fifty smaller islets and cays. The group was acquired from Denmark by the United States in 1917 because of its strategic position in the Caribbean Sea. Remaining under the constitutional and political tutelage of the United States, it was administered by a naval governor until 1931, by a civilian governor appointed by the secretary of the interior from 1931 to 1968, and by an elected governor after 1968. *References*: James A. Bough and Roy C. Macridis, eds., *Virgin Islands, America's Caribbean Outpost—The Evolution of Self-Government* (Wakefield, Mass., 1970); William W. Boyer, *Amer-*

ica's Virgin Islands: A History of Human Rights and Wrongs (Durham, N.C., 1983); Luther H. Evans, *The Virgin Islands: From Naval Base to New Deal* (Ann Arbor, Mich., 1945); John F. Grede, "The New Deal in the Virgin Islands, 1931–1941," Ph.D. diss., University of Chicago, 1963; Gordon K. Lewis, *The Virgin Islands: A Caribbean Lilliput* (Evanston, Ill., 1972); and Hazel M. McFerson, "The Impact of a Changed Racial Tradition: Race, Politics and Society in the U.S. Virgin Islands, 1917–1975," Ph.D. diss., Brandeis University, 1975.

VIRGIN ISLANDS COMPANY (VICO). Chartered in 1934 to manage and give direction to a long-range social, economic, and industrial program for the economic rehabilitation of the Virgin Islands. Sugar and rum production constituted the bulk of its activities until 1949. It was replaced in 1949 by the Virgin Islands Corporation, which officially came to an end in 1966. *Reference*: Isaac Dookhan, "The Virgin Islands Company and Corporation: The Plan for Economic Rehabilitation in the Virgin Islands," *Journal of Caribbean History* 4 (May 1972): 54–76.

VIRGINIUS AFFAIR (1873). The ship *Virginius*, which was blockade running to the Cuban rebels in 1873 during the Ten Years' War in Cuba, was illegally using the American flag for its operations and most of its crew were Americans. It was seized by the Spanish authorities and many of its crew members were shot. *References*: Lawrence C. Allin, "The First Cubic War—the *Virginius* Affair," *AN* 38 (1978): 233–48; and Richard H. Bradford, *The Virginius Affair* (Boulder, Colo., 1980).

VOGELGESANG, CARL THEODORE (1869–1927). Naval officer, born January 11, 1869, in North Branch, Calaveras County, California. Vogelgesang graduated from the U.S. Naval Academy in 1890 and was commissioned an ensign in the U.S. Navy in 1892. He served in the Spanish-American War and was chief of staff of the Asiatic Fleet in 1917–1918 and commandant of the Brooklyn Naval Yard and the Third Naval District in 1921–1922. He was chief of the naval commission to Brazil in 1917 and chief of the U.S. Naval Mission to Brazil and head of the Brazilian War College from 1922 to 1925. He was commander of the scouting fleet in 1926–1927. Died February 16, 1927, in Washington, D.C. *References*: *NYT*, February 17, 1927; and *WWWA*.

VOGT, EVON ZARTMAN, JR. (1918–   ). Anthropologist, born August 20, 1918, in Gallup, New Mexico. Vogt graduated from the University of Chicago. He served in the U.S. Navy during World War II. He was a member of the faculty of Harvard University after 1948. He carried out fieldwork in Zinacantan, Chiapas, Mexico, in 1951–1952 and was director of the Harvard Chiapas Project in San Cristóbal de las Casas from 1957 to 1975. He wrote *Zinacantan: A Maya Community in the Highlands of Chiapas* (Cambridge,

Mass., 1969), *The Zinacantecos of Mexico: A Modern Maya Way of Life* (New York, 1970), *Tortillas for the Gods: A Symbolic Analysis of Zinacanteco Rituals* (Cambridge, Mass., 1976), and an account of his experiences in "The Harvard Chiapas Project: 1957–1975," in *Long-Term Field Research in Social Anthropology*, ed. George M. Foster et al. (New York, 1979). *References*: Victoria R. Bricker and Gary H. Gossen, eds., *Ethnographic Encounters in Southern Mesoamerica: Essays in Honor of Evon Zartman Vogt, Jr.* (Albany, N.Y., 1989); *CA*; and *WWA*.

VON HAGEN, VICTOR WOLFGANG (1908–   ). Author, explorer, and naturalist, born February 29, 1908, in St. Louis, Missouri. Von Hagen attended New York University, University of Quito, and the University of Gottingen. He was a research associate for the Museum of the American Indian in New York City. He participated in expeditions to Mexico from 1931 to 1933 and in 1957, to the Galapagos Islands, Ecuador, the Upper Amazon, and Peru from 1934 to 1936, and to the Mosquito coast of Honduras and Guatemala in 1937–1938, and explored Panama and Costa Rica in 1940. He served in the U.S. Army during World War II. He toured Colombia and Peru in 1947–1948, resided in the British West Indies in 1949–1950, was director of the Inca Highway Expedition to Peru, Bolivia, and Ecuador for the American Geographical Society from 1953 to 1955, and explored Yucatán in 1958–1959. He later investigated Roman roads in Europe and North Africa from 1961 to 1970 and the Royal Persian Road in the Middle East from 1973 to 1975. He wrote *Off with Their Heads* (New York, 1937), *The Tsatchela Indians of Western Ecuador* (New York, 1939), *Ecuador the Unknown: Two and a Half Years: Travels in the Republic of Ecuador and Galapagos Islands* (New York, 1940), *Jungle in the Clouds* (New York, 1940), *Riches of South America* (Boston, 1941), *Riches of Central America* (Boston, 1942), *The Aztecs and Maya Papermakers* (New York, 1943), *The Jicaque (Torrupan) Indians of Honduras* (New York, 1943), *South American Zoo* (New York, 1946), *Maya Explorer: John Lloyd Stephens and the Lost Cities* (Norman, Okla., 1947), *Ecuador and the Galapagos Islands* (Norman, Okla., 1949), *Frederick Catherwood, Archt.* (New York, 1950), *Highway of the Sun* (New York, 1955), *Realm of the Incas* (New York, 1957), *The Aztec: Man and Tribe* (New York, 1958), *World of the Maya* (New York, 1960), *The Ancient Sun Kingdom of the Americas: Aztec, Maya, Inca* (Cleveland, 1961), *The Desert Kingdom of Peru* (New York, 1964), *The Golden Man: A Quest for El Dorado* (New York, 1974), and *The Royal Road of the Inca* (London, 1976), and was coauthor of *Quetzal Quest: The Story of the Capture of the Quetzal, the Sacred Bird of the Aztecs and the Mayas* (New York, 1939). *References*: *CA*; *CB* 1942; *New Yorker* 28 (January 3, 1953): 11–12; and *WWA*.

W

W. R. GRACE AND COMPANY. Formed in Peru by William Russell Grace (1832–1904), a native of Ireland, it developed into an import–export business between Callao, Peru, and New York and then expanded its activities. It controlled sugar estates and sugar-refining plants. In 1871, Grace joined brother Michael P. Grace to form the company of Grace Brothers. In 1894, all the Grace enterprises were consolidated in it. It was also involved in manufacturing and mining in other countries of South America. The sugar plantations were expropriated by the Peruvian government in 1968 and other properties were nationalized in 1974. *References*: W. R. Grace & Company Records, Columbia University Libraries, New York City; "Amazing Grace: The W. R. Grace Corporation," *NACLA's Latin America and Empire Report* 10 (1976): 3–32; Eugene W. Burgess and Frederick H. Harbison, *Casa Grace in Peru* (Washington, D.C., 1954); Lawrence A. Clayton, *Grace: W. R. Grace & Co.: The Formative Years, 1850–1930* (Ottawa, Ill., 1985); Lawrence A. Clayton, "A Shared Prosperity: W. R. Grace & Company and Modern Peru, 1852–1952," in *Dependency Unbends: Case Studies in Inter-American Relations*, ed. Robert H. Claxton (Carrolton, Ga., 1978), pp. 1–12; and *ELA*.

WACHUSETT AFFAIR (1863). The USS *Wachusett* captured the Confederate cruiser *Florida* in the Brazilian port of Bahia in 1863 despite the attempted interference of the Brazilian naval forces, and was taken to Hampton Roads, Virginia. The United States later apologized to Brazil, the commander of the *Wachusett* was court-martialed, and the U.S. consul in Bahia, who was implicated in the affair, was dismissed.

WAGLEY, CHARLES W(ALTER) (1913–   ). Anthropologist, born November 9, 1913, in Clarksville, Texas. Wagley attended the University of Oklahoma and graduated from Columbia University. He was a member of the Institute of Inter-American Affairs field party in Brazil from 1942 to 1945, assistant professor at Columbia University from 1946 to 1949, associate professor from

1949 to 1953, and professor of anthropology from 1953 to 1971. He founded the Institute of Latin American Studies and served as its director from 1961 to 1969. He was professor of anthropology and Latin American Studies at the University of Florida from 1971 to 1983. He was director of a Bahia State–Columbia University study project in 1951–1952. He wrote *Economics of a Guatemalan Village* (Menasha, Wis., 1941), *Social and Religious Life in a Guatemalan Village* (Menasha, Wis., 1949), *Amazon Town: A Study of Man in the Tropics* (New York, 1953), *Welcome of Tears: The Tapirapé Indians of Central Brazil* (New York, 1971), *The Latin American Tradition: Essays on the Unity and the Diversity of Latin American Culture* (New York, 1968), and *An Introduction to Brazil* (New York, 1971). He was coauthor of *The Tenetehara Indians of Brazil* (New York, 1949) and edited *Race and Class in Rural Brazil* (Paris, 1952) and *Man in the Amazon* (Gainesville, Fla., 1974). *References*: *CA*; Maxine L. Margolis and William E. Carter, eds., *Brazil, Anthropological Perspectives: Essays in Honor of Charles Wagley* (New York, 1979).

WAGNER, HENRY R(AUP) (1862–1957). Mining executive, born September 27, 1862, in Philadelphia. Wagner graduated from Yale University and Yale Law School and was admitted to the bar in 1887. He practiced law in Kansas City from 1887 to 1890. He was associated with the Globe Smelting and Refining Company in Denver, Colorado, from 1891 to 1893. He went to Mexico in 1893, managed a branch office for E. P. Allis Company, manufacturers of mining machinery, in Mexico City in 1894–1895, and was engaged in mining in Denver, Spokane, and other parts of the West from 1895 to 1898. He went to South America in 1898 as a representative of the Guggenheim interests as ore buyer in Chile from 1898 to 1902 and was in London from 1902 to 1906, selling silver. He served in Mexico from 1907 to 1911 as a member of the executive committee of southern department of the American Smelting and Refining Company* (ASARCO), and was its general manager in Mexico City. He was resident manager in Santiago, Chile, from 1915 to 1917 for ASARCO, Chile Exploration Company, and the Braden Copper Company. He returned to the United States in 1918, where he was a member of the executive committee of ASARCO from 1918 to 1920 and its vice president in 1920–1921. He retired in 1921 and devoted his time to collecting books and writing historical works, including *Bullion to Books* (Los Angeles, 1942). Died March 28, 1957, in San Marino, California. *References*: Donald C. Dickinson, *Dictionary of American Book Collectors* (Westport, Conn., 1986), pp. 324–25; *HAHR* 37 (1957): 486–94; *NCAB* 45:522; *NYT*, March 29, 1957; and *PHR* 26 (1957): 319–20.

WALKER, HAROLD (1876–1938). Lawyer, born June 5, 1876, in Rutland, Vermont. Walker graduated from Amherst College and the law school of Columbia University and was admitted to the bar in 1901. He practiced law in New York City from 1901 to 1903. He went to Mexico City in 1903 to look after his father's business interests. From 1903 to 1905, he was general manager of the Mexico Asphalt Paving and Construction Company, the first producer of heavy asphalt in commercial quantities and builder of the first asphalt roads in Mexico. In 1905, he became an executive ánd legal adviser of the Mexican Petroleum Company of California, a producer and marketer of petroleum that was owned by Edward L. Doheny* (and which eventually became an affiliate of the Pan American Petroleum and Transport Company), and served various associated companies of the Pan American Petroleum and Transport Company as officer and counsel until 1932. He was prominent in the controversy waged over the Mexican constitution of 1917. He was an executive with Standard Oil Company of New Jersey from 1932 until his death. Died July 8, 1938, in New York City. *References*: *NCAB* 28:76; and *NYT*, July 9, 1938.

WALKER, JOHN GRIMES (1835–1907). Naval officer, born March 20, 1835, in Hillsboro, New Hampshire. Walker was appointed a midshipman in 1850 and graduated from the U.S. Naval Academy in 1856. He served in the Union Navy during the Civil War. He served on the staff of the U.S. Naval Academy from 1866 to 1869 and was secretary of the Lighthouse Board from 1873 to 1878 and chief of the Bureau of Navigation in the Navy Department from 1881 to 1889. He was commander of the South Atlantic station in 1891–1892 and the North Atlantic station in 1892–1893. He retired with the rank of rear admiral in 1897. He was a member of the Nicaragua Canal Commission from 1897 to 1899 and president of the Isthmian Canal Commission, intended to study both the Nicaraguan and Panama routes, from 1899 until 1904. In 1904–1905, he was head of the commission that organized the Canal Zone and operated it. Died September 15, 1907, near Ogunquit, Maine. *References*: *DAB*; *NYT*, September 22, 1907; Frances P. Thomas, *The Career of John Grimes Walker, U.S.N., 1835–1907* (Boston, 1959); Daniel H. Wicks, "New Navy and New Empire: The Life and Times of John Grimes Walker," Ph.D. diss., University of California at Berkeley, 1979; and *WWWA*.

WALKER, WILLIAM (1824–1860). Filibuster, born May 8, 1824, in Nashville, Tennessee. Walker graduated from the universities of Nashville and Pennsylvania and studied medicine in Paris. Finding the practice of medicine distasteful, he studied law and was admitted to the bar. He was editor and proprietor of the New Orleans *Daily Crescent* from 1848 to 1850. He went to California in 1850, practiced law, and was associate editor of the San Francisco *Herald*. In 1853, he fitted an expedition to colonize the Mexican states of Sonora and Lower California. He landed in La Paz, Lower California, proclaimed Lower California an independent state and himself its president, and succeeded in occupying several small towns. In 1854, he was forced out of Mexico. He surrendered to U.S. authorities in San Diego and was tried for violating neutrality laws but was acquitted. In 1855, he went on a filibustering expedition to Nicaragua. He landed at Realejo, won the battle of Virgin Bay, and captured Granada. In 1856, Costa Rica declared war against Walker. He was defeated at

Guanacaste but won the battle at Rivas. He then quarreled with Cornelius Vanderbilt's Accessory Transit Company, revoked its charter, and confiscated its
property, but was then cut off from U.S. reinforcements. He was inaugurated
president of Nicaragua in 1856 and annulled the law prohibiting slavery. His
activities provoked an insurrection, aided by Costa Rica and Honduras and by
agents of Vanderbilt's steamship company. He was forced to surrender to Commander Charles Henry Davis of the U.S. Navy in 1857. He was taken to Panama
and then to New Orleans. He escaped and landed in Punta Arenas, Nicaragua,
but was forced again to surrender to Commander Hiram Pauling of the U.S.
Navy and taken to New York City. In 1857, he sailed to Honduras but was
shipwrecked. He wrote *The War in Nicaragua* (Mobile, Ala., 1860). He went
again to Honduras in 1860, landed at Ruatan and captured Trujillo, and marched
southward. He was arrested at Tinto River by the British Navy and turned over
to the Honduran authorities at Tinto River. He was tried by court-martial and
was executed by a firing squad, September 12, 1860, in Trujillo, Honduras.
References: Alejandro Bolanos Geyer, *William Walker: The Gray-Eyed Man of
Destiny* (Lake Saint Louis, Mo., 1988–1989); Charles H. Brown, *Agents of
Manifest Destiny: The Lives and Times of the Filibusters* (Chapel Hill, N.C.,
1980), chs. 7–19; Albert H. Z. Carr, *The World and William Walker* (New York,
1963); Robert T. Cochran, "Cold-Eyed Soldier of Fortune Who Became a
'President,' " *Smithsonian* 12 (June 1981): 117–28; *ELA*; Laurence Greene, *The
Filibuster: The Career of William Walker* (Indianapolis, 1937); Enrique Guier,
William Walker (San Jose, Costa Rica, 1971); Alejandro Hurtado Chamorro,
William Walker: Ideales y Propositos: Un Ensayo Biografico (Granada, Nica-
ragua, 1965); Frederic Rosengarten, *Freebooters Must Die: The Life and Death
of William Walker, the Most Notorious Filibuster of the Nineteenth Century*
(Wayne, Pa., 1976); Rudolph Wurlitzer, *Walker* (New York, 1987); and Rufus
K. Wyllys, "William Walker's Invasion of Sonora, 1854," *Arizona Historical
Review* 6 (1935): 61–67.

WALLACE, JOHN F(INDLEY) (1852–1921). Civil engineer, born September
10, 1852, in Fall River, Massachusetts. Wallace attended Monmouth College.
He was an assistant engineer in the employ of the United States from 1871 to
1876, working on improvements in the upper Mississippi. He later engaged in
private practice in Monmouth and also served as city engineer and county surveyor. He was chief engineer and superintendent of various railroads from 1878
to 1904 and general manager of the Chicago, Madison and Northern in 1904.
He was the first American chief engineer for the Panama Canal in 1904–1905
and Isthmian Canal commissioner and vice president and general manager of
the Panama Railroad and Steamship Company in 1905. A bitter controversy
ensued over his resignation, which involved a congressional investigation. He
was later connected with a large number of enterprises. Died July 3, 1921, in
Washington, D.C. *References*: *DAB*; *NCAB* 10:168; *NYT*, July 4, 1921; and
WWWA.

WALLER, LITTLETON W(ALTER) T(AZEWELL) (1856–1926). Marine Corps officer, born September 26, 1856, in York County, Virginia. Waller was commissioned second lieutenant in the U.S. Marine Corps in 1880. He served with the European Squadron and in the Spanish-American War in Cuba. He served in the Philippine-American War in 1899–1900 and again from 1900 to 1902, commanded troops in Samar, Philippines, in 1902, and was court-martialed for atrocities and war crimes carried out by his troops in Samar. He served in Panama and Cuba from 1904 to 1911, commanded the marine barracks at Mare Island Navy Yard from 1911 to 1914 and the marine brigade occupying Veracruz, Mexico, in 1914–1915, served in Haiti in 1915–1916, and commanded the advanced base force in Philadelphia. He retired with the rank of major general in 1920. Died July 13, 1926, in Atlantic City, New Jersey. *References*: *NYT*, July 14, 1926; and *WWWA*.

WARFIELD, RALPH MERVINE (1880–1939). Civil engineer, born September 12, 1880, in North Oxford, Massachusetts. Warfield graduated from Worcester Polytechnic Institute. He was an engineer in the Boston Navy Yard, Boston Bridge Works, and the New York Navy Yard from 1901 to 1905, and assistant professor of civil engineering at the University of Vermont from 1905 to 1907. He joined the civil engineer corps of the U.S. Navy in 1907 and served in Charleston, South Carolina, New Orleans, Guam, Puget Sound, Boston, and Pensacola, Florida, until 1919. He was aide to the U.S. military governor of Santo Domingo and U.S. representative to Haiti from 1919 to 1922. He was also secretary of state responsible for public works and communications and secretary of state of agriculture and immigration of the Dominican Republic from 1919 to 1922 and was adviser to the Dominican Republic government in 1922. He later served in Portsmouth, New Hampshire, at the Fifteenth Naval District headquarters in Panama, and in the Nicaraguan national guard where he was involved in road building. Died March 21, 1939, in New York City. *References*: *NCAB* 29:186; and *NYT*, March 23, 1939.

WARREN, JOHN ESAIAS (1827–1896). Traveler, born in Troy, New York. Warren came to St. Paul, Minnesota, in 1852. He was for a time U.S. district attorney for the territory and was mayor of St. Paul after 1863. He traveled in Brazil and wrote *Para, or, Scenes and Adventures on the Banks of the Amazon* (New York, 1851). Died July 6, 1896, in Brussels, Belgium. *Reference*: U. Upham and Rose B. Dunlap, *Minnesota Biographies, 1655–1912* (St. Paul, 1912).

WASHBURN, CHARLES A(MES) (1822–1889). Diplomat, born March 16, 1822, in Livermore, Maine. Washburn graduated from Bowdoin College and was admitted to the bar. He moved to California in 1850, where he edited *Alta California* from 1853 to 1858 and *Daily Times* from 1858 to 1860. He was U.S. commissioner to Paraguay from 1861 to 1863 and U.S. minister to Paraguay from 1863 to 1868. He was an observer of the war between Paraguay and Brazil. In 1868, when the foreign residents were accused of conspiring against President Solano López, he escaped on the USS *Wasp*. He wrote *The History of Paraguay, with Notes of Personal Observations, and Reminiscences of Diplomacy under Difficulties* (Boston, 1871). He later lived in Oakland, California, and Morristown, New Jersey. Died January 26, 1889, in New York City. *References*: *Cutolo*; and *NCAB* 5:255.

WASSON, THERON (1887–1970). Petroleum geologist, born April 23, 1887, in Erie County, New York. Wasson graduated from Carnegie Institute of Technology and studied at Columbia University. He was a field assistant on surveys for coal mines, railroads, oil and gas fields, and pipelines in New York and Pennsylvania from 1903 to 1909 and later in the designing of dams. He was involved in surveys and construction in the oil fields in California from 1913 to 1915. He was a field geologist for the Twin State Oil Company in Tulsa, Oklahoma, and then a topographer for the U.S. Geological Survey. He served in the U.S. Army during World War I. He was chief geologist for the American Oil Engineering Corporation in Fort Worth, Texas, after 1920, and made explorations east of the Andes mountains in Ecuador for the Leonard Exploration Company in 1921. He was chief geologist for the Pure Oil Company (later, a division of the Union Oil Company) from 1922 to 1952 and consulting geologist from 1954 until his retirement in 1962. He made the industry's first offshore seismic survey in the Gulf of Mexico in 1937, directed the successful drilling of the first offshore oil well, discovered Creole Oil Company's oil field in the Gulf of Mexico, and supervised Pure Oil's exploration in South America, especially in Venezuela, through a subsidiary, Orinoco Oil Company. Died August 6, 1970, in Berwyn, Illinois. *References*: *BAAPG* 55 (1971): 2067–68; and *NCAB* 5:423.

WATER WITCH **INCIDENT** (1855–1859). The side-wheel steamer USS *Water Witch*, while exploring the Paraná River, was fired upon by Itapirú, a Paraguay port overlooking the Paraná River, when the vessel proceeded up the river in violation of a Paraguayan decree forbidding such passage. The United States demanded apologies and reparations and sent a U.S. naval expedition to Paraguay in 1858–1859 to obtain redress for its grievances. Paraguay was forced to pay an indemnity. *References*: *ELA*; Oscar P. Fitzgerald, "Profit and Adventure in Paraguay," in *America Spreads Its Sails: U.S. Seapower in the 19th Century*, ed. Clayton R. Barrow, Jr. (Annapolis, Md., 1973), pp. 70–79; Thomas O. Flickema, "The Settlement of the Paraguayan-American Controversy of 1859: A Reappraisal," *TA* 25 (1968): 49–69; Clare V. McKanna, "The *Water Witch* Incident," *AN* 31 (1971): 7–18; and Pablo Max Ynsfrán, *La Expedicion Norteamericana Contra el Paraguay, 1858–1859* (Mexico City, 1954).

WATERMELON RIOT (1856). An American traveler en route to the California gold fields in 1856 refused to pay a local food vendor in Panama City, and the incident degenerated into a fight. Sixteen U.S. citizens and two Panamanians were killed and American businesses were looted. Two U.S. warships landed a detachment of marines in Panama City, and Colombia was forced to pay reparations. *Reference*: *ELA*.

WATERS-PIERCE OIL COMPANY. Directed by Henry Clay Pierce,* it was, before 1900, the most important concern in the petroleum industry in Mexico. It had other Mexican interests, including mining and railroads. It was an affiliate of Standard Oil Company of New Jersey, which owned 65 percent of the company (Pierce owned the rest). It built refineries at Veracruz and Mexico City. It had a monopoly over the sale and distribution of U.S. refined products in Mexico. In 1911, Pierce bought out Standard and became full owner.

WATSON, STEPHEN LAWTON (1880–1966). Missionary, born August 2, 1880, in Marion County, South Carolina. Watson attended Wake Forest College and graduated from Furman University and Southern Baptist Theological Seminary. He was a missionary under the Foreign Mission Board of the Southern Baptist Convention* in Brazil from 1914 until 1950. He directed Baptist seminaries in Rio de Janeiro and Recife and a school in Belo Horizonte. He translated, wrote, and edited books in Portuguese, and edited *O Jornal Batista*. He was a pastor of local churches. Died October 6, 1966, in Columbia, South Carolina. *References*: A. R. Crabtree, *Stephen Lawton Watson of Brazil* (Nashville, Tenn., 1954); and *DSB*.

WAUCHOPE, ROBERT (1909–1979). Archaeologist, born December 10, 1909, in Columbia, South Carolina. Wauchope graduated from the University of South Carolina and Harvard University. He participated in an expedition to Uaxactun, Guatemala, under the auspices of the Carnegie Institution of Washington in 1932. He traveled to the Maya areas of Highland Guatemala, Yucatán, Campeche, and Quintana Roo in 1934 and conducted excavations at Zacualpa, Guatemala, in 1935–1936 and in Kaminaljuyú, Guatemala, in 1936–1937. He wrote *House Mounds of Uaxactun, Guatemala* (Washington, D.C, 1934), *Modern Maya Houses: A Study of Their Archaeological Significance* (Washington, D.C, 1938), *Excavations at Zacualpa, Guatemala* (Washington, D.C., 1948), *Lost Tribes and Sunken Continents: Myth and Method in the Study of American Indians* (Chicago, 1962), and *They Found the Buried Cities: Exploration and Excavation in the American Tropics* (Chicago, 1965). He was editor of *Handbook of Middle American Indians* (Austin, Tex., 1964–1976). He was assistant professor of archaeology at the University of Georgia from 1938 to 1940 and associate professor of anthropology and director of the laboratory of anthropology and archaeology at the University of North Carolina from 1940 to 1944. He served in the U.S. Office of Strategic Services during World War II. He was director of the Middle American Research Institute at Tulane University from 1942 to 1975 and professor of anthropology there from 1942 until 1977. Died January 26, 1979, in New Orleans. *References*: *AmAntiq* 46 (1981): 113–27; and *WWWA*.

WEAVER, PAUL (1888–1964). Petroleum geologist, born May 18, 1888, in Carrollton, Kentucky, and grew up in Brooklyn, New York. Weaver graduated from Columbia University. He served with the U.S. Geological Survey in 1909–1910. He was a geologist for the Bermúdez Corporation of Venezuela in Trinidad and Venezuela and then for the Fred Stark Pearson* interests in Mexico until 1914. He was chief of exploration and technical adviser for the Mexican Eagle Oil Company (Al Águila) from 1915 to 1926. He was a geophysicist with Gulf Oil Corporation in Houston after 1926, and later chief geophysicist, and was a technical assistant to the company's president until his retirement in 1953. He was professor of geology at Texas A&M University from 1953 to 1959. Died June 23, 1964, in Houston, Texas. *References*: *BAAPG* 49 (1965): 317–19; *BGSA* 76 (1965): P37–P41; and *Geophysics* 29 (1964): 870–72.

WEBB, JAMES WATSON (1802–1884). Journalist and diplomat, born February 8, 1802, in Claverack, New York, and grew up in Cooperstown, New York. Webb was commissioned second lieutenant in the U.S. Army in 1819, served on the frontier, and resigned from the army in 1827. He was involved in journalism in New York City, acquired the *Morning Courier* in 1827 and merged it with the *New York Enquirer* in 1829, and was editor and proprietor of the *Morning Courier and New York Enquirer* until 1861, becoming one of the most influential editors of his time. He was U.S. minister to Brazil from 1861 to 1869. He fought against the aid extended by Brazil to Confederate privateers, protected the interests of Americans during the Paraguayan War, and secured the settlement of several long-standing maritime claims. Died June 7, 1884, in New York City. *References*: James L. Crouthamel, *James Watson Webb: A Biography* (Middletown, Conn., 1969); *DAB*; *DADH*; R. B. McCornack, "James Watson Webb and French Withdrawal from Mexico," *HAHR* 31 (1951): 274–86; and *NYT*, June 8, 1884.

WEDDELL, ALEXANDER WILBOURNE (1876–1948). Diplomat, born April 6, 1876, in Richmond, Virginia. Weddell graduated from George Washington University law school. He entered the consular service in 1910, was U.S. consul in Zanzibar and in Catania, Italy, and was consul general in Athens, Calcutta, and Mexico. He resigned from the consular service in 1928 but returned in 1933. He was U.S. ambassador to Argentina from 1933 to 1939 and arranged an armistice in the Chaco War between Paraguay and Bolivia. He was ambassador to Spain from 1939 until his retirement, due to ill health, in 1942. He wrote *Introduction to Argentina* (New York, 1939). Killed January 1, 1948, in a railroad accident, near Sedlia, Missouri. *References*: Alexander W. Weddell Papers,

Virginia Historical Society, Richmond, Va.; *DAB S4*; *DADH*; *NCAB* 35:449; *NYT*, January 2, 1948; and *WWWA*.

WEIR, JAMES R(OBERT) (1881–1943). Plant pathologist, born May 31, 1881, near Scottsburg, Indiana. Weir graduated from Indiana University and the University of Munich. He was a forest pathologist with the Office of Forest Pathology of the Bureau of Plant Industry, U.S. Department of Agriculture, from 1911 to 1923. He was a member of a joint expedition of the departments of agriculture and commerce to study the rubber production possibilities of the Amazon Valley of Brazil and Bolivia in 1923, and then traveled extensively in Argentina, Paraguay, Chile, and the West Indies, studying diseases of tropical plants. He also studied sugar cane disease in Cuba. He was head of the department of plant pathology in the Rubber Research Institute in Kuala Lumpur, Malaya, from 1927 to 1929, and director of the plant research department of the Goodyear Rubber Plantations Company in Sumatra until 1932. He was an agricultural adviser for the Ford Motor Company in its Fordlandia and Belterra plantations along the Tapajoz River in Brazil until 1938. He later traveled extensively in South and Central America and was an agricultural adviser to the government of Venezuela in 1940–1941. He wrote *A Pathological Survey of the Para Rubber Tree (Heavea Brasiliensis) in the Amazon Valley* (Washington, D.C., 1926). Died June 1, 1943, near Scottsburg, Indiana. *Reference*: John A. Stevenson, "James Robert Weir, 1881–1943," *Phytopathology* 36 (1946): 487–92.

WEITZEL, GEORGE T(HOMAS) (1873–1936). Diplomat, born June 23, 1873, in Frankfort, Kentucky. Weitzel graduated from Harvard University and was admitted to the bar in 1898. He practiced law in St. Louis from 1898 to 1906 and served during the Spanish-American War. He was secretary of legation in Costa Rica from 1907 to 1910 and second secretary of embassy in Mexico in 1910 and served in the Latin American division of the State Department in 1910–1911. He was U.S. minister to Nicaragua from 1911 to 1913, and negotiated the Chamorro-Weitzel Treaty in 1913, which gave the United States an option on a canal route and naval base in Fonseca Bay. He wrote *American Policy in Nicaragua* (Washington, D.C., 1916). He served in the Judge Advocate General's Department during World War I, resumed the practice of law in Washington, D.C., from 1921 to 1924, was general counsel to the American Automobile Association from 1924 to 1930. He again practiced law in Washington, D.C., after 1936. Died January 1, 1936, in Washington, D.C. *References*: *NCAB* 45:82; and *WWWA*.

WELLES, (BENJAMIN) SUMNER (1892–1961). Diplomat, born October 14, 1892, in New York City. Welles graduated from Harvard University. He entered the diplomatic service in 1914 and served in Tokyo, Buenos Aires, and at the State Department until 1922. He was delegate or special representative on several international commissions during the 1920s. He was assistant secretary of state from 1933 to 1937 and U.S. ambassador to Cuba in 1933, trying to stabilize the political situation in Cuba and improve U.S.-Cuban relations. He was undersecretary of state from 1937 until his resignation in 1943. He was involved in hemispheric relations and is credited with originating the phrase "Good Neighbor Policy."* Died September 24, 1961, in Bernardsville, New Jersey. *References*: *DADH*; *ELA*; F. Graff, "The Strategy of Involvement: A Diplomatic Biography of Sumner Welles, 1933–1943," Ph.D. diss., University of Michigan, 1971; T. M. Millington, "The Latin American Diplomacy of Sumner Welles," Ph.D. diss., Johns Hopkins University, 1966; *NYT*, September 25, 1961; Louis Perez, "In Defense of Hegemony: Sumner Welles and the Cuban Revolution of 1933," in *Ambassadors in Foreign Policy: The Influence of Individuals on U.S.-Latin American Policy*, ed. C. Neale Ronning and Albert P. Vannucci (New York, 1987), pp. 28–48; William S. Stokes, "The Welles Mission to Cuba," *Central America and Mexico* 1 (December 1953): 3–21; and *WWWA*.

WELLS, R. GIBBON (fl. 1864). Balloonist. Wells came to Argentina in 1864 and conducted several ascensions in balloons that he constructed. He planned to cross South America in a balloon but was unsuccessful in finding the necessary financing for this project. *References*: *Cutolo*; and Ernesto J. Fitte, *La Primera Ascensión en Globo Realizada en el País* (Buenos Aires, 1967).

WELLS, THOMAS (fl. 1827–1833). Printer. Wells came to Chile in 1827 and founded a printing plant in Valparaiso. He published *El Mercurio de Valparaiso*. He returned to the United States in 1833. *Reference*: *Figueroa*.

WELLS, WILLIAM V(INCENT) (1826–1876). Author, born January 2, 1826, in Boston. Wells went to sea at an early age and in 1846 became an officer in the merchant marine. He came to California in 1849 and mined on the Stanislaus and Tuolumne rivers. He was a member of the editorial staff of the *Commercial Advertiser* of San Francisco in 1853–1854. As agent of the Honduras Mining and Trading Company, he went to Honduras in 1854–1855 to explore the gold-bearing regions in eastern Honduras. He wrote *Explorations and Adventures in Honduras, Comprising Sketches of Travel in the Gold Regions of Olancho, and a Review of the History and General Resources of Central America* (New York, 1857). He was U.S. consul for Honduras in San Francisco from 1855 to 1874. He compiled *Walker's Expedition to Nicaragua; a History of the Central American War; and the Sonora and Kinney Expeditions* (New York, 1856). He was associated intermittently with *Alta California* and with the *Daily Times* from 1856 until 1869. He was in Mexico in 1865 and was sent to New York City to conduct a bureau aimed at spreading propaganda favoring the Mexican empire throughout the United States. The fall of Maximilian forced him to return to San Francisco. He was clerk for the mayor of San Francisco from 1869 to 1874. Died June 1, 1876, in Napa, California. *References*: *ACAB*; *DAB*; and *NCAB* 18:292.

WESLEY, ARTHUR (FREDERICK) (1885–1975). Missionary, born October 26, 1885, in North Branch, Michigan. Wesley graduated from Albion College, Northern Baptist Theological Seminary, and the University of Michigan. He studied at Garrett Theological Seminary and was ordained in 1920. He was a missionary under the Board of Foreign Missions of the Methodist Episcopal Church* in Argentina in 1918–1919 and in Montevideo, Uruguay, after 1919. He was founder and pastor of Friendship House in Montevideo, founder of Sweet Memorial Institute in Santiago, and general treasurer of the Methodist Church in Argentina and Uruguay from 1929 to 1944. He was elected bishop in 1944 and served as bishop of the Atlantic area, comprising Argentina, Uruguay, and Bolivia, from 1944 to 1949. He was pastor of the Union Church in Santiago, Chile, from 1949 to 1957. He retired in 1955. He wrote an autobiography, *The Vintage of the Years* (Buenos Aires, 1956). Died August 10, 1975, in Lakeland, Florida. *References*: *EWM*; and *Who's Who in the Methodist Church* (Nashville, Tenn., 1966).

WEST, DUVAL (1861–1949). Judge and diplomat, born in Austin, Texas. West attended Cumberland Law school (Lebanon, Tenn.) and then practiced law. He served as U.S. deputy marshal, clerk, and assistant U.S. attorney. He served during the Spanish-American War. He was a representative of President Woodrow Wilson in Mexico in 1915. He was judge of the Western District of Texas from 1916 until his retirement in 1932. Died May 14, 1949, in San Antonio, Texas. *References*: *Dallas News*, May 15, 1949; *Hill*; and *NYT*, May 15, 1949.

WESTON, EDWARD (1886–1958). Photographer, born March 24, 1886, in Highland Park, Illinois. Weston attended the Illinois College of Photography. He opened his first studio in Tropico (later Glendale), California, in 1911. He ran a studio in Mexico City from 1923 to 1926. He settled in Carmel, California, in 1928. Died January 1, 1958, in Carmel, California. *References*: *The Daybooks of Edward Weston, Vol. I: Mexico*, ed. Nancy Newhall (Rochester, N.Y., 1961); Amy Conger, *Edward Weston in Mexico, 1923–1926* (Albuquerque, N.M., 1983); and Ben Maddow, *Edward Weston: His Life and Photographs* (Millerton, N.Y., 1979).

WESTPHAL, FRANK HENRY (1858–1944). Missionary, born near New London, Wisconsin. Westphal attended Battle Creek College and was ordained in 1883. He was in charge of the city mission in Milwaukee and taught at Union College. He went to South America in 1894, the first ordained Seventh-Day Adventist minister assigned to South America. He served in Crespo, Entre Ríos province and began tent meetings in Diamante in 1895, the first such Seventh-Day Adventist meeting in South America. He established his headquarters in Buenos Aires and returned to the United States in 1901 because of ill health but was back in South America in 1904. He served in Chile until 1920, when he returned to the United States and settled in California. He wrote *Pioneering in the Neglected Continent* (Nashville, Tenn., 1927). *Reference*: *SDAE*.

WHARTON, ROBERT LESLIE (1871–1960). Missionary educator, born September 5, 1871, in McLeansville, North Carolina. Wharton graduated from Davidson College and Union Theological Seminary of Virginia and was ordained in 1898. He was principal of a municipal school in Durham, North Carolina, from 1892 to 1895. He was a missionary under the Board of Foreign Missions of the Presbyterian Church in the United States in Cuba after 1899. He was a pastor in Cárdenas and Caibarien in Cuba from 1901 to 1918, founder of Colegio "La Progressiva" in Cárdenas and Colegio Presbiteriano in Caibarien, and superintendent of educational work for the Presbyterian Church in Cuba from 1918 to 1941. Died August 2, 1960, in Arlington, Virginia. *References*: *MDPC*; and *WWLA*.

WHEAT, CHATAM ROBERDEAU (1826–1862). Soldier, born April 9, 1826, in Alexandria, Virginia, and grew up in New Orleans. Wheat graduated from the University of Nashville and studied law. He participated in the Mexican War, was admitted to the bar in 1847, and practiced law. He served in the state legislature. He accepted a commission as a colonel in the filibustering expedition of Narciso López, commanded a regiment in the battle of Cárdenas in Cuba, and was wounded. In 1856, he joined William Walker* and Charles Frederick Henningsen* and commanded a corps in Nicaragua. When General Juan Álvarez became president of Mexico, he accepted a commission as general of artillery in the Mexican army but resigned his command on Álvarez's retirement. He served briefly in the Italian war of independence. He commanded the "Louisiana Tigers," a battalion of cavalry in the Confederate Army, during the Civil War. Killed June 27, 1862, in the Battle of Gaines' Mill, Virginia. *References*: Charles L. Dufour, *Gentle Tiger: The Gallant Life of Roberdeau Wheat* (Baton Rouge, La., 1957); and *NCAB* 9:168.

WHEELER, JOHN HILL (1806–1882). Lawyer and diplomat, born August 2, 1806, in Murfreesboro, North Carolina. Wheeler graduated from Columbian College (later George Washington University) and the University of North Carolina, studied law, and was admitted to the bar in 1827. He served in the state house of commons from 1827 to 1830. He was superintendent of the Charlotte branch of the U.S. Mint from 1837 to 1841, state treasurer from 1842 to 1844, and again a member of the state house of commons in 1852. He was U.S. minister to Nicaragua from 1854 to 1856. He ignored and went beyond his instructions, favoring William Walker's* attempt to take over Nicaragua. He recognized the Walker government and used his diplomatic position to hinder efforts against Walker. He was recalled in 1856 and forced to resign. He was later involved in historical research and journalism. Died December 7, 1882, in Washington, D.C. *References*: John H. Wheeler Scrapbooks, Manuscript Division, Library of Congress; *DAB*; *DADH*; and Randall O. Hudson, "The Filibuster Minister: The Career of John Hill Wheeler as United States Minister to Nicaragua, 1854–1856," *North Carolina Historical Review* 49 (1972): 280–97.

WHEELWRIGHT, WILLIAM (1798–1873). Entrepreneur, born March 16, 1798, in Newburyport, Massachusetts. He shipped as a cabin boy to the West Indies in 1814. He commanded a bark to Rio in 1817 and the *Rising Star* in 1823, which ran ashore in the Rio de la Plata. He then shipped as a supercargo to Valparaiso. He was U.S. consul in Guayaquil from 1824 to 1829 and engaged successfully in trade. He moved to Valparaiso in 1829 and did much to develop the city, building a lighthouse and other port facilities and constructing gas and water works. In 1838, he obtained a concession for a steamship line along the west coast of South America. He formed the Pacific Steam Navigation Company in 1840, was superintendent of the company, and began service between Valparaiso and Callao. The service was later extended to Panama. Between 1849 and 1852, he built the first railroad in South America, from Caldera, the Chilean port he developed, into the silver and copper mines at Copiapó, and then to Chañarcillo and Tres Puntas. In 1850, he built Chile's (and South America's) first telegraph line. In 1855, he secured a concession from the Argentine government to build a railroad from Rosario to Córdoba, and the Grand Central Argentine Railway was opened in 1870. He created the port of La Plata and, in 1872, completed a railroad from this port to Buenos Aires. He wrote *Statements and Documents Relative to the Establishment of Steam Navigation in the Pacific* (London, 1838), *Mr. Wheelwright's Report on Steam Navigation in the Pacific; with an Account of the Coal Mines of Chile and Panama* (London, 1843), and *Observations on the Isthmus of Panama* (London, 1844). Died September 26, 1873, in London, England. *References*: *Cutolo*; *DAB*; *Drees*; R. E. Duncan, "William Wheelwright and Early Steam Navigation in the Pacific, 1820–1840," *TA* 32 (1975): 257–81; *ELA*; *Figueroa*; Jay Kinsbrunner, "The Business Activities of William Wheelwright in Chile, 1829–1860," Ph.D. diss., New York University, 1965; Jay Kinsbrunner, "Water for Valparaiso: A Case of Entrepreneurial Frustration," *JIAS* 10 (1968): 653–61; and *Udaondo*.

WHITE, ISRAEL C(HARLES) (1848–1927). Geologist, born November 1, 1848, in Monongalia County, Virginia. White graduated from West Virginia University and studied at Columbia University. He was a professor of geology at West Virginia University from 1877 to 1892, in private business from 1892 to 1897, and superintendent of the geological survey of West Virginia from 1897 until his death. He was chief geologist of the Brazilian Coal Commission from 1904 to 1906 and made a survey of the coal fields of the southern part of Brazil. Died November 25, 1927, in Baltimore. *References*: Israel C. White Papers, West Virginia University Library, Morgantown, W.Va.; *BAAPG* 12 (1928): 339–51; *DAB*; *NYT*, November 26, 1927; and *WWWA*.

WHITE, JOHN CAMPBELL (1884–1967). Diplomat, born March 17, 1884, in London, England, to American parents. White graduated from Harvard University. He was a member of the editorial staff of the *Baltimore Sun* from 1910 to 1913. He entered the foreign service in 1913 and was secretary of legation and consul general in Santo Domingo, the Dominican Republic, in 1914–1915. He then served in Russia, Greece, Japan, Siam, Poland, Venezuela, Czechoslovakia, and Latvia, Estonia, and Lithuania until 1927. He was assistant chief of the Eastern European division of the U.S. State Department in 1927–1928; counselor of embassy in Argentina from 1928 to 1933 and in Germany from 1933 to 1935; consul general in Calcutta, India; chargé d'affaires in Kabul, Afghanistan, from 1935 to 1940; and diplomatic agent and consul general to Morocco in 1940–1941. He was U.S. minister to Haiti from 1940 to 1943 and first ambassador to Haiti in 1943–1944. He was ambassador to Peru in 1944–1945. He retired in 1945. Died June 11, 1967, in New York City. *References*: *NCAB* 54:558; and *NYT*, June 12, 1967.

WHITE, ROBERT E(DWARD) (1926–   ). Diplomat, born September 21, 1926, in Stoneham, Massachusetts. White graduated from St. Michaels College and Fletcher School of Law and Diplomacy. He entered the foreign service in 1958; served in Hong Kong, Ecuador, and Honduras; was Latin American director of the Peace Corps* from 1968 to 1970; deputy chief of mission in Nicaragua from 1970 to 1975 and in Colombia in 1975; and deputy U.S. representative to the Organization of American States* from 1975 to 1977. He was U.S. ambassador to Paraguay from 1977 to 1979 and ambassador to El Salvador from 1979 to 1981. He was removed by President Ronald Reagan's administration and was forced to retire from the State Department. He was senior associate of the Carnegie Endowment for International Peace in 1982–1983 and president of the International Center for Development Policy after 1983. *Reference*: *WWAP*.

WHITE, WILLIAM P(ORTER) (1769–1842). Businessman, born October 10, 1769, in Pittsfield, Massachusetts. White graduated from Dartmouth College. He entered the mercantile and shipping business in Boston. He arrived in Buenos Aires in 1803 as a supercargo on a Spanish ship and settled there as merchant and moneylender. In 1806, he acted as interpreter and general agent for the British fleet in Buenos Aires and was forced to flee to Montevideo in 1807 with the retreating British force. He was jailed and his property was confiscated but he was brought back to Buenos Aires in 1808 and released later that year. He entered the yerba maté (a tea-like South American beverage made from the dried leaves of an evergreen tree) business, becoming a leading factor in its import and distribution, and he probably succeeded in cornering the market on yerba maté. In 1813, he was involved in creating an Argentine fleet that destroyed the Spanish fleet and captured Montevideo. He utilized much personal wealth for 'his purpose. Following a revolt in Buenos Aires in 1815, he was forced to flee again to Montevideo and was imprisoned again in 1817–1818. He remained in Buenos Aires, but died there in poverty. *References*: *Cutolo*; Ricardo Piccirilli and Leoncio Gianello, *Biografias Navales* (Buenos Aires, 1963), pp. 311–18; *Udaondo*; and Edward S. Wallace, ''Forgotten Men of Dartmouth: Father of the Argentine Navy, William Porter White, 1790,'' *Dartmouth Alumni Magazine* 27 (March 1935): 22, 74.

WHITTEN, NORMAN E(ARL), JR. (1937–   ). Anthropologist, born May 23, 1937, in Orange, New Jersey. Whitten graduated from Colgate University and the University of North Carolina. He was assistant professor of anthropology at Washington University (St. Louis) from 1965 to 1968 and associate professor there from 1968 to 1970. He was associate professor of anthropology at the University of Illinois from 1970 to 1973 and professor after 1973. He carried out fieldwork in Ecuador and Colombia and wrote *Class, Kinship, and Power in an Ecuadorian Town: The Negroes of San Lorenzo* (Stanford, Calif., 1965), *Black Frontiermen: A South American Case* (New York, 1974), and *Sacha Runa: Ethnicity and Adaptation of Ecuadorian Jungle Quichua* (Urbana, Ill., 1975). *References*: *AMWS*; and *CA*.

WIGHT, WILLIAM FRANKLIN (1874–1954). Botanist. Wight was staff botanist in the Bureau of Plant Industry of the U.S. Department of Agriculture. He went to Buenos Aires, Argentina, in 1912–1913 to assist the Argentine Ministry of Agriculture with the fledgling system of experimental stations, and then criss-crossed the Andes seeking the origins of the primitive white potato. He was a plant explorer for the U.S. Department of Agriculture and crossed the Andes five times. He retired in 1940 and died in California. *Reference*: Michael Morgan, ''South American Odyssey,'' *Americas* 31 (October 1979): 28–34.

WILLARD, THEODORE A(RTHUR) (1862–1943). Manufacturer, born December 10, 1862, in Castle Rock, Minnesota. Willard worked in Minneapolis, began to experiment with batteries, and in 1882 constructed the first storage battery. He was a wood engraver in Cleveland and then worked in New York City, continuing his experiments. He established a laboratory in Norwalk, Ohio, and obtained a patent in 1895. He began manufacturing in Cleveland in 1902. He later organized the Willard Storage Battery Company and was its president until 1928. For several years he spent time in Yucatán, particularly at Chichén Itzá, taking thousands of photographs, studying and translating the Mayan language, and compiling material for his book *The City of the Sacred Well* (New York, 1929). He also wrote *The Lost Empires of the Itzas and Mayas* (Glendale, Calif., 1932) and *Kukulcan, the Bearded Conqueror: New Mayan Discoveries* (Hollywood, Calif., 1942), as well as works of fiction: *Wizard of Zacna: A Lost City of the Mayas* (Boston, 1929) and *Bride of the Rain God: Princess of Chichen-Itza, the Sacred City of the Mayas* (Cleveland, 1930). Died February 3, 1943, in Beverly Hills, California. *References*: *NCAB* 31:83; Edna E. Webster, *T. A.*

Willard: Wizard of the Storage Battery: The Biography of a Famous Inventor (Sherman Oaks, Calif., 1976); and *WWWA*.

WILLEY, GORDON R(ANDOLPH) (1913–   ). Archaeologist, born March 7, 1913, in Chariton, Iowa. Willey graduated from the University of Arizona and Columbia University. He was senior anthropologist with the Bureau of American Ethnology at the Smithsonian Institution from 1943 to 1950 and professor of anthropology at the Peabody Museum of Harvard University after 1950. He conducted archaeological excavations in Guatemala and Central America. He wrote *Prehistoric Settlement Patterns in the Viru Valley, Peru* (Washington, D.C., 1953), *An Introduction to American Archaeology, Vol. I: North and Middle America* (Englewood Cliffs, N.J., 1966), *An Introduction to American Archaeology, Vol. II: South America* (Englewood Cliffs, N.J., 1971), *The Artifacts of Altar de Sacrificios* (Cambridge, Mass., 1972), *The Altar de Sacrificios Excavations: General Summary and Conclusions* (Cambridge, Mass., 1973), *Excavations at Seibal, Department of Petén, Guatemala: Artifacts* (Cambridge, Mass., 1978), and *Portraits in American Archaeology: Remembrances of Some Distinguished Americanists* (Albuquerque, N.M., 1988), and was coauthor of *Early Ancon and Early Supe Culture: Chavin Horizon Sites of the Central Peruvian Coast* (New York, 1954), *The Monagrillo Culture of Panama* (Cambridge, Mass., 1954), *Prehistoric Maya Settlements in the Belize Valley* (Cambridge, Mass., 1965), *The Ruins of Altar de Sacrificios: An Introduction* (Cambridge, Mass., 1969), *Excavations at Seibal: Department of Petén, Guatemala: Introduction: The Site and Its Setting* (Cambridge, Mass., 1975), *A History of American Archaeology* (San Francisco, 1980), and *Essays in Maya Archaeology* (Albuquerque, N.M., 1987). *References*: *DAS*; Richard M. Leventhal and Alan L. Kolara, eds., *Civilization in the Ancient Americas: Essays in Honor of Gordon R. Willey* (Albuquerque, N.M., 1983); Evon Z. Vogt and Richard M. Leventhal, eds., *Prehistoric Settlement Patterns: Essays in Honor of Gordon R. Willey* (Albuquerque, N.M., 1983); and *WWA*.

WILLIAM TAYLOR SELF-SUPPORTING MISSIONS IN SOUTH AMERICA. A system of self-supporting schools organized by William Taylor (1821–1902) in Peru and Chile in 1877–1878 and centered in Coquimbo, Chile. *Reference*: Goodsil F. Arms, *History of the William Taylor Self-Supporting Missions in South America* (New York, 1921).

WILLIAMS, JOSEPH JOHN (1875–1940). Anthropologist, born December 1, 1875, in Boston. Williams joined the Society of Jesus in 1903, attended Boston College, graduated from Woodstock (Md.) College, and was ordained in 1907. He was registrar at St. Francis Xavier College (New York City) from 1897 to 1900. He was one of the original editors of the magazine *America* and its managing editor from 1909 to 1911. He was a missionary in Jamaica from 1912 to 1917. He was treasurer of Holy Cross College (Worcester, Mass.) from

1918 to 1922 and of the New England province of the Jesuits from 1925 to 1928. He was professor of anthropology at Boston College Graduate School after 1934. He wrote *Whisperings of the Caribbean: Reflections of a Missionary* (New York, 1925), *Voodoos and Obeahs: Phases of West India Witchcraft* (New York, 1932), and *Whence the "Black Irish" of Jamaica?* (New York, 1932). Died October 28, 1940, in Lenox, Massachusetts. *Reference: DACB.*

WILLIAMS, LOUIS OTHO (1908–   ). Botanist, born December 16, 1908, in Jackson, Wyoming. Williams graduated from the University of Wyoming and Washington University (St. Louis). He was a research associate at the Botanical Museum of Harvard University from 1937 to 1946 and a botanist with the United Fruit Company* from 1946 to 1957. He was associated with Escuela Agricola Panamericana in Honduras and was economic botanist with the Agricultural Research Service of the U.S. Department of Agriculture in Maryland from 1957 to 1960. He was curator and, later, chief curator of Central American botany at the Field Museum of Natural History from 1960 to 1970, and chairman of the department of botany from 1971 until his retirement in 1974. He was consul of Guatemala in Chicago from 1967 to 1974. He wrote *The Useful Plants of Central America* (Tegucigalpa, Honduras, 1981) and was coauthor of *Flora of Guatemala* (Chicago, 1958–1976). *Reference: AMWS.*

WILLIAMSON, JOHN G(USTAVUS) A(DOLPHUS) (1793–1840). Diplomat, born December 2, 1793, in Person County, North Carolina. Williamson attended the University of North Carolina and studied law. He served in the North Carolina General Assembly from 1823 to 1825. He was U.S. consul in La Guayra, Venezuela, from 1826 to 1835 and chargé d'affaires in Venezuela (the first U.S. diplomatic representative to Venezuela) from 1835 until his death. He negotiated a treaty between Venezuela and the United States. Died August 7, 1840, in Caracas, Venezuela. *References: Caracas Diary, 1835–1840: The Journal of John G. A. Williamson, First Diplomatic Representative of the United States to Venezuela*, ed. J. L. de Grummond (Baton Rouge, La., 1954); and J. L. de Grummond, *Envoy to Caracas: The Story of John G. A. Williamson, Nineteenth Century Diplomat* (Baton Rouge, La., 1951).

WILLIAMSON, SYDNEY BACON (1865–1939). Civil engineer, born April 15, 1865, in Lexington, Virginia. Williamson graduated from the Virginia Military Institute. He was associated with the engineering department of the St. Paul and Duluth and the Northern Pacific railroads from 1886 to 1890, was in general engineering practice in Montgomery, Alabama, from 1890 to 1892, and worked for the U.S. government at the Muscle Shoals canal from 1892 to 1900. He served during the Spanish-American War. He was in civil practice in New York, Baltimore, and other cities from 1903 to 1907. He was a division engineer in the building of the Panama Canal. He was in charge of the Pacific locks and chief of the Pacific Division from 1907 to 1912. He was chief of construction for J. G. White and Company in London from 1912 to 1914, chief of construction for the U.S. Reclamation Service from 1914 to 1916, and consulting engineer for Guggenheim Brothers in Chile and for the Chile Exploration Company from 1916 to 1924. He served in the U.S. Army during World War I. He was in civil practice in Birmingham, Alabama, and Charlottesville, Virginia, from 1924 to 1929. He was consulting engineer for the port of Palm Beach, Florida, from 1926 to 1928 and a member of the Interoceanic Canal Board from 1931 to 1935. Died January 13, 1939, in Lexington, Virginia. *References*: Sydney Bacon Williamson Papers, Virginia Military Institute Library, Lexington, Va.; and *NCAB* 30:187.

WILLIS, BAILEY (1857–1949). Geologist, born May 31, 1857, in Idlewild-on-Hudson, New York. Willis graduated from the Columbia University School of Mines. He became a geologist for the Northern Pacific Railway in 1880 and explored Washington Territory. He was with the U.S. Geological Survey from 1882 to 1915 and conducted geological explorations in China. He helped the Argentine government establish a geological survey and organized and operated a survey of northern Patagonia for the Comisión de Estudios Hidrológicos. He wrote *Northern Patagonia, Character and Resources* (Buenos Aires, 1914). He was professor of geology at Stanford University from 1915 to 1922 and became a consulting engineer in 1922. Died February 9, 1949, in Palo Alto, California. *References*: *BGSA* 73 (1962): 55–72; *BMNAS* 35 (1961): 333–50; *DAB S4*; *DSB*; *NCAB* 37:53; and *WWWA*.

WILSON, HENRY LANE (1857–1932). Diplomat, born November 3, 1857, in Crawfordsville, Indiana. Wilson graduated from Wabash College and studied law. He was owner-editor of the Lafayette *Journal* from 1882 to 1885. He practiced law and was involved in real estate in Spokane, Washington, from 1885 to 1889. He was U.S. minister to Chile from 1897 to 1904, minister to Belgium from 1905 to 1909, and ambassador to Mexico from 1909 to 1913. He defended American interests in Mexico, played a significant and interventionist role in the coup that led to the assassination of Francisco Madero and the rise of Victoriano Huerta, and urged for U.S. recognition of Huerta. He resigned in 1913. He wrote *Diplomatic Episodes in Mexico, Belgium and Chile* (New York, 1927). Died December 22, 1932, in Indianapolis. *References*: *DAB*; *DADH*; *ELA*; Genez Hanrahan, ed., *Documents on the Mexican Revolution, Vol. 2: The Madero Revolution as Reported in the Confidential Dispatches of U.S. Ambassador Henry Lane Wilson and the Embassy in Mexico City, June 1910 to June 1911* (Salisbury, N.C., 1976); Eugene F. Masingill, "The Diplomatic Career of Henry Lane Wilson in Latin America," Ph.D. diss., Louisiana State University, 1957; *NYT*, December 23, 1932; Marjorie C. Parker, "Diary of a Revolution: A United States Ambassador's Involvement in the Intrigue of Mexico's 'Tragic Ten Days,' " *American West* 10 (1973): 4–9, 57–59; Raymond L.

Shoemaker, "Henry Lane Wilson and Republican Policy toward Mexico, 1913–1920," *Indiana Magazine of History* 76 (1980): 103–22; and *WWWA*.

WILSON, LESTER MACLEAN (1885–1937). Educator, born December 15, 1885, in Lamar, Missouri. Wilson graduated from Park College (Parkville, Mo.), University of Chicago, and Columbia University. He taught psychology at the University of Puerto Rico from 1909 to 1912 and at Eastern Illinois State Normal School (Charleston, Ill.) from 1915 to 1921. He was director of examinations and studies in the directorate general of instruction in Lima, Peru, in 1921 and director general of instruction for the Republic of Peru in 1922–1923. He was associate professor of comparative education at Teachers College of Columbia University from 1923 to 1925 and professor from 1925 until his death. Died May 26, 1937, in New York City. *References*: *NYT*, May 27, 1937; and *WWWA*.

WINANS, ROGER S. (1886–1975). Missionary, born December 15, 1886, near Osawkie, Kansas. Winans attended a Bible school. He was a missionary under the Department of Foreign Missions of the Church of the Nazarene* in Peru from 1914 to 1948. He served in Monsefu until 1923, among the Aguaruna Indians in Jaen, Pomera, and later in Sunsuntsa until 1929, and in Yama Yaket until 1944. He translated the gospels of Luke and John into Aguaruna. He retired in 1948. He wrote *Gospel over the Andes: Notes of Roger S. Winans* (Kansas City, Mo., 1955). Died October 26, 1975, in Temple City, Oklahoma.

WINSHIP, BLANTON (1869–1947). Army officer, born November 23, 1869, in Macon, Georgia. Winship graduated from Mercer University (Macon) and the law school of the University of Georgia. He practiced law in Macon from 1893 to 1898. He served during the Spanish-American War, was commissioned first lieutenant in the Judge Advocate's Department in 1899, and served in the Philippines. In 1906, he was a member of the advisory commission headed by General Enoch Herbert Crowder,* which went to Cuba to rewrite the laws and draw up a new constitution. He served as judge advocate of the Army of Cuban Pacification, was a member of the expeditionary force that occupied Veracruz in 1914, and had charge of the civilian administration of the city. He served in France during World War I. He was director general of the Army Claims Settlement Commission in 1918–1919, military aide to President Calvin Coolidge in 1927–1928, legal adviser to Governor-General Henry L. Stimson of the Philippines from 1928 to 1930, and army's advocate general from 1931 to 1933. He retired with the rank of major general in 1933. He was governor of Puerto Rico from 1934 until 1939. He fostered the tourist potential of Puerto Rico but through the use of force tried to prevent discontent and nationalist feelings and activities in the island. He was recalled in World War II and served as a coordinator of the Inter-American Defense Board. Died October 9, 1947, in Washington, D.C. *References*: *DAB S4*; *NCAB* 37:256; *NYT*, October 10, 1947; and *WWWA*.

WIRKUS, FAUSTIN (1896–1945). Marine Corps warrant officer, born in Pittston, Pennsylvania. In 1914, Wirkus ran away from home at age eighteen and joined the Marines. He served in Haiti after 1915. In 1921, as a gunnery sergeant, he was sent to La Gonave, an island north of Port-au-Prince. He served as administrator of the island until 1925. He was crowned King Faustin II and (with Taney Dudley) related his adventures in *The White King of Gonave* (Garden City, N.Y., 1931). He continued to serve in Haiti until 1931, when he left the service. He was later involved in lecturing and selling securities for a Wall Street firm. He reenlisted in the Marines in 1939 and served during World War II. Died October 8, 1945, in Brooklyn, New York. *References*: Eloise Engle, "King Faustin II," *Marine Corps Gazette* 52 (November 1968): 49–54; and *NYT*, October 9, 1945.

WOLFE, BERTRAM D(AVID) (1896–1977). Author, born January 19, 1896, in Brooklyn, New York. Wolfe graduated from the College of the City of New York, University of Mexico, and Columbia University. He was teacher at the Miguel Lerdo High School in Mexico City from 1922 to 1925 and one of the founders of the Mexican Communist party. He was expelled from Mexico in 1925. He was educational director of the Workers School of the American Community Party in New York City from 1926 to 1928, member of the executive committee of the Comintern in Moscow from 1928 to 1930, and a free-lance writer until 1950. He was chief of the ideological advisory unit of the international broadcasting division of the State Department, senior fellow at the Hoover Institution in 1949–1950 and from 1965 to 1968, and senior research fellow there after 1966. He wrote *Portrait of Mexico* (New York, 1937), *Diego Rivera: His Life and Times* (New York, 1939), *The Fabulous Life of Diego Rivera* (New York, 1963), and *A Life in Two Centuries: An Autobiography* (New York, 1981), which was published posthumously. Died February 21, 1977, in Palo Alto, California. *References*: *CA*; *DAS*; *NCAB* 59:85; *NYT*, February 22, 1977; and *WWWA*.

WOOD, LEONARD (1860–1927). Army officer and colonial administrator, born October 9, 1860, in Winchester, New Hampshire. Wood graduated from Harvard Medical School and was commissioned a surgeon with the U.S. Army in 1866. He cooperated with Theodore Roosevelt* in organizing the "Rough Riders"* and served in Cuba during the Spanish-American War. He was military governor of the city of Santiago, Cuba, in 1898, of the province of Santiago in 1898–1899, and of Cuba from 1899 to 1902. He improved sanitation, built roads, established public schools, and reformed the judiciary. He was military governor of the Moro Province in the Philippines from 1903 to 1906, commanded the Philippine Division from 1906 to 1908, and was chief-of-staff of the U.S. Army from 1910 to 1914 and governor general of the Philippines from 1921 to 1927. Died August 7, 1927, in Boston. *References*: *ACAB*; *DAB*; *ELA*; James H. Hitchman, "The American Touch in Imperial Administration: Leonard Wood in Cuba, 1898–1902," *TA* 24 (1968): 394–403; James H. Hitchman, *Leonard Wood and Cuban Independence, 1899–1902* (The Hague, 1971); J. C. Lane, "Leonard Wood and the Shaping of American Defense Policy, 1900–1920," Ph.D. diss., University of Georgia Press, 1963; and *WWWA*.

WOOD, THOMAS BOND (1844–1922). Missionary, born March 18, 1844, in Lafayette, Indiana. Wood graduated from Indiana Asbury (later DePauw) and Wesleyan universities and was ordained in 1868. He was president of Valparaiso (Ind.) College from 1867 to 1869. He was a missionary under the Board of Foreign Missions of the Methodist Episcopal Church* in Argentina from 1870 to 1877. He served in Rosario de Santa Fé from 1870 to 1877 and established a boys' school there. He also served as chairman of the board of the examiners of city schools, as member of the city government, and as a professor of physics and astronomy at the national college from 1875 to 1877. He was president of the national educational commission of Argentina and U.S. consul from 1873 to 1878. He was in Montevideo from 1877 to 1881, where he established and edited *El Evangelista*, the first Spanish evangelical weekly in the world. He was also superintendent of the mission of the Methodist Episcopal Church in South America from 1879 to 1887. He established in Uruguay the first Protestant college south of the United States to grant a degree of B.A. and was in charge of it from 1887 to 1889. He founded the Methodist Theological Seminary in Buenos Aires in 1889 and served as its president until 1891. He served in Peru in 1891 to 1913, championing religious liberty, and was superintendent of all Methodist work in Peru, Ecuador, and Bolivia from 1891 to 1905. In 1891 he founded the Technical School of Commerce in Lima, Peru, and was its president. He established normal schools for the Ecuadoran government and was sent by the president of Ecuador in 1900 to the United States to secure teachers. He was president of the theological seminary in Lima. He founded the Methodist Episcopal Church in Panama in 1903, started the Young Men's Christian Association there, and acted as U.S. chaplain there in 1905–1906. He was superintendent of the North Andes Mission from 1907 to 1913. He founded the Lima High School for girls and was superintendent of public school in Callao. He returned to the United States in 1913 and retired in 1915. Died December 18, 1922, Tacoma, Washington. *References*: Thomas Bond Wood Papers, Archives of DePauw University and Indiana Methodism, Greencastle, Ind.; *DAB*; Paul E. Kuhl, "Gringo in the Andes: Thomas B. Wood and the Normal School System in Ecuador," *Methodist History* 16 (1978): 197–219; and Paul E. Kuhl, "Protestant Missionary Activity and Freedom of Religion in Ecuador, Peru and Bolivia." Ph.D. diss., Southern Illinois University at Carbondale, 1982.

WOODRING, WENDELL P(HILLIPS) (1891–1983). Geologist and paleontologist, born June 13, 1891, in Reading, Pennsylvania. Woodring graduated from Albright College and Johns Hopkins University. He was on the staff of the U.S. Geological Survey from 1916 until his retirement in 1961. He participated in the geological reconnaissance of Hispaniola and was coauthor of *Geology of the Republic of Haiti* (Port-au-Prince, Haiti, 1924). In 1947 he began an extended study of the geology of the Canal Zone and adjoining parts of Panama. Died January 29, 1983, in Santa Barbara, California. *References*: *American Philosophical Society Year Book* 1983, pp. 440–46; *AMWS*; *McGraw-Hill Modern Scientists and Engineers* (New York, 1980); and *WWWA*.

WOODWARD, CLARK H. (1877–1967). Naval officer, born March 4, 1877, in Atlanta. Woodward graduated from the U.S. Naval Academy in 1898. He served during the Spanish-American War, the Philippine-American War, the Boxer Rebellion in China, and World War I. He served on a naval mission to Brazil in 1919 and headed a mission to the Peruvian Navy from 1923 to 1926. He commanded a force of sailors and marines to keep order in Nicaragua in 1927 and returned to Nicaragua in 1932 as President Herbert Hoover's special representative to supervise the presidential elections in that country. He was a member of the Naval General Board from 1933 to 1935 and commander of the Third Naval District in New York from 1935 until his retirement. He retired with the rank of admiral in 1941 but was recalled during World War II. Died May 29, 1967, in Washington, D.C. *Reference*: *NYT*, May 30, 1967.

WOOSTER, CHARLES WHITING (1780–1848). Naval officer, born in New Haven, Connecticut. Wooster ran away to sea in 1791 and commanded a ship in 1801. He commanded a privateer during the War of 1812 and then several merchant ships. He was commissioned captain in the Chilean Navy in 1817, came to Chile in 1818, and commanded a Chilean war ship during its war with Spain. He resigned from the Chilean Navy in 1819 and was captain of a whaler until 1822, when he reentered service as commander in chief of the Chilean navy. He fought the Spanish again in 1825–1826 and 1829, successfully attacking the island of Chiloe, the last stronghold of Spain in Chile. He was commissioned a rear admiral in 1829 but left in 1835 after disagreement with the Chilean government. He returned to the United States in 1835. Died in San Francisco. *References*: *DAB*; *Figueroa*; and Edgar K. Thompson, ''Yankee Admiral under the Chilean Flag,'' *Mariner's Mirror* 64 (1978): 157–62.

WORDEN, J(OHN) HECTOR (1885– ?). Aviator, Cherokee Indian, born in New York City. Worden was educated at Carlisle Indian School (Pa.). He learned to fly at the Blériot school in Etampes, France, and the Moisant Aviation School in Garden City, New York. He was a flight instructor in Galveston, Texas, and then gave exhibition flights in the United States for the Moisant Company. He was sent to Mexico City to demonstrate planes to the Federal government forces. He was one of the first to fly in combat anywhere. During the Mexican revolution, he was engaged by President Francisco I. Madero to fly with the Federal forces operating against the rebels in 1911. He carried out bombing and reconnaissance missions for Madero. In 1912, he became a captain on the staff of General Venustiano Huerta and was assigned to duty in the north, doing scouting and observation work. He wrote of his experiences in the November 16, 1912, issue of *Aero & Hydro*.

WORLD RADIO MISSIONARY FELLOWSHIP, INC. A nondenominational agency, specializing in radio and organized in 1931. It began operations in Ecuador in 1931 and in Panama in 1954. It operates radio station HCJB in Quito, Ecuador. *Reference*: Frank S. Cook, *Seeds in the Wind; the Story of the Voice of the Andes, Radio Station HCJB, Ecuador* (Miami, Fla., 1961).

WORTHINGTON, WILLIAM G. D. (1784– ?). Lawyer and diplomat, born in Baltimore. Worthington served in the Maryland State Senate and then was principal clerk in the office of the controller in the U.S. Department of Treasury. He was a special diplomatic agent to Buenos Aires, Chile, and Peru from 1817 to 1819, with instructions to collect information about the population, resources, and revolutionary factions. He failed to restrict his actions to his instructions, instead negotiating a treaty of commerce and seamen between the United States and Buenos Aires. He was dismissed and recalled. He was secretary of East Florida Territory after 1821 and its acting governor in 1821–1822. *References*: William G. D. Worthington Diaries, Manuscript Division, Library of Congress; Eugenio Pereira Salas, "La Mision Worthington en Chile (1818–1819)," *RCHG* 80 (1936): 91–110; and John C. Pine, "The Role of United States Special Agents in the Development of a Spanish American Policy, 1810–1822," Ph.D. diss., University of Colorado, 1955, ch. 6.

WRIGHT, CHARLES (1811–1885). Plant explorer, born October 29, 1811, in Wethersfield, Connecticut. Wright graduated from Yale University. He went to Texas in 1837. He was a surveyor and teacher in various places in eastern Texas from 1837 to 1845 and explored the botany of that region. He moved to central Texas in 1845, where he was a teacher, private tutor, and schoolmaster. He was a botanist with the U.S.-Mexico boundary commission in 1851–1852 and a botanist with the North Pacific Surveying and Exploring Expedition from 1853 to 1856. He conducted botanical explorations in Cuba from 1856 to 1867 and in Santo Domingo in 1871, and made extensive botanical collections. He retired in 1875. Died August 11, 1885, in Wethersfield, Connecticut. *References*: *DAB*; Samuel W. Geiser, *Naturalists on the Frontier* (Dallas, 1948), pp. 172–98; and Elizabeth A. Shaw, *Charles Wright on the Boundary 1849–1852, or, Plantae Wrightianae Revisitedo* (Westport, Conn., 1987).

WRIGHT, HARRY (1876–1954). Industrialist, born in Bedford, Virginia. Wright was involved in the skins and hides business, and after 1897, in the scrap iron business. He came to Mexico City in 1900 as a buyer of scrap iron. He managed a branch in Mexico City for Isaac Joseph Iron Company from 1900 to 1905. A pioneer in the steel industry in Mexico, he formed Consolidated Iron and Equipment Company, later renamed Consolidated Rolling Milles and Foundries Company, and then La Consolidada, the first steel concern in Mexico, of which he retained control until he sold it in 1942. Died August 15, 1954, in Mexico City. *References*: "Mexican Steel," *Fortune* 22 (October 1940): 81–87, 110–15; and *NYT*, August 17, 1954.

WRIGHT, IRENE ALOHA (1879–1972). Author, born December 19, 1879, in Lake City, Colorado. Wright graduated from Virginia College (Roanoke, Va.) and Stanford University. She was special writer for *Havana Post* in 1904–1905, city editor of Havana *Telegraph* from 1905 to 1907, special agent for the Cuban Department of Agriculture in 1908, and owner and editor of *Cuban Magazine* from 1908 to 1914. She later conducted research in the Archives of the Indies in Seville, Spain, for half a century, and represented the Library of Congress in Spain from 1932 to 1936. She was associate archivist of the U.S. National Archives from 1936 to 1938 and foreign affairs specialist for the State Department, and served as chief of its cultural relations division for Latin America. She retired in 1952. She wrote *The Gem of the Caribbean* (Isle of Pines, Cuba, 1909), *Cuba* (New York, 1910), and *The Isle of Pines* (Havana, Cuba, 1910). Died April 6, 1972, in New Rochelle, New York. *References*: *CA*; *NYT*, April 8, 1972; and *WWAW*.

WRIGHT, JOSHUA BUTLER (1877–1939). Diplomat, born October 18, 1877, in Irvington-on-Hudson, New York. Wright graduated from Princeton University. He was a banker and a rancher, and entered the diplomatic service in 1909. He served in Tegucigalpa, Honduras, Washington, D.C., Brussels, Rio de Janeiro, Petrograd, and London. He was third assistant secretary at the State Department in 1923–1924 and assistant secretary from 1924 to 1927. He was U.S. minister to Hungary from 1927 to 1930, minister to Uruguay from 1930 to 1934, minister to Czechoslovakia from 1934 to 1937, and ambassador to Cuba from 1937 until his death. He was committed to a policy of nonintervention and noninterference and tried to end the practice of the U.S. ambassador's acting as a domestic adviser to the Cuban government. He adopted a formal relationship with Fulgencio Batista, the Cuban dictator, and tried to deal with the problems of Cuban debts and American creditors. Died December 4, 1939, in Havana, Cuba. *References*: *DADH*; *NCAB* 30:196; and *NYT*, December 5, 1939.

WRIGHT, WILLIAM CHARLES (1807–1868). Naval officer, born September 16, 1807, in Philadelphia. Wright came to Buenos Aires in 1825. He joined the forces of Admiral Guillermo Brown and took part in the war against Brazil. He later favored the Unitarists against Juan Manuel de Rosas and was demoted in 1834. He was called back to service in 1845 during the Anglo-French blockade. After the battle of Caseros in 1852, he took part in some of the fighting around Buenos Aires but devoted himself primarily to business and ranching. Died September 30, 1868, in Buenos Aires. *References*: *Cutolo*.

WYCLIFFE BIBLE TRANSLATORS, INC. Interdenominational agency, organized in 1935, to do linguistic analysis and Bible translation. It began operating in Mexico in 1935, in Peru in 1946, in Guatemala in 1952, in Ecuador in 1953, in Bolivia in 1955, in Brazil in 1956, in Honduras in 1960, in Colombia in 1962, in Suriname in 1967, and in Panama in 1970. *References*: *EMCM*; Clarence W. Hall, *Adventures for God* (New York, 1959), 105–55; James and Marti Hefley, *Dawn over Amazonia: The Story of Wycliffe Bible Translators in Peru* (Waco, Tex., 1972); David Stoll, *Fishers of Men or Founders of Empire? The Wycliffe Bible Translators in Latin America* (London, 1982); and Ethel E. Wallis and Mary A. Bennett, *Two Thousand Tongues to Go* (New York, 1959).

WYLIE, HERBERT G(EORGE) (1867–1956). Petroleum producer, born October 20, 1867, in Dublin, Ireland. Wylie came to the United States in 1887 and was naturalized in 1893. He was superintendent of the Petroleum Development Company in Bakersfield, California, from 1898 to 1902. He went to Mexico in 1902 to take charge of the Mexican Petroleum Company, Limited, and developed the vast Mexican oil interests of Edward L. Doheny.* Although it was the Doheny group that provided the capital for the Mexican venture, Wylie is credited with its development into one of the largest oil enterprises at that time. He was vice president and general manager of the company and its president after 1922. Died January 3, 1956, in Los Angeles. *References*: *NYT*, January 5, 1956; and *WWWA*.

Y

YAGER, ARTHUR (1857–1941). Educator and colonial administrator, born October 29, 1857, in Campbellsburg, Kentucky. Yager graduated from Georgetown (Ky.) College and Johns Hopkins University. He was professor of history and economics at Georgetown College from 1884 to 1913, chairman of the faculty from 1898 to 1908, and president of the college from 1908 to 1913. He was also vice president of the Deposit Bank and Trust Company of Georgetown from 1900 to 1907 and vice president of Farmers' Bank and Trust Company of Georgetown from 1907 to 1913. He was governor of Puerto Rico from 1913 to 1921. He established an insular agricultural board, improved the school system, established juvenile courts, sold public lands to laborers, introduced workmen's compensation acts, and extended sanitary services. He oversaw the implementation of the act of 1917 granting U.S. citizenship to the people of Puerto Rico and providing for a new government of a bicameral legislature elected by the voters. He retired in 1921. Died December 24, 1941, in Louisville, Kentucky. *References*: *NCAB* 32:18; *NYT*, December 25, 1941; and *WWWA*.

YANCEY, BENJAMIN C(UDWORTH) (1817–1891). Lawyer and diplomat, born April 27, 1817, in Charleston, South Carolina. Yancey graduated from the University of Georgia and Yale Law School. He practiced law in Alabama from 1837 to 1840 and was master of chancery from 1838 to 1840. He then practiced in Hamburg, South Carolina, from 1841 to 1851, was a member of the state legislature and, later, a member of the state senate from 1855 to 1858. He was U.S. minister to Argentina in 1858–1859. When the president of the Argentina Confederation issued a proclamation decreeing the death penalty to all captains of foreign ships who took their ships into the port of Buenos Aires and then landed at any part of the government of Argentina, he called on the naval force of the United States to resist the decree. He was selected by the contending powers to arbitrate their differences. He served in the Confederate Army during the Civil War. He was president of the Georgia State Agricultural Society from 1867 to 1871 and served in the state legislature in 1878–1879. Died October

24, 1891, in Rome, Georgia. *References*: Beatriz Bosch, "La Mediacion del Coronel Yancey entre la Confederacion Argentina y el Estado de Buenos Aires (1859)," *HAHR* 44 (1964): 568–82; *Cutolo*; and *NCAB* 13:560.

"YANKEE DOODLE ESCADRILLE." A group of American mercenary combat pilots which served in the rebel forces of General J. Gonzalo Escobar during the Escobar Rebellion in Mexico in 1929–1930. *Reference*: Kenneth B. Ragsdale, *Wings over the Mexican Border: Pioneer Military Aviation in the Big Bend* (Austin, Tex., 1984).

YEATMAN, POPE (1861–1953). Mining engineer, born August 3, 1861, in St. Louis. Yeatman graduated from Washington University (St. Louis). He was involved in copper, gold, and silver mining in Missouri, New Mexico, and Colorado. He was manager of gold mining companies in South Africa from 1895 to 1904. He was associated, in a consulting capacity, with the M. Guggenheim Sons' Company from 1906 to 1916 and was involved in developing large mining enterprises in Latin America, including Chuquicamata and Braden copper mines in Chile. He served with the Council of National Defense and War Industries Board during World War I. He was later a consulting engineer in New York City. Died December 4, 1953, in Philadelphia. *References*: *ACAB*; *NCAB* 18:176; *NYT*, December 7, 1953; and *WWWA*.

YOUNG, PIERCE (MANNING BUTLER) (1836–1896). Army officer, politician and diplomat, born November 15, 1836, in Spartanburg, South Carolina, and grew up in Caeterville, Georgia. Young attended the U.S. Military Academy but resigned in 1861. He served in the Confederate Army during the Civil War. He was a member of the U.S. House of Representatives in 1868–1869 and from 1870 to 1875. He was U.S. consul general to St. Petersburg from 1885 to 1887. He was U.S. minister to Guatemala and Honduras from 1893 to 1896 and developed friendly feelings and commercial relations with these countries. He returned to the United States in 1896 because of ill health. Died July 6, 1896, in New York City. *References*: *DAB*; and Lynwood M. Holland, *Pierce M. B. Young: The Warwick of the South* (Athens, Ga., 1964).

YUNGJOHANN, JOHN C(HRISTIAN) (? –1930). Rubber cutter. Yungjohann worked on a coffee plantation in Juiz de Fora, state of Minas Gerais, Brazil, from 1897 until 1906. He was a rubber cutter in Pará from 1906 until 1916, when he returned to the United States. He later worked as tile setter and lived in Brooklyn, Jersey City, and Caldwell, New Jersey. He also served as minister of the New Apostolic Church. His diary was later published as *White Gold: The Diary of a Rubber Cutter in the Amazon 1906–1916*, ed. Ghillean T. Prance (Oracle, Ariz., 1989).

Z

ZAHL, PAUL A(RTHUR) (1910–1985). Explorer, author and photographer, born March 20, 1910, in Bensenville, Illinois. Zahl graduated from Illinois North Central College and Harvard University. He was involved in the establishment of Haskins Laboratories, a research organization in New York, in 1937, as staff physiologist and then as associate director until 1958. He served with the Office of Science Research and Development during World War II. He was a senior natural scientist for the National Geographic Society in Washington, D.C., from 1958 until his retirement in 1975, and was author or photographer for more than fifty articles for the society's magazine. He searched for giant ants in the jungles of Brazil, Venezuela, and British Guiana in the late 1930s and climbed Mount Roraima, at the meeting-point of Brazil, Venezuela, and British Guiana, in 1938. He conducted research on the disappearing Bahamas flamingo in the early 1950s and explored the swampy waterways of tropical Venezuela, looking for the breeding place of the scarlet ibis. He wrote *To the Lost World* (New York, 1939), *Flamingo Hunt* (Indianapolis, 1952), and *Coro-Coro: the World of the Scarlet Ibis* (Indianapolis, 1954). Died October 16, 1985, in Greenwich, Connecticut. *References*: AMWS; CA; *Washington Post*, October 17, 1985; and WWA.

ZAHM, JOHN AUGUSTUS (1851–1921). Clergyman, born September 14, 1851, in New Lexington, Ohio, and grew up in Huntington, Indiana. Zahm graduated from the University of Notre Dame, studied at the seminary of Notre Dame, entered the Congregation of the Holy Cross in 1871, and was ordained in 1875. He was organizer and teacher at the Western Catholic Summer School, procurator general of the Congregation of the Holy Cross in Rome from 1888 to 1898, and provincial of the congregation from 1898 to 1905. He was a writer from 1905 until his death. He made two journeys to South America and wrote *Up the Orinoco and down the Magdalena* (New York, 1910) and *Along the Andes and down the Amazon* (New York, 1911), which were published under the pseudonym J. H. Mozans. He also wrote *Through South America's Southland*

(New York, 1916), about the expedition with Theodore Roosevelt,* and the *Quest of El Dorado* (New York, 1917). Died November 10, 1921, in Munich, Germany. *References*: John A. Zahm Papers, Archives of the Congregation of the Holy Cross, Indiana Province, Notre Dame, Ind.; *DAB*; *NYT*, November 12, 1921; Thomas F. O'Connor, "John A. Zahm, C.S.C.: Scientist and Americanist," *TA* 7 (1951): 435–62; and Ralph E. Weber, *Notre Dame's John Zahm: American Catholic Apologist and Educator* (Notre Dame, Ind., 1961).

ZEMURRAY, SAMUEL (1877–1961). Businessman, born January 18, 1877, in Bessarabia, Russia, came to the United States with his family in 1892, and grew up in Selina, Alabama. Zemurray entered the fruit business in 1899 in Mobile, Alabama, becoming involved in the banana trade. He then moved to New Orleans, and obtained a contract to distribute bananas. In 1900, he began buying cargoes directly in Honduras and selling them in New Orleans and Mobile, and then purchased plantation land in Honduras, formed Cuyamel Fruit Company in 1910, was its president, and expanded its operations. In 1922, he acquired Bluefield Fruit and Steamship Company. He sold Cuyamel to United Fruit Company* in 1929. When stock began to drop after 1929, he took control of that company in 1932 and was its managing director in charge of operations from 1932 to 1938 and president from 1938 until 1951, reorganizing and revamping the company. He became known as "Sam the Banana Man." He became involved in Latin American politics, instigated several revolutions to protect his interests, and had a role in engineering the overthrow of the government of Guatemala in 1954 (*See* GUATEMALAN CRISIS). Died November 30, 1961, in New Orleans. *References*: *BDABL*; *DADH*; John Kobler, "Sam the Banana Man," *Life* 30 (February 19, 1951): 83–94; *NCAB* G:389; *NYT*, December 2, 1961; and Stephen J. Whitfield, "Strange Fruit: The Career of Samuel Zemurray," *American Jewish History* 73 (1984): 307–23.

ZONA LIBRE. Mexican free trade district, established in 1858 to counteract the highly favorable trade conditions enjoyed by American border towns. It was a major stumbling block in the path of U.S. recognition of the government of Porfirio Díaz in the late 1870s. The Mexican government defended the zone's existence even after its economic usefulness had ceased. Its abolition in 1905 led to improved relations between the two countries. *Reference*: Samuel E. Bell and James M. Smallwood, "The Zona Libre: Trade and Diplomacy on the Mexican Border, 1858–1905," *Arizona and the West* 24 (1982): 119–52.

Chiefs of American Diplomatic Missions in Latin America, 1823–1990

ABBREVIATIONS

AE/P	Ambassador Extraordinary and Plenipotentiary
CdA	Chargé d'Affaires
Comm	Commissioner
Comm/CG	Commissioner and Consul General
EE/MP	Envoy Extraordinary and Minister Plenipotentiary
MP	Minister Plenipotentiary
MR	Minister Resident
MR/CG	Minister Resident and Consul General
MR/E	Minister Resident and Extraordinary

Abbott, John True (1850–1914), EE/MP Colombia 1889–1893

Achilles, Theodore Carter (1905–1986), AE/P Peru 1956–1960

Adair, Charles W., Jr. (1914–   ), AE/P Panama 1965–1969; AE/P Uruguay 1969–1972

Adams, Alvin Philip, Jr. (1942–   ), AE/P Haiti 1989–

Adams, Charles (1845–1895), MR/CG Bolivia 1880–1882

Adams, Robert, Jr. (1846–1906), EE/MP Brazil 1889–1890

Ageton, Arthur Ainslie (1900–1971), AE/P Paraguay 1954–1957

*Allen, Heman (1779–1852), MP Chile 1823–1827

*Anderson, Richard Clough (1788–1826), MP Colombia 1823–1826

Anderson, Robert (1922–   ), AE/P Dominican Republic 1982–1985

Anderson, Thomas H., Jr. (1946–   ), AE/P Antigua and Barbuda, Barbados, Dominica, St. Christopher and Nevis, St. Lucia, St. Vincent and the Grenadines, 1984–1986

Anderson, Thomas Henry (1848–1916), MR/CG Bolivia 1889–1890; EE/MP Bolivia 1890–1892

Appleton, John (1815–1864), CdA Bolivia 1848–1849

Aranda, Thomas, Jr. (1934–   ), AE/P Uruguay 1981–1985

Arcos, Crescencio S., Jr. (1943–   ), AE/P Honduras, 1989–

*Armour, Norman (1887–1982), EE/MP Haiti 1932–1935; AE/P Chile 1938–1939; AE/P Argentina 1939–1944; AE/P Venezuela 1950–1951; AE/P Guatemala 1954–1955

Asboth, Alexander (1811–1868), MR Argentina 1866–1868; MR Uruguay 1867–1868

Asencio, Diego Cortes (1931–   ), AE/P Colombia 1977–1980; AE/P Brazil 1983–1986

Bacon, John E. (1830–1897), CdA Paraguay and Uruguay 1885–1886; MR Uruguay 1886–1888; MR Paraguay 1888

Bading, Gerhard Adolph (1870–1946), EE/MP Ecuador 1922–1929

*Bailly-Blanchard, Arthur (1855–1925), EE/MP Haiti 1914–1921

Baker, Jehu (1822–1903), MR Venezuela 1878–1882; MR/CG Venezuela 1882–1885

Baker, Lewis (1832–1899), EE/MP Costa Rica, El Salvador, and Nicaragua 1893–1897

Barbour, Robert E. (1927–   ), AE/P Suriname 1984–1987

Barnebey, Malcolm R. (1927–   ), AE/P Belize 1983–1985

Barnes, Harry George, Jr. (1926–   ), AE/P Chile 1985–1988

*Barrett, John (1866–1938), EE/MP Argentina 1903–1904; EE/MP Panama 1904–1905; EE/MP Colombia 1905–1906

*Barton, Seth (1795–1854), CdA Chile 1847–1849

*Bassett, Ebenezer Don Carlos (1833–1908), MR/CG Haiti 1869–1877

Baxter, Henry (1821–1873), MR Honduras 1869–1873

*Baylies, Francis (1783–1852), CdA Buenos Aires 1832

Beale, Wilson Thomas Moore, Jr. (1909–   ), AE/P Jamaica 1965–1967

*Beaulac, Willard Leon (1899–1990), AE/P Paraguay 1944–1947; AE/P Colombia 1947–1951; AE/P Cuba 1951–1953; AE/P Chile 1953–1956; AE/P Argentina 1956–1960

*Beaupré, Arthur Matthias (1853–1919), EE/MP Colombia 1903; EE/MP Argentina 1904–1908; EE/MP Cuba 1911–1913

Becker, Ralph Elihu (1907–   ), AE/P Honduras 1976–1977

Belcher, Taylor Garrison (1920–1990), AE/P Peru 1969–1974

Bell, John Oscar (1912–   ), AE/P Guatemala 1961–1965

*Bennett, William Tapley, Jr. (1917–   ), AE/P Dominican Republic 1964–1966

Bergold, Harry Early, Jr. (1931–   ), AE/P Nicaragua 1984–1987

*Berle, Adolf Augustus (1895–1971), AE/P Brazil 1945–1946

Bernbaum, Maurice Marshall (1910–   ), AE/P Ecuador 1960–1965; AE/P Venezuela 1965–1969

Biddle, Thomas (1827–1875), MR El Salvador 1871–1873

*Bidlack, Benjamin Alden (1804–1849), CdA New Granada 1845–1849

Bigler, John (1805–1871), EE/MP Chile 1857–1861

Binns, Jack Robert (1933–   ), AE/P Honduras 1980–1981

Bish, Milan D. (1929–   ), AE/P Antigua and Barbuda, Barbados, Dominica, St. Lucia, St. Vincent and the Grenadines 1981–1984

Blackford, William Matthews (1801–1864), CdA New Granada 1842–1844

Blair, Jacob Beeson (1821–1901), MR Costa Rica 1868–1873

Bliss, Robert Woods (1875–1962), AE/P Argentina 1927–1933

Bloomfield, Richard Joseph (1927–   ), AE/P Ecuador 1976–1978

*Blow, Henry Taylor (1817–1875), EE/MP Brazil 1869–1870

*Boal, Pierre de Lagarde (1895–1966), EE/MP Nicaragua 1941–1942; AE/P Bolivia 1942–1944

Boeker, Paul Harold (1938–   ), AE/P Bolivia 1977–1980

*Bonsal, Philip Wilson (1903–   ), AE/P Colombia 1955–1957; AE/P Bolivia 1957–1959; AE/P Cuba 1959–1960

Boonstra, Clarence A. (1914–   ), AE/P Costa Rica 1967–1969

*Borland, Solon (1808–1864), EE/MP Central America 1853–1854

Boster, Davis Eugene (1920–   ), AE/P Guatemala 1976–1979

Bowdler, William Garton (1924–   ), AE/P El Salvador 1968–1971; AE/P Guatemala 1971–1973

*Bowen, Herbert Wolcott (1856–1927), EE/MP Venezuela 1901–1905

*Bowers, Claude Gernade (1878–1958), AE/P Chile 1939–1953

*Bowlin, James Butler (1804–1874), MR New Granada 1854–1857

Boyatt, Thomas David (1933–   ), AE/P Colombia 1980–1983

*Braden, Spruille (1894–1978), AE/P Colombia 1939–1942; AE/P Cuba 1942–1945; AE/P Argentina, 1945

*Bragg, Edward Stuyvesant (1827–1912), EE/MP Mexico 1888–1889

*Brent, William, Jr. (1783–1848), CdA Buenos Aires 1844–1846

Brewster, Robert Charles (1921–   ), AE/P Ecuador 1973–1976

Bridgman, George M. (1853–1925), EE/MP Bolivia 1897–1902

*Briggs, Ellis Ormsbee (1899–1976), AE/P Dominican Republic 1944–1945; AE/P Uruguay 1947–1949; AE/P Peru 1955–1956; AE/P Brazil 1956–1959

Briggs, Everett Ellis (1934–   ), AE/P Panama 1982–1986; AE/P Honduras 1986–1989

Britton, Theodore Roosevelt, Jr. (1925–   ), AE/P Barbados and Grenada 1974–1977

Brown, Aaron Switzer (1913–1969), AE/P Nicaragua 1961–1967

Brown, Ethan Allen (1776–1852), CdA Brazil 1830–1834

Brown, Philip Marshall (1875–1966), EE/MP Honduras 1908–1910

*Bruce, James (1892–1980), AE/P Argentina 1947–1949

Bryan, Charles Page (1856–1918), EE/MP Brazil 1898–1902

Bryan, John Alexander (? – ?), CdA Peru 1844–1845

*Buchanan, William Insco (1852–1909), EE/MP Argentina 1894–1899; EE/MP Panama 1903–1904

Buck, Charles William (1849–1930), EE/MP Peru 1885–1889

Buckalew, Charles Rollin (1821–1899), MR Ecuador 1858–1861

Bunker, Ellsworth (1894–1984), AE/P Argentina 1951–1952

Burgess, Carter Lane (1916–   ), AE/P Argentina 1968–1969

Burke, John Richard (1924–   ), AE/P Guyana 1977–1979

Burns, Findley, Jr. (1917–   ), AE/P Ecuador 1970–1973

Burrows, Charles Robert (1910–   ), AE/P Honduras 1960–1965

Bursley, Herbert S. (1896–1961), AE/P Honduras 1947–1950

Burton, Allan A. (? – ?), MR New Granada 1861–1866

*Butler, Anthony (Wayne) (? – ?), CdA Mexico 1829–1835

Butler, George Howland (1894–1967), AE/P Dominican Republic 1946–1948

Butler, Robert (1897–1955), AE/P Cuba 1948–1951

Cabot, John Moors (1901–1981), AE/P Colombia 1957–1959; AE/P Brazil 1959–1961

*Caffery, Jefferson (1886–1974), EE/MP El Salvador 1926–1928; EE/MP Colombia 1928–1933; AE/P Cuba 1934–1937; AE/P Brazil 1937–1944

Caldwell, John Curtis (1833–1912), MR Paraguay and Uruguay 1874–1876; CdA Paraguay and Uruguay 1876–1882

Caldwell, John Watson (1809–1896), MR Bolivia 1868–1869

Caldwell, Robert Granville (1882– ?), EE/MP Bolivia 1937–1939

Campbell, James Fromharf (1912–), AE/P El Salvador 1974–1976

Carlisle, S. S. (? – ?), MR/CG Bolivia 1887–1889

Carlson, Delmar Richard (1918–), AE/P Guyana 1966–1969

Carlson, Reynold Erland (1912–), AE/P Colombia 1966–1969

Carter, George W. (? – ?), MR Venezuela 1881–1882

Cartter, David Kellogg (1812–1887), MR Bolivia 1861–1862

Castro, Raul Hector (1916–), AE/P El Salvador 1964–1968; AE/P Bolivia 1968–1969; AE/P Argentina 1977–1980

Catto, Henry Edward, Jr. (1930–), AE/P El Salvador 1971–1973

Chapin, Frederick Lincoln (1929–), AE/P Guatemala 1981–1984

Chapin, Selden (1899–1963), AE/P Panama 1953–1955; AE/P Peru 1960

Cheslaw, Irving Gottlieb (1921–), AE/P Trinidad and Tobago 1979–1981

*Christiancy, Isaac Peckham (1812–1890), EE/MP Peru 1879–1881

*Clark, Joshua Reuben, Jr. (1871–1961), AE/P Mexico 1930–1933

Clarke, Beverly Leonides (1809–1860), MR Guatemala 1858–1860; MR Honduras 1858–1860

*Clay, John Randolph (1808—1885), CdA Peru 1847–1853; EE/MP Peru 1853–1860

Clay, Thomas Hart (1803–1871), MR Nicaragua 1862; MR Honduras 1863–1865

*Clayton, Powell (1833–1914), EE/MP Mexico 1897–1898; AE/P Mexico 1898–1905

Clifford, Nathan (1803–1881), EE/MP Mexico 1848–1849

Coerr, Wymberley DeRenne (1913–), AE/P Uruguay 1962–1965; AE/P Ecuador 1965–1967

Coggeshall, William Turner (1824–1867), MR Ecuador 1866–1867

Cole, Charles Woolsey (1906–1978), AE/P Chile 1961–1964

Collier, William Miller (1867–1956), AE/P Chile 1921–1928

Combs, Leslie (1852–1940), EE/MP Guatemala and Honduras 1902–1907; EE/MP Peru 1907–1911

Conger, Edwin Hurd (1843–1907), EE/MP Brazil 1890–1893; EE/MP Brazil 1897–1898; AE/P Mexico 1905

Conkling, Alfred (1789–1874), EE/MP Mexico 1852–1853

Cook, Willis Clifford (1874–1942), EE/MP Venezuela 1921–1929

Cooley, James (1791–1828), CdA Peru 1826–1828

Coolidge, John Gardner (1863–1936), EE/MP Nicaragua 1908

Cooper, James Ford (1935–), AE/P Grenada 1988–

*Cooper, Prentice William, Jr. (1895–1969), AE/P Peru 1946–1948

Corr, Edwin Gharst (1934–), AE/P Peru 1980–1981; AE/P Bolivia 1981–1985; AE/P El Salvador 1985–1988

*Corrigan, Frank [Francis] Patrick (1881–1968), EE/MP El Salvador 1934–1937; EE/MP Panama 1937–1939; AE/P Venezuela 1939–1947

*Corwin, Thomas (1794–1865), EE/MP Mexico 1861–1864

Costello, William Aloysious (1904–1969), AE/P Trinidad and Tobago 1967–1969

Cottrell, Jesse Samuel (1878–1944), EE/MP Bolivia 1921–1928

Coxe, Macgrane (1859–1923), EE/MP Guatemala and Honduras 1896–1897

Crimmins, John Hugh (1919–), AE/P Dominican Republic 1966–1969; AE/P Brazil 1973–1978

Crockett, Kennedy McCampbell (1920–), AE/P Nicaragua 1967–1970

*Crosby, Elisha Oscar (1818–1895), MR Guatemala 1861–1864
*Crowder, Enoch Herbert (1859–1932), AE/P Cuba 1923–1927
Crowley, John Joseph, Jr. (1928–   ), AE/P Suriname 1980–1981
Croxton, John Thomas (1837–1874), MR Bolivia 1872–1874
Crump, William Wood (1819–1897), CdA Chile 1844–1847
*Culbertson, William Smith (1884–1966), AE/P Chile 1928–1933
Culver, Erastus Dean (1803–1889), MR Venezuela 1862–1866
Curtis, Charles Boyd (1878–1962), EE/MP Dominican Republic 1929–1931; EE/MP El
    Salvador 1931–1932
Cushing, Courtland (1809–1856), CdA Ecuador 1850–1853
Cushman, John Franklin (? –1862), MR Argentina 1859–1861
Dana, John Winchester (1808–1867), CdA Bolivia 1853–1854; MR Bolivia 1854–1859
*Daniels, Josephus (1862–1948), AE/P Mexico 1933–1941
Daniels, Paul Clement (1903–1986), AE/P Honduras 1947; AE/P Ecuador 1951–1953
Davis, Arthur H., Jr. (1917–   ), AE/P Paraguay 1982–1985; AE/P Panama 1986–
    1990
Davis, Monnett Bain (1893–1953), AE/P Panama 1948–1951
*Davis, Nathaniel (1925–   ), AE/P Guatemala 1968–1971; AE/P Chile 1971–1973
Davis, Nathaniel Penistone (1895–1973), AE/P Costa Rica 1947–1949
*Davis, Roy Tasco (1889–1975), EE/MP Costa Rica 1922–1930; EE/MP Panama 1929–
    1933; AE/P Haiti 1953–1957
*Dawson, Thomas Cleland (1865—1912), MR/CG Santo Domingo 1904–1907; EE/MP
    Colombia 1907–1909; EE/MP Chile 1909; EE/MP Panama 1910
*Dawson, William, Jr. (1885–1972), EE/MP Ecuador 1930–1935; EE/MP Colombia
    1935–1937; EE/MP Uruguay 1937–1939; AE/P Panama 1939–1941; AE/P Uru-
    guay 1941–1946
*de Roulet, Vincent William (1925–1975), AE/P Jamaica 1969–1973
De Witt, Charles Gerrit (1789–1839), CdA Central America 1833–1839
Dean, Robert William (1920–   ), AE/P Peru 1974–1977
Dearing, Fred Morris (1879–1963), AE/P Peru 1930–1937
DeCourcy, William E. (1894–1981), AE/P Haiti 1948–1950
Des Portes, Fay Allen (1890–1944), EE/MP Bolivia 1933–1936; EE/MP Guatemala 1936–
    1943; AE/P Costa Rica 1943–1944
Devine, Frank James (1922–   ), AE/P El Salvador 1977–1980
Dichman [Dichmann], Ernest [Ernst] (? –1885), MR Colombia 1878–1881
Dickinson, Andrew B. (? – ?), MR/E Nicaragua 1863–1869
*Dimitry, Alexander (1805–1883), MR Costa Rica and Nicaragua 1859–1861
Dobriansky, Lev E. (1918–   ), AE/P The Bahamas 1982–1986
Dodge, Henry Percival (1870–1936), EE/MP Honduras and El Salvador 1907–1909; EE/
    MP El Salvador 1908–1909; EE/MP Panama 1911–1913
Doherty, William Charles (1902–   ), AE/P Jamaica 1962–1964
Donnelley, Walter Joseph (1896–1970), AE/P Costa Rica 1947; AE/P Venezuela 1947-
    1950
Donovan, Eileen Roberta (1915–   ), AE/P Barbados 1969–1974
*Douglass, Frederick Augustus Washington Baily (1817?—1895), CdA Santo Domingo
    1889–1891; MR/CG Haiti 1889–1891
Drew, Gerald Augustin (1903–1970), AE/P Bolivia 1954–1957; AE/P Haiti 1957–1960
DuBois, James Taylor (1851–1920), EE/MP Colombia 1911–1913

Dudley, Irving Bedell (1861–1911), EE/MP Peru 1897–1907; AE/P Brazil 1906–1911

Duemling, Robert Werner (1929–   ), AE/P Suriname 1982–1984

Duke, Angier Biddle (1915–   ), AE/P El Salvador 1952–1953

Dungan, Ralph Anthony (1923–   ), AE/P Chile 1964–1967

Dunn, James Clement (1890–1979), AE/P Brazil 1955–1956

*Durham, John Stephens (1861–1919), CdA Santo Domingo 1891–1893; MR/CG Haiti 1891–1893

Eames, Charles (1812–1867), CdA Venezuela 1854; MR Venezuela 1854–1858

Eberhardt, Charles Christopher (1871–1965), EE/MP Nicaragua 1925–1929; EE/MP Costa Rica 1930–1933

Eddy, Spencer Fayette (1874–1939), EE/MP Argentina 1908–1909

*Egan, Patrick (1841–1919), EE/MP Chile 1889–1893

Einstein, Lewis David (1877–1967), EE/MP Costa Rica 1911

Elbrick, Charles Burke (1908–1983), AE/P Brazil 1969–1970

*Ellis, Powhatan (1790–1863), CdA Mexico 1836; EE/MP Mexico 1839–1842

Ellis, Vespasian (? – ?), CdA Venezuela 1844–1845

Erwin, John Draper (1883– ?), EE/MP Honduras 1937–1943; AE/P Honduras 1943–1947; AE/P Honduras 1951–1954

Evans, Melvin H. (1917–1984), AE/P Trinidad and Tobago 1981–1984

Ewing, John (1857–1923), EE/MP Honduras 1913–1918

*Farland, Joseph Simpson (1914–   ), AE/P Dominican Republic 1957–1960; AE/P Panama 1960–1963

Fay, Albert Bel (1913–   ), AE/P Trinidad and Tobago 1976–1977

Feely, Edward Francis (1880–1964), EE/MP Bolivia 1930–1933

Ferch, John Arthur (1936–   ), AE/P Honduras 1985–1986

Finch, William Rufus (1847–1913), EE/MP Paraguay and Uruguay 1897–1905

*Flack, Joseph (1894–1955), AE/P Bolivia 1946–1949; AE/P Costa Rica 1949–1950

Fleming, Philip Bracken (1887–1955), AE/P Costa Rica 1951–1953

*Fletcher, Henry Prather (1873–1959), EE/MP Chile 1909–1914; AE/P Chile 1914–1916; AE/P Mexico 1916–1919

Florman, Irving (1892–   ), AE/P Bolivia 1949–1951

Foote, Thomas Moses (1808–1858), CdA New Granada 1849–1850

*Forbes, John Murray (1771–1831), CdA Buenos Aires 1825–1831

*Forsyth, John (1812–1879), EE/MP Mexico 1856–1858

*Foster, John Watson (1836–1917), EE/MP Mexico 1873–1880

Fox, Richard Kenneth, Jr. (1925–   ), AE/P Trinidad and Tobago 1977–1979

*Fox, Williams Carlton (1855–1924), EE/MP Ecuador 1907–1911

Frazer, Robert (1878–1947), EE/MP El Salvador 1937–1942

Freeman, Fulton (1915–1974), AE/P Colombia 1961–1964; AE/P Mexico 1964–1969

*Frost, Wesley (1884–1968), EE/MP Paraguay 1941–1942; AE/P Paraguay 1942–1944

*Furniss, Henry Watson (1868–1955), EE/MP Haiti 1905–1913

*Gadsden, James (1788–1858), EE/MP Mexico 1853–1856

*Gardner, Arthur (1889–1967), AE/P Cuba 1953–1957

Gargano, Charles Angelo (1934–   ), AE/P Trinidad and Tobago 1988–

Garrett, John Work (1872–1942), EE/MP Venezuela 1910–1911; EE/MP Argentina 1911–1913

*Gavin, John (1928–   ), AE/P Mexico 1981–1986

Geissler, Arthur H. (1877–1945), EE/MP Guatemala 1922–1930

Gelbard, Robert Sidney (1944–   ), AE/P Bolivia 1988–

Gerard, Sumner (1916–   ), AE/P Jamaica 1974–1977

Gibbs, Richard (1819–1894), EE/MP Peru 1875–1879; MR/CG Bolivia 1883–1885

Gibson, Hugh Simons (1883–1954), AE/P Brazil 1933–1936

Gildred, Theodore Edmunds, Jr. (1935–   ), AE/P Argentina 1986–1989

Gillespie, Charles Anthony, Jr. (1935–   ), AE/P Colombia 1985–1988; AE/P Chile 1988–

*Gonzales, William Elliott (1866–1937), EE/MP Cuba 1913–1919; AE/P Peru 1919–1921

Gonzalez, Antonio Cornelius (1888–1965), EE/MP Panama 1933–1935; EE/MP Ecuador 1935–1938; EE/MP Venezuela 1938–1939

Gonzalez, Raymond Emmanuel (1924–   ), AE/P Ecuador 1978–1982

*Gordon, Abraham Lincoln (1913–   ), AE/P Brazil 1961–1966

Gordon, George Anderson (1885–1959), EE/MP Haiti 1935–1937

Grant, Frederic James (1862–1894), EE/MP Bolivia 1892–1893

Grant-Smith, Ulysses (1870–1959), EE/MP Uruguay 1925–1929

Gray, Isaac Pusey (1828–1895), EE/MP Mexico 1893–1894

Green, James Stephen (1817–1870), CdA New Granada 1853–1854

*Grevstad, Nicolay Andreas (1851–1940), EE/MP Paraguay and Uruguay 1911–1914

Griffis, Stanton (1887–1974), AE/P Argentina 1949–1950

Griscom, Lloyd Carpenter (1872–1959), AE/P Brazil 1906–1907

*Guggenheim, Harry Frank (1890–1971), AE/P Cuba 1929–1933

*Hale, Edward Joseph (1839–1922), EE/MP Costa Rica 1913–1917

Hall, Allen A. (? –1867), CdA Venezuela 1841–1844; MR Bolivia 1863–1867

*Hall, Henry Cook (1820?–1901), MR Costa Rica, El Salvador, Guatemala, Honduras, and Nicaragua 1882; EE/MP Costa Rica, El Salvador, Guatemala, Honduras, and Nicaragua 1882–1889

Hallett, Carol Boyd (1936–   ), AE/P The Bahamas 1986–1989

Hamm, John (1777?–1861), CdA Chile 1830–1833

*Hanna, Bayliss W. (1830–1891), MR/CG Argentina 1885–1887; EE/MP Argentina 1887–1889

*Hanna, Matthew Elting (1873–1936), EE/MP Nicaragua 1929–1933; EE/MP Guatemala 1933–1936

Harrington, Julian Fiske (1901–1984), AE/P Panama 1955–1960

*Harris, William Alexander (1805–1864), CdA Argentina 1846–1851

Harrison, Leland (1883–1951), EE/MP Uruguay 1929–1930

*Harrison, William Henry (1773–1841), EE/MP Colombia 1828–1829

Hart, Charles Burdett (1851–1930), EE/MP Colombia 1897–1903

Hart, Samuel Friedlander (1933–   ), AE/P Ecuador 1982–1985

Hartman, Charles Sampson (1861–1929), EE/MP Ecuador 1913–1922

Haselton, Seneca (1848–1921), EE/MP Venezuela 1894–1895

*Hassaurek, Frederick [Friedrich] (1831–1885), MR Ecuador 1861–1866

Hecht, Chick (1928–   ), AE/P The Bahamas 1989–

Heimké, William (1847–1931), EE/MP Guatemala 1908–1909; EE/MP El Salvador 1909–1914

Henderson, Douglas (1914–   ), AE/P Bolivia 1963–1968

Hernandez, Benigno Carlos (1917–   ), AE/P Paraguay 1967–1969

Hewitt, William Alexander (1914–   ), AE/P Jamaica 1982–1985

Hicks, John (1847–1917), EE/MP Peru 1889–1893; EE/MP Chile 1905–1909

Hill, Robert Charles (1917–1978), AE/P Costa Rica 1953–1954; AE/P El Salvador 1954–1955; AE/P Mexico 1957–1960; AE/P Argentina 1973–1977

*Hilliard, Henry Washington (1808–1892), EE/MP Brazil 1877–1881

Hines, Frank Thomas (1879–1960), AE/P Panama 1945–1948

Hinton, Deane Roesch (1923–   ), AE/P El Salvador 1981–1983; AE/P Costa Rica 1987–1990; AE/P Panama 1990–

*Hise, Elijah (1802–1867), CdA Guatemala 1848–1849

Hitt, Robert Stockwell Reynolds (1876–1938), EE/MP Panama 1909–1910; EE/MP Guatemala 1910–1913

Holden, Glen A. (1927–   ), AE/P Jamaica 1990–

Hollister, Gideon Hiram (1817–1881), MR/CG Haiti 1868–1869

Holwill, Richard Newton (1945–   ), AE/P Ecuador 1988–1989

Hornibrook, William Harrison (1884–1946), EE/MP Costa Rica 1937–1941

Hovey, Alvin Peterson (1821–1891), EE/MP Peru 1865–1870

Howard, Findley Burtch (1885– ?), EE/MP Paraguay 1935–1941

Howard, Henry Clay (1860–1928), EE/MP Peru 1911–1913

Howe, Walter (1907–1966), AE/P Chile 1958–1961

Howland, Richard C. (1934–   ), AE/P Suriname 1988–1990

Hoyt, Henry Augustus (1914–1967), AE/P Uruguay 1965–1967

Hudson, Silas A. (1815–1886), MR Guatemala 1869–1872

Hunter, Whiteside Godfrey (1841–1917), EE/MP Guatemala and Honduras 1897–1903

*Hunter, William, Jr. (1774–1849), CdA Brazil 1834–1841; EE/MP Brazil 1841–1843

*Hurlbut, Stephen Augustus (1815–1882), MR Colombia 1869–1872; EE/MP Peru 1881–1882

Hurwitch, Robert A. (1920–   ), AE/P Dominican Republic 1973–1978

Irving, Frederick (1921–   ), AE/P Jamaica 1977–1978

Isham, Heyward (1926–   ), AE/P Haiti 1973–1977

*Jackson, Henry Rootes (1820–1898), EE/MP Mexico 1885–1886

Jackson, John Brinkerhoff (1862–1920), EE/MP Cuba 1909–1911

Jacob, Charles D. (1838– ?), EE/MP Colombia 1885–1886

Jarimillo, Mari-Luci (1928–   ), AE/P Honduras 1977–1980

*Jarvis, Thomas Jordan (1836–1915), EE/MP Brazil 1885–1888

Jay, Peter Augustus (1877–1933), EE/MP El Salvador 1920–1921; AE/P Argentina 1925–1926

*Jefferson, Benjamin Lafayette (1871–1950), EE/MP Nicaragua 1913–1921

Jeffery, Robert Emmett (1875–1935), EE/MP Uruguay 1915–1921

Jenkins, Douglas (1880–1961), EE/MP Bolivia 1939–1941

Jewett, Albert Gallatin (1802–1885), CdA Peru 1845–1846

Johnson, Hallett (1888–1968), AE/P Costa Rica 1944–1947

Johnson, Herschel Vespasian, II (1894–1966), AE/P Brazil 1948–1953

Jones, George Wallace (1804–1896), MR New Granada 1859–1861

Jones, John Wesley (1907–   ), AE/P Peru 1962–1969

Jones, Thomas Sambola (1859–1933), EE/MP Honduras 1918–1919

Jones, William Bowdoin (1928–   ), AE/P Haiti 1977–1980

Jordan, David C. (1935–   ), AE/P Peru 1984–1986

*Jorden, William John (1923–   ), AE/P Panama 1974–1978

*Jova, Joseph John (1916–   ), AE/P Honduras 1965–1969; AE/P Mexico 1973–1977

*Judah, Noble Brandon (1884–1938), AE/P Cuba 1927–1929
Kalijarvi, Thorsten Valentine (1897–1980), AE/P El Salvador 1957–1960
Kaufman, David E. (1883–1962), EE/MP Bolivia 1928–1929
Keena, Leo John (1878–1967), EE/MP Honduras 1935–1937
Kemper, James Scott (1886–1981), AE/P Brazil 1953–1955
Kerr, John Bozman (1809–1878), CdA Nicaragua 1851–1853
Kilday, Lowell C. (1931–   ), AE/P Dominican Republic 1985–1988
*Kilpatrick, Hugh Judson (1836–1881), EE/MP Chile 1865–1870; EE/MP Chile 1881
Kimelman, Henry L. (1921–   ), AE/P Haiti 1980–1981
King, Spencer Mathews (1917–   ), AE/P Guyana 1969–1974
King, Yelverton P. (1794–1868), CdA New Granada 1851–1853
*Kirk, Robert C. (1821– ?), MR Argentina 1862–1866; MR Argentina 1869–1871; MR
        Uruguay 1869–1870
Knowles, Horace Greeley (1863–1913), MR/CG Dominican Republic 1909–1910; EE/
        MP Bolivia 1910–1913
Knox, Clinton Everett (1908–1980), AE/P Haiti 1969–1973
*Korry, Edward Malcolm (1922–   ), AE/P Chile 1967–1971
Krebs, Max Vance (1916–   ), AE/P Guyana 1974–1976
Kreeck, George Lewis (1882–1945), EE/MP Paraguay 1925–1930
Krys, Sheldon J. (1934–   ), AE/P Trinidad and Tobago 1985–1988
Kyle, Edwin Jackson (1876– ?), AE/P Guatemala 1945–1948
*Lamar, Mirabeau Buonaparte (1798–1859), MR Costa Rica and Nicaragua 1858–1859
Lambert, Paul Christopher (1928–   ), AE/P Ecuador 1990–
Landau, George Walter (1920–   ), AE/P Paraguay 1972–1977; AE/P Chile 1977–
        1982; AE/P Venezuela 1982–1985
*Lane, Arthur Bliss (1894–1956), EE/MP Nicaragua 1933–1936; EE/MP Costa Rica
        1941–1942; EE/MP Colombia 1942–1944
Lane, Lyle Franklin (1926–   ), AE/P Uruguay 1979–1980; AE/P Paraguay 1980–1982
*Langston, John Mercer (1829–1897), MR/CG Haiti 1877–1885; CdA Santo Domingo
        1883–1885
Larned, Samuel (? – ?), CdA Chile 1828–1829; CdA Peru 1828–1839
Lauderdale, Clint Arlen (1932–   ), AE/P Guyana 1984–1987
Lawrence, Albert Gallatin (1836–1887), MR Costa Rica 1866–1868
Lawrence, Loren E. (1926–   ), AE/P Jamaica 1979–1982
Lay, Julius Gareche (1872–1939), EE/MP Honduras 1929–1935; EE/MP Uruguay 1935–
        1937
Leavell, William Hayne (1850–1930), EE/MP Guatemala 1913–1918
Lee, Joseph Wilcox Jenkins (1870–1949), EE/MP Ecuador 1905–1907; EE/MP Guatemala
        1907
Letcher, Robert Perkins (1788–1861), EE/MP Mexico 1849–1852
Livingston, Van Brugh (1792–1868), CdA Ecuador 1848–1849
Lodge, John Davis (1903–1985), AE/P Argentina 1969–1973
Loeb, James Isaac, Jr. (1908–   ), AE/P Peru 1961–1962
*Logan, Cornelius Ambrose (1832–1899), EE/MP Chile 1873–1876; MR Costa Rica, El
        Salvador, Guatemala, Honduras, and Nicaragua 1879–1882; EE/MP Chile 1882–
        1885
*Long, Boaz Walton (1876–1962), EE/MP El Salvador 1914–1917; EE/MP Cuba 1919–
        1921; EE/MP Nicaragua 1936–1938; EE/MP Ecuador 1938–1942; AE/P Ecuador
        1942–1943; AE/P Guatemala 1943–1945

*Loomis, Francis Butler (1861–1948), EE/MP Venezuela 1897–1901
Lord, William Paine (1838–1911), EE/MP Argentina 1899–1903
Lozano, Ignacio E., Jr. (1927–   ), AE/P El Salvador 1976–1977
Lucey, Patrick Joseph (1918–   ), AE/P Mexico 1977–1979
Luers, William Henry (1929–   ), AE/P Venezuela 1978
Lyon, Cecil Burton (1903–   ), AE/P Chile 1956–1958
McAfee, Robert Breckinridge (1784–1849), CdA New Granada 1833–1837
McBride, Robert Henry (1918–1983), AE/P Mexico 1969–1974
McClintock, Robert Mills (1909–1976), AE/P Argentina 1962–1964; AE/P Venezuela
     1970–1975
McClung, Alexander Keith (1811?–1855), CdA Bolivia 1849–1851
McCreery, Fenton Reuben (1866–1940), MR/CG Santo Domingo 1907–1909; EE/MP
     Honduras 1909–1911
McDermott, Michael James (1895–1955), AE/P El Salvador 1953–1954
McGoodwin, Preston Buford (1880–1945), EE/MP Venezuela 1913–1921
McGurk, Joseph F. (1892–1962), AE/P Dominican Republic 1945; AE/P Uruguay 1946–
     1947
McIntosh, Dempster (1896–   ), AE/P Uruguay 1953–1956; AE/P Venezuela 1956–
     1957; AE/P Colombia 1959–1961
McKenzie, James Andrew (1840–1904), EE/MP Peru 1893–1897
McKinley, Brunson (1943–   ), AE/P Haiti 1986–1989
McKinney, Luther Franklin (1841–1922), EE/MP Colombia 1893–1896
*McLane, Robert Milligan (1815–1898), EE/MP Mexico 1859–1860
*McMahon, Martin Thomas (1838–1906), MR Paraguay 1868–1869
McManaway, Clayton E., Jr. (1933–   ), AE/P Haiti 1983–1986
McMillin, Benton (1845–1933), EE/MP Peru 1913–1919; EE/MP Guatemala 1919–1922
McNamara, Thomas Edmund (1940–   ), AE/P Colombia 1988–
McNeil, Francis J. (1932–   ), AE/P Costa Rica 1980–1983
Maginnis, Samuel Abbot (1885–1941), EE/MP Bolivia 1919–1921
*Magoon, Charles Edward (1861–1920), EE/MP Panama 1905–1906
Mahany, Rowland Blennerhassett (1864–1937), EE/MP Ecuador 1892–1893
Mallory, Lester DeWitt (1904–   ), AE/P Guatemala 1958–1959
*Maney, George Earl (1826–1901), MR Colombia 1881–1882; MR/CG Bolivia 1882–
     1883; MR Paraguay and Uruguay 1889–1890; EE/MP Paraguay and Uruguay
     1890–1894
Mann, Frederic Rand (1903–   ), AE/P Barbados 1967–1969
*Mann, Thomas Clifton (1912–   ), AE/P El Salvador 1955–1957; AE/P Mexico 1961–
     1963
Manning, Thomas Courtland (1825–1887), EE/MP Mexico 1886–1887
*Markbreit, Leopold (1842–1909), MR Bolivia 1869–1873
Marling, John Leake (1825–1856), MR Guatemala 1854–1856
Marshall, Anthony Dryden (1924–   ), AE/P Trinidad and Tobago 1972–1973
Martin, Edwin McCammon (1908–   ), AE/P Argentina 1964–1968
*Martin, John Bartlow (1915–1987), AE/P Dominican Republic 1962–1963
Maury, Dabney Herndon (1822–1900), EE/MP Colombia 1886–1889
Mayer, Ferdinand Lathrop (1887– ?), EE/MP Haiti 1937–1940
Meade, Richard Kidder (1803–1862), EE/MP Brazil 1857–1861
*Mein, John Gordon (1913–1968), AE/P Guatemala 1965–1968

Meloy, Francis Edward, Jr. (1917–1976), AE/P Dominican Republic 1969–1973; AE/P Guatemala 1973–1976

Melton, Richard Huntington (1935–   ), AE/P Nicaragua 1987–1989; AE/P Brazil 1989–

*Merry, William Lawrence (1842–1911), EE/MP Costa Rica, El Salvador, and Nicaragua 1897–1907; EE/MP Costa Rica and Nicaragua 1907–1908; EE/MP Costa Rica 1908–1911

*Messersmith, George Strausser (1883–1960), AE/P Cuba 1940–1942; AE/P Mexico 1942–1946; AE/P Argentina 1946–1947

Michel, Jammes H. (1939–   ), AE/P Guatemala 1987–1990

Miller, Horace H. (? – ?), CdA Bolivia 1852–1854

Miller, Lloyd Ivan (1924–   ), AE/P Trinidad and Tobago 1973–1975

Mills, Sheldon Tibbets (1904–   ), AE/P Ecuador 1954–1956

Miner, Robert Graham (1911–   ), AE/P Trinidad and Tobago 1962–1967

*Mizner, Lansing Bond (1825–1893), EE/MP Costa Rica, El Salvador, Guatemala, and Nicaragua 1889–1890

Mooney, Daniel Francis (1865–1930), EE/MP Paraguay 1914–1921

Moonlight, Thomas (1833–1899), EE/MP Bolivia 1894–1898

Moore, Alexander Pollock (1867–1930), AE/P Peru 1928–1929

*Moore, Thomas Patrick (1797–1853), EE/MP Colombia 1829–1833

*Morales, Franklin E. (1884–1962), EE/MP Honduras 1921–1925

*Morgan, Edwin Vernon (1865–1934), EE/MP Cuba 1905–1910; EE/MP Paraguay and Uruguay 1909–1912; AE/P Brazil 1912–1933

*Morgan, Philip Hicky (1825–1900), EE/MP Mexico 1880–1885

*Morrow, Dwight Whitney (1873–1931), AE/P Mexico 1927–1930

Moscoso, Teodoro (1910–   ), AE/P Venezuela 1961

Moss, Ambler Holmes, Jr. (1937–   ), AE/P Panama 1978–1982

Motley, Langhorne A. (1938–   ), AE/P Brazil 1981–1983

Muccio, John Joseph (1900–1989), AE/P Guatemala 1959–1961

*Munro, Dana Gardner (1892–1990), EE/MP Haiti 1930–1932

Nava, Julian (1927–   ), AE/P Mexico 1980–1981

*Negroponte, John Dimitry (1939–   ), AE/P Honduras 1981–1985; AE/P Mexico 1989–

*Nelson, Thomas Henry (1824–1896), EE/MP Chile 1861–1866; EE/MP Mexico 1869–1873

Newbegin, Robert, II (1905–   ), AE/P Honduras 1958–1960; AE/P Haiti 1960–1961

Nicholson, Meredith (1866–1947), EE/MP Paraguay 1933–1935; EE/MP Venezuela 1935–1938; EE/MP Nicaragua 1938–1941

*Northcott, Elliott (1869–1946), EE/MP Colombia 1909–1910; EE/MP Nicaragua 1911; EE/MP Venezuela 1911–1913

Norweb, Raymond Henry (1894–1983), EE/MP Bolivia 1936–1937; EE/MP Dominican Republic 1937–1940; AE/P Peru 1940–1943; AE/P Cuba 1945–1948

Nufer, Albert Frank (1894–1956), AE/P El Salvador 1947–1949; AE/P Argentina 1952–1956

*O'Brien, Edward Charles (1860–1927), EE/MP Paraguay and Uruguay 1905–1909

*O'Dwyer, William (1890–1964), AE/P Mexico 1950–1952

Oliver, Covey Thomas (1913–   ), AE/P Colombia 1964–1966

Olson, Jack B. (1920–   ), AE/P The Bahamas 1976–

O'Rear, John Davis (1868–1918), EE/MP Bolivia 1913–1918

Ortiz, Francis [Frank] Vincent, Jr. (1926–   ), AE/P Barbados and Grenada 1977–1979; AE/P Guatemala 1979–1980; AE/P Argentina 1983–1986

*Osborn, Thomas Andrew (1836–1898), EE/MP Chile 1877–1881; EE/MP Brazil 1881–1885

*Osborn, Thomas Ogden (1832–1904), MR Argentina 1874–1884; MR/CG Argentina 1884–1885

Ostrander, Nancy (1925–   ), AE/P Suriname 1978–1980

O'Toole, William Joseph (1894–1928), EE/MP Paraguay 1922–1924

*Otterbourg, Marcus (1827–1893), EE/MP Mexico 1867

Pacheco, Romualdo (1831–1899), EE/MP Costa Rica, El Salvador, Guatemala, Honduras, and Nicaragua 1890–; EE/MP Guatemala and Honduras 1891–

Palmer, Robert M. (1820–1862), MR Argentina 1861–1862

Partridge, Frank Charles (1861–1943), EE/MP Venezuela 1893–1894

*Partridge, James Rudolph (1823–1884), MR Honduras 1862; MR El Salvador 1863–1866; MR Venezuela 1869–1870

*Patterson, Jefferson (1891–1977), AE/P Uruguay 1956–1958

Patterson, Richard Cunningham, Jr. (1896–1966), AE/P Guatemala 1948–1950

Pawley, William Douglas (1896–1977), AE/P Peru 1945–1946; AE/P Brazil 1946–1948

*Peck, Henry Everard (1821–1867), Comm/CG Haiti 1865–1866; MR/CG Haiti 1866–1867

Peden, James A. (? – ?), MR Republic of Buenos Aires 1854–1857; MR Argentina 1856

*Pendleton, John Strother (1802–1868), CdA Chile 1841–1844; CdA Argentina 1851–1854

Pettis, Solomon Newton (1827–1900), MR/CG Bolivia 1878–1879

*Peurifoy, John Emil (1907–1955), AE/P Guatemala 1953–1954

Peyton, Balie (1803–1878), EE/MP Chile 1848–1853

Pezzulo, Lawrence A. (1926–   ), AE/P Uruguay 1977–1979; AE/P Nicaragua 1979–1981

Pheiffer, William Townsend (1898–   ), AE/P Dominican Republic 1953–1957

Phelps, Phelps (1897–   ), AE/P Dominican Republic 1952–1953

*Phelps, Seth Ledyard (1824–1885), EE/MP Peru 1883–1885

Philip, Hoffman (1872–1951), EE/MP Colombia 1917–1922; EE/MP Uruguay 1922–1925; EE/MP Chile 1935–1937

Pickering, Thomas Reeve (1931–   ), AE/P El Salvador 1983–1985

*Pickett, James Chamberlayne (1793–1872), CdA Peru–Bolivian Confederation 1838–1845

Piedra, Alberto Martinez (1926–   ), AE/P Guatemala 1984–1987

Pile, William Anderson (1829–1889), MR Venezuela 1871–1874

Piles, Samuel Henry (1858–1940), EE/MP Colombia 1922–1928

Pilliod, Charles J., Jr. (1918–   ), AE/P Mexico 1986–1989

*Pitkin, John Robert Graham (1841–1901), EE/MP Argentina 1889–1893

Ploeser, Walter Christian (1907–   ), AE/P Paraguay 1957–1959; AE/P Costa Rica 1970–1972

*Poindexter, Miles (1868–1946), AE/P Peru 1923–1928

*Poinsett, Joel Roberts (1779–1851), EE/MP Mexico 1825–1829

Pollard, Richard (1790–1851), CdA Chile 1834–1842

Popper, David Henry (1912–   ), AE/P Chile 1973–1977
Porter, James Davis (1828–1912), EE/MP Chile 1893–1894
*Powell, William Frank (1848–1920), CdA Santo Domingo 1897–1904; EE/MP Haiti
    1897–1905
Preeg, Ernest Henry (1934–   ), AE/P Haiti 1981–1983
Price, William Jennings (1873–1952), EE/MP Panama 1913–1921
Profitt, George H. (1807–1847), EE/MP Brazil 1843–1844
Quinton, Anthony Cecil Eden (1934–   ), AE/P Nicaragua 1982–1984; AE/P Peru
    1989–
*Raguet, Condy (1784–1842), CdA Brazil 1825–1827
Ramer, John Edward (1870–1926), EE/MP Nicaragua 1921–1925
Ransom, Matthew Whitaker (1826–1904), EE/MP Mexico 1895–1897
Ravndal, Christian Magelssen (1899–1984), AE/P Uruguay 1949–1951; AE/P Ecuador
    1956–1960
Reich, Otto Juan (1945–   ), AE/P Venezuela 1986–1989
Reynolds, Robert McConnell (1826–1885), MR Bolivia 1874–1876
Rich, Robert Graham, Jr. (1930–   ), AE/P Belize 1987–1990
*Riddle, John Wallace (1864–1941), AE/P Argentina 1921–1925
Riotte, Charles N. (? – ?), MR Costa Rica 1861–1867; MR Nicaragua 1869–1873
Robbins, Warren Delano (1885–1935), EE/MP El Salvador 1928–1931
Roberts, George B., Jr. (1930–   ), AE/P Guyana 1979–1981
Roberts, William Randall (1830–1897), EE/MP Chile 1885–1889
*Robinson, Christopher (1806–1889), EE/MP Peru 1861–1865
Roddan, Edward L. (1899–   ), AE/P Uruguay 1951–1953
*Rodney, Caesar Augustus (1772–1824), MP Republic of Buenos Aires 1823–1824
Rondon, Fernando Enrique (1936–   ), AE/P Ecuador 1985–1988
*Root, Joseph Pomeroy (1826–1885), EE/MP Chile 1870–1873
*Rosencrans, William Starke (1819–1898), EE/MP Mexico 1868–1869
Ross, Claude George Anthony (1917–   ), AE/P Haiti 1967–1969
Rountree, William Manning (1917–   ), AE/P Brazil 1970–1973
Rousseau, Richard Hilaire (1815–1872), MR Honduras 1866–1869
Rowell, Edward Morgan (1931–   ), AE/P Bolivia 1985–1988
Rubottom, Roy Richard, Jr. (1912–   ), AE/P Argentina 1960–1961
Russell, Thomas, Jr. (1825–1887), MR Venezuela 1874–1877
*Russell, William Worthington (1859–1944), EE/MP Colombia 1904–1905; EE/MP Ven-
    ezuela 1905–1910; MR/CG Dominican Republic 1910–1911; EE/MP Dominican
    Republic 1911–1913; EE/MP Dominican Republic 1915–1925
Russo, Paul A. (1943–   ), AE/P Antigua and Barbuda, Barbados, Dominica, St.
    Christopher and Nevis, St. Lucia, St. Vincent and the Grenadines, 1986–1988
Ryan, Hewson Anthony (1922–   ), AE/P Honduras 1969–1973
Ryan, Thomas (1837–1914), EE/MP Mexico 1889–1893
Saccio, Leonard John (1911–   ), AE/P Colombia 1970–1973
Sack, Leo R. (1889–1956), EE/MP Costa Rica 1933–1937
Sampson, Archibald Johnson (1839–1921), EE/MP Ecuador 1897–1905
Sanchez, Philip Victor (1929–   ), AE/P Honduras 1973–1976; AE/P Colombia 1976–
    1977
*Sands, William Franklin (1874–1946), EE/MP Guatemala 1909–1910
Sayre, Robert Marion (1924–   ), AE/P Uruguay 1968–1969; AE/P Panama 1969–
    1974; AE/P Brazil 1978–1981

*Schenck, Robert Cumming (1809–1890), EE/MP Brazil 1851–1853

Schoenfeld, Hans Frederick Arthur (1889–1952), EE/MP Dominican Republic 1931–1937

Schoenfeld, Rudolf Emil (1895–1981), AE/P Guatemala 1951–1953; AE/P Colombia 1953–1955

Schuyler, Montgomery, Jr. (1877–1955), EE/MP Ecuador 1913; EE/MP El Salvador 1921–1925

Schwartz, William B. (1921–   ), AE/P The Bahamas 1977–1981

Scott, Charles Lewis (1827–1899), MR/CG Venezuela 1885–1888; EE/MP Venezuela 1888–1889

Scotten, Robert McGregor (1891–1968), EE/MP Dominican Republic 1940–1942; EE/MP Costa Rica 1942–1943; AE/P Ecuador 1943–1947

*Scruggs, William Lindsay (1836–1912), MR Colombia 1873–1876; 1882–1884; EE/MP Colombia 1884–1885; EE/MP Venezuela 1889–1892

Seay, William A. (1831– ?), MR/CG Bolivia 1885–1887

Semple, James (1798–1866), CdA New Grenada 1837–1842

Sessions, Edson Oliver (1902–   ), AE/P Ecuador 1968–1970

Settle, Thomas (1831–1888), EE/MP Peru 1871

Sevier, Henry Hulme (1878–1940), AE/P Chile 1933–1935

Shannon, Richard Cutts (1839–1920), EE/MP Costa Rica, El Salvador, and Nicaragua 1891–1893

*Shannon, Wilson (1802–1877), EE/MP Mexico 1844–1845

Shaw, George Price (1892–1966), AE/P Nicaragua 1948–1949; AE/P El Salvador 1949–1952; AE/P Paraguay 1952–1953

Shea, Joseph Hooker (1863–1928), AE/P Chile 1916–1961

*Sheffield, James Rockwell (1864–1938), AE/P Mexico 1924–1927

Shelton, Sally Angela (1944–   ), AE/P Barbados, Dominica, Grenada, and St. Lucia, 1979–1981

Shelton; Turner Blair (1915–1982), AE/P Nicaragua 1970–1975

Sherrill, Charles Hitchcock (1867–1936), EE/MP Argentina 1909–1910

Shields; Benjamin Glover (1808– ?), CdA Venezuela 1845–1850

Shlaudeman, Harry Walter (1926–   ), AE/P Venezuela 1975–1976; AE/P Peru 1977–1980; AE/P Argentina 1980–1983; AE/P Brazil 1986–1989; AE/P Nicaragua 1990–

Simmons, John Farr (1892–1968), AE/P El Salvador 1944–1947; AE/P Ecuador 1947–1950

Siracusa, Ernest Victor (1918–   ), AE/P Bolivia 1969–1973; AE/P Uruguay 1973–1977

*Smith, Earl Edward Tailer (1903–1991), AE/P Cuba 1957–1959

Smith, John Cotton, II (1810–1879), MR Bolivia 1858–1861

Smith, Madison Roswell (1850–1919), EE/MP Haiti 1913–1914

Smythe, Henry Maxwell (1844–1932), CdA Santo Domingo 1893–1897; MR/CG Haiti 1893–1897

Snow, William Pennell (1907–   ), AE/P Paraguay 1961–1967

Solaun, Mauricio (1935–   ), AE/P Nicaragua 1977–1979

Sorsby, William Brooks (1858–1912), EE/MP Bolivia 1902–1908

Sotirhos, Michael (1928–   ), AE/P Jamaica 1985–1989

South, John Glover (1873–1940), EE/MP Panama 1921–1930

Sparks, Edward John (1897–1976), AE/P Bolivia 1951–1954; AE/P Guatemala 1955–1958; AE/P Venezuela 1958–1961; AE/P Uruguay 1961–1962

Spiers, Ronald Ian (1925–   ), AE/P The Bahamas 1973–1974

*Squiers, Herbert Goldsmith (1859–1911), EE/MP Cuba 1902–1905; EE/MP Panama 1906–1909

Starkweather, David Austin (1802–1876), EE/MP Chile 1854–1857

Stedman, William Perry, Jr. (1923–   ), AE/P Bolivia 1973–1977

Steele, Isaac Nevitt (1809–1891), CdA Venezuela 1849–1853

Steinhardt, Laurence Adolph (1892–1950), AE/P Peru 1937–1939

Stephansky, Ben Solomon (1913–   ), AE/P Bolivia 1961–1963

Stevens, John Leavitt (1820–1895), MR Uruguay 1870–1873; MR Paraguay 1870–1873

Stewart, Charles Allen (1907–1973), AE/P Venezuela 1962–1964

Stewart, James Bolton (1882–1969), EE/MP Nicaragua 1942–1943; AE/P Nicaragua 1943–1945

Stilwell, Thomas Neel (1830–1874), MR Venezuela 1867–1868

Stimpson, Harry Farnum, Jr. (1913–   ), AE/P Paraguay 1959–1961

*Stimson, Frederic Jesup (1855–1943), AE/P Argentina 1914–1921

*Strobel, Edward Henry (1885–1908), EE/MP Ecuador 1894; EE/MP Chile 1894–1897

Strom, Carl Walther (1899–1969), AE/P Bolivia 1959–1961

Stroock, Thomas Frank (1925–   ), AE/P Guatemala 1989–

*Stuart, Granville (1834–1918), EE/MP Paraguay and Uruguay 1894–1898

Stutesman, James Flynn (1860–1917), EE/MP Bolivia 1908–1910

*Sullivan, James Mark (1873–1920), EE/MP Dominican Republic 1913–1915

Sullivan, Peter John (1821–1883), MR Colombia 1867–1869

Summerlin, George Thomas (1872–1947), EE/MP Honduras 1925–1929; EE/MP Venezuela 1929–1935; EE/MP Panama 1935–1937

Symington, John Fife, Jr. (1910–   ), AE/P Trinidad and Tobago 1969–1971

Tambs, Lewis Arthur (1927–   ), AE/P Colombia 1983–1985; AE/P Costa Rica 1985–1987

Taylor, Clyde D. (1937–   ), AE/P Paraguay 1985–1988

Taylor, Paul Daniel (1939–   ), AE/P Dominican Republic 1988–

*Telles, Raymond L., Jr. (1915–   ), AE/P Costa Rica 1961–1967

Tewksbury, Howard Hobson (1895–   ), AE/P Paraguay 1950–1952

Theberge, James Daniel (1930–   ), AE/P Nicaragua 1975–1977; AE/P Chile 1982–1985

Thomas, Allen (1830–1907), EE/MP Venezuela 1895–1897

Thomas, Francis (1799–1876), EE/MP Peru 1872–1875

Thomas, Gerald Eustis (1929–   ), AE/P Guyana 1882–1883

*Thompson, David Eugene (1854–1942), EE/MP Brazil 1902–1905; AE/P Brazil 1905; AE/P Mexico 1906–1909

Thompson, John E. W. (1855– ?), CdA Santo Domingo 1885–1889; MR/CG Haiti 1885–1889

*Thompson, Thomas Larkin (1838–1898), EE/MP Brazil 1893–1897

*Thompson, Waddy, Jr. (1798–1868), EE/MP Mexico 1842–1844

*Thomson, Thaddeus Austin (1853–1927), EE/MP Colombia 1913–1916

Thornton, James B. (1801–1838), CdA Peru 1836–1837

Thurston, Raymond LeRoy (1913–1981), AE/P Haiti 1961–1963

Thurston, Walter Clarence (1894–1974), EE/MP El Salvador 1942–1943; AE/P El Salvador 1943–1944; AE/P Bolivia 1944–1946; AE/P Mexico 1946–1950

Tillman, James Davidson (1841– ?), EE/MP Ecuador 1895–1897

Timmons, Benson Ellison Lane, III (1916–   ), AE/P Haiti 1963–1967

Tittman, Harold Hilgard, Jr. (1893–1980), AE/P Haiti 1946–1948; AE/P Peru 1948–
    1955

Tobriner, Walter Nathan (1902–   ), AE/P Jamaica 1967–1969

Tod, David (1805–1868), EE/MP Brazil 1847–1851

Todman, Terence Alphonso (1926–   ), AE/P Costa Rica 1974–1977; AE/P Argentina
    1989–

Torbet, Alfred Thomas Archimedes (1833–1880), MR El Salvador 1869–1871

Towell, Timothy Lathrop (1934–   ), AE/P Paraguay 1988–

Travers, Howard Karl (1893–1976), AE/P Haiti 1951–1952

Trousdale, William (1790–1872), EE/MP Brazil 1853–1857

*Tudor, William (1779–1830), CdA Brazil 1827–1830

Tull, Theresa Anne (1936–   ), AE/P Guyana 1987–1990

Turpin, Edward A. (? – ?), MR Venezuela 1858–1861

Tuthill, John Wills (1910–   ), AE/P Brazil 1966–1969

Vaky, Viron Peter (1925–   ), AE/P Costa Rica 1972–1974; AE/P Colombia 1973–
    1976; AE/P Venezuela 1976–1978

Van Alen, John Trumbull (? – ?), CdA Ecuador 1849–1850

Vaughn, Jack Hood (1920–   ), AE/P Panama 1964–1965; AE/P Colombia 1969–1970

Walker, William Graham (1935–   ), AE/P El Salvador 1988–

Warren, Avra Milvin (1893–1957), EE/MP Dominican Republic 1942–1943; AE/P Do-
    minican Republic 1943–1944; AE/P Panama 1944–1945

Warren, Charles Beecher (1870–1936), AE/P Mexico 1924

Warren, Fitz Henry (1816–1878), MR Guatemala 1865–1869

Warren, William Fletcher (1896–   ), AE/P Nicaragua 1945–1947; AE/P Paraguay
    1947–1950; AE/P Venezuela 1951–1956

*Washburn, Charles A(mes) (1822–1889), Comm Paraguay 1861–1863; MR Paraguay
    1863–1868

Watson, Alexander Fletcher (1939–   ), AE/P Peru 1986–1989

Watts, Beaufort T. (? – ?), CdA Colombia 1827

Waynick, Capus Miller (1889–   ), AE/P Nicaragua 1949–1951; AE/P Colombia 1951–
    1953

*Webb, James Watson (1802–1884), EE/MP Brazil 1861–1869

*Weddell, Alexander Wilbourne (1876–1948), AE/P Argentina 1933–1938

Weiss, Seymour (1925–   ), AE/P The Bahamas 1974–1976

Weissman, Marvin (1927–   ), AE/P Costa Rica 1977–1980; AE/P Bolivia 1980

*Weitzel, George Thomas (1873–1936), EE/MP Nicaragua 1911–1913

Weller, John B. (1812–1875), EE/MP Mexico 1860–1861

*Welles, Benjamin Sumner (1892–1961), AE/P Cuba 1933

*Wheeler, John Hill (1806–1882), MR Nicaragua 1854–1856

Wheeler, George Post (1869–1956), EE/MP Paraguay 1929–1933

Whidden, Benjamin F. (? – ?), Comm/CG Haiti 1862–1865

White, Charles Dunning (1868–1954), EE/MP Honduras 1911–1913

White, Francis (1892–1961), AE/P Mexico 1953–1957

*White, John Campbell (1884–1967), EE/MP Haiti 1940–1943; AE/P Haiti 1943–1944;
    AE/P Peru 1944–1945

White, Julius (1816–1890), MR Argentina 1872–1873

White, Philo (1796–1874), CdA Ecuador 1853–1854; MR Ecuador 1854–1858
*White, Robert Edward (1926–   ), AE/P Paraguay 1977–1980; AE/P El Salvador 1980–1981
Whitehouse, Sheldon (1883–1965), EE/MP Guatemala 1929–1933; EE/MP Colombia 1933–1934
Wiley, John Cooper (1893–1967), AE/P Colombia 1944–1947; AE/P Panama 1951–1953
Wilkey, Malcolm Richard (1918–   ), AE/P Uruguay 1985–1990
Willauer, Whiting (1906–1962), AE/P Honduras 1954–1958; AE/P Costa Rica 1958–1961
Williams, Alpheus Starkey (1810–1878), MR El Salvador 1866–1869
Williams, John (1778–1837), CdA Central America 1825–1826
Williams, Murat Willis (1914–   ), AE/P El Salvador 1961–1964
Williams, William (1821–1896), CdA Paraguay and Uruguay 1882–1885
Williamson, George McWillie (1829– ?), MR Costa Rica, El Salvador, Guatemala, Honduras, and Nicaragua 1873–1879
*Williamson, John Gustavus Adolphus (1793–1840), CdA Venezuela 1835–1840
Wilson, Edwin Carleton (1893–1972), EE/MP Uruguay 1939–1941; AE/P Panama 1941–1943
*Wilson, Henry Lane (1856–1932), EE/MP Chile 1897–1904; AE/P Mexico 1909–1913
Wilson, James (1825–1867), MR Venezuela 1866–1867
Wilson, Orme, Jr. (1885–1965), AE/P Haiti 1944–1946
Wing, Edward Rumsey (1845–1874), MR Ecuador 1869–1874
Winsor, Curtin, Jr. (1939–   ), AE/P Costa Rica 1983–1985
Wise, Henry Alexander (1806–1876), EE/MP Brazil 1844–1847
Woodward, Robert Forbes (1908–   ), AE/P Costa Rica 1954–1958; AE/P Uruguay 1958–1961; AE/P Chile 1961
Worthington, Henry Gaither (1828–1909), MR Argentina 1868–1869; MR Uruguay 1868–1869
*Wright, Joshua Butler (1877–1939), EE/MP Uruguay 1930–1934; AE/P Cuba 1937–1939
Wullweber, Christian Friedrich Wilhelm Jurgen (1833–1877), MR Ecuador 1875–1876
*Yancey, Benjamin Cudworth (1817–1891), MR Argentina 1858–1859
Ylitalo, John Raymond (1916–   ), AE/P Paraguay 1969–1972
Yost, Robert Lloyd (1922–   ), AE/P Dominican Republic 1978–1982
Young, Evan Erastus (1878–1946), EE/MP Ecuador 1911–1912; EE/MP Dominican Republic 1925–1929
*Young, Pierce Manning Butler (1836–1896), EE/MP Guatemala and Honduras 1893–1896
Zurhellen, Joseph Owen, Jr. (1920–   ), AE/P Suriname 1976–1978

List of Individuals by Profession and Occupation

ACTORS

Gavin, John

ADVENTURERS. *See also* SOLDIERS OF FORTUNE

Cazneau, Jane Maria Eliza (McManus) Storms
Cazneau, William L(esley)
Salm-Salm, Agnes Elisabeth Winona Leclercq Joy, Princess
Thrasher, John Sidney

AGRICULTURISTS

Earle, Franklin Sumner

ANTHROPOLOGISTS

Beals, Ralph L(eon)
Biesanz, John Berry
Boggs, Stanley Harding
Chagnon, Napoleon A(lphonseau)
Coe, Michael D(ouglas)
Ekholm, Gordon Frederick
Farabee, William Curtis
Faron, Louis C.
Foster, George M(cCleland), Jr.
Gillin, John (Philip)
Goldman, Irving
Gordon, George Byron
Harner, Michael J(ames)
Henry, Jules
Herskovitz, Melville J(ean)
Holmberg, Allan Richard
Hutchinson, Harry W(illiam)
Lanning, Edward Putnam
Lewis, Oscar
Longyear, John Munro
Mangin, William Patrick
Mason, Gregory
Mason, John Alden
Murphy, Robert Francis
Pierson, Donald
Price, Richard
Redfield, Robert
Roberts, Henry Buchtel
Rowe, John Howland
Roys, Ralph Loveland
Spinden, Herbert Joseph
Starr, Frederick
Steggerda, Morris
Stirling, Matthew William
Tozzer, Alfred Marston
Tschopik, Harry Schlesinger, Jr.
Vogt, Evon Zartman, Jr.
Wagley, Charles Walter
Whitten, Norman Earl, Jr.
Williams, Joseph John

ARCHAEOLOGISTS

Andrews, E(dward) Wyllys, IV

Bandelier, Adolph Francis
   Alphonse
Bennett, Robert Root
Bennett, Wendell C(lark)
Bird, Junius B(outon)
Blom, Frans Ferdinand
Boggs, Stanley Harding
Borton, Francis
Brainerd, George Walton
Bullard, William R(otch), Jr.
de Booy, Theodoor Hendrick
   Nikolas
Evans, Clifford
Gates, William E(dmond)
Hay, Clarence Leonard
Kelly, Isabel Truesdell
Kidder, Alfred Vincent
Kidder, Alfred II
Le Plongeon, Augustus Henry
   Julius
Le Plongeon, Alice (Dixon)
Lothrop, Samuel Kirkland
Mayer, Brantz
Means, Philip Ainsworth
Meggers, Betty Jane
Mercer, Henry Chapman
Morley, Sylvanus Griswold
Nuttal, Zelia Maria Magdalena
Pollock, Harry Evelyn Dorr
Proskouriakoff, Tatiana Ave-
   nivovna
Rainey, Froelich Gladstone
Ricketson, Oliver Garrison, Jr.
Roberts, Henry Buchtel
Rouse, Irving
Ruppert, Karl
Satterthwaite, Linton
Saville, Marshall Howard
Shook, Edwin Martin
Smith, Augustus Ledyard
Smith, Robert Eliot
Squier, Ephraim George
Stephens, John Lloyd
Stone, Doris Zemurray
Strong, William Duncan
Thompson, Edward Herbert
Thompson, John Eric Sidney
Vaillant, George Clapp

Wauchope, Robert
Willey, Gordon Randolph

ARCHITECTS

Spratling, William Philip

ARMY OFFICERS. *See also* SOL-DIERS, SOLDIERS OF FORTUNE

Allen, Henry Watkins
Black, William Murray
Brooke, John R(utter)
Crowder, Enoch Herbert
Funston, Frederick
Goethals, George Washington
Greble, Edwin St. John
Gulick, John W(iley)
Ingraham, Prentiss
Jordan, Thomas
Kilpatrick, Hugh Judson
Lemly, Henry Rowan
Magruder, John Bankhead
Michler, Nathaniel
Morton, James St. Clair
Osborn, Thomas Ogden
Parker, Frank
Pershing, John Joseph
Price, Sterling
Rosencrans, William Starke
Scott, Hugh Lenox
Shafter, William Rufus
Shelby, Joseph Orville
Slocum, Herbert Jermain
Squiers, Herbert Goldsmith
Stone, Charles Pomeroy
Winship, Blanton
Wood, Leonard
Young, Pierce Manning Butler

ARTISTS. *See also* PAINTERS

Burkhardt, Jacques
Carleton, George Washington
Ferguson, Henry Augustus
Fuertes, Louis Agassiz
Hart, George Overbury
Jacques, Francis Lee

ASSOCIATION OFFICIALS

Harrar, J(acob) George
Jones, Robert Cuba

ASTRONOMERS

Bailey, Solon Irving
Gilliss, James Melville
Gould, Benjamin Apthorp
Perrine, Charles Dillon
Thome, John [Juan] Macon

AUTHORS

Brenner, Anita
Calderón de la Barca, Frances Erskine
    (Inglis)
Dulles, John W(atson) F(oster)
Ewbank, Thomas
Flandrau, Charles Macomb
Franck, Harry A(lverson)
Gill, Richard C(ochran)
Hale, William Bayard
Hastings, Lansford Warren
Helper, Hinton Rowan
Howland, Edward
Howland, Marie (Stevens Case)
Iglehart, Fanny (Chambers) Gooch
Ingraham, Prentiss
Johnson, James Weldon
La Farge, Oliver Hazard Perry
Lekis, Lisa Crichton
Martin, John Bartlow
Mason, Gregory
Mayer, Brantz
Miller, Leo Edward
Norman, Benjamin Moore
Porter, Katherine Anne
Reed, Alma M(arie) (Sullivan)
Rémy, Henry
Robinson, Tracy
Savoy, Gene
Spratling, William Philip
Stephens, John Lloyd
Terry, Thomas Philip
Tiernan, Frances Christine Fisher
Toor, Frances
Von Hagen, Victor Wolfgang

Wells, William Vincent
Wolfe, Bertram David
Wright, Irene Aloha
Zahl, Paul Arthur

AVIATION EXECUTIVES

Faucett, Elmer J.
O'Neill, Ralph A.
Shelton, Cornell Newton

AVIATORS. *See also* AVIATION EXECUTIVES

Andrews, R(ayma) L(aurance)
Angel, James Crawford
Grow, Harold B(artley)
Rihl, George Lawrence
Rowe, Basil Lee
Worden, John Hector

BALLOONISTS

Allen, James
Paulin, William
Wells, R. Gibbon

BANKERS

Allen, Charles H(erbert)
Farnham, Roger L(eslie)
Rosenthal, Louis Samuel Philip
Van Deusen, Walter Merritt

BIOLOGISTS

Carr, Archie Fairly
Noble, Gladwyn Kingsley

BOTANISTS

Archer, William Andrew
Baldwin, William
Brandegee, Townshend Stith
Britton, Nathaniel Lord
Earle, Franklin Sumner
Goodspeed, T(homas) Harper
Harrar, Jacob George
LaRue, Carl Downey
Lundell, Cyrus Longworth
Maguire, Bassett

Millspaugh, Charles Frederick
Prance, Ghillean Tolmie
Rusby, Henry Hurd
Schultes, Richard Evans
Standley, Paul Carpenter
Stork, Harvey Elmer
Wight, William Franklin
Williams, Louis Otho

BUSINESS EXECUTIVES

Cutter, Victor M(acomber)
Dulles, John W(atson) F(oster)

BUSINESSMEN

Blow, Henry Taylor
Braniff, Oscar
Braniff, Thomas
Bruce, James
Burke, Edward A.
Burns, Daniel Monroe
Canfield, C(harles) A(delbert)
Carothers, George C.
Cook, Frederick C.
de Roulet, Vincent W(illiam)
Gardner, Arthur
Guggenheim, Harry Frank
Hale, Samuel B(rown)
Halsey, Thomas Lloyd
Hawley, Robert B(radley)
Hemenway, Augustus
Iglehart, David Stewart
McMillin, Benton
McRae, Colin John
Magoffin, James Wiley
Merrill, John Lenord
Morales, Franklin E.
Morlan, Albert Edmund
Morrow, Dwight Whitney
Phelps, Seth Ledyard
Pierce, Henry Clay
Preston, Andrew Woodbury
Reily, Emmett Montgomery
Ross, Roderick Malcolm
Scrymser, James Alexander
Stabler, Jordan Herbert

Steinhart, Frank (Maximilian)
Stilwell, Arthur Edward
Vincent, Mordelo
White, William Porter
Zemurray, Samuel

CATTLEMEN

Mackenzie, Murdo

CIVIL ENGINEERS

Butterfield, Carlos
Campbell, Allan
Church, George Earl
Corthell, Elmer Lawrence
Craig, Neville B(urgoyne)
Davis, Arthur Powell
Haupt, Lewis M(uhlenberg)
Menocal, Aniceto Garcia
Noble, Alfred
Roberts, William Milnor
Stevens, John Frank
Sutton, Charles Wood
Wallace, John Findley
Warfield, Ralph Mervine
Williamson, Sydney Bacon

CLERGYMEN. *See also* MISSIONARIES

Blenk, James Hubert
Borton, Francis
Byrne, Edwin V(incent)
Carson, Henry Roberts
Currier, Charles Warren
Dunn, Ballard S(mith)
Hamilton, Hiram P(hiletus)
Illich, Ivan D.
Jones, William Ambrose
Kidder, Daniel Parish
Kinsolving, Lucien Lee
Knight, Albion Williamson
McLaughlin, William Patterson
McManus, James Edward
Miller, George Amos
Peterkin, George William
Reinke, Jonathan
Zahm, John Augustus

COLONIAL ADMINISTRATORS

Cramer, Lawrence W(illiam)
Crowder, Enoch Herbert
Hunt, William Henry
Pearson, Paul Martin
Reily, Emmett Montgomery
Wood, Leonard
Yager, Arthur

COLONY PROMOTERS

Dunn, Ballard S(mith)
Gaston, James McFadden
Hastings, Lansford Warren
McMullan, Frank
Murray, William Henry David
Owen, Albert Kimsey

COMPOSERS

Gottschalk, Louis Moreau

CONSULS. *See* DIPLOMATS

DIPLOMATS

Allen, Heman
Anderson, Richard Clough
Andrews, Christopher Columbus
Armour, Norman
Bailly-Blanchard, Arthur
Barrett, John
Barton, Seth
Bassett, Ebenezer Don Carlos
Baylies, Francis
Beaulac, Willard Leon
Beaupré, Arthur Matthias
Belcher, Taylor Garrison
Bennett, W(illiam) Tapley, Jr.
Berle, Adolf Augustus
Bidlack, Benjamin Alden
Bland, Theodorick
Blow, Henry Taylor
Boal, Pierre de Lagarde
Bonsal, Philip W(ilson)
Borland, Solon
Bowen, Herbert Wolcott
Bowers, Claude Gernade

Bowlin, James Butler
Braden, Spruille
Bragg, Edward S(tuyvesant)
Brent, William, Jr.
Briggs, Ellis Ormsbee
Bruce, James
Buchanan, William Insco
Butler, Anthony (Wayne)
Caffery, Jefferson
Carothers, George C.
Christiancy, Isaac Peckham
Clark, J(oshua) Reuben, Jr.
Clay, John Randolph
Clayton, Powell
Cooper, Prentice (William), Jr.
Corrigan, Frank [Francis] Patrick
Corwin, Thomas
Crittenden, Thomas Theodore
Crosby, Elisha O(scar)
Crowder, Enoch Herbert
Culbertson, William S(mith)
Daniels, Josephus, Jr.
Davis, Nathaniel
Davis, Roy Tasco
Dawson, Thomas Cleland
Dawson, William, Jr.
Dennis, Lawrence
de Roulet, Vincent William
Dimitry, Alexander
Douglass, Frederick [Augustus
      Washington Baily]
Dunn, William Edward
Durham, John Stephens
Eberhardt, Charles Christopher
Egan, Patrick
Ellis, Powhatan
Ellsworth, Luther T(homas)
Fabens, Joseph W(arren)
Farland, Joseph S(impson)
Feeley, Edward F(rancis)
Flack, Joseph
Fletcher, Henry P(rather)
Forbes, John Murray
Forsyth, John
Foster, John Watson
Fox, Williams Carlton
Frost, Wesley
Furniss, Henry W(atson)

Gadsden, James
Gardner, Arthur
Gavin, John
Gonzales, William Elliott
Gordon, [Abraham] Lincoln
Graham, John
Green, Benjamin Edwards
Grevstad, Nicolay Andreas
Guggenheim, Harry Frank
Hale, Edward J(oseph)
Hall, Henry C(ook)
Halsey, Thomas Lloyd
Hanna, Bayliss W.
Hanna, Matthew Elting
Harris, William A(lexander)
Harrison, William Henry
Hassaurek, Frederick [Friedrich]
Helm, Charles John
Hill, Robert C(harles)
Hilliard, Henry W(ashington)
Hine, Marquis Lafayette
Hise, Elijah
Howard, Findley Burtch
Hunter, William, Jr.
Hurlbut, Stephen Augustus
Jackson, Henry Rootes
Jarvis, Thomas Jordan
Jefferson, Benjamin Lafayette
Johnson, James Weldon
Jones, William Carey
Jorden, William John
Jova, Joseph John
Judah, Noble Brandon
Kerbey, Joseph Orton
Kilpatrick, Hugh Judson
Kirk, Robert C.
Korry, Edward Malcolm
Lamar, Mirabeau Buonaparte
Lane, Arthur Bliss
Langston, John Mercer
Lee, Fitzhugh
Linowitz, Sol Myron
Litchfield, Franklin
Logan, Cornelius Ambrose
Long, Boaz Walton
Loomis, Francis Butler
McLane, Robert Milligan
McMahon, Martin Thomas

McMillan, Benton
McRae, Colin John
Magoffin, James Wiley
Magoon, Charles Edward
Maney, George Earl
Mann, Thomas Clifton
Manton, Benjamin M.
Markbreit, Leopold
Martin, John Bartlow
Mayer, Brantz
Mein, John Gordon
Merry, William Lawrence
Messersmith, George Strausser
Mizner, Lansing Bond
Montgomery, George Washington
Moore, Thomas Patrick
Morales, Franklin E.
Morgan, Edwin Vernon
Morgan, Philip Hicky
Morlan, Albert Edmund
Morrison, Delesseps Story
Morrow, Dwight Whitney
Munro, Dana Gardner
Negroponte, John Dimitry
Nelson, Thomas Henry
Northcott, Elliott
O'Brien, Edward Charles
O'Dwyer, William
O'Hara, Thomas
Osborn, Thomas Andrew
Osborn, Thomas Ogden
O'Shaughnessy, Nelson Jarvis
    Waterbury
Otterbourg, Marcus
Partridge, James Rudolph
Patterson, Jefferson
Peck, Henry Everard
Pendleton, John Strother
Peurifoy, John Emil
Phelps, Seth Ledyard
Pickett, James Chamberlayne
Pickett, John T.
Pitkin, John Robert Graham
Poindexter, Miles
Poinsett, Joel Roberts
Powell, William Frank
Prevost, John Bartow
Raguet, Condy

Riddle, John Wallace
Robinson, Christopher
Robinson, Jeremy
Rodney, Caesar Augustus
Root, Joseph Pomeroy
Rosencrans, William Starke
Rowe, Leo Stanton
Russell, William Worthington
Sands, William Franklin
Savage, Charles
Schenck, Robert Cumming
Scruggs, William Lindsay
Shaler, William
Shannon, Wilson
Sheffield, James Rockwell
Silliman, John Reid
Smith, Earl Edward Tailer
Smith, Wayne S.
Squier, Ephraim George
Squiers, Herbert Goldsmith
Stabler, Jordan Herbert
Stevens, John Leavitt
Stimson, Frederic Jesup
Strobel, Edward Henry
Stuart, Granville
Sullivan, James Mark
Sumter, Thomas, Jr.
Sutton, Warner Perrin
Tayloe, Edward Thornton
Telles, Raymond L., Jr.
Terrell, Alexander Watkins
Thompson, David Eugene
Thompson, Thomas Larkin
Thompson, Waddy, Jr.
Thomson, Thaddeus Austin
Todd, Charles Stewart
Trist, Nicholas Philip
Tudor, William
Washburn, Charles Ames
Webb, James Watson
Weddell, Alexander Wilbourne
Weitzel, George Thomas
Welles, Benjamin Sumner
West, Duval
Wheeler, John Hill
White, John Campbell
White, Robert Edward

Williamson, John Gustavus
  Adolphus
Wilson, Henry Lane
Worthington, William G. D.
Wright, Joshua Butler
Yancey, Benjamin Cudworth
Young, Pierce Manning Butler

ECONOMIC GEOLOGISTS. *See* GEOLOGISTS

ECONOMISTS

Cumberland, William Wilson
Currie, Lauchlin B(ernard)
Downing, Thomas G.
Eder, George Jackson
Edwards, James Horton
Hollander, Jacob H(arry)
Kemmerer, Edwin W(alter)
Raguet, Condy
Schurz, William L(ytle)

EDITORS. *See also* PUBLISHERS

Daniels, Josephus
Forsyth, John
Gonzales, William Elliott
Hale, Edward J(oseph)
Harris, William A(lexander)
Lowe, D. Warren
Raguet, Condy
Redpath, James
Rémy, Henry
Thrasher, John S(idney)

EDUCATORS. *See also* MISSIONARY EDUCATORS

Armstrong, Clara (Jeanette)
Bard, Harry (Erwin)
Bassett, Ebenezer Don Carlos
Boyd, Sarah M.
Brumbaugh, Martin G(rove)
Conway, Mary E(lizabeth)
Corbitt, Duvon C(lough)
Crone, Frank Linden
Dascomb, Mary P(arker)
Dexter, Edwin G(rant)

Dimitry, Alexander
Eccleston, Sarah (Emily)
  (Chamberlain)
Frye, A(lexis) E(verett)
Giesecke, Albert A(nthony)
Graham, Mary (Olstine)
Howard, Jennie E(liza)
Hunnicutt, Benjamin Harris
Illich, Ivan D.
Inman, Samuel Guy
Johnson, James Weldon
Kidder, Daniel P(arish)
Kuhl, Ella
Langston, John Mercer
Miller, Paul G(erard)
Munro, Dana G(ardner)
Myers, Phillip Van Ness
Pearson, Paul Martin
Peck, Henry Everard
Powell, William Frank
Rowe, Leo Stanton
Stearns, George Albert
Stearns, John William
Tannenbaum, Frank
Wilson, Lester Maclean
Yager, Arthur

ELECTRICAL ENGINEERS

Pearson, Fred(erick) Stark

ENGINEERS

Ashmead, Percy [Percival]
  H(erbert)
Billings, Asa White Kenney
Childs, Orville W(hitmore)
Flanagan, James W(ainwright)
Gaillard, David Dubose
Goethals, George Washington
Hallock, James C.
Harman, Archer
Hart, Francis Russell
Havens, Verne Leroy
Kingman, Lewis
Ludlow, William
McMath, Robert Emmett
Marsh, Richard O(glesby)
Morison, George Shattuck

Morton, James St. Clair
Rock, Miles
Sadler, Everit J(ay)
Schuyler, James Dix
Shunk, William F(indley)
Stevens, Walter H(usted)
Talcott, Andrew
Totten, George Muirson
Trautwine, John Cresson

ENTOMOLOGISTS

Calvert, Philip Powell
Edwards, William Henry
Pallister, John C(lare)
Townsend, Charles H(enry) T(yler)

ENTREPRENEURS. *See also* BUSINESSMEN

Farquhar, Percival
Greene, William C(ornell)
Hopkins, Edward A(ugustus)
Keith, Minor Cooper
Shepherd, Alexander R(obey)
Thompson, Ambrose W(illiam)
Valentine, Washington S(amuel)
Wheelwright, William

EPIDEMIOLOGISTS

Carter, Henry Rose

ETHNOLOGISTS. *See* ANTHROPOLOGISTS

EXPLORERS. *See also* TRAVELERS

Bennett, Robert Root
Bingham, Hiram
Cherrie, Geo(rge) K(ruck)
Church, George Earl
de Booy, Theodoor (Hendrick
  Nikolas)
Elliott, John Henry
Fiala, Anthony
Furlong, Charles Wellington
Gill, Richard C(ochran)
Heath, Edwin R.

Marsh, Richard O(glesby)
Miller, Leo Edward
Newberry, George Harkness
Orton, James
Page, Thomas Jefferson
Rice, [Alexander] Hamilton
Ricketson, Oliver (Garrison, Jr.)
Savoy, Gene
Strain, Isaac G.
Thompson, Edward H(erbert)
Von Hagen, Victor Wolfgang
Zahl, Paul A(rthur)

FILIBUSTERS

Crabb, Henry A(lexander)
Kinney, Henry L(awrence) [or
    Livingston]
Morehead, Joseph C.
Oaksmith, Appleton
Walker, William

FINANCIAL ADVISERS

Lindberg, Abram Frank
Lindberg, Irving A(ugustus)
Millspaugh, Arthur C(hester)
Renwick, William W.
Roddy, William Franklin

FINANCIERS

Garrison, Cornelius Kingsland
Groves, Wallace
Johnson, Lorenzo M(edici)
Sanford, Charles H.

FRUIT GROWERS

Lawrence, G(eorge) O(liver)
    C(rocker)

GEOGRAPHERS

Bowman, Isaiah
Brand, Donald D(ilworth)
Hanson, Earl Parker
Hegen, Edmund Eduard
James, Preston E(verett)

Jefferson, Mark (Sylvester
    William)
Jones, Clarence F(ielden)
McBride, George McC(utchen)
McBryde, F(elix) Webster
Parsons, James J(erome)
Platt, Robert Swanton
Rice, [Alexander] Hamilton
Sauer, Carl O(rtwin)

GEOLOGISTS

Bassler, Harvey
Branner, John Casper
Derby, Orville A(delbert)
Evans, John
Foshag, William Frederick
Hamilton, Charles W(alters)
Hartt, Charles Frederick
Hayes, Charles Willard
Hill, Robert T(homas)
Howe, Ernest
Liddle, Ralph Alexander
Maclure, William
Martin, F(rederick) O(skar)
Meyerhoff, Howard A(ugustus)
Mills, James E(llison)
Schott, Arthur Carl Victor
Singlewald, Joseph (Theophilus, Jr.)
Taylor, Richard Cowling
White, Israel C(harles)
Willis, Bailey
Woodring, Wendell P(hillips)

GOVERNMENT OFFICIALS. *See also*
PUBLIC OFFICIALS

Bishop, Joseph Bucklin
Colton, George R(adcliffe)
Feeley, Edward F(rancis)
Gentry, Irma Ellender
Gordon, [Abraham] Lincoln
Ham, Clifford Dudley
Hill, Robert C(harles)
Hill, Roscoe R.
Klein, Julius
Magoon, Charles E(dward)
Pulliam, William E(llis)
Thatcher, Maurice Hudson

Tugwell, Rexford G(uy)

HERPETOLOGISTS

Ditmars, Raymond Lee

HISTORIANS

Lockey, Joseph B(yrne)

HUMANITARIANS

Ryder, Jeanette (Ford)

HYDROLOGISTS

Oltman, Roy E(dwin)

ICHTHYOLOGISTS

Tee-Van, John

ILLUSTRATORS. *See also* PAINTERS

Howes, Paul G(riswold)

INDUSTRIALISTS. *See also* MANUFACTURERS

Hedges, Dayton
Ross, Roderick Malcolm
Wright, Harry

INVENTORS

Pedrick, Howard A(shley)

IRRIGATION ENGINEERS

Sutton, Charles Wood

JOURNALISTS

Bailly-Blanchard, Arthur
Beach, Moses Y(ale)
Beals, Carleton
Bishop, Joseph Bucklin
Bliss, Porter Cornelius
Bowers, Claude Gernade
Brenner, Anita
Canova, Leon J(oseph)
Clarke, George W.

Curtis, William Elroy
Davis, Richard Harding
Denny, Harold Norman [Hobbs]
Douglass, Frederick [Augustus Washington Baily]
Durham, John Stephens
Finerty, John Frederick
Grevstad, Nicolay Andreas
Gruening, Ernest (Henry)
Hassaurek, Frederick [Friedriech]
Horman, Charles (Edmund)
Irvine, Baptis
Janvier, Thomas Allibone
Jorden, William J(ohn)
Korry, Edward M(alcolm)
Matthews, Herbert L(ionel)
O'Reilly, Edward S(ynnott)
Otterbourg, Marcus
Pepper, Charles M(elville)
Phillips, Ruby Hart
Porter, Robert P(ercival)
Redpath, James
Reed, John
Scovel, Henry Sylvester
Squier, Ephraim George
Steffens, (Joseph) Lincoln
Stevens, John Leavitt
Tannenbaum, Frank
Turner, John Kenneth
Turner, Timothy G(ilman)
Webb, James Watson

JUDGES

West, Duval

LABOR OFFICIALS

Romualdi, Serafino

LAWYERS

Andrews, Christopher Columbus
Barton, Seth
Berle, Adolf Augustus
Bowlin, James Butler
Brackenridge, Henry Marie
Buck, Charles William
Bull, James H(unter)

Campbell, Lewis Davis
Christiancy, Isaac Peckham
Crosby, Elisha O(scar)
Culbertson, William S(mith)
Farrell, James Ambrose
Feuille, Frank
Forbes, John Murray
Fuller, Paul [Francisco]
Hanna, Bayliss W.
Hastings, Lansford Warren
Hilliard, Henry W(ashington)
Hise, Elijah
Hunt, William Henry
Hurlbut, Stephen Augustus
Jackson, Henry Rootes
Jones, William Carey
Judah, Noble Brandon
Lind, John
Linowitz, Sol M(yron)
Magoon, Charles E(dward)
Maney, George Earl
Mizner, Lansing Bond
Momsen, Richard P(aul)
Morgan, Philip H(ickey)
Nelson, Thomas Henry
Northcott, Elliott
O'Hara, Thomas
Osborn, Thomas Andrew
Palmer, Thomas W(averly)
Pendleton, John Strother
Prevost, John B(artow)
Reynolds, Thomas C(aute)
Robinson, Christopher
Rodney, Caesar Augustus
Rubens, Horatio (Seymour)
Schoenrich, Otto
Shannon, Richard C(utts)
Shannon, Wilson
Stimson, Frederic Jesup
Terrell, Alexander Watkins
Thompson, Waddy, Jr.
Todd, Charles Stewart
Towner, Horace M(ann)
Truslow, Francis Adams
Walker, Harold
Wheeler, John Hill
Worthington, William G. D.
Yancey, Benjamin C(udworth)

LINGUISTS

Pike, Eunice Victoria
Townsend, W(illiam) Cameron

MANUFACTURERS. *See also* INDUSTRIALISTS

Atkins, Edwin F(arnsworth)
Bagley, Melville Sewell
Johnston, Benjamin F(rancis)
Willard, Theodore A(rthur)

MARINE CORPS OFFICERS

Beadle, Elias Root
Bearss, Hiram Iddings
Butler, Smedley D(arlington)
Cole, Eli K(elley)
Craige, John H(ouston)
Elliott, George Frank
Feland, Logan
Pendleton, Joseph Henry
Russell, John Henry
Waller, Littleton W(alter) T(azewell)
Wirkus, Faustin

MATADORS

Lee, Harper B.

MEDICAL MISSIONARIES. *See also* MISSIONARIES; PHYSICIANS

Beck, Frank S(purgeon)
Behrhorst, Carroll D(ean) H(enry)
Halliwell, Leo B(lair)
Mellon, William Larimer, Jr.

MERCHANTS

Baker, Lorenzo Dow
Biddle, Charles
De Forest, David Curtis
Devereux, John
Forsyth, Samuel D(ouglas)
Hill, Henry
Horne, Charles Ridgely
Hunt, Benjamin Peter

Lowry, Robert K.
Robinson, William Davis
Ropes, Henry J.
Savage, Charles
Smith, Robert
Taber, Samuel William

METEOROLOGISTS

Bigelow, Frank Hager
Clayton, Henry Helm
Davis, Walter G(ould)
Fassig, Oliver Lanard

MILITARY ENGINEERS

Butterfield, Carlos
Hodges, Garry Foote
Sibert, William Luther

MINE OWNERS

Burns, Daniel Monroe
Dunphy, Charles
Rand, Charles Frederick

MINERALOGISTS

Bandy, Mark Chance
Gordon, Samuel George

MINING ENGINEERS

Barron, George Davis
Braden, William
Corning, Frederick Gleason
Douglas, James
Easley, George A(lbert)
Hewett, D(onnel) Foster
Martin, F(rederick) O(skar)
Newhouse, Edgar L.
Olcott, Eben(ezer) Erskine
Ricketts, Louis D(avidson)
Ross, Louis
Towne, Robert S(afford)
Yeatman, Pope

MINING EXECUTIVES

Clark, Edward Hardy

Wagner, Henry R(aup)

MINING GEOLOGISTS. *See* GEOLOGISTS

MISSIONARIES. *See also* CLERGY-MEN; MEDICAL MISSIONARIES; MISSIONARY EDUCATORS

Bach, T(homas) J(ohannes)
Bagby, William Buck
Bender, Robert H(ermann)
Bishop, Albert Edward
Blackford, Alexander Latimer
Brigham, John C(lark)
Burgess, Paul
Butler, John Wesley
Butler, William
Buyers, Paul Eugene
Case, Alden Buel
Chamberlain, George W(hitehill)
Chastain, James Garvin
Cheavans, John S(elf)
Coan, Titus
Collins, Thomas Patrick
Dale, James G(ary)
Dale, Katherine (Neel)
Danehy, Thomas Joseph
Davis, Jones Edgar
Dempster, John
Dickson, Murray
Drees, Charles W(illiam)
Eaton, James Demarest
Fletcher, James Cooley
Gammon, Samuel R(hea)
Goodfellow, William
Graybill, Anthony (Thomas)
Harrington, Francis Marion
Harris, John Will(iam)
Hart, Joseph Lancaster
Haymaker, Edward M(cIlwain)
Hickey, James
Holly, James Theodore (Augustus)
Howell, John Beatty
Jackson, Henry G.
Jones, Clarence W.
Keener, John C(hristian)
Kidder, Daniel P(arish)

Lane, Edward
Letgers, David Brainerd
McCall, Moses Nathaniel
McConnell, William W(ashington)
MacDonnell, George N(owlands)
Nelson, Erik Alfred
Newman, Junius E.
Norris, William H.
Parvin, Theophilus
Powell, William D(avid)
Pratt, Henry B(arrington)
Pressly, Neill Erskine
Purdie, Samuel A(lexander)
Rankin, Melinda
Ransom, John J(ames)
Reed, Will Eugene
Reno, Loren M(arion)
Simonton, Ashbel Green
Smith, J(ohn) Rockwell
Sowell, Sidney MacFarland
Spaulding, Justin
Stahl, Ferdinand [Fernando] A(nthony)
Strachan, R(obert) Kenneth
Tarboux, John William
Taylor, Zachary Clay
Thomas, William Matthew Merrick
Townsend, W(illiam) Cameron
Trumbull, David
Tucker, Hugh Clarence
Watson, Stephen Lawton
Wesley, Arthur (Frederick)
Westphal, Frank Henry
Winnans, Roger S.
Wood, Thomas Bond

MISSIONARY EDUCATORS. *See also* EDUCATORS; MISSIONARIES

Bardwell, Harry Brown
Graham, (Nora) Agnes
LaFetra, Ira Haynes
Lane, Horace M(anly)
Wharton, Robert Leslie

MORMON LEADERS

Ivins, Anthony W(oodward)
Pratt, Parley Parker
Pratt, Rey L(ucero)

MOUNTAIN CLIMBERS

Peck, Annie Smith

NATURALISTS

Adams, Charles Baker
Agassiz, Jean Louis Rudolphe
Barbour, Thomas
Beebe, (Charles) William
Bull, Charles Livingston
Cherrie, Geo(rge) K(ruck)
Edwards, Charles Lincoln
Gaumer, George F(ranklin)
Howes, Paul G(riswold)
Jacques, Francis Lee
Nelson, Edward W(illiam)
Smith, Herbert H(untington)
Verrill, Alpheus Hyatt
Von Hagen, Victor Wolfgang

NAVAL OFFICERS

Ammen, Daniel
Beach, Edward L(atimer)
Beluche, Renato
Butt, Walter Raleigh
Caperton, William B(anks)
Coe, John Halsted
De Kay, George Colman
Dillingham, Albert Caldwell
Fletcher, Frank Friday
Gilliss, James Melville
Herndon, William Lewis
Hollins, George Nichols
Jeffers, William Nicholson
Jewett, David
Jouett, James E(dward)
Kimball, William W(irt)
Knapp, Harry S(hepard)
Latimer, Julian L(ane)
Lull, Edward Phelps
Manton, Benjamin M.
Maury, Matthew Fontaine
Oliver, James H(arrison)
O'Neil, Charles
Osbon, Bradley Sillick
Page, Thomas Jefferson
Paulding, Hiram

Phelps, Seth Ledyard
Porter, David
Revere, Joseph Warren
Rochelle, James Henry
Selfridge, Thomas Oliver
Shubrick, William B(ranford)
Snowden, Thomas
Spears, William O(scar)
Strain, Isaac G.
Taffinder, Sherwoode Ayerst
Thorne, John
Tucker, John Randolph
Vogelgesang, Carl Theodore
Walker, John Grimes
Woodward, Clark H.
Wooster, Charles Whiting
Wright, William Charles

ORNITHOLOGISTS

Bond, James
Carikker, Melbourne A(rmstrong), Jr.
Chapman, Frank M(ichler)
Cory, Charles B(arney)
Griscom, Ludlow
Hartley, G(eorge) Inness
Holt, Ernest G(oslan)
Murphy, Robert Cushman
Ober, Frederick Albion
Ridgway, Robert
Skutch, Alexander F(rank)
Sutton, George Miksch

PAINTERS. *See also* ARTISTS; ILLUSTRATORS

Bush, Norton
Catlin, George
Chapman, Conrad Wise
Church, Frederick Edwin
Drexel, Francis Martin
Gaul, (William) Gilbert
Hartley, G(eorge) Inness
Heade, Martin Johnson
Homer, Winslow
Mignot, Louis Remy
Turner, Ross Sterling

PALEONTOLOGISTS

Gabb, William M(ore)

Hartt, Charles Frederick
Hatcher, John Bell
Loomis, Frederic B(rewster)
Martin, Handel T(ongue)
Riggs, Elmer S(amuel)
Simpson, George Gaylord
Stirton, Ruben Arthur
Woodring, Wendell P(hillips)

PATHOLOGISTS

Clark, Herbert Charles
Ricketts, Howard Taylor

PETROLEUM EXECUTIVES

Buckley, William F(rank), Sr.
Hamilton, Charles W(alter)
Jarvis, Harry A(ydelotte)
Proudfit, Arthur

PETROLEUM GEOLOGISTS

Arnold, Ralph
DeGolyer, Everette Lee
Dickerson, Roy E(rnest)
Hamilton, Charles W(alter)
Harrington, George Leavitt
Hatfield, Willis Charles
Hedberg, Hollis D(ow)
Hopkins, Edwin Butcher
McArthur, Donald
Macready, George Alexander
Palmer, Robert Hastings
Wasson, Theron
Weaver, Paul

PETROLEUM PRODUCERS

Benedum, M(ichael) L(ate)
Canfield, C(harles) A(delbert)
Doheny, Edward L(awrence)
Gibson, Addison H(oward)
Tweddle, Herbert W(ilkin) C(olguhoun)
Wylie, Herbert G(eorge)

PHARMACISTS

Heyl, James B(ell)

PHOTOGRAPHERS

Aultman, Otis
Fredericks, Charles De Forest
Heyl, James B(ell)
Moulton, Henry De Witt
Muybridge, Eadweard
Pease, Benjamin F(ranklin)
Seager, D. W.
Strand, Paul
Weston, Edward
Zahl, Paul A(rthur)

PHYSICIANS. See also MEDICAL MISSIONARIES

Ashford, Bailey Kelly
Baldwin, William
Barnsley, George S(carborough)
Bush, Ira (Jefferson)
Converse, George M(arquis)
Corrigan, Frank [Francis] Patrick
Forsyth, Samuel D(ouglas)
Furniss, Henry W(atson)
Galt, Francis Land
Gaston, James McFadden
Heath, Edwin R.
Hogan, James
Horner, (Gustavus) R(ichard) B(rown)
Husk, Charles [Carlos] Ellsworth
James, W(illiam) Mc(Cully)
Jefferson, Benjamin Lafayette
Logan, Cornelius Ambrose
Price, Henry Manroe
Rawson, Aman
Redhead, Joseph James Thomas
Root, Joseph Pomeroy
Van Patten, Charles Hansen

PIANISTS

Gottschalk, Louis Moreau

PLANT EXPLORERS

Perrine, Henry
Popenoe, F(rederick) Wilson
Pringle, Cyrus Guernsey
Wright, Charles

PLANT PATHOLOGISTS

Borlaug, Nelson E(rnest)
Orton, William A(llen)
Rupert, Joseph Anthony
Weir, James R(obert)

PLANTERS

Baker, Lorenzo Dow

PREACHERS. See also CLERGYMEN

Liele [or Lisle], George

PRINTERS

Johnston, Samuel B(urr)
Wells, Thomas

PRIVATEERS

Beluche, Renato

PROSPECTORS

Pedrick, Howard A(shley)

PUBLIC HEALTH OFFICIALS. See also SANITARIANS

Hanson, Henry
LePrince, Joseph Albert Augustin
Lloyd, Bolivar Jones
Soper, Fred L(owe)

PUBLIC OFFICIALS. See also GOVERNMENT OFFICIALS

Allen, Heman
Baylies, Francis
Bland, Theodorick
Borland, Solon
Brackenridge, Henry Marie
Bragg, Edward S(tuyvesant)
Churchwell, William M(ontgomery)
Clark, J(oshua) Reuben, Jr.
Clayton, Powell
Cooper, Prentice (William), Jr.
Corwin, Thomas
Crittenden, Thomas Theodore

del Valle, Reginaldo Francisco
Foster, John Watson
Gruening, Ernest (Henry)
Harrison, William Henry
Hoevel, Mathew Arnold
Hunter, William, Jr.
Irvine, Baptis
Jarvis, Thomas Jordan
Kirk, Robert C.
Lamar, Mirabeau Buonaparte
Lind, John
Moore, Thomas Patrick
Morrison, Delesseps S(tory)
Murray, William H(enry) D(avid)
O'Dwyer, William
Poindexter, Miles
Price, Sterling
Rockefeller, Nelson A(ldrich)
Roosevelt, Theodore
Stuart, Granville

PUBLICISTS

Howland, Edward
Howland, Marie Stevens Case

PUBLISHERS

Carleton, George Washington
Gonzales, William Elliott
Hallet, Stephen
Hazard, Samuel
Hoevel, Mathew Arnold
Markbreit, Leopold

RAILROAD BUILDERS

Brown, Edward Norphelt
Harrah, Charles Jefferson
Keith, Minor Cooper
Meiggs, Henry
Palmer, William Jackson
Plumb, Edward Lee
Stilwell, Arthur E(dward)

RUBBER CUTTERS

Yungjohann, John C(hristian)

SANITARIANS. *See also* PUBLIC HEALTH OFFICIALS

Carter, Henry Rose
Gorgas, William Crawford

SCIENTISTS

Scovell, Josiah Thomas

SEA CAPTAINS

Baker, Lorenzo Dow
Chayter, James
Delano, Paul
Fry, Joseph
Merry, William Lawrence
Shaler, William

SHIPPING EXECUTIVES

Lykes, Frederick Eugene

SILVERSMITHS

Spratling, William Philip

SOCIOLOGISTS

Biesanz, John Berry
Nelson, Lowry
Pierson, Donald
Simpson, George Eaton

SOIL SCIENTISTS

Marbut, C(urtis) F(letcher)

SOLDIERS. *See also* ARMY OFFICERS

Barnard, John Gross
Bean, Ellis P(eter)
Crittenden, William Logan
Danells [or Danels], John Daniel
Davis, George Whitefield
Green, George Mason
Henningsen, Charles Frederick
Macauley, Alexander
McMahon, Martin T(homas)
Macomb, Montgomery Meigs

Morgan, William A(lexander)
Shanton, George Reynolds
Sobiesky, John
Villamil, Joseph [José] M.
Wheat, Chatam Roberdeau

SOLDIERS OF FORTUNE

Christmas, Lee
Dreben, Sam
Ingraham, Prentiss
King, J(ohn) Anthony
Lamb, Dean Ivan
O'Reilly, Edward S(ynnott)
Richardson, Tracy
Ryan, William Albert Charles

SURGEONS. *See* PHYSICIANS

SURVEYERS

Anderson, William Marshall
Birbeck, Samuel Braford

TAXIDERMISTS

Batty, Joseph H.
Bull, Charles Livingston

TELEPHONE EXECUTIVES

Vail, Theodore N(ewton)

TRAVELERS. *See also* EXPLORERS

Bull, James H(unter)
Curtis, William Elroy
Flandrau, Charles Macomb
Franck, Harry (Alverson)
Hale, Albert (Barlow)
Hardenburg, Walter Ernest
Hart, Jeanette
Holton, Isaac F(arwell)
Norman, Benjamin Moore
Smith, Edmond Reuel
Smith, Josiah
Stephens, John Lloyd
Warren, John Esaias

VOLCANOLOGISTS

Perret, Frank Alvord

ZOOLOGISTS

Bates, Marston
Eigenmann, Carl H.
Goldman, Edward Alphonso
Nutting, Charles Cleveland
Orton, James
Verrill, Addison Emery

Bibliographical Essay

Reviews of the literature on U.S. relations with Latin America can be found in the following articles: Stephen G. Rabe, "Marching Ahead (Slowly): The Historiography of Inter-American Relations," *Diplomatic History* 13 (1989): 297–316; Richard M. Abrams, "United States Intervention Abroad: The First Quarter Century," *American Historical Review* 79 (1974): 72–102; Gordon Connell-Smith, "Latin America in the Foreign Relations of the United States," *Journal of Latin American Studies* 8 (1976): 137–50; Jorge I. Dominguez, "Consensus and Divergence: The State of the Literature on Inter-American Relations in the 1970s," *Latin American Research Review* 13 (1978): 87–126; Steven W. Hughes and Kenneth J. Mijeski, "Contemporary Paradigms in the Study of Inter-American Relations," in *Latin America, the United States, and the Inter-American System*, ed. John Martz and Lars Schoultz (Boulder, Colo., 1980), pp. 19–43; Abraham F. Lowenthal, "United States Policy toward Latin America: 'Liberal,' 'Radical,' and 'Bureaucratic' Perspectives," *Latin American Research Review* 8 (1973): 3–25; Louis A. Pérez, Jr., "Intervention, Hegemony, and Dependency: The United States in the Circum-Caribbean, 1898–1980," *Pacific Historical Review* 51 (1982): 165–94; David M. Pletcher, "United States Relations with Latin America: Neighborliness and Exploitation," *American Historical Review* 82 (1977): 39–59; Richard V. Salisbury, "Good Neighbors? The United States and Latin America in the Twentieth Century," in *American Foreign Relations: A Historiographical Review*, ed. Gerald K. Haines and J. Samuel Walker (Westport, Conn., 1981), 311–33; and Roger R. Trask, "Inter-American Relations," in *Latin American Scholarship since World War II*, ed. Roberto Esquenazi-Mayo and Michael C. Meyer (Lincoln, Nebr., 1971), pp. 203–21

Comprehensive bibliographies include Richard D. Burns, ed., *Guide to American Foreign Relations Since 1700* (Santa Barbara, Calif.: ABC-Clio, 1983), chs. 7, 9, 13, 15, 34, and 35; David F. Trask, Michael C. Meyer, and Roger R. Trask, comps. and eds., *A Bibliography of United States–Latin American Relations since 1810: A Selected List of Eleven Thousand Published References* (Lincoln: University of Nebraska Press, 1968); and Michael C. Meyer, comp. and ed., *Supplement to a Bibliography of United States–Latin American Relations since 1810* (Lincoln: University of Nebraska Press, 1979). Doctoral dissertations are listed in Carl A. Hanson, *Dissertations on Iberian and Latin American History* (Troy, N.Y.: Whitston Pub. Co., 1975); and Carl W. Dean, *Latin America and the Caribbean: A Dissertation Bibliography* (Ann Arbor, Mich.: University Microfilms International, 1978).

General surveys of U.S. relations with Latin America include Samuel Flagg Bemis, *The Latin American Policy of the United States: An Historical Interpretation* (New York: Harcourt, Brace, 1943); Edwin Lieuwen, *U.S. Policy in Latin America: A Short History* (New York: Praeger, 1965); Edwin Lieuwen, *The United States and the Challenge to Security in Latin America* (Columbus: Ohio State University Press, 1966), Gordon Connell-Smith, *The United States and Latin America* (New York: Wiley, 1974); Federico G. Gil, *Latin America–United States Relations* (New York: Harcourt Brace Jovanovich, 1971); J. Lloyd Mecham, *A Survey of United States–Latin American Relations* (Boston: Houghton Mifflin, 1965); John D. Martz and Lars Schoultz, eds., *Latin America, the United States, and the Inter-American System* (Boulder, Colo.: Westview Press, 1980); Dock Steward, *Money, Marines, and Mission: Recent U.S.–Latin American Policy* (Lanham, Md.: University Press of America, 1980); Margaret D. Hayes, *Latin America and the U.S. National Interest: A Basis for U.S. Foreign Policy* (Boulder, Colo.: Westview Press, 1984); Lester D. Langley, *America and the Americas: The United States in the Western Hemisphere* (Athens: University of Georgia Press, 1989); Michael J. Kryzanek, *U.S.–Latin American Relations* (New York: Praeger, 1990); John J. Johnson, *A Hemisphere Apart: The Foundations of United States Policy toward Latin America* (Baltimore: Johns Hopkins University Press, 1990); Abraham F. Lowenthal, *Exporting Democracy: The United States and Latin America* (Baltimore: Johns Hopkins University Press, 1991); James N. Cortada and James W. Cortada, *U.S. Foreign Policy in the Caribbean, Cuba, and Central America* (New York: Praeger, 1985); and Lars Schoultz, *National Security and United States Policy toward Latin America* (Princeton, N.J.: Princeton University Press, 1987).

Dealing with specific periods are Harry Bernstein, *Origins of Inter-American Interest, 1700–1812* (Philadelphia: University of Pennsylvania Press, 1945); Harry Bernstein, *Making an Inter-American Mind* (Gainesville: University of Florida Press, 1961); T. Ray Shurbutt, ed., *United States–Latin American Relations, 1800–1850: The Formative Generations* (Tuscaloosa: University of Alabama Press, 1991); Charles C. Griffin, *The United States and the Disruption of the Spanish Empire, 1810–1822: A Study of the Relations of the United States with Spain and with the Rebel Spanish Colonies* (New York: Columbia University Press, 1937); Arthur P. Whitaker, *The United States and the Independence of Latin America, 1800–1830* (Baltimore: Johns Hopkins University Press, 1941); Edward B. Billingsley, *In Defense of Neutral Rights: The United States Navy and the Wars of Independence in Chile and Peru* (Chapel Hill: University of North Carolina Press, 1967); Robert E. May, *The Southern Dream of a Caribbean Empire, 1854–1861* (Baton Rouge: Louisiana State University Press, 1973); Charles H. Brown, *Agents of Manifest Destiny: The Lives and Times of the Filibusters* (Chapel Hill: University of North Carolina Press, 1980); Joseph Smith, *Illusions of Conflict: Anglo-American Diplomacy toward Latin America, 1865–1896* (Pittsburgh: University of Pittsburgh Press, 1979); J. Lloyd Mecham, *The United States and Inter-American Security, 1889–1960* (Austin: University of Texas Press, 1961); Cole Blasier, *The Hovering Giant: U.S. Responses to Revolutionary Change in Latin America* (Pittsburgh: University of Pittsburgh Press, 1976); George C. Lodge, *Engines of Change: United States Interests and Revolution in Latin America* (New York: Knopf, 1970); Mark T. Gilderhus, *Pan American Visions: Woodrow Wilson in the Western Hemisphere, 1913–1921* (Tucson: University of Arizona Press, 1986); Joseph S. Tulchin, *The Aftermath of War: World War I and United States Policy toward Latin America* (New York: New York University Press, 1971); Kenneth J. Grieb, *The Latin American Policy of Warren G. Harding* (Fort Worth: Texas Christian University Press, 1977); Alexander

DeConde, *Herbert Hoover's Latin American Policy* (Stanford, Calif.: Stanford University Press, 1951); Donald M. Dozer, *Are We Good Neighbors? Three Decades of Inter-American Relations, 1930–1960* (Gainesville: University of Florida Press, 1959); Irwin F. Gellman, *Good Neighbor Diplomacy: The United States in Latin America 1933–1945* (Baltimore: Johns Hopkins University Press, 1979); David Green, *The Containment of Latin America: A History of the Myths and Realities of the Good Neighbor Policy* (Chicago: Quadrangle Books, 1971); Edward O. Guerrant, *Roosevelt's Good Neighbor Policy* (Albuquerque: University of New Mexico Press, 1950); Bryce Wood, *The Making of the Good Neighbor Policy* (New York: Columbia University Press, 1961); Bryce Wood, *The Dismantling of the Good Neighbor Policy* (Austin: University of Texas Press, 1985); David Haglund, *Latin America and the Transformation of U.S. Strategic Thought, 1936–1940* (Albuquerque: University of New Mexico Press, 1984); J. Manuel Espinosa, *Inter-American Beginnings of U.S. Cultural Diplomacy, 1936–1948* (Washington, D.C.: U.S. Department of State, Bureau of Educational and Cultural Affairs, 1976); John Child, *Unequal Alliance: The Inter-American Military System, 1938–1979* (Boulder, Colo.: Westview Press, 1980); Gary Frank, *Struggle for Hegemony in South America: Argentina, Brazil and the United States during the Second World War* (Coral Gables, Fla.: Center for Advanced International Studies, University of Miami, 1979); Michael J. Francis, *The Limits of Hegemony: United States Relations with Argentina and Chile during World War II* (Notre Dame, Ind.: University of Notre Dame Press, 1977); Samuel L. Baily, *The United States and the Development of South America, 1945–1975* (New York: New Viewpoints, 1976); Stephen G. Rabe, *Eisenhower and Latin America: The Foreign Policy of Anticommunism* (Chapel Hill: University of North Carolina Press, 1988); John D. Martz, ed. *United States Policy in Latin America: A Quarter Century of Crisis and Challenge, 1961–1986* (Lincoln: University of Nebraska Press, 1988); Thomas Carothers, *In the Name of Democracy: U.S. Policy toward Latin America in the Reagan Years* (Berkeley: University of California Press, 1991); Abraham F. Lowenthal, *Partners in Conflict: The United States and Latin America in the 1990s* (Baltimore: Johns Hopkins University Press, 1990); Robert Wesson, ed., *U.S. Influence in Latin America in the 1980s* (New York: Praeger, 1982); and Kevin J. Middlebrook and Carlos Rico, eds., *The United States and Latin America in the 1980's: Contending Perspectives on a Decade of Crisis* (Pittsburgh: University of Pittsburgh Press, 1986).

Studies of U.S. relations with specific regions and countries of Latin America include: *Caribbean*: George C. Calcott, *The Caribbean Policy of the United States, 1890–1920* (Baltimore: Johns Hopkins University Press, 1942); Richard H. Collin, *Theodore Roosevelt's Caribbean: The Panama Canal, the Monroe Doctrine, and the Latin American Context* (Baton Rouge: Louisiana State University Press, 1990); Robert D. Crassweller, *The Caribbean Community: Changing Societies and U.S. Policy* (New York: Praeger, 1972); Carmen D. Deere et al., *In the Shadows of the Sun: Caribbean Development Alternatives and U.S. Policy* (Boulder, Colo.: Westview Press, 1990); Lester D. Langley, *The Banana Wars: An Inner History of American Empire, 1900–1934* (Lexington, Ky.: University Press of Kentucky, 1983); Lester D. Langley, *Struggle for the American Mediterranean: United States–European Rivalry in the Gulf-Caribbean, 1776–1904* (Athens: University of Georgia Press, 1976); Lester D. Langley, *The United States and the Caribbean in the Twentieth Century* (Athens: University of Georgia Press, 1989); John B. Martin, *United States Policy in the Caribbean* (Boulder, Colo.: Westview Press, 1982); Dana G. Munro, *The United States and the Caribbean Republics, 1921–1933* (Princeton, N.J.: Princeton University Press, 1974); Ivan Musicant, *The Banana Wars:*

A History of United States Military Intervention in Latin America from the Spanish-American War to the Invasion of Panama (New York: Macmillan, 1990); Dexter Perkins, *The United States and the Caribbean* (Cambridge, Mass.: Harvard University Press, 1947); Whitney T. Perkins, *Constraints of Empire: The United States and Caribbean Interventions* (Westport, Conn.: Greenwood Press, 1981); and Donald A. Yerxa, *Admirals and Empire: The United States Navy and the Caribbean 1898–1945* (Columbia: University of South Carolina Press, 1991).

Central America: George Black, *The Good Neighbor: How the U.S. Wrote the History of Central America and the Caribbean* (New York: Pantheon, 1988); Roger Burbach and Patricia Flynn, eds., *The Politics of Intervention: The United States in Central America* (New York: Monthly Review, 1984); Don L. Etchison, *The United States and Militarism in Central America* (New York: Praeger, 1975); Jonathan Feldman, *Universities in the Business of Repression: The Academic-Industrial-Military-Complex and Central America* (Boston: South End Press, 1989); John Findling, *Close Neighbors, Distant Friends: United States–Central American Relations* (Westport, Conn.: Greenwood Press, 1987); Rachel Garst and Tom Barry, *Feeding the Crisis: U.S. Food Aid and Farm Policy in Central America* (Lincoln: University of Nebraska Press, 1990); Eugene R. Huck and Edward H. Moseley, eds., *Militarists, Merchants and Missionaries: United States Expansion in Middle America* (University: University of Alabama Press, 1970); Walter LaFeber, *Inevitable Revolutions: The United States in Central America* (New York: W. W. Norton, 1984); Thomas M. Leonard, *Central America and the United States: The Search for Stability* (Athens: University of Georgia Press, 1991); Thomas M. Leonard, *Central America and United States Policies, 1820s–1980s: A Guide to Issues and References* (Claremont, Calif.: Regina Books, 1985); Thomas M. Leonard, *The United States and Central America, 1944–1949: Perceptions of Political Dynamics* (University: University of Alabama Press, 1984); Douglas V. Porpora, *How Holocausts Happen: The United States in Central America* (Philadelphia: Temple University Press, 1990); Richard V. Salisbury, *Anti-Imperialism and International Competition in Central America, 1920–1929* (Wilmington, Del.: SR Books, 1988); and Washington Office on Latin America, *Police Aid and Political Will: U.S. Policy in El Salvador and Honduras (1962–1987)* (Washington, D.C.: Washington Office on Latin America, 1987).

South America: Frederick B. Pike, *The United States and the Andean Republics: Peru, Bolivia, and Ecuador* (Cambridge, Mass.: Harvard University Press, 1977); Arthur P. Whitaker, *The United States and South America, the Northern Republics* (Cambridge, Mass.: Harvard University Press, 1948); and Arthur P. Whitaker, *The United States and the Southern Cone: Argentina, Chile and Uruguay* (Cambridge, Mass.: Harvard University Press, 1976).

Argentina: E. Bradford Burns, *The Unwritten Alliance: Rio Branco and Brazilian-American Relations* (New York: Columbia University Press, 1966); Charles W. Drees, ed., *Americans in Argentina: A Record of Past & Present Activities of Americans in Argentina: Rodney to Riddle* (Buenos Aires: Coni Press, 1922); M. Falcoff, *A Tale of Two Policies: US Relations with the Argentina Junta, 1976–83* (Philadelphia: Foreign Policy Research Institute, 1989); Gary Frank, *Juan Peron vs. Spruille Braden* (Lanham, Md.: University Press of America, 1980); Clarence H. Haring, *Argentina and the United States* (Boston: World Peace Foundation, 1941); Harold F. Peterson, *Argentina and the United States, 1810–1960* (Albany: State University of New York Press, 1964); O. Edmund Smith, *Yankee Diplomacy: U.S. Intervention in Argentina* (Dallas: Southern Methodist University Press, 1953); Joseph S. Tulchin, *Argentina and the United States:*

A Conflicted Relationship (Boston: Twayne Publishers, 1990); Arthur P. Whitaker, *The United States and Argentina* (Cambridge, Mass.: Harvard University Press, 1954); and Randall B. Woods, *The Roosevelt Foreign-Policy Establishment and the "Good Neighbor": The United States and Argentina, 1941–1945* (Lawrence: Regents Press of Kansas, 1979).

Bolivia: James W. Wilkie, *The Bolivian Revolution and U.S. Aid since 1952: Financial Background and Context of Political Decisions* (Los Angeles: Latin American Center, University of California, 1969).

Brazil: Jan K. Black, *United States Penetration of Brazil* (Philadelphia: University of Pennsylvania Press, 1977); Roger W. Fontaine, *Brazil and the United States: Toward a Maturing Relationship* (Washington, D.C.: American Enterprise Institute for Public Policy Research, 1974); Gerald K. Haines, *The Americanization of Brazil: A Study of U.S. Cold War Diplomacy in the Third World, 1945–1954* (Wilmington, Del.: SR Books, 1989); Lawrence F. Hill, *Diplomatic Relations between the United States and Brazil* (Durham, N.C.: Duke University Press, 1932); Ruth Leacock, *Requiem for Revolution: The United States and Brazil, 1961–1969* (Kent, Ohio: Kent State University Press, 1990); Frank D. McCann, Jr., *The Brazilian-American Alliance, 1937–1945* (Princeton, N.J.: Princeton University Press, 1974); and Robert Wesson, *The United States and Brazil: Limits of Influence* (New York: Praeger, 1981).

Chile: Henry C. Evans, *Chile and Its Relations with the United States* (Durham, N.C.: Duke University Press, 1927); F. Petras and Morris Morley, *The United States and Chile: Imperialism and the Overthrow of the Allende Government* (New York: Monthly Review Press, 1975); Frederick B. Pike, *Chile and the United States, 1880–1962: The Emergence of Chile's Social Crisis and the Challenge to United States Diplomacy* (Notre Dame, Ind.: University of Notre Dame Press, 1963); William F. Sater, *Chile and the United States: Empires in Conflict* (Athens: University of Georgia Press, 1990); and William R. Sherman, *The Diplomatic and Commercial Relations of the United States and Chile, 1882–1914* (Boston: Badger, 1926).

Colombia: Richard L. Lael, *Arrogant Diplomacy: U.S. Policy Toward Colombia, 1903–1922* (Wilmington, Del.: Scholarly Resources, 1987); E. Taylor Parks, *Colombia and the United States, 1765–1934* (Durham, N.C.: Duke University Press, 1935); and Stephen J. Randall, *The Diplomacy of Modernization: Colombian-American Relations, 1920–1940* (Toronto: University of Toronto Press, 1977).

Costa Rica: Anita Gregorio Murchie, *Imported Spices: A Study of Anglo-American Settlers in Costa Rica, 1821–1900* (San Jose: Ministerio de Cultura, Juventud y Deportes, Direccion de Publicaciones, 1981).

Cuba: Lynn D. Bender, *The Politics of Hostility: Castro's Revolution and U.S. Policy* (San Juan, P.R.: Inter American University Press, 1975); Jules R. Benjamin, *The United States and Cuba: Hegemony and Dependent Development, 1880–1934* (Pittsburgh: University of Pittsburgh Press, 1977); Jules R. Benjamin, *The United States and the Origins of the Cuban Revolution: An Empire of Liberty in an Age of National Liberation* (Princeton, N.J.: Princeton University Press, 1990); Philip W. Bonsal, *Cuba, Castro, and the United States* (Pittsburgh: University of Pittsburgh Press, 1971); Philip Brenner, *From Confrontation to Negotiation: U.S. Relations with Cuba* (Boulder, Colo.: Westview Press, 1988); Robert D. Crassweller, *Cuba and the United States: The Tangled Relationship* (New York: Foreign Policy Association, 1971); Philip S. Foner, *A History of Cuba and Its Relations with the United States* (New York: International Publishers, 1962–1963); Irwin F. Gellman, *Roosevelt and Batista: Good Neighbor Diplomacy in Cuba, 1933–*

1945 (Albuquerque, N.M.: University of New Mexico Press, 1973); David Healy, *The United States in Cuba: 1898–1902* (Madison: University of Wisconsin Press, 1963); Lester D. Langley, *The Cuban Policy of the United States: A Brief History* (New York: Wiley, 1968); Michael J. Mazarr, *Semper Fidel: America and Cuba, 1776–1988* (Baltimore: Nautical & Aviation Pub. Co. of America, 1988); Allan R. Millett, *The Politics of Intervention: Military Occupation of Cuba, 1906–1909* (Columbus: Ohio State University Press, 1968); Morris H. Morley, *Imperial State and Revolution: The United States and Cuba, 1952–1986* (Urbana: University of Illinois Press, 1987); Louis A. Pérez, Jr., *Cuba and the United States: Ties of Singular Intimacy* (Athens: University of Georgia Press, 1990); Louis A. Pérez, Jr., *Cuba under the Platt Amendment, 1902–1934* (Pittsburgh: University of Pittsburgh Press, 1986); Louis A. Pérez, Jr., *Intervention, Revolution, and Politics in Cuba, 1913–1921* (Pittsburgh: University of Pittsburgh Press, 1978); John Plank, ed., *Cuba and the United States: Long-Range Perspective* (Washington, D.C.: Brookings Institution, 1967); Basil Rauch, *American Interests in Cuba, 1848–1855* (New York: Columbia University Press, 1948); Robert F. Smith, *The United States and Cuba: Business and Diplomacy, 1917–1960* (New York: Bookman Associates, 1960); Wayne S. Smith and Esteban Morales Domínguez, eds., *Subject to Solution: Problems in Cuban–U.S. Relations* (Boulder, Colo.: L. Rienner, 1988); and Richard Welch, Jr., *Response to Revolution: The United States and the Cuban Revolution, 1959–1961* (Chapel Hill: University of North Carolina Press, 1985).

Dominican Republic: G. Pope Atkins and Larman C. Wilson, *The United States and the Trujillo Regime* (New Brunswick, N.J.: Rutgers University Press, 1972); Bruce J. Calder, *The Impact of Intervention: The Dominican Republic during the U.S. Occupation of 1916–1924* (Austin: University of Texas Press, 1984); Earl R. Curry, *Hoover's Dominican Diplomacy and the Origins of the Good Neighbor Policy* (New York: Garland Pub., 1979); and Charles C. Tansill, *The United States and Santo Domingo, 1789–1866: A Chapter in Caribbean Diplomacy* (Baltimore: Johns Hopkins University Press, 1938).

Guatemala: Piero Gleijeses, *Shattered Hope: The Guatemalan Revolution and the United States, 1944–1954* (Princeton, N.J.: Princeton University Press, 1991); and *Report on Guatemala: Findings of the Study Group on United States–Guatemalan Relations* (Boulder, Colo.: Westview Press, with Johns Hopkins University, Foreign Policy Institute, School of Advanced Studies, 1985).

Haiti: David Healy, *Gunboat Diplomacy in the Wilson Era: The U.S. Navy in Haiti, 1915–1916* (Madison: University of Wisconsin Press, 1971); Alfred N. Hunt, *Haiti's Influence on Antebellum America: Slumbering Volcano in the Caribbean* (Baton Rouge: Louisiana State University Press, 1988); Rayford W. Logan, *The Diplomatic Relations of the United States with Haiti, 1776–1891* (Chapel Hill: University of North Carolina Press, 1941); and Ludwell L. Montague, *Haiti and the United States, 1714–1938* (Durham, N.C.: Duke University Press, 1940).

Honduras: Richard Lapper and James Painter, *Honduras, State for Sale* (London: Latin America Bureau, 1985); and Fred Shepherd, *From Banana Cases to Contra Bases: A Chronology of U.S.-Honduran Relations, Jan. 1977 to July 1986* (Washington, D.C.: Georgetown University, Central American Historical Institute, Intercultural Center, 1986).

Mexico: James M. Callahan, *American Foreign Policy in Mexican Relations* (New York: Macmillan, 1932); Clarence C. Clendenen, *Blood on the Border: The United States Army and the Mexican Irregulars* (New York: Macmillan, 1969); Clarence C. Clendenen, *The United States and Pancho Villa: A Study in Unconventional Diplomacy* (Ithaca, N.Y.:

Cornell University Press, 1961); Howard F. Cline, *The United States and Mexico* (Cambridge, Mass.: Harvard University Press, 1958); Don M. Coerver and Linda B. Hall, *Texas and the Mexican Revolution: A Study in State and National Policy* (San Antonio, Tex.: Trinity University Press, 1984); Jules Davids, *American Political and Economic Penetration of Mexico, 1877–1920* (New York: Arno Press, 1976); Richard D. Erb and Stanley R. Ross, eds., *United States Relations with Mexico: Context and Content* (Washington, D.C.: American Enterprise Institute, 1981); Mark T. Gilderhouse, *Diplomacy and Revolution: U.S.–Mexican Relations under Wilson and Carranza* (Tucson: University of Arizona Press, 1977); George W. Grayson, *The United States and Mexico: Patterns of Influence* (New York: Praeger, 1984); Kenneth J. Grieb, *The United States and Huerta* (Lincoln: University of Nebraska Press, 1969); P. Edward Haley, *Revolution and Intervention: The Diplomacy of Taft and Wilson with Mexico, 1910–1917* (Cambridge, Mass.: M.I.T. Press, 1970); Linda B. Hall and Don M. Coerver, *Revolution on the Border: The United States and Mexico, 1910–1920* (Albuquerque: University of New Mexico Press, 1988); Gene Z. Hanrahan, *The Bad Yankee—El Peligro Yankee: American Entrepreneurs and Financiers in Mexico* (Chapel Hill, N.C.: Documentary Publications, 1985); Larry D. Hill, *Emissaries to a Revolution: Woodrow Wilson's Executive Agents to Mexico* (Baton Rouge, La.: Louisiana State University Press, 1973); Daniel James, *Mexico and the Americans* (New York: Praeger, 1963); Gilbert M. Joseph, *Revolution from Without: Yucatan, Mexico, and the United States, 1880–1924* (Cambridge: Cambridge University Press, 1982); Lester D. Langley, *MexAmerican: Two Countries, One Future* (New York: Crown, 1988); Robert R. Miller, *Arms across the Border: United States Aid to Juarez during the French Intervention* (Philadelphia: American Philosophical Society, 1973); Donathon C. Olliff, *Reforma Mexico and the United States: A Search for Alternatives to Annexation, 1854–1861* (University: University of Alabama Press, 1981); Robert A. Pastor and Jorge G. Castañeda, *Limits of Friendship: The United States and Mexico* (New York: Knopf, 1988); Susan K. Purcell, ed., *Mexico–United States Relations* (New York: Praeger, 1981); Clark W. Reynolds and Carlos Tello, eds., *U.S.–Mexico Relations: Economic and Social Aspects* (Stanford, Calif.: Stanford University Press, 1983); J. Fred Rippy, *The United States and Mexico* (New York: Knopf, 1931); Riordan Roett, ed., *Mexico and the United States: Managing the Relationship* (Boulder, Colo.: Westview Press, 1988); Stanley R. Ross, ed., *Views across the Border: The United States and Mexico* (Albuquerque: University of New Mexico Press, 1978); Karl M. Schmitt, *Mexico and the United States, 1821–1973: Conflict and Coexistence* (New York: Wiley, 1974); Thomas D. Schoonover, *Dollars over Dominion: The Triumph of Liberalism in Mexican–United States Relations, 1861–1867* (Baton Rouge: Louisiana State University Press, 1978); Robert J. Shafer and Donald Mobry, *Neighbors—Mexico and the United States Wetbacks and Oil* (Chicago: Nelson-Hall, 1981); Robert F. Smith, *The United States and Revolutionary Nationalism in Mexico, 1916–1932* (Chicago: University of Chicago Press, 1972); Sidney Weintraub, *A Marriage of Convenience: Relations between Mexico and the United States* (New York: Oxford University Press, 1990); and Josefina Zoraida Vazques and Lorenzo Meyer, *The United States and Mexico* (Chicago: University of Chicago Press, 1985).

Nicaragua: Karl Berman, *Under the Big Stick: Nicaragua and the United States since 1848* (Boston: South End, 1986); Lejeune Cummins, *Quijote on a Burro: Sandino and the Marines, a Study in the Formation of Foreign Policy* (Mexico: La Impresora Azteca, 1958); Craig L. Dozier, *Nicaragua's Mosquito Shore: The Years of British and American Presence* (University: University of Alabama Press, 1985); William Kamman, *A Search for Stability: U.S. Diplomacy toward Nicaragua, 1925–1933* (Notre Dame, Ind.: University of Notre Dame Press, 1983); Robert A. Pastor, *Condemned to Repetition: The United States and Nicaragua* (Princeton, N.J.: Princeton University Press, 1988); and Robert F. Turner, *Nicaragua v. United States: A Look at the Facts* (Washington, D.C.: Pergamon-Brassey's, 1987).

Panama: Lawrence O. Early, *Yanqui Politics and the Isthmian Canal* (University Park: Pennsylvania State University Press, 1971); David N. Farnsworth and James W. McKinney, *U.S.–Panama Relations, 1903–1978* (Boulder, Colo.: Westview Press, 1983); J. Michael Hogan, *The Panama Canal in American Politics: Domestic Advocacy and the Evolution of Policy* (Carbondale: Southern Illinois University Press, 1986); and Walter LaFeber, *The Panama Canal: The Crisis in Historical Perspective* (New York: Oxford University Press, 1989).

Paraguay: Michael Grow, *The Good Neighbor Policy and Authoritarianism in Paraguay* (Lawrence: Regents Press of Kansas, 1981).

Peru: James C. Carey, *Peru and the United States, 1900–1962* (Notre Dame, Ind.: University of Notre Dame Press, 1964); Jessica P. Einhorn, *Expropriation Politics* (Lexington, Mass.: Lexington Books, 1974); Charles T. Goodsell, *American Corporations and Peruvian Politics* (Cambridge, Mass.: Harvard University Press, 1974); Richard S. Olson, *The Politics of Earthquake Prediction* (Princeton, N.J.: Princeton University Press, 1989); Ernest H. Preeg, *The Evolution of a Revolution: Peru and Its Relations with the United States, 1968–1980* (Washington, D.C.: NPA Committee on Changing International Realities, 1981); and Daniel A. Sharp, ed., *U.S. Foreign Policy and Peru* (Austin: University of Texas Press for the Institute of Latin American Studies, 1972).

Venezuela: Charles Carreras, *United States Economic Penetration of Venezuela and Its Effects on Diplomacy, 1895–1906* (New York: Garland, 1987); Sheldon B. Liss, *Diplomacy and Dependency: Venezuela, the United States and the Americas* (Salisbury, N.C.: Documentary Publications, 1978); and Stephen G. Rabe, *The Road to OPEC: United States Relations with Venezuela, 1919–1976* (Austin: University of Texas Press, 1982).

Other studies dealing with specific topics include Werner Baer and Donald V. Coes, eds., *United States Policies and the Latin American Economics* (New York: Praeger, 1990); Dick Steward, *Trade and Hemisphere: The Good Neighbor and Reciprocal Trade* (Columbia: University of Missouri Press, 1975); Richard R. Fagen, ed., *Capitalism and the State in U.S.–Latin American Relations* (Stanford, Calif.: Stanford University Press, 1979); Paul E. Sigmund, *Multinationals in Latin America: The Politics of Nationalization* (Madison: University of Wisconsin Press, 1980); Robert H. Swansbrough, *The Embattled Colossus: Economic Nationalism and United States Investors in Latin America* (Gainesville: University Presses of Florida, 1976); Michael R. Czinkota, ed., *U.S.–Latin American Trade Relations: Issues and Concerns* (New York: Praeger, 1983); Eric N. Baklanoff, *Expropriation of U.S. Investments in Cuba, Mexico and Chile* (New York: Praeger, 1975); Remy Montavon, *The Role of Multinational Companies in Latin America: A Case Study in Mexico* (New York: Praeger, 1980); Margaret D. Hayes, *Latin America and the U.S. National Interest: A Basis for U.S. Foreign Policy* (Boulder, Colo.: Westview Press, 1984); James F. Petras, *US Hegemony under Siege: Class, Politics and Development in Latin America* (New York: Verso, 1990); James A. Gardner, *Legal Imperialism: American Lawyers and Foreign Aid in Latin America* (Madison: University of Wisconsin Press, 1980); William E. Kane, *Civil Strife in Latin America: A Legal History of U.S. Involvement* (Baltimore: Johns Hopkins University Press, 1972); Lars Schoultz, *Human Rights and United States Policy toward Latin America* (Princeton, N.J.: Princeton University Press, 1981); Cynthia Brown, ed., *With Friends Like These: The Americas Watch Report on Human Rights and U.S. Policy in Latin America* (New York: Pantheon, 1985); William O. Walker III, *Drug Control in the Americas* (Albuquerque: University of New Mexico Press, 1981); Wesley P. Newton, *The Perilous Sky: U.S. Aviation Diplomacy and Latin America, 1919–1931* (Coral Gables, Fla.: University of Miami Press, 1978); and Fred Fejes, *Imperialism, Media, and the Good Neighbor: New Deal Foreign Policy and United States Shortwave Broadcasting to Latin America* (Norwood, N.J.: Ablex Corp., 1986).

Index

Italicized page numbers indicate the location of the main entry.

About the Author

DAVID SHAVIT is Associate Professor in the Department of Library and Information Studies at Northern Illinois University. He is the author of *The United States in the Middle East: A Historical Dictionary* (Greenwood Press, 1988), *The United States in Africa: A Historical Dictionary* (Greenwood, 1989), and *The United States in Asia: A Historical Dictionary* (Greenwood, 1990).